A treatise on human nature; being an attempt to introduce the experimental method of reasoning into moral subjects; and, Dialogues concerning natural religion

David Hume, Thomas Hill Green, Thomas Hodge Grose

LONDON   PRINTED BY
SPOTTISWOODE AND CO. NEW-STREET SQUARE
AND PARLIAMENT STREET

A TREATISE

ON

HUMAN NATURE

BEING AN

ATTEMPT TO INTRODUCE THE EXPERIMENTAL METHOD

OF REASONING INTO MORAL SUBJECTS

AND

DIALOGUES CONCERNING NATURAL RELIGION

BY DAVID HUME

EDITED, WITH PRELIMINARY DISSERTATIONS AND NOTES, BY

T. H. GREEN AND T. H. GROSE

LATE FELLOW AND TUTOR OF BALLIOL   FELLOW AND TUTOR OF QUEEN'S
COLLEGE, OXFORD   COLLEGE, OXFORD

IN TWO VOLUMES

VOL. II.

NEW EDITION

LONDON

LONGMANS, GREEN, AND CO.

1882

CONTENTS

OF

THE SECOND VOLUME.

———•◇•———

BOOK II.

OF THE PASSIONS.

PART I.

OF PRIDE AND HUMILITY.

PART II.

OF LOVE AND HATRED.

PART III.

OF THE WILL AND DIRECT PASSIONS.

BOOK III.

OF MORALS.

PART I.

OF VIRTUE AND VICE IN GENERAL.

SUMMARY OF THE CONTENTS

OF THE

GENERAL INTRODUCTION TO VOL. II.

———◆◇◆———

INTRODUCTION.

1. In his speculation on morals, no less than on knowledge, Hume follows the lines laid down by Locke. With each there is a precise correspondence between the doctrine of nature and the doctrine of the good. Each gives an account of reason consistent at least in this that, as it allows reason no place in the constitution of real objects, so it allows it none in the constitution of objects that determine desire and, through it, the will. (With each, consequently, the 'moral faculty,' whether regarded as the source of the judgments 'ought and ought not,' or of acts to which these judgments are appropriate, can only be a certain faculty of feeling, a particular susceptibility of pleasure and pain.) The originality of Hume lies in his systematic effort to account for those objects, apparently other than pleasure and pain, which determine desire, and which Locke had taken for granted without troubling himself about their adjustment to his theory, as resulting from the modification of primary feelings by 'associated ideas.' 'Natural relation,' the close and uniform sequence of certain impressions and ideas upon each other, is the solvent by which in the moral world, as in the world of knowledge, he disposes of those ostensibly necessary ideas that seem to regulate impressions without being copied from them; and in regard to the one application of it as much as to the other, the question is whether the efficiency of the solvent does not depend on its secretly including the very ideas of which it seems to get rid.

2. The place held by the 'essay concerning Human Understanding,' as a sort of philosopher's Bible in the last century, is strikingly illustrated by the effect of doctrines that

only appear in it incidentally. It does not profess to be an ethical treatise at all, yet the moral psychology contained in the chapter 'of Power' (II. 21), and the account of moral good and evil contained in the chapter 'of other Relations' (II. 28), furnished the text for most of the ethical speculation that prevailed in England, France, and Scotland for a century later. If Locke's theory was essentially a reproduction of Hobbes', it was yet in the form he gave it that it survived while Hobbes was decried and forgotten. The chapter on Power is in effect an account of determination by motives. More, perhaps, than any other part of the essay it bears the marks of having been written 'currente calamo.' In the second edition a summary was annexed which differs somewhat in the use of terms, but not otherwise, from the original draught. The main course of thought, however, is clear throughout. Will and freedom are at first defined in all but identical terms as each a 'power to begin or forbear action barely by a preference of the mind' (§§ 5, 8, 71). Nor is this identification departed from, except that the term 'will' is afterwards restricted to the 'preference' or 'power of preference,' while freedom is confined to the power of acting upon preference; in which sense it is pointed out that though there cannot be freedom without will, there may be will without freedom, as when, through the breaking of a bridge, a man cannot help falling into the water, though he prefers not to do so. 'Freedom' and 'will' being thus alike powers, if not the same power, it is as improper to ask whether the will is free as whether one power has another power. The proper question is whether man is free (§§ 14, 21), and the answer to this question, according to Locke, is that within certain limits he is free to act, but that he is not free to will. When in any case he has the option of acting or forbearing to act, he cannot help preferring, i.e. willing, one or other alternative. If it is further asked, What determines the will or preference? the answer is that 'nothing sets us upon any new action but some uneasiness' (§ 29), viz., the 'most urgent uneasiness we at any time feel' (§ 40), which again is always 'the uneasiness of desire fixed on some absent good, either negative, as indolence to one in pain, or positive, as enjoyment of pleasure.' In one sense, indeed, it may be said that the will often runs counter to desire, but this merely means that we 'being in this world beset with sundry uneasinesses, distressed with different desires,' the determination of the will by the most pressing desire often implies the counteraction of other desires which would, indeed, under other circumstances, be the most pressing, but at the particular time of the supposed action are not so.

3. So far Locke's doctrine amounts to no more than this, that action is always determined by the strongest motive; and only those who strangely hold that human freedom is to be vindicated by disputing that truism will care to question it. To admit that the strongest desire always moves action (there being, in fact, no test of its strength but its effect on action) and that, since every desire causes uneasiness till it is satisfied, the strongest desire is also the most pressing uneasiness,[1] is compatible with the most opposite views as to the constitution of the objects which determine desire. To understand that it is this constitution of the desired object, not any possible intervention of unmotived willing between the presentation of a strongest motive and action, which forms the central question of ethics, is the condition of all clear thinking on the subject. It is a question, however, which Locke ignores, and popular philosophy, to its great confusion, has not only continued to do the same, but would probably resent as pedantic any attempt at more accurate analysis. When we hear of the strongest 'desire' being the uniform motive to action, we have to ask, in the first place, whether the term is confined to impulses determined by a prior consciousness, or is taken to include those impulses, commonly called 'mere appetites,' which are not so determined, but depend directly and solely on the 'constitution of our bodily organs.' The *appetite* of hunger is obviously quite independent of any remembrance of the pleasure of eating, yet nothing is commoner than to identify with such simple

Two questions Does man always act from the strongest motive? and, What constitutes his motive? The latter the important question

---

[1] Locke's language in regard to 'the most pressing uneasiness' will not be found uniformly consistent. His usual doctrine is that the strength of a desire, as evinced by the resulting action, and the uneasiness which it causes are in exact proportion to each other. According to this view, desire for future happiness can only become a prevalent motive when the uneasiness which it causes has come to outweigh every other (Cf Chap xxi, Secs 43 and 45) On the other hand, he sometimes seems to distinguish the desire for future pleasure from present uneasiness, while at the same time implying that it may be a strongest motive (Cf sec 65) But if so, it follows that there may be a strongest desire which is not the most pressing uneasiness (See below, sec. 13) Hume, distinguishing strong from violent desires, and restricting 'uneasiness' to the latter, is able to hold that it is not alone the present uneasiness which determines action (Book ii , part 3, sec 3, sub fin)

Distinction
between
desires
that are,
and those
that are
not, deter-
mined by
the
conception
of self.
appetite the desire determined by consciousness of some sort, as when we say of a drunkard, who never drinks merely because he is thirsty, that he is governed by his appetite. Upon this distinction, however, since it is recognised by current psychology, it is less important to insist than on that between the kinds of prior consciousness which may determine desire proper. Does this prior consciousness consist simply in the return of an image of past pleasure with consequent hope of its renewal, or is it a conception—the thought of an object under relations to self or of self in relation to certain objects —in a word, self-consciousness as distinct from simple feeling?

4. Of desire determined in the former way we have experience, if at all, in those motives which actuate us, as we say, 'unconsciously'; which means, without our attending to them—feelings which we do not fix even momentarily by reference to self or to a thing. As we cannot set ourselves to recall such feelings without thinking them, without determining them by that reference to self which we suppose them to exclude, they cannot be described; but some of our actions (such as the instinctive recurrence to a sweet smell), seem only to be thus accounted for, and probably those actions of animals which do not proceed from appetite proper are to be accounted for in the same way. But whether such actions are facts in human experience or no, those which make us what we are as men are not so determined. The man whom we Effect of
this
conception
on the
objects of
human
desire call the slave of his appetite, the enlightened pleasure-hunter, the man who lives for his family, the artist, the enthusiast for humanity, are alike in this, that the desire which moves their action is itself determined not by the recurring image of a past pleasure, but by the conception of self. The self may be conceived of simply as a subject to be pleased, or may be a subject of interests, which, indeed, when gratified, produce pleasure but are not produced by it—interests in persons, in beautiful things, in the order of nature and society—but self is still not less the 'punctum stans' whose presence to each passing pleasure renders it a constituent of a happiness which is to be permanently pursued, than it is the focus in which the influences of that world which only self-conscious reason could constitute—the world of science, of art, of human society—must be regathered in order to become the personal interests which move the actions of individuals. It is in this

self-consciousness involved in our motives, in that conversion into a conception by reference to self, which the image even of the merest animal pleasure must undergo before it can become an element in the formation of character, that the possibility of freedom lies. Without it we should be as sinless and as unprogressive, as free from remorse and aspiration, as incapable of selfishness and self-denial as the animals. Each pleasure would be taken as it came. We should have 'the greatest happiness of which our nature is capable,' without possibility of asking ourselves whether we might not have had more. It is only the conception of himself as a permanent subject to be pleased that can set man upon the invention of new pleasures, and then, making each pleasure a disappointment when it comes, produce the 'vicious' temper; only this that can suggest the reflection how much more pleasure he might have had than he has had, and thus produce what the moralists know as 'cool selfishness'; only this, on the other hand, which, as 'enlightened self-love,' perpetually balances the attraction of imagined pleasure by the calculation whether it will be good for one as a whole. Nor less is it the conception of self, with a 'matter' more adequate to its 'form,' taking its content not from imagined pleasure, but from the work of reason in the world of nature and humanity, which determines that personal devotion to a work or a cause, to a state, a church, or mankind, which we call self-sacrifice.

5. If, now, we ask ourselves whether Locke recognised this function of reason, as self-consciousness, in the determination of the will, the answer must be yes and no. His cardinal doctrine, as we have sufficiently seen, forbade him to admit that reason or thought could originate an object. The only possible objects with him are either simple ideas or resoluble into these, and the simple idea, as that which we receive in pure passivity, is virtually feeling. Now no combination of feelings (supposing it possible [1]) can yield the conception of self as a permanent subject even of pleasure, much less as a subject of social claims. It cannot, therefore, yield the objects, ranging from sensual happiness to the moral law, humanity, and God, of which this conception is the correlative condition. Thus, strictly taken, Locke's doctrine excludes every motive to action, but appetite proper and such desire as is deter-

Objects so constituted Locke should consistently exclude.

[1] Cf Introduction to Vol. 1, §§ 215 and 247

But he finds room for them by treating every desire for an object, of which the attainment gives pleasure, as a desire for pleasure

mined by the imagination of animal pleasure or pain, and in doing so renders vice as well as virtue unaccountable—the excessive pursuit of pleasure as well as that dissatisfaction with it which affords the possibility of ordinary reform. On the other hand, the same happy intellectual unscrupulousness, which we have traced in his theory of knowledge, attends him also here. Just as he is ready on occasion to treat any conceived object that determines sense as if it were itself a sensation, so he is ready to treat any object that determines desire, without reference to the work of thought in its construction, as if it were itself the feeling of pleasure, or of uneasiness removed, which arises upon satisfaction of the desire. In this way, without professedly admitting any motive but remembered pleasure—a motive which, if it were our only one, would leave 'man's life as cheap as beasts' '—he can take for granted any objects of recognised interest as accounting for the movement of human life, and as constituents of an utmost possible pleasure which it is his own fault if every one does not pursue.

Confusion covered by calling 'happiness' the general object of desire.

6. The term 'happiness' is the familiar cover for confusion between the animal imagination of pleasure and the conception of personal well-being. It is so when—having raised the question, What moves desire?—Locke answers, 'happiness, and that alone.' What, then, is happiness? 'Good and evil are nothing but pleasure and pain,' and 'happiness in its full extent is the utmost pleasure we are capable of.'[1] This is 'the proper object of desire in general,' but Locke is careful to explain that the happiness which 'moves every particular man's desire' is not the full extent of it, but 'so much of it as is considered and taken to make a necessary part of his happiness.' It is that 'wherewith he in his present thoughts can satisfy himself.' Happiness in this sense 'every one constantly pursues,' and without possibility of error; for 'as to present pleasure the mind never mistakes that which is really good or evil.' Every one 'knows what best pleases him, and that he actually prefers.' That which is the greater pleasure or the greater pain is really just as it appears (Ibid. §§ 43, 58, 63). Now in these statements, if we look closely, we shall find that four different meanings of happiness are mixed up, which we will take leave to distinguish by letters—(a) happiness as an abstract

---

[1] Ibid. sec 42, and cap 28, sec 5.

conception, the sum of possible pleasure; (*b*) happiness as equivalent to the pleasure which at any time survives most strongly in imagination; (*c*) happiness as the object of the self-conscious pleasure-seeker; (*d*) happiness as equivalent to any object at any time most strongly desired, not really a pleasure, but by Locke identified with happiness in sense (*b*) through the fallacy of supposing that the pleasure which arises on satisfaction of any desire, great in proportion to the strength of the desire, is itself the object which excites desire.

7. Happiness ' in its full extent,' as ' the utmost pleasure we are capable of,' is an unreal abstraction if ever there was one It is curious that those who are most forward to deny the reality of universals, in that sense in which they are the condition of all reality, viz., as relations, should yet, having pronounced these to be mere names, be found ascribing reality to a universal, which cannot without contradiction be supposed more than a name. Does this ' happiness in its full extent' mean the 'aggregate of possible enjoyments,' of which modern utilitarians tell us? Such a phrase simply represents the vain attempt to get a definite by addition of indefinites. It has no more meaning than ' the greatest possible quantity of time' would have. Pleasant feelings are not quantities that can be added. Each is over before the next begins, and the man who has been pleased a million times is not really better off—has no more of the supposed chief good in possession—than the man who has only been pleased a thousand times. When we speak of pleasures, then, as forming a possible whole, we cannot mean pleasures as feelings, and what else do we mean? Are we, then, by the 'happiness' in question to understand pleasure *in general*, as might be inferred from Locke's speaking of it as the ' object of desire *in general*' ? But it is in its mere particularity that each pleasure has its being. It is a simple idea, and therefore, as Locke and Hume have themselves taught us, momentary, indefinable, in ' perpetual flux,' changing every moment upon us. Pleasure *in general*, therefore, is not pleasure, and it is nothing else. It is not a conceived reality, as a relation, or a thing determined by relations, is, since pleasure as feeling, in distinction from its conditions which are not feelings, for the same reason that it cannot be defined, cannot be conceived. It is a mere name which utilitarian philosophy

'Greatest sum of pleasure ' and ' Pleasure in general' unmeaning expressions.

has mistaken for a thing; but for which—since no one, whatever his theory of the desirable, can actually desire either the abstraction of pleasure in general or the aggregate of possible pleasures—a practical substitute is apt to be found in any lust of the flesh that may for the time be the strongest.

8. Having begun by making this fiction 'the proper object of desire in general,' Locke saves the appearance of consistency by representing the particular pleasure or removal of uneasiness, which he in fact believed to be the object of every desire, as if it were a certain part of the 'full extent of happiness' which the individual, having this full extent before him, picked out as being what 'in his present thoughts would satisfy him.' Nor does he ever give up the notion of a 'happiness in general,' in distinction from the happiness of each man's actual choice, as a possible motive, which a man who finds himself wretched in consequence of his actions may be told that he ought to have adopted. His real notion, however, of the happiness which is motive to action is a confused result of the three other notions of happiness, distinguished above as (b), (c) and (d). As that about which no one can be mistaken, 'happiness' can only be so in sense (b), as the 'pleasure which survives most strongly in imagination.' Of this it can be said truly, and of this only, that 'it really is just as it appears,' and that 'a man never chooses amiss' since he must 'know what best pleases him' But with this, almost in the same breath, Locke confuses 'happiness' in senses (c) and (d). So soon as it is said of an object that it is 'taken by the individual to make a necessary part of his happiness,' it is implied that it is determined by his conception of self. It is something which, as the result of the action of this conception on his past experience, he has come to present to himself as a constituent of his personal good. Unless he were conscious of himself as a permanent subject, he could have no conception of happiness as a whole from relation to which each present object takes its character as a part. Nor of the objects determined by this relation is it true, as Locke says, that they are always pleasures, or that they 'are really just as they appear.' Our readiness to accept his statements to this effect, is at bottom due to a confusion between the pleasure, or removal of uneasiness,

In what sense of happiness is it true that it 'is really just as it appears'?

incidental to the satisfaction of a desire and the object which excites the desire. If having explained desire, as Locke does, by reference to the good, we then allow ourselves to explain the good by reference to desire, it will indeed be true that no man can be mistaken as to his present good, but only in the sense of the identical proposition that every man most desires what he does most desire ; and true also, that every attained good is pleasure, but only in the sense that what satisfies desire does satisfy it. The man of whom it could be truly said, in any other sense than that of the above identical proposition, that his only objects of desire— the only objects which he ' takes to make a necessary part of his happiness '—were pleasures, would be a man, as we say, of no interests. He would be a man who either lived simply for pleasures incidental to the satisfaction of animal appetite, or one who, having been interested in certain objects in which reason alone enables us to be interested— *e.g.*, persons, pursuits, or works of art—and having found consequent pleasure, afterwards vainly tries to get the pleasure without the interests. To the former type of character, of course, the approximations are numerous enough, though it may be doubted whether such an ideal of sensuality is often fully realised. The latter in its completeness, which would mean a perfect misery that could only issue in suicide, would seem to be an impossibility, though it is constantly being approached in proportion to the unworthiness and fleetingness of the interests by which men allow themselves to be governed, and which, after stimulating an indefinite hunger for good, leave it without an object to satisfy it ; in proportion, too, to the modern habit of hugging and poring over the pleasures which our higher interests cause us till these interests are vitiated, and we find ourselves in restless and hopeless pursuit of the pleasure when the interest which might alone produce it is gone.

In what sense, that it is every one's object ?

9. Just as it is untrue, then, of the object of desire, as ' taken to be part of one's happiness ' or determined by the conception of self, that it is always a pleasure, so it is untrue that it is always really just as it appears, except in the trifling sense that what is most strongly desired is most strongly desired. Rather it is never really what it appears. It is least of all so to the professed pleasure-seeker. Obviously, to the man who seeks the pleasure incidental to

No real object of human desire can ever be just as it appears.

interests which he has lost, there is a contradiction in his quest which for ever prevents what seems to him desirable from satisfying his desire. And even the man who lives for merely animal pleasure, just because he seeks it as part of a happiness, never finds it to be that which he sought. There is no mistake about the pleasure, but he seeks it as that which shall satisfy him, and satisfy him, since he is not an animal, it cannot. Nor are our higher objects of desire ever what they seem. That is too old a topic with poets and moralizers to need enforcing. Each in its turn, we know, promises happiness when it shall have been attained, but when it is attained the happiness has not come. The craving for an object adequate to oneself, which is the source of the desire, is still not quenched; and because it is not, nor can be, even 'the joy of success' has its own bitterness.

Can Locke consistently allow the distinction between true happiness and false?

10. The case, then, stands thus Locke, having too much 'common sense' to reduce all objects of desire to the pleasures incidental to satisfactions of appetite, takes for granted any number of objects which only reason can constitute (or, in other words, which can only exist for a self-conscious subject) without any question as to their origin. It is enough for him that they are not conscious inventions of the individual, and that they are related to feeling—though related as determining it. This being so, they are to him no more the work of thought than are the satisfactions of appetite. The conception of them is of a kind with the simple remembrance or imagination of pleasures caused by such satisfactions. The question how, if only pleasure is the object of desire, they came to be desired before there had been experience of the pleasures incidental to their attainment, is virtually shelved by treating these latter pleasures as if they were themselves the objects originally desired. So far consistency at least is saved. No object but feeling, present or remembered, is ostensibly admitted within human experience. But meanwhile, alongside of this view, comes the account of the strongest motive as determined by the conception of self—as something which a man 'takes to be a necessary part of his happiness,' and which he is 'answerable to himself' for so taking. The inconsistency of such language with the view that every desired object must needs be a pleasure, would have been less noticeable if Locke himself had not frankly admitted, as the corollary of this view,

that the desired good 'is really just as it appears.' The Or respon- necessity of this admission has always been the rock on sibility? which consistent Hedonism has broken. Locke himself has scarcely made it when he becomes aware of its dangerous consequences, and great part of the chapter on Power is taken up by awkward attempts to reconcile it with the distinction between true happiness and false, and with the existence of moral responsibility. If greatest pleasure is the only possible object, and the production of such pleasure the only possible criterion of action, and if 'as to present pleasure and pain the mind never mistakes that which is really good or evil,' with what propriety can any one be told that he might or that he ought to have chosen otherwise than he has done? 'He has missed the true good,' we say, 'which he might and should have found'; but 'good,' according to Locke, is only pleasure, and pleasure, as Locke in any other connexion would be eager to tell us, must mean either some actual present pleasure or a series of pleasures of which each in turn is present. If every one without possibility of mistake has on each occasion chosen the greatest present pleasure, how can the result for him at any time be other than the true good, *i.e.*, the series of greatest pleasures, each in its turn present, that have been hitherto possible for him?

11. A modern utilitarian, if faithful to the principle which Objections excludes any test of pleasure but pleasure itself, will prob- to the ably answer that every one does attain the maximum of answer pleasure possible for him, his character and circumstances to these being what they are; but that with a change in these his questions. choice would be different. He would still choose on each occasion the greatest pleasure of which he was then capable, but this pleasure would be one 'truer'—in the sense of being more intense, more durable, and compatible with a greater quantity of other pleasures—than is that which he actually chooses. But admitting that this answer justifies us in speaking of any sort of pleasure as 'truer' than that at any time chosen by any one—which is a very large admission, for of the intensity of any pleasure we have no test but its being actually preferred, and of durability and compatibility with other pleasures the tests are so vague that a healthy and unrepentant voluptuary would always have the best of it in an attempt to strike the balance between the

pleasures he has actually chosen and any truer sort—it still
only throws us back on a further question. With a better
character, it is said, such as better education and improved
circumstances might have produced, the actually greatest
happiness of the individual—*i. e.*, the series of pleasures
which, because he has chosen them, we know to have been
the greatest possible for him—might have been greater or
'truer.' But the man's character is the result of his previous preferences; and if every one has always chosen the
greatest pleasure of which he was at the time capable, and
if no other motive is possible, how could any other than his
actual character have been produced? How could that conception of a happiness truer than the actual, of something
that should be most pleasant, and therefore preferred,
though it is not—a conception which all education implies—
have been a possible motive among mankind? To say that
the individual is, to begin with, destitute of such a conception, but acquires it through education from others, does not
remove the difficulty. How do the educators come by it?
Common sense assumes them to have found out that more
happiness might have been got by another than the merely
natural course of living, and to wish to give others the
benefit of their experience. But such experience implies
that each has a conception of himself as other than the
subject of a succession of pleasures, of which each has been
the greatest possible at the time of its occurrence; and the
wish to give another the benefit of the experience implies
that this conception, which is no possible image of a feeling,
can originate action. The assumption of common sense,
then, contradicts the two cardinal principles of the Hedon-
istic philosophy; yet, however disguised in the terminology
of development and evolution, it, or some equivalent supposition, is involved in every theory of the progress of mankind.

12. Such difficulties do not suggest themselves to Locke,
because he is always ready to fall back on the language of
common sense without asking whether it is reconcilable

According
to Locke
present
pleasures
may be
compared
with
future,
with his theory. Having asserted, without qualification,
that the will in every case is determined by the strongest
desire, that the strongest desire is desire for the greatest
pleasure, and that 'pleasure is just so great, and no greater,
than it is felt,' he finds a place for moral freedom and responsibility in the 'power a man has to suspend his desires

and stop them from determining his will to any action till he has examined whether it be really of a nature in itself and consequences to make him happy or no.'[1] But how does it happen that there is any need for such suspense, if as to pleasure and pain 'a man never chooses amiss,' and pleasure is the same with happiness or the good? To this Locke answers that it is only present pleasure which is just as it appears, and that in 'comparing present pleasure or pain with future we often make wrong judgments of them;' again, that not only present pleasure and pain, but 'things that draw after them pleasure and pain, are considered as good and evil,' and that of these consequences under the influence of present pleasure or pain we may judge amiss.[2] By these wrong judgments, it will be observed, Locke does not mean mistakes in discovering the proper means to a desired end (Aristotle's ἀγνοία ἡ καθ' ἕκαστα), which it is agreed are not a ground for blame or punishment, but wrong desires—desires for certain pleasures as being the greater, which are not really the greater. Regarding such desires as involving comparisons of one good with another, he counts them judgments, and (the comparison being incorrectly made) *wrong* judgments. A certain present pleasure, and a certain future one, are compared, and though the future would really be the greater, the present is preferred; or a present pleasure, 'drawing after it' a certain amount of pain, is compared with a less amount of present pain, drawing after it a greater pleasure, and the present pleasure preferred. In such cases the man 'may justly incur punishment' for the wrong preference, because having 'the power to suspend his desire' for the present pleasure, he has not done so, but 'by too hasty choice of his own making has imposed on himself wrong measures of good and evil.' 'When he has once chosen it,' indeed, 'and thereby it is become part of his happiness, it raises desire, and that proportionately gives him uneasiness, which determines his will.' But the original wrong choice, having the 'power of suspending his desires,' he might have prevented. In not doing so he 'vitiated his own palate,' and must be 'answerable to himself' for the consequences.[3]

13. Responsibility for evil, then (with its conditions, blame, punishment, and remorse) supposes that a man has

and desire suspended till comparison has been made.

[1] II 21, Sec. 51 and 56.   [2] Ibid., Sec. 61, 63, 67.   [3] Ibid., Sec. 56

What is
meant by
'present'
and
'future'
pleasure ?

gone wrong in the comparison of present with future pleasure or pain, having had the chance of going right.   Upon
this we must remark that as moving desire—and it is the
determination of desire that is here in question—NO pleasure can be present in the sense of actual enjoyment, or (in
Hume's language) as 'impression,' but only in memory or
imagination, as 'idea.'   Otherwise desire would not be
desire.   It would not be that uneasiness which, according
to Locke, implies the absence of good, and alone moves action.
On the other hand, to imagination EVERY pleasure must be
present that is to act as motive at all.   In whatever sense,
then, pleasure, as pleasure, *i.e.* as undetermined by conceptions, can properly be said to move desire, every pleasure is
equally present and equally future [1]   For man, if he only
felt and retained his feelings in memory, or recalled them in
imagination, the only difference among the imagined pleasures which solicit his desires, other than difference of
intensity, would lie in the imagined pains with which each
may have become   associated.   One pleasure might be
imagined in association with a greater amount of the pain
of waiting than another.   In that sense, and only in that,
could one be distinguished from the other as a future pleasure from a present one.   According as the greater imagined
intensity of the future pleasure did or did not outweigh the
imagined pain of waiting for it, the scale of desire would
turn one way or the other.   Or with one pleasure, imagined
as more intense than another, might be associated an expectation of a greater amount of pain to be 'drawn after it.'
Here, again, the question would be whether the greater
imagined intensity of pleasure would have the more effect in
exciting desire, or the greater amount of imagined sequent
pain in quenching it—a question only to be settled by the
action which results.   In whatever sense it is true of the
' present pleasure or pain,' that it is really just as it appears,
it is equally true of the future.   Whenever the determination of desire is in question, the statement that present
pleasure is just as it appears must mean that the pleasure
present in imagination is so, and in this sense all motive
pleasures are equally so present.   Undoubtedly the pleasure

[1] It is noticeable that when Locke takes
to distinguishing the pleasures that
move desire into present and future, he
speaks as if the future pleasure alone
were an absent good, in contradiction
to his previous view that every object
of desire is an absent good   (Cf. sec.
65 with sec 57 of cap 21)

associated with the pain of prolonged expectancy might turn out greater, and that associated with sequent pain less, than was imagined; but so might a pleasure not thus associated. Of every pleasure alike it is as true, that while it is imagined it is just as it is imagined, as that while felt it is just as it is felt; and if man only felt and imagined, there would be no more reason why he should hold himself accountable for his imaginations than for his feelings. Whatever pleasure was most attractive in imagination would determine desire, and, through it, action, which would be the only measure of the amount of the attraction. It would not indeed follow because an action was determined by the pleasure most attractive in imagination, that the ensuing pleasure in actual enjoyment would be greater than might have been attained by a different action—though it would be very hard to show the contrary—but it would follow that the man attained the greatest pleasure of which his nature was capable. There would be no reason why he should blame himself, or be blamed by others, for the result.

By the supposed comparison Locke ought only to have meant the competition of pleasures equally present in imagination

14. Thus on Locke's supposition, that desire is only moved by pleasure—which must mean *imagined* pleasure, since pleasure, determined by conceptions, is excluded by the supposition that pleasure alone is the ultimate motive, and pleasure in actual enjoyment is no longer desired—the 'suspense of desire,' that he speaks of, can only mean an interval, during which a competition of imagined pleasures (one associated with more, another with less, of sequent or antecedent pain) is still going on, and none has become finally the strongest motive. Of such suspense it is unmeaning to say that a man has ' the power of it,' or that, when it terminates in an action which does not produce so much pleasure as another might have done, it is because the man ' has vitiated his palate,' and that therefore he must be ' answerable to himself' for the consequences. This language really implies that pleasures, instead of being ultimate ends, are determined to be ends through reference to an object beyond them which the man himself constitutes; that it is only through his conception of self that every pleasure—not indeed best pleases him, or is most attractive in imagination—but becomes his personal good. It may be that he identifies his personal good with the pleasure most attractive in imagination; but a pleasure so identified is quite a different

and this could give no ground for responsibility.

In order to
do so, it
must be
understood
as imply-
ing deter-
mination
by concep-
tion of
self.

motive from a pleasure simply as imagined. It is no longer
mere pleasure that the man seeks, but self-satisfaction
through the pleasure. The same consciousness of self,
which sets him on the act, continues through the act and its
consequences, carrying with it the knowledge (commonly
called the 'voice of conscience') that it is to himself, as the
ultimate motive, that the act and its consequences, whether
in the shape of natural pains or civil penalties, are due—a
knowledge which breeds remorse, and, through it, the possibility of a better mind. Thus, when Locke finds the ground
of responsibility in a man's power of suspending his desire
till he has considered whether the act, to which it inclines
him, is of a kind to make him happy or no, the value of the
explanation lies in the distinction which it may be taken to
imply, but which Locke could not consistently admit, between
the imagination of pleasure and the conception of self as a
permanent subject of happiness, by reference to which an
imagined pleasure becomes a strongest motive. It is not
really as involving a comparison between imagined pleasures, but as involving the consideration whether the greatest
imagined pleasure will be the best for one in the long run,
that the suspense of desire establishes the responsibility of
man.   Even if we admitted with Locke that nothing entered
into the consideration but an estimate of 'future pleasures'
—and Locke, it will be observed, by supposing the estimate
to include 'pleasures of a sort we are unacquainted with,'[1]
which is as much of a contradiction as to suppose a man influenced by unfelt feelings, renders this restriction unmeaning
—still to be determined by the consideration whether something is good for me on the whole is to be determined, not
by the imagination of pleasure, but by the conception of
self, though it be of self only as a subject to be pleased.

15. The mischief is that, though his language implies this
distinction, he does not himself understand it. 'The care
of ourselves,' he tells us, 'that we mistake not imaginary
for real happiness, is the necessary foundation of our liberty.
The stronger ties we have to an unalterable pursuit of happiness in general, which is our greatest good, and which, as
such, our desires always follow, the more are we free from

---

[1] Cap. 21, sec. 65. He has specially
in view the pleasures of 'another life,'
which 'being intended for a state of
happiness, must certainly be agreeable
to every one's wish and desire; could
we suppose their relishes as different
there as they are here, yet the manna in
heaven will suit every one's palate'

any necessary determination of our will to any particular action, till we have examined whether it has a tendency to, or is inconsistent with, our real happiness.'[1] But he does not see that the *rationale* of the freedom, thus paradoxically, though truly, placed in the strength of a tie, lies in that determination by the conception of self to which the 'unalterable pursuit of happiness' is really equivalent. To him it is not as one mode among others in which that self-determination appears, but simply in itself, that the consideration of what is for our real happiness is the 'foundation of our liberty,' and the consideration itself is no more than a comparison between imagined pleasures and pains. Hence to a reader who refuses to read into Locke an interpretation which he does not himself supply, the range of moral liberty must seem as narrow as its nature is ambiguous. As to its range, the greater part of our actions, and among them those which we are apt to think our best, are not and could not be preceded by any consideration whether they are for our real happiness or no. In truth, they result from a character which the conception of self has rendered possible, or express an interest in objects of which this conception is the condition, and for that reason they represent a will self-determined and free; but they do not rest on the foundation which Locke calls 'the necessary foundation of our liberty.' As to the nature of this liberty, the reader, who takes Locke at his word, would find himself left to choose between the view of it as the condition of a mind 'suspended' between rival presentations of the pleasant, and the equally untenable view of it as that 'liberty of indifference,' which Locke himself is quite ready to deride—as consisting in a choice prior to desire, which determines what the desire shall be.[2]

Locke finds moral freedom in necessity of pursuing happiness

16. This ambiguous deliverance about moral freedom, it must be observed, is the necessary result on a mind, having too strong a practical hold on life to tamper with human responsibility, of a doctrine which denies the originativeness of thought, and in consequence cannot consistently allow any motive to desire, but the image of a past pleasure or pain. The full logical effect of the doctrine, however, does not appear in Locke, because, with his way of taking any

If an action is moved by desire for an object,

---

[1] Cap. 21, sec 51.
[2] Cf. the passage in sec 56 'When he has once chosen it, and thereby it is become part of his happiness, it raises desire,' &c (Cf also sec. 43 sub fin.)

Locke asks
no ques-
tions about
origin of
the object.

desire of which the satisfaction produces pleasure to have
pleasure for its object, he never comes in sight of the question how the manifold objects of actual human interest are
possible for a being who only feels and retains, or combines,
his feelings. An action moved by love of country, love of
fame, love of a friend, love of the beautiful, would cause him
no more difficulty than one moved by desire for the renewal
of some sensual enjoyment, or for that maintenance of
health which is the condition of such enjoyment in the
future. If pressed about them, we may suppose that—avail-
ing himself of the language probably current in the philosophic society in which he lived, though it first became
generally current in England through the writings of his
quasi-pupil, Shaftesbury—he would have said that he found
in his breast affections for public good, as well as for self-
good, the satisfaction of which gave pleasure, and to which
his doctrine, that pleasure is the 'object of desire in general,'
was accordingly applicable. The question—of what feelings
or combinations of feelings are the objects which excite
these several desires copies?—it does not occur to him to

But what
is to be said
of actions,
which we
only do
because we
ought?

ask. It is only when a class of actions presents itself for
which a motive in the way of desire or aversion is not
readily assignable that any difficulty arises, and then it is a
difficulty which the assignment of such a motive, without
any question asked as to its possibility for a merely feeling
and imagining subject, is thought sufficiently to dispose of.
Such a class of actions is that of which we say that we
'ought' to do them, even when we are not compelled and
had rather not. We ought, it is generally admitted, to keep
our promises, even when it is inconvenient to us to do so and
no punishment could overtake us if we did not. We ought
to be just even in ways that the law does not prescribe, and
when we are beyond its ken ; and that, too, in dealing with
men towards whom we have no inclination to be generous.
We ought even—so at least Locke 'on the authority of
Revelation' would have said—to forgive injuries which we
cannot forget, and if not 'to love our enemies' in the literal
sense, which may be an impossibility, yet to act as if we did.
To what motive are such actions to be assigned ?

17. 'To desire for pleasure or aversion from pain,' Locke
would answer, 'but a pleasure and pain other than the
natural consequences of acts and attached to them by some

law.' This is the result of his enquiry into 'Moral Relations' (Book ii., chap. 28). Good and evil, he tells us, being 'nothing but pleasure and pain, moral good or evil is only the conformity or disagreement of our actions to some law, whereby good or evil, *i.e.*, pleasure or pain, is drawn on us by the will and power of the law-maker.' All law according to its 'true nature' is a rule set to the actions of others by an intelligent being, having 'power to reward the compliance with, and punish deviation from, his rule by some good and evil that is not the natural product and consequence of the action itself; for that, being a natural convenience or inconvenience, would operate of itself without a law.' Of such law there are three sorts. 1. Divine Law, 'promulgated to men by the light of nature or voice of revelation, by comparing their actions to which they judge whether, as duties or sins, they are like to procure them happiness or misery from the hands of the Almighty.' 2. Civil Law, 'the rule set by the Commonwealth to the actions of those who belong to it,' reference to which decides 'whether they be criminal or no.' 3. 'The law of opinion or reputation,' according to agreement or disagreement with which actions are reckoned 'virtues or vices.' This law may or may not coincide with the divine law. So far as it does, virtues and vices are really, what they are always supposed to be, actions 'in their own nature' severally right or wrong. It is not as really right or wrong, however, but only as esteemed so, that an act is virtuous or vicious, and thus 'the common measure of virtue and vice is the approbation or dislike, praise or blame, which by a tacit consent establishes itself in the several societies, tribes, and clubs of men in the world, whereby several actions come to find credit or disgrace among them, according to the judgment, maxims, or fashions of the place.' Each sort of law has its own 'enforcement in the way of good and evil.' That of the civil law is obvious. That of the Divine Law lies in the pleasures and pains of 'another world,' which (we have to suppose) render actions 'in their own nature good and evil.' That of the third sort of law lies in those consequences of social reputation and dislike which are stronger motives to most men than are the rewards and punishments either of God or the magistrate (chap. 28, §§ 5–12).

18. 'Moral goodness or evil,' Locke concludes, 'is the

Their object is pleasure, but pleasure given not by nature but by law

c 2

Confor-
mity to
law not
the moral
good but
a means
to it

conformity or non-conformity of any action' to one or other
of the above rules (§ 14). But such conformity or non-conformity is not a feeling, pleasant or painful, at all. If, then,
the account of the good as consisting in pleasure, of which
the morally good is a particular form, is to be adhered to,
we must suppose that, when moral goodness is said to be
conformity to law, it is so called merely with reference to the
specific means of attaining that pleasure in which moral
good consists. Not the conception of conformity to law, but
the imagination of a certain pleasure, will determine the
desire that moves the moral act, as every other desire.
The distinction between the moral act and an act judiciously
done for the sake, let us say, of some pleasure of the palate,
will lie only in the channel through which comes the pleasure
that each is calculated to obtain. If the motive of an act
done for the sake of the pleasure of eating differs from the
motive of an act done for the sake of sexual pleasure on account of the difference of the channels through which the
pleasures are severally obtained, in that sense only can the
motive of either of these acts, upon Locke's principles, be
taken to differ from the motive of an act morally done. The
explanation, then, of the acts not readily assignable to
desire or aversion, of which we say that we only do them
because we ' ought,' has been found. They are so far of a kind
with all actions done to obtain or avoid what Locke calls
' future ' pleasures or pains that the difficulty of assigning
a motive for them only arises from the fact that their
immediate result is not an end but a means. They differ
from these, however, inasmuch as the pleasure they draw
after them is not their ' natural consequence,' any more than
the pain attaching to a contrary act would be, but is only
possible through the action of God, the magistrate, or
society in some of its forms.

Hume has
to derive
from 'im-
pressions'
the objects
which
Locke
took for
granted

19. After the above examination we can easily anticipate
the points on which a candid and clear-headed man, who
accepted the principles of Locke's doctrine, would see that
it needed explanation and development. If all action is
determined by impulse to remove the most pressing uneasiness, as consisting in desire for the greatest pleasure of which
the agent is at the time capable; if this, again, means
desire for the renewal of some ' impression ' previously experienced, and all impressions are either those of sense or

derived from them, how are we to account for those actual objects of human interest and pursuit which seem far removed from any combination of animal pleasures or of the means thereto, and specially for that class of actions determined, as Locke says, by expectation of pain or pleasure other than the 'natural consequence' of the act, to which the term 'moral' is properly applied? Hume, as we have seen,[1] in accepting Locke's principles, clothes them in a more precise terminology, marking the distinction between the feeling as originally felt and the same as returning in memory or imagination as that between 'impression and idea,' and excluding *original* ideas of reflection. 'An impression first strikes upon the senses, and makes us perceive heat or cold, thirst or hunger, pleasure or pain, of some kind or other. Of this impression there is a copy taken by the mind, which remains after the impression ceases; and this we call an idea. This idea of pleasure or pain, when it returns upon the soul, produces the new impressions of desire and aversion, hope and fear, which may properly be called impressions of reflection, because derived from it' (a). These, again, are copied by the memory and imagination, and become ideas; which perhaps in their turn give rise to other impressions' (b). Thus the impressions of reflection, marked (a), will be determined by ideas copied from impressions of sense. If desires, they will be desires for the renewal either of a pleasure incidental to the satisfaction of appetite, or of a pleasant sight or sound, a sweet taste or smell. These desires and their satisfactions will again be copied in ideas, but how can the impressions (b) to which these ideas give rise be other than desires for the renewal of the original animal pleasures? How do they come to be desires as unlike these as are the motives which actuate not merely the saint or the philanthropist, but the ordinary good neighbour or honest citizen or head of a family?

20. During the interval between the publication of Locke's essay and the 'Treatise on Human Nature' there had been much writing on ethical questions in English. The effect of this on Hume is plain enough. He writes with reference to current controversy, and in the moral part of the treatise probably had the views of Clarke, Shaftesbury, Butler, and Hutcheson more consciously before him than Locke's. This does not interfere, however, with the propriety of affiliating

Questions which he found at issue

[1] General Introd., vol i, par 195.

a Is virtue
interested?
b What
is con-
science ?

him in respect of his views on morals, no less than on knowledge, directly to Locke, whose principles and method were
in the main accepted by all the moralists of that age.   His
characteristic lies in his more consistent application of these,
and the effect of current controversy upon him was chiefly
to show him the line which this application must take.   It
was a controversy which turned almost wholly on two points ;
(a) the distinction between 'interested and disinterested,'
selfish and unselfish affections ; (b) the origin and nature of
that 'law,' relation to which, according to Locke, constitutes
our action 'virtuous or vicious.' In the absence of any notion
of thought but as a faculty which puts together simple ideas
into complex ones, of reason but as a faculty which calculates
means and perceives the agreement of ideas mediately, it
could have but one end.

Hobbes'
answer to
first ques-
tion

21. By the generation in which Hume was bred the issue
as to the possible disinterestedness of action was supposed to
lie between the view of Hobbes and that of Shaftesbury.
Hobbes' moral doctrine had not been essentially different
from Locke's, but he had been offensively explicit on questions which Locke left open to more genial views than his
doctrine logically justified.   Each started from the position
that the ultimate motive to every action can only be the
imagination of one's own pleasure or pain, and neither properly left room for the determination of desire by a conceived
object as distinct from remembered pleasure. But while
Locke, as we have seen, illogically took for granted desires
so determined, and thus made it possible for a disciple to
admit any benevolent desires as motives on the strength of
the pleasure which they produce when satisfied, Hobbes had
been more severe in his method, and had explained every
desire, of which the direct motive could not be taken to be
the renewal of some animal pleasure, as desire either for the
power in oneself to command such pleasure at will or for the
pleasure incidental to the contemplation of the signs of such
power.   Hence his peculiar treatment of compassion and the
other 'social affections,' which it is easier to show to be untrue to the facts of the case than to be other than the
proper consequence of principles which Locke had rendered
orthodox.[1] The counter-doctrine of Shaftesbury holds water
just so far as it involves the rejection of the doctrine that

[1] See 'Leviathan,' part 1, chap 6

pleasure is the sole ultimate motive. It becomes confused just because its author had no definite theory of reason, as constitutive of objects, that could justify this rejection.

22. He begins with a doctrine that directly contradicts Locke's identification of the good with pleasure, and of the morally good with pleasure occurring in a particular way. 'In a sensible creature that which is not done through any affection at all makes neither good nor ill in the nature of that creature; who then only is supposed good, when the good or ill of the system to which he has relation is the immediate object of some passion or affection moving him.'[1] This, it will be seen, as against Locke, implies that the good of a man's action lies not in any pleasure sequent upon it to him, but in the nature of the affection from which it proceeds; and that the goodness of this affection depends on its being determined by an object wholly different from imagined pleasure—the *conceived* good of a system to which the man has relation, *i.e.*, of human society, which in Shaftesbury's language is the 'public' as distinct from the 'private' system. It is not enough that an action should result in good to this system; it must proceed from affection for it. 'Whatever is done which happens to be advantageous to the species through an affection merely towards self-good does not imply any more goodness in the creature than as the affection itself is good. Let him in any particular act ever so well; if at the bottom it be that selfish affection alone which moves him, he is in himself still vicious.'[2] Here, then, we seem to have a clear theory of moral evil as consisting in selfish, of moral good as consisting in unselfish affections. But what exactly constitutes a selfish affection, according to Shaftesbury? The answer that first suggests itself, is that as the unselfish affection is an affection for public good, so a selfish one is an affection for 'self-good,' the good of the 'private system.' Shaftesbury, however, does not give this answer. 'Affection for private good' with him is not, as such, selfish; it is so only when 'excessive' and 'inconsistent with the interest of the species or public.'[3] This qualification seems at once to efface the clear line of distinction previously drawn. It puts 'self-affection' on a level with public affection which, according

Counter-
doctrine of
Shaftes-
bury
Vice is
selfishness

[1] 'Inquiry concerning Virtue,' Book I, part 2, sec 1
[2] Ibid, Book I, part 2, sec 2
[3] Ibid, Book II, part I, sec 3.

to Shaftesbury, may equally err on the side of excess. It implies that an affection for self-good, if only it be advantageous to the species, may be good; which is just what had been previously denied. And not only so; although, when the self-affections are under view, they are only allowed a qualified goodness in virtue of their indirect contribution to the good of the species, yet conversely, the superiority of the affections, which have this latter good for their object, is urged specially on the ground of the greater amount of happiness or 'self-good' which they produce.

23. The truth is that the notions which Shaftesbury attached to the terms 'affection for self-good' and 'affection for public good' were not such as allowed of a consistent opposition between them. They can only be so opposed if, on the one hand, self-good is identified with pleasure; and on the other, affection for public good is carefully distinguished from desire for that sort of pleasure of which the gratification of others is a condition. But with Shaftesbury, affections for self-good do not represent merely those desires for pleasure determined by self-consciousness—for pleasure presented as one's personal good—which can alone be properly reckoned sources of moral evil. They include equally mere natural appetites—hunger, the sexual impulse, &c.— which are morally neutral, and they do not clearly exclude any desire for an object which a man has so 'made his own' as to find his happiness—'self-enjoyment' or 'self-good,' according to Shaftesbury's language—in attaining it, though it be as remote from imagined pleasure as possible.[1] On the other hand, 'affections for public good,' as he describes them, are not restricted to such desires for the good of others as are irrespective of pleasure to self. They include not only such natural instincts as 'parental kindness and concern for the nurture and propagation of the young,' which, morally, at any rate, are not to be distinguished from the appetites reckoned as affections for self-good, but also desires for sympathetic pleasure—the pleasure to oneself which arises on consciousness that another is pleased. Shaftesbury's special antipathy, indeed, is the doctrine that benevolent affections are interested in the sense of having for their object a pleasure to oneself, apart from and beyond the pleasure of the person whom they move us to please; but

But no clear account of selfishness.

Confusion in his notions of self-good and public good

---

[1] Book II., part 2, sec. 2

unless he regards them as desires for the pleasure which the subject of them experiences in the pleasure of another, there is no purpose in enlarging, as he does with much unction, on the special pleasantness of the pleasures which they produce. With such vagueness in his notions of what he meant by affections for ' self-good ' and for ' public good,' it is not strange that he should have failed to give any tenable account of the selfishness in which he conceived moral evil to consist. He could not apply such a term of reproach to the ' self-affections ' in general, without condemning as selfish the man who ' finds his own happiness in doing good, and who is in truth indistinguishable from one to whom ' affection for public good ' has become, as we say, the law of his being. Nor could he identify selfishness, as he should have done, with all living for pleasure without a more complete rupture than he was capable of with the received doctrine of his time and without bringing affection for public good, in the form in which it was most generally conceived, and which was, at any rate, one of the forms under which he presented it to himself—as desire, namely, for sympathetic pleasure—into the same condemnation. His way out of the difficulty is, as we have seen, in violation of his own principle to find the characteristic of selfishness not in the motive of any affection but in its result; not in the fact that a man's desire has his own good for its object, which is true of one to whom his neighbour's good is as his own, nor in the fact that it has pleasure for its object, which Shaftesbury, as the child of his age, could scarcely help thinking was the case with every desire, but in the fact that it is stronger than is ' consistent with the interest of the species or public.'

Is all living for pleasure, or only too much of it, selfish ?

24. Neither Butler nor Hutcheson[1] can claim to have carried the ethical controversy much beyond the point at which Shaftesbury left it. Each took for granted that the object of the ' self-affection ' was necessarily one's own happiness, and neither made any distinction between living for happiness and living for pleasure. They could not then identify selfishness with the living for pleasure without con-

What have Butler and Hutcheson to say about it?

[1] The works of Hutcheson, published before Hume's treatise was written, and which strongly affected it, were the ' Enquiry into the Original of our Ideas of Beauty and Virtue ' (1725), and the ' Essay on the Nature and Con- duct of the Passions and Affections ' (1728) In what follows I wrote with direct reference to his posthumous work, not published till after Hume's treatise, but which only reproduces more systematically his earlier views

Chiefly,
that affec-
tions ter-
minate
upon their
objects.

demning the self-affection, and with it the best man's
pursuit of his own highest good in the service of others,
altogether as evil.   Nor in the absence of any better theory
of the object of the self-affection could the social affections,
which, according to Butler, are subject in the developed man
to the direction of self-love, escape the suggestion that they
are one mode of the general desire for pleasure.   Butler and
Hutcheson, indeed, are quite clear that they are 'disinterested' in the sense of 'terminating upon their objects.'[1]
This means, what is sufficiently obvious when once pointed
out, (*a*) that a benevolent desire is not a desire for that
particular pleasure, or rather 'removal of uneasiness,' which
shall ensue when it is satisfied, and (*b*) that it cannot originally arise from the general desire for happiness, since this
creates no pleasures but merely directs us to the pursuit of
objects found pleasant independently of it, and thus, if it
directs us to benevolent acts, presupposes a pleasure previously found in them.   This, however, as Butler points out,
is equally true of all particular desires whatever—of those
styled self-regarding, no less than of the social—and if it is
not incompatible with the former being desires for pleasure,
no more is it with the latter being so.   Much confusion on
the matter, it may be truly said, arises from the loose way
in which the words 'affection' and 'passion' are used by
Butler and his contemporaries, not excluding Hume himself,

But this
does not
exclude
the view
that all
desire is
for plea-
sure.

alike for appetite, desire, and emotion.   In every case a
pleasure other than satisfaction of desire must have been
experienced before desire can be excited by the imagination
of it.   A pleasure incidental to the satisfaction of *appetite*
must have been experienced before imagination of it could
excite the *desire* of the glutton.   In like manner, social
affection, as *desire*, cannot be first excited by the pleasure
which shall arise when it is satisfied; it must previously
exist as the condition of that pleasure being experienced;
but it does not follow that it is other than a desire for
an imagined pleasure, for that sympathetic pleasure in the
pleasure of another in which the social affection as *emotion*
consists.   Now though Butler and Hutcheson sufficiently
showed that it is no other pleasure than this which is the
original object of benevolent desires, they did not attempt
to show that it is not this; and failing such an attempt, the

[1] See in Preface to Butler's Sermons,
the part relating to Sermon XI 'Besides, the only idea of an interested
pursuit' &c , also the early part of
Sermon XI , 'Every man hath a general desire,' &c

received doctrine that the object of all desire, social and self-regarding alike, is pleasure of one sort or another, would naturally be taken to stand. This admitted, there can be nothing in the fact that a certain pleasure depends on the pleasure of another, and that a certain other does not, to entitle an action moved by desire for the former sort of pleasure to be called unselfish in the way of praise, and one moved by desire for the latter sort selfish in the way of reproach. The motive—desire for his own pleasure—is the same to the doer in both cases. The distinction between the acts can only lie in that which Shaftesbury had said could not constitute moral good or ill—in the consequences by which society judges of them, but which do not form the motive of the agent. In other words, it will be a distinction fixed by that law of opinion or reputation, in which Locke had found the common measure of virtue and vice, though he had not entered on the question of the considerations by which that law is formed.

25. Such a conclusion would lie ready to hand for such a reader of Butler and Hutcheson as we may suppose Hume to have been, but it is needless to say that it is not that at which they themselves arrive. Butler, indeed, distinctly refuses to identify moral good and evil respectively with disinterested and interested action,[1] but neither does he admit that desire for pleasure or aversion from pain is the uniform motive of action in such a way as to compel the conclusion that moral good and ill represent a distinction, not of motives, but of consequences of action contemplated by the onlooker. An act is morally good, according to him, when it is approved by the ' reflex faculty of approbation,' bad when it is disapproved, but what it is that this ' faculty ' approves he never distinctly tells us. The good is what ' conscience ' approves, and conscience is what approves the good—that is the circle out of which he never escapes. If we insist on extracting from him any more satisfactory conclusion as to the object of moral approbation, it must be that it is the object which ' self-love ' pursues, i.e., the greatest happiness of the individual, a conclusion which in

Of moral goodness Butler's account circular

---

[1] See preface to Sermons (about four pages from the end in most editions) :— ' The goodness or badness of actions does not arise hence,' &c The conclusion he there arrives at is that a good action is one which 'becomes such creatures as we are', and this, read in the light of the second sermon, must be understood to mean an action 'suitable to our whole nature,' as containing a principle of ' reflex approbation' In other words, the good action is so because approved by conscience.

some places he certainly adopts.[1] Hutcheson, on the other
hand, gives a plain definition of the object which this faculty
approves. It consists in 'affections tending to the happiness
of others and the moral perfection of the mind possessing
them.' If in this definition by 'tending to' may be understood 'of which the motive is'—an interpretation which
the general tenor of Hutcheson's view would justify—it
implies in effect that the morally good lies in desires of
which the object is not pleasure. That desire for moral
perfection, if there is such a thing, is not desire for pleasure
is obvious enough; nor could desire for the happiness of
others be taken to be so except through confusion between
determination by the conception of another's good, to which
his apparent pleasure is rightly or wrongly taken as a
guide, and by the imagination of a pleasure to be experienced
by oneself in sympathy with the pleasure of another. Nor
is it doubtful that Hutcheson himself, though he might
have hesitated to identify moral evil, as selfishness, with the
living for pleasure, yet understood by the morally good the
living for objects wholly different from pleasure. The
question is whether the recognition of such motives is
logically compatible with his doctrine that reason gives no
ends, but is only a 'subservient power' of calculating means.
If feeling, undetermined by thought or reason, can alone
supply motives, and of feeling, thus undetermined, nothing
can be said but that it is pleasant or painful, what motive
can there be but imagination of one's own pleasure or pain
—*one's own*, for if imagination is merely the return of
feeling in fainter form, no one can imagine any feeling, any
more than he can originally feel it, except as his own?

26. The work of reason in constituting the moral judgment
('I ought'), as well as the moral motive ('I must, because I
ought'), could not find due recognition in an age which
took its notion of reason from Locke. The only theory then
known which found the source of moral distinctions in
reason was Clarke's, and Clarke's notion of reason was
essentially the same as that which appears in Locke's
account of demonstrative knowledge.[2] It was in truth

[1] See a passage towards the end of
Sermon III, 'Reasonable self-love and
conscience are the chief,' &c &c, also
a passage towards the end of Sermon
XI, 'Let it be allowed though virtue,'
&c &c.

[2] See Clarke's Boyle Lectures, Vol.
II, proposition 1. The germ of Clarke's
doctrine of morals is to be found in
Locke's occasional assimilation of
moral to mathematical truth and certainty (Cf Essay. Book IV, ch. 4 sec 7,
and ch 12 sec 8

derived from the procedure of mathematics, and only applicable to the comparison of quantities. Clarke talks loftily
about the Eternal Reason of things, but by this he means
nothing definite except the laws of proportion, and when he
finds the virtue of an act to consist in conformity to this
Eternal Reason, the inevitable rejoinder is the question—
Between what quantities is this virtue a proportion?[1]   In
Shaftesbury first appears a doctrine of moral sense. Over
and above the social and self-regarding affections proper to
a 'sensible' creature, the characteristic of man is a 'rational
affection' for goodness as consisting in the proper adjustment of the two orders of 'sensible' affection. This rational
affection is not only a possible motive to action—it is the
only motive that can make that character good of which
human action is the expression ; for with Shaftesbury, though
a balance of the social and self-affections constitutes the
goodness of those affections, yet the man is only good as
actuated by affection for this goodness, and 'should the
sensible affections stand ever so much amiss, yet if they
prevail not because of those other rational affections spoken
of, the person is esteemed virtuous.'[2]   Such a notion, it is
clear, if it had met with a psychology answering it, had only
to be worked out in order to become Kant's doctrine of the
rational will as determined by reverence for law ; but
Shaftesbury had no such psychology, nor, with his aristo-
cratic indifference to completeness of system, does he seem
ever to have felt the want of it. He never asked himself
what precisely was the theory of reason implied in the
admission of an affection 'rational' in the sense, not that
reason calculates the means to its satisfaction, but that it is
determined by an object only possible for a rational as
distinct from a 'sensible' creature ; and just because he did
not do so, he slipped into adaptations to the current view of
the good as pleasure and of desire as determined by the
pleasure incidental to its own satisfaction. Thus, to a
disciple, who wished to extract from Shaftesbury a more
definite system than Shaftesbury had himself formed, the
'rational affection' would become desire for a specific feeling
of pleasure supposed to arise on the view of good actions as
exhibiting a proper balance between social and self-regarding

Marginal notes: reason in-compatible with true view

Marginal notes: Shaftes-bury's doc-trine of rational affection ;

[1] Cf Hume, Vol. II , p 238
[2] 'Inq. concerning Virtue,' Book I pt 2. sec 4   Cf. Sec. 3 sub init.

spoilt by
doctrine of
moral
sense.'
affections. This pleasure is the 'moral sense,' [1] with which Shaftesbury's name has become specially associated, while the doctrine of rational affection, with which he certainly himself connected it, but which it essentially vitiates, has been forgotten.

27. That doctrine is of value as maintaining that those actions only are morally good of which the rational affection is the motive, in the sense that they spring from a character which this affection has fashioned. But if the rational affection is desire for the pleasure of moral sense, we find ourselves in the contradiction of supposing that the only motive which can produce good acts is one that cannot operate till after the good acts have been done. It is desire for a pleasure which yet can only have been experienced as a consequence of the previous existence of the desire. Shaftesbury himself, indeed, treats the moral sense of pleasure in the contemplation of good actions as a pleasure in the view of the right adjustment between the social and self-affections. If, however, on the strength of this, we suppose that certain actions are first done, not from the rational affection, but yet good, and that then remembrance of the pleasure found in the view of their goodness, exciting desire, becomes motive to another set of acts which are thus done from rational affection, we contradict his statement that only the rational affection forms the goodness of man, and are none the nearer to an account of what does form it. To say that it is the 'right adjustment' of the two orders of affection tells us nothing. Except as suggesting an analogy from the world of art, really inapplicable, but by which Shaftesbury was much influenced, this expression means no more than that goodness is a good state of the affections. From such a circle the outlet most consistent

Conse-
quences of
the latter
with the spirit of that philosophy, which had led Shaftesbury himself to bring down the rational affection to the level of a desire for pleasure, would lie in the notion that a state of the affections is good in proportion as it is productive of pleasure; which again would suggest the question whether the specific pleasure of moral sense itself, the supposed object of rational affection, is more than pleasure in that indefinite

---

[1] In using the term 'moral sense,' Shaftesbury himself, no doubt, meant to convey the notion that the moral faculty was one of 'intuition,' in Locke's sense of the word, as opposed to reason, the faculty of demonstration, rather than that it was a susceptibility of pleasure and pain.

anticipation of pleasure which the view of affections so ordered tends to raise in us.

28. Here, again, neither Butler nor Hutcheson, while they avoid the most obvious inconsistency of Shaftesbury's doctrine, do much for its positive development. With each the 'moral faculty,' though it is said to approve and disapprove, is still a 'sense' or 'sentiment,' a specific susceptibility of pleasure in the contemplation of goodness; and each again recognises a 'reflex affection' for—a desire to have—the goodness of which the view conveys this pleasure. But they neither have the merit of stating so explicitly as Shaftesbury does that this rational affection alone constitutes the goodness of man, as man; nor, on the other hand, do they lapse, as he does, into the representation of it as a desire for the pleasure which the view of goodness causes. Butler, indeed, having no account to give of the goodness which is approved or morally pleasing, but the fact that it is so pleasing, could logically have nothing to say against the view that this reflex affection is merely a desire for this particular sort of pleasure; but by representing it as equivalent in its highest form to the love of God, to the longing of the soul after Him as the perfectly good, he in effect gives it a wholly different character. Hutcheson, by his definition of the object of moral approbation,[1] which is also a definition of the object of the reflex affection, is fairly entitled to exclude, as he does, along with the notion that the goodness which we morally approve is the quality of exciting the pleasure of such approval, the notion that 'affection for goodness' means desire for this or any other pleasure. But, in spite of his express rejection of this view, the question will still return, how either a faculty of consciousness of which we only know that it is 'a kind of taste or relish,' or a desire from the determination of which reason is expressly excluded, can have any other object than pleasure or pain.

Is an act done for 'virtue's sake' done for pleasure of moral sense?

29. In contrast with these well-meant efforts to derive that distinction between the selfish and unselfish, between the pleasant and the morally good, which the Christian conscience requires, from principles that do not admit of it, Hume's system has the merit of relative consistency. He sees that the two sides of Locke's doctrine—one that thought originates nothing, but takes its objects as given in feeling, the other that the good which is object of desire is pleasant

Hume excludes every object of desire but pleasure

[1] See above, sec. 25

feeling—are inseparable. Hence he decisively rejects every notion of rational or unselfish affections, which would imply that they are other than desires for pleasure; of virtue, which would imply that it antecedently determines, rather than is constituted by, the specific pleasure of moral sense; and of this pleasure itself, which would imply that anything but the view of tendencies to produce pleasure can excite it. But here his consistency stops. The principle which forbade him to admit any object of desire but pleasure is practically forgotten in his account of the sources of pleasure, and its being so forgotten is the condition of the desire for pleasure being made plausibly to serve as a foundation for morals. It is the assumption of pleasures determined by objects only possible for reason, made in the treatise on the Passions, that prepares the way for the rejection of reason, as supplying either moral motive or moral standard, in the treatise on Morals.

His account of 'direct passions'

30. 'The passions' is Hume's generic term for 'impressions of reflection'—appetites, desires, and emotions alike. He divides them into two main orders, 'direct and indirect,' both 'founded on pain and pleasure.' The *direct* passions are enumerated as 'desire and aversion, grief and joy, hope and fear, along with volition' or will. These 'arise from good and evil' (which are the same as pleasure and pain) 'most naturally and with least preparation.' 'Desire arises from good, aversion from evil, considered simply.' They become will or volition, 'when the good may be attained or evil avoided by any action of the mind or body'—will being simply 'the internal impression we feel and are conscious of, when we knowingly give rise to any new motion of our body or new perception of our mind.' 'When good is certain or probable it produces joy' (which is described also as a pleasure produced by pleasure or by the imagination of pleasure); 'when it is uncertain, it gives rise to hope.' To these the corresponding opposites are grief and fear. We must suppose them to be distinguished from desire and aversion as being what he elsewhere calls 'pure emotions'; such as do not, like desires, 'immediately excite us to action.' Given such an immediate impression of pleasure or pain as excites a 'distinct passion' of one or other of these kinds, and supposing it to 'arise from an object related to ourselves or others,' it excites mediately, through this relation, the new impressions of pride

or humility, love or hatred—pride when the object is related to oneself, love when it is related to another person. These are *indirect* passions. They do not tend to displace the immediate impression which is the condition of their excitement, but being themselves agreeable give it additional force. 'Thus a suit of fine clothes produces pleasure from their beauty; and this pleasure produces the direct passions, or the impressions of volition and desire. Again, when these clothes are considered as belonging to oneself, the double relation conveys to us the sentiment of pride, which is an indirect passion; and the pleasure which attends that passion returns back to the direct affections, and gives new force to our desire or volition, joy or hope.'[1]

All desire is for pleasure

31. Alongside of the unqualified statement that 'the passions, both direct and indirect, are founded on pain and pleasure,' and the consequent theory of them, we find the curiously cool admission that 'beside pain and pleasure, the direct passions frequently arise from a natural impulse or instinct, which is perfectly unaccountable. Of this kind is the desire of punishment to our enemies, and of happiness to our friends; hunger and lust, and a few other bodily appetites. These passions, properly speaking, produce good and evil, and proceed not from them like the other affections.'[2] In this casual way appears the recognition of that difference of the desire for imagined pleasure from appetite proper on the one side, and on the other from desire determined by reason, which it is the point of Hume's system to ignore. The question is, how many of the pleasures in which he finds the springs of human conduct are other than products of a desire which is not itself moved by pleasure, or emotions excited by objects which reason constitutes.

Yet he admits 'passions' which produce pleasure, but proceed not from it.

[1] Vol. ii, pp. 214, 215 Cf. pp 76, 90, 153 and 203.

[2] P. 215 The passage in the 'Dissertation on the Passions' (Vol. iv, 'Dissertation on the Passions,' sub init.), which corresponds to the one here quoted, throws light on the relation in which Hume's later redaction of his theory stands to the earlier, as occasionally disguising, but never removing, its inconsistencies. 'Some objects, by being naturally conformable or contrary to passion, excite an agreeable or painful sensation, and are thence called *good* or *evil*. The punishment of an adversary, by gratifying revenge, is good the sickness of a companion, by affecting friendship, is evil' Here he avoids the inconsistency of admitting in so many words a 'desire' which is not for a pleasure. But the inconsistency really remains What is the passion, the 'conformability' to which of an object in the supposed cases constitutes pleasure? Since it is neither an appetite (such as hunger), nor an emotion (such as pride), it remains that it is a desire, and a desire which, though the 'gratification' of it is a pleasure, canno be a desire for that or any other pleasure.

Desire for
objects, as
he under-
stands it,
excluded
by his
theory of
impres-
sions and
ideas.

32. In what sense, we have first to ask, do Hume's principles justify him in speaking of desire *for an object* at all.
'The appearance of an object to the senses' is the same
thing as 'an impression becoming present to the mind,'[1] and
if this is true of impressions of sense it cannot be less true
of impressions of reflection. If sense 'offers not its object
as anything distinct from itself,' neither can desire. Its
object, according to Hume, is an idea of a past impression;
but this, if we take him at his word, can merely mean that
a feeling which, when at its liveliest, was pleasant, has
passed into a fainter stage, which, in contrast with the
livelier, is pain—the pain of want, which is also a wish for
the renewal of the original pleasure. In fact, however, when
Hume or anyone else (whether he admit the possibility of
desiring an object not previously found pleasant, or no),
speaks of desire for an object, he means something different
from this. He means either desire for an object that causes
pleasure, which is impossible except so far as the original
pleasure has been—consciously to the subject feeling it—
pleasure caused by an object, *i.e*, a feeling determined by
the conception of a thing under relations to self; or else
desire for pleasure as an object, *i.e.*, not merely desire for
the revival of some feeling which, having been pleasant as
'impression,' survives without being pleasant as 'idea,' but
desire determined by the consciousness of self as a permanent subject that has been pleased, and is to be pleased again.
It is here, then, as in the case of the attempted derivation
of space, or of identity and substance, from impressions of
sense. In order to give rise to such an impression of reflection as desire for an object is, either the original impression
of sense, or the idea of this, must be other than Hume could
allow it to be. Either the original impression must be other
than a satisfaction of appetite, other than a sight, smell,
sound, &c., or the idea must be other than a copy of the impression. One or other must be determined by conceptions
not derived from feeling, the correlative conceptions of self
and thing. Thus, in order to be able to interpret his
primary class of impressions of reflection[2] as desires for
objects, or for pleasures as good, Hume has already made
the assumption that is needed for the transition to that

[1] See General Introduction, paragraph 208.   [2] See above, sec. 19.

secondary class of impressions through which he has to account for morality. He has assumed that thought determines feeling, and not merely reproduces it. Even if the materials out of which it constructs the determining object be merely remembered pleasures, the object is no more to be identified with these materials than the living body with its chemical constituents.

33. In the account of the 'indirect passions' the term *object* is no longer applied, as in the account of the direct ones, to the pleasure or pain which excites desire or aversion. It is expressly transferred to the self or other person, to whom the 'exciting causes' of pride and love must be severally related. 'Pride and humility, though directly contrary, have yet the same object,' viz., self; but since they are contrary, ''tis impossible this object can be their cause, or sufficient alone to excite them. . . . . We must therefore make a distinction betwixt that idea which excites them, and that to which they direct their view when excited. . . . . The first idea that is presented to the mind is that of the cause or productive principle. This excites the passion connected with it; and that passion, when excited, turns our view to another idea, which is that of self. . . . . The first idea represents the *cause*, the second the *object* of the passion.'[1] Again a further distinction must be made 'in the causes of the passion betwixt that *quality* which operates, and the *subject* on which it is placed. A man, for instance, is vain of a beautiful house which belongs to him, or which he has himself built or contrived. Here the object of the passion is himself, and the cause is the beautiful house; which cause again is subdivided into two parts, viz., the quality which operates upon the passion, and the subject in which the quality inheres. The quality is the beauty, and the subject is the house, considered as his property or contrivance.'[2] It is next found that the operative qualities which produce pride, however various, agree in this, that they produce pleasure—a 'separate pleasure,' independent of the resulting pride. In all cases, again, 'the subjects to which these qualities adhere are either parts of ourselves or something nearly related to us.' The conclusion is that 'the cause, which excites the passion, is related to the

Pride determined by reference to self.

---

[1] Vol. ii., pp. 77 and 78   [2] Ibid., p. 79.

object which nature has attributed to the passion; the
sensation, which the cause separately produces, is related to
the sensation of the passion: from this double relation of
ideas and impressions the passion is derived.'[1] The ideas,
it will be observed, are severally those of the exciting
'subject' (in the illustrative case quoted, the beautiful
house) and of the 'object' self; the impressions are severally
the pleasure immediately caused by the 'subject' (in the
case given, the pleasure of feeling beauty) and the pleasure
of pride. The relation between the ideas may be any of the
'natural ones' that regulate association.[2] In the supposed
case it is that of cause and effect, since a man's property
'produces effects on him and he on it.' The relation between
the impressions must be that of resemblance—this, as we are
told by the way (somewhat strangely, if impressions are
only stronger ideas), being the only possible relation between
impressions—the resemblance of one pleasure to another.

This
means that
it takes its
character
from that
which is
not a
possible
'impres-
sion'

34. Pride, then, is a special sort of pleasure excited by
another special sort of pleasure, and the distinction of the
two sorts of pleasure from each other depends on the
character which each derives from an idea—one from the
idea of self, the other from the idea of some 'quality in a
subject,' which may be the beauty of a picture, or the
achievement of an ancestor, or any other quality as unlike
these as these are unlike each other, so long as the idea of it
is capable of association with the idea of self. Apart from
such determination by ideas, the pleasure of pride itself and
the pleasure which excites it, on the separateness of which
from each other Hume insists, could only be separate in
time and degree of liveliness—a separation which might
equally obtain between successive feelings of pride. Of
neither could anything be said but that it was pleasant—
more or less pleasant than the other, before or after it, as
the case might be. Is the idea, then, that gives each impression its character, itself an impression grown fainter?
It should be so, of course, if Hume's theory of consciousness
is to hold good, either in its general form, or in its application to morals, according to which all actions, those moved
by pride among the rest, have pleasure for their ultimate
motive; and no doubt he would have said that it was so.

' Vol II., pp 84, 85.   ² Book I., part 1, secs 4 and 5.

The idea of the beauty of a picture, for instance, is the original impression which it 'makes on the senses' as more faintly retained by the mind. But is the original impression *merely* an impression—an impression undetermined by conceptions, and of which, therefore, as it is to the subject of it, nothing can be said, but simply that it is pleasant? This, too, in the particular instance of beauty, Hume seems to hold;[1] but if it is so, the idea of beauty, as determined by reference to the impression, is determined by reference to the indeterminate, and we know no more of the separate pleasure that excites the pleasure of pride, when we are told that its source is an impression of beauty, than we did before. Apart from any other reference, we only know that pride is a pleasure excited by a pleasure which is itself excited by a pleasure grown fainter. Of effect, proximate cause, and ultimate cause, only one and the same thing can be said, viz., that each feels pleasant. Meanwhile in regard to that other relation from which the pleasure of pride, on its part, is supposed to take its character, the same question arises. This pleasure 'has self for its object.' Is self, then, an impression stronger or fainter? Can one feeling be said without nonsense to have another feeling for its object? If it can, what specification is gained for a pleasure or pain by reference to an object of which, as a mere feeling, nothing more can be said than that it is a pleasure or pain? If, on the other hand, the idea of self, relation to which makes the feeling of pride what it is, and through it determines action, is not a copy of any impression of sense or reflection—not a copy of any sight or sound, any passion or emotion[2]—how can it be true that the ultimate determination of action in all cases arises from pleasure or pain?

35. From the pressure of such questions as these Hume offers us two main subterfuges. One is furnished by his account of the self, as 'that succession of related ideas and impressions of which we have an intimate memory and consciousness'[3]—an account which, to an incurious reader, conveys the notion that 'self,' if not exactly an impression, is something in the nature of an impression, while yet it seems to give the required determination to the impression which has this for its 'object.' It is evident, however, that

Hume's attempt to represent idea of self as derived from impression.

---

[1] Vol. ii , p. 96 , iv , 'Dissertation on the Passions,' ii. 7.

[2] Intr to Vol i., paragraph 208.

[3] Vol. ii., p 77, &c

its plausibility depends entirely on the qualification of the
'succession, &c.,' as that of which we have an 'intimate consciousness.' The succession of impressions, simply as such,
and in the absence of relation to a single subject, is nothing
intelligible at all. Hume, indeed, elsewhere represents it as
constituting time, which, as we have previously shown,[1] by
itself it could not properly be said to do; but if it could,
the characterisation of pleasure as having time for its object
would not be much to the purpose. The successive impressions and ideas are further said to be 'related,' *i.e.*,
naturally related, according to Hume's sense of the term;
but this we have found means no more than that when two
feelings have been often felt to be either like each other or
'contiguous,' the recurrence of one is apt to be followed by
the recurrence in fainter form of the other. This characteristic of the succession brings it no nearer to the intelligible unity which it must have, in order to be an object of
which the idea makes the pleasure of pride what it is. The
notion of its having such unity is really conveyed by the
statement that we have an 'intimate consciousness' of it.
It is through these words, so to speak, that we read into the
definition of self that conception of it which we carry with
us, but of which it states the reverse. Now, however
difficult it may be to say what this intimate consciousness is,
it is clear that it cannot be one of the feelings, stronger or
fainter—impressions or ideas—which the first part of the
definition tells us form a succession, for this would imply
that one of them was at the same time all the rest. Nor
yet can it be a compound of them all, for the fact that they
are a succession is incompatible with their forming a compound. Here, then, is a consciousness, which is not an
impression, and which we can only take to be derived from
impressions by supposing these to be what they first become
in relation to this consciousness. In saying that we have
such a consciousness of the succession of impressions, we
say in effect that we are other than the succession. How,
then, without contradiction, can our self be said to *be* the
succession of impressions, &c.—a succession which in the very
next word has to be qualified in a way that implies we are
other than it? This question, once put, will save us from

[1] Intr to Vol 1, sec 261

surprise at finding that in one place, among frequent repetitions of the account of self already given, the 'succession &c.' is dropped, and for it substituted '*the individual person* of whose actions and sentiments each of us is intimately conscious.'[1]

36. The other way of gaining an apparent determination for the impression, pride, without making it depend on relation to that which is not an impression at all, corresponds to that appeal to the 'anatomist' by the suggestion of which, it will be remembered, Hume avoids the troublesome question, how the simple impressions of sense, undetermined by relation, can have that definite character which they must have if they are to serve as the elements of knowledge. The question in that case being really one that concerns the simple impression, as it is for the consciousness of the subject of it, Hume's answer is in effect a reference to what it is for the physiologist. So in regard to pride; the question being what character it can have, for the conscious subject of it, to distinguish it from any other pleasant feeling, except such as is derived from a conception which is not an impression, Hume is ready on occasion to suggest that it has the distinctive character which for the physiologist it would derive from the nerves organic to it, if such nerves could be traced. 'We must suppose that nature has given to the organs of the human mind a certain disposition fitted to produce a peculiar impression or emotion, which we call PRIDE: to this emotion she has assigned a certain idea, viz., that of SELF, which it never fails to produce. This contrivance of nature is easily conceived. We have many instances of such a situation of affairs. The nerves of the nose and palate are so disposed, as in certain circumstances to convey such peculiar sensations to the mind; the sensations of lust and hunger always produce in us the idea of those peculiar objects, which are suitable to each appetite. These two circumstances are united in pride. The organs are so disposed as to produce the passion; and the passion, after its production, naturally produces a certain idea.'[2]

Another device is to suggest a physiological account of pride.

37. Here, it will be noticed, the doctrine, that the pleasant emotion of pride derives its specific character from relation to the idea of self, is dropped. The emotion we call pride is

Fallacy of this.

[1] Vol. II, p. 84.　　　[2] Vol. II., p. 85.

It does not
tell us
what pride
is to the
subject of
it.
supposed to be first produced, and then, in virtue of its
specific character as pride, to *produce* the idea of self.[1] If
the idea of self, then, does not give the pleasure its specific
character, what does? 'That disposition fitted to produce
it,' Hume answers, which belongs to the 'organs of the
human mind.' Now either this is the old story of explaining
the soporific qualities of opium by its *vis soporifica*, or it means
that the distinction of the pleasure of pride from other
pleasures, like the distinction of a smell from a taste, is
due to a particular kind of nervous irritation that conditions
it, and may presumably be ascertained by the physiologist.
Whether such a physical condition of pride can be discovered or no, it is not to the purpose to dispute. The point
to observe is that, if discovered, it would not afford an
answer to the question to which an answer is being sought
—to the question, namely, what the emotion of pride is to
the conscious subject of it. If it were found to be condi-
tioned by as specific a nervous irritation as the sensations of
smell and taste to which Hume assimilates it, it would yet
be no more the consciousness of such irritation than is the
smell of a rose to the person smelling it. In the one case
as in the other, the feeling, as it is to the subject of it, can
only be determined by relation to other feelings or other
modes of consciousness. It is by such a relation that, according to Hume's general account of it, pride is determined,
but the relation is to the consciousness of an object which,
not being any form of feeling, has no proper place in his
psychology. Hence in the passage before us he tries to substitute for it a physical determination of the emotion, which
for the subject of it is no determination at all; and, having
gained an apparent specification for it in this way, to represent as its product that idea of a distinctive object which
he had previously treated as necessary to constitute it. Pride
produces the idea of self, just as 'the sensations of hunger
and lust always produce in us the idea of those peculiar
objects, which are suitable to each appetite.' Now it is a
large assumption in regard to animals other than men, that,
because hunger and lust move them to eat and generate,
they so move them through the intervention of any ideas *of
objects* whatever—an assumption which in the absence of

[1] Cf. Vol. IV, 'Dissertation on the Passions,' II. 2.

language on the part of the animals it is impossible to verify —and one still more questionable, that the ideas of objects which these appetites (if it be so) produce in the animals, except as determined by self-consciousness, are ideas in the same sense as the idea of self. But at any rate, if such feelings produce ideas of peculiar objects, it must be in virtue of the distinctive character which, as feelings, they have for the subjects of them. The withdrawal, however, of determination by the idea of self from the emotion of pride, leaves it with no distinctive character whatever, and therefore with nothing by which we may explain its production of that idea as analogous to the production by hunger, if we admit such to take place, of the 'idea of the peculiar object suited to it.'

38. If, in Hume's account of pride, for *pleasure*, wherever it occurs, is substituted *pain*, it becomes his account of humility. A criticism of one account is equally a criticism of the other; and with him every passion that ' has self for its object,' according as it is pleasant or painful, is included under one or other of these designations. In like manner, every passion that has ' some other thinking being' for its object, according as it is pleasant or painful, is either love or hatred. To these the key is to be found in the same ' double relation of impressions and ideas' by which pride and humility are explained. If beautiful pictures, for instance, belong not to oneself but to another person, they tend to excite not pride but esteem, which is a form of love. The idea of them is ' naturally related' to the idea of the person to whom they belong, and they cause a separate pleasure which naturally excites the resembling impression of which this other person is the object. Write ' other person,' in short, where before was written ' self,' and the account of pride and humility becomes the account of love and hatred. Of this pleasure determined by the idea of another person, or of which such a person ' is the object,' Hume gives no *rationale*, and, failing this, it must be taken to imply the same power of determining feeling on the part of a conception not derived from feeling, which we have found to be implied in the pleasure of which self is the object. All his pains and ingenuity in the second part of the book ' on the Passions,' are spent on illustrating the ' double relation of impressions and ideas '—on characteris-

Account of love involves the same difficulties;

and a
further one
as to
nature of
sympathy.
ing the separate pleasures which excite the pleasure of love,
and showing how the idea of the object of the exciting
pleasure is related to the idea of the beloved person. The
objection to this part of his theory, which most readily suggests itself to a reader, arises from the essential discrepancy
which in many cases seems to lie between the exciting and
the excited pleasure. The drinking of fine wine, and the
feeling of love, are doubtless 'resembling impressions,' so
far as each is pleasant, and from the idea of the wine the
transition is natural to that of the person who gives it; but
is there really anything, it will be asked, in my enjoyment
of a rich man's wine, that tends to make me love him, even
in the wide sense of 'love' which Hume admits? This
objection, it will be found, is so far anticipated by Hume,
that in most cases he treats the exciting pleasure as taking
its character from sympathy. Thus it is not chiefly the
pleasure of ear, sight, and palate, caused by the rich man's
music, and gardens, and wine, that excites our love for him,
but the pleasure we experience through sympathy with his
pleasure in them.[1] The explanation of love being thus
thrown back on sympathy (which had previously served to
explain that form of pride which is called 'love of fame'), we
have to ask whether sympathy is any less dependent than we
have found pride to be on an originative, as distinct from a
merely reproductive, reason.

Hume's ac-
count of
sympathy.
39. 'When any affection is infused by sympathy, it is at
first known only by its effects, and by those external signs
in the countenance and conversation which convey an idea
of it.' By inference from effect to cause, 'we are convinced
of the reality of the passion,' conceiving it 'to belong to
another person, as we conceive any other matter of fact.'
This idea of another's affection 'is presently converted into
an impression, and acquires such a degree of force and vivacity as to become the very passion itself, and produce an
equal emotion as any original affection.' The conversion is
not difficult to account for when we reflect that 'all ideas
are borrowed from impressions, and that these two kinds of
perceptions differ only in the degrees of force and vivacity
with which they strike upon the soul. . . . As this difference
may be removed in some measure by a relation between the

[1] Vol. II., p. 147

impressions and ideas '—in the case before us, the relation between the impression of one's own person and the idea of another's, by which the vivacity of the former may be conveyed to the latter—''tis no wonder an idea of a sentiment or passion may by this means be so enlivened as to become the very sentiment or passion.'[1]

40. Upon this it must be remarked that the inference from the external signs of an affection, according to Hume's doctrine of inference, can only mean that certain impressions of the other person's words and gestures call up the ideas of their 'usual attendants'; which, again, must mean either that they convey the belief in certain exciting circumstances experienced by the other man, and the expectation of certain acts to follow upon his words and gestures; or else that they suggest to the spectator the memory of certain like manifestations on his own part and through these of the emotion which in his own case was their antecedent. Either way, the spectator's idea of the other person's affection is in no sense a copy of it, or that affection in a fainter form. If it is an idea of an impression *of reflection* at all, it is of such an impression as experienced by the spectator himself, and determined, as Hume admits, by his consciousness of himself; nor could any conveyance of vivacity to the idea make it other than that impression. How it should become to the spectator consciously at once another's impression and his own, remains unexplained. Hume only seems to explain it by means of the equivocation lurking in the phrase, 'idea of another's affection.' The reader, not reflecting that, according to the copying theory, so far as the idea is a copy of anything *in the other*, it can only be a copy of certain 'external signs, &c.,' and so far as it is a copy *of an affection*, only of an affection experienced by the man who has the idea, thinks of it as being to the spectator the other's affection minus a certain amount of vivacity—the restoration of which will render it an impression at once his own and the other's. It can in truth only be so in virtue (*a*) of an interpretation of words and gestures, as related to a person, which no suggestion by impressions of their usual attendants can account for, and in virtue (*b*) of there being such a conceived identity, or unity in difference, between the spectator's own

It implies a self-consciousness not reducible to impressions.

---

[1] Vol II., pp. 111–114.

person and the person of the other that the same impression, in being determined by his consciousness of himself, is determined also by his consciousness of the other as an 'alter ego.' Thus sympathy, according to Hume's account of it, so soon as that account is rationalized, is found to involve the determination of pleasure and pain, not merely by self-consciousness, but by a self-consciousness which is also self-identification with another. If self-consciousness cannot in any of its functions be reduced to an impression or succession of impressions, least of all can it in this. On the other hand, if it is only through its constitutive action, its reflection of itself, upon successive impressions of sense that these become the permanent objects which we know, we can understand how by a like action on certain impressions of reflection, certain emotions and desires, it constitutes those objects of interest which we love as ourselves.

Ambiguity in his account of benevolence.

41. Pride, love, and sympathy, then, are the motives which Hume must have granted him, if his moral theory is to march. Sympathy is not only necessary to his explanation of that most important form of pride which is the motive to a man in maintaining a character with his neighbours when 'nothing is to be gained by it'—nothing, that is, beyond the immediate pleasure it gives—and of all forms of 'love,' except those of which the exciting cause lies in the pleasures of beauty and sexual appetite: he finds in it also the ground of benevolence. Where he first treats of benevolence, indeed, this does not appear. Unlike pride and humility, we are told, which 'are pure emotions of the soul, unattended with any desire, and not immediately exciting us to action, love and hatred are not completed within themselves. . . Love is always followed by a desire of the happiness of the person beloved, and an aversion to his misery; as hatred produces a desire of the misery, and an aversion to the happiness, of the person hated.'[1] This actual sequence of 'benevolence' and 'anger' severally upon love and hatred is due, it appears, to 'an original constitution of the mind' which

It is a desire, and therefore has pleasure for its object.

cannot be further accounted for. That benevolence is no essential part of love is clear from the fact that the latter passion 'may express itself in a hundred ways, and may subsist a considerable time, without our reflecting on the

---

[1] Vol. ii., p 153.

happiness of its object.' Doubtless, when we do reflect on it, we desire the happiness; but, 'if nature had so pleased, love might have been unattended with any such desire.[1] So far, the view given tallies with what we have already quoted from the summary account of the direct and indirect passions, where the 'desire of punishment to our enemies and happiness to our friends' is expressly left outside the general theory of the passions as a 'natural impulse wholly unaccountable,' a 'direct passion' which yet does not proceed from pleasure.' With his instinct for consistency, however, Hume could scarcely help seeking to assimilate this alien element to his definition of desire as universally for pleasure; and accordingly, while the above view of benevolence is never in so many words given up, an essentially different one appears a little further on, which by help of the doctrine of sympathy at once makes the connection of benevolence with love more accountable, and brings it under the general definition of desire. 'Benevolence,' we are there told, 'is an original pleasure arising from the pleasure of the person beloved, and a pain proceeding from his pain, from which correspondence of impressions there arises a subsequent desire of his pleasure and aversion to his pain.'[2]

What pleasure?

42. Now, strictly construed, this passage seems to efface the one clear distinction of benevolence that had been previously insisted on—that it is a desire, namely, as opposed to a pure emotion. If benevolence *is* an 'original pleasure arising from the pleasure of the person beloved,' it is identical with love, so far as sympathy is an exciting cause of love, instead of being distinguished from it as desire from emotion. We must suppose, however, that the sentence was carelessly put together, and that Hume did not really mean to identify benevolence with the pleasure spoken of in the former part of it (for which his proper term is simply sympathy), but with the desire for that pleasure, spoken of in the latter part. In that case we find that benevolence forms no exception to the general definition of

Pleasure of sympathy with the pleasure of another.

[1] Vol ii, p 154.

[2] Vol. ii, p. 170 Compare Vol iv., 'Inquiry concerning the Principles of Morals,' Appendix ii, *note* 3, where 'general benevolence,' also called 'humanity,' is identified with sympathy.' 'Benevolence is naturally divided into two kinds, the *general* and the *particular*. The first is, where we have no friendship, or connection, or esteem for the person, but feel only a general sympathy with him, or a compassion for his pains, and a congratulation with his pleasures,' &c. &c.

desire. It is desire for one's own pleasure, but for a pleasure received through the communication by sympathy of the pleasure of another. In like manner, the sequence of benevolence upon love, instead of being an unaccountable 'disposition of nature,' would seem explicable, as merely the ordinary sequence upon a pleasant emotion of a desire for its renewal. Though it be not strictly the pleasant emotion of love, but that of sympathy, for which benevolence is the desire, yet if sympathy is necessary to the excitement of love, it will equally follow that benevolence attends on love. Pleasure sympathised with, we may suppose, first excites the secondary emotion of love, and afterwards, when reflected on, that desire for its continuance or renewal, which is benevolence. That love 'should express itself in a hundred ways, and subsist a considerable time' without any consciousness of benevolence, will merely be the natural relation of emotion to desire. When a pleasure is in full enjoyment, it cannot be so reflected on as to excite desire ; and thus, if benevolence is desire for that pleasure in the pleasure of another, which is an exciting cause of love, the latter emotion must naturally subsist and express itself for some time before it reaches the stage in which reflection on its cause, and with it benevolent desire, ensues.

All 'passions' equally interested or disinterested.

43. This *rationale*, however, of the relation between love and benevolence is not explicitly given by Hume himself. He nowhere expressly withdraws the exception, made in favour of benevolence, to the rule that all desire is for pleasure—an exception which, once admitted, undermines his whole system—or tells us in so many words that benevolence is desire for pleasure to oneself in the pleasure of another. In an important note to the Essays,[1] indeed, he distinctly puts benevolence on the same footing with such desires as avarice or ambition. 'A man is no more interested when he seeks his own glory, than when the happiness of his friend is the object of his wishes ; nor is he any more disinterested when he sacrifices his own ease and quiet to public good, than when he labours for the gratification of avarice or ambition.' . . . 'Though the satisfaction of these latter passions gives us enjoyment, yet the prospect of this enjoyment is not the cause of the passion, but, on the

---

[1] 'Inquiry concerning Human Understanding,' note to sec. 1. In the editions after the second, this note was omitted.

contrary, the passion is antecedent to the enjoyment, and without the former the latter could not possibly exist.' In other words, if 'passion' means *desire*—and, as applied to *emotion*, the designation 'interested' or 'disinterested' has no meaning—every passion is equally disinterested in the sense of presupposing an 'enjoyment' a pleasant emotion, antecedent to that which consists in its satisfaction; but at the same time equally interested in the sense of being a desire for such enjoyment. Whether from a wish to find acceptance, however, or because forms of man's good-will to man forced themselves on his notice which forbade the consistent development of his theory, Hume is always much more explicit about the disinterestedness of benevolence in the former sense than about its interestedness in the latter.[1] Accordingly he does not avail himself of such an explanation of its relation to love as that above indicated, which by avowedly reducing benevolence to a desire for pleasure, while it simplified his system, might have revolted the 'common sense' even of the eighteenth century. He prefers —as his manner is, when he comes upon a question which he cannot face—to fall back on a 'disposition of nature' as the ground of the 'conjunction' of benevolence with love. There is a form of benevolence, however, which would seem as little explicable by such natural conjunction as by reduction to a desire for sympathetic pleasure. How is it that active good-will is shown towards those whom, according to Hume's theory of love, it should be impossible to love—towards those with whom intercourse is impossible, or from whom, if intercourse is possible, we can derive no such pleasure as is supposed necessary to excite that pleasant emotion, but rather such pain, in sympathy with their pain, as according to the theory should excite hatred? To this question Hume in effect finds an answer in the simple device of using the same terms, 'pity' and 'compassion,' alike for the painful *emotion* produced by the spectacle of another's

Margin notes:

Confusion arises from use of 'passion' alike for desire and emotion.

Of this Hume avails himself in his account of active pity.

---

[1] Attention should be called to a passage at the end of the account of 'self-love' in the Essays, where he seems to revert to the view of benevolence as a desire not *originally* produced by pleasure, but productive of it, and thus passing into a secondary stage in which it is combined with desire for pleasure. He suggests tentatively that 'from the original frame of our temper we may feel a desire for another's happiness or good, which, by means of that affection, becomes our own good, and is afterwards pursued from the combined motives of benevolence and self-enjoyment.'
The passage might have been written by Butler. (Vol IV, 'Inquiry concerning Principles of Morals,' Appendix II)

pain and for 'desire for the happiness of another and
aversion to his misery.'[1] According to the latter account
of it, pity is already 'the same desire' as benevolence,
though 'proceeding from a different principle,' and thus
has a resemblance to the love with which benevolence is
conjoined—a 'resemblance not of feeling or sentiment but
of tendency or direction.'[2] Hence, whereas 'pity' in the
former sense would make us hate those whose pain gives us
pain, by understanding it in the latter sense we can explain
how it leads us to love them, on the principle that one
resembling passion excites another.

Explana-
tion of
apparent
conflict
between
reason and
passion.

44. We are now in a position to review the possible
motives of human action according to Hume. Reason, constituting no objects, affords no motives. 'It is only the
slave of the passions, and can never pretend to any other
office than to serve and obey them.'[3] To any logical thinker
who accepted Locke's doctrine of reason, as having no
other function but to 'lay in order intermediate ideas,' this
followed of necessity. It is the clearness with which Hume
points out that, as it cannot move, so neither can it restrain,
action, that in this regard chiefly distinguishes him from
Locke. The check to any passion, he points out, can only
proceed from some counter-motive, and such a motive
reason, 'having no original influence,' cannot give. Strictly
speaking, then, a passion can only be called unreasonable,
as accompanied by some false judgment, which on its part
must consist in 'disagreement of ideas, considered as copies,
with those objects which they represent;' and 'even then it
is not the passion, properly speaking, which is unreasonable,
but the judgment.' It is nothing against reason—not, as
Locke had inadvertently said, a wrong judgment—'to prefer
my own acknowledged lesser good to my greater.' The only
unreasonableness would lie in supposing that 'my own
acknowledged lesser good,' being preferred, could be attained
by means that would not really lead to it. Hence 'we speak
not strictly when we talk of the combat of reason and
passion.' They can in truth never oppose each other. The
supposition that they do so arises from a confusion between

---

[1] Book ii., part 2, secs 7 and 9.
Within a few lines of each other will
be found the statements (a) that 'pity
is an uneasiness arising from the misery
of others,' and (b) that 'pity is

desire for the happiness of another,'
&c

[2] 'Dissertation on the Passions' (in the
Essays), sec 3, sub-sec 5.

[3] Vol ii, p 195.

'calm passions' and reason—a confusion founded on the fact that the former 'produce little emotion in the mind, while the operation of reason produces none at all.'[1] Calm passions, undoubtedly, do often conflict with the violent ones and even prevail over them, and thus, as the violent passion causes most uneasiness, it is untrue to say with Locke[2] that it is the most pressing uneasiness which always determines action. The calmness of a passion is not to be confounded with weakness, nor its violence with strength. A desire may be calm either because its object is remote, or because it is customary. In the former case, it is true, the desire is likely to be relatively weak; but in the latter case, the calmer the desire, the greater is likely to be its strength, since the repetition of a desire has the twofold effect, on the one hand of diminishing the 'sensible emotion' that accompanies it, on the other hand of 'bestowing a facility in the performance of the action' corresponding to the desire, which in turn creates a new inclination or tendency that combines with the original desire.[3]

45. The distinction, then, between 'reasonable' and 'unreasonable' desires—and it is only *desires* that can be referred to when will, or the determination to action, is in question—in the only sense in which Hume can admit it, is a distinction not of objects but of our situation in regard to them. The object of desire in every case—whether near or remote, whether either by its novelty or by its contrariety to other passions it excites more or less 'sensible emotion'—is still 'good,' *i.e.* pleasure. The greater the pleasure in prospect, the stronger the desire.[4] The only proper question, then, according to Hume, as to the pleasure which in any particular case is an object of desire will be whether it

A 'reasonable' desire means one that excites little emotion.

---

[1] Vol. ii., pp 195, 196.
[2] Above, sec 3.
[3] Vol ii pp 198-200
It will be found that here Hume might have stated his case much more succinctly by avoiding the equivocal use of 'passion' at once for 'desire' and 'emotion.' When a 'passion' is designated as 'calm' or 'violent,' 'passion' means emotion When the terms 'strong' and 'weak' are applied to it, it means 'desire' Since of the strength of any desire there is in truth no test but the resulting action, and habit

facilitates action, if we will persist in asking the idle question about the relative strength of desires we must suppose that the most habitual is the strongest

[4] Cf p 198 'The same good, when near, will cause a violent passion, which, when remote, produces only a calm one' The expression, here, is obviously inaccurate It cannot be the *same good* in Hume's sense, *i e.* equally pleasant in prospect, when remote as when near

Enumeration of possible motives.

is (*a*) an immediate impression of sense, or (*b*) a pleasure of pride, or (*c*) one of sympathy. Under the first head, apparently, he would include pleasures incidental to the satisfaction of appetite, and pleasures corresponding to the several senses—not only the smells and tastes we call 'sweet,' but the sights and sounds we call 'beautiful.'[1] Pleasures of this sort, we must suppose, are the *ultimate* 'exciting causes'[2] of all those secondary ones, which are distinguished from their 'exciting causes' as determined by the ideas either of self or of another thinking person—the pleasures, namely, of pride and sympathy. Sympathetic pleasure, again, will be of two kinds, according as the pleasure in the pleasure of another does or does not excite the further pleasure of love for the other person. If the object desired is none of these pleasures, nor the means to them, it only remains for the follower of Hume to suppose that it is 'pleasure in general'—the object of 'self love.'

If pleasure sole motive, what is the distinction of self-love ?

46. Anyone reading the 'Treatise on Human Nature' alongside of Shaftesbury or Butler would be surprised to find that while sympathy and benevolence fill a very large place in it, self-love 'eo nomine' has a comparatively small one. At first, perhaps, he would please himself with thinking that he had come upon a more 'genial' system of morals. The true account of the matter, however, he will find to be that, whereas with Shaftesbury and his followers the notion of self-love was really determined by opposition to those desires for other objects than pleasure, in the existence of which they really believed, however much the current psychology may have embarrassed their belief, on the other hand with Hume's explicit reduction of all desire to desire for pleasure self-love loses the significance which this opposition gave it, and can have no meaning except as desire for 'pleasure in general' in distinction from this or that particular pleasure.

---

[1] No other account of pleasure in beauty can be extracted from Hume than this—that it is either a 'primary impression of sense,' so far co-ordinate with any pleasant taste or smell that but for an accident of language the term 'beautiful' might be equally applicable to these, or else a pleasure in that indefinite anticipation of pleasure which is called the contemplation of utility.

[2] *Ultimate* because according to Hume the *immediate* exciting cause of a pleasure of pride may be one of love, and *vice versâ* In that case, however a more remote 'exciting cause' of the exciting pleasure must be found in some impressions of sense, if the doctrine that these are the sole 'original impressions' is to be maintained.

Passages from the Essays may be adduced, it is true, where self-love is spoken of under the same opposition under which Shaftesbury and Hutcheson conceived of it, but in these, it will be found, advantage is taken of the ambiguity between 'emotion' and 'desire,' covered by the term 'passion.' That there are sympathetic *emotions*—pleasures occasioned by the pleasure of others—is, no doubt, as cardinal a point in Hume's system as that all *desire* is for pleasure to self; but between such emotions and self-love there is no co-ordination. No emotion, as he points out, determines action directly, but only by exciting desire; which with him can only mean that the image of the pleasant emotion excites desire for its renewal. In other words, no emotion amounts to volition or will. Self-love, on the other hand, if it means anything, means desire and a possibly strongest desire, or will. It can thus be no more determined by opposition to generous or sympathetic *emotions* than can these by opposition to hunger and thirst. Hume, however, when he insists on the existence of generous 'passions' as showing that self-love is not our uniform motive, though he cannot consistently mean more than that desire for 'pleasure in general,' or desire for the satisfaction of desire, is not the uniform motive—which might equally be shown (as he admits) by pointing to such self-regarding 'passions' as love of fame, or such appetites as hunger—is yet apt, through the reader's interpretation of 'generous passions' as *desires* for something other than pleasure, to gain credit for recognising a possibility of living for others, in distinction from living for pleasure, which was in truth as completely excluded by his theory as by that of Hobbes. If he himself meant to convey any other distinction between self-love and the generous passions than one which would hold no less between it and every emotion whatever, it was through a fresh intrusion upon him of that notion of benevolence, as a 'desire not founded on pleasure,' which was in too direct contradiction to the first principles of his theory to be acquiesced in.[1]

Its opposition to disinterested desires, as commonly understood, disappears.

It is desire for pleasure in general.

[1] Cf II. p. 197, where, speaking of 'calm desires,' he says they 'are of two kinds: either certain instincts originally implanted in our natures, such as benevolence and resentment, the love of life, and kindness to children; or the general appetite to good and aversion to evil, considered merely as such' This seems to imply a twofold distinction of the 'general appetite to good' (a) from desires for particular pleasures, which are commonly not

47. Such desire, then, being excluded, what other motive than 'interest' remains, by contrast with which the latter may be defined? It has been explained above (§ 7) that since pleasure as such, or as a feeling, does not admit of generality, 'pleasure in general' is an impossible object. When the motive of an action is said to be 'pleasure in general,' what is really meant is that the action is determined by the conception of pleasure, or, more properly, of self as a subject to be pleased. Such determination, again, is distinguished by opposition to two other kinds—(a) to that sort of determination which is not by conception, but either by animal want, or by the animal *imagination* of pleasure, and (b) to determination by the conception of other objects than pleasure. By an author, however, who expressly excluded the latter sort of determination, and who did not recognise any distinction between the thinking and the animal subject, the motive in question could not thus be defined. Hence the difficulty of extracting from Hume himself any clear and consistent account of that which he variously describes as the 'general appetite for good, considered merely as such,' as 'interest,' and as 'self-love.' To say that he understood by it a desire for pleasure which is yet not a desire for any pleasure in particular, may seem a strange interpretation to put on one who regarded himself as a great liberator from abstractions, but there is no other which his statements, taken together, would justify. This desire for nothing, however, he converts into a desire for something by identify-

calm, and (b) from certain desires, which resemble the 'general appetite' in being calm but are not for pleasure at all. See above, sec. 31. In that section of the Essays where 'self-love' is expressly treated of, there is a still clearer appearance of the doctrine, that there are desires (in that instance called 'mental passions') which have not pleasure for their object any more than have such 'bodily wants' as hunger and thirst. From these self-love, as desire for pleasure, is distinguished, though, when the pleasure incidental to their satisfaction is discovered and reflected on, it is supposed to combine with them. (Vol iv. Appendix on Self-love, near the end. See above, sec 43 and note.)

This amounts, in fact, to a complete withdrawal from Hume's original position and the adoption of one which is most clearly stated in Hutcheson's posthumous treatise—the position, namely, that we begin with a multitude of 'particular' or 'violent' desires, severally 'terminating upon objects' which are not pleasures at all, and that, as reason developes, these gradually blend with, or are superseded by, the 'calm' desire for pleasure; so that moral growth means the access of conscious pleasure-seeking. This in effect seems to be Butler's view, and Hutcheson reckons it 'a lovely represent-ation of human nature' though he himself holds that benevolence may exist, not merely as one of the 'particular desires' controlled by self-love, but as itself a 'calm' and controlling principle, co-ordinate with self-love. (System of Moral Philosophy,' Vol i p. 51, &c.)

ing it on occasion, (1) with any desire for a pleasure of which the attainment is regarded as sufficiently remote to allow of calmness in the desire, and (2) with desire for the means of having all pleasures indifferently at command. It is in one or other of these senses—either as desire for some particular pleasure distinguished only by its calmness, or as desire for power—that he always understands 'interest' or 'self-love,' except where he gains a more precise meaning for it by the admission of desires, not for pleasure at all, to which it may be opposed. Now taken in the former sense, its difference from the desires for the several pleasures of 'sense,' 'pride,' and 'sympathy,' of which Hume's account has already been examined, cannot lie in the object, but— as he himself says of the distinction, which he regarded as an equivalent one, between 'reasonable and unreasonable' desires—in our situation with regard to it. If then the object of each of these desires, as we have shown to be implied in Hume's account of them, is one which only reason, as self-consciousness, can constitute, it cannot be less so when the desire is calm enough to be called self-love. Still more plainly is the desire in question determined by reason—by the conception of self as a permanent suscepti-bility of pleasure—if it is understood to be desire for power.

'Interest, like other motives described, implies de-termina-tion by reason.

48. Having now before us a complete view of the possible motives to human action which Hume admits, we find that while he has carried to its furthest limit, and with the least verbal inconsistency possible, the effort to make thought deny its own originativeness in action, he has yet not suc-ceeded. He has made abstraction of everything in the objects of human interest but their relation to our nervous irritability—he has left nothing of the beautiful in nature or art but that which it has in common with a sweetmeat, nothing of that which is lovely and of good report to the saint or statesman but what they share with the dandy or diner-out—yet he cannot present even this poor residuum of an object, by which all action is to be explained, except under the character it derives from the thinking soul, which looks before and after, and determines everything by relation to itself. Thus if, as he says, the distinction between reasonable and unreasonable desires does not lie in the object, this will not be because reason has never anything to

Thus Hume, having de-graded morality for the sake of consis-tency, after all is not consistent.

do with the constitution of the object, but because it has always so much to do with it as renders selfishness—the self-conscious pursuit of pleasure—possible. Sensuality then will have been vindicated, the distinction between the 'higher' and 'lower' modes of life will have been erased, and after all the theoretic consistency—for the sake of which, and not, of course, to gratify any sinister interest, Hume made his philosophic venture—will not have been attained. Man will still not be ultimately passive, nor human action natural. Reason may be the 'slave of the passions,' but it will be a self-imposed subjection.

If all good is pleasure, what is *moral* good?

49. We have still, however, to explain how Hume himself completes the assimilation of the moral to the natural; how, on the supposition that the 'good' can only mean the 'pleasant,' he accounts for the apparent distinction between moral and other good, for the intrusion of the 'ought and ought not' of ethical propositions upon the 'is and is not' of truth concerning nature.[1] Here again he is faithful to his *rôle* as the expander and expurgator of Locke. With Locke, it will be remembered, the distinction of *moral* good lay in the channel through which the pleasure, that consti-tutes it, is derived. It was pleasure accruing through the intervention of law, as opposed to the operation of nature: and from the pleasure thus accruing the term 'morally good' was transferred to the act which, as 'conformable to some law,' occasions it.[2] This view Hume retains, merely remedying Locke's omissions and inconsistencies. Locke, as

Ambiguity in Locke's view.

we saw, not only neglected to derive the existence of the laws, whose intervention he counted necessary to constitute the morally good, from the operation of that desire for pleasure which he pronounced the only motive of man; in speaking of moral goodness as consisting in conformity to law, he might, if taken at his word, be held to admit some-thing quite different from pleasure alike as the standard and the motive of morality. Hume then had, in the first place, to account for the laws in question, and so account for them as to remove that absolute opposition between them and the operation of nature which Locke had taken for granted; secondly, to exhibit that conformity to law, in which the moral goodness of an act was held to consist, as

[1] Vol. ii p 245   [2] Above, secs. 16–18.

itself a mode of pleasure—pleasure, namely, to the contemplator of the act; and thirdly, to show that not the moral goodness of the act, even thus understood, but pleasure to himself was the motive to the doer of it.[1]

50. It was a necessary incident of this process that Locke's notion of a Law of God, conformity to which rendered actions 'in their own nature right and wrong,' should disappear. The existence of such a law cannot be explained as a result of any desire for pleasure, nor conformity to it as a mode of pleasure. Locke, indeed, tries to bring the goodness, consisting in such conformity, under his general definition by treating it as equivalent to the production of pleasure in another world. This, however, is to seek refuge from the contradictory in the unmeaning. The question—Is it the pleasure it produces, or its conformity to law, that constitutes the goodness of an act?—remains unanswered, while the further one is suggested—What meaning has pleasure except as the pleasure we experience?[2] Between pleasure, then, and a 'conformity' irreducible to pleasure, as the moral standard, the reader of Locke had to chose. Clarke, supported by Locke's occasional assimilation of moral to mathematical truth, had elaborated the notion of conformity. To him an action was 'in its own nature right' when it conformed to the 'reason of things'—i.e. to certain 'eternal proportions,' by which God, 'qui omnia numero, ordine, mensurâ posuit,' obliges Himself to govern the world, and of which reason in us is 'the appearance.'[3] Thus reason, as an eternal 'agreement or disagreement of ideas,' was the standard to which action ought to conform, and, as our consciousness of such agreement, at once the judge of and motive to conformity. To this Hume's reply is in effect the challenge to instance any act, of which the morality consists either in any of those four relations, 'depending on the nature of the ideas related,' which he regarded as alone admitting of demonstration, or in any other of those relations (contiguity, identity, and cause and effect) which, as 'matters of fact,' can be 'discovered by the understanding.'[4] Such a challenge

Margin notes: Development of it by Clarke, which breaks down for want of true view of reason.

---

[1] Of the three problems here specified, Hume's treatment of the *second* is discussed in the following secs. 50–54, of the *first* in secs 55–58, of the *third* in secs. 60 to the end

[2] Above, sec. 14.
[3] Boyle Lectures, Vol. II. prop. 1. secs 1–4.
[4] Book III part 1, sec. 1. (Cf Book I part 3, sec 1, and Introduction to

admits of no reply, and no other function but the perception of such relations being allowed to reason or understanding in the school of Locke, it follows that it is not this faculty which either constitutes, or gives the consciousness of, the morally good. Reason excluded, feeling remains. No action, then, can be called ' right in its own nature,' if that is taken to imply (as ' conformity to divine law ' must be), relation to something else than our feeling. It could only be so called with propriety in the sense of *exciting some pleasure immediately,* as distinct from an act which may be a condition of the attainment of pleasure, but does not directly convey it.

With Hume, moral good is pleasure excited in a particular way,

51. So far, however, there is nothing to distinguish the moral act either from any ' inanimate object,' which may equally excite immediate pleasure, or from actions which have no character, as virtuous or vicious, at all. Some further limitation, then, must be found for the immediate pleasure which constitutes the goodness called ' moral,' and of which praise is the expression. This Hume finds in the exciting object which must be (*a*) ' considered in general and without reference to our particular interest,' and (*b*) an object so ' related ' (in the sense above [1] explained) to oneself or to another as that the pleasure which it excites shall cause the further pleasure either of pride or love.[2] The precise effect of such limitation he does not explain in detail. A man's pictures, gardens, and clothes, we have been told, tend to excite pride in himself and love in others. If then we can ' consider them in general and without reference to our particular interest,' and in such ' mere survey' find pleasure, this pleasure, according to Hume's showing, will constitute them morally good.[3] He usually takes for granted, however, a further limitation of the pleasure in

Vol I. secs 283 and ff) It will be observed that throughout the polemic against Clarke and his congeners Hume writes as if there were a difference between objects of reason and feeling, which he could not consistently admit He begins by putting the question thus (page 234), ' whether 'tis by means of our ideas or impressions we distinguish betwixt vice and virtue:' but if, as he tells us, ' the idea is merely the weaker impression, and the impression the stronger idea,' such a question has no meaning. In like manner he concludes by saying (page

245) that ' vice and virtue may be compared to sounds, colours, heat and cold, which are not qualities in objects, but perceptions in the mind' But, since the whole drift of Book I. is to show that all ' objective relations' are such ' perceptions' or their succession, this still leaves us without any distinction between science and morality that shall be tenable according to his own doctrine.

[1] Sec. 33.

[2] Vol II pp 247 and 248

[3] Hume treats them as such in Book III. part 3, sec. 5.

question, as excited only by 'actions, sentiments, and characters,' and thus finds virtue to consist in the 'satisfaction produced to the spectator of an act or character by the mere view of it.'[1] Virtues and vices then mean, as Locke well said, the usual likes and dislikes of society. If we choose with him to call that virtue of an act, which really consists in the pleasure experienced by the spectator of it, 'conformity to the law of their opinion,' we may do so, provided we do not suppose that there is some other law, which this imperfectly reflects, and that the virtue is something other than the pleasure, but to be inferred from it. 'We do not infer a character to be virtuous, because it pleases; but in feeling that it pleases after such a particular manner, we in effect feel that it is virtuous.'[2]

viz. in the spectator of the 'good' act, and by the view of its tendency to produce pleasure.

52. Some further explanation, however, of the 'particular manner' of this pleasure was clearly needed in order at once to adjust it to the doctrine previously given of the passions (of which this, as a pleasant emotion, must be one), and to account for our speaking of the actions which excite it—at least of some of them—as actions which we *ought* to do. If we revert to the account of the passions, we can have no difficulty in fixing on that of which this peculiar pleasure, excited by the 'mere survey' of an action without reference to the spectator's 'particular interest,' must be a mode. It must be a kind of sympathy—pleasure felt by the spectator in the pleasure of another, as distinct from what might be felt in the prospect of pleasure to himself.[3] On the other hand, there seem to be certain discrepancies between pleasure and moral sentiment. We sympathise where we neither approve nor disapprove; and, conversely, we express approbation where it would seem there was no pleasure to sympathise with, *e.g.*, in regard to an act of simple justice, or where the person experiencing it was one with whom we could have no fellow-feeling—an enemy, a stranger, a character in history—or where the experience, being one not of pleasure but of pain (say, that of a martyr at the stake), should excite the reverse of approbation in the spectator, if approbation means pleasure sympathised with. Our sympathies, moreover, are highly variable, but our moral sentiments on the whole constant. How must 'sym-

---

[1] Vol II. p 251. Cf. p. 225   [2] Vol. II p. 247   [3] Vol. II. pp. 335–337.

pathy' be qualified, in order that, when we identify moral sentiment with it, these objections may be avoided?

Moral sense is thus sympathy with pleasure qualified by consideration of general tendencies.

53. Hume's answer, in brief, is that the sympathy, which constitutes moral sentiment, is sympathy qualified by the consideration of 'general tendencies.' Thus we sympathise with the pleasure arising from any casual action, but the sympathy does not become moral approbation unless the act is regarded as a sign of some quality or character, generally permanently agreeable or useful (*sc.* and productive of pleasure directly or indirectly) to the agent or others. An act of justice may not be productive of any immediate pleasure with which we can sympathise; nay, taken singly, it may cause pain both in itself and in its results, as when a judge 'takes from the poor to give to the rich, or bestows on the dissolute the labour of the industrious;' but we sympathise with the general satisfaction resulting to society from 'the whole scheme of law and justice,' to which the act in question belongs, and approve it accordingly. The constancy which leads to a dungeon is a painful commodity to its possessor, but sympathy with his pain need not incapacitate a spectator for that other sympathy with the general pleasure caused by such a character to others, which constitutes it virtuous. Again, though remote situation or the state of one's temper may at any time modify or suppress sympathy with the pleasure caused by the good qualities of any particular person, we may still apply to him terms expressive of our liking. 'External beauty is determined merely by pleasure; and 'tis evident a beautiful countenance cannot give so much pleasure, when seen at a distance of twenty paces, as when it is brought nearer to us. We say not, however, that it appears to us less beautiful; because we know what effect it will have in such a position, and by that reflection we correct its momentary appearance.' As with the beautiful, so with the morally good. 'In order to correct the continual contradictions' in our judgment of it, that would arise from changes in personal temper or situation, 'we fix on some steady and general points of view, and always in our thoughts place ourselves in them, whatever may be our present situation.' Such a point of view is furnished by the consideration of 'the interest or pleasure of the person himself whose character is examined, and of the persons who have a connection with

him,' as distinct from the spectator's own. The imagination
in time learns to ' adhere to these general views, and distinguishes the feelings they produce from those which arise
from our particular and momentary situation.' Thus a certain
constancy is introduced into sentiments of blame and praise,
and the variations, to which they continue subject, do not
appear in language, which ' experience teaches us to
correct, even where our sentiments are more stubborn and
unalterable.' [1]

54. It thus appears that though the virtue of an act means
the pleasure which it causes to a spectator, and though this
again arises from sympathy with imagined pleasure of the
doer or others, yet the former may be a pleasure which no
particular spectator at any given time does actually feel—
he need only know that under other conditions on his part
he would feel it—and the latter pleasure may be one either
not felt at all by any existing person, or only felt as the
opposite of the uneasiness with which society witnesses a
departure from its general rules. Of the essential distinction between a feeling of pleasure or pain and a knowledge
of the conditions under which a pleasure or pain is generally
felt, Hume shows no suspicion; nor, while he admits that
without substitution of the knowledge for the feeling there
could be no general standard of praise or blame, does he ask
himself what the quest for such a standard implies. As little
does he trouble himself to explain how there can be such
sympathy with an unfelt feeling—with a pleasure which no
one actually feels but which is possible for posterity— as will
explain our approval of the virtue which defies the world,
and which is only assumed, for the credit of a theory, to
bring pleasure to its possessor, because it certainly brings
pleasure to no one else. For the ' artificial' virtue, however, of acts done in conformity with the ' general scheme of
justice,' or other social conventions, he accounts at length in
part II. of his Second Book—that entitled ' Of Justice and
Injustice.'

In order to account for the facts, it has to become sympathy with unfelt feelings.

55. To a generation which has sufficiently freed itself
from all ' mystical' views of law—which is aware that
' natural right,' if it means a right that existed in a ' state
of nature,' is a contradiction in terms; that, since contracts

Can the distinction between the 'moral' and

[1] Book III vol. ii part 3, sec. 1. Specially pp. 339, 342, 346, 349.

'natural' be maintained by Hume?

could not be made, or property exist apart from social convention, any question about a primitive obligation to respect them is unmeaning—the negative side of this part of the treatise can have little interest. That all rights and obligations are in some sense 'artificial,' we are as much agreed as that without experience there can be no knowledge. The question is, how the artifice, which constitutes them, is to be understood, and what are its conditions. If we ask what Hume understood by it, we can get no other answer than that the artificial is the opposite of the natural. If we go on to ask for the meaning of the natural, we only learn that we must distinguish the senses in which it is opposed to the miraculous and to the unusual from that in which it is opposed to the artificial,[1] but not what the latter sense is.

What is 'artificial virtue'?

The truth is that, if the first book of Hume's treatise has fulfilled its purpose, the only conception of the natural, which can give meaning to the doctrine that the obligation to observe contracts and respect property is artificial, must disappear. There are, we shall find, two different negations which in different contexts this doctrine conveys. Sometimes it means that such an obligation did not exist for man in a 'state of nature,' *i.e.*, as man was to begin with. But in that sense the law of cause and effect, without which there would be no nature at all, is, according to Hume, not natural, for it—not merely our recognition of it, but the law itself—is a habit of imagination, gradually formed. Sometimes it conveys an opposition to Clarke's doctrine of obligation as constituted by certain 'eternal relations and proportions,' which also form the order of nature, and are other than, though regulative of, the succession of our feelings. Nature, however, having been reduced by Hume to the succession of our feelings, the 'artifice,' by which he supposes obligations to be formed, cannot be determined by opposition to it, unless the operation of motives, which explains the artifice, is something else than a succession of feelings. But that it is nothing else is just what it is one great object of the moral part of his treatise to show.

56. He is nowhere more happy than in exposing the fallacies by which 'liberty of indifference'—the liberty supposed to consist in a possibility of unmotived action—was

---

[1] BOOK II part 1, sec 2.

defended.[1] Every act, he shows, is determined by a strongest motive, and the relation between motive and act is no other than that between any cause and effect in nature. In one case, as in the other, 'necessity' lies not in an 'esse' but in a 'percipi.' It is the 'determination of the thought of any intelligent being, who considers' an act or event, 'to infer its existence from some preceding objects;'[2] and such determination is a habit formed by, and having a strength proportionate to, the frequency with which certain phenomena —actions or events—have followed certain others. The weakness in this part of Hume's doctrine lies, not in the assumption of an equal uniformity in the sequence of act upon motive with that which obtains in nature, but in his inability consistently to justify the assumption of an absolute uniformity in either case. When there is an apparent irregularity in the consequences of a given motive—when according to one 'experiment' action (a) follows upon it, according to another action (b), and so on—although 'these contrary experiments are entirely equal, we remove not the notion of causes and necessity; but, supposing that the usual contrariety proceeds from the operation of contrary and concealed causes, we conclude that the chance or indifference lies only in our judgment on account of our imperfect knowledge, not in the things themselves, which are in every case equally necessary, though to appearance not equally constant or uniform.'[3] But we have already seen that, if necessary connection were in truth only a habit arising from the frequency with which certain phenomena follow certain others, the cases of exception to a usual sequence, or in which the balance of chances did not incline one way more than another, could only so far weaken the habit. The explanation of them by the 'operation of concealed causes' implies, as he here says, an opposition of real necessity to apparent inconstancy, which, if necessity were such a habit as he says it is, would be impossible.[4] This difficulty, however, applying equally to moral and natural sequences, can constitute no difference between them. It cannot therefore be in the relation between motive and act that the followers of Hume can find any ground for a dis-

Nor of such distinction in relation and act.

[1] BOOK II part 3, secs. 1 and 2.
[2] Vol II p. 189.
[3] Ibid., p 185.

[4] See Introduction to Vol. I. secs. 323 and 336.

tinction between the process by which the conventions of
society are formed, and that succession of feelings which he
calls nature.   May he then find it in the character of the
motive itself by which the 'invention' of justice is to be
accounted for ?   Is this other than a feeling determined by a
previous, and determining a sequent, one ?   Not, we must
answer, as Hume himself understood his own account of it,
which is as follows :—

Motive to
artificial
virtues.

57. He will examine, he says, 'two questions, viz., concerning the manner in which the rules of justice are
established by the artifice of men ; and concerning the
reasons which determine us to attribute to the observance or
neglect of these rules a moral beauty and deformity.'[1]   Of
the motives which he recognises (§ 45) it is clear that only
two—'benevolence' and 'interest'—can be thought of in
this connection, and a little reflection suffices to show that
benevolence cannot account for the artifice in question.
Benevolence with Hume means either sympathy with pleasure—and this (though Hume could forget it on occasion [2])
must be a particular pleasure of some particular person—or
desire for the pleasure of such sympathy.   Even if a benevolence may be admitted, which is not a desire for pleasure at
all but an impulse to please, still this can only be an impulse
to please some particular person, and the only effect of
thought upon it, which Hume recognises, is not to widen
its object but to render it 'interested.'[3]   'There is no such
passion in human minds as the love of mankind, merely as
such, independent of personal qualities, of services, or of
relation to ourself.'[4]   The motive, then, to the institution
of rules of justice cannot be found in general benevolence.[5]
As little can it be found in private benevolence, for the
person to whom I am obliged to be just may be an object of
merited hatred.   It is true that, 'though it be rare to meet
with one who loves any single person better than himself,
yet 'tis as rare to meet with one in whom all the kind affections, taken together, do not overbalance all the selfish'; but
they are affections to his kinsfolk and acquaintance, and the
generosity which they prompt will constantly conflict with
justice.[6]   'Interest,' then, must be the motive we are in quest

[1] Book iii part 2, sec. 2.
[2] Cf sec. 54.
[3] Cf secs. 42, 43, and 46.
[4] Vol. ii p. 255.
[5] For the sense in which Hume did
admit a 'general benevolence,' see sec.
41, note.
[6] Vol. ii. pp. 256 and 260.

of. Of the 'three species of goods which we are possessed
of—the satisfaction of our minds, the advantages of our
body, and the enjoyment of such possessions as we have
acquired by our industry and good fortune '—the last only
' may be transferred without suffering any loss or alteration;
while at the same time there is not sufficient quantity of
them to supply every one's desires and necessities.' Hence
a special instability in their possession. Reflection on the
general loss caused by such instability leads to a 'tacit convention, entered into by all the members of a society, to
abstain from each other's possessions;' and thereupon 'immediately arise the ideas of justice and injustice; as also
those of property, right, and obligation.' It is not to be
supposed, however, that the 'convention' is of the nature of
a promise, for all promises presuppose it. 'It is only a
general sense of common interest; which sense all the members of the society express to one another, and which induces
them to regulate their conduct by certain rules;' and this
' general sense of common interest,' it need scarcely be said,
is every man's sense of his own interest, as in fact coincid-
ing with that of his neighbours. In short, ''tis only from
the selfishness and confined generosity of man, along with
the scanty provision nature has made for his wants, that
justice derives its origin.'[1]

58. Thus the origin of rules of justice is explained, but How
the obligation to observe them so far appears only as artificial
' interested,' not as ' moral.' In order that it may become become
' moral,' a pleasure must be generally experienced in the moral.
spectacle of their observance, and a pain in that of their
breach, apart from reference to any gain or loss likely to
arise to the spectator himself from that observance or breach.
In accounting for this experience Hume answers the second
of the questions, proposed above. 'To the imposition and
observance of these rules, both in general and in every
particular instance, men are at first induced only by a regard
to interest; and this motive, on the first formation of
society, is sufficiently strong and forcible. But when society
has become numerous, and has increased to a tribe or nation,
this interest is more remote; nor do men so readily perceive
that disorder and confusion follow upon each breach of these

[1] Vol. II. pp. 261, 263, 268.

rules, as in a more narrow and contracted society. But though, in our own actions, we may frequently lose sight of that interest which we have in maintaining order, and may follow a lesser and more present interest, we never fail to observe the prejudice we receive, either mediately or immediately, from the injustice of others. . . . . Nay, when the injustice is so distant from us, as no way to affect our interest, it still displeases us, because we consider it as prejudicial to human society, and pernicious to every one that approaches the person guilty of it. We partake of their uneasiness by *sympathy*; and as everything which gives uneasiness in human actions, upon the general survey, is called vice, and whatever produces satisfaction, in the same manner, denominated virtue, this is the reason why the sense of moral good and evil follows upon justice and injustice. And though this sense, in the present case, be derived only from contemplating the actions of others, yet we fail not to extend it even to our own actions. The *general rule* reaches beyond those instances from which it arose, while at the same time we naturally *sympathise* with others in the sentiments they entertain of us.'[1]

Interest and sympathy account for all obligations, civil and moral.

59. To this account of the process by which rules of justice have not only come into being, but come to bind our 'conscience' as they do, the modern critic will be prompt to object that it is still affected by the 'unhistorical' delusions of the systems against which it was directed. In expression, at any rate, it bears the marks of descent from Hobbes, and, if read without due allowance, might convey the notion that society first existed without any sort of justice, and that afterwards its members, finding universal war inconvenient, said to themselves, 'Go to; let us abstain from each other's goods.' It would be hard, however, to expect from Hume the full-blown terminology of development. He would probably have been the first to admit that rules of justice, as well as our feelings towards them, were not made but grew; and in his view of the 'passions,' whose operation this growth exhibits, he does not seriously differ from the ordinary exponents of the 'natural history' of ethics. These passions, we have seen, are 'Interest' and 'Sympathy,' which with Hume only differ from the pleasures

---

[1] Vol. II. p. 271.

and desires we call 'animal' as any one of these differs
from another—the pleasure of eating, for instance, from that
of drinking, or desire for the former pleasure from desire for
the latter. Nor do their effects in the regulation of society,
and in the growth of 'artificial' virtues and vices, differ
according to his account of them from sentiments which,
because they 'occur to us whether we will or no,' he reckons
purely natural, save in respect of the further extent to
which the modifying influence of imagination—itself reacted
on by language—must have been carried in order to their
existence; and since this in his view is a merely 'natural'
influence, there can only be a relative difference between the
'artificiality' of its more complex, and the 'naturalness' of
its simpler, products. Locke's opposition, then, of 'moral'
to other good, on the ground that other than natural instru-
mentality is implied in its attainment, will not hold even in
regard to that good which, it is admitted, would not be
what it is, *i.e.*, not a pleasure, but for the intervention of
civil law.

60. The doctrine, which we have now traversed, of
'interested' and 'moral' obligation, implicitly answers the
question as to the origin and significance of the ethical
copula 'ought.' It originally expresses, we must suppose,
obligation by positive law, or rather by that authoritative
custom in which (as Hume would probably have been ready
to admit) the 'general sense of common interest' first
embodies itself. In this primitive meaning it already
implies an opposition between the 'interest which each man
has in maintaining order' and his 'lesser and more present
interests.' Its meaning will be modified in proportion as
the direct interest in maintaining order is reinforced or
superseded by sympathy with the general uneasiness which
any departure from the rules of justice causes. And as this
uneasiness is not confined to cases where the law is directly
or in the letter violated, the judgment, that an act *ought* to
be done, not only need not imply a belief that the person,
so judging, will himself gain anything by its being done or
lose anything by its omission; it need not imply that any
positive law requires it. Whether it is applicable to every
act 'causing pleasure on the mere survey'—whether the
range of 'imperfect obligation' is as wide as that of moral
sentiment—Hume does not make clear. That every action

*What is
meant by
an action
which
ought to
be done*

representing a quality 'fitted to give immediate pleasure to its possessor' should be virtuous—as according to Hume's account of the exciting cause of moral sentiment it must be—seems strange enough, but it would be stranger that we should judge of it as an act which *ought* to be done. It is less difficult, for instance, to suppose that it is virtuous to be witty, than that one ought to be so. Perhaps it would be open to a disciple of Hume to hold that as, according to his master's showing, an opposition between permanent and present interest is implied in the judgment of obligation as at first formed, so it is when the pleasure to be produced by an act, which gratifies moral sense, is remote rather than near, and a pleasure to others rather than to the doer, that the term 'ought' is appropriate to it.

Sense of morality no motive. 61. But though Hume leaves some doubt on this point, he leaves none in regard to the sense in which alone any one can be said to do an action *because he ought*. This must mean that he does it to avoid either a legal penalty or that pain of shame which would arise upon the communication through sympathy of such uneasiness as a contrary act would excite in others upon the survey. So far from its being true that an act, in order to be thoroughly virtuous, must be done for virtue's sake, 'no action can be virtuous or morally good unless there is some motive to produce it, distinct from the sense of its morality.'[1] An act is virtuous on account of the pleasure which supervenes when it is contemplated as proceeding from a motive fitted to produce pleasure to the agent or to others. The presence of this motive, then, being the antecedent condition of the act's being regarded as virtuous, the motive cannot itself have been a regard to the virtue. It may be replied, indeed, that though this shows 'regard to virtue' or 'sense of morality' to be not the primary or only virtuous motive, it does not follow that it cannot be a motive at all. An action cannot be prompted for the first time by desire for a pleasure which can only be felt as a consequence of the action having been done, but it may be repeated, after experience of this pleasure, from desire for its renewal. In like manner, since with Hume the 'sense of morality' is not a desire at all but an emotion, and an emotion which cannot be felt till an

[1] Vol. II., p. 253.

act of a certain kind has been done, it cannot be the original motive to such an action; but why may not desire for so pleasant an emotion, when once it has been experienced, lead to a repetition of the act? The answer to this question is that the pleasure of moral sentiment, as Hume thinks of it, is essentially a pleasure experienced by a spectator of an act who is other than the doer of it. If the doer and spectator were regarded as one person, there would be no meaning in the rule that the tendency to produce pleasure, which excites the sentiment of approbation, must be a tendency to produce it to the doer himself or others, as distinct from the spectator himself. Thus pleasure, in the specific form in which Hume would call it 'moral sentiment,' is not what any one could attain by his own action, and consequently cannot be a motive to action. Transferred by sympathy to the consciousness of the man whose act is approved, 'moral sentiment' becomes 'pride,' and desire for the pleasure of pride—otherwise called 'love of fame'—is one of the 'virtuous' motives on which Hume dwells most. When an action, however, is done for the sake of any such positive pleasure, he would not allow apparently that the agent does it 'from a sense of duty' or 'because he ought.' He would confine this description to cases where the object was rather the avoidance of humiliation. 'I ought' means 'it is expected of me.' 'When any virtuous motive 'or principle is common in human nature, a person who feels his heart devoid of that motive may hate himself' (strictly, according to Hume's usage of terms, 'despise himself') 'on that account, and may perform the action without the motive from a certain sense of duty, in order to acquire by practice that virtuous principle, or at least to disguise to himself as much as possible his want of it.'[1]

When it seems so, the motive is really pride

62. What difference, then, we have finally to ask, does Hume leave between one motive and another, which can give any significance to the assertion that an act, to be virtuous, must proceed from a virtuous motive? When a writer has so far distinguished between motive and action as to tell us that the moral value of an action depends on its motive—which is what Hume is on occasion ready to tell us—we naturally suppose that any predicate, which he pro-

Distinction between virtuous and vicious motive does not exist for person moved.

[1] Vol. ii., p 253.

ceeds to apply to the motive, is meant to represent what it
is in relation to the subject of it. It cannot be so, however,
when Hume calls a motive virtuous. This predicate, as he
explains, refers not to an 'esse' but to a 'percipi;' which
means that it does not represent what the motive is to the
person whom it moves, but a pleasant feeling excited in the
spectator of the act. To the excitement of this feeling it
is necessary that the action should not merely from some
temporary combination of circumstances produce pleasure
for that time and turn, but that the desire, to which the
spectator ascribes it, should be one according to his expectation 'fitted to produce pleasure to the agent or to others.'
In this sense only can Hume consistently mean that virtue
in the motive is the condition of virtue in the act, and in this
sense the qualification has not much significance for the
spectator of the act, and none at all in relation to the doer.
It has not much for the spectator, because, according to it,
no supposed desire will excite his displeasure and consequently be vicious unless in its general operation it produces
a distinct overbalance of pain to the subject of it *and* to
others;[1] and by this test it would be more difficult to show
that an unseasonable passion for reforming mankind was *not*
vicious than that moderate lechery was so. It has no
significance at all for the person to whom vice or virtue is
imputed, because a difference in the results, which others
anticipate from any desire that moves him to action, makes
no difference in that desire, as he feels and is moved by it.
To him, according to Hume, it is simply desire for the
pleasure of which the idea is for the time most lively, and,
being most lively, cannot but excite the strongest desire. In
this—in the character which they severally bear for the
subjects of them—the virtuous motive and the vicious are
alike. Hume, it is true, allows that the subject of a vicious
desire may become conscious through sympathy of the
uneasiness which the contemplation of it causes to others,
but if this sympathy were strong enough to neutralize the

---

[1] I write 'AND to others' not 'OR,'
because according to Hume the production of pleasure to the agent alone is
enough to render an action virtuous, if
it proceeds from some permanent quality.
Thus an action could not be unmistak-
ably vicious unless it tended to produce
pain *both* to the doer and to others. If,
though tending to bring pain to others,
it had a contrary tendency for the agent
himself, there would be nothing to decide whether the viciousness of the former tendency was, or was not, balanced
by the virtuousness of the latter

imagination which excites the desire, the desire would not move him to act. That predominance of anticipated pain over pleasure in the effects of a motive, which renders it vicious to the spectator, cannot be transferred to the imagination of the subject of it without making it cease to be his motive because no longer his strongest desire. A vicious motive, in short, would be a contradiction in terms, if that productivity of pain, which belongs to the motive in the imagination of the spectator, belonged to it also in the imagination of the agent.

63. Thus the consequence, which we found to be involved in Locke's doctrine of motives, is virtually admitted by its most logical exponent. Locke's confusions began when he tried to reconcile his doctrine with the fact of self-condemnation, with the individual's consciousness of vice as a condition of himself; or, in his own words, to explain how the vicious man could be 'answerable to himself' for his vice. Consciousness of vice could only mean consciousness of pleasure wilfully foregone, and since pleasure could not be wilfully foregone, there could be no such consciousness. Hume, as we have seen, cuts the knot by disposing of the consciousness of vice, as a relation in which the individual stands to himself, altogether. A man's vice is someone else's displeasure with him, and, if we wish to be precise, we must not speak of self-condemnation or desire for excellence as influencing human conduct, but of aversion from the pain of humiliation and desire for the pleasure of pride—humiliation and pride of that sort of which each man's sympathy with the feeling of others about him is the condition.

'Consciousness of sin disappears

64. That such a doctrine leaves large fields of human experience unexplained, few will now dispute. Wesley, Wordsworth, Fichte, Mazzini, and the German theologians, lie between us and the generation in which, to so healthy a nature as Hume's, and in so explicit a form, it could be possible. Enthusiasm—religious, political, and poetic—if it has not attained higher forms, has been forced to understand itself better since the time when Shaftesbury's thin and stilted rhapsody was its most intelligent expression. It is now generally agreed that the saint is not explained by being called a fanatic, that there is a patriotism which is not 'the last refuge of a scoundrel,' and that we know no more about the poet, when we have been told that he seeks

Only respectability remains.

the beautiful, and that what is beautiful is pleasant, than we
did before.   This admitted, Hume's Hedonism needs only to
be clearly stated to be found 'unsatisfactory.'   If it ever
tends to find acceptance with serious people, it is through
confusion with that hybrid, though beneficent, utilitarianism
which finds the moral good in the 'greatest happiness of the
greatest number' without reflecting that desire for such an
object, not being for a feeling of pleasure to be experienced
by the subject of the desire, is with Hume impossible.   Understood as he himself understood his doctrine, it is only
'respectability'—the temper of the man who 'naturally,'
i.e., without definite expectation of ulterior gain, seeks to
stand well with his neighbours—that it will explain ; and
this it can only treat as a fixed quantity.   Taking for
granted the heroic virtue, for which it cannot account, it
still must leave it a mystery how the heroic virtue of an
earlier age can become the respectability of a later one.
Recent literary fashion has led us perhaps unduly to
depreciate respectability, but the avowed insufficiency of a
moral theory to explain anything beyond it may fairly
entitle us to enquire whether it can consistently explain
even that.   The reason, as we have sufficiently seen, why
Hume's ethical speculation has such an issue is that he does
not recognize the constitutive action of self-conscious
thought.   Misunderstanding our passivity in experience—
unaware that it has no meaning except in relation to an
object which thought itself projects, yet too clear-sighted
to acquiesce in the vulgar notion of either laws of matter or
laws of action, as simply thrust upon us from an unaccountable without—he seeks in the mere abstraction of passivity,
of feeling which is a feeling of nothing, the explanation of
the natural and moral world.   Nature is a sequence of
sensations, morality a succession of pleasures and pains.
It is under the pressure of this abstraction that he so
empties morality of its actual content as to leave only the
residuum we have described.   Yet to account even for this
he has to admit such motives as 'pride,' 'love,' and 'interest ;'
and each of these, as we have shown, implies that very
constitutive action of reason, by ignoring which he compels
himself to reduce all morality to that of the average man in
his least exalted moments.   The formative power of thought,
as exhibited in such motives, only differs in respect of the

And even
this not
consis-
tently ac-
counted
for.

lower degree, to which it has fashioned its matter, from the same power as the source of the 'desire for excellence,' of the will autonomous in the service of mankind, of the forever (to us) unfilled ideal of a perfect society. It is because Hume de-rationalizes respectability, that he can find no *rationale*, and therefore no room, for the higher morality. This might warn us that an 'ideal' theory of ethics tampers with its only sure foundation when it depreciates respectability; and if it were our business to extract a practical lesson from him, it would be that there is no other genuine 'enthusiasm of humanity' than one which has travelled the common highway of reason—the life of the good neighbour and honest citizen—and can never forget that it is still only on a further stage of the same journey. Our business, however, has not been to moralise, but to show that the philosophy based on the abstraction of feeling, in regard to morals no less than to nature, was with Hume played out, and that the next step forward in speculation could only be an effort to re-think the process of nature and human action from its true beginning in thought. If this object has been in any way attained, so that the attention of Englishmen 'under five-and-twenty' may be diverted from the anachronistic systems hitherto prevalent among us to the study of Kant and Hegel, an irksome labour will not have been in vain.

T. H. GREEN.

A

TREATISE

OF

Human Nature:

BEING

An ATTEMPT to introduce the experimental
Method of Reasoning

INTO

MORAL SUBJECTS.

*Rara temporum felicitas, ubi sentire, quæ velis; & quæ sentias,
dicere licet.* TACIT.

VOL. II.

OF THE

PASSIONS.

LONDON:

Printed for JOHN NOON, at the *White-Hart*, near *Mercers-
Chapel*, in *Cheapside*.

MDCCXXXIX.

A TREATISE

OF

HUMAN NATURE.

———◦⋈◦———

BOOK II.

OF THE PASSIONS.

———

PART I.

OF PRIDE AND HUMILITY.

SECT. I.—*Division of the Subject.*

As all the perceptions of the mind may be divided into *impressions* and *ideas*, so the impressions admit of another division into *original* and *secondary*. This division of the impressions is the same with that which[1] I formerly made use of when I distinguish'd them into impressions of *sensation* and *reflection*. Original impressions or impressions of sensation are such as without any antecedent perception arise in the soul, from the constitution of the body, from the animal spirits, or from the application of objects to the external organs. Secondary, or reflective impressions are such as proceed from some of these original ones, either immediately or by the interposition of its idea. Of the first kind are all the impressions of the senses, and all bodily pains

SECT
I
Division of
the sub-
ject.

———

[1] Book I. Part I. Sect. 2.

and pleasures: Of the second are the passions, and other emotions resembling them.

'Tis certain, that the mind, in its perceptions, must begin somewhere; and that since the impressions precede their correspondent ideas, there must be some impressions, which without any introduction make their appearance in the soul. As these depend upon natural and physical causes, the examination of them wou'd lead me too far from my present subject, into the sciences of anatomy and natural philosophy. For this reason I shall here confine myself to those other impressions, which I have call'd secondary and reflective, as arising either from the original impressions, or from their ideas. Bodily pains and pleasures are the source of many passions, both when felt and consider'd by the mind; but arise originally in the soul, or in the body, whichever you please to call it, without any preceding thought or perception. A fit of the gout produces a long train of passions, as grief, hope, fear; but is not deriv'd immediately from any affection or idea.

The reflective impressions may be divided into two kinds, *viz.* the *calm* and the *violent.* Of the first kind is the sense of beauty and deformity in action, composition, and external objects. Of the second are the passions of love and hatred, grief and joy, pride and humility. This division is far from being exact. The raptures of poetry and music frequently rise to the greatest height; while those other impressions, properly call'd *passions*, may decay into so soft an emotion, as to become, in a manner, imperceptible. But as in general the passions are more violent than the emotions arising from beauty and deformity, these impressions have been commonly distinguish'd from each other. The subject of the human mind being so copious and various, I shall here take advantage of this vulgar and specious division, that I may proceed with the greater order; and having said all I thought necessary concerning our ideas, shall now explain those violent emotions or passions, their nature, origin, causes, and effects.

When we take a survey of the passions, there occurs a division of them into *direct* and *indirect.* By direct passions I understand such as arise immediately from good or evil, from pain or pleasure. By indirect such as proceed from the same principles, but by the conjunction of other qualities.

This distinction I cannot at present justify or explain any farther. I can only observe in general, that under the indirect passions I comprehend pride, humility, ambition, vanity, love, hatred, envy, pity, malice, generosity, with their dependants. And under the direct passions, desire, aversion, grief, joy, hope, fear, despair and security. I shall begin with the former.

SECT
I
⌇
Division of
the subject

SECT. II.—*Of Pride and Humility; their Objects and Causes.*[1]

The passions of PRIDE and HUMILITY being simple and uniform impressions, 'tis impossible we can ever, by a multitude of words, give a just definition of them, or indeed of any of the passions. The utmost we can pretend to is a description of them, by an enumeration of such circumstances, as attend them : But as these words, *pride* and *humility*, are of general use, and the impressions they represent the most common of any, every one, of himself, will be able to form a just idea of them, without any danger of mistake. For which reason, not to lose time upon preliminaries, I shall immediately enter upon the examination of these passions.

'Tis evident, that pride and humility, tho' directly contrary, have yet the same OBJECT. This object is self, or that succession of related ideas and impressions, of which we have an intimate memory and consciousness. Here the view always fixes when we are actuated by either of these passions. According as our idea of ourself is more or less advantageous, we feel either of those opposite affections, and are elated by pride, or dejected with humility. Whatever other objects may be comprehended by the mind, they are always consider'd with a view to ourselves ; otherwise they wou'd never be able either to excite these passions, or produce the smallest encrease or diminution of them. When self enters not into the consideration, there is no room either for pride or humility.

But tho' that connected succession of perceptions, which we call *self*,[2] be always the object of these two passions, 'tis impossible it can be their CAUSE, or be sufficient alone to excite them. For as these passions are directly contrary, and have the same object in common ; were their object also their cause ; it cou'd never produce any degree of the one

[1 Introd. sects 33 and 34.—Ed]   [2 Introd. sect. 35.—Ed.]

passion, but at the same time it must excite an equal degree of the other; which opposition and contrariety must destroy both. 'Tis impossible a man can at the same time be both proud and humble; and where he has different reasons for these passions, as frequently happens, the passions either take place alternately; or if they encounter, the one annihilates the other, as far as its strength goes, and the remainder only of that, which is superior, continues to operate upon the mind. But in the present case neither of the passions cou'd ever become superior; because supposing it to be the view only of ourself, which excited them, that being perfectly indifferent to either, must produce both in the very same proportion; or in other words, can produce neither. To excite any passion, and at the same time raise an equal share of its antagonist, is immediately to undo what was done, and must leave the mind at last perfectly calm and indifferent.

We must, therefore, make a distinction betwixt the cause and the object of these passions; betwixt that idea, which excites them, and that to which they direct their view, when excited. Pride and humility, being once rais'd, immediately turn our attention to ourself, and regard that as their ultimate and final object; but there is something farther requisite in order to raise them: Something, which is peculiar to one of the passions, and produces not both in the very same degree. The first idea, that is presented to the mind, is that of the cause or productive principle. This excites the passion, connected with it; and that passion, when excited, turns our view to another idea, which is that of self. Here then is a passion plac'd betwixt two ideas, of which the one produces it, and the other is produc'd by it. The first idea, therefore, represents the *cause*, the second the *object* of the passion.

To begin with the causes of pride and humility; we may observe, that their most obvious and remarkable property is the vast variety of *subjects*, on which they may be plac'd. Every valuable quality of the mind, whether of the imagination, judgment, memory or disposition; wit, good-sense, learning, courage, justice, integrity; all these are the causes of pride; and their opposites of humility. Nor are these passions confin'd to the mind, but extend their view to the body likewise. A man may be proud of his beauty, strength, agility, good mien, address in dancing, riding, fencing, and of his dexterity in any manual business or manufacture. But this is not all. The passion looking farther, comprehends whatever objects are in the least ally'd or related to us. Our country, family, children, relations, riches, houses, gardens, horses, dogs, cloaths; any of these may become a cause either of pride or of humility.

SECT
II

Of pride
and humi-
lity; their
objects and
causes.

From the consideration of these causes, it appears necessary we shou'd make a new distinction in the causes of the passion, betwixt that *quality*, which operates, and the *subject*, on which it is plac'd. A man, for instance, is vain of a beautiful house, which belongs to him, or which he has himself built and contriv'd. Here the object of the passion is himself, and the cause is the beautiful house: Which cause again is sub-divided into two parts, *viz.* the quality, which operates upon the passion, and the subject, in which the quality inheres. The quality is the beauty, and the subject is the house, consider'd as his property or contrivance. Both these parts are essential, nor is the distinction vain and chimerical. Beauty, consider'd merely as such, unless plac'd upon something related to us, never produces any pride or vanity; and the strongest relation alone, without beauty, or something else in its place, has as little influence on that passion. Since, therefore, these two particulars are easily separated, and there is a necessity for their conjunction, in order to produce the passion, we ought to consider them as component parts of the cause; and infix in our minds an exact idea of this distinction.

Sect. III.—*Whence these Objects and Causes are Deriv'd.*

Being so far advanc'd as to observe a difference betwixt the *object* of the passions and their *cause*, and to distinguish in the cause the *quality*, which operates on the passions, from the *subject*, in which it inheres; we now proceed to examine what determines each of them to be what it is, and assigns such a particular object, and quality, and subject to these affections. By this means we shall fully understand the origin of pride and humility.

'Tis evident in the first place, that these passions are determin'd to have self for their *object*, not only by a natural but also by an original property. No one can doubt but this property is *natural* from the constancy and steadiness of its operations. 'Tis always self, which is the object of pride and humility; and whenever the passions look beyond, 'tis still with a view to ourselves, nor can any person or object otherwise have any influence upon us.

That this proceeds from an *original* quality or primary impulse, will likewise appear evident, if we consider that 'tis the distinguishing characteristic of these passions. Unless nature had given some original qualities to the mind, it cou'd never have any secondary ones; because in that case it wou'd have no foundation for action, nor cou'd ever begin to exert itself. Now these qualities, which we must consider as original, are such as are most inseparable from the soul, and can be resolv'd into no other: And such is the quality, which determines the object of pride and humility.

We may, perhaps, make it a greater question, whether the *causes*, that produce the passion, be as *natural* as the object, to which it is directed, and whether all that vast variety proceeds from caprice or from the constitution of the mind. This doubt we shall soon remove, if we cast our eye upon human nature, and consider that in all nations and ages, the same objects still give rise to pride and humility; and that upon the view even of a stranger, we can know pretty nearly, what will either encrease or diminish his passions of this kind. If there be any variation in this particular, it proceeds from nothing but a difference in the tempers and complexions of men; and is besides very inconsiderable. Can we imagine it possible, that while human nature remains the same, men will ever become entirely indifferent to their power, riches, beauty or personal merit, and that their pride and vanity will not be affected by these advantages?

But tho' the causes of pride and humility be plainly *natural*, we shall find upon examination, that they are not *original*, and that 'tis utterly impossible they shou'd each of them be adapted to these passions by a particular provision, and primary constitution of nature. Beside their prodigious number, many of them are the effects of art, and arise partly from the industry, partly from the caprice, and partly from the good fortune of men. Industry produces houses, furniture, cloaths. Caprice determines their particular kinds and qualities. And good fortune frequently contributes to all this, by discovering the effects that result from the different mixtures and combinations of bodies. 'Tis absurd, therefore, to imagine, that each of these was foreseen and provided for by nature, and that every new production of art, which causes pride or humility; instead of adapting itself to the passion by partaking of some general quality, that naturally operates on the mind; is itself the object of an original principle, which till then lay conceal'd in the soul, and is only by accident at last brought to light. Thus the first mechanic, that invented a fine scritoire, produc'd pride in him, who became possest of it, by principles different from those, which made him proud of handsome chairs and tables. As this appears evidently ridiculous, we must conclude, that each cause of pride and humility is not adapted to the passions by a distinct original quality; but that there are some one or more circumstances common to all of them, on which their efficacy depends.

Sect.
III

Whence
these ob-
jects and
causes are
deriv'd.

Besides, we find in the course of nature, that tho' the effects be many, the principles, from which they arise, are commonly but few and simple, and that 'tis the sign of an unskilful naturalist to have recourse to a different quality, in order to explain every different operation. How much more must this be true with regard to the human mind, which being so confin'd a subject may justly be thought incapable of containing such a monstrous heap of principles, as wou'd be necessary to excite the passions of pride and humility, were each distinct cause adapted to the passion by a distinct set of principles?

Here, therefore, moral philosophy is in the same condition as natural, with regard to astronomy before the time of *Copernicus*. The antients, tho' sensible of that maxim, *that nature does nothing in vain*, contriv'd such intricate systems of the heavens, as seem'd inconsistent with true philosophy, and gave place at last to something more simple and natural. To invent without scruple a new principle to every new phænomenon, instead of adapting it to the old; to overload our hypotheses with a variety of this kind; are certain proofs, that none of these principles is the just one, and that we only desire, by a number of falsehoods, to cover our ignorance of the truth.

Sect. IV.—*Of the Relations of Impressions and Ideas.*

Thus we have establish'd two truths without any obstacle or difficulty, *that 'tis from natural principles this variety of*

causes excite pride and humility, and *that 'tis not by a different
principle each different cause is adapted to its passion.* We
shall now proceed to enquire how we may reduce these principles to a lesser number, and find among the causes something common, on which their influence depends.

In order to this we must reflect on certain properties of
human nature, which tho' they have a mighty influence on
every operation both of the understanding and passions, are
not commonly much insisted on by philosophers. The *first*
of these is the association of ideas, which I have so often
observ'd and explain'd. 'Tis impossible for the mind to fix
itself steadily upon one idea for any considerable time; nor
can it by its utmost efforts ever arrive at such a constancy.
But however changeable our thoughts may be, they are not
entirely without rule and method in their changes. The
rule, by which they proceed, is to pass from one object to
what is resembling, contiguous to, or produc'd by it. When
one idea is present to the imagination, any other, united by
these relations, naturally follows it, and enters with more
facility by means of that introduction.

The *second* property I shall observe in the human mind
is a like association of impressions. All resembling impressions are connected together, and no sooner one arises
than the rest immediately follow. Grief and disappointment
give rise to anger, anger to envy, envy to malice, and malice
to grief again, till the whole circle be compleated. In like
manner our temper, when elevated with joy, naturally throws
itself into love, generosity, pity, courage, pride, and the
other resembling affections. 'Tis difficult for the mind,
when actuated by any passion, to confine itself to that
passion alone, without any change or variation. Human
nature is too inconstant to admit of any such regularity.
Changeableness is essential to it. And to what can it so
naturally change as to affections or emotions, which are
suitable to the temper, and agree with that set of passions,
which then prevail? 'Tis evident, then, there is an attraction or association among impressions, as well as among
ideas; tho' with this remarkable difference, that ideas are
associated by resemblance, contiguity, and causation; and
impressions only by resemblance.

In the *third* place, 'tis observable of these two kinds of
association, that they very much assist and forward each

other, and that the transition is more easily made where they both concur in the same object. Thus a man, who, by any injury from another, is very much discompos'd and ruffled in his temper, is apt to find a hundred subjects of discontent, impatience, fear, and other uneasy passions; especially if he can discover these subjects in or near the person, who was the cause of his first passion. Those principles, which forward the transition of ideas, here concur with those, which operate on the passions; and both uniting in one action, bestow on the mind a double impulse. The new passion, therefore, must arise with so much greater violence, and the transition to it must be render'd so much more easy and natural.

Upon this occasion I may cite the authority of an elegant writer, who expresses himself in the following manner. 'As the fancy delights in every thing that is great, strange, or beautiful, and is still more pleas'd the more it finds of these perfections in the *same* object, so it is capable of receiving a new satisfaction by the assistance of another sense. Thus any continu'd sound, as the music of birds, or a fall of waters, awakens every moment the mind of the beholder, and makes him more attentive to the several beauties of the place, that lie before him. Thus if there arises a fragrancy of smells or perfumes, they heighten the pleasure of the imagination, and make even the colours and verdure of the landschape appear more agreeable; for the ideas of both senses recommend each other, and are pleasanter together than when they enter the mind separately: As the different colours of a picture, when they are well disposed, set off one another, and receive an additional beauty from the advantage of the situation.'[1] In this phænomenon we may remark the association both of impressions and ideas, as well as the mutual assistance they lend each other.

Sect. V.—*Of the Influence of these Relations on Pride and Humility.*

These principles being establish'd on unquestionable experience, I begin to consider how we shall apply them, by revolving over all the causes of pride and humility, whether these causes be regarded, as the qualities, that operate, or

[1] The 'Spectator,' No 412 —Ed]

G 2

as the subjects, on which the qualities are plac'd. In examining these *qualities* I immediately find many of them to concur in producing the sensation of pain and pleasure, independent of those affections, which I here endeavour to explain. Thus the beauty of our person, of itself, and by its very appearance, gives pleasure, as well as pride; and its deformity, pain as well as humility. A magnificent feast delights us, and a sordid one displeases. What I discover to be true in some instances, I *suppose* to be so in all; and take it for granted at present, without any farther proof, that every cause of pride, by its peculiar qualities, produces a separate pleasure, and of humility a separate uneasiness.

Again, in considering the *subjects*, to which these qualities adhere, I make a new *supposition*, which also appears probable from many obvious instances, *viz.* that these subjects are either parts of ourselves, or something nearly related to us. Thus the good and bad qualities of our actions and manners constitute virtue and vice, and determine our personal character, than which nothing operates more strongly on these passions. In like manner, 'tis the beauty or deformity of our person, houses, equipage, or furniture, by which we are render'd either vain or humble. The same qualities, when transfer'd to subjects, which bear us no relation, influence not in the smallest degree either of these affections.

Having thus in a manner suppos'd two properties of the causes of these affections, *viz.* that the *qualities* produce a separate pain or pleasure, and that the *subjects*, on which the qualities are plac'd, are related to self; I proceed to examine the passions themselves, in order to find something in them, correspondent to the suppos'd properties of their causes. *First*, I find, that the peculiar object of pride and humility is determin'd by an original and natural instinct, and that 'tis absolutely impossible, from the primary constitution of the mind, that these passions shou'd ever look beyond self, or that individual person, of whose actions and sentiments each of us is intimately conscious.[1] Here at last the view always rests, when we are actuated by either of these passions; nor can we, in that situation of mind, ever lose sight of this object. For this I pretend not to give

[¹ Introd. Sect. 35.—Ed.]

any reason; but consider such a peculiar direction of the thought as an original quality.

The *second* quality, which I discover in these passions, and which I likewise consider as an original quality, is their sensations, or the peculiar emotions they excite in the soul, and which constitute their very being and essence. Thus pride is a pleasant sensation, and humility a painful; and upon the removal of the pleasure and pain, there is in reality no pride nor humility. Of this our very feeling convinces us; and beyond our feeling, 'tis here in vain to reason or dispute.

If I compare, therefore, these two *establish'd* properties of the passions, *viz.* their object, which is self, and their sensation, which is either pleasant or painful, to the two *suppos'd* properties of the causes, *viz.* their relation to self, and their tendency to produce a pain or pleasure, independent of the passion; I immediately find, that taking these suppositions to be just, the true system breaks in upon me with an irresistible evidence. That cause, which excites the passion, is related to the object, which nature has attributed to the passion; the sensation, which the cause separately produces, is related to the sensation of the passion : From this double relation of ideas and impressions, the passion is deriv'd.[1] The one idea is easily converted into its cor-relative; and the one impression into that, which resembles and corresponds to it : With how much greater facility must this transition be made, where these movements mutually assist each other, and the mind receives a double impulse from the relations both of its impressions and ideas?

That we may comprehend this the better, we must suppose, that nature has given to the organs of the human mind, a certain disposition fitted to produce a peculiar impression or emotion, which we call *pride*: To this emotion she has assign'd a certain idea, *viz.* that of *self*, which it never fails to produce. This contrivance of nature is easily conceiv'd. We have many instances of such a situation of affairs. The nerves of the nose and palate are so dispos'd, as in certain circumstances to convey such peculiar sensations to the mind : The sensations of lust and hunger always produce in us the idea of those peculiar objects, which are

[¹ Introd. Sect. 33.—Ed.]

suitable to each appetite. These two circumstances are united in pride. The organs are so dispos'd as to produce the passion; and the passion, after its production, naturally produces a certain idea.[1] All this needs no proof. 'Tis evident we never shou'd be possest of that passion, were there not a disposition of mind proper for it; and 'tis as evident, that the passion always turns our view to ourselves, and makes us think of our own qualities and circumstances.

This being fully comprehended, it may now be ask'd, *Whether nature produces the passion immediately, of herself; or whether she must be assisted by the co-operation of other causes?* For 'tis observable, that in this particular her conduct is different in the different passions and sensations. The palate must be excited by an external object, in order to produce any relish: But hunger arises internally, without the concurrence of any external object. But however the case may stand with other passions and impressions, 'tis certain, that pride requires the assistance of some foreign object, and that the organs, which produce it, exert not themselves like the heart and arteries, by an original internal movement. For *first*, daily experience convinces us, that pride requires certain causes to excite it, and languishes when unsupported by some excellency in the character, in bodily accomplishments, in cloaths, equipage or fortune. *Secondly*, 'tis evident pride wou'd be perpetual, if it arose immediately from nature; since the object is always the same, and there is no disposition of body peculiar to pride, as there is to thirst and hunger. *Thirdly*, Humility is in the very same situation with pride; and therefore, either must, upon this supposition, be perpetual likewise, or must destroy the contrary passion from the very first moment; so that none of them cou'd ever make its appearance. Upon the whole, we may rest satisfy'd with the foregoing conclusion, that pride must have a cause, as well as an object, and that the one has no influence without the other.

The difficulty, then, is only to discover this cause, and find what it is that gives the first motion to pride, and sets those organs in action, which are naturally fitted to produce that emotion. Upon my consulting experience, in order to resolve this difficulty, I immediately find a hundred different

[1 Introd. Sects. 36 and 37 —Ed]

causes, that produce pride; and upon examining these causes, I suppose, what at first I perceive to be probable, that all of them concur in two circumstances; which are, that of themselves they produce an impression, ally'd to the passion, and are plac'd on a subject, ally'd to the object of the passion.   When I consider after this the nature of *relation*, and its effects both on the passions and ideas, I can no longer doubt, upon these suppositions, that 'tis the very principle, which gives rise to pride, and bestows motion on those organs, which being naturally dispos'd to produce that affection, require only a first impulse or beginning to their action.   Any thing, that gives a pleasant sensation, and is related to self, excites the passion of pride, which is also agreeable, and has self for its object.

What I have said of pride is equally true of humility. The sensation of humility is uneasy, as that of pride is agreeable; for which reason the separate sensation, arising from the causes, must be revers'd, while the relation to self continues the same.   Tho' pride and humility are directly contrary in their effects, and in their sensations, they have notwithstanding the same object; so that 'tis requisite only to change the relation of impressions, without making any change upon that of ideas.   Accordingly we find, that a beautiful house, belonging to ourselves, produces pride; and that the same house, still belonging to ourselves, produces humility, when by any accident its beauty is chang'd into deformity, and thereby the sensation of pleasure, which corresponded to pride, is transform'd into pain, which is related to humility.   The double relation between the ideas and impressions subsists in both cases, and produces an easy transition from the one emotion to the other.

In a word, nature has bestow'd a kind of attraction on certain impressions and ideas, by which one of them, upon its appearance, naturally introduces its correlative.   If these two attractions or associations of impressions and ideas concur on the same object, they mutually assist each other, and the transition of the affections and of the imagination is made with the greatest ease and facility.   When an idea produces an impression, related to an impression, which is connected with an idea, related to the first idea, these two impressions must be in a manner inseparable, nor will the one in any case be unattended with the other.   'Tis after this manner, that the particular causes of pride and humility are determin'd. The quality, which operates on the passion, produces separately an impression resembling it; the subject, to which the quality adheres, is related to self, the object of the passion: No wonder the whole cause, consisting of a quality and of a subject, does so unavoidably give rise to the passion.

To illustrate this hypothesis, we may compare it to that, by which I have already explain'd the belief attending the judgments, which we form from causation. I have observ'd, that in all judgments of this kind, there is always a present impression, and a related idea; and that the present impression gives a vivacity to the fancy, and the relation conveys this vivacity, by an easy transition, to the related idea. Without the present impression, the attention is not fix'd, nor the spirits excited. Without the relation, this attention rests on its first object, and has no farther consequence. There is evidently a great analogy betwixt that hypothesis, and our present one of an impression and idea, that transfuse themselves into another impression and idea by means of their double relation: Which analogy must be allow'd to be no despicable proof of both hypotheses.

Sect. VI.—*Limitations of this System.*

But before we proceed farther in this subject, and examine particularly all the causes of pride and humility, 'twill be proper to make some limitations to the general system, *that all agreeable objects, related to ourselves, by an association of ideas and of impressions, produce pride, and disagreeable ones, humility:* And these limitations are deriv'd from the very nature of the subject.

I. Suppose an agreeable object to acquire a relation to self, the first passion, that appears on this occasion, is joy; and this passion discovers itself upon a slighter relation than pride and vain-glory. We may feel joy upon being present at a feast, where our senses are regal'd with delicacies of every kind: But 'tis only the master of the feast, who, beside the same joy, has the additional passion of self-applause and vanity. 'Tis true, men sometimes boast of a great entertainment, at which they have only been present; and by so small a relation convert their pleasure into pride:

But however, this must in general be own'd, that joy arises from a more inconsiderable relation than vanity, and that many things, which are too foreign to produce pride, are yet able to give us a delight and pleasure. The reason of the difference may be explain'd thus. A relation is requisite to joy, in order to approach the object to us, and make it give us any satisfaction. But beside this, which is common to both passions, 'tis requisite to pride, in order to produce a transition from one passion to another, and convert the satisfaction into vanity. As it has a double task to perform, it must be endow'd with double force and energy. To which we may add, that where agreeable objects bear not a very close relation to ourselves, they commonly do to some other person; and this latter relation not only excels, but even diminishes, and sometimes destroys the former, as we shall see afterwards.[1]

SECT.
VI.

Limita-
tions of
this sys-
tem.

Here then is the first limitation, we must make to our general position, *that every thing related to us, which produces pleasure or pain, produces likewise pride or humility.* There is not only a relation requir'd, but a close one, and a closer than is requir'd to joy.

II. The second limitation is, that the agreeable or disagreeable object be not only closely related, but also peculiar to ourselves, or at least common to us with a few persons. 'Tis a quality observable in human nature, and which we shall endeavour to explain afterwards, that every thing, which is often presented, and to which we have been long accustom'd, loses its value in our eyes, and is in a little time despis'd and neglected. We likewise judge of objects more from comparison than from their real and intrinsic merit; and where we cannot by some contrast enhance their value, we are apt to overlook even what is essentially good in them. These qualities of the mind have an effect upon joy as well as pride; and 'tis remarkable, that goods, which are common to all mankind, and have become familiar to us by custom, give us little satisfaction; tho' perhaps of a more excellent kind, than those on which, for their singularity, we set a much higher value. But tho' this circumstance operates on both these passions, it has a much greater influence on vanity. We are rejoic'd for many goods, which, on

[1] Part II. Sect. 4.

account of their frequency, give us no pride. Health, when it returns after a long absence, affords us a very sensible satisfaction; but is seldom regarded as a subject of vanity, because 'tis shar'd with such vast numbers.

The reason, why pride is so much more delicate in this particular than joy, I take to be, as follows. In order to excite pride, there are always two objects we must contemplate, *viz.* the *cause* or that object which produces pleasure; and self, which is the real object of the passion. But joy has only one object necessary to its production, *viz.* that which gives pleasure; and tho' it be requisite, that this bear some relation to self, yet that is only requisite in order to render it agreeable; nor is self, properly speaking, the object of this passion. Since, therefore, pride has in a manner two objects, to which it directs our view; it follows, that where neither of them have any singularity, the passion must be more weaken'd upon that account, than a passion, which has only one object. Upon comparing ourselves with others, as we are every moment apt to do, we find we are not in the least distinguish'd; and upon comparing the object we possess, we discover still the same unlucky circumstance. By two comparisons so disadvantageous the passion must be entirely destroy'd.

III. The third limitation is, that the pleasant or painful object be very discernible and obvious, and that not only to ourselves, but to others also. This circumstance, like the two foregoing, has an effect upon joy, as well as pride. We fancy ourselves more happy, as well as more virtuous or beautiful, when we appear so to others; but are still more ostentacious of our virtues than of our pleasures. This proceeds from causes, which I shall endeavour to explain afterwards.

IV. The fourth limitation is deriv'd from the inconstancy of the cause of these passions, and from the short duration of its connexion with ourselves. What is casual and inconstant gives but little joy, and less pride. We are not much satisfy'd with the thing itself; and are still less apt to feel any new degrees of self-satisfaction upon its account. We foresee and anticipate its change by the imagination; which makes us little satisfy'd with the thing: We compare it to ourselves, whose existence is more durable; by which means its inconstancy appears still greater. It seems ridiculous to

infer an excellency in ourselves from an object, which is of
so much shorter duration, and attends us during so small a
part of our existence. 'Twill be easy to comprehend the
reason, why this cause operates not with the same force in
joy as in pride; since the idea of self is not so essential to
the former passion as to the latter.

V. I may add as a fifth limitation, or rather enlargement
of this system, that *general rules* have a great influence upon
pride and humility, as well as on all the other passions.
Hence we form a notion of different ranks of men, suitable
to the power or riches they are possest of; and this notion
we change not upon account of any peculiarities of the
health or temper of the persons, which may deprive them of
all enjoyment in their possessions. This may be accounted
for from the same principles, that explain'd the influence of
general rules on the understanding. Custom readily carries
us beyond the just bounds in our passions, as well as in our
reasonings.

It may not be amiss to observe on this occasion, that the
influence of general rules and maxims on the passions very
much contributes to facilitate the effects of all the principles,
which we shall explain in the progress of this treatise. For
'tis evident, that if a person full-grown, and of the same
nature with ourselves, were on a sudden transported into our
world, he wou'd be very much embarrass'd with every object,
and wou'd not readily find what degree of love or hatred,
pride or humility, or any other passion he ought to attribute
to it. The passions are often vary'd by very inconsiderable
principles; and these do not always play with a perfect regularity, especially on the first trial. But as custom and practice have brought to light all these principles, and have
settled the just value of every thing; this must certainly
contribute to the easy production of the passions, and guide
us, by means of general establish'd maxims, in the proportions we ought to observe in preferring one object to another.
This remark may, perhaps, serve to obviate difficulties, that
may arise concerning some causes, which I shall hereafter
ascribe to particular passions, and which may be esteem'd
too refin'd to operate so universally and certainly, as they
are found to do.

I shall close this subject with a reflection deriv'd from
these five limitations. This reflection is, that the persons,

who are proudest, and who in the eye of the world have most reason for their pride, are not always the happiest; nor the most humble always the most miserable, as may at first sight be imagin'd from this system. An evil may be real, tho' its cause has no relation to us: It may be real, without being peculiar: It may be real, without shewing itself to others: It may be real, without being constant: And it may be real, without falling under the general rules. Such evils as these will not fail to render us miserable, tho' they have little tendency to diminish pride: And perhaps the most real and the most solid evils of life will be found of this nature.

SECT. VII.—*Of Vice and Virtue.*

Taking these limitations along with us, let us proceed to examine the causes of pride and humility; and see, whether in every case we can discover the double relations, by which they operate on the passions. If we find that all these causes are related to self, and produce a pleasure or uneasiness separate from the passion, there will remain no farther scruple with regard to the present system. We shall principally endeavour to prove the latter point; the former being in a manner self-evident.

To begin with VICE and VIRTUE, which are the most obvious causes of these passions; 'twou'd be entirely foreign to my present purpose to enter upon the controversy, which of late years has so much excited the curiosity of the publick, *whether these moral distinctions be founded on natural and original principles, or arise from interest and education.* The examination of this I reserve for the following book; and in the mean time shall endeavour to show, that my system maintains its ground upon either of these hypotheses; which will be a strong proof of its solidity.

For granting that morality had no foundation in nature, it must still be allow'd, that vice and virtue, either from self-interest or the prejudices of education, produce in us a real pain and pleasure; and this we may observe to be strenuously asserted by the defenders of that hypothesis. Every passion, habit, or turn of character (say they) which has a tendency to our advantage or prejudice, gives a delight or uneasiness; and 'tis from thence the approbation or dis-approbation arises. We easily gain from the liberality of others, but are

always in danger of losing by their avarice : Courage defends
us, but cowardice lays us open to every attack : Justice is the
support of society, but injustice, unless check'd, wou'd quickly
prove its ruin : Humility exalts ; but pride mortifies us. For
these reasons the former qualities are esteem'd virtues, and
the latter regarded as vices.   Now since 'tis granted there is
a delight or uneasiness still attending merit or demerit of
every kind, this is all that is requisite for my purpose.

But I go farther, and observe, that this moral hypothesis
and my present system not only agree together, but also that,
allowing the former to be just, 'tis an absolute and invincible
proof of the latter.   For if all morality be founded on the
pain or pleasure, which arises from the prospect of any loss
or advantage, that may result from our own characters, or
from those of others, all the effects of morality must be deriv'd from the same pain or pleasure, and among the rest,
the passions of pride and humility.   The very essence of
virtue, according to this hypothesis, is to produce pleasure,
and that of vice to give pain.   The virtue and vice must be
part of our character in order to excite pride or humility.
What farther proof can we desire for the double relation of
impressions and ideas ?

The same unquestionable argument may be deriv'd from
the opinion of those, who maintain that morality is something real, essential, and founded on nature.   The most probable hypothesis, which has been advanc'd to explain the
distinction betwixt vice and virtue, and the origin of moral
rights and obligations, is, that from a primary constitution
of nature certain characters and passions, by the very view
and contemplation, produce a pain, and others in like manner
excite a pleasure.   The uneasiness and satisfaction are not
only inseparable from vice and virtue, but constitute their
very nature and essence.   To approve of a character is to
feel an original delight upon its appearance.   To disapprove
of it is to be sensible of an uneasiness.   The pain and
pleasure, therefore, being the primary causes of vice and
virtue, must also be the causes of all their effects, and consequently of pride and humility, which are the unavoidable
attendants of that distinction.[1]

But supposing this hypothesis of moral philosophy shou'd

[1 Cf Book III. Part I. Sect. 2, and Part III. Sect. 1 ; and Introd. Sect.
51 —Ed]

be allow'd to be false, 'tis still evident, that pain and pleasure, if not the causes of vice and virtue, are at least inseparable from them. A generous and noble character affords a satisfaction even in the survey; and when presented to us, tho' only in a poem or fable, never fails to charm and delight us. On the other hand cruelty and treachery displease from their very nature; nor is it possible ever to reconcile us to these qualities, either in ourselves or others. Thus one hypothesis of morality is an undeniable proof of the foregoing system, and the other at worst agrees with it.

But pride and humility arise not from these qualities alone of the mind, which, according to the vulgar systems of ethicks, have been comprehended as parts of moral duty, but from any other that has a connexion with pleasure and uneasiness. Nothing flatters our vanity more than the talent of pleasing by our wit, good humour, or any other accomplishment; and nothing gives us a more sensible mortification than a disappointment in any attempt of that nature. No one has ever been able to tell what *wit* is, and to shew why such a system of thought must be receiv'd under that denomination, and such another rejected. 'Tis only by taste we can decide concerning it, nor are we possest of any other standard, upon which we can form a judgment of this kind. Now what is this *taste*, from which true and false wit in a manner receive their being, and without which no thought can have a title to either of these denominations? 'Tis plainly nothing but a sensation of pleasure from true wit, and of uneasiness from false, without our being able to tell the reasons of that pleasure or uneasiness. The power of bestowing these opposite sensations is, therefore, the very essence of true and false wit; and consequently the cause of that pride or humility, which arises from them.

There may, perhaps, be some, who being accustom'd to the style of the schools and pulpit, and having never consider'd human nature in any other light, than that in which *they* place it, may here be surpriz'd to hear me talk of virtue as exciting pride, which they look upon as a vice; and of vice as producing humility, which they have been taught to consider as a virtue. But not to dispute about words, I observe, that by *pride* I understand that agreeable impression, which arises in the mind, when the view either of our virtue, beauty, riches or power makes us satisfy'd with ourselves:

And that by *humility* I mean the opposite impression. 'Tis evident the former impression is not always vicious, nor the latter virtuous. The most rigid morality allows us to receive a pleasure from reflecting on a generous action; and 'tis by none esteem'd a virtue to feel any fruitless remorses upon the thoughts of past villainy and baseness. Let us, therefore, examine these impressions, consider'd in themselves; and enquire into their causes, whether plac'd on the mind or body, without troubling ourselves at present with that merit or blame, which may attend them.

SECT.
VII.

Of vice and
virtue

Sect. VIII.—*Of Beauty and Deformity.*

Whether we consider the body as a part of ourselves, or assent to those philosophers, who regard it as something external, it must still be allow'd to be near enough connected with us to form one of these double relations, which I have asserted to be necessary to the causes of pride and humility. Wherever, therefore, we can find the other relation of impressions to join to this of ideas, we may expect with assurance either of these passions, according as the impression is pleasant or uneasy. But *beauty* of all kinds gives us a peculiar delight and satisfaction; as *deformity* produces pain, upon whatever subject it may be plac'd, and whether survey'd in an animate or inanimate object. If the beauty or deformity, therefore, be plac'd upon our own bodies, this pleasure or uneasiness must be converted into pride or humility, as having in this case all the circumstances requisite to produce a perfect transition of impressions or ideas. These opposite sensations are related to the opposite passions. The beauty or deformity is closely related to self, the object of these passions. No wonder, then our own beauty becomes an object of pride, and deformity of humility.

But this effect of personal and bodily qualities is not only a proof of the present system, by shewing that the passions arise not in this case without all the circumstances I have requir'd, but may be employ'd as a stronger and more convincing argument. If we consider all the hypotheses, which have been form'd either by philosophy or common reason, to explain the difference betwixt beauty and deformity, we shall find that all of them resolve into this, that beauty is such an order and construction of parts, as either by the *primary constitution* of our nature, by *custom*, or by *caprice*, is fitted to give a pleasure and satisfaction to the soul.[1] This is the distinguishing character of beauty, and forms all the difference betwixt it and deformity, whose natural tendency is to produce uneasiness. Pleasure and pain, therefore, are not only necessary attendants of beauty and deformity, but constitute their very essence. And indeed, if we consider, that a great part of the beauty, which we admire either in animals or in other objects, is deriv'd from the idea of convenience and utility, we shall make no scruple to assent to this opinion. That shape, which produces strength, is beautiful in one animal; and that which is a sign of agility in another. The order and convenience of a palace are no less essential to its beauty, than its mere figure and appearance. In like manner the rules of architecture require, that the top of a pillar shou'd be more slender than its base, and that because such a figure conveys to us the idea of security, which is pleasant; whereas the contrary form gives us the apprehension of danger, which is uneasy. From innumerable instances of this kind, as well as from considering that beauty like wit, cannot be defin'd, but is discern'd only by a taste or sensation, we may conclude, that beauty is nothing but a form, which produces pleasure, as deformity is a structure of·parts, which conveys pain; and since the power of producing pain and pleasure make in this manner the essence of beauty and deformity, all the effects of these qualities must be deriv'd from the sensation; and among the rest pride and humility, which of all their effects are the most common and remarkable.

This argument I esteem just and decisive; but in order to give greater authority to the present reasoning, let us suppose it false for a moment, and see what will follow. 'Tis certain, then, that if the power of producing pleasure and pain forms not the essence of beauty and deformity, the sensations are at least inseparable from the qualities, and 'tis even difficult to consider them apart. Now there is nothing common to natural and moral beauty, (both of which are the causes of pride) but this power of producing pleasure; and as a common effect supposes always a common cause, 'tis plain the pleasure must in both cases be the real and in-

[¹ Introd. Sect. 34.—Ed.]

fluencing cause of the passion. Again; there is nothing originally different betwixt the beauty of our bodies and the beauty of external and foreign objects, but that the one has a near relation to ourselves, which is wanting in the other. This original difference, therefore, must be the cause of all their other differences, and among the rest, of their different influence upon the passion of pride, which is excited by the beauty of our person, but is not affected in the least by that of foreign and external objects. Placing, then, these two conclusions together, we find they compose the preceding system betwixt them, *viz.* that pleasure, as a related or resembling impression, when plac'd on a related object, by a natural transition, produces pride; and its contrary, humility. This system, then, seems already sufficiently confirm'd by experience; tho' we have not yet exhausted all our arguments.

'Tis not the beauty of the body alone that produces pride, but also its strength and force. Strength is a kind of power; and therefore the desire to excel in strength is to be consider'd as an inferior species of *ambition.* For this reason the present phænomenon will be sufficiently accounted for, in explaining that passion.

Concerning all other bodily accomplishments we may observe in general, that whatever in ourselves is either useful, beautiful, or surprising, is an object of pride; and it's contrary, of humility. Now 'tis obvious, that every thing useful, beautiful or surprising, agrees in producing a separate pleasure, and agrees in nothing else. The pleasure, therefore, with the relation to self must be the cause of the passion.

Tho' it shou'd be question'd, whether beauty be not something real, and different from the power of producing pleasure, it can never be disputed, that as surprize is nothing but a pleasure arising from novelty, it is not, properly speaking, a quality in any object, but merely a passion or impression in the soul. It must, therefore, be from that impression, that pride by a natural transition arises. And it arises so naturally, that there is nothing *in us or belonging to us,* which produces surprize, that does not at the same time excite that other passion. Thus we are vain of the surprising adventures we have met with, the escapes we have made, and dangers we have been expos'd to. Hence the origin of vulgar lying; where men without any interest, and merely out of vanity, heap up a number of extraordinary events, which are either the fictions of their brain, or if true, have at least no connexion with themselves. Their fruitful invention supplies them with a variety of adventures; and where that talent is wanting, they appropriate such as belong to others, in order to satisfy their vanity.

In this phænomenon are contain'd two curious experiments, which if we compare them together, according to the known rules, by which we judge of cause and effect in anatomy, natural philosophy, and other sciences, will be an undeniable argument for that influence of the double relations above-mention'd. By one of these experiments we find, that an object produces pride merely by the interposition of pleasure; and that because the quality, by which it produces pride, is in reality nothing but the power of producing pleasure. By the other experiment we find, that the pleasure produces the pride by a transition along related ideas; because when we cut off that relation the passion is immediately destroy'd. A surprising adventure, in which we have been ourselves engag'd, is related to us, and by that means produces pride: But the adventures of others, tho' they may cause pleasure, yet for want of this relation of ideas, never excite that passion. What farther proof can be desired for the present system?

There is only one objection to this system with regard to our body; which is, that tho' nothing be more agreeable than health, and more painful than sickness, yet commonly men are neither proud of the one, nor mortify'd with the other. This will easily be accounted for, if we consider the *second* and *fourth* limitations, propos'd to our general system. It was observ'd, that no object ever produces pride or humi-lity, if it has not something *peculiar* to ourself; as also, that every cause of that passion must be in some measure *constant*, and hold some proportion to the duration of ourself, which is its object. Now as health and sickness vary incessantly to all men, and there is none, who is *solely* or *certainly* fix'd in either, these accidental blessings and calamities are in a manner separated from us, and are never consider'd as con-nected with our being and existence. And that this account is just appears hence, that wherever a malady of any kind is so rooted in our constitution, that we no longer entertain any hopes of recovery, from that moment it becomes an object of humility; as is evident in old men, whom nothing mortifies more than the consideration of their age and infirmities. They endeavour, as long as possible, to conceal their blindness and deafness, their rheums and gouts; nor do they ever confess them without reluctance and uneasiness. And tho' young men are not asham'd of every head-ach or cold they fall into, yet no topic is so proper to mortify human pride, and make us entertain a mean opinion of our nature, than this, that we are every moment of our lives subject to such infirmities. This sufficiently proves that bodily pain and sickness are in themselves proper causes of humility; tho' the custom of estimating every thing by comparison more than by its intrinsic worth and value, makes us overlook these calamities, which we find to be incident to every one, and causes us to form an idea of our merit and character independent of them.

We are asham'd of such maladies as affect others, and are either dangerous or disagreeable to them. Of the epilepsy; because it gives a horror to every one present: Of the itch; because it is infectious: Of the king's-evil; because it commonly goes to posterity. Men always consider the sentiments of others in their judgment of themselves. This has evidently appear'd in some of the foregoing reasonings; and will appear still more evidently, and be more fully explain'd afterwards.

Sect. IX.—*Of External Advantages and Disadvantages.*

But tho' pride and humility have the qualities of our mind and body, that is *self*, for their natural and more immediate causes, we find by experience, that there are many other objects, which produce these affections, and that the primary one is, in some measure, obscur'd and lost by the multiplicity of foreign and extrinsic. We found a vanity upon houses, gardens, equipages, as well as upon personal merit and accomplishments; and tho' these external advantages be in themselves widely distant from thought or a person, yet they considerably influence even a passion, which is directed to that as its ultimate object. This happens when external objects acquire any particular relation to ourselves, and are associated or connected with us. A beautiful fish in the ocean, an animal in a desart, and indeed any thing that neither belongs, nor is related to us, has no manner of influence on our vanity, whatever extraordinary qualities it may be endow'd with, and whatever degree of surprize and admiration it may naturally occasion. It must be some way associated with us in order to touch our pride. Its idea must hang in a manner, upon that of ourselves; and the transition from the one to the other must be easy and natural.

But here 'tis remarkable, that tho' the relation of *resemblance* operates upon the mind in the same manner as contiguity and causation, in conveying us from one idea to another, yet 'tis seldom a foundation either of pride or of humility. If we resemble a person in any of the valuable parts of his character, we must, in some degree, possess the quality, in which we resemble him; and this quality we always chuse to survey directly in ourselves rather than by reflexion in another person, when we wou'd found upon it any degree of vanity. So that tho' a likeness may occasionally produce that passion by suggesting a more advantageous idea of ourselves, 'tis there the view fixes at last, and the passion finds its ultimate and final cause.

There are instances, indeed, wherein men shew a vanity in resembling a great man in his countenance, shape, air, or other minute circumstances, that contribute not in any degree to his reputation; but it must be confess'd, that this extends not very far, nor is of any considerable moment in these affections. For this I assign the following reason. We can never have a vanity of resembling in trifles any person, unless he be possess'd of very shining qualities, which give us a respect and veneration for him. These qualities, then, are, properly speaking, the causes of our vanity, by means of their relation to ourselves. Now after what manner are they related to ourselves? They are parts of the person we value, and consequently connected with these trifles; which are also suppos'd to be parts of him. These trifles are connected with the resembling qualities in us; and these qualities in us, being parts, are connected with the whole; and by that means form a chain of several links betwixt ourselves and the shining qualities of the person we resemble. But besides that this multitude of relations must weaken the connexion; 'tis evident the mind, in passing from the shining qualities to the trivial ones, must by that contrast the better perceive the minuteness of the latter, and be in some measure asham'd of the comparison and resemblance.

SECT.
IX.

Of exter-
nal advan
tages and
disadvan-
tages.

The relation, therefore, of contiguity, or that of causation, betwixt the cause and object of pride and humility, is alone requisite to give rise to these passions; and these relations are nothing else but qualities, by which the imagination is convey'd from one idea to another. Now let us consider what effect these can possibly have upon the mind, and by what means they become so requisite to the production of the passions. 'Tis evident, that the association of ideas operates in so silent and imperceptible a manner, that we are scarce sensible of it, and discover it more by its effects than by any immediate feeling or perception. It produces no emotion, and gives rise to no new impression of any kind, but only modifies those ideas, of which the mind was formerly possess'd, and which it cou'd recal upon occasion. From this reasoning, as well as from undoubted experience, we may conclude, that an association of ideas, however necessary, is not alone sufficient to give rise to any passion.

'Tis evident, then, that when the mind feels the passion either of pride or humility upon the appearance of a related object, there is, beside the relation or transition of thought, an emotion or original impression produc'd by some other principle. The question is, whether the emotion first produc'd be the passion itself, or some other impression related to it. This question we cannot be long in deciding. For besides all the other arguments, with which this subject abounds, it must evidently appear, that the relation of ideas, which experience shews to be so requisite a circumstance to the production of the passion, wou'd be entirely superfluous, were it not to second a relation of affections, and facilitate the transition from one impression to another. If nature produc'd immediately the passion of pride or humility, it wou'd be compleated in itself, and wou'd require no farther addition or encrease from any other affection. But supposing the first emotion to be only related to pride or humility, 'tis easily conceiv'd to what purpose the relation of objects may serve, and how the two different associations, of impressions and ideas, by uniting their forces, may assist each other's operation. This is not only easily conceiv'd, but I will venture to affirm 'tis the only manner, in which we can conceive this subject. An easy transition of ideas, which, of itself, causes no emotion, can never be necessary, or even useful to the passions, but by forwarding the transition betwixt some related impressions. Not to mention, that the same object causes a greater or smaller degree of pride, not only in proportion to the encrease or decrease of its qualities, but also to the distance or nearness of the relation; which is a clear argument for the transition of affections along the relation of ideas; since every change in the relation produces a proportionable change in the passion. Thus one part of the preceding system, concerning the relations of ideas is a sufficient proof of the other, concerning that of impressions; and is itself so evidently founded on experience, that 'twou'd be lost time to endeavour farther to prove it.

This will appear still more evidently in particular instances. Men are vain of the beauty of their country, of their county, of their parish. Here the idea of beauty plainly produces a pleasure. This pleasure is related to pride. The object or cause of this pleasure is, by the supposition, related to self, or the object of pride. By this double relation of impressions or ideas, a transition is made from the one impression to the other.

Men are also vain of the temperature of the climate, in which they were born; of the fertility of their native soil; of the goodness of the wines, fruits or victuals, produc'd by it; of the softness or force of their language; with other particulars of that kind. These objects have plainly a reference to the pleasures of the senses, and are originally consider'd as agreeable to the feeling, taste or hearing. How is it possible they cou'd ever become objects of pride, except by means of that transition above-explain'd?

There are some, that discover a vanity of an opposite kind, and affect to depreciate their own country, in comparison of those, to which they have travell'd. These persons find, when they are at home, and surrounded with their countrymen, that the strong relation betwixt them and their own nation is shar'd with so many, that 'tis in a manner lost to them; whereas their distant relation to a foreign country, which is form'd by their having seen it and liv'd in it, is augmented by their considering how few there are who have done the same. For this reason they always admire the beauty, utility and rarity of what is abroad, above what is at home.

SECT.
IX.

Of exter-
nal advan
tages and
disadvan-
tages.

Since we can be vain of a country, climate or any inanimate object, which bears a relation to us, 'tis no wonder we are vain of the qualities of those, who are connected with us by blood or friendship. Accordingly we find, that the very same qualities, which in ourselves produce pride, produce also in a lesser degree the same affection, when discover'd in persons related to us. The beauty, address, merit, credit and honours of their kindred are carefully display'd by the proud, as some of the most considerable sources of their vanity.

As we are proud of riches in ourselves, so to satisfy our vanity we desire that every one, who has any connexion with us, shou'd likewise be possest of them, and are asham'd of any one, that is mean or poor, among our friends and relations. For this reason we remove the poor as far from us as possible; and as we cannot prevent poverty in some distant collaterals, and our forefathers are taken to be our nearest relations; upon this account every one affects to be of a good family, and to be descended from a long succession of rich and honourable ancestors.

I have frequently observ'd, that those, who boast of the antiquity of their families, are glad when they can join this circumstance, that their ancestors for many generations have been uninterrupted proprietors of the same portion of land, and that their family has never chang'd its possessions, or been transplanted into any other county or province. I have also observ'd, that 'tis an additional subject of vanity, when they can boast, that these possessions have been transmitted thro' a descent compos'd entirely of males, and that the honours and fortune have never past thro' any female. Let us endeavour to explain these phænomena by the foregoing system.

'Tis evident, that when any one boasts of the antiquity of his family, the subjects of his vanity are not merely the extent of time and number of ancestors, but also their riches and credit, which are suppos'd to reflect a lustre on himself on account of his relation to them. He first considers these objects; is affected by them in an agreeable manner; and then returning back to himself, thro' the relation of parent and child, is elevated with the passion of pride, by means of the double relation of impressions and ideas. Since therefore the passion depends on these relations, whatever strengthens any of the relations must also encrease the passion, and whatever weakens the relations must diminish the passion. Now 'tis certain the identity of the possession strengthens the relation of ideas arising from blood and kindred, and conveys the fancy with greater facility from one generation to another, from the remotest ancestors to their posterity, who are both their heirs and their descendants. By this facility the impression is transmitted more entire, and excites a greater degree of pride and vanity.

The case is the same with the transmission of the honours and fortune thro' a succession of males without their passing thro' any female. 'Tis a quality of human nature, which we shall consider[1] afterwards, that the imagination naturally turns to whatever is important and considerable; and where two objects are presented to it, a small and a great one, usually leaves the former, and dwells entirely upon the latter. As in the society of marriage, the male sex has the advantage above the female, the husband first engages our attention; and whether we consider him directly, or reach him by passing thro' related objects, the thought both rests upon him with greater satisfaction, and arrives at him with greater facility than his consort. 'Tis easy to see, that this property must strengthen the child's relation to the father, and weaken that to the mother. For as all relations are nothing but a propensity to pass from one idea to another, whatever strengthens the propensity strengthens the relation; and as we have a stronger propensity to pass from the idea of the children to that of the father, than from the same idea to that of the mother, we ought to regard the former relation as the closer and more considerable. This is the reason why children commonly bear their father's name, and are esteem'd to be of nobler or baser birth, according to *his* family. And tho' the mother shou'd be possest of a superior spirit and genius to the father, as often happens, the *general rule* prevails, notwithstanding the exception, according to the doctrine above-explain'd. Nay even when a superiority of any kind is so great, or when any other reasons have such an effect, as to make the children rather

[1] Part II. Sect. 2.

this be strictly true in a just and *philosophical* way of thinking, 'tis certain it is not *the philosophy* of our passions ; but
that many things operate upon them by means of the idea
and supposition of power, independent of its actual exercise.
We are pleas'd when we acquire an ability of procuring
pleasure, and are displeas'd when another acquires a power
of giving pain. This is evident from experience ; but in
order to give a just explication of the matter, and account
for this satisfaction and uneasiness, we must weigh the following reflections.

'Tis evident the error of distinguishing power from its exercise proceeds not entirely from the scholastic doctrine of
free-will, which, indeed, enters very little into common life,
and has but small influence on our vulgar and popular ways
of thinking. According to that doctrine, motives deprive us
not of free-will, nor take away our power of performing or
forbearing any action. But according to common notions
a man has no power, where very considerable motives lie
betwixt him and the satisfaction of his desires, and determine him to forbear what he wishes to perform. I do not
think I have fallen into my enemy's power, when I see him
pass me in the streets with a sword by his side, while I am
unprovided of any weapon. I know that the fear of the
civil magistrate is as strong a restraint as any of iron, and
that I am in as perfect safety as if he were chain'd or im-
prison'd. But when a person acquires such an authority
over me, that not only there is no external obstacle to his
actions ; but also that he may punish or reward me as he
pleases, without any dread of punishment in his turn, I then
attribute a full power to him, and consider myself as his
subject or vassal.

Now if we compare these two cases, that of a person, who
has very strong motives of interest or safety to forbear any
action, and that of another, who lies under no such obligation, we shall find, according to the philosophy explain'd in
the foregoing book, that the only *known* difference betwixt
them lies in this, that in the former case we conclude from
past experience, that the person never will perform that
action, and in the latter, that he possibly or probably will
perform it. Nothing is more fluctuating and inconstant on
many occasions, than the will of man ; nor is there any
thing but strong motives, which can give us an absolute

certainty in pronouncing concerning any of his future actions. When we see a person free from these motives, we suppose a possibility either of his acting or forbearing; and tho' in general we may conclude him to be determin'd by motives and causes, yet this removes not the uncertainty of our judgment concerning these causes, nor the influence of that uncertainty on the passions. Since therefore we ascribe a power of performing an action to every one, who has no very powerful motive to forbear it, and refuse it to such as have; it may justly be concluded, that *power* has always a reference to its *exercise*, either actual or probable, and that we consider a person as endow'd with any ability when we find from past experience, that 'tis probable, or at least possible he may exert it. And indeed, as our passions always regard the real existence of objects, and we always judge of this reality from past instances; nothing can be more likely of itself, without any farther reasoning, than that power consists in the possibility or probability of any action, as discover'd by experience and the practice of the world.

Now 'tis evident, that wherever a person is in such a situation with regard to me, that there is no very powerful motive to deter him from injuring me, and consequently 'tis *uncertain* whether he will injure me or not, I must be uneasy in such a situation, and cannot consider the possibility or probability of that injury without a sensible concern. The passions are not only affected by such events as are certain and infallible, but also in an inferior degree by such as are possible and contingent. And tho' perhaps I never really feel any harm, and discover by the event, that, philosophically speaking, the person never had any power of harming me; since he did not exert any; this prevents not my uneasiness from the preceding uncertainty. The agreeable passions may here operate as well as the uneasy, and convey a pleasure when I perceive a good to become either possible or probable by the possibility or probability of another's bestowing it on me, upon the removal of any strong motives, which might formerly have hinder'd him.

But we may farther observe, that this satisfaction encreases, when any good approaches in such a manner that it is in one's *own* power to take or leave it, and there neither is any physical impediment, nor any very strong motive to hinder our enjoyment. As all men desire pleasure, nothing can be

more probable, than its existence when there is no external
obstacle to the producing it, and men perceive no danger in
following their inclinations.   In that case their imagination
easily anticipates the satisfaction, and conveys the same joy,
as if they were perswaded of its real and actual existence.

But this accounts not sufficiently for the satisfaction,
which attends riches.   A miser receives delight from his
money; that is, from the *power* it affords him of procuring
all the pleasures and conveniences of life, tho' he knows he
has enjoy'd his riches for forty years without ever employing
them; and consequently cannot conclude by any species of
reasoning, that the real existence of these pleasures is nearer,
than if he were entirely depriv'd of all his possessions.   But
tho' he cannot form any such conclusion in a way of reasoning concerning the nearer approach of the pleasure, 'tis
certain he *imagines* it to approach nearer, whenever all
external obstacles are remov'd, along with the more powerful
motives of interest and danger, which oppose it.   For
farther satisfaction on this head I must refer to my account
of the will, where I shall[1] explain that false sensation of
liberty, which makes us imagine we can perform any thing,
that is not very dangerous or destructive.   Whenever any
other person is under no strong obligations of interest to
forbear any pleasure, we judge from *experience*, that the
pleasure will exist, and that he will probably obtain it.   But
when ourselves are in that situation, we judge from an
illusion of the fancy, that the pleasure is still closer and
more immediate.   The will seems to move easily every way,
and casts a shadow or image of itself, even to that side, on
which it did not settle.   By means of this image the enjoyment seems to approach nearer to us, and gives us the same
lively satisfaction, as if it were perfectly certain and unavoidable.

'Twill now be easy to draw this whole reasoning to a point,
and to prove, that when riches produce any pride or vanity
in their possessors, as they never fail to do, 'tis only by
means of a double relation of impression and ideas.   The
very essence of riches consists in the power of procuring the
pleasures and conveniences of life.   The very essence of
this power consists in the probability of its exercise, and in

[1] Part III. Sect. 2

its causing us to anticipate, by a *true* or *false* reasoning, the real existence of the pleasure. This anticipation of pleasure is, in itself, a very considerable pleasure; and as its cause is some possession or property, which we enjoy, and which is thereby related to us, we here clearly see all the parts of the foregoing system most exactly and distinctly drawn out before us.

For the same reason, that riches cause pleasure and pride, and poverty excites uneasiness and humility, power must produce the former emotions, and slavery the latter. Power or an authority over others makes us capable of satisfying all our desires; as slavery, by subjecting us to the will of others, exposes us to a thousand wants, and mortifications.

'Tis here worth observing, that the vanity of power, or shame of slavery, are much augmented by the consideration of the persons, over whom we exercise our authority, or who exercise it over us. For supposing it possible to frame statues of such an admirable mechanism, that they cou'd move and act in obedience to the will; 'tis evident the possession of them wou'd give pleasure and pride, but not to such a degree, as the same authority, when exerted over sensible and rational creatures, whose condition, being compar'd to our own, makes it seem more agreeable and honourable. Comparison is in every case a sure method of augmenting our esteem of any thing. A rich man feels the felicity of his condition better by opposing it to that of a beggar. But there is a peculiar advantage in power, by the contrast, which is, in a manner, presented to us, betwixt ourselves and the person we command. The comparison is obvious and natural: The imagination finds it in the very subject: The passage of the thought to its conception is smooth and easy. And that this circumstance has a considerable effect in augmenting its influence, will appear afterwards in examining the nature of *malice* and *envy*.

SECT. XI.—*Of the Love of Fame.*

But beside these original causes of pride and humility, there is a secondary one in the opinions of others, which has an equal influence on the affections. Our reputation, our character, our name are considerations of vast weight and importance; and even the other causes of pride; virtue, beauty and riches; have little influence, when not seconded by the opinions and sentiments of others. In order to account for this phænomenon 'twill be necessary to take some compass, and first explain the nature of *sympathy*.

No quality of human nature is more remarkable, both in itself and in its consequences, than that propensity we have to sympathize with others, and to receive by communication their inclinations and sentiments, however different from, or even contrary to our own. This is not only conspicuous in children, who implicitly embrace every opinion propos'd to them; but also in men of the greatest judgment and understanding, who find it very difficult to follow their own reason or inclination, in opposition to that of their friends and daily companions. To this principle we ought to ascribe the great uniformity we may observe in the humours and turn of thinking of those of the same nation; and 'tis much more probable, that this resemblance arises from sympathy, than from any influence of the soil and climate, which, tho' they continue invariably the same, are not able to preserve the character of a nation the same for a century together. A good-natur'd man finds himself in an instant of the same humour with his company; and even the proudest and most surly take a tincture from their countrymen and acquaintance. A chearful countenance infuses a sensible complacency and serenity into my mind; as an angry or sorrowful one throws a sudden damp upon me. Hatred, resentment, esteem, love, courage, mirth and melancholy; all these passions I feel more from communication than from my own natural temper and disposition. So remarkable a phænomenon merits our attention, and must be trac'd up to its first principles.

When any affection is infus'd by sympathy, it is at first known only by its effects, and by those external signs in the countenance and conversation, which convey an idea of it. This idea is presently converted into an impression, and acquires such a degree of force and vivacity, as to become the very passion itself, and produce an equal emotion, as any original affection.[1] However instantaneous this change of the idea into an impression may be, it proceeds from certain views and reflections, which will not escape the strict scrutiny of a philosopher, tho' they may the person himself, who makes them.

[1 Introd. Sect. 40.—ED]

'Tis evident, that the idea, or rather impression of ourselves is always intimately present with us, and that our consciousness gives us so lively a conception of our own person, that 'tis not possible to imagine, that any thing can in this particular go beyond it. Whatever object, therefore, is related to ourselves must be conceived with a like vivacity of conception, according to the foregoing principles; and tho' this relation shou'd not be so strong as that of causation, it must still have a considerable influence. Resemblance and contiguity are relations not to be neglected; especially when by an inference from cause and effect, and by the observation of external signs, we are inform'd of the real existence of the object, which is resembling or contiguous.

Now 'tis obvious, that nature has preserv'd a great resemblance among all human creatures, and that we never remark any passion or principle in others, of which, in some degree or other, we may not find a parallel in ourselves. The case is the same with the fabric of the mind, as with that of the body. However the parts may differ in shape or size, their structure and composition are in general the same. There is a very remarkable resemblance, which preserves itself amidst all their variety; and this resemblance must very much contribute to make us enter into the sentiments of others, and embrace them with facility and pleasure. Accordingly we find, that where, beside the general resemblance of our natures, there is any peculiar similarity in our manners, or character, or country, or language, it facilitates the sympathy. The stronger the relation is betwixt ourselves and any object, the more easily does the imagination make the transition, and convey to the related idea the vivacity of conception, with which we always form the idea of our own person.

Nor is resemblance the only relation, which has this effect, but receives new force from other relations, that may accompany it. The sentiments of others have little influence, when far remov'd from us, and require the relation of contiguity, to make them communicate themselves entirely. The relations of blood, being a species of causation, may sometimes contribute to the same effect; as also acquaintance, which operates in the same manner with education and custom; as we shall see more fully [1] afterwards. All these relations,

[1] Part II Sect. 4

when united together, convey the impression or consciousness of our own person to the idea of the sentiments or passions of others, and makes us conceive them in the strongest and most lively manner.

It has been remark'd in the beginning of this treatise, that all ideas are borrow'd from impressions, and that these two kinds of perceptions differ only in the degrees of force and vivacity, with which they strike upon the soul. The component parts of ideas and impressions are precisely alike. The manner and order of their appearance may be the same. The different degrees of their force and vivacity are, therefore, the only particulars, that distinguish them : And as ,this difference may be remov'd, in some measure, by a relation betwixt the impressions and ideas, 'tis no wonder an idea of a sentiment or passion, may by this means be so inliven'd as to become the very sentiment or passion The lively idea of any object always approaches its impression ; and 'tis certain we may feel sickness and pain from the mere force of imagination, and make a malady real by often thinking of it. But this is most remarkable in the opinions and affections ; and 'tis there principally that a lively idea is converted into an impression. Our affections depend more upon ourselves, and the internal operations of the mind, than any other impressions ; for which reason they arise more naturally from the imagination, and from every lively idea we form of them. This is the nature and cause of sympathy ; and 'tis after this manner we enter so deep into the opinions and affections of others, whenever we discover them.

What is principally remarkable in this whole affair is the strong confirmation these phænomena give to the foregoing system concerning the understanding, and consequently to the present one concerning the passions ; since these are analogous to each other. 'Tis indeed evident, that when we sympathize with the passions and sentiments of others, these movements appear at first in *our* mind as mere ideas, and are conceiv'd to belong to another person, as we conceive any other matter of fact.[1] 'Tis also evident, that the ideas of the affections of others are converted into the very impressions they represent, and that the passions arise in conformity to the images we form of them. All this is an object of the plainest experience, and depends not on any hypothesis of

[1 Introd Sect 40 —Ed]

philosophy. That science can only be admitted to explain
the phænomena; tho' at the same time it must be confest,
they are so clear of themselves, that there is but little occasion to employ it. For besides the relation of cause and
effect, by which we are convinc'd of the reality of the passion,
with which we sympathize; besides this, I say, we must be
assisted by the relations of resemblance and contiguity, in
order to feel the sympathy in its full perfection. And since
these relations can entirely convert an idea into an impression, and convey the vivacity of the latter into the former,
so perfectly as to lose nothing of it in the transition, we may
easily conceive how the relation of cause and effect alone,
may serve to strengthen and inliven an idea. In sympathy
there is an evident conversion of an idea into an impression.
This conversion arises from the relation of objects to ourself.
Ourself is always intimately present to us. Let us compare
all these circumstances, and we shall find, that sympathy is
exactly correspondent to the operations of our understanding; and even contains something more surprising and
extraordinary.

'Tis now time to turn our view from the general consideration of sympathy, to its influence on pride and humility,
when thèse passions arise from praise and blame, from reputation and infamy. We may observe, that no person is ever
prais'd by another for any quality, which wou'd not, if real,
produce, of itself, a pride in the person possest of it. The
elogiums either turn upon his power, or riches, or family,
or virtue; all of which are subjects of vanity, that we have
already explain'd and accounted for. 'Tis certain, then, that
if a person consider'd himself in the same light, in which he
appears to his admirer, he wou'd first receive a separate
pleasure, and afterwards a pride or self-satisfaction, according
to the hypothesis above explain'd. Now nothing is more
natural than for us to embrace the opinions of others in this
particular; both from *sympathy*, which renders all their sentiments intimately present to us; and from *reasoning*, which
makes us regard their judgment, as a kind of argument for
what they affirm. These two principles of authority and
sympathy influence almost all our opinions; but must have
a peculiar influence, when we judge of our own worth and
character. Such judgments are always attended with passion;[1]

[1] Book I Part III Sect. 10

and nothing tends more to disturb our understanding, and
precipitate us into any opinions, however unreasonable, than
their connexion with passion; which diffuses itself over the
imagination, and gives an additional force to every related
idea. To which we may add, that being conscious of great
partiality in our own favour, we are peculiarly pleas'd with
any thing, that confirms the good opinion we have of ourselves, and are easily shock'd with whatever opposes it.

All this appears very probable in theory; but in order to
bestow a full certainty on this reasoning, we must examine
the phænomena of the passions, and see if they agree with it.

Among these phænomena we may esteem it a very favourable one to our present purpose, that tho' fame in general be
agreeable, yet we receive a much greater satisfaction from the
approbation of those, whom we ourselves esteem and approve
of, than of those, whom we hate and despise. In like manner
we are principally mortify'd with the contempt of persons,
upon whose judgment we set some value, and are, in a great
measure, indifferent about the opinions of the rest of mankind. But if the mind receiv'd from any original instinct a
desire of fame, and aversion to infamy, fame and infamy
wou'd influence us without distinction; and every opinion,
according as it were favourable or unfavourable, wou'd equally
excite that desire or aversion. The judgment of a fool is the
judgment of another person, as well as that of a wise man,
and is only inferior in its influence on our own judgment.

We are not only better pleas'd with the approbation of a
wise man than with that of a fool, but receive an additional
satisfaction from the former, when 'tis obtain'd after a long
and intimate acquaintance. This is accounted for after the
same manner.

The praises of others never give us much pleasure, unless
they concur with our own opinion, and extol us for those
qualities, in which we chiefly excel. A mere soldier little
values the character of eloquence: A gownman of courage:
A bishop of humour: Or a merchant of learning. Whatever
esteem a man may have for any quality, abstractedly consider'd; when he is conscious he is not possest of it; the
opinions of the whole world will give him little pleasure in
that particular, and that because they never will be able to
draw his own opinion after them.

Nothing is more usual than for men of good families, but

narrow circumstances, to leave their friends and country, and
rather seek their livelihood by mean and mechanical employments among strangers, than among those, who are
acquainted with their birth and education. We shall be unknown, say they, where we go. No body will suspect from
what family we are sprung. We shall be remov'd from all
our friends and acquaintance, and our poverty and meanness
will by that means sit more easy upon us. In examining
these sentiments, I find they afford many very convincing
arguments for my present purpose.

First, We may infer from them, that the uneasiness of
being contemn'd depends on sympathy, and that sympathy
depends on the relation of objects to ourselves; since we are
most uneasy under the contempt of persons, who are both
related to us by blood, and contiguous in place. Hence we
seek to diminish this sympathy and uneasiness by separating
these relations, and placing ourselves in a contiguity to
strangers, and at a distance from relations.

Secondly, We may conclude, that relations are requisite to
sympathy, not absolutely consider'd as relations, but by their
influence in converting our ideas of the sentiments of others
into the very sentiments, by means of the association betwixt
the idea of their persons, and that of our own. For here the
relations of kindred and contiguity both subsist; but not
being united in the same persons, they contribute in a less
degree to the sympathy.

Thirdly, This very circumstance of the diminution of sympathy by the separation of relations is worthy of our attention. Suppose I am plac'd in a poor condition among
strangers, and consequently am but lightly treated; I yet
find myself easier in that situation, than when I was every
day expos'd to the contempt of my kindred and countrymen.
Here I feel a double contempt; from my relations, but they
are absent; from those about me, but they are strangers.
This double contempt is likewise strengthen'd by the two
relations of kindred and contiguity. But as the persons are
not the same, who are connected with me by those two relations, this difference of ideas separates the impressions arising
from the contempt, and keeps them from running into each
other. The contempt of my neighbours has a certain influence; as has also that of my kindred: But these influences
are distinct, and never unite; as when the contempt proceeds

from persons who are at once both my neighbours and kindred. This phænomenon is analogous to the system of pride and humility above-explain'd, which may seem so extraordinary to vulgar apprehensions.

Fourthly, A person in these circumstances naturally conceals his birth from those among whom he lives, and is very uneasy, if any one suspects him to be of a family, much superior to his present fortune and way of living. Every thing in this world is judg'd of by comparison. What is an immense fortune for a private gentleman is beggary for a prince. A peasant wou'd think himself happy in what cannot afford necessaries for a gentleman. When a man has either been accustom'd to a more splendid way of living, or thinks himself intitled to it by his birth and quality, every thing below is disagreeable and even shameful; and 'tis with the greatest industry he conceals his pretensions to a better fortune. Here he himself knows his misfortunes; but as those, with whom he lives, are ignorant of them, he has the disagreeable reflection and comparison suggested only by his own thoughts, and never receives it by a sympathy with others; which must contribute very much to his ease and satisfaction.

If there be any objections to this hypothesis, *that the pleasure, which we receive from praise, arises from a communication of sentiments,* we shall find, upon examination, that these objections, when taken in a proper light, will serve to confirm it. Popular fame may be agreeable even to a man, who despises the vulgar; but 'tis because their multitude gives them additional weight and authority. Plagiaries are delighted with praises, which they are conscious they do not deserve; but this is a kind of castle-building, where the imagination amuses itself with its own fictions, and strives to render them firm and stable by a sympathy with the sentiments of others. Proud men are most shock'd with contempt, tho' they do not most readily assent to it; but 'tis because of the opposition betwixt the passion, which is natural to them, and that receiv'd by sympathy. A violent lover in like manner is very much displeas'd when you blame and condemn his love; tho' 'tis evident your opposition can have no influence, but by the hold it takes of himself, and by his sympathy with you. If he despises you, or perceives you are in jest, whatever you say has no effect upon him.

SECT. XII.—*Of the Pride and Humility of Animals.*

Thus in whatever light we consider this subject, we may still observe, that the causes of pride and humility correspond exactly to our hypothesis, and that nothing can excite either of these passions, unless it be both related to ourselves, and produces a pleasure or pain independent of the passion. We have not only prov'd, that a tendency to produce pleasure or pain is common to all the causes of pride or humility, but also that 'tis the only thing, which is common; and consequently is the quality, by which they operate. We have farther prov'd, that the most considerable causes of these passions are really nothing but the power of producing either agreeable or uneasy sensations; and therefore that all their effects, and amongst the rest, pride and humility, are deriv'd solely from that origin. Such simple and natural principles, founded on such solid proofs, cannot fail to be receiv'd by philosophers, unless oppos'd by some objections, that have escap'd me.

'Tis usual with anatomists to join their observations and experiments on human bodies to those on beasts, and from the agreement of these experiments to derive an additional argument for any particular hypothesis. 'Tis indeed certain, that where the structure of parts in brutes is the same as in men, and the operation of these parts also the same, the causes of that operation cannot be different, and that whatever we discover to be true of the one species, may be concluded without hesitation to be certain of the other. Thus tho' the mixture of humours and the composition of minute parts may justly be presum'd to be somewhat different in men from what it is in mere animals; and therefore any experiment we make upon the one concerning the effects of medicines will not always apply to the other; yet as the structure of the veins and muscles, the fabric and situation of the heart, of the lungs, the stomach, the liver and other parts, are the same or nearly the same in all animals, the very same hypothesis, which in one species explains muscular motion, the progress of the chyle, the circulation of the blood, must be applicable to every one; and according as it agrees or disagrees with the experiments we may make in any species of creatures, we may draw a proof of its truth or falshood on the whole. Let us, therefore, apply this method of enquiry, which is found so just and useful in reasonings concerning the body, to our present anatomy of the mind, and see what discoveries we can make by it.

SECT
XII

Of the
pride and
humility of
animals.

In order to this we must first shew the correspondence of *passions* in men and animals, and afterwards compare the *causes*, which produce these passions.

'Tis plain, that almost in every species of creatures, but especially of the nobler kind, there are many evident marks of pride and humility. The very port and gait of a swan, or turkey, or peacock show the high idea he has entertain'd of himself, and his contempt of all others. This is the more remarkable, that in the two last species of animals, the pride always attends the beauty, and is discover'd in the male only. The vanity and emulation of nightingales in singing have been commonly remark'd; as likewise that of horses in swiftness, of hounds in sagacity and smell, of the bull and cock in strength, and of every other animal in his particular excellency. Add to this, that every species of creatures, which approach so often to man, as to familiarize themselves with him, show an evident pride in his approbation, and are pleas'd with his praises and caresses, independent of every other consideration. Nor are they the caresses of every one without distinction, which give them this vanity, but those principally of the persons they know and love; in the same manner as that passion is excited in mankind. All these are evident proofs, that pride and humility are not merely human passions, but extend themselves over the whole animal creation.

The *causes* of these passions are likewise much the same in beasts as in us, making a just allowance for our superior knowledge and understanding. Thus animals have little or no sense of virtue or vice; they quickly lose sight of the relations of blood; and are incapable of that of right and property: For which reason the causes of their pride and humility must lie solely in the body, and can never be plac'd either in the mind or external objects. But so far as regards the body, the same qualities cause pride in the animal as in the human kind; and 'tis on beauty, strength, swiftness or some other useful or agreeable quality that this passion is always founded.

The next question is, whether, since those passions are the same, and arise from the same causes thro' the whole

creation, the *manner*, in which the causes operate, be also the
same. According to all rules of analogy, this is justly to be
expected; and if we find upon trial, that the explication of
these phænomena, which we make use of in one species, will
not apply to the rest, we may presume that that explication,
however specious, is in reality without foundation.

In order to decide this question, let us consider, that there
is evidently the same *relation* of ideas, and deriv'd from the
same causes, in the minds of animals as in those of men.
A dog, that has hid a bone, often forgets the place; but
when brought to it, his thought passes easily to what he formerly conceal'd, by means of the contiguity, which produces
a relation among his ideas. In like manner, when he has
been heartily beat in any place, he will tremble on his approach to it, even tho' he discover no signs of any present
danger. The effects of resemblance are not so remarkable;
but as that relation makes a considerable ingredient in
causation, of which all animals shew so evident a judgment,
we may conclude that the three relations of resemblance,
contiguity and causation operate in the same manner upon
beasts as upon human creatures.

There are also instances of the relation of impressions,
sufficient to convince us, that there is an union of certain
affections with each other in the inferior species of creatures
as well as in the superior, and that their minds are frequently
convey'd thro' a series of connected emotions. A dog, when
elevated with joy, runs naturally into love and kindness,
whether of his master or of the sex. In like manner, when
full of pain or sorrow, he becomes quarrelsome and ill-
natur'd; and that passion, which at first was grief, is by the
smallest occasion converted into anger.

Thus all the internal principles, that are necessary in us to
produce either pride or humility, are common to all creatures; and since the causes, which excite these passions, are
likewise the same, we may justly conclude, that these causes
operate after the same *manner* thro' the whole animal creation. My hypothesis is so simple, and supposes so little
reflection and judgement, that 'tis applicable to every sensible creature; which must not only be allow'd to be a convincing proof of its veracity, but, I am confident, will be
found an objection to every other system.

PART II.

OF LOVE AND HATRED.

Sect. I.—*Of the Object and Causes of Love and Hatred.*[1]

'Tis altogether impossible to give any definition of the passions of *love* and *hatred;* and that because they produce merely a simple impression, without any mixture or composition. 'Twou'd be as unnecessary to attempt any description of them, drawn from their nature, origin, causes and objects; and that both because these are the subjects of our present enquiry, and because these passions of themselves are sufficiently known from our common feeling and experience. This we have already observ'd concerning pride and humility, and here repeat it concerning love and hatred; and indeed there is so great a resemblance betwixt these two sets of passions, that we shall be oblig'd to begin with a kind of abridgment of our reasonings concerning the former, in order to explain the latter.

As the immediate *object* of pride and humility is self or that identical person, of whose thoughts, actions, and sensations we are intimately conscious; so the *object* of love and hatred is some other person, of whose thoughts, actions, and sensations we are not conscious. This is sufficiently evident from experience. Our love and hatred are always directed to some sensible being external to us; and when we talk of *self-love,* 'tis not in a proper sense, nor has the sensation it produces any thing in common with that tender emotion, which is excited by a friend or mistress. 'Tis the same case with hatred. We may be mortified by our own faults and follies; but never feel any anger or hatred, except from the injuries of others.

Side note: SECT. 1 — Of the object and causes of love and hatred.

[¹ Introd Sect 38 —Ed]

But tho' the object of love and hatred be always some
other person, 'tis plain that the object is not, properly
speaking, the *cause* of these passions, or alone sufficient to
excite them.   For since love and hatred are directly contrary in their sensation, and have the same object in common,
if that object were also their cause, it wou'd produce these
opposite passions in an equal degree; and as they must, from
the very first moment, destroy each other, none of them
wou'd ever be able to make its appearance.   There must,
therefore, be some cause different from the object.

If we consider the causes of love and hatred, we shall find
they are very much diversify'd, and have not many things
in common.   The virtue, knowledge, wit, good sense, good
humour of any person, produce love and esteem; as the
opposite qualities, hatred and contempt.   The same passions
arise from bodily accomplishments, such as beauty, force,
swiftness, dexterity; and from their contraries; as likewise
from the external advantages and disadvantages of family,
possessions, cloaths, nation and climate.   There is not one
of these objects, but what by its different qualities may
produce love and esteem, or hatred and contempt.

From the view of these causes we may derive a new
distinction betwixt the *quality* that operates, and the *subject*
on which it is plac'd.   A prince, that is possess'd of a stately
palace, commands the esteem of the people upon that
account; and that *first*, by the beauty of the palace, and
secondly, by the relation of property, which connects it with
him.   The removal of either of these destroys the passion;
which evidently proves that the cause is a compounded one.

'Twou'd be tedious to trace the passions of love and
hatred, thro' all the observations which we have form'd
concerning pride and humility, and which are equally
applicable to both sets of passions.   'Twill be sufficient to
remark in general, that the object of love and hatred is
evidently some thinking person; and that the sensation of
the former passion is always agreeable, and of the latter
uneasy. We may also *suppose* with some shew of probability,
*that the cause of both these passions is always related to a
thinking being,* and *that the cause of the former produces a
separate pleasure, and of the latter a separate uneasiness.*

One of these suppositions, *viz.* that the cause of love and
hatred must be related to a person or thinking being, in

order to produce these passions, is not only probable, but too evident to be contested. Virtue and vice, when consider'd in the abstract; beauty and deformity, when plac'd on inanimate objects; poverty and riches, when belonging to a third person, excite no degree of love or hatred, esteem or contempt towards those, who have no relation to them. A person looking out at a window, sees me in the street, and beyond me a beautiful palace, with which I have no concern : I believe none will pretend, that this person will pay me the same respect, as if I were owner of the palace.

SECT. I

Of the object and causes of love and hatred.

'Tis not so evident at first sight, that a relation of impressions is requisite to these passions, and that because in the transition the one impression is so much confounded with the other, that they become in a manner undistinguishable. But as in pride and humility, we have easily been able to make the separation, and to prove, that every cause of these passions produces a separate pain or pleasure, I might here observe the same method with the same success, in examining particularly the several causes of love and hatred. But as I hasten to a full and decisive proof of these systems, I delay this examination for a moment: And in the mean time shall endeavour to convert to my present purpose all my reasonings concerning pride and humility, by an argument that is founded on unquestionable experience.

There are few persons, that are satisfy'd with their own character, or genius, or fortune, who are not desirous of shewing themselves to the world, and of acquiring the love and approbation of mankind. Now 'tis evident, that the very same qualities and circumstances, which are the causes of pride or self-esteem, are also the causes of vanity or the desire of reputation; and that we always put to view those particulars with which in ourselves we are best satisfy'd. But if love and esteem were not produc'd by the same qualities as pride, according as these qualities are related to ourselves or others, this method of proceeding wou'd be very absurd, nor cou'd men expect a correspondence in the sentiments of every other person, with those themselves have entertain'd. 'Tis true, few can form exact systems of the passions, or make reflections on their general nature and resemblances. But without such a progress in philosophy, we are not subject to many mistakes in this particular, but are sufficiently guided by common experience, as well as by a kind of *presentation;* which tells us what will operate on others, by what we feel immediately in ourselves. Since then the same qualities that produce pride or humility, cause love or hatred; all the arguments that have been employ'd to prove, that the causes of the former passions excite a pain or pleasure independent of the passion, will be applicable with equal evidence to the causes of the latter.

SECT. II.—*Experiments to Confirm this System.*

Upon duly weighing these arguments, no one will make any scruple to assent to that conclusion I draw from them, concerning the transition along related impressions and ideas, especially as 'tis a principle, in itself, so easy and natural. But that we may place this system beyond doubt both with regard to love and hatred, pride and humility, 'twill be proper to make some new experiments upon all these passions, as well as to recal a few of these observations, which I have formerly touch'd upon.

In order to make these experiments, let us suppose I am in company with a person, whom I formerly regarded without any sentiments either of friendship or enmity. Here I have the natural and ultimate object of all these four passions plac'd before me. Myself am the proper object of pride or humility, the other person of love or hatred.

Regard now with attention the nature of these passions, and their situation with respect to each other. 'Tis evident here are four affections, plac'd, as it were, in a square or regular connexion with, and distance from each other. The passions of pride and humility, as well as those of love and hatred, are connected together by the identity of their object, which to the first set of passions is self, to the second some other person. These two lines of communication or connexion form two opposite sides of the square. Again, pride and love are agreeable passions; hatred and humility uneasy. This similitude of sensation betwixt pride and love, and that betwixt humility and hatred form a new connexion, and may be consider'd as the other two sides of the square. Upon the whole, pride is connected with humility, love with hatred, by their objects or ideas: Pride with love, humility with hatred, by their sensations or impressions.

I say then, that nothing can produce any of these passions without bearing it a double relation, *viz.* of ideas to the object of the passion, and of sensation to the passion itself. This we must prove by our experiments.

First Experiment. To proceed with the greater order in these experiments, let us first suppose, that being plac'd in the situation above-mention'd, *viz.* in company with some other person, there is an object presented, that has no relation either of impressions or ideas to any of these passions. Thus suppose we regard together an ordinary stone, or other common object, belonging to neither of us, and causing of itself no emotion, or independent pain and pleasure: 'Tis evident such an object will produce none of these four passions. Let us try it upon each of them successively. Let us apply it to love, to hatred, to humility, to pride; none of them ever arises in the smallest degree imaginable. Let us change the object, as oft as we please; provided still we choose one, that has neither of these two relations. Let us repeat the experiment in all the dispositions, of which the mind is susceptible. No object, in the vast variety of nature, will, in any disposition, produce any passion without these relations.

Second Experiment. Since an object, that wants both these relations can never produce any passion, let us bestow on it only one of these relations; and see what will follow. Thus suppose, I regard a stone or any common object, that belongs either to me or my companion, and by that means acquires a relation of ideas to the object of the passions: 'Tis plain, that to consider the matter *a priori*, no emotion of any kind can reasonably be expected. For besides, that a relation of ideas operates secretly and calmly on the mind, it bestows an equal impulse towards the opposite passions of pride and humility, love and hatred, according as the object belongs to ourselves or others; which opposition of the passions must destroy both, and leave the mind perfectly free from any affection or emotion. This reasoning *a priori* is confirm'd by experience. No trivial or vulgar object, that causes not a pain or pleasure, independent of the passion, will ever, by its property or other relations, either to ourselves or others, be able to produce the affections of pride or humility, love or hatred.

Third Experiment. 'Tis evident, therefore, that a relation

of ideas is not able alone to give rise to these affections. Let us now remove this relation, and in its stead place a relation of impressions, by presenting an object, which is agreeable or disagreeable, but has no relation either to ourself or companion; and let us observe the consequences. To consider the matter first *a priori*, as in the preceding experiment; we may conclude, that the object will have a small, but an uncertain connexion with these passions. For besides, that this relation is not a cold and imperceptible one, it has not the inconvenience of the relation of ideas, nor directs us with equal force to two contrary passions, which by their opposition destroy each other. But if we consider, on the other hand, that this transition from the sensation to the affection is not forwarded by any principle, that produces a transition of ideas; but, on the contrary, that tho' the one impression be easily transfus'd into the other, yet the change of objects is suppos'd contrary to all the principles, that cause a transition of that kind; we may from thence infer, that nothing will ever be a steady or durable cause of any passion, that is connected with the passion merely by a relation of impressions. What our reason wou'd conclude from analogy, after ballancing these arguments, wou'd be, that an object, which produces pleasure or uneasiness, but has no manner of connexion either with ourselves or others, may give such a turn to the disposition, as that it may naturally fall into pride or love, humility or hatred, and search for other objects, upon which, by a double relation, it can found these affections; but that an object, which has only one of these relations, tho' the most advantageous one, can never give rise to any constant and establish'd passion.

Most fortunately all this reasoning is found to be exactly conformable to experience, and the phænomena of the passions. Suppose I were travelling with a companion thro' a country, to which we are both utter strangers; 'tis evident, that if the prospects be beautiful, the roads agreeable, and the inns commodious, this may put me into good humour both with myself and fellow-traveller. But as we suppose, that this country has no relation either to myself or friend, it can never be the immediate cause of pride or love; and therefore if I found not the passion on some other object, that bears either of us a closer relation, my emotions are rather to be consider'd as the overflowings of an elevate or humane disposition, than as an establish'd passion. The case is the same where the object produces uneasiness.

Fourth Experiment. Having found, that neither an object without any relation of ideas or impressions, nor an object, that has only one relation, can ever cause pride or humility, love or hatred; reason alone may convince us, without any farther experiment, that whatever has a double relation must necessarily excite these passions; since 'tis evident they must have some cause. But to leave as little room for doubt as possible, let us renew our experiments, and see whether the event in this case answers our expectation. I choose an object, such as virtue, that causes a separate satisfaction: On this object I bestow a relation to self; and find, that from this disposition of affairs, there immediately arises a passion. But what passion? That very one of pride, to which this object bears a double relation. Its idea is related to that of self, the object of the passion: The sensation it causes resembles the sensation of the passion. That I may be sure I am not mistaken in this experiment, I remove first one relation; then another; and find, that each removal destroys the passion, and leaves the object perfectly indifferent. But I am not content with this. I make a still farther trial; and instead of removing the relation, I only change it for one of a different kind. I suppose the virtue to belong to my companion, not to myself; and observe what follows from this alteration. I immediately perceive the affections to wheel about, and leaving pride, where there is only one relation, *viz.* of impressions, fall to the side of love, where they are attracted by a double relation of impressions and ideas. By repeating the same experiment, in changing anew the relation of ideas, I bring the affections back to pride; and by a new repetition I again place them at love or kindness. Being fully convinc'd of the influence of this relation, I try the effects of the other; and by changing virtue for vice, convert the pleasant impression, which arises from the former, into the disagreeable one, which proceeds from the latter. The effect still answers expectation. Vice, when plac'd on another, excites, by means of its double relations, the passion of hatred, instead of love, which for the same reason arises from virtue. To continue the experiment, I change anew the relation of ideas, and suppose the

vice to belong to myself. What follows? What is usual.
A subsequent change of the passion from hatred to humility.
This humility I convert into pride by a new change of the
impression; and find after all that I have compleated the
round, and have by these changes brought back the passion
to that very situation, in which I first found it.

But to make the matter still more certain, I alter the
object; and instead of vice and virtue, make the trial upon
beauty and deformity, riches and poverty, power and servi-
tude.   Each of these objects runs the circle of the passions
in the same manner, by a change of their relations: And in
whatever order we proceed, whether thro' pride, love, hatred,
humility, or thro' humility, hatred, love, pride, the experiment is not in the least diversify'd.   Esteem and contempt, indeed, arise on some occasions instead of love and
hatred; but these are at the bottom the same passions, only
diversify'd by some causes, which we shall explain afterwards.

Fifth Experiment.   To give greater authority to these
experiments, let us change the situation of affairs as much
as possible, and place the passions and objects in all the
different positions, of which they are susceptible. Let us
suppose, beside the relations above-mention'd, that the person, along with whom I make all these experiments, is
closely connected with me either by blood or friendship. He
is, we shall suppose, my son or brother, or is united to me
by a long and familiar acquaintance. Let us next suppose,
that the cause of the passion acquires a double relation of
impressions and ideas to this person; and let us see what
the effects are of all these complicated attractions and relations.

Before we consider what they are in fact, let us determine
what they ought to be, conformable to my hypothesis. 'Tis
plain, that, according as the impression is either pleasant
or uneasy, the passion of love or hatred must arise towards
the person, who is thus connected to the cause of the impression by these double relations, which I have all along
requir'd. The virtue of a brother must make me love him;
as his vice or infamy must excite the contrary passion. But
to judge only from the situation of affairs, I shou'd not
expect, that the affections wou'd rest there, and never transfuse themselves into any other impression. As there is here

SECT
II

Experi-
ments to
confirm
this sys-
tem.

a person, who by means of a double relation is the object
of my passion, the very same reasoning leads me to think
the passion will be carry'd farther. The person has a relation of ideas to myself, according to the supposition; the
passion, of which he is the object, by being either agreeable
or uneasy, has a relation of impressions to pride or humility.
'Tis evident, then, that one of these passions must arise
from the love or hatred.

This is the reasoning I form in conformity to my hypothesis; and am pleas'd to find upon trial that every thing
answers exactly to my expectation. The virtue or vice of
a son or brother not only excites love or hatred, but by a
new transition, from similar causes, gives rise to pride or
humility. Nothing causes greater vanity than any shining
quality in our relations; as nothing mortifies us more than
their vice or infamy. This exact conformity of experience
to our reasoning is a convincing proof of the solidity of that
hypothesis, upon which we reason.

Sixth Experiment. This evidence will be still augmented,
if we reverse the experiment, and preserving still the same
relations, begin only with a different passion. Suppose,
that instead of the virtue or vice of a son or brother, which
causes first love or hatred, and afterwards pride or humility,
we place these good or bad qualities on ourselves, without
any immediate connexion with the person, who is related
to us: Experience shews us, that by this change of situation
the whole chain is broke, and that the mind is not convey'd from one passion to another, as in the preceding
instance. We never love or hate a son or brother for the
virtue or vice we discern in ourselves; tho' 'tis evident the
same qualities in him give us a very sensible pride or
humility. The transition from pride or humility to love or
hatred is not so natural as from love or hatred to pride or
humility. This may at first sight be esteem'd contrary to
my hypothesis; since the relations of impressions and ideas
are in both cases precisely the same. Pride and humility
are impressions related to love and hatred. Myself am related to the person. It shou'd, therefore, be expected, that
like causes must produce like effects, and a perfect transition
arise from the double relation, as in all other cases. This
difficulty we may easily solve by the following reflections.

'Tis evident, that as we are at all times intimately conscious of ourselves, our sentiments and passions, their ideas must strike upon us with greater vivacity than the ideas of the sentiments and passions of any other person. But every thing, that strikes upon us with vivacity, and appears in a full and strong light, forces itself, in a manner, into our consideration, and becomes present to the mind on the smallest hint and most trivial relation. For the same reason, when it is once present, it engages the attention, and keeps it from wandering to other objects, however strong may be their relation to our first object. The imagination passes easily from obscure to lively ideas, but with difficulty from lively to obscure. In the one case the relation is aided by another principle : In the other case, 'tis oppos'd by it.

Now I have observ'd, that those two faculties of the mind, the imagination and passions, assist each other in their operation, when their propensities are similar, and when they act upon the same object. The mind has always a propensity to pass from a passion to any other related to it; and this propensity is forwarded when the object of the one passion is related to that of the other. The two impulses concur with each other, and render the whole transition more smooth and easy. But if it shou'd happen, that while the relation of ideas, strictly speaking, continues the same, its influence, in causing a transition of the imagination, shou'd no longer take place, 'tis evident its influence on the passions must also cease, as being dependent entirely on that transition. This is the reason why pride or humility is not transfus'd into love or hatred with the same ease, that the latter passions are chang'd into the former. If a person be my brother I am his likewise : But tho' the relations be reciprocal, they have very different effects on the imagination. The passage is smooth and open from the consideration of any person related to us to that of ourself, of whom we are every moment conscious. But when the affections are once directed to ourself, the fancy passes not with the same facility from that object to any other person, how closely so ever connected with us. This easy or difficult transition of the imagination operates upon the passions, and facilitates or retards their transition; which is a clear proof, that these two faculties of the passions and imagination are connected together, and that the relations of ideas have an influence upon the affections. Besides innumerable experiments that prove this, we here find, that even when the relation remains; if by any particular circumstance its usual effect upon the fancy in producing an association or transition of ideas, is prevented; its usual effect upon the passions, in conveying us from one to another, is in like manner prevented.

Some may, perhaps, find a contradiction betwixt this phænomenon and that of sympathy, where the mind passes easily from the idea of ourselves to that of any other object related to us. But this difficulty will vanish, if we consider that in sympathy our own person is not the object of any passion, nor is there any thing, that fixes our attention on ourselves; as in the present case, where we are suppos'd to be actuated with pride or humility. Ourself, independent of the perception of every other object, is in reality nothing: For which reason we must turn our view to external objects; and 'tis natural for us to consider with most attention such as lie contiguous to us, or resemble us. But when self is the object of a passion, 'tis not natural to quit the consideration of it, till the passion be exhausted; in which case the double relations of impressions and ideas can no longer operate.

Seventh Experiment. To put this whole reasoning to a farther trial, let us make a new experiment; and as we have already seen the effects of related passions and ideas, let us here suppose an identity of passions along with a relation of ideas; and let us consider the effects of this new situation. 'Tis evident a transition of the passions from the one object to the other is here in all reason to be expected; since the relation of ideas is suppos'd still to continue, and an identity of impressions must produce a stronger connexion, than the most perfect resemblance, that can be imagin'd. If a double relation, therefore, of impressions and ideas is able to produce a transition from one to the other, much more an identity of impressions with a relation of ideas. Accordingly we find, that when we either love or hate any person, the passions seldom continue within their first bounds; but extend themselves towards all the contiguous objects, and comprehend the friends and relations of him we love or hate. Nothing is more natural than to bear a kindness to one brother on account of our friendship for another, without any farther examination of his character. A quarrel with one person gives us a hatred for the whole family, tho' entirely innocent of that, which displeases us. Instances of this kind are every where to be met with.

There is only one difficulty in this experiment, which it will be necessary to account for, before we proceed any farther. 'Tis evident, that tho' all passions pass easily from one object to another related to it, yet this transition is made with greater facility, where the more considerable object is first presented, and the lesser follows it, than where this order is revers'd, and the lesser takes the precedence. Thus 'tis more natural for us to love the son upon account of the father, than the father upon account of the son; the servant for the master, than the master for the servant; the subject for the prince, than the prince for the subject. In like manner we more readily contract a hatred against a whole family, where our first quarrel is with the head of it, than where we are displeas'd with a son, or servant, or some inferior member. In short, our passions, like other objects, descend with greater facility than they ascend.

That we may comprehend, wherein consists the difficulty of explaining this phænomenon, we must consider, that the very same reason, which determines the imagination to pass from remote to contiguous objects, with more facility than from contiguous to remote, causes it likewise to change with more ease, the less for the greater, than the greater for the less. Whatever has the greatest influence is most taken notice of; and whatever is most taken notice of, presents itself most readily to the imagination. We are more apt to over-look in any subject, what is trivial, than what appears of considerable moment; but especially if the latter takes the precedence, and first engages our attention. Thus if any accident makes us consider the *Satellites* of *Jupiter*, our fancy is naturally determin'd to form the idea of that planet; but if we first reflect on the principal planet, 'tis more natural for us to overlook its attendants. The mention of the provinces of any empire conveys our thought to the seat of the empire; but the fancy returns not with the same facility to the consideration of the provinces. The idea of the servant makes us think of the master; that of the subject carries our view to the prince. But the same relation has not an equal influence in conveying us back again. And on this is founded that reproach of *Cornelia* to her sons, that they ought to be asham'd she shou'd be more known by the title of the

daughter of *Scipio*, than by that of the mother of the
Gracchi. This was, in other words, exhorting them to
render themselves as illustrious and famous as their grand-
father, otherwise the imagination of the people, passing from
her who was intermediate, and plac'd in an equal relation to
both, wou'd always leave them, and denominate her by what
was more considerable and of greater moment. On the same
principle is founded that common custom of making wives
bear the name of their husbands, rather than husbands that
of their wives; as also the ceremony of giving the prece-
dency to those, whom we honour and respect. We might
find many other instances to confirm this principle, were it
not already sufficiently evident.

SECT.
II

Experi-
ments to
confirm
this sys-
tem.

Now since the fancy finds the same facility in passing
from the lesser to the greater, as from remote to contiguous,
why does not this easy transition of ideas assist the transition of passions in the former case, as well as in the latter?
The virtues of a friend or brother produce first love, and then
pride; because in that case the imagination passes from
remote to contiguous, according to its propensity. Our own
virtues produce not first pride, and then love to a friend or
brother; because the passage in that case wou'd be from
contiguous to remote, contrary to its propensity. But the
love or hatred of an inferior causes not readily any passion
to the superior, tho' that be the natural propensity of the
imagination: While the love or hatred of a superior, causes
a passion to the inferior, contrary to its propensity. In
short, the same facility of transition operates not in the
same manner upon superior and inferior as upon contiguous
and remote. These two phænomena appear contradictory,
and require some attention to be reconcil'd.

As the transition of ideas is here made contrary to the
natural propensity of the imagination, that faculty must be
overpower'd by some stronger principle of another kind; and
as there is nothing ever present to the mind but impressions
and ideas, this principle must necessarily lie in the impressions. Now it has been observ'd, that impressions or passions
are connected only by their resemblance, and that where any
two passions place the mind in the same or in similar dispositions, it very naturally passes from the one to the other:
As on the contrary, a repugnance in the dispositions produces a difficulty in the transition of the passions. But 'tis

observable, that this repugnance may arise from a difference of degree as well as of kind   nor do we experience a greater difficulty in passing suddenly from a small degree of love to a small degree of hatred, than from a small to a great degree of either of these affections.   A man, when calm or only moderately agitated, is so different, in every respect, from himself, when disturbed with a violent passion, that no two persons can be more unlike; nor is it easy to pass from the one extreme to the other, without a considerable interval betwixt them.

The difficulty is not less, if it be not rather greater, in passing from the strong passion to the weak, than in passing from the weak to the strong, provided the one passion upon its appearance destroys the other, and they do not both of them exist at once.   But the case is entirely alter'd, when the passions unite together, and actuate the mind at the same time.   A weak passion, when added to a strong, makes not so considerable change in the disposition, as a strong when added to a weak; for which reason there is a closer connexion betwixt the great degree and the small, than betwixt the small degree and the great.

The degree of any passion depends upon the nature of its object; and an affection directed to a person, who is considerable in our eyes, fills and possesses the mind much more than one, which has for its object a person we esteem of less consequence.   Here then the contradiction betwixt the propensities of the imagination and passion displays itself. When we turn our thought to a great and a small object, the imagination finds more facility in passing from the small to the great, than from the great to the small; but the affections find a greater difficulty: And as the affections are a more powerful principle than the imagination, no wonder they prevail over it, and draw the mind to their side.   In spite of the difficulty of passing from the idea of great to that of little, a passion directed to the former, produces always a similar passion towards the latter; when the great and little are related together.   The idea of the servant conveys our thought most readily to the master; but the hatred or love of the master produces with greater facility anger or good-will to the servant.   The strongest passion in this case takes the precedence; and the addition of the weaker making no considerable change on the disposition, the passage is by that means render'd more easy and natural betwixt them.

As in the foregoing experiment we found, that a relation of ideas, which, by any particular circumstance, ceases to produce its usual effect of facilitating the transition of ideas, ceases likewise to operate on the passions; so in the present experiment we find the same property of the impressions. Two different degrees of the same passion are surely related together; but if the smaller be first present, it has little or no tendency to introduce the greater; and that because the addition of the great to the little, produces a more sensible alteration on the temper, than the addition of the little to the great. These phænomena, when duly weigh'd, will be found convincing proofs of this hypothesis.

And these proofs will be confirm'd, if we consider the manner in which the mind here reconciles the contradiction, I have observ'd betwixt the passions and the imagination. The fancy passes with more facility from the less to the greater, than from the greater to the less: But on the contrary a violent passion produces more easily a feeble, than that does a violent. In this opposition the passion in the end prevails over the imagination; but 'tis commonly by complying with it, and by seeking another quality, which may counter-ballance that principle, from whence the opposition arises. When we love the father or master of a family, we little think of his children or servants. But when these are present with us, or when it lies any ways in our power to serve them, the nearness and contiguity in this case encreases their magnitude, or at least removes that opposition, which the fancy makes to the transition of the affections. If the imagination finds a difficulty in passing from greater to less, it finds an equal facility in passing from remote to contiguous, which brings the matter to an equality, and leaves the way open from the one passion to the other.

Eighth Experiment. I have observ'd that the transition from love or hatred to pride or humility, is more easy than from pride or humility to love or hatred; and that the difficulty, which the imagination finds in passing from contiguous to remote, is the cause why we scarce have any instance of the latter transition of the affections. I must, however make one exception, viz. when the very cause of the pride and humility is plac'd in some other person. For in that case the imagination is necessitated to consider the person, nor can it possibly confine its view to ourselves. Thus nothing more readily produces kindness and affection to any person, than his approbation of our conduct and character: As on the other hand, nothing inspires us with a stronger hatred, than his blame or contempt. Here 'tis evident, that the original passion is pride or humility, whose object is self; and that this passion is transfus'd into love or hatred, whose object is some other person, notwithstanding the rule I have already establish'd, *that the imagination passes with difficulty from contiguous to remote.* But the transition in this case is not made merely on account of the relation betwixt ourselves and the person; but because that very person is the real cause of our first passion, and of consequence is intimately connected with it. 'Tis his approbation that produces pride; and disapprobation, humility. No wonder, then, the imagination returns back again attended with the related passions of love and hatred. This is not a contradiction, but an exception to the rule; and an exception that arises from the same reason with the rule itself.

Such an exception as this is, therefore, rather a confirmation of the rule. And indeed, if we consider all the eight experiments I have explain'd, we shall find that the same principle appears in all of them, and that 'tis by means of a transition arising from a double relation of impressions and ideas, pride and humility, love and hatred are produc'd. An object without[1] a relation, or[2] with but one, never produces either of these passions; and 'tis[3] found that the passion always varies in conformity to the relation. Nay we may observe, that where the relation, by any particular circumstance, has not its usual effect of producing a transition either of[4] ideas or of impressions, it ceases to operate upon the passions, and gives rise neither to pride nor love, humility nor hatred. This rule we find still to hold good,[5] even under the appearance of its contrary; and as relation is frequently experienc'd to have no effect; which upon examination is found to proceed from some particular circumstance, that prevents the transition; so even in instances, where that circumstance, tho' present, prevents not the

[1] First Experiment.
[2] Second and Third Experiments.
[3] Fourth Experiment
[4] Sixth Experiment
[5] Seventh and Eighth Experiments.

transition, 'tis found to arise from some other circumstance, which counter-ballances it. Thus not only the variations resolve themselves into the general principle, but even the variations of these variations.

Sect. III.—*Difficulties Solv'd.*

After so many and such undeniable proofs drawn from daily experience and observation, it may seem superfluous to enter into a particular examination of all the causes of love and hatred. I shall, therefore, employ the sequel of this part, *First*, In removing some difficulties, concerning particular causes of these passions. *Secondly*, In examining the compound affections, which arise from the mixture of love and hatred with other emotions.

Nothing is more evident, than that any person acquires our kindness, or is expos'd to our ill-will, in proportion to the pleasure or uneasiness we receive from him, and that the passions keep pace exactly with the sensations in all their changes and variations. Whoever can find the means either by his services, his beauty, or his flattery, to render himself useful or agreeable to us, is sure of our affections: As on the other hand, whoever harms or displeases us never fails to excite our anger or hatred. When our own nation is at war with any other, we detest them under the character of cruel, perfidious, unjust and violent: But always esteem ourselves and allies equitable, moderate, and merciful. If the general of our enemies be successful, 'tis with difficulty we allow him the figure and character of a man. He is a sorcerer: He has a communication with dæmons; as is reported of *Oliver Cromwell,* and the *Duke of Luxembourg :* He is bloody-minded, and takes a pleasure in death and destruction. But if the success be on our side, our commander has all the opposite good qualities, and is a pattern of virtue, as well as of courage and conduct. His treachery we call policy: His cruelty is an evil inseparable from war. In short, every one of his faults we either endeavour to extenuate, or dignify it with the name of that virtue, which approaches it. 'Tis evident the same method of thinking runs thro' common life.

There are some, who add another condition, and require not only that the pain and pleasure arise from the person, but likewise that it arise knowingly, and with a particular design and intention. A man, who wounds and harms us by accident, becomes not our enemy upon that account, nor do we think ourselves bound by any ties of gratitude to one, who does us any service after the same manner. By the intention we judge of the actions, and according as that is good or bad, they become causes of love or hatred.

But here we must make a distinction. If that quality in another, which pleases or displeases, be constant and inherent in his person and character, it will cause love or hatred independent of the intention : But otherwise a knowledge and design is requisite, in order to give rise to these passions. One that is disagreeable by his deformity or folly is the object of our aversion, tho' nothing be more certain, than that he has not the least intention of displeasing us by these qualities. But if the uneasiness proceed not from a quality, but an action, which is produc'd and annihilated in a moment, 'tis necessary, in order to produce some relation, and connect this action sufficiently with the person, that it be deriv'd from a particular fore-thought and design. 'Tis not enough, that the action arise from the person, and have him for its immediate cause and author. This relation alone is too feeble and inconstant to be a foundation for these passions. It reaches not the sensible and thinking part, and neither proceeds from any thing *durable* in him, nor leaves any thing behind it; but passes in a moment, and is as if it had never been. On the other hand, an intention shews certain qualities, which remaining after the action is perform'd, connect it with the person, and facilitate the transition of ideas from one to the other. We can never think of him without reflecting on these qualities ; unless repentance and a change of life have produc'd an alteration in that respect : In which case the passion is likewise alter'd. This therefore is one reason, why an intention is requisite to either love or hatred.

But we must farther consider, that an intention, besides its strengthening the relation of ideas, is often necessary to produce a relation of impressions, and give rise to pleasure and uneasiness. For 'tis observable, that the principal part of an injury is the contempt and hatred, which it shews in the person, that injures us ; and without that, the mere harm gives us a less sensible uneasiness. In like manner, a good office is agreeable, chiefly because it flatters our vanity, and is a proof of the kindness and esteem of the person, who performs it. The removal of the intention, removes the mortification in the one case, and vanity in the other; and must of course cause a remarkable diminution in the passions of love and hatred.

I grant, that these effects of the removal of design, in diminishing the relations of impressions and ideas, are not entire, nor able to remove every degree of these relations. But then I ask, if the removal of design be able entirely to remove the passion of love and hatred? Experience, I am sure, informs us of the contrary, nor is there any thing more certain, than that men often fall into a violent anger for injuries, which they themselves must own to be entirely involuntary and accidental. This emotion, indeed, cannot be of long continuance; but still is sufficient to shew, that there is a natural connexion betwixt uneasiness and anger, and that the relation of impressions will operate upon a very small relation of ideas. But when the violence of the impression is once a little abated, the defect of the relation begins to be better felt; and as the character of a person is no wise interested in such injuries as are casual and involuntary, it seldom happens that on their account, we entertain a lasting enmity.

To illustrate this doctrine by a parallel instance, we may observe, that not only the uneasiness, which proceeds from another by accident, has but little force to excite our passion, but also that which arises from an acknowledg'd necessity and duty. One that has a real design of harming us, proceeding not from hatred and ill-will, but from justice and equity, draws not upon him our anger, if we be in any degree reasonable; notwithstanding he is both the cause, and the knowing cause of our sufferings. Let us examine a little this phænomenon.

'Tis evident in the first place, that this circumstance is not decisive; and tho' it may be able to diminish the passions, 'tis seldom it can entirely remove them. How few criminals are there, who have no ill-will to the person, that accuses them, or to the judge, that condemns them, even tho' they be conscious of their own deserts? In like manner our antagonist in a law-suit, and our competitor for an office, are commonly regarded as our enemies; tho' we must acknowledge, if we won'd but reflect a moment, that their motive is entirely as justifiable as our own.

Besides we may consider, that when we receive harm from any person, we are apt to imagine him criminal, and 'tis with extreme difficulty we allow of his justice and innocence. This is a clear proof, that, independent of the opinion of iniquity, any harm or uneasiness has a natural tendency to excite our hatred, and that afterwards we seek for reasons upon which we may justify and establish the passion. Here the idea of injury produces not the passion, but arises from it.

Nor is it any wonder that passion shou'd produce the opinion of injury; since otherwise it must suffer a considerable diminution, which all the passions avoid as much as possible. The removal of injury may remove the anger, without proving that the anger arises only from the injury. The harm and the justice are two contrary objects, of which the one has a tendency to produce hatred, and the other love; and 'tis according to their different degrees, and our particular turn of thinking, that either of the objects prevails, and excites its proper passion.

SECT. IV.—*Of the Love of Relations.*

Having given a reason, why several actions, that cause a real pleasure or uneasiness, excite not any degree, or but a small one, of the passion of love or hatred towards the actors; 'twill be necessary to shew, wherein consists the pleasure or uneasiness of many objects, which we find by experience to produce these passions.

According to the preceding system there is always requir'd a double relation of impressions and ideas betwixt the cause and effect, in order to produce either love or hatred. But tho' this be universally true, 'tis remarkable that the passion of love may be excited by only one *relation* of a different kind, *viz.*, betwixt ourselves and the object; or more properly speaking, that this relation is always attended with both the others. Whoever is united to us by any connexion is always sure of a share of our love, proportion'd to the connexion, without enquiring into his other qualities. Thus the relation of blood produces the strongest tie the mind is

capable of in the love of parents to their children, and a
lesser degree of the same affection, as the relation lessens.
Nor has consanguinity alone this effect, but any other relation without exception. We love our country-men, our
neighbours, those of the same trade, profession, and even
name with ourselves. Every one of these relations is esteem'd some tie, and gives a title to a share of our affection.

There is another phænomenon, which is parallel to this,
viz. that *acquaintance*, without any kind of relation, gives
rise to love and kindness. When we have contracted a
habitude and intimacy with any person; tho' in frequenting
his company we have not been able to discover any very
valuable quality, of which he is possess'd; yet we cannot
forbear preferring him to strangers, of whose superior merit
we are fully convinc'd. These two phænomena of the effects
of relation and acquaintance will give mutual light to each
other, and may be both explain'd from the same principle.

Those, who take a pleasure in declaiming against human
nature, have observ'd, that man is altogether insufficient to
support himself; and that when you loosen all the holds,
which he has of external objects, he immediately drops down
into the deepest melancholy and despair. From this, say
they, proceeds that continual search after amusement in
gaming, in hunting, in business; by which we endeavour to
forget ourselves, and excite our spirits from the languid
state, into which they fall, when not sustain'd by some brisk
and lively emotion. To this method of thinking I so far
agree, that I own the mind to be insufficient, of itself, to its
own entertainment, and that it naturally seeks after foreign
objects, which may produce a lively sensation, and agitate
the spirits. On the appearance of such an object it awakes,
as it were, from a dream: The blood flows with a new tide:
The heart is elevated: And the whole man acquires a
vigour, which he cannot command in his solitary and calm
moments. Hence company is naturally so rejoicing, as
presenting the liveliest of all objects, *viz.* a rational and
thinking Being like ourselves, who communicates to us all
the actions of his mind; makes us privy to his inmost
sentiments and affections; and lets us see, in the very instant
of their production, all the emotions, which are caus'd by
any object. Every lively idea is agreeable, but especially
that of a passion, because such an idea becomes a kind of

passion, and gives a more sensible agitation to the mind, than any other image or conception.

This being once admitted, all the rest is easy. For as the company of strangers is agreeable to us for *a short time,* by inlivening our thought; so the company of our relations and acquaintance must be peculiarly agreeable, because it has this effect in a greater degree, and is of more *durable* influence. Whatever is related to us is conceiv'd in a lively manner by the easy transition from ourselves to the related object. Custom also, or acquaintance facilitates the entrance, and strengthens the conception of any object. The first case is parallel to our reasonings from cause and effect; the second to education. And as reasoning and education concur only in producing a lively and strong idea of any object; so is this the only particular, which is common to relation and acquaintance. This must, therefore, be the influencing quality, by which they produce all their common effects; and love or kindness being one of these effects, it must be from the force and liveliness of conception, that the passion is deriv'd. Such a conception is peculiarly agreeable, and makes us have an affectionate regard for every thing, that produces it, when the proper object of kindness and good-will.

'Tis obvious, that people associate together according to their particular tempers and dispositions, and that men of gay tempers naturally love the gay; as the serious bear an affection to the serious. This not only happens, where they remark this resemblance betwixt themselves and others, but also by the natural course of the disposition, and by a certain sympathy, which always arises betwixt similar characters. Where they remark the resemblance, it operates after the manner of a relation, by producing a connexion of ideas. Where they do not remark it, it operates by some other principle; and if this latter principle be similar to the former, it must be received as a confirmation of the foregoing reasoning.

The idea of ourselves is always intimately present to us, and conveys a sensible degree of vivacity to the idea of any other object, to which we are related. This lively idea changes by degrees into a real impression; these two kinds of perception being in a great measure the same, and differing only in their degrees of force and vivacity. But this change must be produc'd with the greater ease, that our natural temper gives us a propensity to the same impression, which we observe in others, and makes it arise upon any slight occasion. In that case resemblance converts the idea into an impression, not only by means of the relation, and by transfusing the original vivacity into the related idea; but also by presenting such materials as take fire from the least spark. And as in both cases a love or affection arises from the resemblance, we may learn that a sympathy with others is agreeable only by giving an emotion to the spirits, since an easy sympathy and correspondent emotions are alone common to *relation, acquaintance,* and *resemblance.*

The great propensity men have to pride may be consider'd as another similar phænomenon. It often happens, that after we have liv'd a considerable time in any city; however at first it might be disagreeable to us; yet as we become familiar with the objects, and contract an acquaintance, tho' merely with the streets and buildings, the aversion diminishes by degrees, and at last changes into the opposite passion. The mind finds a satisfaction and ease in the view of objects, to which it is accustom'd, and naturally prefers them to others, which, tho', perhaps, in themselves more valuable, are less known to it. By the same quality of the mind we are seduc'd into a good opinion of ourselves, and of all objects, that belong to us. They appear in a stronger light; are more agreeable; and consequently fitter subjects of pride and vanity, than any other.

It may not be amiss, in treating of the affection we bear our acquaintance and relations, to observe some pretty curious phænomena, which attend it. 'Tis easy to remark in common life, that children esteem their relation to their mother to be weaken'd, in a great measure, by her second marriage, and no longer regard her with the same eye, as if she had continu'd in her state of widow-hood. Nor does this happen only, when they have felt any inconveniencies from her second marriage, or when her husband is much her inferior; but even without any of these considerations, and merely because she has become part of another family. This also takes place with regard to the second marriage of a father; but in a much less degree: And 'tis certain the ties of blood are not so much loosen'd in the latter case as by the marriage of a mother. These two phænomena are remarkable in themselves, but much more so when compar'd.

In order to produce a perfect relation betwixt two objects, 'tis requisite, not only that the imagination be convey'd from one to the other by resemblance, contiguity or causation, but also that it return back from the second to the first, with the same ease and facility. At first sight this may seem a necessary and unavoidable consequence. If one object resemble another, the latter object must necessarily resemble the former. If one object be the cause of another, the second object is effect to its cause. 'Tis the same case with contiguity: And therefore the relation being always reciprocal, it may be thought, that the return of the imagination from the second to the first must also, in every case, be equally natural as its passage from the first to the second. But upon farther examination we shall easily discover our mistake. For supposing the second object, beside its reciprocal relation to the first, to have also a strong relation to a third object; in that case the thought, passing from the first object to the second, returns not back with the same facility, tho' the relation continues the same; but is readily carry'd on to the third object, by means of the new relation, which presents itself, and gives a new impulse to the imagination. This new relation, therefore, weakens the tie betwixt the first and second objects. The fancy is by its very nature wavering and inconstant; and considers always two objects as more strongly related together, where it finds the passage equally easy both in going and returning, than where the transition is easy only in one of these motions. The double motion is a kind of a double tie, and binds the objects together in the closest and most intimate manner.

The second marriage of a mother breaks not the relation of child and parent; and that relation suffices to convey my imagination from myself to her with the greatest ease and facility. But after the imagination is arrived at this point of view, it finds its object to be surrounded with so many other relations, which challenge its regard, that it knows not which to prefer, and is at a loss what new object to pitch upon. The ties of interest and duty bind her to another family, and prevent that return of the fancy from her to myself, which is necessary to support the union. The thought has no longer the vibration, requisite to set it perfectly at ease, and indulge its inclination to change. It goes with facility, but returns with difficulty; and by that interruption finds the relation much weaken'd from what it wou'd be were the passage open and easy on both sides.

Now to give a reason, why this effect follows not in the same degree upon the second marriage of a father: we may reflect on what has been prov'd already, that tho' the imagination goes easily from the view of a lesser object to that of a greater, yet it returns not with the same facility from the greater to the less. When my imagination goes from myself to my father, it passes not so readily from him to his second wife, nor considers him as entering into a different family, but as continuing the head of that family, of which I am myself a part. His superiority prevents the easy transition of the thought from him to his spouse, but keeps the passage still open for a return to myself along the same relation of child and parent. He is not sunk in the new relation he acquires; so that the double motion or vibration of thought is still easy and natural. By this indulgence of the fancy in its inconstancy, the tie of child and parent still preserves its full force and influence.

A mother thinks not her tie to a son weaken'd, because 'tis shar'd with her husband: Nor a son his with a parent, because 'tis shar'd with a brother. The third object is here related to the first, as well as to the second; so that the imagination goes and comes along all of them with the greatest facility.

Sect. V.—*Of our Esteem for the Rich and Powerful.*

Nothing has a greater tendency to give us an esteem for any person, than his power and riches; or a contempt, than his poverty and meanness: And as esteem and contempt are to be consider'd as species of love and hatred, 'twill be proper in this place to explain these phænomena.

Here it happens most fortunately, that the greatest difficulty is not to discover a principle capable of producing such an effect, but to choose the chief and predominant among several, that present themselves. The *satisfaction* we take in the riches of others, and the *esteem* we have for the possessors may be ascrib'd to three different causes. *First,* To the objects they possess; such as houses, gardens, equipages;

which, being agreeable in themselves, necessarily produce a
sentiment of pleasure in every one, that either considers or
surveys them. *Secondly*, To the expectation of advantage
from the rich and powerful by our sharing their possessions.
Thirdly, To sympathy, which makes us partake of the satisfaction of every one, that approaches us. All these principles may concur in producing the present phænomenon.
The question is, to which of them we ought principally to
ascribe it.

'Tis certain, that the first principle, *viz.* the reflection on
agreeable objects, has a greater influence, than what, at first
sight, we may be apt to imagine. We seldom reflect on what
is beautiful or ugly, agreeable or disagreeable, without an
emotion of pleasure or uneasiness ; and tho' these sensations
appear not much in our common indolent way of thinking,
'tis easy, either in reading or conversation, to discover them.
Men of wit always turn the discourse on subjects that are
entertaining to the imagination; and poets never present
any objects but such as are of the same nature. Mr. *Philips*
has chosen *Cyder* for the subject of an excellent poem. Beer
wou'd not have been so proper, as being neither so agreeable
to the taste nor eye. But he wou'd certainly have preferr'd
wine to either of them, cou'd his native country have afforded
him so agreeable a liquor. We may learn from thence, that
every thing, which is agreeable to the senses, is also in some
measure agreeable to the fancy, and conveys to the thought
an image of that satisfaction, which it gives by its real application to the bodily organs.

But tho' these reasons may induce us to comprehend this
delicacy of the imagination among the causes of the respect,
which we pay the rich and powerful, there are many other
reasons, that may keep us from regarding it as the sole or
principal. For as the ideas of pleasure can have an influence
only by means of their vivacity, which makes them approach
impressions, 'tis most natural those ideas shou'd have that
influence, which are favour'd by most circumstances, and
have a natural tendency to become strong and lively ; such
as our ideas of the passions and sensations of any human
creature. Every human creature resembles ourselves, and
by that means has an advantage above any other object, in
operating on the imagination.

Besides, if we consider the nature of that faculty, and the

great influence which all relations have upon it, we shall easily be perswaded, that however the ideas of the pleasant wines, music, or gardens, which the rich man enjoys, may become lively and agreeable, the fancy will not confine itself to them, but will carry its view to the related objects; and in particular, to the person, who possesses them. And this is the more natural, that the pleasant idea or image produces here a passion towards the person, by means of his relation to the object; so that 'tis unavoidable but he must enter into the original conception, since he makes the object of the derivative passion. But if he enters into the original conception, and is consider'd as enjoying these agreeable objects, 'tis *sympathy*, which is properly the cause of the affection; and the *third* principle is more powerful and universal than the *first*.[1]

Add to this, that riches and power alone, even tho' unemploy'd, naturally cause esteem and respect: And consequently these passions arise not from the idea of any beautiful or agreeable objects. 'Tis true; money implies a kind of representation of such objects, by the power it affords of obtaining them; and for that reason may still be esteem'd proper to convey those agreeable images, which may give rise to the passion. But as this prospect is very distant, 'tis more natural for us to take a contiguous object, *viz.* the satisfaction, which this power affords the person, who is possest of it. And of this we shall be farther satisfy'd, if we consider, that riches represent the goods of life, only by means of the will; which employs them; and therefore imply in their very nature an idea of the person, and cannot be consider'd without a kind of sympathy with his sensations and enjoyments.

This we may confirm by a reflection, which to some will, perhaps, appear too subtile and refin'd. I have already observ'd, that power, as distinguish'd from its exercise, has either no meaning at all, or is nothing but a possibility or probability of existence; by which any object approaches to reality, and has a sensible influence on the mind. I have also observ'd, that this approach, by an illusion of the fancy, appears much greater, when we ourselves are possest of the power, than when it is enjoy'd by another; and that in the former case the objects seem to touch upon the very verge

SECT.
V.
Of our esteem for the rich and powerful

[1 Introd Sect 38.—Ed]

of reality, and convey almost an equal satisfaction, as if actually in our possession. Now I assert, that where we esteem a person upon account of his riches, we must enter into this sentiment of the proprietor, and that without such a sympathy the idea of the agreeable objects, which they give him the power to produce, wou'd have but a feeble influence upon us. An avaritious man is respected for his money, tho' he scarce is possest of a *power*; that is, there scarce is a *probability* or even *possibility* of his employing it in the acquisition of the pleasures and conveniences of life. To himself alone this power seems perfect and entire; and therefore we must receive his sentiments by sympathy, before we can have a strong intense idea of these enjoyments, or esteem him upon account of them.

Thus we have found, that the *first* principle, *viz. the agreeable idea of those objects, which riches afford the enjoyment of;* resolves itself in a great measure into the *third*, and becomes a *sympathy* with the person we esteem or love. Let us now examine the *second* principle, *viz. the agreeable expectation of advantage*, and see what force we may justly attribute to it.

'Tis obvious, that tho' riches and authority undoubtedly give their owner a power of doing us service, yet this power is not to be consider'd as on the same footing with that, which they afford him, of pleasing himself, and satisfying his own appetites. Self-love approaches the power and exercise very near each other in the latter case; but in order to produce a similar effect in the former, we must suppose a friendship and good-will to be conjoin'd with the riches. Without that circumstance 'tis difficult to conceive on what we can found our hope of advantage from the riches of others, tho' there is nothing more certain, than that we naturally esteem and respect the rich, even before we discover in them any such favourable disposition towards us.

But I carry this farther, and observe, not only that we respect the rich and powerful, where they shew no inclination to serve us, but also when we lie so much out of the sphere of their activity, that they cannot even be suppos'd to be endow'd with that power. Prisoners of war are always treated with a respect suitable to their condition; and 'tis certain riches go very far towards fixing the condition of any person. If birth and quality enter for a share, this still affords us an argument of the same kind. For what is it we call a man of birth, but one who is descended from a long succession of rich and powerful ancestors, and who acquires our esteem by his relation to persons whom we esteem? His ancestors, therefore, tho' dead, are respected, in some measure, on account of their riches, and consequently without any kind of expectation.

But not to go so far as prisoners of war and the dead to find instances of this disinterested esteem for riches, let us observe with a little attention those phænomena that occur to us in common life and conversation. A man, who is himself of a competent fortune, upon coming into a company of strangers, naturally treats them with different degrees of respect and deference, as he is inform'd of their different fortunes and conditions; tho' 'tis impossible he can ever propose, and perhaps wou'd not accept of any advantage from them. A traveller is always admitted into company, and meets with civility, in proportion as his train and equipage speak him a man of great or moderate fortune. In short, the different ranks of men are, in a great measure, regulated by riches, and that with regard to superiors as well as inferiors, strangers as well as acquaintance.

There is, indeed, an answer to these arguments, drawn from the influence of *general rules*. It may be pretended, that being accustom'd to expect succour and protection from the rich and powerful, and to esteem them upon that account, we extend the same sentiments to those, who resemble them in their fortune, but from whom we can never hope for any advantage. The general rule still prevails, and by giving a bent to the imagination draws along the passion, in the same manner as if its proper object were real and existent.

But that this principle does not here take place, will easily appear, if we consider, that in order to establish a general rule, and extend it beyond its proper bounds, there is requir'd a certain uniformity in our experience, and a great superiority of those instances, which are conformable to the rule, above the contrary. But here the case is quite otherwise. Of a hundred men of credit and fortune I meet with, there is not, perhaps, one from whom I can expect advantage; so that 'tis impossible any custom can ever prevail in the present case.

Upon the whole, there remains nothing, which can give

us an esteem for power and riches, and a contempt for meanness and poverty, except the principle of *sympathy*, by which we enter into the sentiments of the rich and poor, and partake of their pleasure and uneasiness. Riches give satisfaction to their possessor; and this satisfaction is convey'd to the beholder by the imagination, which produces an idea resembling the original impression in force and vivacity. This agreeable idea or impression is connected with love, which is an agreeable passion. It proceeds from a thinking conscious being, which is the very object of love. From this relation of impressions, and identity of ideas, the passion arises, according to my hypothesis.

The best method of reconciling us to this opinion is to take a general survey of the universe, and observe the force of sympathy thro' the whole animal creation, and the easy communication of sentiments from one thinking being to another. In all creatures, that prey not upon others, and are not agitated with violent passions, there appears a remarkable desire of company, which associates them together, without any advantages they can ever propose to reap from their union. This is still more conspicuous in man, as being the creature of the universe, who has the most ardent desire of society, and is fitted for it by the most advantages. We can form no wish, which has not a reference to society. A perfect solitude is, perhaps, the greatest punishment we can suffer. Every pleasure languishes when enjoy'd a-part from company, and every pain becomes more cruel and intolerable. Whatever other passions we may be actuated by; pride, ambition, avarice, curiosity, revenge or lust; the soul or animating principle of them all is sympathy; nor wou'd they have any force, were we to abstract entirely from the thoughts and sentiments of others. Let all the powers and elements of nature conspire to serve and obey one man: Let the sun rise and set at his command: The sea and rivers roll as he pleases, and the earth furnish spontaneously whatever may be useful or agreeable to him: He will still be miserable, till you give him some one person at least, with whom he may share his happiness, and whose esteem and friendship he may enjoy.

This conclusion from a general view of human nature, we may confirm by particular instances, wherein the force of sympathy is very remarkable. Most kinds of beauty are deriv'd from this origin; and tho' our first object be some senseless inanimate piece of matter, 'tis seldom we rest there, and carry not our view to its influence on sensible and rational creatures. A man, who shews us any house or building, takes particular care among other things to point out the convenience of the apartments, the advantages of their situation, and the little room lost in the stairs, antichambers and passages; and indeed 'tis evident, the chief part of the beauty consists in these particulars. The observation of convenience gives pleasure, since convenience is a beauty. But after what manner does it give pleasure? 'Tis certain our own interest is not in the least concern'd; and as this is a beauty of interest, not of form, so to speak, it must delight us merely by communication, and by our sympathizing with the proprietor of the lodging. We enter into his interest by the force of imagination, and feel the same satisfaction, that the objects naturally occasion in him.

This observation extends to tables, chairs, scritoires, chimneys, coaches, sadles, ploughs, and indeed to every work of art; it being an universal rule, that their beauty is chiefly deriv'd from their utility, and from their fitness for that purpose, to which they are destin'd. But this is an advantage, that concerns only the owner, nor is there any thing but sympathy, which can interest the spectator.

'Tis evident, that nothing renders a field more agreeable than its fertility, and that scarce any advantages of ornament or situation will be able to equal this beauty. 'Tis the same case with particular trees and plants, as with the field on which they grow. I know not but a plain, overgrown with furze and broom, may be, in itself, as beautiful as a hill cover'd with vines or olive-trees; tho' it will never appear so to one, who is acquainted with the value of each. But this is a beauty merely of imagination, and has no foundation in what appears to the senses. Fertility and value have a plain reference to use; and that to riches, joy, and plenty; in which tho' we have no hope of partaking, yet we enter into them by the vivacity of the fancy, and share them, in some measure, with the proprietor.

There is no rule in painting more reasonable than that of ballancing the figures, and placing them with the greatest exactness on their proper center of gravity. A figure, which is not justly ballanc'd, is disagreeable; and that because it conveys the ideas of its fall, of harm, and of pain: Which ideas are painful, when by sympathy they acquire any degree of force and vivacity.

Add to this, that the principal part of personal beauty is an air of health and vigour, and such a construction of members as promises strength and activity. This idea of beauty cannot be accounted for but by sympathy.

In general we may remark, that the minds of men are mirrors to one another, not only because they reflect each other's emotions, but also because those rays of passions, sentiments and opinions may be often reverberated, and may decay away by insensible degrees. Thus the pleasure, which the rich man receives from his possessions, being thrown upon the beholder, causes a pleasure and esteem; which sentiments again, being perceiv'd and sympathiz'd with, encrease the pleasure of the possessor; and being once more reflected, become a new foundation for pleasure and esteem in the beholder. There is certainly an original satisfaction in riches deriv'd from that power, which they bestow, of enjoying all the pleasures of life; and as this is their very nature and essence, it must be the first source of all the passions, which arise from them. One of the most considerable of these passions is that of love or esteem in others, which therefore proceeds from a sympathy with the pleasure of the possessor. But the possessor has also a secondary satisfaction in riches arising from the love and esteem he acquires by them, and this satisfaction is nothing but a second reflexion of that original pleasure, which proceeded from himself. This secondary satisfaction or vanity becomes one of the principal recommendations of riches, and is the chief reason, why we either desire them for ourselves, or esteem them in others. Here then is a third rebound of the original pleasure; after which 'tis difficult to distinguish the images and reflexions, by reason of their faintness and confusion.

Sect. VI.—*Of Benevolence and Anger.*

Ideas may be compar'd to the extension and solidity of matter, and impressions, especially reflective ones, to colours, tastes, smells and other sensible qualities. Ideas never admit of a total union, but are endowed with a kind of impenetrability, by which they exclude each other, and are capable of forming a compound by their conjunction, not by their mixture. On the other hand, impressions and passions are susceptible of an entire union ; and like colours, may be blended so perfectly together, that each of them may lose itself, and contribute only to vary that uniform impression, which arises from the whole. Some of the most curious phænomena of the human mind are deriv'd from this property of the passions.

In examining those ingredients, which are capable of uniting with love and hatred, I begin to be sensible, in some measure, of a misfortune, that has attended every system of philosophy, with which the world has been yet acquainted. 'Tis commonly found, that in accounting for the operations of nature by any particular hypothesis ; among a number of experiments, that quadrate exactly with the principles we wou'd endeavour to establish ; there is always some phænomenon, which is more stubborn, and will not so easily bend to our purpose. We need not be surpriz'd, that this shou'd happen in natural philosophy. The essence and composition of external bodies are so obscure, that we must necessarily, in our reasonings, or rather conjectures concerning them, involve ourselves in contradictions and absurdities. But as the perceptions of the mind are perfectly known, and I have us'd all imaginable caution in forming conclusions concerning them, I have always hop'd to keep clear of those contradictions, which have attended every other system. Accordingly the difficulty, which I have at present in my eye, is no-wise contrary to my system ; but only departs a little from that simplicity, which has been hitherto its principal force and beauty.

The passions of love and hatred are always follow'd by, or rather conjoin'd with benevolence and anger. 'Tis this conjunction, which chiefly distinguishes these affections from pride and humility. For pride and humility are pure emotions in the soul, unattended with any desire, and not immediately exciting us to action. But love and hatred are not compleated within themselves, nor rest in that emotion, which they produce, but carry the mind to something farther. Love is always follow'd by a desire of the happiness of the person belov'd, and an aversion to his misery : As hatred produces a desire of the misery and an aversion to the happiness of the person hated. So remarkable a difference betwixt these two sets of passions of pride and humility, love and hatred, which in so many other particulars correspond to each other, merits our attention.[1]

The conjunction of this desire and aversion with love and hatred may be accounted for by two different hypotheses. The first is, that love and hatred have not only a *cause*, which excites them, *viz.* pleasure and pain; and an *object*, to which they are directed, *viz.* a person or thinking being; but likewise an *end*, which they endeavour to attain, *viz.* the happiness or misery of the person belov'd or hated; all which views, mixing together, make only one passion. According to this system, love is nothing but the desire of happiness to another person, and hatred that of misery. The desire and aversion constitute the very nature of love and hatred. They are not only inseparable but the same.

But this is evidently contrary to experience. For tho' 'tis certain we never love any person without desiring his happiness, nor hate any without wishing his misery, yet these desires arise only upon the ideas of the happiness or misery of our friend or enemy being presented by the imagination, and are not absolutely essential to love and hatred. They are the most obvious and natural sentiments of these affections, but not the only ones. The passions may express themselves in a hundred ways, and may subsist a considerable time, without our reflecting on the happiness or misery of their objects; which clearly proves, that these desires are not the same with love and hatred, nor make any essential part of them.

We may, therefore, infer, that benevolence and anger are passions different from love and hatred, and only conjoin'd with them, by the original constitution of the mind. As nature has given to the body certain appetites and inclinations, which she encreases, diminishes, or changes according to the situation of the fluids or solids; she has proceeded in the same manner with the mind. According as we are possess'd with love or hatred, the correspondent desire of the happiness or misery of the person, who is the object of these passions, arises in the mind, and varies with each variation of these opposite passions. This order of things, abstractedly consider'd, is not necessary. Love and hatred

[1 Introd Sect 41 —Ed]

might have been unattended with any such desires, or their
particular connexion might have been entirely revers'd.   If
nature had so pleas'd, love might have had the same effect
as hatred, and hatred as love.   I see no contradiction in
supposing a desire of producing misery annex'd to love, and
of happiness to hatred.   If the sensation of the passion and
desire be opposite, nature cou'd have alter'd the sensation
without altering the tendency of the desire, and by that
means made them compatible with each other.

SECT. VII.—*Of Compassion.*

But tho' the desire of the happiness or misery of others,
according to the love or hatred we bear them, be an arbitrary
and original instinct implanted in our nature, we find it may
be counterfeited on many occasions, and may arise from
secondary principles.   *Pity* is a concern for, and *malice* a joy
in the misery of others, without any friendship or enmity to
occasion this concern or joy.[1]   We pity even strangers, and
such as are perfectly indifferent to us: And if our ill-will
to another proceed from any harm or injury, it is not, properly speaking, malice, but revenge.   But if we examine
these affections of pity and malice, we shall find them to be
secondary ones, arising from original affections, which are
varied by some particular turn of thought and imagination.

'Twill be easy to explain the passion of *pity*, from the
precedent reasoning concerning *sympathy*.   We have a lively
idea of every thing related to us.   All human creatures are
related to us by resemblance.   Their persons, therefore,
their interests, their passions, their pains and pleasures must
strike upon us in a lively manner, and produce an emotion
similar to the original one; since a lively idea is easily converted into an impression.   If this be true in general, it
must be more so of affliction and sorrow.   These have always
a stronger and more lasting influence than any pleasure or
enjoyment.

A spectator of a tragedy passes thro' a long train of grief,
terror, indignation, and other affections, which the poet
represents in the persons he introduces.   As many tragedies
end happily, and no excellent one can be compos'd without
some reverses of fortune, the spectator must sympathize with
all these changes, and receive the fictitious joy as well as

[¹ Introd. Sect. 43 —ED]

every other passion. Unless, therefore, it be asserted, that every distinct passion is communicated by a distinct original quality, and is not deriv'd from the general principle of sympathy above-explained, it must be allow'd, that all of them arise from that principle. To except any one in particular must appear highly unreasonable. As they are all first present in the mind of one person, and afterwards appear in the mind of another; and as the manner of their appearance, first as an idea, then as an impression, is in every case the same, the transition must arise from the same principle. I am at least sure, that this method of reasoning wou'd be consider'd as certain, either in natural philosophy or common life.

Add to this, that pity depends, in a great measure, on the contiguity, and even sight of the object; which is a proof, that 'tis deriv'd from the imagination. Not to mention that women and children are most subject to pity, as being most guided by that faculty. The same infirmity, which makes them faint at the sight of a naked sword, tho' in the hands of their best friend, makes them pity extremely those, whom they find in any grief or affliction. Those philosophers, who derive this passion from I know not what subtile reflections on the instability of fortune, and our being liable to the same miseries we behold, will find this observation contrary to them among a great many others, which it were easy to produce.

There remains only to take notice of a pretty remarkable phænomenon of this passion; which is, that the communicated passion of sympathy sometimes acquires strength from the weakness of its original, and even arises by a transition from affections, which have no existence. Thus when a person obtains any honourable office, or inherits a great fortune, we are always the more rejoic'd for his prosperity, the less sense he seems to have of it, and the greater equanimity and indifference he shews in its enjoyment. In like manner a man, who is not dejected by misfortunes, is the more lamented on account of his patience; and if that virtue extends so far as utterly to remove all sense of uneasiness, it still farther encreases our compassion. When a person of merit falls into what is vulgarly esteem'd a great misfortune, we form a notion of his condition; and carrying our fancy from the cause to the usual effect, first conceive a lively idea of his sorrow, and then feel an impression of it, entirely over-looking that greatness of mind, which elevates him above such emotions, or only considering it so far as to encrease our admiration, love and tenderness for him. We find from experience, that such a degree of passion is usually connected with such a misfortune; and tho' there be an exception in the present case, yet the imagination is affected by the *general rule*, and makes us conceive a lively idea of the passion, or rather feel the passion itself, in the same manner, as if the person were really actuated by it. From the same principles we blush for the conduct of those, who behave themselves foolishly before us; and that tho' they shew no sense of shame, nor seem in the least conscious of their folly. All this proceeds from sympathy; but 'tis of a partial kind, and views its objects only on one side, without considering the other, which has a contrary effect, and wou'd entirely destroy that emotion, which arises from the first appearance.

We have also instances, wherein an indifference and insensibility under misfortune encreases our concern for the misfortunate, even tho' the indifference proceed not from any virtue and magnanimity. 'Tis an aggravation of a murder, that it was committed upon persons asleep and in perfect security; as historians readily observe of any infant prince, who is captive in the hands of his enemies, that he is more worthy of compassion the less sensible he is of his miserable condition. As we ourselves are here acquainted with the wretched situation of the person, it gives us a lively idea and sensation of sorrow, which is the passion that *generally* attends it; and this idea becomes still more lively, and the sensation more violent by a contrast with that security and indifference, which we observe in the person himself. A contrast of any kind never fails to affect the imagination, especially when presented by the subject; and 'tis on the imagination that pity entirely depends.[1]

---

[1] To prevent all ambiguity, I must observe, that where I oppose the imagination to the memory, I mean in general the faculty that presents our fainter ideas. In all other places, and particularly when it is oppos'd to the understanding, I understand the same faculty, excluding only our demonstrative and probable reasonings.[1]

[[1] Cf. Vol I. Part III. Sect 9, note.—ED]

Sect. VIII.—*Of Malice and Envy.*

We must now proceed to account for the passion of *malice*, which imitates the effects of hatred, as pity does those of love; and gives us a joy in the sufferings and miseries of others, without any offence or injury on their part.

So little are men govern'd by reason in their sentiments and opinions, that they always judge more of objects by comparison than from their intrinsic worth and value. When the mind considers, or is accustom'd to, any degree of perfection, whatever falls short of it, tho' really esteemable, has notwithstanding the same effect upon the passions, as what is defective and ill. This is an *original* quality of the soul, and similar to what we have every day experience of in our bodies. Let a man heat one hand and cool the other; the same water will, at the same time, seem both hot and cold, according to the disposition of the different organs. A small degree of any quality, succeeding a greater, produces the same sensation, as if less than it really is, and even sometimes as the opposite quality. Any gentle pain, that follows a violent one, seems as nothing, or rather becomes a pleasure; as on the other hand a violent pain, succeeding a gentle one, is doubly grievous and uneasy.

This no one can doubt of with regard to our passions and sensations. But there may arise some difficulty with regard to our ideas and objects. When an object augments or diminishes to the eye or imagination from a comparison with others, the image and idea of the object are still the same, and are equally extended in the *retina*, and in the brain or organ of perception. The eyes refract the rays of light, and the optic nerves convey the images to the brain in the very same manner, whether a great or small object has preceded; nor does even the imagination alter the dimensions of its object on account of a comparison with others. The question then is, how from the same impression and the same idea we can form such different judgments concerning the same object, and at one time admire its bulk, and at another despise its littleness. This variation in our judgments must certainly proceed from a variation in some perception; but as the variation lies not in the immediate impression or idea of the object, it must lie in some other impression, that accompanies it.

In order to explain this matter, I shall just touch upon two
principles, one of which shall be more fully explain'd in the
progress of this treatise; the other has been already accounted for.   I believe it may safely be establish'd for a
general maxim, that no object is presented to the senses, nor
image form'd in the fancy, but what is accompany'd with
some emotion or movement of spirits proportion'd to it; and
however custom may make us insensible of this sensation,
and cause us to confound it with the object or idea, 'twill be
easy, by careful and exact experiments, to separate and distinguish them.   For to instance only in the cases of extension and number; 'tis evident, that any very bulky object,
such as the ocean, an extended plain, a vast chain of moun-
tains, a wide forest; or any very numerous collection of objects,
such as an army, a fleet, a crowd, excite in the mind a sensible emotion; and that the admiration, which arises on the
appearance of such objects, is one of the most lively pleasures,
which human nature is capable of enjoying.   Now as this
admiration encreases or diminishes by the encrease or diminution of the objects, we may conclude, according to our foregoing [1] principles, that 'tis a compound effect, proceeding
from the conjunction of the several effects, which arise from
each part of the cause.   Every part, then, of extension, and
every unite of number has a separate emotion attending it,
when conceiv'd by the mind; and tho' that emotion be not
always agreeable, yet by its conjunction with others, and by
its agitating the spirits to a just pitch, it contributes to the
production of admiration, which is always agreeable.   If
this be allow'd with respect to extension and number, we
can make no difficulty with respect to virtue and vice, wit
and folly, riches and poverty, happiness and misery, and
other objects of that kind, which are always attended with
an evident emotion.

The second principle I shall take notice of is that of our
adherence to *general rules*; which has such a mighty influence
on the actions and understanding, and is able to impose on
the very senses.   When an object is found by experience to be
always accompany'd with another; whenever the first object
appears, tho' chang'd in very material circumstances; we
naturally fly to the conception of the second, and form an
idea of it in as lively and strong a manner, as if we had

[1] Book I Part III. Sect 15

infer'd its existence by the justest and most authentic con-clusion of our understanding. Nothing can undeceive us, not even our senses, which, instead of correcting this false judgment, are often perverted by it, and seem to authorize its errors.

The conclusion I draw from these two principles, join'd to the influence of comparison above-mention'd, is very short and decisive. Every object is attended with some emotion proportion'd to it; a great object with a great emotion, a small object with a small emotion. A great *object*, therefore, succeeding a small one makes a great *emotion* succeed a small one. Now a great emotion succeeding a small one becomes still greater, and rises beyond its ordinary proportion. But as there is a certain degree of an emotion, which commonly attends every magnitude of an object; when the emotion encreases, we naturally imagine that the object has likewise encreas'd. The effect conveys our view to its usual cause, a certain degree of emotion to a certain magnitude of the object; nor do we consider, that comparison may change the emotion without changing any thing in the object. Those, who are acquainted with the metaphysical part of optics, and know how we transfer the judgments and con-clusions of the understanding to the senses, will easily con-ceive this whole operation.

But leaving this new discovery of an impression, that secretly attends every idea; we must at least allow of that principle, from whence the discovery arose, *that objects appear greater or less by a comparison with others.* We have so many instances of this, that it is impossible we can dispute its veracity; and 'tis from this principle I derive the passions of malice and envy.

'Tis evident we must receive a greater or less satisfaction or uneasiness from reflecting on our own condition and circumstances, in proportion as they appear more or less fortunate or unhappy, in proportion to the degrees of riches, and power, and merit, and reputation, which we think our-selves possest of. Now as we seldom judge of objects from their intrinsic value, but form our notions of them from a comparison with other objects; it follows, that according as we observe a greater or less share of happiness or misery in others, we must make an estimate of our own, and feel a consequent pain or pleasure. The misery of another gives us a more lively idea of our happiness, and his happiness of our misery. The former, therefore, produces delight; and the latter uneasiness.

Here then is a kind of pity reverst, or contrary sensations arising in the beholder, from those which are felt by the person, whom he considers. In general we may observe, that in all kinds of comparison an object makes us always receive from another, to which it is compar'd, a sensation contrary to what arises from itself in its direct and immediate survey. A small object makes a great one appear still greater. A great object makes a little one appear less. Deformity of itself produces uneasiness; but makes us receive new pleasure by its contrast with a beautiful object, whose beauty is augmented by it; as on the other hand, beauty, which of itself produces pleasure, makes us receive a new pain by the contrast with any thing ugly, whose deformity it augments. The case, therefore, must be the same with happiness and misery. The direct survey of another's pleasure naturally gives us pleasure, and therefore produces pain when compar'd with our own. His pain, consider'd in itself, is painful to us, but augments the idea of our own happiness, and gives us pleasure.

Nor will it appear strange, that we may feel a reverst sensation from the happiness and misery of others; since we find the same comparison may give us a kind of malice against ourselves, and make us rejoice for our pains, and grieve for our pleasures. Thus the prospect of past pain is agreeable, when we are satisfied with our present condition; as on the other hand our past pleasures give us uneasiness, when we enjoy nothing at present equal to them. The comparison being the same, as when we reflect on the sentiments of others, must be attended with the same effects.

Nay a person may extend this malice against himself, even to his present fortune, and carry it so far as designedly to seek affliction, and encrease his pains and sorrows. This may happen upon two occasions. *First*, Upon the distress and misfortune of a friend, or person dear to him. *Secondly*, Upon the feeling any remorses for a crime, of which he has been guilty. 'Tis from the principle of comparison that both these irregular appetites for evil arise. A person, who indulges himself in any pleasure, while his friend lies under affliction, feels the reflected uneasiness from his friend more sensibly by a comparison with the original pleasure, which he himself enjoys. This contrast, indeed, ought also to inliven the present pleasure. But as grief is here suppos'd to be the predominant passion, every addition falls to that side, and is swallow'd up in it, without operating in the least upon the contrary affection. 'Tis the same case with those penances, which men inflict on themselves for their past sins and failings. When a criminal reflects on the punishment he deserves, the idea of it is magnify'd by a comparison with his present ease and satisfaction; which forces him, in a manner, to seek uneasiness, in order to avoid so disagreeable a contrast.

This reasoning will account for the origin of *envy* as well as of malice. The only difference betwixt these passions lies in this, that envy is excited by some present enjoyment of another, which by comparison diminishes our idea of our own: Whereas malice is the unprovok'd desire of producing evil to another, in order to reap a pleasure from the comparison. The enjoyment, which is the object of envy, is commonly superior to our own. A superiority naturally seems to overshade us, and presents a disagreeable comparison. But even in the case of an inferiority, we still desire a greater distance, in order to augment still more the idea of ourself. When this distance diminishes, the comparison is less to our advantage; and consequently gives us less pleasure, and is even disagreeable. Hence arises that species of envy, which men feel, when they perceive their inferiors approaching or overtaking them in the pursuit of glory or happiness. In this envy we may see the effects of comparison twice repeated. A man, who compares himself to his inferior, receives a pleasure from the comparison: And when the inferiority decreases by the elevation of the inferior, what shou'd only have been a decrease of pleasure, becomes a real pain, by a new comparison with its preceding condition.

'Tis worthy of observation concerning that envy, which arises from a superiority in others, that 'tis not the great disproportion betwixt ourselves and another, which produces it; but on the contrary, our proximity. A common soldier bears no such envy to his general as to his sergeant or corporal; nor does an eminent writer meet with so great jealousy in common hackney scriblers, as in authors, that more nearly approach him.   It may, indeed, be thought, that the greater the disproportion is, the greater must be the uneasiness from the comparison.   But we may consider on the other hand, that the great disproportion cuts off the relation, and either keeps us from comparing ourselves with what is remote from us, or diminishes the effects of the comparison.   Resemblance and proximity always produce a relation of ideas; and where you destroy these ties, however other accidents may bring two ideas together; as they have no bond or connecting quality to join them in the imagination; 'tis impossible they can remain long united, or have any considerable influence on each other.

I have observ'd in considering the nature of ambition, that the great feel a double pleasure in authority from the comparison of their own condition with that of their slaves; and this comparison has a double influence, because 'tis natural, and presented by the subject.   When the fancy, in the comparison of objects, passes not easily from the one object to the other, the action of the mind is, in a great measure, broke, and the fancy, in considering the second object, begins, as it were, upon a new footing.   The impression, which attends every object, seems not greater in that case by succeeding a less of the same kind; but these two impressions are distinct, and produce their distinct effects, without any communication together.   The want of relation in the ideas breaks the relation of the impressions, and by such a separation prevents their mutual operation and influence.

To confirm this we may observe, that the proximity in the degree of merit is not alone sufficient to give rise to envy, but must be assisted by other relations.   A poet is not apt to envy a philosopher, or a poet of a different kind, of a different nation, or of a different age.   All these differences prevent or weaken the comparison, and consequently the passion.

This too is the reason, why all objects appear great or little, merely by a comparison with those of the same species.   A mountain neither magnifies nor diminishes a horse in our eyes; but when a *Flemish* and a *Welsh* horse are seen together, the one appears greater and the other less, than when view'd apart.

From the same principle we may account for that remark of historians, that any party in a civil war always choose to call in a foreign enemy at any hazard rather than submit to their fellow-citizens. *Guicciardin* applies this remark to the wars in *Italy*, where the relations betwixt the different states are, properly speaking, nothing but of name, language, and contiguity. Yet even these relations, when join'd with superiority, by making the comparison more natural, make it likewise more grievous, and cause men to search for some other superiority, which may be attended with no relation, and by that means may have a less sensible influence on the imagination. The mind quickly perceives its several advantages and disadvantages; and finding its situation to be most uneasy, where superiority is conjoin'd with other relations, seeks its repose as much as possible, by their separation, and by breaking that association of ideas, which renders the comparison so much more natural and efficacious. When it cannot break the association, it feels a stronger desire to remove the superiority; and this is the reason why travellers are commonly so lavish of their praises to the *Chinese* and *Persians*, at the same time, that they depreciate those neighbouring nations, which may stand upon a foot of rivalship with their native country

These examples from history and common experience are rich and curious; but we may find parallel ones in the arts, which are no less remarkable. Shou'd an author compose a treatise, of which one part was serious and profound, another light and humorous, every one wou'd condemn so strange a mixture, and wou'd accuse him of the neglect of all rules of art and criticism. These rules of art are founded on the qualities of human nature; and the quality of human nature, which requires a consistency in every performance, is that which renders the mind incapable of passing in a moment from one passion and disposition to a quite different one. Yet this makes us not blame Mr. *Prior* for joining his *Alma* and his *Solomon* in the same volume, tho' that admirable poet has succeeded perfectly well in the gaiety of the one, as well as in the melancholy of the other. Even supposing the reader shou'd peruse these two compositions without any interval, he wou'd feel little or no difficulty in the change of passions: Why, but because he considers these performances as entirely different, and by this break in the ideas, breaks the progress of the affections, and hinders the one from influencing or contradicting the other?

An heroic and burlesque design, united in one picture, wou'd be monstrous; tho' we place two pictures of so opposite a character in the same chamber, and even close by each other, without any scruple or difficulty.

In a word, no ideas can affect each other, either by comparison, or by the passions they separately produce, unless they be united together by some relation, which may cause an easy transition of the ideas, and consequently of the emotions or impressions, attending the ideas; and may preserve the one impression in the passage of the imagination to the object of the other. This principle is very remarkable, because it is analogous to what we have observ'd both concerning the *understanding* and the *passions*. Suppose two objects to be presented to me, which are not connected by any kind of relation. Suppose that each of these objects separately produces a passion; and that these two passions are in themselves contrary: We find from experience, that the want of relation in the objects or ideas hinders the natural contrariety of the passions, and that the break in the transition of the thought removes the affections from each other, and prevents their opposition. 'Tis the same case with comparison; and from both these phænomena we may safely conclude, that the relation of ideas must forward the transition of impressions; since its absence alone is able to prevent it, and to separate what naturally shou'd have operated upon each other. When the absence of an object or quality removes any usual or natural effect, we may certainly conclude that its presence contributes to the production of the effect.

SECT. IX.—*Of the Mixture of Benevolence and Anger with Compassion and Malice.*

Thus we have endeavour'd to account for *pity* and *malice.* Both these affections arise from the imagination, according to the light, in which it places its object. When our fancy considers directly the sentiments of others, and enters deep into them, it makes us sensible of all the passions it surveys, but in a particular manner of grief or sorrow. On the contrary, when we compare the sentiments of others to our own, we feel a sensation directly opposite to the original one, *viz.* a joy from the grief of others, and a grief from their joy.

But these are only the first foundations of the affections of pity and malice. Other passions are afterwards confounded with them. There is always a mixture of love or tenderness with pity, and of hatred or anger with malice. But it must be confess'd, that this mixture seems at first sight to be contradictory to my system. For as pity is an uneasiness, and malice a joy, arising from the misery of others, pity shou'd naturally, as in all other cases, produce hatred; and malice, love.[1] This contradiction I endeavour to reconcile, after the following manner.

In order to cause a transition of passions, there is requir'd a double relation of impressions and ideas, nor is one relation sufficient to produce this effect. But that we may understand the full force of this double relation, we must consider, that 'tis not the present sensation alone or momentary pain or pleasure, which determines the character of any passion, but the whole bent or tendency of it from the beginning to the end. One impression may be related to another, not only when their sensations are resembling, as we have all along suppos'd in the preceding cases; but also when their impulses or directions are similar and correspondent. This cannot take place with regard to pride and humility; because these are only pure sensations, without any direction or tendency to action. We are, therefore, to look for instances of this peculiar relation of impressions only in such affections, as are attended with a certain appetite or desire; such as those of love and hatred.

Benevolence or the appetite, which attends love, is a desire of the happiness of the person belov'd, and an aversion to his misery; as anger or the appetite, which attends hatred, is a desire of the misery of the person hated, and an aversion to his happiness. A desire, therefore, of the happiness of another, and aversion to his misery, are similar to benevolence; and a desire of his misery and aversion to his happiness are correspondent to anger. Now pity is a desire of happiness to another, and aversion to his misery; as malice is the contrary appetite. Pity, then, is related to benevolence; and malice to anger: And as benevolence has been already found to be connected with love, by a natural and original quality, and anger with hatred; 'tis by this chain

[¹ Introd. Sect 43 —ED.]

the passions of pity and malice are connected with love and hatred.[1]

This hypothesis is founded on sufficient experience. A man, who from any motives has entertain'd a resolution of performing an action, naturally runs into every other view or motive, which may fortify that resolution, and give it authority and influence on the mind. To confirm us in any design, we search for motives drawn from interest, from honour, from duty. What wonder, then, that pity and benevolence, malice and anger, being the same desires arising from different principles, shou'd so totally mix together as to be undistinguishable? As to the connexion betwixt benevolence and love, anger and hatred, being *original* and primary, it admits of no difficulty.

We may add to this another experiment, *viz.* that benevolence and anger, and consequently love and hatred, arise when our happiness or misery have any dependance on the happiness or misery of another person, without any farther relation. I doubt not but this experiment will appear so singular as to excuse us for stopping a moment to consider it.

Suppose, that two persons of the same trade shou'd seek employment in a town, that is not able to maintain both, 'tis plain the success of one is perfectly incompatible with that of the other, and that whatever is for the interest of either is contrary to that of his rival, and so *vice versa.* Suppose again, that two merchants, tho' living in different parts of the world, shou'd enter into co-partnership together, the advantage or loss of one becomes immediately the advantage or loss of his partner, and the same fortune necessarily attends both. Now 'tis evident, that in the first case, hatred always follows upon the contrariety of interests; as in the second, love arises from their union. Let us consider to what principle we can ascribe these passions.

'Tis plain they arise not from the double relations of impressions and ideas, if we regard only the present sensation. For taking the first case of rivalship; tho' the pleasure and advantage of an antagonist necessarily causes my pain and loss, yet to counter-ballance this, his pain and loss causes my pleasure and advantage; and supposing him to be unsuccessful, I may by this means receive from him a superior degree

SECT.
IX.

Of the
mixture of
benevo-
lence, &c

[1 Introd Sect. 43.—Ed.]

of satisfaction. In the same manner the success of a partner rejoices me, but then his misfortunes afflict me in an equal proportion; and 'tis easy to imagine, that the latter sentiment may in many cases preponderate. But whether the fortune of a rival or partner be good or bad, I always hate the former and love the latter.

This love of a partner cannot proceed from the relation or connexion betwixt us; in the same manner as I love a brother or countryman. A rival has almost as close a relation to me as a partner. For as the pleasure of the latter causes my pleasure, and his pain my pain; so the pleasure of the former causes my pain, and his pain my pleasure. The connexion, then, of cause and effect is the same in both cases; and if in the one case, the cause and effect has a farther relation of resemblance, they have that of contrariety in the other; which, being also a species of resemblance, leaves the matter pretty equal.

The only explication, then, we can give of this phænomenon is deriv'd from that principle of a parallel direction above-mention'd. Our concern for our own interest gives us a pleasure in the pleasure, and a pain in the pain of a partner, after the same manner as by sympathy we feel a sensation correspondent to those, which appear in any person, who is present with us. On the other hand, the same concern for our interest makes us feel a pain in the pleasure, and a pleasure in the pain of a rival; and in short the same contrariety of sentiments as arises from comparison and malice. Since, therefore, a parallel direction of the affections, proceeding from interest, can give rise to benevolence or anger, no wonder the same parallel direction, deriv'd from sympathy and from comparison, shou'd have the same effect.

In general we may observe, that 'tis impossible to do good to others, from whatever motive, without feeling some touches of kindness and good-will towards 'em; as the injuries we do, not only cause hatred in the person, who suffers them, but even in ourselves. These phænomena, indeed, may in part be accounted for from other principles.

But here there occurs a considerable objection, which 'twill be necessary to examine before we proceed any farther. I have endeavour'd to prove, that power and riches, or poverty and meanness; which give rise to love or hatred, without producing any original pleasure or uneasiness; operate upon us by means of a secondary sensation deriv'd from a sympathy with that pain or satisfaction, which they produce in the person, who possesses them. From a sympathy with his pleasure there arises love; from that with his uneasiness, hatred. But 'tis a maxim, which I have just now establish'd, and which is absolutely necessary to the explication of the phænomena of pity and malice, "That 'tis not the present "sensation or momentary pain or pleasure, which determines "the character of any passion, but the general bent or ten- "dency of it from the beginning to the end." For this reason, pity or a sympathy with pain produces love, and that because it interests us in the fortunes of others, good or bad, and gives us a secondary sensation correspondent to the primary: in which it has the same influence with love and benevolence. Since then this rule holds good in one case, why does it not prevail throughout, and why does sympathy in uneasiness ever produce any passion beside good-will and kindness? Is it becoming a philosopher to alter his method of reasoning, and run from one principle to its contrary, according to the particular phænomenon, which he wou'd explain?

I have mention'd two different causes, from which a transition of passion may arise, *viz.* a double relation of ideas and impressions, and what is similar to it, a conformity in the tendency and direction of any two desires, which arise from different principles. Now I assert, that when a sympathy with uneasiness is weak, it produces hatred or contempt by the former cause; when strong, it produces love or tenderness by the latter. This is the solution of the foregoing difficulty, which seems so urgent; and this is a principle founded on such evident arguments, that we ought to have establish'd it, even tho' it were not necessary to the explication of any phænomenon.

'Tis certain, that sympathy is not always limited to the present moment, but that we often feel by communication the pains and pleasures of others, which are not in being, and which we only anticipate by the force of imagination. For supposing I saw a person perfectly unknown to me, who, while asleep in the fields, was in danger of being trod under foot by horses, I shou'd immediately run to his assistance; and in this I shou'd be actuated by the same principle of sympathy, which makes me concern'd for the present sorrows of a stranger. The bare mention of this is sufficient. Sympathy being nothing but a lively idea converted into an impression, 'tis evident, that, in considering the future possible or probable condition of any person, we may enter into it with so vivid a conception as to make it our own concern; and by that means be sensible of pains and pleasures, which neither belong to ourselves, nor at the present instant have any real existence.

But however we may look forward to the future in sympathizing with any person, the extending of our sympathy depends in a great measure upon our sense of his present condition. 'Tis a great effort of imagination, to form such lively ideas even of the present sentiments of others as to feel these very sentiments; but 'tis impossible we cou'd extend this sympathy to the future, without being aided by some circumstance in the present, which strikes upon us in a lively manner. When the present misery of another has any strong influence upon me, the vivacity of the conception is not confin'd merely to its immediate object, but diffuses its influence over all the related ideas, and gives me a lively notion of all the circumstances of that person, whether past, present, or future; possible, probable or certain. By means of this lively notion I am interested in them; take part with them; and feel a sympathetic motion in my breast, conformable to whatever I imagine in his. If I diminish the vivacity of the first conception, I diminish that of the related ideas; as pipes can convey no more water than what arises at the fountain. By this diminution I destroy the future prospect, which is necessary to interest me perfectly in the fortunes of another. I may feel the present impression, but carry my sympathy no farther, and never transfuse the force of the first conception into my ideas of the related objects. If it be another's misery, which is presented in this feeble manner, I receive it by communication, and am affected with all the passions related to it: But as I am not so much interested as to concern myself in his good fortune, as well as his bad, I never feel the extensive sympathy, nor the passions related to *it*.

Now in order to know what passions are related to these different kinds of sympathy, we must consider, that benevolence is an original pleasure arising from the pleasure of the person belov'd, and a pain proceeding from his pain: From which correspondence of impressions there arises a subsequent desire of his pleasure, and aversion to his pain.[1] In order, then, to make a passion run parallel with benevolence, 'tis requisite we should feel these double impressions, correspondent to those of the person, whom we consider; nor is any one of them alone sufficient for that purpose. When we sympathize only with one impression, and that a painful one, this sympathy is related to anger and to hatred, upon account of the uneasiness it conveys to us. But as the extensive or limited sympathy depends upon the force of the first sympathy; it follows, that the passion of love or hatred depends upon the same principle. A strong impression, when communicated, gives a double tendency of the passions; which is related to benevolence and love by a similarity of direction; however painful the first impression might have been. A weak impression, that is painful, is related to anger and hatred by the resemblance of sensations. Benevolence, therefore, arises from a great degree of misery, or any degree strongly sympathiz'd with : Hatred or contempt from a small degree, or one weakly sympathiz'd with; which is the principle I intended to prove and explain.

Nor have we only our reason to trust to for this principle, but also experience. A certain degree of poverty produces contempt; but a degree beyond causes compassion and goodwill. We may under-value a peasant or servant; but when the misery of a beggar appears very great, or is painted in very lively colours, we sympathize with him in his afflictions, and feel in our heart evident touches of pity and benevolence. The same object causes contrary passions according to its different degrees. The passions, therefore, must depend upon principles, that operate in such certain degrees, according to my hypothesis. The encrease of the sympathy has evidently the same effect as the encrease of the misery.

A barren and desolate country always seems ugly and disagreeable, and commonly inspires us with contempt for the inhabitants. This deformity, however, proceeds in a great measure from a sympathy with the inhabitants, as has been already observ'd; but it is only a weak one, and reaches no farther than the immediate sensation, which is disagreeable. The view of a city in ashes conveys benevolent sentiments; because we there enter so deep into the interests of the

SECT.
. IX.
Of the
mixture of
benevo-
lence, &c.

[¹ Introd Sect. 42 —Ed]

miserable inhabitants, as to wish for their prosperity, as well as feel their adversity.

But tho' the force of the impression generally produces pity and benevolence, 'tis certain, that being carry'd too far it ceases to have that effect. This, perhaps, may be worth our notice. When the uneasiness is either small in itself, or remote from us, it engages not the imagination, nor is able to convey an equal concern for the future and contingent good, as for the present and real evil. Upon its acquiring greater force, we become so interested in the concerns of the person, as to be sensible both of his good and bad fortune; and from that compleat sympathy there arises pity and benevolence. But 'twill easily be imagin'd, that where the present evil strikes with more than ordinary force, it may entirely engage our attention, and prevent that double sympathy, abovemention'd. Thus we find, that tho' every one, but especially women, are apt to contract a kindness for criminals, who go to the scaffold, and readily imagine them to be uncommonly handsome and well-shap'd; yet one, who is present at the cruel execution of the rack, feels no such tender emotions; but is in a manner overcome with horror, and has no leisure to temper this uneasy sensation by any opposite sympathy.

But the instance, which makes the most clearly for my hypothesis, is that wherein by a change of the objects we separate the double sympathy even from a midling degree of the passion; in which case we find, that pity, instead of producing love and tenderness as usual, always gives rise to the contrary affection. When we observe a person in misfortunes, we are affected with pity and love: but the author of that misfortune becomes the object of our strongest hatred, and is the more detested in proportion to the degree of our compassion. Now for what reason shou'd the same passion of pity produce love to the person, who suffers the misfortune, and hatred to the person, who causes it; unless it be because in the latter case the author bears a relation only to the misfortune; whereas in considering the sufferer we carry our view on every side, and wish for his prosperity, as well as are sensible of his affliction?

I shall just observe, before I leave the present subject, that this phænomenon of the double sympathy, and its tendency to cause love, may contribute to the production of the kindness, which we naturally bear our relations and ac-

quaintance.   Custom and relation make us enter deeply into
the sentiments of others; and whatever fortune we suppose
to attend them, is render'd present to us by the imagination,
and operates as if originally our own.   We rejoice in their
pleasures, and grieve for their sorrows, merely from the force
of sympathy.   Nothing that concerns them is indifferent to
us; and as this correspondence of sentiments is the natural
attendant of love, it readily produces that affection.

SECT. X.—*Of Respect and Contempt.*

There now remains only to explain the passions of *respect*
and *contempt,* along with the *amorous* affection, in order to
understand all the passions which have any mixture of love
or hatred.   Let us begin with respect and contempt.

In considering the qualities and circumstances of others,
we may either regard them as they really are in themselves;
or may make a comparison betwixt them and our own qualities and circumstances; or may join these two methods of
consideration.   The good qualities of others, from the first
point of view, produce love; from the second, humility; and
from the third, respect; which is a mixture of these two
passions.   Their bad qualities, after the same manner, cause
either hatred, or pride, or contempt, according to the light
in which we survey them.

That there is a mixture of pride in contempt, and of
humility in respect, is, I think, too evident, from their very
feeling or appearance, to require any particular proof.   That
this mixture arises from a tacit comparison of the person
contemn'd or respected with ourselves is no less evident.
The same man may cause either respect, love, or contempt by
his condition and talents, according as the person, who considers him, from his inferior becomes his equal or superior.
In changing the point of view, tho' the object may remain
the same, its proportion to ourselves entirely alters, which
is the cause of an alteration in the passions.   These passions,
therefore, arise from our observing the proportion; that is,
from a comparison.

I have already observ'd, that the mind has a much stronger
propensity to pride than to humility, and have endeavour'd,
from the principles of human nature, to assign a cause for
this phænomenon.   Whether my reasoning be received or

not, the phænomenon is undisputed, and appears in many instances. Among the rest, 'tis the reason why there is a much greater mixture of pride in contempt, than of humility in respect, and why we are more elevated with the view of one below us, than mortify'd with the presence of one above us. Contempt or scorn has so strong a tincture of pride, that there scarce is any other passion discernable: Whereas in esteem or respect, love makes a more considerable ingredient than humility. The passion of vanity is so prompt, that it rouzes at the least call; while humility requires a stronger impulse to make it exert itself.

But here it may reasonably be ask'd, why this mixture takes place only in some cases, and appears not on every occasion. All those objects, which cause love, when plac'd on another person, are the causes of pride, when transfer'd to ourselves; and consequently ought to be causes of humility, as well as love, while they belong to others, and are only compar'd to those, which we ourselves possess. In like manner every quality, which, by being directly consider'd, produces hatred, ought always to give rise to pride by comparison, and by a mixture of these passions of hatred and pride ought to excite contempt or scorn. The difficulty then is, why any objects ever cause pure love or hatred, and produce not always the mixt passions of respect and contempt.

I have suppos'd all along, that the passions of love and pride, and those of humility and hatred are similar in their sensations, and that the two former are always agreeable, and the two latter painful. But tho' this be universally true, 'tis observable, that the two agreeable, as well as the two painful passions, have some differences, and even contrarieties, which distinguish them. Nothing invigorates and exalts the mind equally with pride and vanity; tho' at the same time love or tenderness is rather found to weaken and infeeble it The same difference is observable betwixt the uneasy passions. Anger and hatred bestow a new force on all our thoughts and actions; while humility and shame deject and discourage us. Of these qualities of the passions, 'twill be necessary to form a distinct idea. Let us remember, that pride and hatred invigorate the soul; and love and humility infeeble it.

From this it follows, that tho' the conformity betwixt love and hatred in the agreeableness of their sensation makes them always be excited by the same objects, yet this other contrariety is the reason, why they are excited in very different degrees. Genius and learning are *pleasant* and *magnificent* objects, and by both these circumstances are adapted to pride and vanity; but have a relation to love by their pleasure only. Ignorance and simplicity are *disagreeable* and *mean*, which in the same manner gives them a double connexion with humanity, and a single one with hatred. We may, therefore, consider it as certain, that tho' the same object always produces love and pride, humility and hatred, according to its different situations, yet it seldom produces either the two former or the two latter passions in the same proportion.

'Tis here we must seek for a solution of the difficulty abovemention'd, why any object ever excites pure love or hatred, and does not always produce respect or contempt, by a mixture of humility or pride. No quality in another gives rise to humility by comparison, unless it wou'd have produc'd pride by being plac'd in ourselves; and *vice versa* no object excites pride by comparison, unless it wou'd have produc'd humility by the direct survey. This is evident, objects always produce by *comparison* a sensation directly contrary to their *original* one. Suppose, therefore, an object to be presented, which is peculiarly fitted to produce love, but imperfectly to excite pride; this object, belonging to another, gives rise directly to a great degree of love, but to a small one of humility by comparison and consequently that latter passion is scarce felt in the compound, nor is able to convert the love into respect. This is the case with good nature, good humour, facility, generosity, beauty, and many other qualities. These have a peculiar aptitude to produce love in others; but not so great a tendency to excite pride in ourselves: For which reason the view of them, as belonging to another person, produces pure love, with but a small mixture of humility and respect. 'Tis easy to extend the same reasoning to the opposite passions.

Before we leave this subject, it may not be amiss to account for a pretty curious phænomenon, *viz.* why we commonly keep at a distance such as we contemn, and allow not our inferiors to approach too near even in place and situation. It has already been observ'd, that almost every kind of idea is attended with some emotion, even the ideas of number and extension, much more those of such objects as are esteem'd of consequence in life, and fix our attention. 'Tis not with entire indifference we can survey either a rich man or a poor one, but must feel some faint touches, at least, of respect in the former case, and of contempt in the latter. These two passions are contrary to each other; but in order to make this contrariety be felt, the objects must be some way related, otherwise the affections are totally separate and distinct, and never encounter. The relation takes place wherever the persons become contiguous; which is a general reason why we are uneasy at seeing such disproportioned objects, as a rich man and a poor one, a nobleman and a porter, in that situation.

This uneasiness, which is common to every spectator, must be more sensible to the superior; and that because the near approach of the inferior is regarded as a piece of ill-breeding, and shews that he is not sensible of the disproportion, and is no way affected by it. A sense of superiority in another breeds in all men an inclination to keep themselves at a distance from him, and determines them to redouble the marks of respect and reverence, when they are oblig'd to approach him; and where they do not observe that conduct, 'tis a proof they are not sensible of his superiority. From hence too it proceeds, that any great *difference* in the degrees of any quality is call'd a *distance* by a common metaphor, which, however trivial it may appear, is founded on natural principles of the imagination. A great difference inclines us to produce a distance. The ideas of distance and difference are, therefore, connected together. Connected ideas are readily taken for each other; and this is in general the source of the metaphor, as we shall have occasion to observe afterwards.

Sect. XI.—*Of the Amorous Passion, or Love betwixt the Sexes.*

Of all the compound passions, which proceed from a mixture of love and hatred with other affections, no one better deserves our attention, than that love, which arises betwixt the sexes, as well on account of its force and violence, as those curious principles of philosophy, for which it affords us an uncontestable argument. 'Tis plain, that this affection, in its most natural state, is deriv'd from the conjunction of three different impressions or passions, *viz.* The pleasing sensation arising from beauty; the bodily appetite for generation;

and a generous kindness or good-will.　The origin of kindness from beauty may be explain'd from the foregoing reasoning.　The question is how the bodily appetite is excited by it.

The appetite of generation, when confin'd to a certain degree, is evidently of the pleasant kind, and has a strong connexion with all the agreeable emotions.　Joy, mirth, vanity, and kindness are all incentives to this desire; as well as music, dancing, wine, and good cheer.　On the other hand, sorrow, melancholy, poverty, humility are destructive of it.　From this quality 'tis easily conceiv'd why it shou'd be connected with the sense of beauty.

But there is another principle that contributes to the same effect.　I have observ'd that the parallel direction of the desires is a real relation, and no less than a resemblance in their sensation, produces a connexion among them.　That we may fully comprehend the extent of this relation, we must consider, that any principal desire may be attended with subordinate ones, which are connected with it, and to which if other desires are parallel, they are by that means related to the principal one.　Thus hunger may oft be consider'd as the primary inclination of the soul, and the desire of approaching the meat as the secondary one; since 'tis absolutely necessary to the satisfying that appetite.　If an object, therefore, by any separate qualities, inclines us to approach the meat, it naturally encreases our appetite; as on the contrary, whatever inclines us to set our victuals at a distance, is contradictory to hunger, and diminishes our inclination to them.　Now 'tis plain that beauty has the first effect, and deformity the second: Which is the reason why the former gives us a keener appetite for our victuals, and the latter is sufficient to disgust us at the most savoury dish, that cookery has invented.　All this is easily applicable to the appetite for generation.

From these two relations, *viz.* resemblance and a parallel desire, there arises such a connexion betwixt the sense of beauty, the bodily appetite, and benevolence, that they become in a manner inseparable: And we find from experience, that 'tis indifferent which of them advances first; since any of them is almost sure to be attended with the related affections.　One, who is inflam'd with lust, feels at least a momentary kindness towards the object of it, and at the same time fancies her more beautiful than ordinary; as there

are many, who begin with kindness and esteem for the wit
and merit of the person, and advance from that to the other
passions. But the most common species of love is that
which first arises from beauty, and afterwards diffuses itself
into kindness and into the bodily appetite. Kindness or
esteem, and the appetite to generation, are too remote to
unite easily together. The one is, perhaps, the most refin'd
passion of the soul, the other the most gross and vulgar.
The love of beauty is plac'd in a just medium betwixt them,
and partakes of both their natures: From whence it proceeds, that 'tis so singularly fitted to produce both.

This account of love is not peculiar to my system, but is
unavoidable on any hypothesis. The three affections, which
compose this passion, are evidently distinct, and has each of
them its distinct object. 'Tis certain, therefore, that 'tis
only by their relation they produce each other. But the relation of passions is not alone sufficient. 'Tis likewise necessary, there shou'd be a relation of ideas. The beauty of
one person never inspires us with love for another. This
then is a sensible proof of the double relation of impressions
and ideas. From one instance so evident as this we may
form a judgment of the rest.

This may also serve in another view to illustrate what I
have insisted on concerning the origin of pride and humility,
love and hatred. I have observ'd, that tho' self be the object of the first set of passions, and some other person of the
second, yet these objects cannot alone be the causes of the
passions; as having each of them a relation to two contrary
affections, which must from the very first moment destroy
each other. Here then is the situation of the mind, as I
have already describ'd it. It has certain organs naturally
fitted to produce a passion; that passion, when produc'd,
naturally turns the view to a certain object. But this not
being sufficient to produce the passion, there is requir'd some
other emotion, which by a double relation of impressions and
ideas[1] may set these principles in action, and bestow on them
their first impulse. This situation is still more remarkable
with regard to the appetite of generation. Sex is not only the
object, but also the cause of the appetite. We not only turn
our view to it, when actuated by that appetite; but the reflecting on it suffices to excite the appetite. But as this

[¹ Introd Sect 33 – Ed.]

cause loses its force by too great frequency, 'tis necessary it
shou'd be quicken'd by some new impulse; and that impulse
we find to arise from the *beauty* of the *person* ; that is, from
a double relation of impressions and ideas. Since this double
relation is necessary where an affection has both a distinct
cause, and object, how much more so, where it has only a
distinct object, without any determinate cause ?

Sect. XII.—*Of the Love and Hatred of Animals.*

But to pass from the passions of love and hatred, and
from their mixtures and compositions, as they appear in
man, to the same affections, as they display themselves in
brutes ; we may observe, not only that love and hatred are
common to the whole sensitive creation, but likewise that
their causes, as above-explain'd, are of so simple a nature,
that they may easily be suppos'd to operate on mere animals.
There is no force of reflection or penetration requir'd.
Every thing is conducted by springs and principles, which
are not peculiar to man, or any one species of animals.   The
conclusion from this is obvious in favour of the foregoing
system.

Love in animals has not for its only object animals of
the same species, but extends itself farther, and comprehends almost every sensible and thinking being. A dog
naturally loves a man above his own species, and very commonly meets with a return of affection.

As animals are but little susceptible either of the pleasures
or pains of the imagination, they can judge of objects only
by the sensible good or evil, which they produce, and from
that must regulate their affections towards them.   Accordingly we find, that by benefits or injuries we produce their
love or hatred; and that by feeding and cherishing any
animal, we quickly acquire his affections; as by beating and
abusing him we never fail to draw on us his enmity and ill-
will.

Love in beasts is not caus'd so much by relation, as in
our species; and that because their thoughts are not so
active as to trace relations, except in very obvious instances.
Yet 'tis easy to remark, that on some occasions it has a considerable influence upon them.   Thus acquaintance, which
has the same effect as relation, always produces love in

animals either to men or to each other. For the same
reason any likeness among them is the source of affection.
An ox confin'd to a park with horses, will naturally join
their company, if I may so speak, but always leaves it to
enjoy that of his own species, where he has the choice of
both.

The affection of parents to their young proceeds from a
peculiar instinct in animals, as well as in our species.

'Tis evident, that *sympathy*, or the communication of
passions, takes place among animals, no less than among
men. Fear, anger, courage and other affections are frequently communicated from one animal to another, without
their knowledge of that cause, which produc'd the original
passion. Grief likewise is receiv'd by sympathy; and produces almost all the same consequences, and excites the
same emotions as in our species. The howlings and lamen-
tations of a dog produce a sensible concern in his fellows.
And 'tis remarkable, that tho' almost all animals use in play
the same member, and nearly the same action as in fighting;
a lion, a tyger, a cat their paws; an ox his horns; a dog
his teeth; a horse his heels: Yet they most carefully avoid
harming their companion, even tho' they have nothing to
fear from his resentment; which is an evident proof of the
sense brutes have of each other's pain and pleasure.

Every one has observ'd how much more dogs are animated when they hunt in a pack, than when they pursue
their game apart; and 'tis evident this can proceed from
nothing but from sympathy. 'Tis also well known to
hunters, that this effect follows in a greater degree, and
even in too great a degree, where two packs, that are
strangers to each other, are join'd together. We might,
perhaps, be at a loss to explain this phænomenon, if we had
not experience of a similar in ourselves.

Envy and malice are passions very remarkable in animals.
They are perhaps more common than pity; as requiring less
effort of thought and imagination.

PART III.

OF THE WILL AND DIRECT PASSIONS.

SECT. I.—*Of Liberty and Necessity.*

WE come now to explain the *direct* passions, or the impressions, which arise immediately from good or evil, from pain or pleasure. Of this kind are, *desire and aversion, grief and joy, hope and fear.*

Of all the immediate effects of pain and pleasure, there is none more remarkable than the WILL; and tho', properly speaking, it be not comprehended among the passions, yet as the full understanding of its nature and properties, is necessary to the explanation of them, we shall here make it the subject of our enquiry. I desire it may be observ'd, that by the *will*, I mean nothing but *the internal impression we feel and are conscious of, when we knowingly give rise to any new motion of our body, or new perception of our mind.* This impression, like the preceding ones of pride and humility, love and hatred, 'tis impossible to define, and needless to describe any farther; for which reason we shall cut off all those definitions and distinctions, with which philosophers are wont to perplex rather than clear up this question; and entering at first upon the subject, shall examine that long disputed question concerning *liberty and necessity*; which occurs so naturally in treating of the will.

'Tis universally acknowledg'd, that the operations of external bodies are necessary, and that in the communication of their motion, in their attraction, and mutual cohesion, there are not the least traces of indifference or liberty. Every object is determin'd by an absolute fate to a certain degree and direction of its motion, and can no more depart from that precise line, in which it moves, than it can convert itself into an angel, or spirit, or any superior substance. The actions, therefore, of matter are to be regarded as

SECT.
I.

Of liberty
and necessity.

instances of necessary actions; and whatever is in this respect on the same footing with matter, must be acknowledg'd to be necessary. That we may know whether this be
the case with the actions of the mind, we shall begin with
examining matter, and considering on what the ideas of a
necessity in its operations are founded, and why we conclude
one body or action to be the infallible cause of another.

It has been observ'd already, that in no single instance
the ultimate connexion of any objects is discoverable, either
by our senses or reason, and that we can never penetrate so
far into the essence and construction of bodies, as to perceive
the principle, on which their mutual influence depends. 'Tis
their constant union alone, with which we are acquainted;
and 'tis from the constant union the necessity arises. If
objects had not an uniform and regular conjunction with
each other, we shou'd never arrive at any idea of cause
and effect; and even after all, the necessity, which enters
into that idea, is nothing but a determination of the mind to
pass from one object to its usual attendant, and infer the
existence of one from that of the other. Here then are
two particulars, which we are to consider as essential to
necessity, *viz.* the constant *union* and the *inference* of the
mind; and wherever we discover these we must acknowledge
a necessity. As the actions of matter have no necessity, but
what is deriv'd from these circumstances, and it is not by
any insight into the essence of bodies we discover their connexion, the absence of this insight, while the union and
inference remain, will never, in any case, remove the necessity. 'Tis the observation of the union, which produces
the inference; for which reason it might be thought sufficient, if we prove a constant union in the actions of the
mind, in order to establish the inference, along with the
necessity of these actions. But that I may bestow a greater
force on my reasoning, I shall examine these particulars
apart, and shall first prove from experience, that our actions
have a constant union with our motives, tempers, and
circumstances, before I consider the inferences we draw
from it.

To this end a very slight and general view of the common
course of human affairs will be sufficient. There is no light,
in which we can take them, that does not confirm this
principle. Whether we consider mankind according to the

difference of sexes, ages, governments, conditions, or methods of education; the same uniformity and regular operation of natural principles are discernible. Like causes still produce like effects; in the same manner as in the mutual action of the elements and powers of nature.

There are different trees, which regularly produce fruit, whose relish is different from each other; and this regularity will be admitted as an instance of necessity and causes in external bodies. But are the products of *Guienne* and of *Champagne* more regularly different than the sentiments, actions, and passions of the two sexes, of which the one are distinguish'd by their force and maturity, the other by their delicacy and softness?

Are the changes of our body from infancy to old age more regular and certain than those of our mind and conduct? And wou'd a man be more ridiculous, who wou'd expect that an infant of four years old will raise a weight of three hundred pound, than one, who from a person of the same age, wou'd look for a philosophical reasoning, or a prudent and well-concerted action?

We must certainly allow, that the cohesion of the parts of matter arises from natural and necessary principles, whatever difficulty we may find in explaining them: And for a like reason we must allow, that human society is founded on like principles; and our reason in the latter case, is better than even that in the former; because we not only observe, that men *always* seek society, but can also explain the principles, on which this universal propensity is founded. For is it more certain, that two flat pieces of marble will unite together, than that two young savages of different sexes will copulate? Do the children arise from this copulation more uniformly, than does the parents' care for their safety and preservation? And after they have arriv'd at years of discretion by the care of their parents, are the inconveniencies attending their separation more certain than their foresight of these inconveniencies, and their care of avoiding them by a close union and confederacy?

The skin, pores, muscles, and nerves of a day-labourer are different from those of a man of quality: So are his sentiments, actions and manners. The different stations of life influence the whole fabric, external and internal; and these different stations arise necessarily, because uniformly, from the necessary and uniform principles of human nature. Men cannot live without society, and cannot be associated without government. Government makes a distinction of property, and establishes the different ranks of men. This produces industry, traffic, manufactures, law-suits, war, leagues, alliances, voyages, travels, cities, fleets, ports, and all those other actions and objects, which cause such a diversity, and at the same time maintain such an uniformity in human life.

Shou'd a traveller, returning from a far country, tell us, that he had seen a climate in the fiftieth degree of northern latitude, where all the fruits ripen and come to perfection in the winter, and decay in the summer, after the same manner as in *England* they are produc'd and decay in the contrary seasons, he wou'd find few so credulous as to believe him. I am apt to think a traveller wou'd meet with as little credit, who shou'd inform us of people exactly of the same character with those in *Plato's* republic on the one hand, or those in *Hobbes's Leviathan* on the other. There is a general course of nature in human actions, as well as in the operations of the sun and the climate. There are also characters peculiar to different nations and particular persons, as well as common to mankind. The knowledge of these characters is founded on the observation of an uniformity in the actions, that flow from them; and this uniformity forms the very essence of necessity.

I can imagine only one way of eluding this argument, which is by denying that uniformity of human actions, on which it is founded. As long as actions have a constant union and connexion with the situation and temper of the agent, however we may in words refuse to acknowledge the necessity, we really allow the thing. Now some may, perhaps, find a pretext to deny this regular union and connexion. For what is more capricious than human actions? What more inconstant than the desires of man? And what creature departs more widely, not only from right reason, but from his own character and disposition? An hour, a moment is sufficient to make him change from one extreme to another, and overturn what cost the greatest pain and labour to establish. Necessity is regular and certain. Human conduct is irregular and uncertain. The one, therefore, proceeds not from the other.

To this I reply, that in judging of the actions of men we must proceed upon the same maxims, as when we reason concerning external objects. When any phænomena are constantly and invariably conjoin'd together, they acquire such a connexion in the imagination, that it passes from one to the other, without any doubt or hesitation. But below this there are many inferior degrees of evidence and probability, nor does one single contrariety of experiment entirely destroy all our reasoning. The mind ballances the contrary experiments, and deducting the inferior from the superior, proceeds with that degree of assurance or evidence, which remains. Even when these contrary experiments are entirely equal, we remove not the notion of causes and necessity; but supposing that the usual contrariety proceeds from the operation of contrary and conceal'd causes, we conclude, that the chance or indifference lies only in our judgment on account of our imperfect knowledge, not in the things themselves, which are in every case equally necessary, tho' to appearance not equally constant or certain.[1] No union can be more constant and certain, than that of some actions with some motives and characters; and if in other cases the union is uncertain, 'tis no more than what happens in the operations of body, nor can we conclude any thing from the one irregularity, which will not follow equally from the other.

'Tis commonly allow'd that mad-men have no liberty. But were we to judge by their actions, these have less regularity and constancy than the actions of wise-men, and consequently are farther remov'd from necessity. Our way of thinking in this particular is, therefore, absolutely inconsistent; but is a natural consequence of these confus'd ideas and undefin'd terms, which we so commonly make use of in our reasonings, especially on the present subject

We must now shew, that as the *union* betwixt motives and actions has the same constancy, as that in any natural operations, so its influence on the understanding is also the same, in *determining* us to infer the existence of one from that of another. If this shall appear, there is no known circumstance, that enters into the connexion and production of the actions of matter, that is not to be found in all the operations of the mind; and consequently we cannot, without

[1 Introd Sect. 56, cf also Introd. to Vol I Sect. 6, 336.—ED]

a manifest absurdity, attribute necessity to the one, and refuse it to the other.

There is no philosopher, whose judgment is so riveted to this fantastical system of liberty, as not to acknowledge the force of *moral evidence*, and both in speculation and practice proceed upon it, as upon a reasonable foundation. Now moral evidence is nothing but a conclusion concerning the actions of men, deriv'd from the consideration of their motives, temper and situation. Thus when we see certain characters or figures describ'd upon paper, we infer that the person, who produc'd them, wou'd affirm such facts, the death of *Cæsar*, the success of *Augustus*, the cruelty of *Nero*; and remembering many other concurrent testimonies we conclude, that those facts were once really existent, and that so many men, without any interest, wou'd never conspire to deceive us; especially since they must, in the attempt, expose themselves to the derision of all their contemporaries, when these facts were asserted to be recent and universally known. The same kind of reasoning runs thro' politics, war, commerce, oeconomy, and indeed mixes itself so entirely in human life, that 'tis impossible to act or subsist a moment without having recourse to it. A prince, who imposes a tax upon his subjects, expects their compliance. A general, who conducts an army, makes account of a certain degree of courage. A merchant looks for fidelity and skill in his factor or super-cargo. A man, who gives orders for his dinner, doubts not of the obedience of his servants. In short, as nothing more nearly interests us than our own actions and those of others, the greatest part of our reasonings is employ'd in judgments concerning them. Now I assert, that whoever reasons after this manner, does *ipso facto* believe the actions of the will to arise from necessity, and that he knows not what he means, when he denies it.

All those objects, of which we call the one *cause* and the other *effect*, consider'd in themselves, are as distinct and separate from each other, as any two things in nature, nor can we ever, by the most accurate survey of them, infer the existence of the one from that of the other. 'Tis only from experience and the observation of their constant union, that we are able to form this inference; and even after all, the inference is nothing but the effects of custom on

the imagination. We must not here be content with
saying, that the idea of cause and effect arises from objects
constantly united; but must affirm, that 'tis the very
same with the idea of these objects, and that the *necessary
connexion* is not discover'd by a conclusion of the understanding, but is merely a perception of the mind. Wherever,
therefore, we observe the same union, and wherever the
union operates in the same manner upon the belief and
opinion, we have the idea of causes and necessity, tho'
perhaps we may avoid those expressions. Motion in one
body in all past instances, that have fallen under our observation, is follow'd upon impulse by motion in another.
'Tis impossible for the mind to penetrate farther. From
this constant union it *forms* the idea of cause and effect,
and by its influence *feels* the necessity. As there is the
same constancy, and the same influence in what we call
moral evidence, I ask no more. What remains can only be
a dispute of words.

And indeed, when we consider how aptly *natural* and
moral evidence cement together, and form only one chain
of argument betwixt them, we shall make no scruple to
allow, that they are of the same nature, and deriv'd from
the same principles. A prisoner, who has neither money
nor interest, discovers the impossibility of his escape, as well
from the obstinacy of the gaoler, as from the walls and bars
with which he is surrounded; and in all attempts for his
freedom chuses rather to work upon the stone and iron
of the one, than upon the inflexible nature of the other.
The same prisoner, when conducted to the scaffold, fore-
sees his death as certainly from the constancy and fidelity
of his guards as from the operation of the ax or wheel.
His mind runs along a certain train of ideas: The refusal
of the soldiers to consent to his escape, the action of the
executioner; the separation of the head and body; bleeding,
convulsive motions, and death. Here is a connected chain
of natural causes and voluntary actions; but the mind
feels no difference betwixt them in passing from one link to
another; nor is less certain of the future event than if it
were connected with the present impressions of the memory
and senses by a train of causes cemented together by what
we are pleas'd to call a *physical necessity*. The same experienc'd union has the same effect on the mind, whether

the united objects be motives, volitions and actions; or figure and motion. We may change the names of things; but their nature and their operation on the understanding never change.

I dare be positive no one will ever endeavour to refute these reasonings otherwise than by altering my definitions, and assigning a different meaning to the terms of *cause, and effect, and necessity, and liberty, and chance.* According to my definitions, necessity makes an essential part of causation; and consequently liberty, by removing necessity, removes also causes, and is the very same thing with chance. As chance is commonly thought to imply a contradiction, and is at least directly contrary to experience, there are always the same arguments against liberty or free-will. If any one alters the definitions, I cannot pretend to argue with him, 'till I know the meaning he assigns to these terms.

SECT. II.—*The same Subject continu'd.*

I believe we may assign the three following reasons for the prevalence of the doctrine of liberty, however absurd it may be in one sense, and unintelligible in any other. First, After we have perform'd any action; tho' we confess we were influenc'd by particular views and motives; 'tis diffi-cult for us to perswade ourselves we were govern'd by necessity, and that 'twas utterly impossible for us to have acted otherwise; the idea of necessity seeming to imply something of force, and violence, and constraint, of which we are not sensible. Few are capable of distinguishing betwixt the liberty of *spontaneity*, as it is call'd in the schools, and the liberty of *indifference*; betwixt that which is oppos'd to violence, and that which means a negation of necessity and causes. The first is even the most common sense of the word; and as 'tis only that species of liberty, which it concerns us to preserve, our thoughts have been principally turn'd towards it, and have almost universally confounded it with the other.

Secondly, There is a *false sensation or experience* even of the liberty of indifference, which is regarded as an argu-ment for its real existence. The necessity of any action, whether of matter or of the mind, is not properly a quality in the agent, but in any thinking or intelligent being, who may consider the action, and consists in the determination of his thought to infer its existence from some preceding objects:[1] As liberty or chance, on the other hand, is nothing but the want of that determination, and a certain loose-ness, which we feel in passing or not passing from the idea of one to that of the other. Now we may observe, that tho' in reflecting on human actions we seldom feel such a looseness or indifference, yet it very commonly happens, that in performing the actions themselves we are sensible of something like it: And as all related or resembling objects are readily taken for each other, this has been employ'd as a demonstrative or even an intuitive proof of human liberty. We feel that our actions are subject to our will on most occasions, and imagine we feel that the will itself is subject to nothing; because when by a denial of it we are provok'd to try, we feel that it moves easily every way, and produces an image of itself even on that side, on which it did not settle. This image or faint motion, we perswade ourselves, cou'd have been compleated into the thing itself; because, shou'd that be deny'd, we find, upon a second trial, that it can. But these efforts are all in vain; and whatever capri-cious and irregular actions we may perform; as the desire of showing our liberty is the sole motive of our actions; we can never free ourselves from the bonds of necessity. We may imagine we feel a liberty within ourselves; but a spec-tator can commonly infer our actions from our motives and character; and even where he cannot, he concludes in general, that he might, were he perfectly acquainted with every circumstance of our situation and temper, and the most secret springs of our complexion and disposition. Now this is the very essence of necessity, according to the fore-going doctrine.

A third reason why the doctrine of liberty has generally been better receiv'd in the world, than its antagonist, pro-ceeds from *religion*, which has been very unnecessarily in-terested in this question. There is no method of reasoning more common, and yet none more blameable, than in philosophical debates to endeavour to refute any hypothesis by a pretext of its dangerous consequences to religion and morality. When any opinion leads us into absurdities, 'tis certainly false; but 'tis not certain an opinion is false,

SECT
II

The same subject continu'd.

[1 Introd Sect 56 —Ed]

because 'tis of dangerous consequence. Such topics, therefore, ought entirely to be foreborn, as serving nothing to the
discovery of truth, but only to make the person of an antagonist odious. This I observe in general, without pretending
to draw any advantage from it.   I submit myself frankly to
an examination of this kind, and dare venture to affirm, that
the doctrine of necessity, according to my explication of it,
is not only innocent, but even advantageous to religion and
morality.

I define necessity two ways, conformable to the two definitions of *cause*, of which it makes an essential part. I place
it either in the constant union and conjunction of like
objects, or in the inference of the mind from the one to the
other.   Now necessity, in both these senses, has universally,
tho' tacitely, in the schools, in the pulpit, and in common
life, been allow'd to belong to the will of man, and no one
has ever pretended to deny, that we can draw inferences
concerning human actions, and that those inferences are
founded on the experienc'd union of like actions with like
motives and circumstances. The only particular in which
any one can differ from me, is either, that perhaps he will
refuse to call this necessity.   But as long as the meaning is
understood, I hope the word can do no harm.   Or that he
will maintain there is something else in the operations of
matter.   Now whether it be so or not is of no consequence
to religion, whatever it may be to natural philosophy.   I
may be mistaken in asserting, that we have no idea of any
other connexion in the actions of body, and shall be glad to
be farther instructed on that head : But sure I am, I ascribe
nothing to the actions of the mind, but what must readily
be allow'd of.   Let no one, therefore, put an invidious construction on my words, by saying simply, that I assert the
necessity of human actions, and place them on the same
footing with the operations of senseless matter.   I do not
ascribe to the will that unintelligible necessity, which is
suppos'd to lie in matter.   But I ascribe to matter, that
intelligible quality, call it necessity or not, which the most
rigorous orthodoxy does or must allow to belong to the will.
I change, therefore, nothing in the receiv'd systems, with
regard to the will, but only with regard to material objects.

Nay I shall go farther, and assert, that this kind of necessity is so essential to religion and morality, that without

it there must ensue an absolute subversion of both, and that every other supposition is entirely destructive to all laws both *divine* and *human*. 'Tis indeed certain, that as all human laws are founded on rewards and punishments, 'tis suppos'd as a fundamental principle, that these motives have an influence on the mind, and both produce the good and prevent the evil actions. We may give to this influence what name we please; but as 'tis usually conjoin'd with the action, common sense requires it shou'd be esteem'd a cause, and be look'd upon as an instance of that necessity, which I wou'd establish.

This reasoning is equally solid, when apply'd to *divine* laws, so far as the deity is consider'd as a legislator, and is suppos'd to inflict punishment and bestow rewards with a design to produce obedience. But I also maintain, that even where he acts not in his magisterial capacity, but is regarded as the avenger of crimes merely on account of their odiousness and deformity, not only 'tis impossible, without the necessary connexion of cause and effect in human actions, that punishments cou'd be inflicted compatible with justice and moral equity; but also that it cou'd ever enter into the thoughts of any reasonable being to inflict them. The constant and universal object of hatred or anger is a person or creature endow'd with thought and consciousness; and when any criminal or injurious actions excite that passion, 'tis only by their relation to the person or connexion with him. But according to the doctrine of liberty or chance, this connexion is reduc'd to nothing, nor are men more accountable for those actions, which are design'd and premeditated, than for such as are the most casual and accidental. Actions are by their very nature temporary and perishing; and where they proceed not from some cause in the characters and disposition of the person, who perform'd them, they infix not themselves upon him, and can neither redound to his honour, if good, nor infamy, if evil. The action itself may be blameable; it may be contrary to all the rules of morality and religion: But the person is not responsible for it; and as it proceeded from nothing in him, that is durable or constant, and leaves nothing of that nature behind it, 'tis impossible he can, upon its account, become the object of punishment or vengeance. According to the hypothesis of liberty, therefore, a man is as pure and untainted, after having committed the most horrid crimes, as at the first moment of his birth, nor is his character any way concern'd in his actions; since they are not deriv'd from it, and the wickedness of the one can never be us'd as a proof of the depravity of the other. 'Tis only upon the principles of necessity, that a person acquires any merit or demerit from his actions, however the common opinion may incline to the contrary.

But so inconsistent are men with themselves, that tho' they often assert, that necessity utterly destroys all merit and demerit either towards mankind or superior powers, yet they continue still to reason upon these very principles of necessity in all their judgments concerning this matter. Men are not blam'd for such evil actions as they perform ignorantly and casually, whatever may be their consequences. Why? but because the cause of these actions are only momentary, and terminate in them alone. Men are less blam'd for such evil actions as they perform hastily and unpremeditatedly, than for such as proceed from thought and deliberation. For what reason? but because a hasty temper, tho' a constant cause in the mind, operates only by intervals, and infects not the whole character. Again, repentance wipes off every crime, especially if attended with an evident reformation of life and manners. How is this to be accounted for, but by asserting that actions render a person criminal, merely as they are proofs of criminal passions or principles in the mind; and when by any alteration of these principles they cease to be just proofs, they likewise cease to be criminal? But according to the doctrine of *liberty* or *chance* they never were just proofs, and consequently never were criminal.

Here then I turn to my adversary, and desire him to free his own system from these odious consequences before he charge them upon others. Or if he rather chuses, that this question should be decided by fair arguments before philosophers, than by declamations before the people, let him return to what I have advanc'd to prove that liberty and chance are synonimous; and concerning the nature of moral evidence and the regularity of human actions. Upon a review of these reasonings, I cannot doubt of an entire victory; and therefore having prov'd, that all actions of the will have particular causes, I proceed to explain what these causes are, and how they operate.

Sect. III.—*Of the Influencing Motives of the Will.*

SECT
III

Of the in-
fluencing
motives of
the will

Nothing is more usual in philosophy, and even in common life, than to talk of the combat of passion and reason, to give the preference to reason, and assert that men are only so far virtuous as they conform themselves to its dictates. Every rational creature, 'tis said, is oblig'd to regulate his actions by reason; and if any other motive or principle challenge the direction of his conduct, he ought to oppose it, 'till it be entirely subdu'd, or at least brought to a conformity with that superior principle. On this method of thinking the greatest part of moral philosophy, ancient and modern, seems to be founded; nor is there an ampler field, as well for metaphysical arguments, as popular declamations, than this suppos'd pre-eminence of reason above passion. The eternity, invariableness, and divine origin of the former have been display'd to the best advantage: The blindness, unconstancy, and deceitfulness of the latter have been as strongly insisted on. In order to shew the fallacy of all this philosophy, I shall endeavour to prove *first*, that reason alone can never be a motive to any action of the will; and *secondly*, that it can never oppose passion in the direction of the will.[1]

The understanding exerts itself after two different ways, as it judges from demonstration or probability; as it regards the abstract relations of our ideas, or those relations of objects, of which experience only gives us information. I believe it scarce will be asserted, that the first species of reasoning alone is ever the cause of any action. As it's proper province is the world of ideas, and as the will always places us in that of realities, demonstration and volition seem, upon that account, to be totally remov'd, from each other. Mathematics, indeed, are useful in all mechanical operations, and arithmetic in almost every art and profession: But 'tis not of themselves they have any influence. Mechanics are the art of regulating the motions of bodies *to some design'd end or purpose*, and the reason why we employ arithmetic in fixing the proportions of numbers, is only that we may discover the proportions of their influence and operation. A merchant is desirous of knowing the sum total of his accounts with any person: Why? but that he may learn what sum will

[¹ Introd § 44 — Ed]

have the same *effects* in paying his debt, and going to market, as all the particular articles taken together. Abstract or demonstrative reasoning, therefore, never influences any of our actions, but only as it directs our judgment concerning causes and effects ; which leads us to the second operation of the understanding.

'Tis obvious, that when we have the prospect of pain or pleasure from any object, we feel a consequent emotion of aversion or propensity, and are carry'd to avoid or embrace what will give us this uneasiness or satisfaction. 'Tis also obvious, that this emotion rests not here, but making us cast our view on every side, comprehends whatever objects are connected with its original one by the relation of cause and effect. Here then reasoning takes place to discover this relation ; and according as our reasoning varies, our actions receive a subsequent variation. But 'tis evident in this case, that the impulse arises not from reason, but is only directed by it. 'Tis from the prospect of pain or pleasure that the aversion or propensity arises towards any object : And these emotions extend themselves to the causes and effects of that object, as they are pointed out to us by reason and experience. It can never in the least concern us to know, that such objects are causes, and such others effects, if both the causes and effects be indifferent to us. Where the objects themselves do not affect us, their connexion can never give them any influence ; and 'tis plain, that as reason is nothing but the discovery of this connexion, it cannot be by its means that the objects are able to affect us.

Since reason alone can never produce any action, or give rise to volition, I infer, that the same faculty is as incapable of preventing volition, or of disputing the preference with any passion or emotion. This consequence is necessary. 'Tis impossible reason cou'd have the latter effect of preventing volition, but by giving an impulse in a contrary direction to our passion ; and that impulse, had it operated alone, wou'd have been able to produce volition. Nothing can oppose or retard the impulse of passion, but a contrary impulse ; and if this contrary impulse ever arises from reason, that latter faculty must have an original influence on the will, and must be able to cause, as well as hinder any act of volition. But if reason has no original influence, 'tis impossible it can withstand any principle, which has such an efficacy, or ever keep the mind in suspence a moment. Thus it appears, that the principle, which opposes our passion, cannot be the same with reason, and is only call'd so in an improper sense. We speak not strictly and philosophically when we talk of the combat of passion and of reason. Reason is, and ought only to be the slave of the passions, and can never pretend to any other office than to serve and obey them. As this opinion may appear somewhat extraordinary, it may not be improper to confirm it by some other considerations.[1]

A passion is an original existence, or, if you will, modification of existence, and contains not any representative quality, which renders it a copy of any other existence or modification. When I am angry, I am actually possest with the passion, and in that emotion have no more a reference to any other object, than when I am thirsty, or sick, or more than five foot high. 'Tis impossible, therefore, that this passion can be oppos'd by, or be contradictory to truth and reason; since this contradiction consists in the disagreement of ideas, consider'd as copies, with those objects, which they represent.

What may at first occur on this head, is, that as nothing can be contrary to truth or reason, except what has a reference to it, and as the judgments of our understanding only have this reference, it must follow, that passions can be contrary to reason only so far as they are *accompany'd* with some judgment or opinion. According to this principle, which is so obvious and natural, 'tis only in two senses, that any affection can be call'd unreasonable. First, When a passion, such as hope or fear, grief or joy, despair or security, is founded on the supposition of the existence of objects, which really do not exist. Secondly, When in exerting any passion in action, we chuse means insufficient for the design'd end, and deceive ourselves in our judgment of causes and effects. Where a passion is neither founded on false suppositions, nor chuses means insufficient for the end, the understanding can neither justify nor condemn it. 'Tis not contrary to reason to prefer the destruction of the whole world to the scratching of my finger. 'Tis not contrary to reason for me to chuse my total ruin, to prevent the least uneasi-

[¹ Introd. § 44.—Ed]

ness of an *Indian* or person wholly unknown to me. 'Tis as little contrary to reason to prefer even my own acknowledg'd lesser good to my greater, and have a more ardent affection for the former than the latter. A trivial good may, from certain circumstances, produce a desire superior to what arises from the greatest and most valuable enjoyment; nor is there anything more extraordinary in this, than in mechanics to see one pound weight raise up a hundred by the advantage of its situation. In short, a passion must be accompany'd with some false judgment, in order to its being unreasonable; and even then 'tis not the passion, properly speaking, which is unreasonable, but the judgment.

The consequences are evident. Since a passion can never, in any sense, be call'd unreasonable, but when founded on a false supposition, or when it chuses means insufficient for the design'd end, 'tis impossible, that reason and passion can ever oppose each other, or dispute for the government of the will and actions. The moment we perceive the falshood of any supposition, or the insufficiency of any means, our passions yield to our reason without any opposition. I may desire any fruit as of an excellent relish, but whenever you convince me of my mistake, my longing ceases. I may will the performance of certain actions as means of obtaining any desir'd good; but as my willing of these actions is only secondary, and founded on the supposition, that they are causes of the propos'd effect; as soon as I discover the falshood of that supposition, they must become indifferent to me.

'Tis natural for one, that does not examine objects with a strict philosophic eye, to imagine, that those actions of the mind are entirely the same, which produce not a different sensation, and are not immediately distinguishable to the feeling and perception. Reason, for instance, exerts itself without producing any sensible emotion, and except in the more sublime disquisitions of philosophy, or in the frivolous subtilties of the schools, scarce ever conveys any pleasure or uneasiness. Hence it proceeds, that every action of the mind, which operates with the same calmness and tranquillity, is confounded with reason by all those, who judge of things from the first view and appearance. Now 'tis certain, there are certain calm desires and tendencies, which, tho' they be real passions, produce little emotion in the mind, and are more known by their effects than by the immediate feeling or sensation. These desires are of two kinds; either certain instincts originally implanted in our natures, such as benevolence and resentment, the love of life, and kindness to children; or the general appetite to good, and aversion to evil, consider'd merely as such.[1] When any of these passions are calm, and cause no disorder in the soul, they are very readily taken for the determinations of reason, and are suppos'd to proceed from the same faculty, with that, which judges of truth and falshood. Their nature and principles have been suppos'd the same, because their sensations are not evidently different.

Beside these calm passions, which often determine the will, there are certain violent emotions of the same kind, which have likewise a great influence on that faculty. When I receive any injury from another, I often feel a violent passion of resentment, which makes me desire his evil and punishment, independent of all considerations of pleasure and advantage to myself When I am immediately threaten'd with any grievous ill, my fears, apprehensions, and aversions rise to a great height, and produce a sensible emotion.

The common error of metaphysicians has lain in ascribing the direction of the will entirely to one of these principles, and supposing the other to have no influence. Men often act knowingly against their interest: For which reason the view of the greatest possible good does not always influence them. Men often counter-act a violent passion in prosecution of their interests and designs: 'Tis not therefore the present uneasiness alone, which determines them.[2] In general we may observe, that both these principles operate on the will; and where they are contrary, that either of them prevails, according to the *general* character or *present* disposition of the person. What we call strength of mind, implies the prevalence of the calm passions above the violent; tho' we may easily observe, there is no man so constantly possess'd of this virtue, as never on any occasion to yield to the sollicitations of passion and desire. From these variations of temper proceeds the great difficulty of deciding concerning the actions and resolutions of men, where there is any contrariety of motives and passions.

[1 Introd § 46, and note   ED]
[2 Cf Locke, Essay, Book II cap 21, § 31, and Introd to this vol § 3—ED]

SECT. IV.—*Of the Causes of the Violent Passions.*[1]

There is not in philosophy a subject of more nice speculation than this of the different *causes* and *effects* of the calm
and violent passions. 'Tis evident passions influence not the
will in proportion to their violence, or the disorder they
occasion in the temper; but on the contrary, that when a
passion has once become a settled principle of action, and is
the predominant inclination of the soul, it commonly produces no longer any sensible agitation. As repeated custom
and its own force have made every thing yield to it, it directs
the actions and conduct without that opposition and emotion,
which so naturally attend every momentary gust of passion.
We must, therefore, distinguish betwixt a calm and a weak
passion; betwixt a violent and a strong one. But notwithstanding this, 'tis certain, that when we wou'd govern a man,
and push him to any action, 'twill commonly be better policy
to work upon the violent than the calm passions, and rather
take him by his inclination, than what is vulgarly call'd his
reason. We ought to place the object in such particular
situations as are proper to encrease the violence of the
passion. For we may observe, that all depends upon the
situation of the object, and that a variation in this particular
will be able to change the calm and the violent passions into
each other. Both these kinds of passions pursue good, and
avoid evil, and both of them are encreas'd or diminish'd by
the encrease or diminution of the good or evil. But herein
lies the difference betwixt them: The same good, when near,
will cause a violent passion, which, when remote, produces only
a calm one.[2] As this subject belongs very properly to the
present question concerning the will, we shall here examine
it to the bottom, and shall consider some of those circumstances and situations of objects, which render a passion
either calm or violent.

'Tis a remarkable property of human nature, that any
emotion, which attends a passion, is easily converted into it,
tho' in their natures they be originally different from, and
even contrary to each other. 'Tis true; in order to make a
perfect union among passions, there is always requir'd a
double relation of impressions and ideas; nor is one relation

[' Introd. 44 —ED]　　　　　　[² Introd § 45 —ED]

sufficient for that purpose.   But tho' this be confirm'd by
undoubted experience, we must understand it with its proper
limitations, and must regard the double relation, as requisite
only to make one passion produce another.   When two
passions are already produc'd by their separate causes, and
are both present in the mind, they readily mingle and unite,
tho' they have but one relation, and sometimes without any.
The predominant passion swallows up the inferior, and converts it into itself.   The spirits, when once excited, easily
receive a change in their direction; and 'tis natural to
imagine this change will come from the prevailing affection.
The connection is in many respects closer betwixt any two
passions, than betwixt any passion and indifference.

When a person is once heartily in love, the little faults
and caprice of his mistress, the jealousies and quarrels, to
which that commerce is so subject; however unpleasant and
related to anger and hatred; are yet found to give additional
force to the prevailing passion.   'Tis a common artifice of
politicians, when they wou'd affect any person very much by
a matter of fact, of which they intend to inform him, first to
excite his curiosity; delay as long as possible the satisfying
it; and by that means raise his anxiety and impatience to
the utmost, before they give him a full insight into the
business.   They know that his curiosity will precipitate him
into the passion they desire to raise, and assist the object in
its influence on the mind.   A soldier advancing to the battle,
is naturally inspir'd with courage and confidence, when he
thinks on his friends and fellow-soldiers; and is struck with
fear and terror, when he reflects on the enemy.   Whatever
new emotion, therefore, proceeds from the former naturally
encreases the courage; as the same emotion, proceeding from
the latter, augments the fear; by the relation of ideas, and
the conversion of the inferior emotion into the predominant.
Hence it is that in martial discipline, the uniformity and
lustre of our habit, the regularity of our figures and motions,
with all the pomp and majesty of war, encourage ourselves
and allies; while the same objects in the enemy strike terror
into us, tho' agreeable and beautiful in themselves.

Since passions, however independent, are naturally transfus'd into each other, if they are both present at the same
time; it follows, that when good or evil is plac'd in such a
situation, as to cause any particular emotion, beside its direct

passion of desire or aversion, that latter passion must acquire new force and violence.

This happens, among other cases, whenever any object excites contrary passions. For 'tis observable that an opposition of passions commonly causes a new emotion in the spirits, and produces more disorder, than the concurrence of any two affections of equal force. This new emotion is easily converted into the predominant passion, and encreases its violence, beyond the pitch it wou'd have arriv'd at had it met with no opposition. Hence we naturally desire what is forbid, and take a pleasure in performing actions, merely because they are unlawful. The notion of duty, when opposite to the passions, is seldom able to overcome them; and when it fails of that effect, is apt rather to encrease them, by producing an opposition in our motives and principles.

The same effect follows whether the opposition arises from internal motives or external obstacles. The passion commonly acquires new force and violence in both cases. The efforts, which the mind makes to surmount the obstacle, excite the spirits and inliven the passion.

Uncertainty has the same influence as opposition. The agitation of the thought; the quick turns it makes from one view to another, the variety of passions, which succeed each other, according to the different views: All these produce an agitation in the mind, and transfuse themselves into the predominant passion.

There is not in my opinion any other natural cause, why security diminishes the passions, than because it removes that uncertainty, which encreases them. The mind, when left to itself, immediately languishes; and in order to preserve its ardour, must be every moment supported by a new flow of passion. For the same reason, despair, tho' contrary to security, has a like influence.

'Tis certain nothing more powerfully animates any affection, than to conceal some part of its object by throwing it into a kind of shade, which at the same time that it shews enough to pre-possess us in favour of the object, leaves still some work for the imagination. Besides that obscurity is always attended with a kind of uncertainty; the effort, which the fancy makes to compleat the idea, rouzes the spirits, and gives an additional force to the passion.

As despair and security, tho' contrary to each other, produce the same effects; so absence is observ'd to have contrary effects, and in different circumstances either encreases or diminishes our affections. The *Duc de la Rochefoucault* has very well observ'd, that absence destroys weak passions, but encreases strong; as the wind extinguishes a candle, but blows up a fire. Long absence naturally weakens our idea, and diminishes the passion: But where the idea is so strong and lively as to support itself, the uneasiness, arising from absence, encreases the passion, and gives it new force and violence.

SECT. V.—*Of the Effects of Custom.*

But nothing has a greater effect both to encrease and diminish our passions, to convert pleasure into pain, and pain into pleasure, than custom and repetition. Custom has two *original* effects upon the mind, in bestowing a *facility* in the performance of any action or the conception of any object; and afterwards a *tendency or inclination* towards it; and from these we may account for all its other effects, however extraordinary.

When the soul applies itself to the performance of any action, or the conception of any object, to which it is not accustom'd, there is a certain unpliableness in the faculties, and a difficulty of the spirits' moving in their new direction. As this difficulty excites the spirits, 'tis the source of wonder, surprise, and of all the emotions, which arise from novelty; and is in itself very agreeable, like every thing, which inlivens the mind to a moderate degree. But tho' surprize be agreeable in itself, yet as it puts the spirits in agitation, it not only augments our agreeable affections, but also our painful, according to the foregoing principle, *that every emotion, which precedes or attends a passion, is easily converted into it* Hence every thing, that is new, is most affecting, and gives us either more pleasure or pain, than what, strictly speaking, naturally belongs to it. When it often returns upon us, the novelty wears off; the passions subside; the hurry of the spirits is over; and we survey the objects with greater tranquillity.

By degrees the repetition produces a facility, which is another very powerful principle of the human mind, and an infallible source of pleasure, where the facility goes not beyond a certain degree. And here 'tis remarkable that the pleasure, which arises from a moderate facility, has not the same tendency with that which arises from novelty, to augment the painful, as well as the agreeable affections. The pleasure of facility does not so much consist in any ferment of the spirits, as in their orderly motion ; which will sometimes be so powerful as even to convert pain into pleasure, and give us a relish in time for what at first was most harsh and disagreeable.

But again, as facility converts pain into pleasure, so it often converts pleasure into pain, when it is too great, and renders the actions of the mind so faint and languid, that they are no longer able to interest and support it. And indeed, scarce any other objects become disagreeable thro' custom ; but such as are naturally attended with some emotion or affection, which is destroyed by the too frequent repetition. One can consider the clouds, and heavens, and trees, and stones, however frequently repeated, without ever feeling any aversion. But when the fair sex, or music, or good cheer, or any thing, that naturally ought to be agreeable, becomes indifferent, it easily produces the opposite affection.

But custom not only gives a facility to perform any action, but likewise an inclination and tendency towards it, where it is not entirely disagreeable, and can never be the object of inclination. And this is the reason why custom encreases all *active* habits, but diminishes *passive*, according to the observation of a late eminent philosopher.[1] The facility takes off from the force of the passive habits by rendering the motion of the spirits faint and languid. But as in the active, the spirits are sufficiently supported of themselves, the tendency of the mind gives them new force, and bends them more strongly to the action.

SECT. VI.—*Of the Influence of the Imagination on the Passions.*

'Tis remarkable, that the imagination and affections have a close union together, and that nothing, which affects the former, can be entirely indifferent to the latter. Wherever our ideas of good or evil acquire a new vivacity, the passions

[1 The reference apparently must be to Butler (Analogy, Part I ch 5 'Practical habits are formed and strengthened by repeated acts, but passive impressions grow weaker by being repeated'), but he was still living when Hume wrote —ED]

become more violent; and keep pace with the imagination in all its variations. Whether this proceeds from the principle above-mention'd, *that any attendant emotion is easily converted into the predominant,* I shall not determine. 'Tis sufficient for my present purpose, that we have many instances to confirm this influence of the imagination upon the passions.

Any pleasure, with which we are acquainted, affects us more than any other, which we own to be superior, but of whose nature we are wholly ignorant. Of the one we can form a particular and determinate idea: The other we conceive under the general notion of pleasure; and 'tis certain, that the more general and universal any of our ideas are, the less influence they have upon the imagination. A general idea, tho' it be nothing but a particular one consider'd in a certain view,[1] is commonly more obscure; and that because no particular idea, by which we represent a general one, is ever fix'd or determinate, but may easily be chang'd for other particular ones, which will serve equally in the representation.

There is a noted passage in the history of *Greece,* which may serve for our present purpose. *Themistocles* told the *Athenians,* that he had form'd a design, which wou'd be highly useful to the public, but which 'twas impossible for him to communicate to them without ruining the execution, since its success depended entirely on the secrecy with which it shou'd be conducted. The *Athenians,* instead of granting him full power to act as he thought fitting, order'd him to communicate his design to *Aristides,* in whose prudence they had an entire confidence, and whose opinion they were resolv'd blindly to submit to. The design of *Themistocles* was secretly to set fire to the fleet of all the *Grecian* commonwealths, which was assembled in a neighbouring port, and which being once destroy'd, would give the *Athenians* the empire of the sea without any rival. *Aristides* returned to the assembly, and told them, that nothing cou'd be more advantageous than the design of *Themistocles*; but at the same time that nothing cou'd be more unjust: Upon which the people unanimously rejected the project.

A late celebrated [2] historian admires this passage of antient history, as one of the most singular that is any where to be

[1 Cf Vol 1 Part 1, § 7, sub fin —Ed]   [2] Mons. *Rollin*

met with. *Here,* says he, *they are not philosophers, to whom 'tis easy in their schools to establish the finest maxims and most sublime rules of morality, who decide that interest ought never to prevail above justice. 'Tis a whole people interested in the proposal, which is made to them, who consider it as of importance to the public good, and who notwithstanding reject it unanimously, and without hesitation, merely because it is contrary to justice.* For my part I see nothing so extraordinary in this proceeding of the *Athenians.* The same reasons, which render it so easy for philosophers to establish these sub'ime maxims, tend, in part, to diminish the merit of such a conduct in that people. Philosophers never ballance betwixt profit and honesty, because their decisions are general, and neither their passions nor imaginations are interested in the objects. And tho' in the present case the advantage was immediate to the *Athenians,* yet as it was known only under the general notion of advantage, without being conceiv'd by any particular idea, it must have had a less considerable influence on their imaginations, and have been a less violent temptation, than if they had been acquainted with all its circumstances: Otherwise 'tis difficult to conceive, that a whole people, unjust and violent as men commonly are, shou'd so unanimously have adher'd to justice, and rejected any considerable advantage.

Any satisfaction, which we lately enjoy'd, and of which the memory is fresh and recent, operates on the will with more violence, than another of which the traces are decay'd, and almost obliterated. From whence does this proceed, but that the memory in the first case assists the fancy, and gives an additional force and vigour to its conceptions? The image of the past pleasure being strong and violent, bestows these qualities on the idea of the future pleasure, which is connected with it by the relation of resemblance.

A pleasure, which is suitable to the way of life, in which we are engag'd, excites more our desires and appetites than another, which is foreign to it. This phænomenon may be explain'd from the same principle.

Nothing is more capable of infusing any passion into the mind, than eloquence, by which objects are represented in their strongest and most lively colours. We may of ourselves acknowledge, that such an object is valuable, and such another odious; but 'till an orator excites the imagination,

and gives force to these ideas, they may have but a feeble influence either on the will or the affections.

SECT
VI.

Of the in-
fluence of
the imagi-
nation, &c.

But eloquence is not always necessary. The bare opinion
of another, especially when inforc'd with passion, will cause
an idea of good or evil to have an influence upon us, which
wou'd otherwise have been entirely neglected. This proceeds
from the principle of sympathy or communication; and
sympathy, as I have already observ'd, is nothing but the
conversion of an idea into an impression by the force of
imagination.

'Tis remarkable, that lively passions commonly attend a
lively imagination. In this respect, as well as others, the
force of the passion depends as much on the temper of the
person, as the nature or situation of the object.

I have already observ'd, that belief is nothing but a lively
idea related to a present impression. This vivacity is a
requisite circumstance to the exciting all our passions, the
calm as well as the violent; nor has a mere fiction of the
imagination any considerable influence upon either of them.
'Tis too weak to take any hold of the mind, or be attended
with emotion.

Sect. VII.—*Of Contiguity and Distance in Space and Time.*

There is an easy reason, why every thing contiguous to us,
either in space or time, shou'd be conceiv'd with a peculiar
force and vivacity, and excel every other object, in its influence on the imagination. Ourself is intimately present
to us, and whatever is related to self must partake of that
quality. But where an object is so far remov'd as to have
lost the advantage of this relation, why, as it is farther remov'd, its idea becomes still fainter and more obscure, wou'd,
perhaps, require a more particular examination.

'Tis obvious, that the imagination can never totally forget
the points of space and time, in which we are existent; but
receives such frequent advertisements of them from the passions and senses, that however it may turn its attention to
foreign and remote objects, it is necessitated every moment to
reflect on the present. 'Tis also remarkable, that in the conception of those objects, which we regard as real and existent, we take them in their proper order and situation, and
never leap from one object to another, which is distant from

it, without running over, at least in a cursory manner, all those objects, which are interpos'd betwixt them. When we reflect, therefore, on any object distant from ourselves, we are oblig'd not only to reach it at first by passing thro' all the intermediate space betwixt ourselves and the object, but also to renew our progress every moment; being every moment recall'd to the consideration of ourselves and our present situation. 'Tis easily conceiv'd, that this interruption must weaken the idea by breaking the action of the mind, and hindering the conception from being so intense and continu'd, as when we reflect on a nearer object. The *fewer* steps we make to arrive at the object, and the *smoother* the road is, this diminution of vivacity is less sensibly felt, but still may be observ'd more or less in proportion to the degrees of distance and difficulty.

Here then we are to consider two kinds of objects, the contiguous and remote; of which the former, by means of their relation to ourselves, approach an impression in force and vivacity; the latter by reason of the interruption in our manner of conceiving them, appear in a weaker and more imperfect light. This is their effect on the imagination. If my reasoning be just, they must have a proportionable effect on the will and passions. Contiguous objects must have an influence much superior to the distant and remote. Accordingly we find in common life, that men are principally concern'd about those objects, which are not much remov'd either in space or time, enjoying the present, and leaving what is afar off to the care of chance and fortune. Talk to a man of his condition thirty years hence, and he will not regard you. Speak of what is to happen to-morrow, and he will lend you attention. The breaking of a mirror gives us more concern when at home, than the burning of a house, when abroad, and some hundred leagues distant.

But farther; tho' distance both in space and time has a considerable effect on the imagination, and by that means on the will and passions, yet the consequences of a removal in *space* are much inferior to those of a removal in *time*. Twenty years are certainly but a small distance of time in comparison of what history and even the memory of some may inform them of, and yet I doubt if a thousand leagues, or even the greatest distance of place this globe can admit of, will so remarkably weaken our ideas, and diminish our passions.   A *West-India* merchant will tell you, that he is not without concern about what passes in *Jamaica*; tho' few extend their views so far into futurity, as to dread very remote accidents.

SECT.
VII.

Of conti-
guity, and
distance in
space and
time.

The cause of this phænomenon must evidently lie in the different properties of space and time.   Without having recourse to metaphysics, any one may easily observe, that space or extension consists of a number of co-existent parts dispos'd in a certain order, and capable of being at once present to the sight or feeling.   On the contrary, time or succession, tho' it consists likewise of parts, never presents to us more than one at once; nor is it possible for any two of them ever to be co-existent.   These qualities of the objects have a suitable effect on the imagination.   The parts of extension being susceptible of an union to the senses, acquire an union in the fancy; and as the appearance of one part excludes not another, the transition or passage of the thought thro' the contiguous parts is by that means render'd more smooth and easy.   On the other hand, the incompatibility of the parts of time in their real existence separates them in the imagination, and makes it more *difficult* for that faculty to trace any long succession or series of events. Every part must appear single and alone, nor can regularly have entrance into the fancy without banishing what is suppos'd to have been immediately precedent.   By this means any distance in time causes a greater interruption in the thought than an equal distance in space, and consequently weakens more considerably the idea, and consequently the passions; which depend in a great measure, on the imagination, according to my system.

There is another phænomenon of a like nature with the foregoing, viz. *the superior effects of the same distance in futurity above that in the past.*   This difference with respect to the will is easily accounted for.   As none of our actions can alter the past, 'tis not strange it shou'd never determine the will.   But with respect to the passions the question is yet entire, and well worth the examining.

Besides the propensity to a gradual progression thro' the points of space and time, we have another peculiarity in our method of thinking, which concurs in producing this phænomenon.   We always follow the succession of time in placing our ideas, and from the consideration of any object pass more easily to that, which follows immediately after it, than to that which went before it. We may learn this, among other instances, from the order, which is always observ'd in historical narrations. Nothing but an absolute necessity can oblige an historian to break the order of time, and in his *narration* give the precedence to an event, which was in *reality* posterior to another.

This will easily be apply'd to the question in hand, if we reflect on what I have before observ'd, that the present situation of the person is always that of the imagination, and that 'tis from thence we proceed to the conception of any distant object. When the object is past, the progression of the thought in passing to it from the present is contrary to nature, as proceeding from one point of time to that which is preceding, and from that to another preceding, in opposition to the natural course of the succession. On the other hand, when we turn our thought to a future object, our fancy flows along the stream of time, and arrives at the object by an order, which seems most natural, passing always from one point of time to that which is immediately posterior to it. This *easy* progression of ideas favours the imagination, and makes it conceive its object in a stronger and fuller light, than when we are continually oppos'd in our passage, and are oblig'd to overcome the difficulties arising from the natural propensity of the fancy. A small degree of distance in the past has, therefore, a greater effect, in interrupting and weakening the conception, than a much greater in the future. From this effect of it on the imagination is deriv'd its influence on the will and passions.

There is another cause, which both contributes to the same effect, and proceeds from the same quality of the fancy, by which we are determin'd to trace the succession of time by a similar succession of ideas. When from the present instant we consider two points of time equally distant in the future and in the past, 'tis evident, that, abstractedly consider'd, their relation to the present is almost equal. For as the future will *sometime* be present, so the past was *once* present. If we cou'd, therefore, remove this quality of the imagination, an equal distance in the past and in the future, wou'd have a similar influence. Nor is this only true, when the fancy remains fix'd, and from the present instant surveys the future and the past; but also when it changes its situation, and places us in different periods of time. For as on the one hand, in supposing ourselves existent in a point of time interpos'd betwixt the present instant and the future object, we find the future object approach to us, and the past retire, and become more distant: So on the other hand, in supposing ourselves existent in a point of time interpos'd betwixt the present and the past, the past approaches to us, and the future becomes more distant. But from the property of the fancy above-mention'd we rather chuse to fix our thought on the point of time interpos'd betwixt the present and the future, than on that betwixt the present and the past. We advance, rather than retard our existence; and following what seems the natural succession of time, proceed from past to present, and from present to future. By which means we conceive the future as flowing every moment nearer us, and the past as retiring. An equal distance, therefore, in the past and in the future, has not the same effect on the imagination; and that because we consider the one as continually encreasing, and the other as continually diminishing. The fancy anticipates the course of things, and surveys the object in that condition, to which it tends, as well as in that, which is regarded as the present.

SECT. VII

Of contiguity, and distance in space and time.

Sect. VIII.—*The same Subject continu'd.*

Thus we have accounted for three phænomena, which seem pretty remarkable. Why distance weakens the conception and passion: Why distance in time has a greater effect than that in space: And why distance in past time has still a greater effect than that in future. We must now consider three phænomena, which seem to be, in a manner, the reverse of these: Why a very great distance encreases our esteem and admiration for an object: Why such a distance in time encreases it more than that in space: And a distance in past time more than that in future. The curiousness of the subject will, I hope, excuse my dwelling on it for some time.

To begin with the first phænomenon, why a great distance encreases our esteem and admiration for an object; 'tis evident that the mere view and contemplation of any greatness, whether successive or extended, enlarges the soul, and gives it a sensible delight and pleasure. A wide plain, the ocean, eternity, a succession of several ages; all these are entertaining objects, and excel every thing, however beautiful, which accompanies not its beauty with a suitable greatness. Now when any very distant object is presented to the imagination, we naturally reflect on the interpos'd distance, and by that means, conceiving something great and magnificent, receive the usual satisfaction. But as the fancy passes easily from one idea to another related to it, and transports to the second all the passions excited by the first, the admiration, which is directed to the distance, naturally diffuses itself over the distant object. Accordingly we find, that 'tis not necessary the object shou'd be actually distant from us, in order to cause our admiration; but that 'tis sufficient, if, by the natural association of ideas, it conveys our view to any considerable distance. A great traveller, tho' in the same chamber, will pass for a very extraordinary person; as a *Greek* medal, even in our cabinet, is always esteem'd a valuable curiosity. Here the object, by a natural transition, conveys our view to the distance; and the admiration, which arises from that distance, by another natural transition, returns back to the object.

But tho' every great distance produces an admiration for the distant object, a distance in time has a more considerable effect than that in space. Antient busts and inscriptions are more valu'd than *Japan* tables: And not to mention the *Greeks* and *Romans*, 'tis certain we regard with more veneration the old *Chaldeans* and *Egyptians*, than the modern *Chinese* and *Persians*, and bestow more fruitless pains to clear up the history and chronology of the former, than it wou'd cost us to make a voyage, and be certainly inform'd of the character, learning and government of the latter. I shall be oblig'd to make a digression in order to explain this phænomenon.

'Tis a quality very observable in human nature, that any opposition, which does not entirely discourage and intimidate us, has rather a contrary effect, and inspires us with a more than ordinary grandeur and magnanimity. In collecting our force to overcome the opposition, we invigorate the soul, and give it an elevation with which otherwise it wou'd never have been acquainted. Compliance, by rendering our strength useless, makes us insensible of it; but opposition awakens and employs it.

This is also true in the inverse. Opposition not only enlarges the soul; but the soul, when full of courage and magnanimity, in a manner seeks opposition.

> *Spumantemque dari pecora inter inertia votis*
> *Optat aprum, aut fulvum descendere monte leonem.*

Whatever supports and fills the passions is agreeable to us; as on the contrary, what weakens and infeebles them is uneasy. As opposition has the first effect, and facility the second, no wonder the mind, in certain dispositions, desires the former, and is averse to the latter.

These principles have an effect on the imagination as well as on the passions. To be convinc'd of this we need only consider the influence of *heights* and *depths* on that faculty. Any great elevation of place communicates a kind of pride or sublimity of imagination, and gives a fancy'd superiority over those that lie below; and, *vice versá*, a sublime and strong imagination conveys the idea of ascent and elevation. Hence it proceeds, that we associate, in a manner, the idea of whatever is good with that of height, and evil with lowness. Heaven is suppos'd to be above, and hell below. A noble genius is call'd an elevate and sublime one. *Atque udam spernit humum fugiente penna.* On the contrary, a vulgar and trivial conception is stil'd indifferently low or mean. Prosperity is denominated ascent, and adversity descent. Kings and princes are suppos'd to be plac'd at the top of human affairs; as peasants and day-labourers are said to be in the lowest stations. These methods of thinking, and of expressing ourselves, are not of so little consequence as they may appear at first sight.

'Tis evident to common sense, as well as philosophy, that there is no natural nor essential difference betwixt high and low, and that this distinction arises only from the gravitation of matter, which produces a motion from the one to the other. The very same direction, which in this part of the globe is call'd *ascent*, is denominated *descent* in our antipodes; which can proceed from nothing but the contrary tendency of bodies. Now 'tis certain, that the tendency of bodies, continually operating upon our senses, must produce, from custom, a like tendency in the fancy, and that when we consider any object situated in an ascent, the idea of its weight gives us a propensity to transport it from the place, in which it is situated, to the place immediately below it, and so on, 'till we come to the ground, which equally stops the body and our imagination. For a like reason we feel a difficulty in mounting, and pass not without a kind of reluctance from the inferior to that which is situated above it; as if our ideas acquir'd a kind of gravity from their objects. As a proof of this, do we not find, that the facility, which is so much study'd in music and poetry, is call'd the fall or cadency of the harmony or period; the idea of facility communicating to us that of descent, in the same manner as descent produces a facility?

Since the imagination, therefore, in running from low to high, finds an opposition in its internal qualities and principles, and since the soul, when elevated with joy and courage, in a manner seeks opposition, and throws itself with alacrity into any scene of thought or action, where its courage meets with matter to nourish and employ it; it follows, that everything, which invigorates and inlivens the soul, whether by touching the passions or imagination, naturally conveys to the fancy this inclination for ascent, and determines it to run against the natural stream of its thoughts and conceptions. This aspiring progress of the imagination suits the present disposition of the mind; and the difficulty, instead of extinguishing its vigour and alacrity, has the contrary effect, of sustaining and encreasing it. Virtue, genius, power, and riches are for this reason associated with height and sublimity; as poverty, slavery, and folly are conjoin'd with descent and lowness. Were the case the same with us as *Milton* represents it to be with the angels, to whom *descent is adverse*, and who *cannot sink without labour and compulsion*, this order of things wou'd be entirely inverted; as appears hence, that the very nature of ascent and descent is deriv'd from the difficulty and propensity, and consequently every one of their effects proceeds from that origin.

All this is easily apply'd to the present question, why a considerable distance in time produces a greater veneration for the distant objects than a like removal in space. The imagination moves with more difficulty in passing from one portion of time to another, than in a transition thro' the parts of space; and that because space or extension appears united to our senses, while time or succession is always broken and divided. This difficulty, when join'd with a small distance, interrupts and weakens the fancy: But has a contrary effect in a great removal. The mind, elevated by the vastness of its object, is still farther elevated by the difficulty of the conception; and being oblig'd every moment to renew its efforts in the transition from one part of time to another, feels a more vigorous and sublime disposition, than in a transition thro' the parts of space, where the ideas flow along with easiness and facility. In this disposition, the imagination, passing, as is usual, from the consideration of the distance to the view of the distant objects, gives us a proportionable veneration for it: and this is the reason why all the relicts of antiquity are so precious in our eyes, and appear more valuable than what is brought even from the remotest parts of the world.

The third phænomenon I have remark'd will be a full confirmation of this. 'Tis not every removal in time, which has the effect of producing veneration and esteem. We are not apt to imagine our posterity will excel us, or equal our ancestors. This phænomenon is the more remarkable, because any distance in futurity weakens not our ideas so much as an equal removal in the past. Tho' a removal in the past, when very great, encreases our passions beyond a like removal in the future, yet a small removal has a greater influence in diminishing them.

In our common way of thinking we are plac'd in a kind of middle station betwixt the past and future; and as our imagination finds a kind of difficulty in running along the former, and a facility in following the course of the latter, the difficulty conveys the notion of ascent, and the facility of the contrary. Hence we imagine our ancestors to be, in a manner, mounted above us, and our posterity to lie below us. Our fancy arrives not at the one without effort, but easily reaches the other: Which effort weakens the conception, where the distance is small; but enlarges and elevates the imagination, when attended with a suitable object. As on the other hand, the facility assists the fancy in a small removal, but takes off from its force when it contemplates any considerable distance.

It may not be improper, before we leave this subject of the will, to resume, in a few words, all that has been said concerning it, in order to set the whole more distinctly before the eyes of the reader. What we commonly understand by

SECT VIII

The same subject continu'd.

passion is a violent and sensible emotion of mind, when any good or evil is presented, or any object, which, by the original formation of our faculties, is fitted to excite an appetite. By *reason* we mean affections of the very same kind with the former; but such as operate more calmly, and cause no disorder in the temper: Which tranquillity leads us into a mistake concerning them, and causes us to regard them as conclusions only of our intellectual faculties. Both the *causes* and *effects* of these violent and calm passions are pretty variable, and depend, in a great measure, on the peculiar temper and disposition of every individual. Generally speaking, the violent passions have a more powerful influence on the will; tho' 'tis often found, that the calm ones, when corroborated by reflection, and seconded by resolution, are able to controul them in their most furious movements. What makes this whole affair more uncertain, is, that a calm passion may easily be chang'd into a violent one, either by a change of temper, or of the circumstances and situation of the object, as by the borrowing of force from any attendant passion, by custom, or by exciting the imagination. Upon the whole, this struggle of passion and of reason, as it is call'd, diversifies human life, and makes men so different not only from each other, but also from themselves in different times. Philosophy can only account for a few of the greater and more sensible events of this war; but must leave all the smaller and more delicate revolutions, as dependent on principles too fine and minute for her comprehension.

SECT. IX.—*Of the Direct Passions.*[1]

'Tis easy to observe, that the passions, both direct and indirect, are founded on pain and pleasure, and that in order to produce an affection of any kind, 'tis only requisite to present some good or evil. Upon the removal of pain and pleasure.there immediately follows a removal of love and hatred, pride and humility, desire and aversion, and of most of our reflective or secondary impressions.

The impressions, which arise from good and evil most naturally, and with the least preparation, are the *direct* passions of desire and aversion, grief and joy, hope and fear, along with volition. The mind by an *original* instinct tends

[1 Introd. sect. 30.—ED]

to unite itself with the good, and to avoid the evil, tho' they
be conceiv'd merely in idea, and be consider'd as to exist in
any future period of time.

But supposing that there is an immediate impression of
pain or pleasure, and *that* arising from an object related to
ourselves or others, this does not prevent the propensity or
aversion, with the consequent emotions, but by concurring
with certain dormant principles of the human mind, excites
the new impressions of pride or humility, love or hatred.
That propensity, which unites us to the object, or separates
us from it, still continues to operate, but in conjunction with
the *indirect* passions, which arise from a double relation of
impressions and ideas.[1]

These indirect passions, being always agreeable or uneasy, give in their turn additional force to the direct passions,
and encrease our desire and aversion to the object.   Thus a
suit of fine cloaths produces pleasure from their beauty ; and
this pleasure produces the direct passions, or the impressions
of volition and desire.   Again, when these cloaths are consider'd as belonging to ourself, the double relation conveys
to us the sentiment of pride, which is an indirect passion ;
and the pleasure, which attends that passion, returns back to
the direct affections, and gives new force to our desire or
volition, joy or hope.

When good is certain or probable, it produces JOY. When
evil is in the same situation there arises GRIEF or SORROW.

When either good or evil is uncertain, it gives rise to FEAR
or HOPE, according to the degrees of uncertainty on the one
side or the other.

Desire arises from good consider'd simply, and AVERSION
is deriv'd from evil.   The WILL exerts itself, when either the
good or the absence of the evil may be attain'd by any action
of the mind or body.

Beside good and evil, or in other words, pain and pleasure, the direct passions frequently arise from a natural impulse or instinct, which is perfectly unaccountable.[2]   Of this
kind is the desire of punishment to our enemies, and of happiness to our friends ; hunger, lust, and a few other bodily
appetites.   These passions, properly speaking, produce good
and evil, and proceed not from them, like the other affections.

[1 Introd. sect 30.—Ed]   [2 Introd. sect. 31 —Ed]

None of the direct affections seem to merit our particular attention, except hope and fear, which we shall here endeavour to account for. 'Tis evident that the very same event, which by its certainty wou'd produce grief or joy, gives always rise to fear or hope, when only probable and uncertain. In order, therefore, to understand the reason why this circumstance makes such a considerable difference, we must reflect on what I have already advanc'd in the preceding book concerning the nature of probability.

Probability arises from an opposition of contrary chances or causes, by which the mind is not allow'd to fix on either side, but is incessantly tost from one to another, and at one moment is determin'd to consider an object as existent, and at another moment as the contrary. The imagination or understanding, call it which you please, fluctuates betwixt the opposite views; and tho' perhaps it may be oftner turn'd to the one side than the other, 'tis impossible for it, by reason of the opposition of causes or chances, to rest on either. The *pro* and *con* of the question alternately prevail; and the mind, surveying the object in its opposite principles, finds such a contrariety as utterly destroys all certainty and establish'd opinion.

Suppose, then, that the object, concerning whose reality we are doubtful, is an object either of desire or aversion, 'tis evident, that, according as the mind turns itself either to the one side or the other, it must feel a momentary impression of joy or sorrow. An object, whose existence we desire, gives satisfaction, when we reflect on those causes, which produce it; and for the same reason excites grief or uneasiness from the opposite consideration: So that as the understanding, in all probable questions, is divided betwixt the contrary points of view, the affections must in the same manner be divided betwixt opposite emotions.

Now if we consider the human mind, we shall find, that with regard to the passions, 'tis not of the nature of a wind-instrument of music, which in running over all the notes immediately loses the sound after the breath ceases; but rather resembles a string-instrument, where after each stroke the vibrations still retain some sound, which gradually and insensibly decays. The imagination is extreme quick and agile; but the passions are slow and restive: For which reason, when any object is presented, that affords a variety

of views to the one, and emotions to the other; tho' the
fancy may change its views with great celerity; each stroke
will not produce a clear and distinct note of passion, but the
one passion will always be mixt and confounded with the
other. According as the probability inclines to good or evil,
the passion of joy or sorrow predominates in the composition :
Because the nature of probability is to cast a superior number of views or chances on one side; or, which is the same
thing, a superior number of returns of one passion; or since
the dispers'd passions are collected into one, a superior
degree of that passion. That is, in other words, the grief
and joy being intermingled with each other, by means of the
contrary views of the imagination, produce by their union
the passions of hope and fear.

Upon this head there may be started a very curious question
concerning that contrariety of passions, which is our present
subject. 'Tis observable, that where the objects of contrary
passions are presented at once, beside the encrease of the
predominant passion (which has been already explain'd, and
commonly arises at their first shock or rencounter) it sometimes happens, that both the passions exist successively, and
by short intervals; sometimes, that they destroy each other,
and neither of them takes place; and sometimes that both of
them remain united in the mind. It may, therefore, be ask'd,
by what theory we can explain these variations, and to what
general principle we can reduce them.

When the contrary passions arise from objects entirely
different, they take place alternately, the want of relation in
the ideas separating the impressions from each other, and
preventing their opposition. Thus when a man is afflicted
for the loss of a law-suit, and joyful for the birth of a son, the
mind running from the agreeable to the calamitous object,
with whatever celerity it may perform this motion, can
scarcely temper the one affection with the other, and remain
betwixt them in a state of indifference.

It more easily attains that calm situation, when the same
event is of a mixt nature, and contains something adverse
and something prosperous in its different circumstances. For
in that case, both the passions, mingling with each other by
means of the relation, become mutually destructive, and leave
the mind in perfect tranquillity.

But suppose, in the third place, that the object is not a

compound of good or evil, but is consider'd as probable or improbable in any degree; in that case I assert, that the contrary passions will both of them be present at once in the soul, and instead of destroying and tempering each other, will subsist together, and produce a third impression or affection by their union. Contrary passions are not capable of destroying each other, except when their contrary movements exactly rencounter, and are opposite in their direction, as well as in the sensation they produce. This exact rencounter depends upon the relations of those ideas, from which they are deriv'd, and is more or less perfect, according to the degrees of the relation. In the case of probability the contrary chances are so far related, that they determine concerning the existence or non-existence of the same object. But this relation is far from being perfect; since some of the chances lie on the side of existence, and others on that of non-existence; which are objects altogether incompatible. 'Tis impossible by one steady view to survey the opposite chances, and the events dependent on them; but 'tis necessary, that the imagination shou'd run alternately from the one to the other. Each view of the imagination produces its peculiar passion, which decays away by degrees, and is follow'd by a sensible vibration after the stroke. The incompatibility of the views keeps the passions from shocking in a direct line, if that expression may be allow'd; and yet their relation is sufficient to mingle their fainter emotions. 'Tis after this manner that hope and fear arise from the different mixture of these opposite passions of grief and joy, and from their imperfect union and conjunction.

Upon the whole, contrary passions succeed each other alternately, when they arise from different objects: They mutually destroy each other, when they proceed from different parts of the same: And they subsist both of them, and mingle together, when they are deriv'd from the contrary and incompatible chances or possibilities, on which any one object depends. The influence of the relations of ideas is plainly seen in this whole affair. If the objects of the contrary passions be totally different, the passions are like two opposite liquors in different bottles, which have no influence on each other. If the objects be intimately connected, the passions are like an *alcali* and an *acid*, which, being mingled, destroy each other. If the relation be more imperfect, and consists in the contradictory views of the same object, the passions are like oil and vinegar, which, however mingled, never perfectly unite and incorporate.

As the hypothesis concerning hope and fear carries its own evidence along with it, we shall be the more concise in our proofs. A few strong arguments are better than many weak ones.

The passions of fear and hope may arise when the chances are equal on both sides, and no superiority can be discovered in the one above the other. Nay, in this situation the passions are rather the strongest, as the mind has then the least foundation to rest upon, and is toss'd with the greatest uncertainty. Throw in a superior degree of probability to the side of grief, you immediately see that passion diffuse itself over the composition, and tincture it into fear. Encrease the probability, and by that means the grief, the fear prevails still more and more, till at last it runs insensibly, as the joy continually diminishes, into pure grief. After you have brought it to this situation, diminish the grief, after the same manner that you encreas'd it; by diminishing the probability on that side, and you'll see the passion clear every moment, 'till it changes insensibly into hope; which again runs, after the same manner, by slow degrees, into joy, as you encrease that part of the composition by the encrease of the probability. Are not these as plain proofs, that the passions of fear and hope are mixtures of grief and joy, as in optics 'tis a proof, that a colour'd ray of the sun passing thro' a prism, is a composition of two others, when, as you diminish or encrease the quantity of either, you find it prevail proportionably more or less in the composition? I am sure neither natural nor moral philosophy admits of stronger proofs.

Probability is of two kinds, either when the object is really in itself uncertain, and to be determin'd by chance; or when, tho' the object be already certain, yet 'tis uncertain to our judgment, which finds a number of proofs on each side of the question. Both these kinds of probabilities cause fear and hope; which can only proceed from that property, in which they agree, viz. the uncertainty and fluctuation they bestow on the imagination by that contrariety of views, which is common to both.

'Tis a probable good or evil, that commonly produces

hope or fear; because probability, being a wavering and unconstant method of surveying an object, causes naturally a like mixture and uncertainty of passion. But we may observe, that wherever from other causes this mixture can be produc'd, the passions of fear and hope will arise, even tho' there be no probability; which must be allow'd to be a convincing proof of the present hypothesis.

We find that an evil, barely conceiv'd as *possible*, does sometimes produce fear; especially if the evil be very great. A man cannot think of excessive pains and tortures without trembling, if he be in the least danger of suffering them. The smallness of the probability is compensated by the greatness of the evil; and the sensation is equally lively, as if the evil were more probable. One view or glimpse of the former, has the same effect as several of the latter.

But they are not only possible evils, that cause fear, but even some allow'd to be *impossible*; as when we tremble on the brink of a precipice, tho' we know ourselves to be in perfect security and have it in our choice whether we will advance a step farther. This proceeds from the immediate presence of the evil, which influences the imagination in the same manner as the certainty of it wou'd do; but being encounter'd by the reflection on our security, is immediately retracted, and causes the same kind of passion, as when from a contrariety of chances contrary passions are produc'd.

Evils, that are *certain*, have sometimes the same effect in producing fear, as the possible or impossible. Thus a man in a strong prison well-guarded, without the least means of escape, trembles at the thought of the rack to which he is sentenc'd. This happens only when the certain evil is terrible and confounding; in which case the mind continually rejects it with horror, while it continually presses in upon the thought. The evil is there fix'd and establish'd, but the mind cannot endure to fix upon it; from which fluctuation and uncertainty there arises a passion of much the same appearance with fear.

But 'tis not only where good or evil is uncertain, as to its *existence*, but also as to its *kind*, that fear or hope arises. Let one be told by a person, whose veracity he cannot doubt of, that one of his sons is suddenly kill'd, 'tis evident the passion this event wou'd occasion, wou'd not settle into pure grief, till he got certain information, which of his sons he had lost.   Here there is an evil certain, but the kind of it uncertain : Consequently the fear we feel on this occasion is without the least mixture of joy, and arises merely from the fluctuation of the fancy betwixt its objects.   And tho' each side of the question produces here the same passion, yet that passion cannot settle, but receives from the imagination a tremulous and unsteady motion, resembling in its cause, as well as in its sensation, the mixture and contention of grief and joy.

From these principles we may account for a phænomenon in the passions, which at first sight seems very extraordinary, *viz.* that surprize is apt to change into fear, and every thing that is unexpected affrights us.   The most obvious conclusion from this is, that human nature is in general pusilanimous; since upon the sudden appearance of any object we immediately conclude it to be an evil, and without waiting till we can examine its nature, whether it be good or bad, are at first affected with fear.   This I say is the most obvious conclusion ; but upon farther examination we shall find that the phænomenon is otherwise to be accounted for.   The suddenness and strangeness of an appearance naturally excite a commotion in the mind, like every thing for which we are not prepar'd, and to which we are not accustom'd.   This commotion, again, naturally produces a curiosity or inquisitiveness, which being very violent, from the strong and sudden impulse of the object, becomes uneasy, and resembles, in its fluctuation and uncertainty, the sensation of fear or the mix'd passions of grief and joy.   This image of fear naturally converts into the thing itself, and gives us a real apprehension of evil, as the mind always forms its judgments more from its present disposition than from the nature of its objects.

Thus all kinds of uncertainty have a strong connexion with fear, even tho' they do not cause any opposition of passions by the opposite views and considerations they present to us.   A person, who has left his friend in any malady, will feel more anxiety upon his account, than if he were present, tho' perhaps he is not only incapable of giving him assistance, but likewise of judging of the event of his sickness. In this case, tho' the principal object of the passion, *viz.* the life or death of his friend, be to him equally uncertain when present as when absent ; yet there are a thousand little cir-

cumstances of his friend's situation and condition, the knowledge of which fixes the idea, and prevents that fluctuation and
uncertainty so near ally'd to fear.   Uncertainty is, indeed,
in one respect as near ally'd to hope as to fear, since it makes
an essential part in the composition of the former passion;
but the reason, why it inclines not to that side, is, that uncertainty alone is uneasy, and has a relation of impressions
to the uneasy passions.

'Tis thus our uncertainty concerning any minute circumstance relating to a person encreases our apprehensions
of his death or misfortune.   *Horace* has remark'd this
phænomenon.

> *Ut assidens implumibus pullis avis*
> *Serpentium allapsus timet,*
> *Magis relictis, non, ut adsit, auxili*
> *Latura plus præsentibus.*

But this principle of the connexion of fear with uncertainty
I carry farther, and observe that any doubt produces that
passion, even tho' it presents nothing to us on any side but
what is good and desireable.   A virgin, on her bridal-night,
goes to bed full of fears and apprehensions, tho' she expects
nothing but pleasure of the highest kind, and what she has
long wish'd for.   The newness and greatness of the event,
the confusion of wishes and joys, so embarrass the mind,
that it knows not on what passion to fix itself; from whence
arises a fluttering or unsettledness of the spirits, which
being, in some degree, uneasy, very naturally degenerates
into fear.

Thus we still find, that whatever causes any fluctuation or
mixture of passions, with any degree of uneasiness, always
produces fear, or at least a passion so like it, that they are
scarcely to be distinguish'd.

I have here confin'd myself to the examination of hope
and fear in their most simple and natural situation, without
considering all the variations they may receive from the
mixture of different views and reflections.   *Terror, consternation, astonishment, anxiety,* and other passions of that kind,
are nothing but different species and degrees of fear.   'Tis
easy to imagine how a different situation of the object, or a
different turn of thought, may change even the sensation of
a passion; and this may in general account for all the
particular sub-divisions of the other affections, as well as of

fear. Love may shew itself in the shape of *tenderness, friend-ship, intimacy, esteem, good-will,* and in many other appear-ances; which at the bottom are the same affections, and arise from the same causes, tho' with a small variation, which it is not necessary to give any particular account of. 'Tis for this reason I have all along confin'd myself to the principal passion.

The same care of avoiding prolixity is the reason why I wave the examination of the will and direct passions, as they appear in animals; since nothing is more evident, than that they are of the same nature, and excited by the same causes as in human creatures. I leave this to the reader's own observation; desiring him at the same time to consider the additional force this bestows on the present system.

SECT. X.—*Of Curiosity, or the Love of Truth.*

But methinks we have been not a little inattentive to run over so many different parts of the human mind, and examine so many passions, without taking once into the consideration that love of truth, which was the first source of all our enquiries. 'Twill therefore be proper, before we leave this subject, to bestow a few reflections on that passion, and shew its origin in human nature. 'Tis an affection of so peculiar a kind, that 'twou'd have been impossible to have treated of it under any of those heads, which we have examin'd, without danger of obscurity and confusion.

Truth is of two kinds, consisting either in the discovery of the proportions of ideas, consider'd as such, or in the con-formity of our ideas of objects to their real existence. 'Tis certain, that the former species of truth, is not desir'd merely as truth, and that 'tis not the justness of our conclusions, which alone gives the pleasure. For these conclusions are equally just, when we discover the equality of two bodies by a pair of compasses, as when we learn it by a mathematical demonstration; and tho' in the one case the proofs be demonstrative, and in the other only sensible, yet generally speaking, the mind acquiesces with equal assurance in the one as in the other. And in an arithmetical operation, where both the truth and the assurance are of the same nature, as in the most profound algebraical problem, the pleasure is very inconsiderable, if rather it does not degenerate into pain: Which is an evident proof, that the satisfaction, which we sometimes receive from the discovery of truth, proceeds not from it, merely as such, but only as endow'd with certain qualities.

The first and most considerable circumstance requisite to render truth agreeable, is the genius and capacity, which is employ'd in its invention and discovery. What is easy and obvious is never valu'd; and even what is *in itself* difficult, if we come to the knowledge of it without difficulty, and without any stretch of thought or judgment, is but little regarded. We love to trace the demonstrations of mathematicians; but shou'd receive small entertainment from a person, who shou'd barely inform us of the proportions of lines and angles, tho' we repos'd the utmost confidence both in his judgment and veracity. In this case 'tis sufficient to have ears to learn the truth. We never are oblig'd to fix our attention or exert our genius; which of all other exercises of the mind is the most pleasant and agreeable.

But tho' the exercise of genius be the principal source of that satisfaction we receive from the sciences, yet I doubt, if it be alone sufficient to give us any considerable enjoyment. The truth we discover must also be of some importance. 'Tis easy to multiply algebraical problems to infinity, nor is there any end in the discovery of the proportions of conic sections; tho' few mathematicians take any pleasure in these researches, but turn their thoughts to what is more useful and important. Now the question is, after what manner this utility and importance operate upon us? The difficulty on this head arises from hence, that many philosophers have consum'd their time, have destroy'd their health, and neglected their fortune, in the search of such truths, as they esteem'd important and useful to the world, tho' it appear'd from their whole conduct and behaviour, that they were not endow'd with any share of public spirit, nor had any concern for the interests of mankind. Were they convinc'd, that their discoveries were of no consequence, they wou'd entirely lose all relish for their studies, and that tho' the consequences be entirely indifferent to them; which seems to be a contradiction.

To remove this contradiction, we must consider, that there are certain desires and inclinations, which go no farther than the imagination, and are rather the faint shadows and images of passions, than any real affections. Thus, suppose a man, who takes a survey of the fortifications of any city; considers their strength and advantages, natural or acquir'd; observes the disposition and contrivance of the bastions, ramparts, mines, and other military works; 'tis plain, that in proportion as all these are fitted to attain their ends, he will receive a suitable pleasure and satisfaction. This pleasure, as it arises from the utility, not the form of the objects, can be no other than a sympathy with the inhabitants, for whose security all this art is employ'd; tho' 'tis possible, that this person, as a stranger or an enemy, may in his heart have no kindness for them, or may even entertain a hatred against them.

It may indeed be objected, that such a remote sympathy is a very slight foundation for a passion, and that so much industry and application, as we frequently observe in philosophers, can never be deriv'd from so inconsiderable an original. But here I return to what I have already remark'd, that the pleasure of study consists chiefly in the action of the mind, and the exercise of the genius and understanding in the discovery or comprehension of any truth. If the importance of the truth be requisite to compleat the pleasure, 'tis not on account of any considerable addition, which of itself it brings to our enjoyment, but only because 'tis, in some measure, requisite to fix our attention. When we are careless and inattentive, the same action of the understanding has no effect upon us, nor is able to convey any of that satisfaction, which arises from it, when we are in another disposition.

But beside the action of the mind, which is the principal foundation of the pleasure, there is likewise requir'd a degree of success in the attainment of the end, or the discovery of that truth we examine. Upon this head I shall make a general remark, which may be useful on many occasions, *viz.* that where the mind pursues any end with passion; tho' that passion be not deriv'd originally from the end, but merely from the action and pursuit; yet by the natural course of the affections, we acquire a concern for the end itself, and are uneasy under any disappointment we meet with in the pursuit of it. This proceeds from the relation and parallel direction of the passions above-mention'd.

To illustrate all this by a similar instance, I shall observe, that there cannot be two passions more nearly resembling each other, than those of hunting and philosophy, whatever disproportion may at first sight appear betwixt them. 'Tis evident, that the pleasure of hunting consists in the action of the mind and body; the motion, the attention, the difficulty, and the uncertainty. 'Tis evident likewise, that these actions must be attended with an idea of utility, in order to their having any effect upon us. A man of the greatest fortune, and the farthest removed from avarice, tho' he takes a pleasure in hunting after partridges and pheasants, feels no satisfaction in shooting crows and magpies; and that because he considers the first as fit for the table, and the other as entirely useless. Here 'tis certain, that the utility or importance of itself causes no real passion, but is only requisite to support the imagination; and the same person, who overlooks a ten times greater profit in any other subject, is pleas'd to bring home half a dozen woodcocks or plovers, after having employ'd several hours in hunting after them. To make the parallel betwixt hunting and philosophy more compleat, we may observe, that tho' in both cases the end of our action may in itself be despis'd, yet in the heat of the action we acquire such an attention to this end, that we are very uneasy under any disappointments, and are sorry when we either miss our game, or fall into any error in our reasoning.

If we want another parallel to these affections, we may consider the passion of gaming, which affords a pleasure from the same principles as hunting and philosophy. It has been remark'd, that the pleasure of gaming arises not from interest alone; since many leave a sure gain for this entertainment: Neither is it deriv'd from the game alone; since the same persons have no satisfaction, when they play for nothing: But proceeds from both these causes united, tho' separately they have no effect. 'Tis here, as in certain chymical preparations, where the mixture of two clear and transparent liquids produces a third, which is opaque and colour'd.

The interest, which we have in any game, engages our attention, without which we can have no enjoyment, either in that or in any other action. Our attention being once engag'd, the difficulty, variety, and sudden reverses of fortune, still farther interest us; and 'tis from that concern our satisfaction arises. Human life is so tiresome a scene, and

men generally are of such indolent dispositions, that whatever amuses them, tho' by a passion mixt with pain, does in
the main give them a sensible pleasure. And this pleasure
is here encreas'd by the nature of the objects, which being
sensible, and of a narrow compass, are enter'd into with
facility, and are agreeable to the imagination.

The same theory, that accounts for the love of truth in
mathematics and algebra, may be extended to morals, politics, natural philosophy, and other studies, where we consider not the abstract relations of ideas, but their real connexions and existence. But beside the love of knowledge, which
displays itself in the sciences, there is a certain curiosity
implanted in human nature, which is a passion deriv'd from
a quite different principle. Some people have an insatiable
desire of knowing the actions and circumstances of their
neighbours, tho' their interest be no way concern'd in them,
and they must entirely depend on others for their information; in which case there is no room for study or application.
Let us search for the reason of this phænomenon.

It has been prov'd at large, that the influence of belief is
at once to inliven and infix any idea in the imagination, and
prevent all kind of hesitation and uncertainty about it.
Both these circumstances are advantageous. By the vivacity
of the idea we interest the fancy, and produce, tho' in a
lesser degree, the same pleasure, which arises from a moderate passion. As the vivacity of the idea gives pleasure, so
its certainty prevents uneasiness, by fixing one particular
idea in the mind, and keeping it from wavering in the choice
of its objects. 'Tis a quality of human nature, which is conspicuous on many occasions, and is common both to the
mind and body, that too sudden and violent a change is unpleasant to us, and that however any objects may in themselves be indifferent, yet their alteration gives uneasiness.
As 'tis the nature of doubt to cause a variation in the thought,
and transport us suddenly from one idea to another, it must
of consequence be the occasion of pain. This pain chiefly
takes place, where interest, relation, or the greatness and
novelty of any event interests us in it. 'Tis not every matter
of fact, of which we have a curiosity to be inform'd; neither
are they such only as we have an interest to know. 'Tis
sufficient if the idea strikes on us with such force, and concerns us so nearly, as to give us an uneasiness in its instabi-

lity and inconstancy. A stranger, when he arrives first at any town, may be entirely indifferent about knowing the history and adventures of the inhabitants ; but as he becomes farther acquainted with them, and has liv'd any considerable time among them, he acquires the same curiosity as the natives. When we are reading the history of a nation, we may have an ardent desire of clearing up any doubt or difficulty, that occurs in it ; but become careless in such researches, when the ideas of these events are, in a great measure, obliterated.

A TREATISE

OF

Human Nature:

BEING

An ATTEMPT to introduce the experimental
Method of Reasoning

INTO

MORAL SUBJECTS.

―――――― *Duræ semper virtutis amator,*
Quære quid est virtus, et posce exemplar honesti.

LUCAN

WITH AN

APPENDIX.

Wherein some Passages of the foregoing Volumes
are illustrated and explain'd.

VOL. III.

OF

MORALS.

LONDON,

Printed for THOMAS LONGMAN, at the *Ship* in
Pater-noster-Row, MDCCXL.

ADVERTISEMENT.

I think it proper to inform the public, that tho' this be a third volume of the Treatise of Human Nature, yet 'tis in some measure independent of the other two, and requires not that the reader shou'd enter into all the abstract reasonings contain'd in them. I am hopeful it may be understood by ordinary readers, with as little attention as is usually given to any books of reasoning. It must only be observ'd, that I continue to make use of the terms, *impressions* and *ideas*, in the same sense as formerly; and that by impressions I mean our stronger perceptions, such as our sensations, affections and sentiments; and by ideas the fainter perceptions, or the copies of these in the memory and imagination.

A TREATISE

OF

HUMAN NATURE.

BOOK III.
OF MORALS.

PART I.

OF VIRTUE AND VICE IN GENERAL.

SECT. I.—*Moral Distinctions not deriv'd from Reason.*

THERE is an inconvenience which attends all abstruse reasoning, that it may silence, without convincing an antagonist, and requires the same intense study to make us sensible of its force, that was at first requisite for its invention. When we leave our closet, and engage in the common affairs of life, its conclusions seem to vanish, like the phantoms of the night on the appearance of the morning; and 'tis difficult for us to retain even that conviction, which we had attain'd with difficulty. This is still more conspicuous in a long chain of reasoning, where we must preserve to the end the evidence of the first propositions, and where we often lose sight of all the most receiv'd maxims, either of philosophy or common life. I am not, however, without hopes, that the present system of philosophy will acquire new force as it advances; and that our reasonings concerning *morals* will corroborate whatever has been said concerning the *under-standing* and the *passions*. Morality is a subject that interests us above all others: We fancy the peace of society to be at stake in every decision concerning it; and 'tis evident, that this concern must make our speculations appear more real and solid, than where the subject is, in a great measure, indifferent to us. What affects us, we conclude can never be a chimera; and as our passion is engag'd on the one side or the other, we naturally think that the question lies within human comprehension; which, in other cases of this nature, we are apt to entertain some doubt of. Without this ad-vantage I never should have ventur'd upon a third volume of such abstruse philosophy, in an age, wherein the greatest part of men seem agreed to convert reading into an amuse-ment, and to reject every thing that requires any considerable degree of attention to be comprehended.

It has been observ'd, that nothing is ever present to the mind but its perceptions; and that all the actions of seeing, hearing, judging, loving, hating, and thinking, fall under this denomination. The mind can never exert itself in any action, which we may not comprehend under the term of *perception*; and consequently that term is no less applicable to those judgments, by which we distinguish moral good and evil, than to every other operation of the mind. To approve of one character, to condemn another, are only so many different perceptions.

Now as perceptions resolve themselves into two kinds, viz. *impressions* and *ideas*, this distinction gives rise to a question, with which we shall open up our present enquiry concerning morals, *Whether 'tis by means of our* ideas *or im-*pressions *we distinguish betwixt vice and virtue, and pronounce an action blameable or praiseworthy?*[1] This will immediately cut off all loose discourses and declamations, and reduce us to something precise and exact on the present subject.

Those who affirm that virtue is nothing but a conformity to reason; that there are eternal fitnesses and unfitnesses of things, which are the same to every rational being that con-siders them; that the immutable measures of right and wrong impose an obligation, not only on human creatures, but also on the Deity himself: All these systems concur in the opinion, that morality, like truth, is discern'd merely by

[1 Introd. sect 50 —ED]

ideas, and by their juxta-position and comparison.   In order, therefore, to judge of these systems, we need only consider, whether it be possible, from reason alone, to distinguish betwixt moral good and evil, or whether there must concur some other principles to enable us to make that distinction.

If morality had naturally no influence on human passions and actions, 'twere in vain to take such pains to inculcate it ; and nothing wou'd be more fruitless than that multitude of rules and precepts, with which all moralists abound.   Philosophy is commonly divided into *speculative* and *practical* ; and as morality is always comprehended under the latter division, 'tis supposed to influence our passions and actions, and to go beyond the calm and indolent judgments of the understanding.   And this is confirm'd by common experience, which informs us, that men are often govern'd by their duties, and are deter'd from some actions by the opinion of injustice, and impell'd to others by that of obligation.

Since morals, therefore, have an influence on the actions and affections, it follows, that they cannot be deriv'd from reason ; and that because reason alone, as we have already prov'd, can never have any such influence.   Morals excite passions, and produce or prevent actions.   Reason of itself is utterly impotent in this particular.   The rules of morality, therefore, are not conclusions of our reason.

No one, I believe, will deny the justness of this inference ; nor is there any other means of evading it, than by denying that principle, on which it is founded.   As long as it is allow'd, that reason has no influence on our passions and actions, 'tis in vain to pretend, that morality is discover'd only by a deduction of reason.   An active principle can never be founded on an inactive ; and if reason be inactive in itself, it must remain so in all its shapes and appearances, whether it exerts itself in natural or moral subjects, whether it considers the powers of external bodies, or the actions of rational beings.

It would be tedious to repeat all the arguments, by which I have prov'd,[1] that reason is perfectly inert, and can never either prevent or produce any action or affection.   'Twill be easy to recollect what has been said upon that subject.   I shall only recal on this occasion one of these arguments,

[1 Book II. Part III. Sect 3]

which I shall endeavour to render still more conclusive, and more applicable to the present subject.

Reason is the discovery of truth or falshood. Truth or falshood consists in an agreement or disagreement either to the *real* relations of ideas, or to *real* existence and matter of fact. Whatever, therefore, is not susceptible of this agreement or disagreement, is incapable of being true or false, and can never be an object of our reason. Now 'tis evident our passions, volitions, and actions, are not susceptible of any such agreement or disagreement; being original facts and realities, compleat in themselves, and implying no reference to other passions, volitions, and actions. 'Tis impossible, therefore, they can be pronounced either true or false, and be either contrary or conformable to reason.

This argument is of double advantage to our present purpose. For it proves *directly*, that actions do not derive their merit from a conformity to reason, nor their blame from a contrariety to it; and it proves the same truth more *indirectly*, by shewing us, that as reason can never immediately prevent or produce any action by contradicting or approving of it, it cannot be the source of moral good and evil, which are found to have that influence. Actions may be laudable or blameable; but they cannot be reasonable or unreasonable: Laudable or blameable, therefore, are not the same with reasonable or unreasonable. The merit and demerit of actions frequently contradict, and sometimes controul our natural propensities. But reason has no such influence. Moral distinctions, therefore, are not the offspring of reason. Reason is wholly inactive, and can never be the source of so active a principle as conscience, or a sense of morals.

But perhaps it may be said, that tho' no will or action can be immediately contradictory to reason, yet we may find such a contradiction in some of the attendants of the action, that is, in its causes or effects. The action may cause a judgment, or may be *obliquely* caus'd by one, when the judgment concurs with a passion; and by an abusive way of speaking, which philosophy will scarce allow of, the same contrariety may, upon that account, be ascrib'd to the action. How far this truth or falshood may be the source of morals, 'twill now be proper to consider.

It has been observ'd, that reason, in a strict and philosophical sense, can have an influence on our conduct only after two ways: Either when it excites a passion by informing us of the existence of something which is a proper object of it; or when it discovers the connexion of causes and effects, so as to afford us means of exerting any passion. These are the only kinds of judgment, which can accompany our actions, or can be said to produce them in any manner; and it must be allow'd, that these judgments may often be false and erroneous. A person may be affected with passion, by supposing a pain or pleasure to lie in an object, which has no tendency to produce either of these sensations, or which produces the contrary to what is imagin'd. A person may also take false measures for the attaining his end, and may retard, by his foolish conduct, instead of forwarding the execution of any project. These false judgments may be thought to affect the passions and actions, which are connected with them, and may be said to render them unreasonable, in a figurative and improper way of speaking. But tho' this be acknowledg'd, 'tis easy to observe, that these errors are so far from being the source of all immorality, that they are commonly very innocent, and draw no manner of guilt upon the person who is so unfortunate as to fall into them. They extend not beyond a mistake of *fact*, which moralists have not generally suppos'd criminal, as being perfectly involuntary. I am more to be lamented than blam'd, if I am mistaken with regard to the influence of objects in producing pain or pleasure, or if I know not the proper means of satisfying my desires. No one can ever regard such errors as a defect in my moral character. A fruit, for instance, that is really disagreeable, appears to me at a distance, and thro' mistake I fancy it to be pleasant and delicious. Here is one error. I choose certain means of reaching this fruit, which are not proper for my end. Here is a second error; nor is there any third one, which can ever possibly enter into our reasonings concerning actions. I ask, therefore, if a man, in this situation, and guilty of these two errors, is to be regarded as vicious and criminal, however unavoidable they might have been? Or if it be possible to imagine, that such errors are the sources of all immorality?

And here it may be proper to observe, that if moral distinctions be deriv'd from the truth or falshood of those

SECT.
I.

Moral distinctions not deriv'd from reason.

judgments, they must take place wherever we form the judgments; nor will there be any difference, whether the question be concerning an apple or a kingdom, or whether the error be avoidable or unavoidable. For as the very essence of morality is suppos'd to consist in an agreement or disagreement to reason, the other circumstances are entirely arbitrary, and can never either bestow on any action the character of virtuous or vicious, or deprive it of that character. To which we may add, that this agreement or disagreement, not admitting of degrees, all virtues and vices wou'd of course be equal.

Shou'd it be pretended, that tho' a mistake of *fact* be not criminal, yet a mistake of *right* often is; and that this may be the source of immorality: I would answer, that 'tis impossible such a mistake can ever be the original source of immorality, since it supposes a real right and wrong; that is, a real distinction in morals, independent of these judgments. A mistake, therefore, of right may become a species of immorality; but 'tis only a secondary one, and is founded on some other, antecedent to it.

As to those judgments which are the *effects* of our actions, and which, when false, give occasion to pronounce the actions contrary to truth and reason; we may observe, that our actions never cause any judgment, either true or false, in ourselves, and that 'tis only on others they have such an influence. 'Tis certain, that an action, on many occasions, may give rise to false conclusions in others; and that a person, who thro' a window sees any lewd behaviour of mine with my neighbour's wife, may be so simple as to imagine she is certainly my own. In this respect my action resembles somewhat a lye or falshood; only with this difference, which is material, that I perform not the action with any intention of giving rise to a false judgment in another, but merely to satisfy my lust and passion. It causes, however, a mistake and false judgment by accident; and the falshood of its effects may be ascribed, by some odd figurative way of speaking, to the action itself. But still I can see no pretext of reason for asserting, that the tendency to cause such an error is the first spring or original source of all immorality.[a]

* One might think it were entirely superfluous to prove this, if a late author,[1] who has had the good fortune to obtain some reputation, had not

['1' Wollaston, in the 'Religion of Nature Delineated,' sect 1.—ED]

Thus upon the whole, 'tis impossible, that the distinction betwixt moral good and evil, can be made by reason; since that distinction has an influence upon our actions, of which reason alone is incapable. Reason and judgment may, indeed, be the mediate cause of an action, by prompting,

seriously affirmed, that such a falshood is the foundation of all guilt and moral deformity. That we may discover the fallacy of his hypothesis, we need only consider, that a false conclusion is drawn from an action, only by means of an obscurity of natural principles, which makes a cause be secretly interrupted in its operation, by contrary causes, and renders the connection betwixt two objects uncertain and variable. Now, as a like uncertainty and variety of causes take place, even in natural objects, and produce a like error in our judgment, if that tendency to produce error were the very essence of vice and immorality, it shou'd follow, that even inanimate objects might be vicious and immoral.

'Tis in vain to urge, that inanimate objects act without liberty and choice. For as liberty and choice are not necessary to make an action produce in us an erroneous conclusion, they can be, in no respect, essential to morality; and I do not readily perceive, upon this system, how they can ever come to be regarded by it. If the tendency to cause error be the origin of immorality, that tendency and immorality wou'd in every case be inseparable.

Add to this, that if I had used the precaution of shutting the windows, while I indulg'd myself in those liberties with my neighbour's wife, I should have been guilty of no immorality; and that because my action, being perfectly conceal'd, wou'd have had no tendency to produce any false conclusion.

For the same reason, a thief, who steals in by a ladder at a window, and takes all imaginable care to cause no disturbance, is in no respect criminal. For either he will not be perceiv'd, or if he be, 'tis impossible he can produce any error, nor will any one, from these circumstances, take him to be other than what he really is.

'Tis well known, that those who are squint-sighted, do very readily cause mistakes in others, and that we imagine they salute or are talking to one person, while they address themselves to

another. Are they therefore, upon that account, immoral?

Besides, we may easily observe, that in all those arguments there is an evident reasoning in a circle. A person who takes possession of *another's* goods, and uses them as his *own*, in a manner declares them to be his own, and this falshood is the source of the immorality of injustice. But is property, or right, or obligation, intelligible, without an antecedent morality?

A man that is ungrateful to his benefactor, in a manner affirms, that he never received any favours from him. But in what manner? Is it because 'tis his duty to be grateful? But this supposes, that there is some antecedent rule of duty and morals. Is it because human nature is generally grateful, and makes us conclude, that a man who does any harm never received any favour from the person he harm'd? But human nature is not so generally grateful, as to justify such a conclusion. Or if it were, is an exception to a general rule in every case criminal, for no other reason than because it is an exception?

But what may suffice entirely to destroy this whimsical system is, that it leaves us under the same difficulty to give a reason why truth is virtuous and falshood vicious, as to account for the merit or turpitude of any other action. I shall allow, if you please, that all immorality is deriv'd from this supposed falshood in action, provided you can give me any plausible reason, why such a falshood is immoral. If you consider rightly of the matter, you will find yourself in the same difficulty as at the beginning.

This last argument is very conclusive, because, if there be not an evident merit or turpitude annex'd to this species of truth or falshood, it can never have any influence upon our actions. For, who ever thought of forbearing any action, because others might possibly draw false conclusions from it? Or, who ever perform'd any, that he might give rise to true conclusions?

or by directing a passion : But it is not pretended, that a judgment of this kind, either in its truth or falshood, is attended with virtue or vice. And as to the judgments, which are caused by our judgments, they can still less bestow those moral qualities on the actions, which are their causes.

But to be more particular, and to shew, that those eternal immutable fitnesses and unfitnesses of things cannot be defended by sound philosophy, we may weigh the following considerations.

If the thought and understanding were alone capable of fixing the boundaries of right and wrong, the character of virtuous and vicious either must lie in some relations of objects, or must be a matter of fact, which is discovered by our reasoning. This consequence is evident. As the operations of human understanding divide themselves into two kinds, the comparing of ideas, and the inferring of matter of fact; were virtue discover'd by the understanding; it must be an object of one of these operations, nor is there any third operation of the understanding, which can discover it. There has been an opinion very industriously propagated by certain philosophers, that morality is susceptible of demonstration ; and tho' no one has ever been able to advance a single step in those demonstrations; yet 'tis taken for granted, that this science may be brought to an equal certainty with geometry or algebra. Upon this supposition, vice and virtue must consist in some relations; since 'tis allow'd on all hands, that no matter of fact is capable of being demonstrated. Let us, therefore, begin with examining this hypothesis, and endeavour, if possible, to fix those moral qualities, which have been so long the objects of our fruitless researches. Point out distinctly the relations, which constitute morality or obligation, that we may know wherein they consist, and after what manner we must judge of them.

If you assert, that vice and virtue consist in relations susceptible of certainty and demonstration, you must confine yourself to those *four* relations, which alone admit of that degree of evidence; and in that case you run into absurdities, from which you will never be able to extricate yourself. For as you make the very essence of morality to lie in the relations, and as there is no one of these relations but what is applicable, not only to an irrational, but also to an inanimate object; it follows, that even such objects must be susceptible of merit or demerit. *Resemblance, contrariety, degrees in quality,* and *proportions in quantity and number*; [1] all these relations belong as properly to matter, as to our actions, passions, and volitions. 'Tis unquestionable, therefore, that morality lies not in any of these relations, nor the sense of it in their discovery. [2]

Shou'd it be asserted, that the sense of morality consists in the discovery of some relation, distinct from these, and that our enumeration was not compleat, when we comprehended all demonstrable relations under four general heads: To this I know not what to reply, till some one be so good as to point out to me this new relation. 'Tis impossible to refute a system, which has never yet been explain'd. In such a manner of fighting in the dark, a man loses his blows in the air, and often places them where the enemy is not present.

I must, therefore, on this occasion, rest contented with requiring the two following conditions of any one that wou'd undertake to clear up this system. *First,* As moral good and evil belong only to the actions of the mind, and are deriv'd from our situation with regard to external objects, the relations from which these moral distinctions arise, must lie only betwixt internal actions, and external objects, and must not be applicable either to internal actions, compared among themselves, or to external objects, when placed in opposition to other external objects. For as morality is supposed to attend certain relations, if these relations cou'd belong to internal actions consider'd singly, it wou'd follow, that we might be guilty of crimes in ourselves, and independent of

---

[1 Introd. sect 50 Cf vol i. part iii. sect. i —ED]

2 As a proof, how confus'd our way of thinking on this subject commonly is, we may observe, that those who assert, that morality is demonstrable, do not say, that morality lies in the relations, and that the relations are distinguishable by reason They only say, that reason can discover such an action, in such relations, to be virtuous, and such another vicious It seems they thought it sufficient, if they cou'd bring the word, Relation, into the proposition, without troubling themselves whether it was to the purpose or not But here, I think, is plain argument Demonstrative reason discovers only relations But that reason, according to this hypothesis, discovers also vice and virtue. These moral qualities, therefore, must be relations When we blame any action, in any situation, the whole complicated object, of action and situation, must form certain relations, wherein the essence of vice consists This hypothesis is not otherwise intelligible For what does reason discover, when it pronounces any action vicious? Does it discover a relation or a matter of fact? These questions are decisive, and must not be eluded.

our situation, with respect to the universe : And in like manner, if these moral relations cou'd be apply'd to external objects, it wou'd follow, that even inanimate beings wou'd be susceptible of moral beauty and deformity. Now it seems difficult to imagine, that any relation can be discover'd betwixt our passions, volitions and actions, compared to external objects, which relation might not belong either to these passions and volitions, or to these external objects, compar'd among *themselves*.

But it will be still more difficult to fulfil the *second* condition, requisite to justify this system. According to the principles of those who maintain an abstract rational difference betwixt moral good and evil, and a natural fitness and unfitness of things, 'tis not only suppos'd that these relations, being eternal and immutable, are the same, when consider'd by every rational creature, but their *effects* are also suppos'd to be necessarily the same ; and 'tis concluded they have no less, or rather a greater, influence in directing the will of the deity, than in governing the rational and virtuous of our own species. These two particulars are evidently distinct. 'Tis one thing to know virtue, and another to conform the will to it. In order, therefore, to prove, that the measures of right and wrong are eternal laws, *obligatory* on every rational mind, 'tis not sufficient to shew the relations upon which they are founded : We must also point out the connexion betwixt the relation and the will ; and must prove that this connexion is so necessary, that in every well-disposed mind, it must take place and have its influence ; tho' the difference betwixt these minds be in other respects immense and infinite. Now besides what I have already prov'd, that even in human nature no relation can ever alone produce any action ; besides this, I say, it has been shewn, in treating of the understanding, that there is no connexion of cause and effect, such as this is suppos'd to be, which is discoverable otherwise than by experience, and of which we can pretend to have any security by the simple consideration of the objects. All beings in the universe, consider'd in themselves, appear entirely loose and independent of each other. 'Tis only by experience we learn their influence and connexion ; and this influence we ought never to extend beyond experience.

Thus it will be impossible to fulfil the *first* condition required to the system of eternal rational measures of right and wrong; because it is impossible to shew those relations, upon which such a distinction may be founded: And 'tis as impossible to fulfil the *second* condition; because we cannot prove *a priori*, that these relations, if they really existed and were perceiv'd, wou'd be universally forcible and obligatory.

But to make these general reflections more clear and convincing, we may illustrate them by some particular instances, wherein this character of moral good or evil is the most universally acknowledged. Of all crimes that human creatures are capable of committing, the most horrid and unnatural is ingratitude, especially when it is committed against parents, and appears in the more flagrant instances of wounds and death. This is acknowledg'd by all mankind, philosophers as well as the people; the question only arises among philosophers, whether the guilt or moral deformity of this action be discover'd by demonstrative reasoning, or be felt by an internal sense, and by means of some sentiment, which the reflecting on such an action naturally occasions. This question will soon be decided against the former opinion, if we can shew the same relations in other objects, without the notion of any guilt or iniquity attending them. Reason or science is nothing but the comparing of ideas, and the discovery of their relations; and if the same relations have different characters, it must evidently follow, that those characters are not discover'd merely by reason. To put the affair, therefore, to this trial, let us chuse any inanimate object, such as an oak or elm; and let us suppose, that by the dropping of its seed, it produces a sapling below it, which springing up by degrees, at last overtops and destroys the parent tree: I ask, if in this instance there be wanting any relation, which is discoverable in parricide or ingratitude? Is not the one tree the cause of the other's existence; and the latter the cause of the destruction of the former, in the same manner as when a child murders his parent? 'Tis not sufficient to reply, that a choice or will is wanting. For in the case of parricide, a will does not give rise to any *different* relations, but is only the cause from which the action is deriv'd; and consequently produces the *same* relations, that in the oak or elm arise from some other principles. 'Tis a will or choice, that determines a man to kill his parent; and they are the laws of matter and motion, that determine a sapling to destroy the oak, from which it sprung. Here then the same relations have different causes; but still the relations are the same: And as their discovery is not in both cases attended with a notion of immorality, it follows, that that notion does not arise from such a discovery.

But to chuse an instance, still more resembling; I would fain ask any one, why incest in the human species is criminal, and why the very same action, and the same relations in animals have not the smallest moral turpitude and deformity? If it be answer'd, that this action is innocent in animals, because they have not reason sufficient to discover its turpitude; but that man, being endow'd with that faculty, which *ought* to restrain him to his duty, the same action instantly becomes criminal to him; should this be said, I would reply, that this is evidently arguing in a circle. For before reason can perceive this turpitude, the turpitude must exist; and consequently is independent of the decisions of our reason, and is their object more properly than their effect. According to this system, then, every animal, that has sense, and appetite, and will; that is, every animal must be susceptible of all the same virtues and vices, for which we ascribe praise and blame to human creatures. All the difference is, that our superior reason may serve to discover the vice or virtue, and by that means may augment the blame or praise: But still this discovery supposes a separate being in these moral distinctions, and a being, which depends only on the will and appetite, and which, both in thought and reality, may be distinguish'd from the reason. Animals are susceptible of the same relations, with respect to each other, as the human species, and therefore wou'd also be susceptible of the same morality, if the essence of morality consisted in these relations. Their want of a sufficient degree of reason may hinder them from perceiving the duties and obligations of morality, but can never hinder these duties from existing; since they must antecedently exist, in order to their being perceiv'd. Reason must find them, and can never produce them. This argument deserves to be weigh'd, as being, in my opinion, entirely decisive.

Nor does this reasoning only prove, that morality consists not in any relations, that are the objects of science; but if examin'd will prove with equal certainty, that it consists not in any *matter of fact*, which can be discover'd by the understanding.[1]   This is the *second* part of our argument; and if it can be made evident, we may conclude, that morality is not an object of reason.   But can there be any difficulty in proving, that vice and virtue are not matters of fact, whose existence we can infer by reason?   Take any action allow'd to be vicious: Wilful murder, for instance.   Examine it in all lights, and see if you can find that matter of fact, or real existence, which you call *vice*.   In which-ever way you take it, you find only certain passions, motives, volitions and thoughts.   There is no other matter of fact in the case.   The vice entirely escapes you, as long as you consider the object.   You never can find it, till you turn your reflection into your own breast, and find a sentiment of disapprobation, which arises in you, towards this action.   Here is a matter of fact; but 'tis the object of feeling, not of reason.   It lies in yourself, not in the object.   So that when you pronounce any action or character to be vicious, you mean nothing, but that from the constitution of your nature you have a feeling or sentiment of blame from the contemplation of it.   Vice and virtue, therefore, may be compar'd to sounds, colours, heat and cold, which, according to modern philosophy, are not qualities in objects, but perceptions in the mind:[2]   And this discovery in morals, like that other in physics, is to be regarded as a considerable[3] advancement of the speculative sciences; tho', like that too, it has little or no influence on practice.   Nothing can be more real, or concern us more, than our own sentiments of pleasure and uneasiness; and if these be favourable to virtue, and unfavourable to vice, no more can be requisite to the regulation of our conduct and behaviour.

I cannot forbear adding to these reasonings an observation, which may, perhaps, be found of some importance.   In every system of morality, which I have hitherto met with, I have always remark'd, that the author proceeds for some time in the ordinary way of reasoning, and establishes the being of a God, or makes observations concerning human affairs; when of a sudden I am surpriz'd to find, that instead of the usual copulations of propositions, *is*, and *is not*, I meet with no proposition that is not connected with an *ought*, or an

---

[1 Introd sect 50 —Ed]
[2 Introd. sect. 50, note 4.—Ed]

[3 For the history of this sentence, see vol iii p 31.—Ed]

ought not.[1] This change is imperceptible ; but is, however, of the last consequence. For as this *ought*, or *ought not*, expresses some new relation or affirmation, 'tis necessary that it shou'd be observ'd and explain'd ; and at the same time that a reason should be given, for what seems altogether inconceivable, how this new relation can be a deduction from others, which are entirely different from it. But as authors do not commonly use this precaution, I shall presume to recommend it to the readers ; and am persuaded, that this small attention wou'd subvert all the vulgar systems of morality, and let us see, that the distinction of vice and virtue is not founded merely on the relations of objects, nor is perceiv'd by reason.

Sect. II.—*Moral distinctions deriv'd from a moral sense.*

Thus the course of the argument leads us to conclude, that since vice and virtue are not discoverable merely by reason, or the comparison of ideas, it must be by means of some impression or sentiment they occasion, that we are able to mark the difference betwixt them. Our decisions concerning moral rectitude and depravity are evidently perceptions ; and as all perceptions are either impressions or ideas, the exclusion of the one is a convincing argument for the other. Morality, therefore, is more properly felt than judg'd of ; tho' this feeling or sentiment is commonly so soft and gentle, that we are apt to confound it with an idea, according to our common custom of taking all things for the same, which have any near resemblance to each other.

The next question is, Of what nature are these impressions, and after what manner do they operate upon us ? Here we cannot remain long in suspense, but must pronounce the impression arising from virtue, to be agreeable, and that proceeding from vice to be uneasy. Every moment's experience must convince us of this. There is no spectacle so fair and beautiful as a noble and generous action ; nor any which gives us more abhorrence than one that is cruel and treacherous. No enjoyment equals the satisfaction we receive from the company of those we love and esteem ; as the greatest of all punishments is to be oblig'd to pass our lives with those we hate or contemn. A very play or romance

[1 Introd. sect. 49.—Ed]

may afford us instances of this pleasure, which virtue conveys to us; and pain, which arises from vice.

SECT.
II.

Moral dis-
tinctions
deriv'd
from a
moral
sense

Now since the distinguishing impressions, by which moral good or evil is known, are nothing but *particular* pains or pleasures; it follows, that in all enquiries concerning these moral distinctions, it will be sufficient to shew the principles, which make us feel a satisfaction or uneasiness from the survey of any character, in order to satisfy us why the character is laudable or blameable. An action, or sentiment, or character is virtuous or vicious; why? because its view causes a pleasure or uneasiness of a particular kind. In giving a reason, therefore, for the pleasure or uneasiness, we sufficiently explain the vice or virtue. To have the sense of virtue, is nothing but to *feel* a satisfaction of a particular kind from the contemplation of a character. The very *feeling* constitutes our praise or admiration. We go no farther, nor do we enquire into the cause of the satisfaction. We do not infer a character to be virtuous, because it pleases: But in feeling that it pleases after such a particular manner, we in effect feel that it is virtuous.[1] The case is the same as in our judgments concerning all kinds of beauty, and tastes, and sensations. Our approbation is imply'd in the immediate pleasure they convey to us.

I have objected to the system, which establishes eternal rational measures of right and wrong, that 'tis impossible to shew, in the actions of reasonable creatures, any relations, which are not found in external objects; and therefore, if morality always attended these relations, 'twere possible for inanimate matter to become virtuous or vicious. Now it may, in like manner, be objected to the present system, that if virtue and vice be determin'd by pleasure and pain, these qualities must, in every case, arise from the sensations; and consequently any object, whether animate or inanimate, rational or irrational, might become morally good or evil, provided it can excite a satisfaction or uneasiness. But tho' this objection seems to be the very same, it has by no means the same force, in the one case as in the other. For, *first*, 'tis evident, that under the term *pleasure*, we comprehend sensations, which are very different from each other, and which have only such a distant resemblance, as is requisite to make them be express'd by the same abstract term. A

[¹ Introd. sect 51 —Ed]

good composition of music and a bottle of good wine equally produce pleasure; and what is more, their goodness is determin'd merely by the pleasure. But shall we say upon that account, that the wine is harmonious, or the music of a good flavour? In like manner an inanimate object, and the character or sentiments of any person may, both of them, give satisfaction; but as the satisfaction is different, this keeps our sentiments concerning them from being confounded, and makes us ascribe virtue to the one, and not to the other. Nor is every sentiment of pleasure or pain, which arises from characters and actions, of that *peculiar* kind, which makes us praise or condemn. The good qualities of an enemy are hurtful to us; but may still command our esteem and respect. 'Tis only when a character is considered in general, without reference to our particular interest, that it causes such a feeling or sentiment, as denominates it morally good or evil.[1] 'Tis true, those sentiments, for interest and morals, are apt to be confounded, and naturally run into one another. It seldom happens, that we do not think an enemy vicious, and can distinguish betwixt his opposition to our interest and real villainy or baseness. But this hinders not, but that the sentiments are, in themselves, distinct; and a man of temper and judgment may preserve himself from these illusions. In like manner, tho' 'tis certain a musical voice is nothing but one that naturally gives a *particular* kind of pleasure; yet 'tis difficult for a man to be sensible, that the voice of an enemy is agreeable, or to allow it to be musical. But a person of a fine ear, who has the command of himself, can separate these feelings, and give praise to what deserves it.

Secondly, We may call to remembrance the preceding system of the passions, in order to remark a still more considerable difference among our pains and pleasures. Pride and humility, love and hatred are excited, when there is any thing presented to us, that both bears a relation to the object of the passion, and produces a separate sensation related to the sensation of the passion. Now virtue and vice are attended with these circumstances. They must necessarily be plac'd either in ourselves or others, and excite either pleasure or uneasiness; and therefore must give rise to one of these four passions; which clearly distinguishes them from the pleasure and pain arising from inanimate

[1 Introd. sect. 51.— Ed]

SECT.
II.

Moral dis-
tinctions
deriv'd
from a
moral
sense.

objects, that often bear no relation to us: And that is, perhaps, the most considerable effect that virtue and vice have upon the human mind.

It may now be ask'd *in general*, concerning this pain or pleasure, that distinguishes moral good and evil, *From what principles is it derived, and whence does it arise in the human mind?* To this I reply, *first*, that 'tis absurd to imagine, that in every particular instance, these sentiments are produc'd by an *original* quality and *primary* constitution. For as the number of our duties is, in a manner, infinite, 'tis impossible that our original instincts should extend to each of them, and from our very first infancy impress on the human mind all that multitude of precepts, which are contain'd in the compleatest system of ethics. Such a method of proceeding is not conformable to the usual maxims, by which nature is conducted, where a few principles produce all that variety we observe in the universe, and every thing is carry'd on in the easiest and most simple manner. 'Tis necessary, therefore, to abridge these primary impulses, and find some more general principles, upon which all our notions of morals are founded.

But in the *second* place, should it be ask'd, Whether we ought to search for these principles in *nature*, or whether we must look for them in some other origin? I wou'd reply, that our answer to this question depends upon the definition of the word, Nature, than which there is none more ambiguous and equivocal. If *nature* be oppos'd to miracles, not only the distinction betwixt vice and virtue is natural, but also every event, which has ever happen'd in the world, *excepting those miracles, on which our religion is founded*. In saying, then, that the sentiments of vice and virtue are natural in this sense, we make no very extraordinary discovery.

But *nature* may also be opposed to rare and unusual; and in this sense of the word, which is the common one, there may often arise disputes concerning what is natural or unnatural; and one may in general affirm, that we are not possess'd of any very precise standard, by which these disputes can be decided. Frequent and rare depend upon the number of examples we have observ'd; and as this number may gradually encrease or diminish, 'twill be impossible to fix any exact boundaries betwixt them. We may only affirm on this head, that if ever there was any thing, which cou'd be call'd natural in this sense, the sentiments of morality certainly may; since there never was any nation of the world, nor any single person in any nation, who was utterly depriv'd of them, and who never, in any instance, shew'd the least approbation or dislike of manners. These sentiments are so rooted in our constitution and temper, that without entirely confounding the human mind by disease or madness, 'tis impossible to extirpate and destroy them.

But *nature* may also be opposed to artifice, as well as to what is rare and unusual; and in this sense it may be disputed, whether the notions of virtue be natural or not. We readily forget, that the designs, and projects, and views of men are principles as necessary in their operation as heat and cold, moist and dry: But taking them to be free and entirely our own, 'tis usual for us to set them in opposition to the other principles of nature. Shou'd it, therefore, be demanded, whether the sense of virtue be natural or artificial, I am of opinion, that 'tis impossible for me at present to give any precise answer to this question. Perhaps it will appear afterwards, that our sense of some virtues is artificial, and that of others natural. The discussion of this question will be more proper, when we enter upon an exact detail of each particular vice and virtue.[1]

Mean while it may not be amiss to observe from these definitions of *natural* and *unnatural*, that nothing can be more unphilosophical than those systems, which assert, that virtue is the same with what is natural, and vice with what is unnatural. For in the first sense of the word, Nature, as opposed to miracles, both vice and virtue are equally natural, and in the second sense, as oppos'd to what is unusual, perhaps virtue will be found to be the most unnatural. At least it must be own'd, that heroic virtue, being as unusual, is as little natural as the most brutal barbarity. As to the third sense of the word, 'tis certain, that both vice and virtue are equally artificial, and out of nature. For however it may be disputed, whether the notion of a merit or

---

[1] In the following discourse *natural* is also opposed sometimes to *civil*, sometimes to *moral*.* The opposition will always discover the sense, in which it is taken

---

[* As in Part II. sect 8-10.—Ed]

demerit in certain actions be natural or artificial, 'tis evident, that the actions themselves are artificial, and are perform'd with a certain design and intention; otherwise they cou'd never be rank'd under any of these denominations. 'Tis impossible, therefore, that the character of natural and un-natural can ever, in any sense, mark the boundaries of vice and virtue.

SECT. II.

Moral distinctions deriv'd from a moral sense.

Thus we are still brought back to our first position, that virtue is distinguished by the pleasure, and vice by the pain, that any action, sentiment or character gives us by the mere view and contemplation. This decision is very commodious; because it reduces us to this simple question, *Why any action or sentiment upon the general view or survey, gives a certain satisfaction or uneasiness*, in order to shew the origin of its moral rectitude or depravity, without looking for any incomprehensible relations and qualities, which never did exist in nature, nor even in our imagination, by any clear and distinct conception. I flatter myself I have executed a great part of my present design by a statement of the question, which appears to me so free from ambiguity and obscurity.

PART II.

OF JUSTICE AND INJUSTICE.

SECT. I.—*Justice, whether a natural or artificial virtue?*

I HAVE already hinted, that our sense of every kind of virtue is not natural; but that there are some virtues, that produce pleasure and approbation by means of an artifice or contrivance, which arises from the circumstances and necessity of mankind. Of this kind I assert *justice* to be; and shall endeavour to defend this opinion by a short, and, I hope, convincing argument, before I examine the nature of the artifice, from which the sense of that virtue is derived.

'Tis evident, that when we praise any actions, we regard only the motives that produced them, and consider the actions as signs or indications of certain principles in the mind and temper. The external performance has no merit. We must look within to find the moral quality. This we cannot do directly; and therefore fix our attention on actions, as on external signs. But these actions are still considered as signs; and the ultimate object of our praise and approbation is the motive, that produc'd them.

After the same manner, when we require any action, or blame a person for not performing it, we always suppose, that one in that situation shou'd be influenc'd by the proper motive of that action, and we esteem it vicious in him to be regardless of it. If we find, upon enquiry, that the virtuous motive was still powerful over his breast, tho' check'd in its operation by some circumstances unknown to us, we retract our blame, and have the same esteem for him, as if he had actually perform'd the action, which we require of him.

It appears, therefore, that all virtuous actions derive their merit only from virtuous motives, and are consider'd merely as signs of those motives. From this principle I conclude, that the first virtuous motive, which bestows a merit on any action, can never be a regard to the virtue of that action,

SECT
I.
_____
Justice,
whether a
natural or
artificial
virtue?

but must be some other natural motive or principle. To suppose, that the mere regard to the virtue of the action, may be the first motive, which produc'd the action, and render'd it virtuous, is to reason in a circle. Before we can have such a regard, the action must be really virtuous; and this virtue must be deriv'd from some virtuous motive: And consequently the virtuous motive must be different from the regard to the virtue of the action. A virtuous motive is requisite to render an action virtuous. An action must be virtuous, before we can have a regard to its virtue. Some virtuous motive, therefore, must be antecedent to that regard.

Nor is this merely a metaphysical subtilty; but enters into all our reasonings in common life, tho' perhaps we may not be able to place it in such distinct philosophical terms. We blame a father for neglecting his child. Why? because it shews a want of natural affection, which is the duty of every parent. Were not natural affection a duty, the care of children cou'd not be a duty; and 'twere impossible we cou'd have the duty in our eye in the attention we give to our offspring. In this case, therefore, all men suppose a motive to the action distinct from a sense of duty.

Here is a man, that does many benevolent actions; relieves the distress'd, comforts the afflicted, and extends his bounty even to the greatest strangers. No character can be more amiable and virtuous. We regard these actions as proofs of the greatest humanity. This humanity bestows a merit on the actions. A regard to this merit is, therefore, a secondary consideration, and deriv'd from the antecedent principle of humanity, which is meritorious and laudable.

In short, it may be establish'd as an undoubted maxim, *that no action can be virtuous, or morally good, unless there be* *in human nature some motive to produce it, distinct from the* *sense of its morality.*[1]

But may not the sense of morality or duty produce an action, without any other motive? I answer, It may: But this is no objection to the present doctrine. When any virtuous motive or principle is common in human nature, a person, who feels his heart devoid of that motive, may hate himself upon that account, and may perform the action without the motive, from a certain sense of duty, in order to acquire by practice, that virtuous principle, or at least, to disguise to himself, as much as possible, his want of it. A

[1] Introd sect 61 —Ed]

man that really feels no gratitude in his temper, is still pleas'd to perform grateful actions, and thinks he has, by that means, fulfill'd his duty. Actions are at first only consider'd as signs of motives: But 'tis usual, in this case, as in all others, to fix our attention on the signs, and neglect, in some measure, the thing signify'd. But tho', on some occasions, a person may perform an action merely out of regard to its moral obligation, yet still this supposes in human nature some distinct principles, which are capable of producing the action, and whose moral beauty renders the action meritorious.

Now to apply all this to the present case; I suppose a person to have lent me a sum of money, on condition that it be restor'd in a few days; and also suppose, that after the expiration of the term agreed on, he demands the sum: I ask, *What reason or motive have I to restore the money?* It will, perhaps, be said, that my regard to justice, and abhorrence of villainy and knavery, are sufficient reasons for me, if I have the least grain of honesty, or sense of duty and obligation. And this answer, no doubt, is just and satisfactory to man in his civiliz'd state, and when train'd up according to a certain discipline and education. But in his rude and more *natural* condition, if you are pleas'd to call such a condition natural, this answer wou'd be rejected as perfectly unintelligible and sophistical. For one in that situation wou'd immediately ask you, *Wherein consists this honesty and justice, which you find in restoring a loan, and abstaining from the property of others?* It does not surely lie in the external action. It must, therefore be plac'd in the motive, from which the external action is deriv'd. This motive can never be a regard to the honesty of the action. For 'tis a plain fallacy to say, that a virtuous motive is requisite to render an action honest, and at the same time that a regard to the honesty is the motive of the action. We can never have a regard to the virtue of an action, unless the action be antecedently virtuous. No action can be virtuous, but so far as it proceeds from a virtuous motive. A virtuous motive, therefore, must precede the regard to the virtue; and 'tis impossible, that the virtuous motive and the regard to the virtue can be the same.

'Tis requisite, then, to find some motive to acts of justice and honesty, distinct from our regard to the honesty; and in this lies the great difficulty. For shou'd we say, that a concern for our private interest or reputation is the legitimate motive to all honest actions; it wou'd follow, that wherever that concern ceases, honesty can no longer have place. But 'tis certain, that self-love, when it acts at its liberty, instead of engaging us to honest actions, is the source of all injustice and violence; nor can a man ever correct those vices, without correcting and restraining the *natural* movements of that appetite.

SECT
I

Justice,
whether a
natural or
artificial
virtue?

But shou'd it be affirm'd, that the reason or motive of such actions is the *regard to publick interest,* to which nothing is more contrary than examples of injustice and dishonesty; shou'd this be said, I wou'd propose the three following considerations, as worthy of our attention. *First,* public interest is not naturally attach'd to the observation of the rules of justice; but is only connected with it, after an artificial convention for the establishment of these rules, as shall be shewn more at large hereafter. *Secondly,* if we suppose, that the loan was secret, and that it is necessary for the interest of the person, that the money be restor'd in the same manner (as when the lender wou'd conceal his riches), in that case the example ceases, and the public is no longer interested in the actions of the borrower; tho' I suppose there is no moralist, who will affirm, that the duty and obligation ceases. *Thirdly,* experience sufficiently proves, that men, in the ordinary conduct of life, look not so far as the public interest, when they pay their creditors, perform their promises, and abstain from theft, and robbery, and injustice of every kind. That is a motive too remote and too sublime to affect the generality of mankind, and operate with any force in actions so contrary to private interest as are frequently those of justice and common honesty.

In general, it may be affirm'd, that there is no such passion in human minds, as the love of mankind, merely as such, independent of personal qualities, of services, or of relation to ourself.[1] 'Tis true, there is no human, and indeed no sensible, creature, whose happiness or misery does not, in some measure, affect us, when brought near to us, and represented in lively colours: But this proceeds merely from sympathy, and is no proof of such an universal affection to mankind, since this concern extends itself beyond our own species. An affection betwixt the sexes is a passion evidently implanted in human nature; and this passion not only appears

[1 Introd. sect. 57.—Ed.]

in its peculiar symptoms, but also in inflaming every other principle of affection, and raising a stronger love from beauty, wit, kindness, than what wou'd otherwise flow from them. Were there an universal love among all human creatures, it wou'd appear after the same manner. Any degree of a good quality wou'd cause a stronger affection than the same degree of a bad quality wou'd cause hatred; contrary to what we find by experience. Men's tempers are different, and some have a propensity to the tender, and others to the rougher, affections: But in the main, we may affirm, that man in general, or human nature, is nothing but the object both of love and hatred, and requires some other cause, which by a double relation of impressions and ideas, may excite these passions. In vain would we endeavour to elude this hypothesis. There are no phænomena that point out any such kind affection to men, independent of their merit, and every other circumstance. We love company in general; but 'tis as we love any other amusement. An *Englishman* in *Italy* is a friend: A *Europæan* in *China*; and perhaps a man wou'd be belov'd as such, were we to meet him in the moon. But this proceeds only from the relation to ourselves; which in these cases gathers force by being confined to a few persons.

If public benevolence, therefore, or a regard to the interests of mankind, cannot be the original motive to justice, much less can *private benevolence*, or a *regard to the interests of the party concern'd*, be this motive. For what if he be my enemy, and has given me just cause to hate him? What if he be a vicious man, and deserves the hatred of all mankind? What if he be a miser, and can make no use of what I would deprive him of? What if he be a profligate debauchee, and wou'd rather receive harm than benefit from large possessions? What if I be in necessity, and have urgent motives to acquire something to my family? In all these cases, the original motive to justice wou'd fail; and consequently the justice itself, and along with it all property, right, and obligation.

A rich man lies under a moral obligation to communicate to those in necessity a share of his superfluities. Were private benevolence the original motive to justice, a man wou'd not be oblig'd to leave others in the possession of more than he is oblig'd to give them. At least the difference wou'd be very inconsiderable. Men generally fix their affections more on what they are possess'd of, than on what they never en-joy'd : For this reason, it wou'd be greater cruelty to dis-possess a man of any thing, than not to give it him. But who will assert, that this is the only foundation of justice ?

SECT.
I
Justice,
whether a
natural or
artificial
virtue ?

Besides, we must consider, that the chief reason, why men attach themselves so much to their possessions is, that they consider them as their property, and as secur'd to them inviolably by the laws of society. But this is a secondary con-sideration, and dependent on the preceding notions of justice and property.

A man's property is suppos'd to be fenc'd against every mortal, in every possible case. But private benevolence is, and ought to be, weaker in some persons, than in others : And in many, or indeed in most persons, must absolutely fail. Private benevolence, therefore, is not the original mo-tive of justice.

From all this it follows, that we have no real or universal motive for observing the laws of equity, but the very equity and merit of that observance ; and as no action can be equit-able or meritorious, where it cannot arise from some separate motive, there is here an evident sophistry and reasoning in a circle. Unless, therefore, we will allow, that nature has establish'd a sophistry, and render'd it necessary and un-avoidable, we must allow, that the sense of justice and injustice is not deriv'd from nature, but arises artificially, tho' neces-sarily from education, and human conventions.

I shall add, as a corollary to this reasoning, that since no action can be laudable or blameable, without some motives or impelling passions, distinct from the sense of morals, these distinct passions must have a great influence on that sense. 'Tis according to their general force in human nature, that we blame or praise. In judging of the beauty of animal bodies, we always carry in our eye the œconomy of a certain species ; and where the limbs and features observe that proportion, which is common to the species, we pronounce them hand-some and beautiful. In like manner we always consider the *natural* and *usual* force of the passions, when we determine concerning vice and virtue ; and if the passions depart very much from the common measures on either side, they are always disapprov'd as vicious. A man naturally loves his children better than his nephews, his nephews better than his cousins, his cousins better than strangers, where every

thing else is equal. Hence arise our common measures of
duty, in preferring the one to the other. Our sense of duty always follows the common and natural course of our passions.

To avoid giving offence, I must here observe, that when I
deny justice to be a natural virtue, I make use of the word,
natural, only as oppos'd to *artificial*. In another sense of the
word; as no principle of the human mind is more natural
than a sense of virtue; so no virtue is more natural
than justice. Mankind is an inventive species; and where
an invention is obvious and absolutely necessary, it may as
properly be said to be natural as any thing that proceeds
immediately from original principles, without the intervention
of thought or reflection. Tho' the rules of justice be *artificial*,
they are not *arbitrary*. Nor is the expression improper to
call them *Laws of Nature*; if by natural we understand what
is common to any species, or even if we confine it to mean
what is inseparable from the species.

Sect. II.—*Of the origin of justice and property.*

We now proceed to examine two questions, viz. *concerning
the manner, in which the rules of justice are establish'd by the
artifice of men*; and *concerning the reasons, which determine
us to attribute to the observance or neglect of these rules a moral
beauty and deformity.*[1] These questions will appear afterwards to be distinct. We shall begin with the former.

Of all the animals, with which this globe is peopled, there
is none towards whom nature seems, at first sight, to have
exercis'd more cruelty than towards man, in the numberless
wants and necessities, with which she has loaded him, and
in the slender means, which she affords to the relieving these
necessities. In other creatures these two particulars generally
compensate each other. If we consider the lion as a voracious
and carnivorous animal, we shall easily discover him to be
very necessitous; but if we turn our eye to his make and
temper, his agility, his courage, his arms, and his force, we
shall find, that his advantages hold proportion with his
wants. The sheep and ox are depriv'd of all these advantages; but their appetites are moderate, and their food is of
easy purchase. In man alone, this unnatural conjunction of
infirmity, and of necessity, may be observ'd in its greatest
perfection. Not only the food, which is requir'd for his sus-

[¹ Introd sect 57 —Ed]

tenance, flies his search and approach, or at least requires his
labour to be produc'd, but he must be possess'd of cloaths
and lodging, to defend him against the injuries of the
weather; tho' to consider him only in himself, he is provided
neither with arms, nor force, nor other natural abilities,
which are in any degree answerable to so many necessities.

'Tis by society alone he is able to supply his defects, and
raise himself up to an equality with his fellow-creatures, and
even acquire a superiority above them. By society all his
infirmities are compensated; and tho' in that situation his
wants multiply every moment upon him, yet his abilities are
still more augmented, and leave him in every respect more
satisfied and happy, than 'tis possible for him, in his savage
and solitary condition, ever to become. When every individual person labours a-part, and only for himself, his force
is too small to execute any considerable work; his labour
being employ'd in supplying all his different necessities, he
never attains a perfection in any particular art; and as his
force and success are not at all times equal, the least failure
in either of these particulars must be attended with inevitable
ruin and misery. Society provides a remedy for these *three*
inconveniences. By the conjunction of forces, our power is
augmented: By the partition of employments, our ability
encreases: And by mutual succour we are less expos'd to
fortune and accidents. 'Tis by this additional *force, ability,*
and *security,* that society becomes advantageous.

But in order to form society, 'tis requisite not only that it
be advantageous, but also that men be sensible of these
advantages; and 'tis impossible, in their wild uncultivated
state, that by study and reflection alone, they should ever be
able to attain this knowledge. Most fortunately, therefore,
there is conjoin'd to those necessities, whose remedies are
remote and obscure, another necessity, which having a present and more obvious remedy, may justly be regarded as the
first and original principle of human society. This necessity
is no other than that natural appetite betwixt the sexes,
which unites them together, and preserves their union, till a
new tye takes place in their concern for their common
offspring. This new concern becomes also a principle of
union betwixt the parents and offspring, and forms a more
numerous society; where the parents govern by the advantage of their superior strength and wisdom, and at the same

time are restrain'd in the exercise of their authority by that
natural affection, which they bear their children. In a little
time, custom and habit operating on the tender minds of the
children, makes them sensible of the advantages, which they
may reap from society, as well as fashions them by degrees
for it, by rubbing off those rough corners and untoward
affections, which prevent their coalition.

For it must be confest, that however the circumstances of
human nature may render an union necessary, and however
those passions of lust and natural affection may seem to
render it unavoidable; yet there are other particulars in our
natural temper, and in our *outward circumstances*, which are
very incommodious, and are even contrary to the requisite
conjunction. Among the former, we may justly esteem our
selfishness to be the most considerable. I am sensible, that,
generally speaking, the representations of this quality have
been carried much too far; and that the descriptions, which
certain philosophers delight so much to form of mankind in
this particular, are as wide of nature as any accounts of
monsters, which we meet with in fables and romances. So
far from thinking, that men have no affection for any thing
beyond themselves, I am of opinion, that tho' it be rare to
meet with one, who loves any single person better than himself; yet 'tis as rare to meet with one, in whom all the kind
affections, taken together, do not over-balance all the selfish.
Consult common experience: Do you not see, that tho' the
whole expence of the family be generally under the direction
of the master of it, yet there are few that do not bestow the
largest part of their fortunes on the pleasures of their wives,
and the education of their children, reserving the smallest
portion for their own proper use and entertainment This
is what we may observe concerning such as have those en-
dearing ties; and may presume, that the case would be the
same with others, were they plac'd in a like situation.

But tho' this generosity must be acknowledg'd to the
honour of human nature, we may at the same time remark,
that so noble an affection, instead of fitting men for large
societies, is almost as contrary to them, as the most narrow
selfishness. For while each person loves himself better than
any other single person, and in his love to others bears the
greatest affection to his relations and acquaintance, this
must necessarily produce an opposition of passions, and a

consequent opposition of actions, which cannot but be dangerous to the new-establish'd union.

'Tis however worth while to remark, that this contrariety of passions wou'd be attended with but small danger, did it not concur with a peculiarity in our *outward circumstances*, which affords it an opportunity of exerting itself. There are three different species of goods, which we are possess'd of; the internal satisfaction of our minds, the external advantages of our body, and the enjoyment of such possessions as we have acquir'd by our industry and good fortune. We are perfectly secure in the enjoyment of the first. The second may be ravish'd from us, but can be of no advantage to him who deprives us of them. The last only are both expos'd to the violence of others, and may be transferr'd without suffering any loss of alteration; while at the same time, there is not a sufficient quantity of them to supply every one's desires and necessities. As the improvement, therefore, of these goods is the chief advantage of society, so the *instability* of their possession, along with their *scarcity*, is the chief impediment.[1]

In vain shou'd we expect to find, in *uncultivated nature*, a remedy to this inconvenience; or hope for any inartificial principle of the human mind, which might controul those partial affections, and make us overcome the temptations arising from our circumstances. The idea of justice can never serve to this purpose, or be taken for a natural principle, capable of inspiring men with an equitable conduct towards each other. That virtue, as it is now understood, wou'd never have been dream'd of among rude and savage men. For the notion of injury or injustice implies an immorality or vice committed against some other person: And as every immorality is deriv'd from some defect or unsoundness of the passions, and as this defect must be judg'd of, in a great measure, from the ordinary course of nature in the constitution of the mind; 'twill be easy to know, whether we be guilty of any immorality, with regard to others, by considering the natural, and usual force of those several affections, which are directed towards them. Now it appears, that in the original frame of our mind, our strongest attention is confin'd to ourselves; our next is extended to our relations and acquaintance; and 'tis only the weakest

[1 Introd sect 57 —Ed.]

which reaches to strangers and indifferent persons. This partiality, then, and unequal affection, must not only have an influence on our behaviour and conduct in society, but even on our ideas of vice and virtue; so as to make us regard any remarkable transgression of such a degree of partiality, either by too great an enlargement, or contraction of the affections, as vicious and immoral. This we may observe in our common judgments concerning actions, where we blame a person, who either centers all his affections in his family, or is so regardless of them, as, in any opposition of interest, to give the preference to a stranger, or mere chance acquaintance. From all which it follows, that our natural uncultivated ideas of morality, instead of providing a remedy for the partiality of our affections, do rather conform themselves to that partiality, and give it an additional force and influence.

The remedy, then, is not deriv'd from nature, but from *artifice*; or more properly speaking, nature provides a remedy in the judgment and understanding, for what is irregular and incommodious in the affections. For when men, from their early education in society, have become sensible of the infinite advantages that result from it, and have besides acquir'd a new affection to company and conversation; and when they have observ'd, that the principal disturbance in society arises from those goods, which we call external, and from their looseness and easy transition from one person to another; they must seek for a remedy, by putting these goods, as far as possible, on the same footing with the fix'd and constant advantages of the mind and body. This can be done after no other manner, than by a convention enter'd into by all the members of the society to bestow stability on the possession of those external goods, and leave every one in the peaceable enjoyment of what he may acquire by his fortune and industry. By this means, every one knows what he may safely possess; and the passions are restrain'd in their partial and contradictory motions. Nor is such a restraint contrary to these passions; for if so, it cou'd never be enter'd into, nor maintain'd; but it is only contrary to their heedless and impetuous movement. Instead of departing from our own interest, or from that of our nearest friends, by abstaining from the possessions of others, we cannot better consult both these interests, than by such a conven-

tion; because it is by that means we maintain society, which
is so necessary to their well-being and subsistence, as well
as to our own.

SECT.
II.

Of the
origin of
justice and
property.

This convention is not of the nature of a *promise*: For
even promises themselves, as we shall see afterwards, arise
from human conventions. It is only a general sense of common interest; which sense all the members of the society
express to one another, and which induces them to regulate
their conduct by certain rules. I observe, that it will be for
my interest to leave another in the possession of his goods,
provided he will act in the same manner with regard to me.
He is sensible of a like interest in the regulation of his conduct. When this common sense of interest is mutually express'd, and is known to both, it produces a suitable resolution
and behaviour. And this may properly enough be call'd a
convention or agreement betwixt us, tho' without the interposition of a promise; since the actions of each of us have a
reference to those of the other, and are perform'd upon the
supposition, that something is to be perform'd on the other
part. Two men, who pull the oars of a boat, do it by an
agreement or convention, tho' they have never given promises
to each other. Nor is the rule concerning the stability of
possession the less deriv'd from human conventions, that it
arises gradually, and acquires force by a slow progression,
and by our repeated experience of the inconveniences of
transgressing it. On the contrary, this experience assures
us still more, that the sense of interest has become common
to all our fellows, and gives us a confidence of the future
regularity of their conduct: And 'tis only on the expectation
of this, that our moderation and abstinence are founded. In
like manner are languages gradually establish'd by human
conventions without any promise. In like manner do gold
and silver become the common measures of exchange, and are
esteem'd sufficient payment for what is of a hundred times
their value.

After this convention, concerning abstinence from the
possessions of others, is enter'd into, and every one has acquir'd a stability in his possessions, there immediately arise
the ideas of justice and injustice; as also those of *property*,
right, and *obligation*. The latter are altogether unintelligible
without first understanding the former. Our property is
nothing but those goods, whose constant possession is estab-

lish'd by the laws of society; that is, by the laws of justice.
Those, therefore, who make use of the words *property*,or *right*,
or *obligation*, before they have explain'd the origin of justice,
or even make use of them in that explication, are guilty of
a very gross fallacy, and can never reason upon any solid
foundation. A man's property is some object related to him.
This relation is not natural, but moral, and founded on
justice. 'Tis very preposterous, therefore, to imagine, that
we can have any idea of property, without fully comprehending the nature of justice, and shewing its origin in
the artifice and contrivance of men. The origin of justice
explains that of property. The same artifice gives rise to
both. As our first and most natural sentiment of morals is
founded on the nature of our passions, and gives the preference to ourselves and friends, above strangers, 'tis impossible there can be naturally any such thing as a fix'd
right or property, while the opposite passions of men impel
them in contrary directions, and are not restrain'd by any
convention or agreement.

No one can doubt, that the convention for the distinction
of property, and for the stability of possession, is of all circumstances the most necessary to the establishment of human
society, and that after the agreement for the fixing and
observing of this rule, there remains little or nothing to be
done towards settling a perfect harmony and concord. All
the other passions, beside this of interest, are either easily
restrain'd, or are not of such pernicious consequence, when
indulg'd. *Vanity* is rather to be esteem'd a social passion,
and a bond of union among men. *Pity* and *love* are to be
consider'd in the same light. And as to *envy* and *revenge*,
tho' pernicious, they operate only by intervals, and are
directed against particular persons, whom we consider as our
superiors or enemies. This avidity alone, of acquiring goods
and possessions for ourselves and our nearest friends, is insatiable, perpetual, universal, and directly destructive of
society. There scarce is any one, who is not actuated by it;
and there is no one, who has not reason to fear from it, when
it acts without any restraint, and gives way to its first and
most natural movements. So that upon the whole, we are
to esteem the difficulties in the establishment of society, to
be greater or less, according to those we encounter in regulating and restraining this passion.

'Tis certain, that no affection of the human mind has both
a sufficient force, and a proper direction to counter-balance
the love of gain, and render men fit members of society, by
making them abstain from the possessions of others.   Benevolence to strangers is too weak for this purpose ; and as to
the other passions, they rather inflame this avidity, when we
observe, that the larger our possessions are, the more ability
we have of gratifying all our appetites.   There is no passion,
therefore, capable of controlling the interested affection, but
the very affection itself, by an alteration of its direction.
Now this alteration must necessarily take place upon the
least reflection ; since 'tis evident, that the passion is much
better satisfy'd by its restraint, than by its liberty, and that
in preserving society, we make much greater advances in the
acquiring possessions, than in the solitary and forlorn condition, which must follow upon violence and an universal
licence.   The question, therefore, concerning the wickedness
or goodness of human nature, enters not in the least into
that other question concerning the origin of society ; nor is
there any thing to be consider'd but the degrees of men's
sagacity or folly.   For whether the passion of self-interest
be esteemed vicious or virtuous, 'tis all a case ; since itself
alone restrains it : So that if it be virtuous, men become
social by their virtue ; if vicious, their vice has the same
effect.

Now as 'tis by establishing the rule for the stability of
possession, that this passion restrains itself ; if that rule be
very abstruse, and of difficult invention ; society must be
esteem'd, in a manner, accidental, and the effect of many
ages.   But if it be found, that nothing can be more simple
and obvious than that rule ; that every parent, in order to
preserve peace among his children, must establish it ; and
that these first rudiments of justice must every day be im-
prov'd, as the society enlarges : If all this appear evident,
as it certainly must, we may conclude, that 'tis utterly
impossible for men to remain any considerable time in that
savage condition, which precedes society ; but that his very
first state and situation may justly be esteem'd social.   This,
however, hinders not, but that philosophers may, if they
please, extend their reasoning to the suppos'd *state of nature*;
provided they allow it to be a mere philosophical fiction,
which never had, and never cou'd have any reality.   Human

nature being compos'd of two principal parts, which are requisite in all its actions, the affections and understanding; 'tis certain, that the blind motions of the former, without the direction of the latter, incapacitate men for society: And it may be allow'd us to consider separately the effects, that result from the separate operations of these two component parts of the mind. The same liberty may be permitted to moral, which is allow'd to natural philosophers; and 'tis very usual with the latter to consider any motion as compounded and consisting of two parts separate from each other, tho' at the same time they acknowledge it to be in itself uncompounded and inseparable.

This *state of nature*, therefore, is to be regarded as a mere fiction, not unlike that of the *golden age*, which poets have invented; only with this difference, that the former is describ'd as full of war, violence and injustice; whereas the latter is painted out to us, as the most charming and most peaceable condition, that can possibly be imagin'd. The seasons, in that first age of nature, were so temperate, if we may believe the poets, that there was no necessity for men to provide themselves with cloaths and houses as a security against the violence of heat and cold. The rivers flow'd with wine and milk: The oaks yielded honey; and nature spontaneously produc'd her greatest delicacies. Nor were these the chief advantages of that happy age. The storms and tempests were not alone remov'd from nature; but those more furious tempests were unknown to human breasts, which now cause such uproar, and engender such confusion. Avarice, ambition, cruelty, selfishness, were never heard of: Cordial affection, compassion, sympathy, were the only movements, with which the human mind was yet acquainted. Even the distinction of *mine* and *thine* was banish'd from that happy race of mortals, and carry'd with them the very notions of property and obligation, justice and injustice.

This, no doubt, is to be regarded as an idle fiction; but yet deserves our attention, because nothing can more evidently shew the origin of those virtues, which are the subjects of our present enquiry. I have already observ'd, that justice takes its rise from human conventions; and that these are intended as a remedy to some inconveniences, which proceed from the concurrence of certain *qualities* of the human mind with the *situation* of external objects. The qualities of the mind are *selfishness* and *limited generosity*: And the situation of external objects is their *easy change*, join'd to their *scarcity* in comparison of the wants and desires of men. But however philosophers may have been bewilder'd in those speculations, poets have been guided more infallibly, by a certain taste or common instinct, which in most kinds of reasoning goes farther than any of that art and philosophy, with which we have been yet acquainted. They easily perceiv'd, if every man had a tender regard for another, or if nature supplied abundantly all our wants and desires, that the jealousy of interest, which justice supposes, could no longer have place; nor would there be any occasion for those distinctions and limits of property and possession, which at present are in use among mankind. Encrease to a sufficient degree the benevolence of men, or the bounty of nature, and you render justice useless, by supplying its place with much nobler virtues, and more valuable blessings. The selfishness of men is animated by the few possessions we have, in proportion to our wants; and 'tis to restrain this selfishness, that men have been oblig'd to separate themselves from the community, and to distinguish betwixt their own goods and those of others.

Nor need we have recourse to the fictions of poets to learn this; but beside the reason of the thing, may discover the same truth by common experience and observation. 'Tis easy to remark, that a cordial affection renders all things common among friends; and that married people in particular mutually lose their property, and are unacquainted with the *mine* and *thine*, which are so necessary, and yet cause such disturbance in human society. The same effect arises from any alteration in the circumstances of mankind; as when there is such a plenty of any thing as satisfies all the desires of men: In which case the distinction of property is entirely lost, and every thing remains in common. This we may observe with regard to air and water, tho' the most valuable of all external objects; and may easily conclude, that if men were supplied with every thing in the same abundance, or if *every one* had the same affection and tender regard for *every one* as for himself; justice and injustice would be equally unknown among mankind.

Here then is a proposition, which, I think, may be regarded as certain, *that 'tis only from the selfishness and confin'd gene-*

SECT
II.

Of the
origin of
justice and
property.

rosity of men, along with the scanty provision nature has made for his wants, that justice derives its origin. If we look backward we shall find, that this proposition bestows an additional force on some of those observations, which we have already made on this subject.

First, we may conclude from it, that a regard to public interest, or a strong extensive benevolence, is not our first and original motive for the observation of the rules of justice; since 'tis allow'd, that if men were endow'd with such a benevolence, these rules would never have been dreamt of.

Secondly, we may conclude from the same principle, that the sense of justice is not founded on reason, or on the discovery of certain connexions and relations of ideas, which are eternal, immutable, and universally obligatory. For since it is confest, that such an alteration as that above-mention'd, in the temper and circumstances of mankind, wou'd entirely alter our duties and obligations, 'tis necessary upon the common system, *that the sense of virtue is deriv'd from reason,* to shew the change which this must produce in the relations and ideas. But 'tis evident, that the only cause, why the extensive generosity of man, and the perfect abundance of every thing, wou'd destroy the very idea of justice, is because they render it useless; and that, on the other hand, his confin'd benevolence, and his necessitous condition, give rise to that virtue, only by making it requisite to the publick interest, and to that of every individual. 'Twas therefore a concern for our own, and the publick interest, which made us establish the laws of justice; and nothing can be more certain, than that it is not any relation of ideas, which gives us this concern, but our impressions and sentiments, without which every thing in nature is perfectly indifferent to us, and can never in the least affect us. The sense of justice, therefore, is not founded on our ideas, but on our impressions.

Thirdly, we may farther confirm the foregoing proposition, *that those impressions, which give rise to this sense of justice, are not natural to the mind of man, but arise from artifice and human conventions.* For since any considerable alteration of temper and circumstances destroys equally justice and injustice; and since such an alteration has an effect only by changing our own and the publick interest; it follows, that the first establishment of the rules of justice depends on these different interests. But if men pursu'd the publick interest naturally, and with a hearty affection, they wou'd never have dream'd of restraining each other by these rules; and if they pursu'd their own interest, without any precaution, they wou'd run head-long into every kind of injustice and violence. These rules, therefore, are artificial, and seek their end in an oblique and indirect manner; nor is the interest, which gives rise to them, of a kind that cou'd be pursu'd by the natural and inartificial passions of men.

To make this more evident, consider, that tho' the rules of justice are establish'd merely by interest, their connexion with interest is somewhat singular, and is different from what may be observ'd on other occasions. A single act of justice is frequently contrary to *public interest*; and were it to stand alone, without being follow'd by other acts, may, in itself, be very prejudicial to society. When a man of merit, of a beneficent disposition, restores a great fortune to a miser, or a seditious bigot, he has acted justly and laudably, but the public is a real sufferer. Nor is every single act of justice, consider'd apart, more conducive to private interest, than to public; and 'tis easily conceiv'd how a man may impoverish himself by a signal instance of integrity, and have reason to wish, that with regard to that single act, the laws of justice were for a moment suspended in the universe. But however single acts of justice may be contrary, either to public or private interest, 'tis certain, that the whole plan or scheme is highly conducive, or indeed absolutely requisite, both to the support of society, and the well-being of every individual. 'Tis impossible to separate the good from the ill. Property must be stable, and must be fix'd by general rules. Tho' in one instance the public be a sufferer, this momentary ill is amply compensated by the steady prosecution of the rule, and by the peace and order, which it establishes in society. And even every individual person must find himself a gainer, on ballancing the account; since, without justice, society must immediately dissolve, and every one must fall into that savage and solitary condition, which is infinitely worse than the worst situation that can possibly be suppos'd in society. When therefore men have had experience enough to observe, that whatever may be the consequence of any single act of justice, perform'd by a single person, yet the whole system of actions, concurr'd in by the whole society, is infinitely advantageous to the whole, and to every part; it is not long before justice and property take place. Every member of society is sensible of this interest: Every one expresses this sense to his fellows, along with the resolution he has taken of squaring his actions by it, on condition that others will do the same. No more is requisite to induce any one of them to perform an act of justice, who has the first opportunity. This becomes an example to others. And thus justice establishes itself by a kind of convention or agreement; that is, by a sense of interest, suppos'd to be common to all, and where every single act is perform'd in expectation that others are to perform the like. Without such a convention, no one wou'd ever have dream'd, that there was such a virtue as justice, or have been induc'd to conform his actions to it. Taking any single act, my justice may be pernicious in every respect; and 'tis only upon the supposition, that others are to imitate my example, that I can be induc'd to embrace that virtue; since nothing but this combination can render justice advantageous, or afford me any motives to conform myself to its rules.

We come now to the *second* question we propos'd, *viz. Why we annex the idea of virtue to justice, and of vice to injustice.* This question will not detain us long after the principles, which we have already establish'd. All we can say of it at present will be dispatch'd in a few words: And for farther satisfaction, the reader must wait till we come to the *third* part of this book. The *natural* obligation to justice, *viz.* interest, has been fully explain'd; but as to the *moral* obligation, or the sentiment of right and wrong, 'twill first be requisite to examine the natural virtues, before we can give a full and satisfactory account of it.

After men have found by experience, that their selfishness and confin'd generosity, acting at their liberty, totally incapacitate them for society; and at the same time have observ'd, that society is necessary to the satisfaction of those very passions, they are naturally induc'd to lay themselves under the restraint of such rules, as may render their commerce more safe and commodious. To the imposition then, and observance of these rules, both in general, and in every particular instance, they are at first induc'd only by a regard to interest; and this motive, on the first formation of society, is sufficiently strong and forcible. But when society has

become numerous, and has encreas'd to a tribe or nation, this
interest is more remote; nor do men so readily perceive, that
disorder and confusion follow upon every breach of these
rules, as in a more narrow and contracted society. But tho'
in our own actions we may frequently lose sight of that interest, which we have in maintaining order, and may follow
a lesser and more present interest, we never fail to observe
the prejudice we receive, either mediately or immediately,
from the injustice of others; as not being in that case either
blinded by passion, or byass'd by any contrary temptation.
Nay when the injustice is so distant from us, as no way to
affect our interest, it still displeases us; because we consider
it as prejudicial to human society, and pernicious to every one
that approaches the person guilty of it. We partake of their
uneasiness by *sympathy*, and as every thing, which gives
uneasiness in human actions, upon the general survey, is
call'd Vice, and whatever produces satisfaction, in the same
manner, is denominated Virtue, this is the reason why
the sense of moral good and evil follows upon justice and
injustice. And tho' this sense, in the present case, be deriv'd
only from contemplating the actions of others, yet we fail
not to extend it even to our own actions. The *general rule*
reaches beyond those instances, from which it arose; while
at the same time we naturally *sympathize* with others in the
sentiments they entertain of us. *Thus self-interest is the
original motive to the* establishment *of justice*: *but a* sympathy
with public interest is the source of the moral approbation,
which attends that virtue.[1]

Tho' this progress of the sentiments be *natural*, and even
necessary, 'tis certain, that it is here forwarded by the artifice
of politicians, who, in order to govern men more easily,
and preserve peace in human society, have endeavour'd to
produce an esteem for justice, and an abhorrence of injustice.
This, no doubt, must have its effect; but nothing can be
more evident, than that the matter has been carry'd too far
by certain writers on morals, who seem to have employ'd
their utmost efforts to extirpate all sense of virtue from
among mankind. Any artifice of politicians may assist
nature in the producing of those sentiments, which she suggests to us, and may even on some occasions, produce alone
an approbation or esteem for any particular action; but 'tis

SECT
II

Of the
origin of
justice and
property.

[1 Introd sect. 58 and ff —Ed.]

impossible it should be the sole cause of the distinction we make betwixt vice and virtue. For if nature did not aid us in this particular, 'twou'd be in vain for politicians to talk of *honourable* or *dishonourable, praiseworthy* or *blameable.* These words wou'd be perfectly unintelligible, and wou'd no more have any idea annex'd to them, than if they were of a tongue perfectly unknown to us. The utmost politicians can perform, is, to extend the natural sentiments beyond their original bounds; but still nature must furnish the materials, and give us some notion of moral distinctions.

As publick praise and blame encrease our esteem for justice; so private education and instruction contribute to the same effect. For as parents easily observe, that a man is the more useful, both to himself and others, the greater degree of probity and honour he is endow'd with; and that those principles have greater force, when custom and education assist interest and reflection: For these reasons they are induc'd to inculcate on their children, from their earliest infancy, the principles of probity, and teach them to regard the observance of those rules, by which society is maintain'd, as worthy and honourable, and their violation as base and infamous. By this means the sentiments of honour may take root in their tender minds, and acquire such firmness and solidity, that they may fall little short of those principles, which are the most essential to our natures, and the most deeply radicated in our internal constitution.

What farther contributes to encrease their solidity, is the interest of our reputation, after the opinion, *that a merit or demerit attends justice or injustice,* is once firmly establish'd among mankind. There is nothing, which touches us more nearly than our reputation, and nothing on which our reputation more depends than our conduct, with relation to the property of others. For this reason, every one, who has any regard to his character, or who intends to live on good terms with mankind, must fix an inviolable law to himself, never, by any temptation, to be induc'd to violate those principles, which are essential to a man of probity and honour.

I shall make only one observation before I leave this subject, *viz.* that tho' I assert, that in the *state of nature,* or that imaginary state, which preceded society, there be neither justice nor injustice, yet I assert not, that it was allowable, in such a state, to violate the property of others. I only maintain, that there was no such thing as property; and consequently cou'd be no such thing as justice or injustice. I shall have occasion to make a similar reflection with regard to *promises*, when I come to treat of them; and I hope this reflection, when duly weigh'd, will suffice to remove all odium from the foregoing opinions, with regard to justice and injustice.

SECT. III.—*Of the Rules, which determine Property.*

Tho' the establishment of the rule, concerning the stability of possession, be not only useful, but even absolutely necessary to human society, it can never serve to any purpose, while it remains in such general terms. Some method must be shewn, by which we may distinguish what particular goods are to be assign'd to each particular person, while the rest of mankind are excluded from their possession and enjoyment. Our next business, then, must be to discover the reasons which modify this general rule, and fit it to the common use and practice of the world.

'Tis obvious, that those reasons are not deriv'd from any utility or advantage, which either the *particular* person or the public may reap from his enjoyment of any *particular* goods, beyond what wou'd result from the possession of them by any other person. 'Twere better, no doubt, that every one were possess'd of what is most suitable to him, and proper for his use: But besides, that this relation of fitness may be common to several at once, 'tis liable to so many controversies, and men are so partial and passionate in judging of these controversies, that such a loose and uncertain rule wou'd be absolutely incompatible with the peace of human society. The convention concerning the stability of possession is enter'd into, in order to cut off all occasions of discord and contention; and this end wou'd never be attain'd, were we allow'd to apply this rule differently in every particular case, according to every particular utility, which might be discover'd in such an application. Justice, in her decisions, never regards the fitness or unfitness of objects to particular persons, but conducts herself by more extensive views. Whether a man be generous, or a miser, he is equally well receiv'd by her, and obtains with the same facility a decision in his favour, even for what is entirely useless to him.

It follows, therefore, that the general rule, *that possession
must be stable,* is not apply'd by particular judgments, but by
other general rules, which must extend to the whole society,
and be inflexible either by spite or favour. To illustrate this,
I propose the following instance. I first consider men in
their savage and solitary condition; and suppose, that being
sensible of the misery of that state, and foreseeing the
advantages that wou'd result from society, they seek each
other's company, and make an offer of mutual protection and
assistance. I also suppose, that they are endow'd with such
sagacity as immediately to perceive, that the chief impediment
to this project of society and partnership lies in the avidity
and selfishness of their natural temper; to remedy which,
they enter into a convention for the stability of possession,
and for mutual restraint and forbearance. I am sensible,
that this method of proceeding is not altogether natural;
but besides that I here only suppose those reflections to be
form'd at once, which in fact arise insensibly and by degrees;
besides this, I say, 'tis very possible, that several persons,
being by different accidents separated from the societies, to
which they formerly belong'd, may be oblig'd to form a new
society among themselves; in which case they are entirely
in the situation above-mention'd

'Tis evident, then, that their first difficulty, in this situation, after the general convention for the establishment of
society, and for the constancy of possession, is, how to separate their possessions, and assign to each his particular
portion, which he must for the future inalterably enjoy.
This difficulty will not detain them long; but it must immediately occur to them, as the most natural expedient, that
every one continue to enjoy what he is at present master of,
and that property or constant possession be conjoin'd to the
immediate possession. Such is the effect of custom, that it
not only reconciles us to anything we have long enjoy'd, but
even gives us an affection for it, and makes us prefer it to
other objects, which may be more valuable, but are less
known to us. What has long lain under our eye, and has
often been employed to our advantage, *that* we are always the
most unwilling to part with; but can easily live without
possessions, which we never have enjoy'd, and are not accustom'd to. 'Tis evident, therefore, that men wou'd easily
acquiesce in this expedient, *that every one continue to enjoy*

what he is at present possess'd of; and this is the reason, why they wou'd so naturally agree in preferring it.[1]

But we may observe, that tho' the rule of the assignment of property to the present possessor be natural, and by that means useful, yet its utility extends not beyond the first formation of society; nor wou'd anything be more pernicious, than the constant observance of it; by which restitution

[1] No questions in philosophy are more difficult, than when a number of causes present themselves for the same phænomenon, to determine which is the principal and predominant There seldom is any very precise argument to fix our choice, and men must be contented to be guided by a kind of taste or fancy, arising from analogy, and a comparison of similar instances Thus, in the present case, there are, no doubt, motives of public interest for most of the rules, which determine property, but still I suspect, that these rules are principally fix'd by the imagination, or the more frivolous properties of our thought and conception I shall continue to explain these causes, leaving it to the reader's choice, whether he will prefer those deriv'd from publick utility, or those deriv'd from the imagination. We shall begin with the right of the present possessor.

'Tis a quality, which (a) I have already observ'd in human nature, that when two objects appear in a close relation to each other, the mind is apt to ascribe to them any additional relation, in order to compleat the union, and this inclination is so strong, as often to make us run into errors (such as that of the conjunction of thought and matter) if we find that they can serve to that purpose Many of our impressions are incapable of place or local position, and yet those very impressions we suppose to have a local conjunction with the impressions of sight and touch, merely because they are conjoin'd by causation, and are already united in the imagination Since, therefore, we can feign a new relation, and even an absurd one, in order to compleat any union, 'twill easily be imagin'd, that if there be any relations, which depend on the mind, 'twill readily conjoin them to any preceding relation,

and unite, by a new bond, such objects as have already an union in the fancy Thus for instance, we never fail, in our arrangement of bodies, to place those which are *resembling* in *contiguity* to each other, or at least in *correspondent* points of view . because we feel a satisfaction in joining the relation of contiguity to that of resemblance, or the resemblance of situation to that of qualities And this is easily accounted for from the known properties of human nature When the mind is determin'd to join certain objects but undetermin'd in its choice of the particular objects, it naturally turns its eye to such as are related together They are already united in the mind They present themselves at the same time to the conception , and instead of requiring any new reason for their conjunction, it wou'd require a very powerful reason to make us over-look this natural affinity This we shall have occasion to explain more fully afterwards, when we come to treat of *beauty* In the mean time, we may content ourselves with observing, that the same love of order and uniformity, which arranges the books in a library, and the chairs in a parlour, contribute to the formation of society, and to the well-being of mankind, by modifying the general rule concerning the stability of possession And as property forms a relation betwixt a person and an object, 'tis natural to found it on some preceding relation; and as property is nothing but a constant possession, secur'd by the laws of society, 'tis natural to add it to the present possession, which is a relation that resembles it For this also has its influence. If it be natural to conjoin all sorts of relations, 'tis more so, to conjoin such relations as are resembling, and are related together

---

(a) Book I. Part IV. Sect. 5.

wou'd be excluded, and every injustice wou'd be authoriz'd
and rewarded.   We must, therefore, seek for some other circumstance, that may give rise to property after society is
once establish'd ; and of this kind, I find four most considerable, *viz.* Occupation, Prescription, Accession, and Succession.   We shall briefly examine each of these, beginning
with *Occupation*.

The possession of all external goods is changeable and
uncertain ; which is one of the most considerable impediments
to the establishment of society, and is the reason why, by
universal agreement, express or tacite, men restrain themselves by what we now call the rules of justice and equity.
The misery of the condition, which precedes this restraint, is
the cause why we submit to that remedy as quickly as possible ; and this affords us an easy reason, why we annex the
idea of property to the first possession, or to *occupation*.
Men are unwilling to leave property in suspence, even for
the shortest time, or open the least door to violence and disorder.   To which we may add, that the first possession
always engages the attention most ; and did we neglect it,
there wou'd be no colour of reason for assigning property to
any succeeding possession.[1]

There remains nothing, but to determine exactly, what is
meant by possession ; and this is not so easy as may at first
sight be imagin'd.   We are said to be in possession of anything, not only when we immediately touch it, but also when
we are so situated with respect to it, as to have it in our
power to use it; and may move, alter, or destroy it, according
to our present pleasure or advantage.   This relation, then,
is a species of cause and effect ; and as property is nothing
but a stable possession, deriv'd from the rules of justice, or
the conventions of men, 'tis to be consider'd as the same
species of relation.   But here we may observe, that as the
power of using any object becomes more or less certain,

[1] Some philosophers account for the
right of occupation, by saying, that
every one has a property in his own
labour , and when he joins that labour
to any thing, it gives him the property
of the whole   But, 1 There are several
kinds of occupation, where we cannot
be said to join our labour to the object
we acquire   As when we possess a
meadow by grazing our cattle upon it

2 This accounts for the matter by
means of *accession* , which is taking a
needless circuit 3 We cannot be said
to join our labour to any thing but in a
figurative sense Properly speaking, we
only make an alteration on it by our
labour   This forms a relation betwixt
us and the object , and thence arises the
property, according to the preceding
principles.

according as the interruptions we may meet with are more or less probable; and as this probability may increase by insensible degrees; 'tis in many cases impossible to determine when possession begins or ends; nor is there any certain standard, by which we can decide such controversies. A wild boar, that falls into our snares, is deem'd to be in our possession, if it be impossible for him to escape. But what do we mean by impossible? How do we separate this impossibility from an improbability? And how distinguish that exactly from a probability? Mark the precise limits of the one and the other, and shew the standard, by which we may decide all disputes that may arise, and, as we find by experience, frequently do arise upon this subject.[1]

[1] If we seek a solution of these difficulties in reason and public interest, we never shall find satisfaction, and if we look for it in the imagination, 'tis evident, that the qualities, which operate upon that faculty, run so insensibly and gradually into each other, that 'tis impossible to give them any precise bounds or termination. The difficulties on this head must encrease, when we consider, that our judgment alters very sensibly, according to the subject, and that the same power and proximity will be deem'd possession in one case, which is not esteem'd such in another. A person, who has hunted a hare to the last degree of weariness, wou'd look upon it as an injustice for another to rush in before him, and seize his prey. But the same person, advancing to pluck an apple, that hangs within his reach, has no reason to complain, if another, more alert, passes him, and takes possession. What is the reason of this difference, but that immobility, not being natural to the hare, but the effect of industry, forms in that case a strong relation with the hunter, which is wanting in the other? Here then it appears, that a certain and infallible power of enjoyment, without touch or some other sensible relation, often produces not property. And I farther observe, that a sensible relation, without any present power, is sometimes sufficient to give a title to any object. The sight of a thing is seldom a considerable relation, and is only regarded as such, when the object is hidden, or very obscure, in which case we find, that the view alone conveys a property, according to that maxim, *that even a whole continent belongs to the nation, which first discover'd it.* 'Tis however remarkable, that both in the case of discovery and that of possession, the first discoverer and possessor must join to the relation an intention of rendering himself proprietor, otherwise the relation will not have its effect, and that because the connexion in our fancy betwixt the property and the relation is not so great, but that it requires to be help'd by such an intention.

From all these circumstances, 'tis easy to see how perplex'd many questions may become concerning the acquisition of property by occupation; and the least effort of thought may present us with instances, which are not susceptible of any reasonable decision. If we prefer examples, which are real, to such as are feign'd, we may consider the following one, which is to be met with in almost every writer, that has treated of the laws of nature. Two *Grecian* colonies, leaving their native country, in search of new seats, were inform'd that a city near them was deserted by its inhabitants. To know the truth of this report, they dispatch'd at once two messengers, one from each colony; who finding on their approach, that their information was true, begun a race together with an intention to take possession of the city, each of them for his countrymen. One of these messengers, finding that he was not an equal match for the other, launch'd his spear at the gates of the city, and was so fortunate as to fix it there before the arrival of his companion. This produc'd a dispute betwixt

But such disputes may not only arise concerning the real existence of property and possession, but also concerning their extent; and these disputes are often susceptible of no decision, or can be decided by no other faculty than the imagination. A person who lands on the shore of a small island, that is desart and uncultivated, is deem'd its possessor from the very first moment, and acquires the property of the whole; because the object is there bounded and circumscrib'd in the fancy, and at the same time is proportion'd to the new possessor. The same person landing on a desart island, as large as *Great Britain*, extends his property no farther than his immediate possession; tho' a numerous colony are esteem'd the proprietors of the whole from the instant of their debarkment.

But it often happens, that the title of first possession becomes obscure thro' time; and that 'tis impossible to determine many controversies, which may arise concerning it. In that case long possession or *prescription* naturally takes place, and gives a person a sufficient property in anything he enjoys. The nature of human society admits not of any great accuracy; nor can we always remount to the first origin of things, in order to determine their present condition. Any considerable space of time sets objects at such a distance, that they seem, in a manner, to lose their reality, and have as little influence on the mind, as if they never had been in being. A man's title, that is clear and certain at present, will seem obscure and doubtful fifty years hence, even tho' the facts, on which it is founded, shou'd be

the two colonies, which of them was the proprietor of the empty city, and this dispute still subsists among philosophers For my part I find the dispute impossible to be decided, and that because the whole question hangs upon the fancy which in this case is not possess'd of any precise or determinate standard, upon which it can give sentence To make this evident, let us consider that if these two persons had been simply members of the colonies, and not messengers or deputies, their actions wou'd not have been of any consequence, since in that case their relation to the colonies wou'd have been but feeble and imperfect Add to this that nothing determin'd them to run to the gates rather than the walls

or any other part of the city, but that the gates, being the most obvious and remarkable part satisfy the fancy best in taking them for the whole, as we find by the poets, who frequently draw their images and metaphors from them. Besides we may consider, that the touch or contact of the one messenger is not properly possession, no more than the piercing the gates with a spear; but only forms a relation, and there is a relation, in the other case, equally obvious, tho' not, perhaps, of equal force Which of these relations, then, conveys a right and property, or whether any of them be sufficient for that effect, I leave to the decision of such as are wiser than myself prov'd with the greatest evidence and certainty. The same facts have not the same influence after so long an interval of time. And this may be receiv'd as a convincing argument for our preceding doctrine with regard to property and justice. Possession during a long tract of time conveys a title to any object. But as 'tis certain, that, however every thing be produc'd in time, there is nothing real, that is produc'd by time; it follows, that property being produc'd by time, is not anything real in the objects, but is the offspring of the sentiments, on which alone time is found to have any influence.[1]

We acquire the property of objects by *accession*, when they are connected in an intimate manner with objects that are already our property, and at the same time are inferior to them. Thus the fruits of our garden, the offspring of our cattle, and the work of our slaves, are all of them esteem'd our property, even before possession. Where objects are connected together in the imagination, they are apt to be put on the same footing, and are commonly suppos'd to be endow'd with the same qualities. We readily pass from one to the other, and make no difference in our judgments concerning them; especially if the latter be inferior to the former.[2]

[1] Present possession is plainly a relation betwixt a person and an object, but it is not sufficient to counter-ballance the relation of first possession, unless the former be long and uninterrupted: In which case the relation is encreas'd on the side of the present possession, by the extent of time, and diminish'd on that of first possession, by the distance. This change in the relation produces a consequent change in the property.

[2] This source of property can never be explain'd but from the imaginations, and one may affirm, that the causes are here unmix'd. We shall proceed to explain them more particularly, and illustrate them by examples from common life and experience.

It has been observ'd above, that the mind has a natural propensity to join relations, especially resembling ones, and finds a kind of fitness and uniformity in such an union. From this propensity are deriv'd these laws of nature, *that upon the first formation of society property always follows the present possession*, and afterwards, *that it arises from first or from long possession*. Now we may easily observe, that relation is not confin'd merely to one degree, but that from an object, that is related to us, we acquire a relation to every other object, which is related to it, and so on, till the thought loses the chain by too long a progress. However the relation may weaken by each remove, 'tis not immediately destroy'd, but frequently connects two objects by means of an intermediate one, which is related to both. And this principle is of such force as to give rise to the right of *accession*, and causes us to acquire the property not only of such objects as we are immediately possess'd of, but also of such as are closely connected with them.

Suppose a *German*, a *Frenchman*, and a *Spaniard* to come into a room, where there are plac'd upon the table three bottles of wine, *Rhenish*, *Burgundy* and *Port*, and suppose they shou'd fall a quarrelling about the division of them; a person, who was chosen for umpire,

The right of *succession* is a very natural one, from the pre-sum'd consent of the parent or near relation, and from the general interest of mankind, which requires, that men's pos-

wou'd naturally, to shew his impartiality, give every one the product of his own country. And this from a principle, which, in some measure, is the source of those laws of nature, that ascribe pro-perty to occupation, prescription and accession.

In all these cases, and particularly that of accession, there is first a *natural* union betwixt the idea of the person and that of the object, and afterwards a new and *moral* union produc'd by that right or property, which we ascribe to the person. But here there occurs a difficulty, which merits our attention, and may afford us an opportunity of putting to tryal that singular method of reasoning, which has been employ'd on the present subject. I have already observ'd, that the imagination passes with greater facility from little to great, than from great to little; and that the transition of ideas is always easier and smoother in the former case than in the latter. Now as the right of accession arises from the easy transition of ideas, by which related objects are connected together, it shou'd naturally be imagin'd, that the right of accession must encrease in strength, in proportion as the transi-tion of ideas is perform'd with greater facility. It may, therefore, be thought, that when we have acquir'd the property of any small object, we shall readily consider any great object related to it as an accession, and as belonging to the proprietor of the small one, since the transition is in that case very easy from the small object to the great one, and shou'd connect them together in the closest manner. But in fact the case is always found to be otherwise. The em-pire of *Great Britain* seems to draw along with it the dominion of the *Orkneys*, the *Hebrides*, the isle of *Man*, and the isle of *Wight*, but the authority over those lesser islands does not naturally imply any title to *Great Britain*. In short, a small object naturally follows a great one as its accession; but a great one is never suppos'd to belong to the proprietor of a small one related to it, merely on account of that pro-perty and relation. Yet in this latter case the transition of ideas is smoother from the proprietor to the small object

which is his property, and from the small object to the great one, than in the former case from the proprietor to the great object, and from the great one to the small. It may therefore be thought, that these phænomena are ob-jections to the foregoing hypothesis, *that the ascribing of property to acces-sion is nothing but an effect of the rela-tions of ideas, and of the smooth transi-tion of the imagination.*

'Twill be easy to solve this objection, if we consider the agility and unsteadi-ness of the imagination, with the dif-ferent views, in which it is continually placing its objects. When we attribute to a person a property in two objects, we do not always pass from the person to one object, and from that to the other related to it. The objects being here to be consider'd as the property of the person, we are apt to join them to-gether, and place them in the same light. Suppose, therefore, a great and a small object to be related together; if a per-son be strongly related to the great ob-ject, he will likewise be strongly related to both the objects, consider'd together, because he is related to the most con-siderable part. On the contrary, if he be only related to the small object, he will not be strongly related to both, consider'd together, since his relation lies only with the most trivial part, which is not apt to strike us in any great degree, when we consider the whole. And this is the reason, why small objects become accessions to great ones, and not great to small.

'Tis the general opinion of philoso-phers and civilians, that the sea is in-capable of becoming the property of any nation; and that because 'tis im-possible to take possession of it, or form any such distinct relation with it as may be the foundation of property. Where this reason ceases, property im-mediately takes place. Thus the most strenuous advocates for the liberty of the seas universally allow, that friths and bays naturally belong as an acces-sion to the proprietors of the surround-ing continent. These have properly no more bond or union with the land, than the *Pacific* ocean wou'd have; but having an union in the fancy, and being sessions shou'd pass to those, who are dearest to them, in order to render them more industrious and frugal. Perhaps these causes are seconded by the influence of *relation*, or the

at the same time *inferior*, they are of course regarded as an accession

The property of rivers, by the laws of most nations, and by the natural turn of our thought, is attributed to the proprietors of their banks, excepting such vast rivers as the *Rhine* or the *Danube*, which seem too large to the imagination to follow as an accession the property of the neighbouring fields. Yet even these rivers are consider'd as the property of that nation, thro' whose dominions they run, the idea of a nation being of a suitable bulk to correspond with them, and bear them such a relation in the fancy

The accessions, which are made to lands bordering upon rivers, follow the land, say the civilians, provided it be made by what they call *alluvion*, that is, insensibly and imperceptibly, which are circumstances that mightily assist the imagination in the conjunction. Where there is any considerable portion torn at once from one bank, and join'd to another, it becomes not his property, whose land it falls on, till it unite with the land, and till the trees or plants have spread their roots into both Before that, the imagination does not sufficiently join them

There are other cases, which somewhat resemble this of accession, but which at the bottom, are considerably different, and merit our attention. Of this kind is the conjunction of the properties of different persons, after such a manner as not to admit of *separation* The question is, to whom the united mass must belong.

Where this conjunction is of such a nature as to admit of *division*, but not of *separation* the decision is natural and easy The whole mass must be suppos'd to be common betwixt the proprietors of the several parts, and afterwards must be divided according to the proportions of these parts But here I cannot forbear taking notice of a remarkable subtilty of the *Roman* law, in distinguishing betwixt *confusion* and *commixtion* Confusion is an union of two bodies, such as different liquors, where the parts become entirely undistinguishable Commixtion is the

blending of two bodies, such as two bushels of corn, where the parts remain separate in an obvious and visible manner As in the latter case the imagination discovers not so entire an union as in the former, but is able to trace and preserve a distinct idea of the property of each, this is the reason, why the *civil* law, tho' it establish'd an entire community in the case of *confusion*, and after that a proportional division, yet in the case of *commixtion*, supposes each of the proprietors to maintain a distinct right, however necessity may at last force them to submit to the same division

Quod si frumentum Titii frumento tuo mistum fuerit siquidem ex voluntate vestra, commune est quia singula corpora, id est, singula grana, quæ cujusque propria fuerunt, ex consensu vestro communicata sunt. Quod si casu id mistum fuerit, vel Titius id miscuerit sine tua voluntate, non videtur id commune esse, quia singula corpora in sua substantia durant. Sed nec magis istis casibus commune sit frumentum quam grex intelligitur esse communis, si pecora Titii tuis pecoribus mista fuerint Sed si ab alterutro vestrûm totum id frumentum retineatur, in rem quidem actio pro modo frumenti cujusque competit Arbitrio autem judicis, ut ipse æstimet quale cujusque frumentum fuerit. Inst. Lib. II Tit 1 § 28

Where the properties of two persons are united after such a manner as neither to admit of *division* nor *separation*, as when one builds a house on another's ground, in that case, the whole must belong to one of the proprietors And here I assert, that it naturally is conceiv'd to belong to the proprietor of the most considerable part For however the compound object may have a relation to two different persons, and carry our view at once to both of them, yet as the most considerable part principally engages our attention, and by the strict union draws the inferior along it, for this reason, the whole bears a relation to the proprietor of that part, and is regarded as his property. The only difficulty is, what we shall be pleas'd to call the most considerable part, and most attractive to the imagination.

association of ideas, by which we are naturally directed to consider the son after the parent's decease, and ascribe to him a title to his father's possessions. Those goods must become the property of some body: But *of whom* is the question. Here 'tis evident the person's children naturally present themselves to the mind; and being already connected to those possessions by means of their deceas'd parent, we are apt to connect them still farther by the relation of property. Of this there are many parallel instances.[1]

This quality depends on several different circumstances, which have little connexion with each other. One part of a compound object may become more considerable than another, either because it is more constant and durable, because it is of greater value, because it is more obvious and remarkable, because it is of greater extent, or because its existence is more separate and independent. 'Twill be easy to conceive that, as these circumstances may be conjoin'd and oppos'd in all the different ways, and according to all the different degrees, which can be imagin'd, there will result many cases, where the reasons on both sides are so equally ballanc'd, that 'tis impossible for us to give any satisfactory decision. Here then is the proper business of municipal laws, to fix what the principles of human nature have left undetermin'd.

The superficies yields to the soil, says the civil law. The writing to the paper. The canvas to the picture. These decisions do not well agree together, and are a proof of the contrariety of those principles, from which they are deriv'd.

But of all the questions of this kind the most curious is that, which for so many ages divided the disciples of *Proculus* and *Sabinus*. Suppose a person shou'd make a cup from the metal of another, or a ship from his wood, and suppose the proprietor of the metal or wood shou'd demand his goods, the question is, whether he acquires a title to the cup or ship. *Sabinus* maintain'd the affirmative, and asserted that the substance or matter is the foundation of all the qualities; that it is incorruptible and immortal, and therefore superior to the form, which is casual and dependent. On the other hand, *Proculus* observ'd, that the form is the most obvious and remarkable part, and that from it bodies are denominated of this

or that particular species. To which he might have added, that the matter or substance is in most bodies so fluctuating and uncertain, that 'tis utterly impossible to trace it in all its changes. For my part, I know not from what principles such a controversy can be certainly determin'd. I shall therefore content my self with observing, that the decision of *Trebonian* seems to me pretty ingenious; that the cup belongs to the proprietor of the metal, because it can be brought back to its first form: But that the ship belongs to the author of its form for a contrary reason: But however ingenious this reason may seem, it plainly depends upon the fancy, which by the possibility of such a reduction, finds a closer connexion and relation betwixt a cup and the proprietor of its metal, than betwixt a ship and the proprietor of its wood, where the substance is more fix'd and unalterable.

[1] In examining the different titles to authority in government, we shall meet with many reasons to convince us, that the right of succession depends, in a great measure, on the imagination. Mean while I shall rest contented with observing one example, which belongs to the present subject. Suppose that a person die without children, and that a dispute arises among his relations concerning his inheritance; 'tis evident, that if his riches be deriv'd partly from his father, partly from his mother, the most natural way of determining such a dispute, is, to divide his possessions, and assign each part to the family, from whence it is deriv'd. Now as the person is suppos'd to have been once the full and entire proprietor of those goods, I ask, what is it makes us find a certain equity and natural reason in this partition, except it be the imagination? His affection to these families does not depend upon his possessions

SECT. IV.—*Of the transference of property by consent.*

SECT.
IV.

Of the
transfer
ence of
property
by consent.

However useful, or even necessary, the stability of possession may be to human society, 'tis attended with very considerable inconveniences. The relation of fitness or suitableness ought never to enter into consideration, in distributing the properties of mankind; but we must govern ourselves by rules, which are more general in their application, and more free from doubt and uncertainty. Of this kind is *present* possession upon the first establishment of society; and afterwards *occupation, prescription, accession,* and *succession.* As these depend very much on chance, they must frequently prove contradictory both to men's wants and desires; and persons and possessions must often be very ill adjusted. This is a grand inconvenience, which calls for a remedy. To apply one directly, and allow every man to seize by violence what he judges to be fit for him, wou'd destroy society; and therefore the rules of justice seek some medium betwixt a rigid stability, and this changeable and uncertain adjustment. But there is no medium better than that obvious one, that possession and property shou'd always be stable, except when the proprietor consents to bestow them on some other person. This rule can have no ill consequence, in occasioning wars and dissentions; since the proprietor's consent, who alone is concern'd, is taken along in the alienation: And it may serve to many good purposes in adjusting property to persons. Different parts of the earth produce different commodities; and not only so, but different men both are by nature fitted for different employments, and attain to greater perfection in any one, when they confine themselves to it alone. All this requires a mutual exchange and commerce; for which reason the translation of property by consent is founded on a law of nature, as well as its stability without such a consent.

So far is determin'd by a plain utility and interest. But perhaps 'tis from more trivial reasons, that *delivery,* or a sensible transference of the object is commonly requir'd by civil laws, and also by the laws of nature, according to most authors, as a requisite circumstance in the translation of property. The property of an object, when taken for some-

for which reason his consent can never be presum'd precisely for such a partıtıon And as to the public interest, it seems not to be in the least concern'd on the one side or the other.

thing real, without any reference to morality, or the sentiments of the mind, is a quality perfectly insensible, and
even inconceivable; nor can we form any distinct notion,
either of its stability or translation. This imperfection of
our ideas is less sensibly felt with regard to its stability, as it
engages less our attention, and is easily past over by the
mind, without any scrupulous examination. But as the
translation of property from one person to another is a more
remarkable event, the defect of our ideas becomes more
sensible on that occasion, and obliges us to turn ourselves on
every side in search of some remedy. Now as nothing more
enlivens any idea than a present impression, and a relation
betwixt that impression and the idea; 'tis natural for us to
seek some false light from this quarter. In order to aid the
imagination in conceiving the transference of property, we
take the sensible object, and actually transfer its possession
to the person, on whom we wou'd bestow the property. The
suppos'd resemblance of the actions, and the presence of
this sensible delivery, deceive the mind, and make it fancy,
that it conceives the mysterious transition of the property.
And that this explication of the matter is just, appears
hence, that men have invented a *symbolical* delivery, to satisfy
the fancy, where the real one is impracticable. Thus the
giving the keys of a granary is understood to be the delivery
of the corn contain'd in it: The giving of stone and earth
represents the delivery of a mannor. This is a kind of
superstitious practice in civil laws, and in the laws of nature,
resembling the *Roman catholic* superstitions in religion. As
the *Roman catholics* represent the inconceivable mysteries of
the *Christian* religion, and render them more present to the
mind, by a taper, or habit, or grimace, which is suppos'd to
resemble them; so lawyers and moralists have run into like
inventions for the same reason, and have endeavour'd by
those means to satisfy themselves concerning the transference
of property by consent.

SECT. V.—*Of the obligation of promises.*

That the rule of morality, which enjoins the performance
of promises, is not *natural,* will sufficiently appear from these
two propositions, which I proceed to prove, viz. *that a promise wou'd not be intelligible, before human conventions had*

establish'd it; and *that even if it were intelligible, it wou'd not be attended with any moral obligation.*

I say, *first*, that a promise is not intelligible naturally, nor antecedent to human conventions; and that a man, unacquainted with society, could never enter into any engagements with another, even tho' they could perceive each other's thoughts by intuition. If promises be natural and intelligible, there must be some act of the mind attending these words, *I promise*; and on this act of the mind must the obligation depend. Let us, therefore, run over all the faculties of the soul, and see which of them is exerted in our promises.

The act of the mind, exprest by a promise, is not a *resolution* to perform any thing: For that alone never imposes any obligation. Nor is it a *desire* of such a performance: For we may bind ourselves without such a desire, or even with an aversion, declar'd and avow'd. Neither is it the *willing* of that action, which we promise to perform: For a promise always regards some future time, and the will has an influence only on present actions. It follows, therefore, that since the act of the mind, which enters into a promise, and produces its obligation, is neither the resolving, desiring, nor willing any particular performance, it must necessarily be the *willing* of that *obligation*, which arises from the promise. Nor is this only a conclusion of philosophy; but is entirely conformable to our common ways of thinking and of expressing ourselves, when we say that we are bound by our own consent, and that the obligation arises from our mere will and pleasure. The only question, then, is, whether there be not a manifest absurdity in supposing this act of the mind, and such an absurdity as no man cou'd fall into, whose ideas are not confounded with prejudice and the fallacious use of language.

All morality depends upon our sentiments; and when any action, or quality of the mind, pleases us *after a certain manner*, we say it is virtuous; and when the neglect, or non-performance of it, displeases us *after a like manner*, we say that we lie under an obligation to perform it. A change of the obligation supposes a change of the sentiment; and a creation of a new obligation supposes some new sentiment to arise. But 'tis certain we can naturally no more change our own sentiments, than the motions of the heavens; nor by a single act of our will, that is, by a promise, render any action agreeable or disagreeable, moral or immoral ; which, without that act, wou'd have produc'd contrary impressions, or have been endowed with different qualities. It wou'd be absurd, therefore, to will any new obligation, that is, any new sentiment of pain or pleasure ; nor is it possible, that men cou'd naturally fall into so gross an absurdity. A promise, therefore, is *naturally* something altogether unintelligible ; nor is there any act of the mind belonging to it.[1]

But, *secondly*, if there was any act of the mind belonging to it, it could not *naturally* produce any obligation. This appears evidently from the foregoing reasoning. A promise creates a new obligation. A new obligation supposes new sentiments to arise. The will never creates new sentiments. There could not naturally, therefore, arise any obligation from a promise, even supposing the mind could fall into the absurdity of willing that obligation.

The same truth may be prov'd still more evidently by that reasoning, which proved justice in general to be an artificial virtue. No action can be requir'd of us as our duty, unless there be implanted in human nature some actuating passion or motive, capable of producing the action. This motive cannot be the sense of duty. A sense of duty supposes an antecedent obligation : And where an action is not requir'd by any natural passion, it cannot be requir'd by any natural obligation ; since it may be omitted without proving any

---

[1] Were morality discoverable by reason, and not by sentiment, 'twou'd be still more evident, that promises cou'd make no alteration upon it. Morality is suppos'd to consist in relation. Every new imposition of morality therefore, must arise from some new relation of objects ; and consequently the will cou'd not produce *immediately* any change in morals, but cou'd have that effect only by producing a change upon the objects. But as the moral obligation of a promise is the pure effect of the will, without the least change in any part of the universe, it follows, that promises have no *natural* obligation.

Shou'd it be said, that this act of the will being in effect a new object, produces new relations and new duties, I wou'd answer, that this is a pure sophism, which may be detected by a very moderate share of accuracy and exactness. To will a new obligation, is to will a new relation of objects ; and therefore, if this new relation of objects were form'd by the volition itself, we shou'd in effect will the volition, which is plainly absurd and impossible. The will has here no object to which it cou'd tend, but must return upon itself *in infinitum*. The new obligation depends upon new relations. The new relations depend upon a new volition. The new volition has for object a new obligation, and consequently new relations, and consequently a new volition, which volition again has in view a new obligation, relation and volition, without any termination. 'Tis impossible, therefore, we cou'd ever will a new obligation, and consequently 'tis impossible the will cou'd ever accompany a promise, or produce a new obligation of morality.

defect or imperfection in the mind and temper, and conse-

quently without any vice. Now 'tis evident we have no
motive leading us to the performance of promises, distinct
from a sense of duty. If we thought, that promises had no
moral obligation, we never shou'd feel any inclination to
observe them. This is not the case with the natural virtues.
Tho' there was no obligation to relieve the miserable, our
humanity wou'd lead us to it; and when we omit that duty,
the immorality of the omission arises from its being a proof,
that we want the natural sentiments of humanity. A father
knows it to be his duty to take care of his children: But he
has also a natural inclination to it. And if no human
creature had that inclination, no one cou'd lie under any such
obligation. But as there is naturally no inclination to
observe promises, distinct from a sense of their obligation;
it follows, that fidelity is no natural virtue, and that promises
have no force antecedent to human conventions.

If any one dissent from this, he must give a regular proof
of these two propositions, viz. *that there is a peculiar act of
the mind, annext to promises;* and *that consequent to this act
of the mind, there arises an inclination to perform, distinct from
a sense of duty.* I presume, that it is impossible to prove
either of these two points; and therefore I venture to conclude, that promises are human inventions, founded on the
necessities and interests of society.

In order to discover these necessities and interests, we
must consider the same qualities of human nature, which
we have already found to give rise to the preceding laws of
society. Men being naturally selfish, or endow'd only with
a confin'd generosity, they are not easily induc'd to perform
any action for the interest of strangers, except with a view
to some reciprocal advantage, which they had no hope of
obtaining but by such a performance. Now as it frequently
happens, that these mutual performances cannot be finish'd
at the same instant, 'tis necessary, that one party be contented to remain in uncertainty, and depend upon the gratitude of the other for a return of kindness. But so much
corruption is there among men, that, generally speaking,
this becomes but a slender security; and as the benefactor
is here suppos'd to bestow his favours with a view to self-
interest, this both takes off from the obligation, and sets an
example of selfishness, which is the true mother of ingrati-

tude. Were we, therefore, to follow the natural course of our passions and inclinations, we shou'd perform but few actions for the advantage of others, from disinterested views; because we are naturally very limited in our kindness and affection : And we shou'd perform as few of that kind, out of a regard to interest; because we cannot depend upon their gratitude. Here then is the mutual commerce of good offices in a manner lost among mankind, and every one reduc'd to his own skill and industry for his well-being and subsistence. The invention of the law of nature, concerning the *stability* of possession, has already render'd men tolerable to each other; that of the *transference* of property and possession by consent has begun to render them mutually advantageous : But still these laws of nature, however strictly observ'd, are not sufficient to render them so serviceable to each other, as by nature they are fitted to become. Tho' possession be *stable*, men may often reap but small advantage from it, while they are possess'd of a greater quantity of any species of goods than they have occasion for, and at the same time suffer by the want of others. The *transference* of property, which is the proper remedy for this inconvenience, cannot remedy it entirely; because it can only take place with regard to such objects as are *present* and *individual*, but not to such as are *absent* or *general*. One cannot transfer the property of a particular house, twenty leagues distant; because the consent cannot be attended with delivery, which is a requisite circumstance. Neither can one transfer the property of ten bushels of corn, or five hogsheads of wine, by the mere expression and consent; because these are only general terms, and have no direct relation to any particular heap of corn, or barrels of wine. Besides, the commerce of mankind is not confin'd to the barter of commodities, but may extend to services and actions, which we may exchange to our mutual interest and advantage. Your corn is ripe to-day; mine will be so to-morrow. 'Tis profitable for us both, that I shou'd labour with you to-day, and that you shou'd aid me to-morrow. I have no kindness for you, and know you have as little for me. I will not, therefore, take any pains upon your account; and should I labour with you upon my own account, in expectation of a return, I know I shou'd be disappointed, and that I shou'd in vain depend upon your gratitude. Here then I leave you to labour alone:

You treat me in the same manner. The seasons change; and both of us lose our harvests for want of mutual confidence and security.

All this is the effect of the natural and inherent principles and passions of human nature; and as these passions and principles are inalterable, it may be thought, that our conduct, which depends on them, must be so too, and that 'twou'd be in vain, either for moralists or politicians, to tamper with us, or attempt to change the usual course of our actions, with a view to public interest. And indeed, did the success of their designs depend upon their success in correcting the selfishness and ingratitude of men, they wou'd never make any progress, unless aided by omnipotence, which is alone able to new-mould the human mind, and change its character in such fundamental articles. All they can pretend to, is, to give a new direction to those natural passions, and teach us that we can better satisfy our appetites in an oblique and artificial manner, than by their headlong and impetuous motion. Hence I learn to do a service to another, without bearing him any real kindness; because I foresee, that he will return my service, in expectation of another of the same kind, and in order to maintain the same correspondence of good offices with me or with others. And accordingly, after I have serv'd him, and he is in possession of the advantage arising from my action, he is induc'd to perform his part, as foreseeing the consequences of his refusal.

But tho' this self-interested commerce of men begins to take place, and to predominate in society, it does not entirely abolish the more generous and noble intercourse of friendship and good offices. I may still do services to such persons as I love, and am more particularly acquainted with, without any prospect of advantage; and they may make me a return in the same manner, without any view but that of recompensing my past services. In order, therefore, to distinguish those two different sorts of commerce, the interested and the disinterested, there is a *certain form of words* invented for the former, by which we bind ourselves to the performance of any action. This form of words constitutes what we call a *promise*, which is the sanction of the interested commerce of mankind. When a man says *he promises any thing*, he in effect expresses a *resolution* of performing it; and along with that, by making use of this *form of words*, subjects himself to the penalty of never being trusted again in case of failure. A resolution is the natural act of the mind, which promises express: But were there no more than a resolution in the case, promises wou'd only declare our former motives, and wou'd not create any new motive or obligation. They are the conventions of men, which create a new motive, when experience has taught us, that human affairs wou'd be conducted much more for mutual advantage, were their certain *symbols* or *signs* instituted, by which we might give each other security of our conduct in any particular incident. After these signs are instituted, whoever uses them is immediately bound by his interest to execute his engagements, and must never expect to be trusted any more, if he refuse to perform what he promis'd.

Nor is that knowledge, which is requisite to make mankind sensible of this interest in the *institution* and *observance* of promises, to be esteem'd superior to the capacity of human nature, however savage and uncultivated. There needs but a very little practice of the world, to make us perceive all these consequences and advantages. The shortest experience of society discovers them to every mortal; and when each individual perceives the same sense of interest in all his fellows, he immediately performs his part of any contract, as being assur'd, that they will not be wanting in theirs. All of them, by concert, enter into a scheme of actions, calculated for common benefit, and agree to be true to their word; nor is there any thing requisite to form this concert or convention, but that every one have a sense of interest in the faithful fulfilling of engagements, and express that sense to other members of the society. This immediately causes that interest to operate upon them; and interest is the *first* obligation to the performance of promises.

Afterwards a sentiment of morals concurs with interest, and becomes a new obligation upon mankind. This sentiment of morality, in the performance of promises, arises from the same principles as that in the abstinence from the property of others. *Public interest, education,* and *the artifices of politicians,* have the same effect in both cases. The difficulties, that occur to us, in supposing a moral obligation to attend promises, we either surmount or elude. For instance; the expression of a resolution is not commonly suppos'd to be obligatory; and we cannot readily conceive how the making use of a certain form of words shou'd be able to cause any material difference. Here, therefore, we *feign* a new act of the mind, which we call the *willing* an obligation; and on this we suppose the morality to depend. But we have prov'd already, that there is no such act of the mind, and consequently that promises impose no natural obligation.

To confirm this, we may subjoin some other reflections concerning that will, which is suppos'd to enter into a promise, and to cause its obligation. 'Tis evident, that the will alone is never suppos'd to cause the obligation, but must be express'd by words or signs, in order to impose a tye upon any man. The expression being once brought in as subservient to the will, soon becomes the principal part of the promise; nor will a man be less bound by his word, tho' he secretly give a different direction to his intention, and withhold himself both from a resolution, and from willing an obligation. But tho' the expression makes on most occasions the whole of the promise, yet it does not always so; and one, who shou'd make use of any expression, of which he knows not the meaning, and which he uses without any intention of binding himself, wou'd not certainly be bound by it. Nay, tho' he knows its meaning, yet if he uses it in jest only, and with such signs as shew evidently he has no serious intention of binding himself, he wou'd not lie under any obligation of performance; but 'tis necessary, that the words be a perfect expression of the will, without any contrary signs. Nay, even this we must not carry so far as to imagine, that one, whom, by our quickness of understanding, we conjecture, from certain signs, to have an intention of deceiving us, is not bound by his expression or verbal promise, if we accept it; but must limit this conclusion to those cases, where the signs are of a different kind from those of deceit. All these contradictions are easily accounted for, if the obligation of promises be merely a human invention for the convenience of society; but will never be explain'd, if it be something *real* and *natural*, arising from any action of the mind or body.

I shall farther observe, that since every new promise imposes a new obligation of morality on the person who promises, and since this new obligation arises from his will; 'tis one of the most mysterious and incomprehensible operations that can possibly be imagin'd, and may even be compar'd to *transubstantiation*, or *holy orders*,[1] where a certain form of words, along with a certain intention, changes entirely the nature of an external object, and even of a human creature. But tho' these mysteries be so far alike, 'tis very remarkable, that they differ widely in other particulars, and that this difference may be regarded as a strong proof of the difference of their origins. As the obligation of promises is an invention for the interest of society, 'tis warp'd into as many different forms as that interest requires, and even runs into direct contradictions, rather than lose sight of its object. But as those other monstrous doctrines are mere priestly inventions, and have no public interest in view, they are less disturb'd in their progress by new obstacles; and it must be own'd, that, after the first absurdity, they follow more directly the current of reason and good sense. Theologians clearly perceiv'd, that the external form of words, being mere sound, require an intention to make them have any efficacy; and that this intention being once consider'd as a requisite circumstance, its absence must equally prevent the effect, whether avow'd or conceal'd, whether sincere or deceitful. Accordingly they have commonly determin'd, that the intention of the priest makes the sacrament, and that when he secretly withdraws his intention, he is highly criminal in himself; but still destroys the baptism, or communion, or holy orders. The terrible consequences of this doctrine were not able to hinder its taking place; as the inconveniences of a similar doctrine, with regard to promises, have prevented that doctrine from establishing itself. Men are always more concern'd about the present life than the future; and are apt to think the smallest evil, which regards the former, more important than the greatest, which regards the latter.

We may draw the same conclusion, concerning the origin of promises, from the *force*, which is suppos'd to invalidate all contracts, and to free us from their obligation. Such a principle is a proof, that promises have no natural obligation, and are mere artificial contrivances for the convenience and advantage of society. If we consider aright of the matter,

---

[1] I mean so far, as holy orders are suppos'd to produce the *indelible character*. In other respects they are only a legal qualification.

force is not essentially different from any other motive of
hope or fear, which may induce us to engage our word, and
lay ourselves under any obligation.   A man, dangerously
wounded, who promises a competent sum to a surgeon to
cure him, wou'd certainly be bound to performance ; tho'
the case be not so much different from that of one, who promises a sum to a robber, as to produce so great a difference
in our sentiments of morality, if these sentiments were not
built entirely on public interest and convenience.

Sect. VI.—*Some farther reflections concerning justice and injustice.*

We have now run over the three fundamental laws of
nature, *that of the stability of possession, of its transference by
consent,* and *of the performance of promises.*   'Tis on the strict
observance of those three laws, that the peace and security
of human society entirely depend ; nor is there any possibility
of establishing a good correspondence among men, where
these are neglected.   Society is absolutely necessary for the
well-being of men ; and these are as necessary to the support
of society.   Whatever restraint they may impose on the
passions of men, they are the real offspring of those passions,
and are only a more artful and more refin'd way of satisfying
them.   Nothing is more vigilant and inventive than our
passions ; and nothing is more obvious, than the convention
for the observance of these rules.   Nature has, therefore,
trusted this affair entirely to the conduct of men, and has
not plac'd in the mind any peculiar original principles, to
determine us to a set of actions, into which the other principles of our frame and constitution were sufficient to lead us.
And to convince us the more fully of this truth, we may here
stop a moment, and from a review of the preceding reasonings may draw some new arguments, to prove that those
laws, however necessary, are entirely artificial, and of human
invention ; and consequently that justice is an artificial, and
not a natural virtue.

I. The first argument I shall make use of is deriv'd from
the vulgar definition of justice.   Justice is commonly defin'd
to be *a constant and perpetual will of giving every one his due.*
In this definition 'tis supposed, that there are such things as

right and property, independent of justice, and antecedent to it; and that they wou'd have subsisted, tho' men had never dreamt of practising such a virtue. I have already observ'd, in a cursory manner, the fallacy of this opinion, and shall here continue to open up a little more distinctly my sentiments on that subject.

I shall begin with observing, that this quality, which we call *property*, is like many of the imaginary qualities of the *peripatetic* philosophy, and vanishes upon a more accurate inspection into the subject, when consider'd a-part from our moral sentiments. 'Tis evident property does not consist in any of the sensible qualities of the object. For these may continue invariably the same, while the property changes. Property, therefore, must consist in some relation of the object. But 'tis not in its relation with regard to other external and inanimate objects. For these may also continue invariably the same, while the property changes. This quality, therefore, consists in the relations of objects to intelligent and rational beings. But 'tis not the external and corporeal relation, which forms the essence of property. For that relation may be the same betwixt inanimate objects, or with regard to brute creatures; tho' in those cases it forms no property. 'Tis, therefore, in some internal relation, that the property consists; that is, in some influence, which the external relations of the object have on the mind and actions. Thus the external relation, which we call *occupation* or first possession, is not of itself imagin'd to be the property of the object, but only to cause its property. Now 'tis evident, this external relation causes nothing in external objects, and has only an influence on the mind, by giving us a sense of duty in abstaining from that object, and in restoring it to the first possessor. These actions are properly what we call *justice*; and consequently 'tis on that virtue that the nature of property depends, and not the virtue on the property.

If any one, therefore, wou'd assert, that justice is a natural virtue, and injustice a natural vice, he must assert, that abstracting from the notions of *property*, and *right* and *obligation*, a certain conduct and train of actions, in certain external relations of objects, has naturally a moral beauty or deformity, and causes an original pleasure or uneasiness. Thus the restoring a man's goods to him is consider'd as virtuous, not because nature has annex'd a certain sentiment of pleasure to such a conduct, with regard to the property of others, but because she has annex'd that sentiment to such a conduct, with regard to those external objects, of which others have had the first or long possession, or which they have receiv'd by the consent of those, who have had the first or long possession. If nature has given us no such sentiment, there is not, naturally, nor antecedent to human conventions, any such thing as property. Now, tho' it seems sufficiently evident, in this dry and accurate consideration of the present subject, that nature has annex'd no pleasure or sentiment of approbation to such a conduct; yet that I may leave as little room for doubt as possible, I shall subjoin a few more arguments to confirm my opinion.

SECT VI.

Some farther reflections concerning justice and injustice.

First, If nature had given us a pleasure of this kind, it wou'd have been as evident and discernible as on every other occasion; nor shou'd we have found any difficulty to perceive, that the consideration of such actions, in such a situation, gives a certain pleasure and sentiment of approbation. We shou'd not have been oblig'd to have recourse to notions of property in the definition of justice, and at the same time make use of the notions of justice in the definition of property. This deceitful method of reasoning is a plain proof, that there are contain'd in the subject some obscurities and difficulties, which we are not able to surmount, and which we desire to evade by this artifice.

Secondly, Those rules, by which properties, rights, and obligations are determin'd, have in them no marks of a natural origin, but many of artifice and contrivance. They are too numerous to have proceeded from nature: They are changeable by human laws: And have all of them a direct and evident tendency to public good, and the support of civil society. This last circumstance is remarkable upon two accounts. *First,* because, tho' the cause of the establishment of these laws had been a *regard* for the public good, as much as the public good is their natural tendency, they wou'd still have been artificial, as being purposely contriv'd and directed to a certain end. *Secondly,* because, if men had been endow'd with such a strong regard for public good, they wou'd never have restrain'd themselves by these rules: so that the laws of justice arise from natural principles in a manner still more oblique and artificial. 'Tis self-love which is their real origin; and as the self-love of one person is naturally contrary to that of another, these several interested passions are oblig'd to adjust themselves after such a manner as to concur in some system of conduct and behaviour. This system, therefore, comprehending the interest of each individual, is of course advantageous to the public; tho' it be not intended for that purpose by the inventors.

II. In the second place we may observe, that all kinds of vice and virtue run insensibly into each other, and may approach by such imperceptible degrees as will make it very difficult, if not absolutely impossible, to determine when the one ends, and the other begins; and from this observation we may derive a new argument for the foregoing principle. For whatever may be the case, with regard to all kinds of vice and virtue, 'tis certain, that rights, and obligations, and property, admit of no such insensible gradation, but that a man either has a full and perfect property, or none at all; and is either entirely oblig'd to perform any action, or lies under no manner of obligation. However civil laws may talk of a perfect *dominion*, and of an imperfect, 'tis easy to observe, that this arises from a fiction, which has no foundation in reason, and can never enter into our notions of natural justice and equity. A man that hires a horse, tho' but for a day, has as full a right to make use of it for that time, as he whom we call its proprietor has to make use of it any other day; and 'tis evident, that however the use may be bounded in time or degree, the right itself is not susceptible of any such gradation, but is absolute and entire, so far as it extends. Accordingly we may observe, that this right both arises and perishes in an instant; and that a man entirely acquires the property of any object by occupation, or the consent of the proprietor; and loses it by his own consent; without any of that insensible gradation, which is remarkable in other qualities and relations. Since, therefore, this is the case with regard to property, and rights, and obligations, I ask, how it stands with regard to justice and injustice? After whatever manner you answer this question, you run into inextricable difficulties. If you reply, that justice and injustice admit of no degree, and run insensibly into each other, you expressly contradict the foregoing position, that obligation and property are not susceptible of such a gradation.　These depend entirely upon justice and injustice, and follow them in all their variations.　Where the justice is entire, the property is also entire : Where the justice is imperfect, the property must also be imperfect.　And *vice versa*, if the property admit of no such variations, they must also be incompatible with justice.　If you assent, therefore, to this last proposition, and assert, that justice and injustice are not susceptible of degrees, you in effect assert, that they are not *naturally* either vicious or virtuous ; since vice and virtue, moral good and evil, and indeed all *natural* qualities, run insensibly into each other, and are, on many occasions, undistinguishable.

SECT.
VI.

Some farther reflections concerning justice and injustice.

And here it may be worth while to observe, that tho' abstract reasoning, and the general maxims of philosophy and law establish this position, *that property, and right, and obligation admit not of degrees,* yet in our common and negligent way of thinking, we find great difficulty to entertain that opinion, and do even *secretly* embrace the contrary principle.　An object must either be in the possession of one person or another.　An action must either be perform'd or not.　The necessity there is of choosing one side in these dilemmas, and the impossibility there often is of finding any just medium, oblige us, when we reflect on the matter, to acknowledge, that all property and obligations are entire. But on the other hand, when we consider the origin of property and obligation, and find that they depend on public utility, and sometimes on the propensities of the imagination, which are seldom entire on any side ; we are naturally inclin'd to imagine, that these moral relations admit of an insensible gradation.　Hence it is, that in references, where the consent of the parties leave the referees entire masters of the subject, they commonly discover so much equity and justice on both sides, as induces them to strike a medium, and divide the difference betwixt the parties.　Civil judges, who have not this liberty, but are oblig'd to give a decisive sentence on some one side, are often at a loss how to determine, and are necessitated to proceed on the most frivolous reasons in the world.　Half rights and obligations, which seem so natural in common life, are perfect absurdities in their tribunal ; for which reason they are often oblig'd to take half arguments for whole ones, in order to terminate the affair one way or other.

III. The third argument of this kind I shall make use of may be explain'd thus. If we consider the ordinary course of human actions, we shall find, that the mind restrains not itself by any general and universal rules; but acts on most occasions as it is determin'd by its present motives and inclination. As each action is a particular individual event, it must proceed from particular principles and from our immediate situation within ourselves, and with respect to the rest of the universe. If on some occasions we extend our motives beyond those very circumstances, which gave rise to them, and form something like *general rules* for our conduct, 'tis easy to observe, that these rules are not perfectly inflexible, but allow of many exceptions. Since, therefore, this is the ordinary course of human actions, we may conclude, that the laws of justice, being universal and perfectly inflexible, can never be deriv'd from nature, nor be the immediate offspring of any natural motive or inclination. No action can be either morally good or evil, unless there be some natural passion or motive to impel us to it, or deter us from it; and 'tis evident, that the morality must be susceptible of all the same variations, which are natural to the passion. Here are two persons, who dispute for an estate; of whom one is rich, a fool, and a batchelor; the other poor, a man of sense, and has a numerous family: The first is my enemy; the second my friend. Whether I be actuated in this affair by a view to public or private interest, by friendship or enmity, I must be induc'd to do my utmost to procure the estate to the latter. Nor wou'd any consideration of the right and property of the persons be able to restrain me, were I actuated only by natural motives, without any combination or convention with others. For as all property depends on morality; and as all morality depends on the ordinary course of our passions and actions; and as these again are only directed by particular motives; 'tis evident, such a partial conduct must be suitable to the strictest morality, and cou'd never be a violation of property. Were men, therefore, to take the liberty of acting with regard to the laws of society, as they do in every other affair, they wou'd conduct themselves, on most occasions, by particular judgments, and wou'd take into consideration the characters and circumstances of the persons, as well as the general nature of the question. But 'tis easy to observe, that this wou'd produce an infinite confusion in human

society, and that the avidity and partiality of men wou'd
quickly bring disorder into the world, if not restrain'd by
some general and inflexible principles.   'Twas, therefore,
with a view to this inconvenience, that men have establish'd
those principles, and have agreed to restrain themselves by
general rules, which are unchangeable by spite and favour,
and by particular views of private or public interest.   These
rules, then, are artificially invented for a certain purpose,
and are contrary to the common principles of human nature,
which accommodate themselves to circumstances, and have
no stated invariable method of operation.

SECT.
VI
Some far-
ther re-
flections
concerning
justice and
injustice

Nor do I perceive how I can easily be mistaken in this
matter. I see evidently, that when any man imposes on
himself general inflexible rules in his conduct with others, he
considers certain objects as their property, which he supposes
to be sacred and inviolable.   But no proposition can be more
evident, than that property is perfectly unintelligible without
first supposing justice and injustice; and that these virtues
and vices are as unintelligible, unless we have motives, independent of the morality, to impel us to just actions, and
deter us from unjust ones.   Let those motives, therefore, be
what they will, they must accommodate themselves to circumstances, and must admit of all the variations, which
human affairs, in their incessant revolutions, are susceptible
of. They are consequently a very improper foundation for such
rigid inflexible rules as the laws of nature; and 'tis evident
these laws can only be deriv'd from human conventions, when
men have perceiv'd the disorders that result from following
their natural and variable principles.

Upon the whole, then, we are to consider this distinction
betwixt justice and injustice, as having two different foundations, _viz._ that of _interest_, when men observe, that 'tis impossible to live in society without restraining themselves by
certain rules; and that of _morality_, when this interest is
once observ'd, and men receive a pleasure from the view of
such actions as tend to the peace of society, and an uneasiness
from such as are contrary to it.   'Tis the voluntary convention and artifice of men, which makes the first interest take
place; and therefore those laws of justice are so far to be
consider'd as _artificial_.   After that interest is once establish'd
and acknowledg'd, the sense of morality in the observance of

these rules follows *naturally*, and of itself; tho' 'tis certain, that it is also augmented by a new *artifice*, and that the public instructions of politicians, and the private education of parents, contribute to the giving us a sense of honour and duty in the strict regulation of our actions with regard to the properties of others.

SECT. VII.—*Of the origin of government.*

Nothing is more certain, than that men are, in a great measure, govern'd by interest, and that even when they extend their concern beyond themselves, 'tis not to any great distance; nor is it usual for them, in common life, to look farther than their nearest friends and acquaintance. 'Tis no less certain, that 'tis impossible for men to consult their interest in so effectual a manner, as by an universal and in-flexible observance of the rules of justice, by which alone they can preserve society, and keep themselves from falling into that wretched and savage condition, which is commonly represented as the *state of nature.* And as this interest, which all men have in the upholding of society, and the observation of the rules of justice, is great, so is it palpable and evident, even to the most rude and uncultivated of the human race; and 'tis almost impossible for any one, who has had experience of society, to be mistaken in this particular. Since, therefore, men are so sincerely attach'd to their interest, and their interest is so much concern'd in the ob-servance of justice, and this interest is so certain and avow'd; it may be ask'd, how any disorder can ever arise in society, and what principle there is in human nature so *powerful* as to overcome so strong a passion, or so *violent* as to obscure so clear a knowledge?

It has been observ'd, in treating of the passions, that men are mightily govern'd by the imagination, and proportion their affections more to the light, under which any object appears to them, than to its real and intrinsic value. What strikes upon them with a strong and lively idea commonly prevails above what lies in a more obscure light; and it must be a great superiority of value, that is able to com-pensate this advantage. Now as every thing, that is con-tiguous to us, either in space or time, strikes upon us with such an idea, it has a proportional effect on the will and passions, and commonly operates with more force than any object, that lies in a more distant and obscure light. Tho' we may be fully convinc'd, that the latter object excels the former, we are not able to regulate our actions by this judgment; but yield to the sollicitations of our passions, which always plead in favour of whatever is near and contiguous.

This is the reason why men so often act in contradiction to their known interest; and in particular why they prefer any trivial advantage, that is present, to the maintenance of order in society, which so much depends on the observance of justice. The consequences of every breach of equity seem to lie very remote, and are not able to counterballance any immediate advantage, that may be reap'd from it. They are, however, never the less real for being remote; and as all men are, in some degree, subject to the same weakness, it necessarily happens, that the violations of equity must become very frequent in society, and the commerce of men, by that means, be render'd very dangerous and uncertain. You have the same propension, that I have, in favour of what is contiguous above what is remote. You are, therefore, naturally carried to commit acts of injustice as well as me. Your example both pushes me forward in this way by imitation, and also affords me a new reason for any breach of equity, by shewing me, that I should be the cully of my integrity, if I alone shou'd impose on myself a severe restraint amidst the licentiousness of others.

This quality, therefore, of human nature, not only is very dangerous to society, but also seems, on a cursory view, to be incapable of any remedy. The remedy can only come from the consent of men; and if men be incapable of themselves to prefer remote to contiguous, they will never consent to any thing, which wou'd oblige them to such a choice, and contradict, in so sensible a manner, their natural principles and propensities. Whoever chuses the means, chuses also the end; and if it be impossible for us to prefer what is remote, 'tis equally impossible for us to submit to any necessity, which would oblige us to such a method of acting.

But here 'tis observable, that this infirmity of human nature becomes a remedy to itself, and that we provide against our negligence about remote objects, merely because we are naturally inclin'd to that negligence. When we consider any objects at a distance, all their minute distinctions vanish, and we always give the preference to whatever is in itself preferable, without considering its situation and circumstances. This gives rise to what in an improper sense we call *reason*, which is a principle, that is often contradictory to those propensities that display themselves upon the approach of the object. In reflecting on any action, which I am to perform a twelve-month hence, I always resolve to prefer the greater good, whether at that time it will be more contiguous or remote; nor does any difference in that particular make a difference in my present intentions and resolutions. My distance from the final determination makes all those minute differences vanish, nor am I affected by any thing, but the general and more discernable qualities of good and evil. But on my nearer approach, those circumstances, which I at first over-look'd, begin to appear, and have an influence on my conduct and affections. A new inclination to the present good springs up, and makes it difficult for me to adhere inflexibly to my first purpose and resolution. This natural infirmity I may very much regret, and I may endeavour, by all possible means, to free myself from it. I may have recourse to study and reflection within myself; to the advice of friends; to frequent meditation, and repeated resolution: And having experienc'd how ineffectual all these are, I may embrace with pleasure any other expedient, by which I may impose a restraint upon myself, and guard against this weakness.

The only difficulty, therefore, is to find out this expedient, by which men cure their natural weakness, and lay themselves under the necessity of observing the laws of justice and equity, notwithstanding their violent propension to prefer contiguous to remote. 'Tis evident such a remedy can never be effectual without correcting this propensity; and as 'tis impossible to change or correct any thing material in our nature, the utmost we can do is to change our circumstances and situation, and render the observance of the laws of justice our nearest interest, and their violation our most remote. But this being impracticable with respect to all mankind, it can only take place with respect to a few, whom we thus immediately interest in the execution of justice. These are the persons, whom we call civil magistrates, kings and their ministers, our governors and rulers, who being in-

different persons to the greatest part of the state, have no
interest, or but a remote one, in any act of injustice; and
being satisfied with their present condition, and with their
part in society, have an immediate interest in every execution of justice, which is so necessary to the upholding of
society. Here then is the origin of civil government and
society. Men are not able radically to cure, either in themselves or others, that narrowness of soul, which makes them
prefer the present to the remote. They cannot change their
natures. All they can do is to change their situation, and
render the observance of justice the immediate interest of
some particular persons, and its violation their more remote.
These persons, then, are not only induc'd to observe those
rules in their own conduct, but also to constrain others to a
like regularity, and enforce the dictates of equity thro' the
whole society. And if it be necessary, they may also interest
others more immediately in the execution of justice, and
create a number of officers, civil and military, to assist them
in their government.

But this execution of justice, tho' the principal, is not the
only advantage of government. As violent passion hinders
men from seeing distinctly the interest they have in an
equitable behaviour towards others; so it hinders them from
seeing that equity itself, and gives them a remarkable partiality in their own favours. This inconvenience is corrected
in the same manner as that above-mention'd. The same
persons, who execute the laws of justice, will also decide all
controversies concerning them; and being indifferent to the
greatest part of society, will decide them more equitably
than every one wou'd in his own case.

By means of these two advantages, in the *execution* and
decision of justice, men acquire a security against each others
weakness and passion, as well as against their own, and under
the shelter of their governors, begin to taste at ease the
sweets of society and mutual assistance. But government
extends farther its beneficial influence; and not contented
to protect men in those conventions they make for their
mutual interest, it often obliges them to make such conventions, and forces them to seek their own advantage, by a
concurrence in some common end or purpose. There is no
quality in human nature, which causes more fatal errors in
our conduct, than that which leads us to prefer whatever is

SECT.
VII.

Of the
origin of
govern-
ment.

present to the distant and remote, and makes us desire objects more according to their situation than their intrinsic value. Two neighbours may agree to drain a meadow, which they possess in common; because 'tis easy for them to know each others mind; and each must perceive, that the immediate consequence of his failing in his part, is, the abandoning the whole project. But 'tis very difficult, and indeed impossible, that a thousand persons shou'd agree in any such action; it being difficult for them to concert so complicated a design, and still more difficult for them to execute it; while each seeks a pretext to free himself of the trouble and expence, and wou'd lay the whole burden on others. Political society easily remedies both these inconveniences. Magistrates find an immediate interest in the interest of any considerable part of their subjects. They need consult no body but themselves to form any scheme for the promoting of that interest. And as the failure of any one piece in the execution is connected, tho' not immediately, with the failure of the whole, they prevent that failure, because they find no interest in it, either immediate or remote. Thus bridges are built; harbours open'd; ramparts rais'd; canals form'd; fleets equip'd; and armies disciplin'd; every where, by the care of government, which, tho' compos'd of men subject to all human infirmities, becomes, by one of the finest and most subtle inventions imaginable, a composition, which is, in some measure, exempted from all these infirmities.

SECT. VIII.—*Of the source of allegiance.*

Though government be an invention very advantageous, and even in some circumstances absolutely necessary to mankind; it is not necessary in all circumstances, nor is it impossible for men to preserve society for some time, without having recourse to such an invention. Men, 'tis true, are always much inclin'd to prefer present interest to distant and remote; nor is it easy for them to resist the temptation of any advantage, that they may immediately enjoy, in apprehension of an evil, that lies at a distance from them: But still this weakness is less conspicuous, where the possessions, and the pleasures of life are few, and of little value, as they always are in the infancy of society. An *Indian* is but little tempted to dispossess another of his hut, or to steal his bow, as being already provided of the same advantages ; and as to any superior fortune, which may attend one above another in hunting and fishing, 'tis only casual and temporary, and will have but small tendency to disturb society. And so far am I from thinking with some philosophers, that men are utterly incapable of society without government, that I assert the first rudiments of government to arise from quarrels, not among men of the same society, but among those of different societies. A less degree of riches will suffice to this latter effect, than is requisite for the former. Men fear nothing from public war and violence but the resistance they meet with, which, because they share it in common, seems less terrible ; and because it comes from strangers, seems less pernicious in its consequences, than when they are expos'd singly against one whose commerce is advantageous to them, and without whose society 'tis impossible they can subsist. Now foreign war to a society without government necessarily produces civil war. Throw any considerable goods among men, they instantly fall a quarrelling, while each strives to get possession of what pleases him, without regard to the consequences. In a foreign war the most considerable of all goods, life and limbs, are at stake ; and as every one shuns dangerous ports, seizes the best arms, seeks excuse for the slightest wounds, the laws, which may be well enough observ'd, while men were calm, can now no longer take place, when they are in such commotion.

This we find verified in the *American* tribes, where men live in concord and amity among themselves without any establish'd government ; and never pay submission to any of their fellows, except in time of war, when their captain enjoys a shadow of authority, which he loses after their return from the field, and the establishment of peace with the neighbouring tribes. This authority, however, instructs them in the advantages of government, and teaches them to have recourse to it, when either by the pillage of war, by commerce, or by any fortuitous inventions, their riches and possessions have become so considerable as to make them forget, on every emergence, the interest they have in the preservation of peace and justice. Hence we may give a plausible reason, among others, why all governments are at first monarchical, without any mixture and variety ; and why republics arise only from the abuses of monarchy and despotic power. Camps are the true mothers of cities; and as war cannot be administered, by reason of the suddenness of every exigency, without some authority in a single person, the same kind of authority naturally takes place in that civil government, which succeeds the military. And this reason I take to be more natural, than the common one deriv'd from patriarchal government, or the authority of a father, which is said first to take place in one family, and to accustom the members of it to the government of a single person. The state of society without government is one of the most natural states of men, and must subsist with the conjunction of many families, and long after the first generation. No thing but an encrease of riches and possessions cou'd oblige men to quit it; and so barbarous and uninstructed are all societies on their first formation, that many years must elapse before these can encrease to such a degree, as to disturb men in the enjoyment of peace and concord.

But tho' it be possible for men to maintain a small uncultivated society without government, 'tis impossible they shou'd maintain a society of any kind without justice, and the observance of those three fundamental laws concerning the stability of possession, its translation by consent, and the performance of promises. These are, therefore, antecedent to government, and are suppos'd to impose an obligation before the duty of allegiance to civil magistrates has once been thought of. Nay, I shall go farther, and assert, that government, *upon its first establishment*, wou'd naturally be suppos'd to derive its obligation from those laws of nature, and, in particular, from that concerning the performance of promises. When men have once perceived the necessity of government to maintain peace, and execute justice, they wou'd naturally assemble together, wou'd chuse magistrates, determine their power, and *promise* them obedience. As a promise is suppos'd to be a bond or security already in use, and attended with a moral obligation, 'tis to be consider'd as the original sanction of government, and as the source of the first obligation to obedience. This reason appears so natural, that it has become the foundation of our fashionable system of politics, and is in a manner the creed of a party amongst us, who pride themselves, with reason, on the soundness of their philosophy, and their liberty

of thought. *All men, say they, are born free and equal*
Government and superiority can only be establish'd by consent:
The consent of men, in establishing government, imposes on them
a new obligation, unknown to the laws of nature. *Men, there-*
fore, are bound to obey their magistrates, only because they
promise it; and if they had not given their word, either expressly
or tacitly, to preserve allegiance, it would never have become a
part of their moral duty. This conclusion, however, when
carried so far as to comprehend government in all its ages
and situations, is entirely erroneous; and I maintain, that
tho' the duty of allegiance be at first grafted on the obligation of promises, and be for some time supported by that
obligation, yet it quickly takes root of itself, and has an
original obligation and authority, independent of all contracts. This is a principle of moment, which we must
examine with care and attention, before we proceed any
farther.

'Tis reasonable for those philosophers, who assert justice
to be a natural virtue, and antecedent to human conventions,
to resolve all civil allegiance into the obligation of a promise,
and assert that 'tis our own consent alone, which binds us to
any submission to magistracy. For as all government is
plainly an invention of men, and the origin of most governments is known in history, 'tis necessary to mount higher,
in order to find the source of our political duties, if we wou'd
assert them to have any *natural* obligation of morality.
These philosophers, therefore, quickly observe, that society
is as antient as the human species, and those three fundamental laws of nature as antient as society: So that taking
advantage of the antiquity, and obscure origin of these laws,
they first deny them to be artificial and voluntary inventions
of men, and then seek to ingraft them on those other duties,
which are more plainly artificial. But being once undeceiv'd
in this particular, and having found that *natural*, as well as
civil justice, derives its origin from human conventions, we
shall quickly perceive, how fruitless it is to resolve the one
into the other, and seek, in the laws of nature, a stronger
foundation for our political duties than interest, and human
conventions; while these laws themselves are built on the
very same foundation. On which ever side we turn this
subject, we shall find, that these two kinds of duty are
exactly on the same footing, and have the same source both

of their *first invention* and *moral obligation*. They are contriv'd to remedy like inconveniences, and acquire their moral
sanction in the same manner, from their remedying those
inconveniences. These are two points, which we shall endeavour to prove as distinctly as possible

We have already shewn, that men *invented* the three fundamental laws of nature, when they observ'd the necessity
of society to their mutual subsistance, and found, that 'twas
impossible to maintain any correspondence together, without
some restraint on their natural appetites. The same self-
love, therefore, which renders men so incommodious to each
other, taking a new and more convenient direction, produces
the rules of justice, and is the *first* motive of their observance.
But when men have observ'd, that tho' the rules of justice
be sufficient to maintain any society, yet 'tis impossible for
them, of themselves, to observe those rules, in large and
polish'd societies ; they establish government, as a new invention to attain their ends, and preserve the old, or procure
new advantages, by a more strict execution of justice. So
far, therefore, our *civil* duties are connected with our *natural*,
that the former are invented chiefly for the sake of the latter ;
and that the principal object of government is to constrain
men to observe the laws of nature. In this respect, however,
that law of nature, concerning the performance of promises,
is only compriz'd along with the rest ; and its exact observance is to be considered as an effect of the institution of
government, and not the obedience to government as an
effect of the obligation of a promise. Tho' the object of our
civil duties be the enforcing of our natural, yet the[1] *first*
motive of the invention, as well as performance of both, is
nothing but self-interest : And since there is a separate interest in the obedience to government, from that in the performance of promises, we must also allow of a separate
obligation. To obey the civil magistrate is requisite to
preserve order and concord in society. To perform promises
is requisite to beget mutual trust and confidence in the
common offices of life. The ends, as well as the means,
are perfectly distinct ; nor is the one subordinate to the
other.

To make this more evident, let us consider, that men will
often bind themselves by promises to the performance of

---

[1] First in time, not in dignity or force.

what it wou'd have been their interest to perform, independent of these promises; as when they wou'd give others a fuller security, by super-adding a new obligation of interest to that which they formerly lay under. The interest in the performance of promises, besides its moral obligation, is general, avow'd, and of the last consequence in life. Other interests may be more particular and doubtful; and we are apt to entertain a greater suspicion, that men may indulge their humour, or passion, in acting contrary to them. Here, therefore, promises come naturally in play, and are often requir'd for fuller satisfaction and security. But supposing those other interests to be as general and avow'd as the interest in the performance of a promise, they will be regarded as on the same footing, and men will begin to repose the same confidence in them. Now this is exactly the case with regard to our civil duties, or obedience to the magistrate; without which no government cou'd subsist, nor any peace or order be maintain'd in large societies, where there are so many possessions on the one hand, and so many wants, real or imaginary, on the other. Our civil duties, therefore, must soon detach themselves from our promises, and acquire a separate force and influence. The interest in both is of the very same kind: 'Tis general, avow'd, and prevails in all times and places. There is, then, no pretext of reason for founding the one upon the other; while each of them has a foundation peculiar to itself. We might as well resolve the obligation to abstain from the possessions of others, into the obligation of a promise, as that of allegiance. The interests are not more distinct in the one case than the other. A regard to property is not more necessary to natural society, than obedience is to civil society or government; nor is the former society more necessary to the being of mankind, than the latter to their well-being and happiness. In short, if the performance of promises be advantageous, so is obedience to government: If the former interest be general, so is the latter: If the one interest be obvious and avow'd, so is the other. And as these two rules are founded on like obligations of interest, each of them must have a peculiar authority, independent of the other.

But 'tis not only the *natural* obligations of interest, which are distinct in promises and allegiance; but also the *moral* obligations of honour and conscience: Nor does the merit or demerit of the one depend in the least upon that of the other. And indeed, if we consider the close connexion there is betwixt the natural and moral obligations, we shall find this conclusion to be entirely unavoidable. Our interest is always engag'd on the side of obedience to magistracy; and there is nothing but a great present advantage, that can lead us to rebellion, by making us over-look the remote interest, which we have in the preserving of peace and order in society. But tho' a present interest may thus blind us with regard to our own actions, it takes not place with regard to those of others; nor hinders them from appearing in their true colours, as highly prejudicial to public interest, and to our own in particular. This naturally gives us an uneasiness, in considering such seditious and disloyal actions, and makes us attach to them the idea of vice and moral deformity. 'Tis the same principle, which causes us to disapprove of all kinds of private injustice, and in particular of the breach of promises. We blame all treachery and breach of faith; because we consider, that the freedom and extent of human commerce depend entirely on a fidelity with regard to promises. We blame all disloyalty to magistrates; because we perceive, that the execution of justice, in the stability of possession, its translation by consent, and the performance of promises, is impossible, without submission to government. As there are here two interests entirely distinct from each other, they must give rise to two moral obligations, equally separate and independent. Tho' there was no such thing as a promise in the world, government wou'd still be necessary in all large and civiliz'd societies; and if promises had only their own proper obligation, without the separate sanction of government, they wou'd have but little efficacy in such societies. This separates the boundaries of our public and private duties, and shews that the latter are more dependent on the former, than the former on the latter. *Education*, and *the artifice of politicians*, concur to bestow a farther morality on loyalty, and to brand all rebellion with a greater degree of guilt and infamy. Nor is it a wonder, that politicians shou'd be very industrious in inculcating such notions, where their interest is so particularly concern'd.

Lest those arguments shou'd not appear entirely conclusive (as I think they are) I shall have recourse to authority, and shall prove, from the universal consent of mankind, that the obligation of submission to government is not deriv'd from any promise of the subjects. Nor need any one wonder, that tho' I have all along endeavour'd to establish my system on pure reason, and have scarce ever cited the judgment even of philosophers or historians on any article, I shou'd now appeal to popular authority, and oppose the sentiments of the rabble to any philosophical reasoning. For it must be observ'd, that the opinions of men, in this case, carry with them a peculiar authority, and are, in a great measure, infallible. The distinction of moral good and evil is founded on the pleasure or pain, which results from the view of any sentiment, or character; and as that pleasure or pain cannot be unknown to the person who feels it, it follows,[1] that there is just so much vice or virtue in any character, as every one places in it, and that 'tis impossible in this particular we can ever be mistaken. And tho' our judgments concerning the *origin* of any vice or virtue, be not so certain as those concerning their *degrees*; yet, since the question in this case regards not any philosophical origin of an obligation, but a plain matter of fact, 'tis not easily conceiv'd how we can fall into an error. A man, who acknowledges himself to be bound to another, for a certain sum, must certainly know whether it be by his own bond, or that of his father; whether it be of his mere good-will, or for money lent him; and under what conditions, and for what purposes he has bound himself. In like manner, it being certain, that there is a moral obligation to submit to government, because every one thinks so; it must be as certain, that this obligation arises not from a promise; since no one, whose judgment has not been led astray by too strict adherence to a system of philosophy, has ever yet dreamt of ascribing it to that origin. Neither magistrates nor subjects have form'd this idea of our civil duties.

We find, that magistrates are so far from deriving their authority, and the obligation to obedience in their subjects, from the foundation of a promise or original contract, that they conceal, as far as possible, from their people, especially

---

[1] This proposition must hold strictly true, with regard to every quality, that is determin'd merely by sentiment In what sense we can talk either of a *right* or a *wrong* taste in morals, eloquence, or beauty, shall be consider'd afterwards. In the mean time, it may be observ'd, that there is such an uniformity in the *general* sentiments of mankind, as to render such questions of but small importance

from the vulgar, that they have their origin from thence. Were this the sanction of government, our rulers wou'd never receive it tacitly, which is the utmost that can be pretended; since what is given tacitly and insensibly can never have such influence on mankind, as what is perform'd expressly and openly.   A tacit promise is, where the will is signified by other more diffuse signs than those of speech; but a will there must certainly be in the case, and that can never escape the person's notice, who exerted it, however silent or tacit.   But were you to ask the far greater part of the nation, whether they had ever consented to the authority of their rulers, or promis'd to obey them, they wou'd be inclin'd to think very strangely of you; and wou'd certainly reply, that the affair depended not on their consent, but that they were born to such an obedience.   In consequence of this opinion, we frequently see them imagine such persons to be their natural rulers, as are at that time depriv'd of all power and authority, and whom no man, however foolish, wou'd voluntarily chuse; and this merely because they are in that line, which rul'd before, and in that degree of it, which us'd to succeed; tho' perhaps in so distant a period, that scarce any man alive cou'd ever have given any promise of obedience. Has a government, then, no authority over such as these, because they never consented to it, and wou'd esteem the very attempt of such a free choice a piece of arrogance and impiety?   We find by experience, that it punishes them very freely for what it calls treason and rebellion, which, it seems, according to this system, reduces itself to common injustice. If you say, that by dwelling in its dominions, they in effect consented to the establish'd government; I answer, that this can only be, where they think the affair depends on their choice, which few or none, beside those philosophers, have ever yet imagin'd.   It never was pleaded as an excuse for a rebel, that the first act he perform'd, after he came to years of discretion, was to levy war against the sovereign of the state; and that while he was a child he cou'd not bind himself by his own consent, and having become a man, show'd plainly, by the first act he perform'd, that he had no design to impose on himself any obligation to obedience.   We find, on the contrary, that civil laws punish this crime at the same age as any other, which is criminal, of itself, without our consent; that is, when the person is come to the full use of

reason : Whereas to this crime they ought in justice to allow
some intermediate time, in which a tacit consent at least
might be suppos'd.   To which we may add, that a man
living under an absolute government, wou'd owe it no allegiance; since, by its very nature, it depends not on consent.
But as that is as *natural* and *common* a government as any, it
must certainly occasion some obligation; and 'tis plain from
experience, that men, who are subjected to it, do always
think so.   This is a clear proof, that we do not commonly
esteem our allegiance to be deriv'd from our consent or promise; and a farther proof is, that when our promise is upon
any account expressly engag'd, we always distinguish exactly
betwixt the two obligations, and believe the one to add more
force to the other, than in a repetition of the same promise.
Where no promise is given, a man looks not on his faith as
broken in private matters, upon account of rebellion; but
keeps those two duties of honour and allegiance perfectly
distinct and separate.   As the uniting of them was thought
by these philosophers a very subtile invention, this is a convincing proof, that 'tis not a true one; since no man can
either give a promise, or be restrain'd by its sanction and
obligation unknown to himself.

SECT. IX.—*Of the measures of allegiance.*

Those political writers, who have had recourse to a promise, or original contract, as the source of our allegiance to
government, intended to establish a principle, which is perfectly just and reasonable; tho' the reasoning, upon which
they endeavour'd to establish it, was fallacious and sophistical.
They wou'd prove, that our submission to government admits
of exceptions, and that an egregious tyranny in the rulers is
sufficient to free the subjects from all ties of allegiance.
Since men enter into society, say they, and submit themselves to government, by their free and voluntary consent, they
must have in view certain advantages, which they propose to
reap from it, and for which they are contented to resign
their native liberty.   There is, therefore, something mutual
engag'd on the part of the magistrate, *viz.* protection and
security; and 'tis only by the hopes he affords of these advantages, that he can ever persuade men to submit to him.
But when instead of protection and security, they meet with

tyranny and oppression, they are free'd from their promises,
(as happens in all conditional contracts) and return to that
state of liberty, which preceded the institution of government. Men wou'd never be so foolish as to enter into such
engagements as shou'd turn entirely to the advantage of
others, without any view of bettering their own condition.
Whoever proposes to draw any profit from our submission,
must engage himself, either expressly or tacitly, to make us
reap some advantage from his authority; nor ought he to
expect, that without the performance of his part we will ever
continue in obedience.

I repeat it: This conclusion is just, tho' the principles be
erroneous; and I flatter myself, that I can establish the same
conclusion on more reasonable principles. I shall not take
such a compass, in establishing our political duties, as to
assert, that men perceive the advantages of government;
that they institute government with a view to those advantages; that this institution requires a promise of obedience;
which imposes a moral obligation to a certain degree, but
being conditional, ceases to be binding, whenever the other
contracting party performs not his part of the engagement.
I perceive, that a promise itself arises entirely from human
conventions, and is invented with a view to a certain interest.
I seek, therefore, some such interest more immediately connected with government, and which may be at once the
original motive to its institution, and the source of our
obedience to it. This interest I find to consist in the security and protection, which we enjoy in political society,
and which we can never attain, when perfectly free and independent. As interest, therefore, is the immediate sanction
of government, the one can have no longer being than the
other; and whenever the civil magistrate carries his oppression so far as to render his authority perfectly intolerable,
we are no longer bound to submit to it. The cause ceases;
the effect must cease also.

So far the conclusion is immediate and direct, concerning
the *natural* obligation which we have to allegiance.[1] As to
the *moral* obligation, we may observe, that the maxim wou'd
here be false, that *when the cause ceases, the effect must cease
also.* For there is a principle of human nature, which we

[1] The antithesis of 'natural' and
'moral' corresponds to that of 'interest'
and 'morality' in sect 6 of Part I.
sect 2 Note near the end —ED

have frequently taken notice of, that men are mightily addicted to *general rules*, and that we often carry our maxims beyond those reasons, which first induc'd us to establish them. Where cases are similar in many circumstances, we are apt to put them on the same footing, without considering, that they differ in the most material circumstances, and that the resemblance is more apparent than real. It may, therefore, be thought, that in the case of allegiance our moral obligation of duty will not cease, even tho' the natural obligation of interest, which is its cause, has ceas'd; and that men may be bound by *conscience* to submit to a tyrannical government against their own and the public interest. And indeed, to the force of this argument I so far submit, as to acknowledge, that general rules commonly extend beyond the principles, on which they are founded; and that we seldom make any exception to them, unless that exception have the qualities of a general rule, and be founded on very numerous and common instances. Now this I assert to be entirely the present case. When men submit to the authority of others, 'tis to procure themselves some security against the wickedness and injustice of men, who are perpetually carried, by their unruly passions, and by their present and immediate interest, to the violation of all the laws of society. But as this imperfection is inherent in human nature, we know that it must attend men in all their states and conditions; and that those, whom we chuse for rulers, do not immediately become of a superior nature to the rest of mankind, upon account of their superior power and authority. What we expect from them depends not on a change of their nature but of their situation, when they acquire a more immediate interest in the preservation of order and the execution of justice. But besides that this interest is only more immediate in the execution of justice among their subjects; besides this, I say, we may often expect, from the irregularity of human nature, that they will neglect even this immediate interest, and be transported by their passions into all the excesses of cruelty and ambition. Our general knowledge of human nature, our observation of the past history of mankind, our experience of present times; all these causes must induce us to open the door to exceptions, and must make us conclude, that we may resist the more violent effects of supreme power, without any crime or injustice.

Accordingly we may observe, that this is both the general practice and principle of mankind, and that no nation, that cou'd find any remedy, ever yet suffer'd the cruel ravages of a tyrant, or were blam'd for their resistance. Those who took up arms against *Dionysius* or *Nero*, or *Philip the second*, have the favour of every reader in the perusal of their history; and nothing but the most violent perversion of common sense can ever lead us to condemn them. 'Tis certain, therefore, that in all our notions of morals we never entertain such an absurdity as that of passive obedience, but make allowances for resistance in the more flagrant instances of tyranny and oppression The general opinion of mankind has some authority in all cases; but in this of morals 'tis perfectly infallible. Nor is it less infallible, because men cannot distinctly explain the principles, on which it is founded. Few persons can carry on this train of reasoning: 'Government 'is a mere human invention for the interest of society. 'Where the tyranny of the governor removes this interest, it 'also removes the natural obligation to obedience. The 'moral obligation is founded on the natural, and therefore 'must cease where *that* ceases; especially where the subject 'is such as makes us foresee very many occasions wherein the 'natural obligation may cease, and causes us to form a kind 'of general rule for the regulation of our conduct in such 'occurrences.' But tho' this train of reasoning be too subtile for the vulgar, 'tis certain, that all men have an implicit notion of it, and are sensible, that they owe obedience to government merely on account of the public interest; and at the same time, that human nature is so subject to frailties and passions, as may easily pervert this institution, and change their governors into tyrants and public enemies. If the sense of common interest were not our original motive to obedience, I wou'd fain ask, what other principle is there in human nature capable of subduing the natural ambition of men, and forcing them to such a submission? Imitation and custom are not sufficient. For the question still recurs, what motive first produces those instances of submission, which we imitate, and that train of actions, which produces the custom? There evidently is no other principle than common interest; and if interest first produces obedience to government, the obligation to obedience must cease, whenever the interest ceases, in any great degree, and in a considerable number of instances.

Sect. X.—*Of the objects of allegiance.*

But tho', on some occasions, it may be justifiable, both in sound politics and morality, to resist supreme power, 'tis certain, that in the ordinary course of human affairs nothing can be more pernicious and criminal; and that besides the convulsions, which always attend revolutions, such a practice tends directly to the subversion of all government, and the causing an universal anarchy and confusion among mankind. As numerous and civiliz'd societies cannot subsist without government, so government is entirely useless without an exact obedience. We ought always to weigh the advantages, which we reap from authority, against the disadvantages; and by this means we shall become more scrupulous of putting in practice the doctrine of resistance. The common rule requires submission; and 'tis only in cases of grievous tyranny and oppression, that the exception can take place.

Since then such a blind submission is commonly due to magistracy, the next question is, *to whom it is due, and whom we are to regard as our lawful magistrates?* In order to answer this question, let us recollect what we have already establish'd concerning the origin of government and political society. When men have once experienc'd the impossibility of preserving any steady order in society, while every one is his own master, and violates or observes the laws of society, according to his present interest or pleasure, they naturally run into the invention of government, and put it out of their own power, as far as possible, to transgress the laws of society. Government, therefore, arises from the voluntary convention of men; and 'tis evident, that the same convention, which establishes government, will also determine the persons who are to govern, and will remove all doubt and ambiguity in this particular. And the voluntary consent of men must here have the greater efficacy, that the authority of the magistrates does *at first* stand upon the foundation of a promise of the subjects, by which they bind themselves to obedience; as in every other contract or engagement. The same promise, then, which binds them to obedience, ties them down to a particular person, and makes him the object of their allegiance.

But when government has been establish'd on this footing for some considerable time, and the separate interest, which we have in submission has produc'd a separate sentiment of morality, the case is entirely alter'd, and a promise is no longer able to determine the particular magistrate; since it is no longer consider'd as the foundation of government. We naturally suppose ourselves born to submission; and imagine, that such particular persons have a right to command. as we on our part are bound to obey. These notions of right and obligation are deriv'd from nothing but the *advantage* we reap from government, which gives us a repugnance to practise resistance ourselves, and makes us displeas'd with any instance of it in others. But here 'tis remarkable, that in this new state of affairs, the original sanction of government, which is *interest*, is not admitted to determine the persons whom we are to obey, as the original sanction did at first, when affairs were on the footing of a *promise*. A *promise* fixes and determines the persons, without any uncertainty : But 'tis evident, that if men were to regulate their conduct in this particular, by the view of a peculiar *interest*, either public or private, they wou'd involve themselves in endless confusion, and wou'd render all government, in a great measure, ineffectual. The private interest of every one is different ; and tho' the public interest in itself be always one and the same, yet it becomes the source of as great dissentions, by reason of the different opinions of particular persons concerning it. The same interest, therefore, which causes us to submit to magistracy, makes us renounce itself in the choice of our magistrates, and binds us down to a certain form of government, and to particular persons, without allowing us to aspire to the utmost perfection in either. The case is here the same as in that law of nature concerning the stability of possession. 'Tis highly advantageous, and even absolutely necessary to society, that possession shou'd be stable ; and this leads us to the establishment of such a rule : But we find, that were we to follow the same advantage, in assigning particular possessions to particular persons, we shou'd disappoint our end, and perpetuate the confusion, which that rule is intended to prevent. We must, therefore, proceed by general rules, and regulate ourselves by general interests, in modifying the law of nature concerning the stability of possession. Nor need we fear, that our attachment to this law will diminish upon account of the seeming frivolousness of those interests, by which it is

determin'd.   The impulse of the mind is deriv'd from a very
strong interest; and those other more minute interests serve
only to direct the motion, without adding anything to it, or
diminishing from it.   'Tis the same case with government.
Nothing is more advantageous to society than such an invention; and this interest is sufficient to make us embrace it
with ardour and alacrity; tho' we are oblig'd afterwards to
regulate and direct our devotion to government by several
considerations, which are not of the same importance, and
to chuse our magistrates without having in view any particular advantage from the choice.

The *first* of those principles I shall take notice of, as a
foundation of the right of magistracy, is that which gives
authority to all the most establish'd governments of the
world without exception : I mean, *long possession* in any one
form of government, or succession of princes.   'Tis certain,
that if we remount to the first origin of every nation, we
shall find, that there scarce is any race of kings, or form of a
commonwealth, that is not primarily founded on usurpation
and rebellion, and whose title is not at first worse than
doubtful and uncertain.   Time alone gives solidity to their
right; and operating gradually on the minds of men, reconciles them to any authority, and makes it seem just and
reasonable.   Nothing causes any sentiment to have a greater
influence upon us than custom, or turns our imagination more
strongly to any object.   When we have been long accustom'd
to obey any set of men, that general instinct or tendency,
which we have to suppose a moral obligation attending
loyalty, takes easily this direction, and chuses that set of
men for its objects.   'Tis interest which gives the general
instinct; but 'tis custom which gives the particular direction.

And here 'tis observable, that the same length of time has
a different influence on our sentiments of morality, according
to its different influence on the mind.   We naturally judge
of everything. by comparison; and since in considering the
fate of kingdoms and republics, we embrace a long extent of
time, a small duration has not in this case a like influence
on our sentiments, as when we consider any other object.
One thinks he acquires a right to a horse, or a suit of cloaths,
in a very short time; but a century is scarce sufficient to
establish any new government, or remove all scruples in the
minds of the subjects concerning it.   Add to this, that a

shorter period of time will suffice to give a prince a title to any additional power he may usurp, than will serve to fix his right, where the whole is an usurpation. The kings of *France* have not been possess'd of absolute power for above two reigns; and yet nothing will appear more extravagant to *Frenchmen* than to talk of their liberties. If we consider what has been said concerning *accession*, we shall easily account for this phænomenon.

When there is no form of government establish'd by *long* possession, the *present* possession is sufficient to supply its place, and may be regarded as the *second* source of all public authority. Right to authority is nothing but the constant possession of authority, maintain'd by the laws of society and the interests of mankind; and nothing can be more natural than to join this constant possession to the present one, according to the principles above-mention'd. If the same principles did not take place with regard to the property of private persons, 'twas because these principles were counter-ballanc'd by very strong considerations of interest; when we observ'd, that all restitution wou'd by that means be prevented, and every violence be authoriz'd and protected. And tho' the same motives may seem to have force, with regard to public authority, yet they are oppos'd by a contrary interest; which consists in the preservation of peace, and the avoiding of all changes, which, however they may be easily produc'd in private affairs, are unavoidably attended with bloodshed and confusion, where the public is interested.

Any one, who finding the impossibility of accounting for the right of the present possessor, by any receiv'd system of ethics, shou'd resolve to deny absolutely that right, and assert, that it is not authoriz'd by morality, wou'd be justly thought to maintain a very extravagant paradox, and to shock the common sense and judgment of mankind. No maxim is more conformable, both to prudence and morals, than to submit quietly to the government, which we find establish'd in the country where we happen to live, without enquiring too curiously into its origin and first establishment Few governments will bear being examin'd so rigorously. How many kingdoms are there at present in the world, and how many more do we find in history, whose governors have no better foundation for their authority than that of present possession? To confine ourselves to the *Roman* and *Grecian* empire; is it not evident, that the long succession of emperors, from the dissolution of the *Roman* liberty, to the final extinction of that empire by the *Turks*, cou'd not so much as pretend to any other title to the empire? The election of the senate was a mere form, which always follow'd the choice of the legions; and these were almost always divided in the different provinces, and nothing but the sword was able to terminate the difference. 'Twas by the sword, therefore, that every emperor acquir'd, as well as defended his right; and we must either say, that all the known world, for so many ages, had no government, and ow'd no allegiance to any one, or must allow, that the right of the stronger, in public affairs, is to be receiv'd as legitimate, and authoriz'd by morality, when not oppos'd by any other title.

The right of *conquest* may be consider'd as a *third* source of the title of sovereigns. This right resembles very much that of present possession; but has rather a superior force, being seconded by the notions of glory and honour, which we ascribe to *conquerors*, instead of the sentiments of hatred and detestation, which attend *usurpers*. Men naturally favour those they love; and therefore are more apt to ascribe a right to successful violence, betwixt one sovereign and another, than to the successful rebellion of a subject against his sovereign.[1]

When neither long possession, nor present possession, nor conquest take place, as when the first sovereign, who founded any monarchy, dies; in that case, the right of *succession* naturally prevails in their stead, and men are commonly induc'd to place the son of their late monarch on the throne, and suppose him to inherit his father's authority. The presum'd consent of the father; the imitation of the succession to private families, the interest, which the state has in chusing the person, who is most powerful, and has the most numerous followers; all these reasons lead men to prefer the son of their late monarch to any other person.[2]

---

[1] It is not here asserted, that *present possession* or *conquest* are sufficient to give a title against *long possession* and *positive laws* But only that they have some force, and will be able to cast the ballance where the titles are otherwise equal, and will even be sufficient *sometimes* to sanctify the weaker title What degree of force they have is difficult to determine I believe all moderate men will allow, that they have great force in all disputes concerning the rights of princes

[2] To prevent mistakes I must observe, that this case of succession is not the same with that of hereditary monarchies, where custom has fix'd the right of succession These depend upon the principle of long possession above explain'd.

These reasons have some weight; but I am persuaded, that to one, who considers impartially of the matter, 'twill appear, that there concur some principles of the imagination, along with those views of interest. The royal authority seems to be connected with the young prince even in his father's lifetime, by the natural transition of the thought; and still more after his death: So that nothing is more natural than to compleat this union by a new relation, and by putting him actually in possession of what seems so naturally to belong to him.

To confirm this we may weigh the following phænomena, which are pretty curious in their kind. In elective monarchies the right of succession has no place by the laws and settled custom; and yet its influence is so natural, that 'tis impossible entirely to exclude it from the imagination, and render the subjects indifferent to the son of their deceas'd monarch. Hence in some governments of this kind, the choice commonly falls on one or other of the royal family, and in some governments they are all excluded. Those contrary phænomena proceed from the same principle. Where the royal family is excluded, 'tis from a refinement in politics, which makes people sensible of their propensity to chuse a sovereign in that family, and gives them a jealousy of their liberty, lest their new monarch, aided by this propensity, shou'd establish his family, and destroy the freedom of elections for the future.

The history of *Artaxerxes*, and the younger *Cyrus*, may furnish us with some reflections to the same purpose. *Cyrus* pretended a right to the throne above his elder brother, because he was born after his father's accession. I do not pretend, that this reason was valid. I wou'd only infer from it, that he wou'd never have made use of such a pretext, were it not for the qualities of the imagination above-mention'd, by which we are naturally inclin'd to unite by a new relation whatever objects we find already united. *Artaxerxes* had an advantage above his brother, as being the eldest son, and the first in succession: But *Cyrus* was more closely related to the royal authority, as being begot after his father was invested with it.

Shou'd it here be pretended, that the view of convenience may be the source of all the right of succession, and that men gladly take advantage of any rule, by which they can fix the successor of their late sovereign, and prevent that anarchy and confusion, which attends all new elections : To this I wou'd answer, that I readily allow, that this motive may contribute something to the effect ; but at the same time I assert, that without another principle, 'tis impossible such a motive shou'd take place.   The interest of a nation requires, that the succession to the crown shou'd be fix'd one way or other ; but 'tis the same thing to its interest in what way it be fix'd : So that if the relation of blood had not an effect independent of public interest, it would never have been regarded, without a positive law ; and 'twou'd have been impossible, that so many positive laws of different nations could ever have concur'd precisely in the same views and intentions.

This leads us to consider the *fifth* source of authority, viz. *positive laws* ; when the legislature establishes a certain form of government and succession of princes. At first sight it may be thought, that this must resolve into some of the preceding titles of authority. The legislative power, whence the positive law is deriv'd, must either be establish'd by original contract, long possession, present possession, conquest, or succession ; and consequently the positive law must derive its force from some of those principles. But here 'tis remarkable, that tho' a positive law can only derive its force from these principles, yet it acquires not all the force of the principle from whence it is deriv'd, but loses considerably in the transition ; as it is natural to imagine. For instance ; a government is establish'd for many centuries on a certain system of laws, forms, and methods of succession. The legislative power, established by this long succession, changes all on a sudden the whole system of government, and introduces a new constitution in its stead. I believe few of the subjects will think themselves bound to comply with this alteration, unless it have an evident tendency to the public good : But will think themselves still at liberty to return to the antient government. Hence the notion of *fundamental laws*; which are suppos'd to be inalterable by the will of the sovereign : And of this nature the *Salic* law is understood to be in *France*. How far these fundamental laws extend is not determin'd in any government; nor is it possible it ever shou'd. There is such an insensible gradation from the most material laws to the most trivial, and from the most antient laws to the most modern, that 'twill be impossible to set bounds to the legislative power, and determine how far it may innovate in the principles of government. That is the work more of imagination and passion than of reason.

Whoever considers the history of the several nations of the world ; their revolutions, conquests, increase, and diminution ; the manner in which their particular governments are establish'd, and the successive right transmitted from one person to another, will soon learn to treat very lightly all disputes concerning the rights of princes, and will be convinc'd, that a strict adherence to any general rules, and the rigid loyalty to particular persons and families, on which some people set so high a value, are virtues that hold less of reason, than of bigotry and superstition. In this particular, the study of history confirms the reasonings of true philosophy ; which, shewing us the original qualities of human nature, teaches us to regard the controversies in politics as incapable of any decision in most cases, and as entirely subordinate to the interests of peace and liberty. Where the public good does not evidently demand a change ; 'tis certain that the concurrence of all those titles, *original contract, long possession, present possession, succession,* and *positive laws,* forms the strongest title to sovereignty, and is justly regarded as sacred and inviolable. But when these titles are mingled and oppos'd in different degrees, they often occasion perplexity ; and are less capable of solution from the arguments of lawyers and philosophers, than from the swords of the soldiery. Who shall tell me, for instance, whether *Germanicus* or *Drusus,* ought to have succeeded *Tiberius,* had he died while they were both alive, without naming any of them for his successor ? Ought the right of adoption to be receiv'd as equivalent to that of blood in a nation, where it had the same effect in private families, and had already, in two instances, taken place in public ? Ought *Germanicus* to be esteem'd the eldest son, because he was born before *Drusus ;* or the younger, because he was adopted after the birth of his brother ? Ought the right of the elder to be regarded in a nation, where the eldest brother had no advantage in the succession to private families ? Ought the *Roman* empire at that time to be esteem'd hereditary, because of two examples ; or ought it, even so early, to be regarded as belonging to the stronger, or the present possessor, as being founded on so

recent an usurpation? Upon whatever principles we may
pretend to answer these and such like questions, I am afraid
we shall never be able to satisfy an impartial enquirer, who
adopts no party in political controversies, and will be satisfied with nothing but sound reason and philosophy.

But here an *English* reader will be apt to enquire concerning that famous *revolution*, which has had such a happy
influence on our constitution, and has been attended with
such mighty consequences. We have already remark'd, that
in the case of enormous tyranny and oppression, 'tis lawful
to take arms even against supreme power; and that as
government is a mere human invention for mutual advantage
and security, it no longer imposes any obligation, either
natural or moral, when once it ceases to have that tendency.
But 'tho this *general* principle be authoriz'd by common
sense, and the practice of all ages, 'tis certainly impossible
for the laws, or even for philosophy, to establish any *particular* rules, by which we may know when resistance is
lawful; and decide all controversies, which may arise on that
subject. This may not only happen with regard to supreme
power; but 'tis possible, even in some constitutions, where
the legislative authority is not lodg'd in one person, that
there may be a magistrate so eminent and powerful, as
to oblige the laws to keep silence in this particular. Nor
wou'd this silence be an effect only of their *respect*, but also
of their *prudence;* since 'tis certain, that in the vast variety
of circumstances, which occur in all governments, an exercise
of power, in so great a magistrate, may at one time be beneficial to the public, which at another time wou'd be pernicious
and tyrannical. But notwithstanding this silence of the
laws in limited monarchies, 'tis certain, that the people still
retain the right of resistance; since 'tis impossible, even in
the most despotic governments, to deprive them of it. The
same necessity of self-preservation, and the same motive of
public good, give them the same liberty in the one case as in
the other. And we may farther observe, that in such mix'd
governments, the cases, wherein resistance is lawful, must
occur much oftener, and greater indulgence be given to the
subjects to defend themselves by force of arms, than in
arbitrary governments. Not only where the chief magistrate
enters into measures, in themselves, extremely pernicious to

PART
II.
──────
Of justice
and in-
justice.

the public, but even when he wou'd encroach on the other parts of the constitution, and extend his power beyond the legal bounds, it is allowable to resist and dethrone him ; tho' such resistance and violence may, in the general tenor of the laws, be deem'd unlawful and rebellious.   For besides that nothing is more essential to public interest, than the preservation of public liberty ; 'tis evident, that if such a mix'd government be once suppos'd to be establish'd, every part or member of the constitution must have a right of self-defence, and of maintaining its antient bounds against the encroachment of every other authority.   As matter wou'd have been created in vain, were it depriv'd of a power of resistance, without which no part of it cou'd preserve a distinct existence, and the whole might be crowded up into a single point : So 'tis a gross absurdity to suppose, in any government, a right without a remedy, or allow, that the supreme power is shar'd with the people, without allowing, that 'tis lawful for them to defend their share against every invader.   Those, therefore, who wou'd seem to respect our free government, and yet deny the right of resistance, have renounc'd all pretensions to common sense, and do not merit a serious answer.

It does not belong to my present purpose to shew, that these general principles are applicable to the late *revolution ;* and that all the rights and privileges, which ought to be sacred to a free nation, were at that time threaten'd with the utmost danger.   I am better pleas'd to leave this controverted subject, if it really admits of controversy ; and to indulge myself in some philosophical reflections, which naturally arise from that important event.

First, We may observe, that shou'd the *lords* and *commons* in our constitution, without any reason from public interest, either depose the king in being, or after his death exclude the prince, who, by laws and settled custom, ought to succeed, no one wou'd esteem their proceedings legal, or think themselves bound to comply with them.   But shou'd the king, by his unjust practices, or his attempts for a tyrannical and despotic power, justly forfeit his legal, it then not only becomes morally lawful and suitable to the nature of political society to dethrone him ; but what is more, we are apt likewise to think, that the remaining members of the constitution acquire a right of excluding his next heir, and of chusing whom they please for his successor.   This is founded on a very singular quality of our thought and imagination. When a king forfeits his authority, his heir ought naturally to remain in the same situation, as if the king were remov'd by death; unless by mixing himself in the tyranny, he forfeit it for himself.   But tho' this may seem reasonable, we easily comply with the contrary opinion.   The deposition of a king, in such a government as ours, is certainly an act beyond all common authority, and an illegal assuming a power for public good, which, in the ordinary course of government, can belong to no member of the constitution.   When the public good is so great and so evident as to justify the action, the commendable use of this licence causes us naturally to attribute to the *parliament* a right of using farther licences; and the antient bounds of the laws being once transgressed with approbation, we are not apt to be so strict in confining ourselves precisely within their limits.   The mind naturally runs on with any train of action, which it has begun; nor do we commonly make any scruple concerning our duty, after the first action of any kind, which we perform.   Thus at the *revolution*, no one who thought the deposition of the father justifiable, esteem'd themselves to be confin'd to his infant son; tho' had that unhappy monarch died innocent at that time, and had his son, by any accident, been convey'd beyond seas, there is no doubt but a regency wou'd have been appointed till he shou'd come to age, and cou'd be restor'd to his dominions.   As the slightest properties of the imagination have an effect on the judgments of the people, it shews the wisdom of the laws and of the parliament to take advantage of such properties, and to chuse the magistrates either in or out of a line, according as the vulgar will most naturally attribute authority and right to them.

Secondly, Tho' the accession of the *Prince* of *Orange* to the throne might at first give occasion to many disputes, and his title be contested, it ought not now to appear doubtful, but must have acquir'd a sufficient authority from those three princes, who have succeeded him upon the same title. Nothing is more usual, tho' nothing may, at first sight, appear more unreasonable, than this way of thinking. Princes often *seem* to acquire a right from their successors, as well as from their ancestors; and a king, who during his life-time might justly be deem'd an usurper, will be regarded by posterity as a lawful prince, because he has had the good fortune to settle his family on the throne, and entirely change the antient form of government. *Julius Cæsar* is regarded as the first *Roman* emperor; while *Sylla* and *Marius,* whose titles were really the same as his, are treated as tyrants and usurpers. Time and custom give authority to all forms of government, and all successions of princes; and that power, which at first was founded only on injustice and violence, becomes in time legal and obligatory. Nor does the mind rest there; but returning back upon its footsteps, transfers to their predecessors and ancestors that right, which it naturally ascribes to the posterity, as being related together, and united in the imagination. The present *king* of *France* makes *Hugh Capet* a more lawful prince than *Cromwell;* as the establish'd liberty of the *Dutch* is no inconsiderable apology for their obstinate resistance to *Philip* the second.

Sect. XI.—*Of the laws of nations*

When civil government has been establish'd over the greatest part of mankind, and different societies have been form'd contiguous to each other, there arises a new set of duties among the neighbouring states, suitable to the nature of that commerce, which they carry on with each other. Political writers tell us, that in every kind of intercourse, a body politic is to be consider'd as one person; and indeed this assertion is so far just, that different nations, as well as private persons, require mutual assistance; at the same time that their selfishness and ambition are perpetual sources of war and discord. But tho' nations in this particular resemble individuals, yet as they are very different in other respects, no wonder they regulate themselves by different maxims, and give rise to a new set of rules, which we call *the laws of nations.* Under this head we may comprize the sacredness of the persons of ambassadors, the declaration of war, the abstaining from poison'd arms, with other duties of that kind, which are evidently calculated for the commerce, that is peculiar to different societies.

But tho' these rules be super-added to the laws of nature, the former do not entirely abolish the latter; and one may safely affirm, that the three fundamental rules of justice, the stability of possession, its transference by consent, and the performance of promises, are duties of princes, as well as of subjects. The same interest produces the same effect in both cases. Where possession has no stability, there must be perpetual war. Where property is not transferr'd by consent, there can be no commerce. Where promises are not observ'd, there can be no leagues nor alliances. The advantages, therefore, of peace, commerce, and mutual succour, make us extend to different kingdoms the same notions of justice, which take place among individuals.

There is a maxim very current in the world, which few politicians are willing to avow, but which has been authoriz'd by the practice of all ages, *that there is a system of morals calculated for princes, much more free than that which ought to govern private persons.* 'Tis evident this is not to be understood of the lesser *extent* of public duties and obligations; nor will any one be so extravagant as to assert, that the most solemn treaties ought to have no force among princes. For as princes do actually form treaties among themselves, they must propose some advantage from the execution of them; and the prospect of such advantage for the future must engage them to perform their part, and must establish that law of nature. The meaning, therefore, of this political maxim is, that tho' the morality of princes has the same *extent*, yet it has not the same *force* as that of private persons, and may lawfully be transgress'd from a more trivial motive. However shocking such a proposition may appear to certain philosophers, 'twill be easy to defend it upon those principles, by which we have accounted for the origin of justice and equity.

When men have found by experience, that 'tis impossible to subsist without society, and that 'tis impossible to maintain society, while they give free course to their appetites; so urgent an interest quickly restrains their actions, and imposes an obligation to observe those rules, which we call *the laws of justice.* This obligation of interest rests not here; but by the necessary course of the passions and sentiments, gives rise to the moral obligation of duty; while we approve of such actions as tend to the peace of society, and disapprove of such as tend to its disturbance. The same *natural* obligation of interest takes place among independent kingdoms, and gives rise to the same *morality*; so that no one of ever so corrupt morals will approve of a prince, who voluntarily, and of his own accord, breaks his word, or violates any treaty.   But here we may observe, that tho' the intercourse of different states be advantageous, and even sometimes necessary, yet it is not so necessary nor advantageous as that among individuals, without which 'tis utterly impossible for human nature ever to subsist.   Since, therefore, the *natural* obligation to justice, among different states, is not so strong as among individuals, the *moral* obligation, which arises from it, must partake of its weakness; and we must necessarily give a greater indulgence to a prince or minister, who deceives another; than to a private gentleman, who breaks his word of honour.

Shou'd it be ask'd, *what proportion these two species of morality bear to each other?* I wou'd answer, that this is a question, to which we can never give any precise answer; nor is it possible to reduce to numbers the proportion, which we ought to fix betwixt them.   One may safely affirm, that this proportion finds itself, without any art or study of men; as we may observe on many other occasions.   The practice of the world goes farther in teaching us the degrees of our duty, than the most subtile philosophy, which was ever yet invented.   And this may serve as a convincing proof, that all men have an implicit notion of the foundation of those moral rules concerning natural and civil justice, and are sensible, that they arise merely from human conventions, and from the interest, which we have in the preservation of peace and order.   For otherwise the diminution of the interest wou'd never produce a relaxation of the morality, and reconcile us more easily to any transgression of justice among princes and republics, than in the private commerce of one subject with another.

Sect. XII.—*Of chastity and modesty.*

If any difficulty attend this system concerning the laws of nature and nations, 'twill be with regard to the universal approbation or blame, which follows their observance or transgression, and which some may not think sufficiently explain'd from the general interests of society.   To remove, as far as possible, all scruples of this kind, I shall here consider another set of duties, *viz.* the *modesty* and *chastity* which belong to the fair sex: And I doubt not but these virtues will be found to be still more conspicuous instances of the operation of those principles, which I have insisted on.

There are some philosophers, who attack the female virtues with great vehemence, and fancy they have gone very far in detecting popular errors, when they can show, that there is no foundation in nature for all that exterior modesty, which we require in the expressions, and dress, and behaviour of the fair sex. I believe I may spare myself the trouble of insisting on so obvious a subject, and may proceed, without farther preparation, to examine after what manner such notions arise from education, from the voluntary conventions of men, and from the interest of society.

Whoever considers the length and feebleness of human infancy, with the concern which both sexes naturally have for their offspring, will easily perceive, that there must be an union of male and female for the education of the young, and that this union must be of considerable duration. But in order to induce the men to impose on themselves this restraint, and undergo chearfully all the fatigues and expences, to which it subjects them, they must believe, that the children are their own, and that their natural instinct is not directed to a wrong object, when they give a loose to love and tenderness. Now if we examine the structure of the human body, we shall find, that this security is very difficult to be attain'd on our part; and that since, in the copulation of the sexes, the principle of generation goes from the man to the woman, an error may easily take place on the side of the former, tho' it be utterly impossible with regard to the latter. From this trivial and anatomical observation is deriv'd that vast difference betwixt the education and duties of the two sexes.

Were a philosopher to examine the matter à priori, he wou'd reason after the following manner. Men are induc'd to labour for the maintenance and education of their children, by the persuasion that they are really their own; and therefore 'tis reasonable, and even necessary, to give them some security in this particular. This security cannot consist entirely in the imposing of severe punishments on any transgressions of conjugal fidelity on the part of the wife; since the public punishments cannot be inflicted without legal proof, which 'tis difficult to meet with in this subject. What restraint, therefore, shall we impose on women, in order to counter-balance so strong a temptation as they have to infidelity? There seems to be no restraint possible, but in the punishment of bad fame or reputation ; a punishment, which has a mighty influence on the human mind, and at the same time is inflicted by the world upon surmizes, and conjectures, and proofs, that wou'd never be receiv'd in any court of judicature. In order, therefore, to impose a due restraint on the female sex, we must attach a peculiar degree of shame to their infidelity, above what arises merely from its injustice, and must bestow proportionable praises on their chastity.

But tho' this be a very strong motive to fidelity, our philosopher wou'd quickly discover, that it wou'd not alone be sufficient to that purpose. All human creatures, especially of the female sex, are apt to over-look remote motives in favour of any present temptation : The temptation is here the strongest imaginable : Its approaches are insensible and seducing : And a woman easily finds, or flatters herself she shall find, certain means of securing her reputation, and preventing all the pernicious consequences of her pleasures. 'Tis necessary, therefore, that, beside the infamy attending such licences, there shou'd be some preceding backwardness or dread, which may prevent their first approaches, and may give the female sex a repugnance to all expressions, and postures, and liberties, that have an immediate relation to that enjoyment.

Such wou'd be the reasonings of our speculative philosopher : But I am persuaded, that if he had not a perfect knowledge of human nature, he wou'd be apt to regard them as mere chimerical speculations, and wou'd consider the infamy attending infidelity, and backwardness to all its approaches, as principles that were rather to be wish'd than hop'd for in the world. For what means, wou'd he say, of persuading mankind, that the transgressions of conjugal duty are more infamous than any other kind of injustice, when 'tis evident they are more excusable, upon account of the greatness of the temptation? And what possibility of giving a backwardness to the approaches of a pleasure, to which nature has inspir'd so strong a propensity ; and a propensity that 'tis absolutely necessary in the end to comply with, for the support of the species?

But speculative reasonings, which cost so much pains to philosophers, are often form'd by the world naturally, and without reflection : As difficulties, which seem unsurmountable in theory, are easily got over in practice. Those, who have an interest in the fidelity of women, naturally disapprove of their infidelity, and all the approaches to it. Those, who have no interest, are carried along with the stream. Education takes possession of the ductile minds of the fair sex in their infancy. And when a general rule of this kind is once establish'd, men are apt to extend it beyond those principles, from which it first arose. Thus batchelors, however debauch'd, cannot chuse but be shock'd with any instance of lewdness or impudence in women. And tho' all these maxims have a plain reference to generation, yet women past child-bearing have no more privilege in this respect than those who are in the flower of their youth and beauty. Men have undoubtedly an implicit notion, that all those ideas of modesty and decency have a regard to generation; since they impose not the same laws, *with the same force*, on the male sex, where that reason takes not place. The exception is there obvious and extensive, and founded on a remarkable difference, which produces a clear separation and disjunction of ideas. But as the case is not the same with regard to the different ages of women, for this reason, tho' men know, that these notions are founded on the public interest, yet the general rule carries us beyond the original principle, and makes us extend the notions of modesty over the whole sex, from their earliest infancy to their extremest old-age and infirmity.

Courage, which is the point of honour among men, derives its merit, in a great measure, from artifice, as well as the chastity of women; tho' it has also some foundation in nature, as we shall see afterwards.

As to the obligations which the male sex lie under, with regard to chastity, we may observe, that according to the general notions of the world, they bear nearly the same proportion to the obligations of women, as the obligations of the law of nations do to those of the law of nature. 'Tis contrary to the interest of civil society, that men shou'd have an *entire* liberty of indulging their appetites in venereal enjoyment: But as this interest is weaker than in the case of the female sex, the moral obligation, arising from it, must be proportionably weaker. And to prove this we need only appeal to the practice and sentiments of all nations and ages.

PART III.

OF THE OTHER VIRTUES AND VICES.

Sect. I.—*Of the origin of the natural virtues and vices.*

PART
III

Of the
other
virtues
and vices.

We come now to the examination of such virtues and vices as are entirely natural, and have no dependance on the artifice and contrivance of men. The examination of these will conclude this system of morals.

The chief spring or actuating principle of the human mind is pleasure or pain; and when these sensations are remov'd both from our thought and feeling, we are, in a great measure, incapable of passion or action, of desire or volition. The most immediate effects of pleasure and pain are the propense and averse motions of the mind; which are diversified into volition, into desire and aversion, grief and joy, hope and fear, according as the pleasure or pain changes its situation, and becomes probable or improbable, certain or uncertain, or is consider'd as out of our power for the present moment. But when along with this, the objects, that cause pleasure or pain, acquire a relation to ourselves or others; they still continue to excite desire and aversion, grief and joy: But cause, at the same time, the indirect passions of pride or humility, love or hatred, which in this case have a double relation of impressions and ideas to the pain or pleasure.

We have already observ'd, that moral distinctions depend entirely on certain peculiar sentiments of pain and pleasure, and that whatever mental quality in ourselves or others gives us a satisfaction, by the survey or reflection, is of course virtuous; as everything of this nature, that gives uneasiness, is vicious. Now since every quality in ourselves or others, which gives pleasure, always causes pride or love; as every one, that produces uneasiness, excites humility or hatred.

It follows, that these two particulars are to be consider'd as equivalent, with regard to our mental qualities, *virtue* and the power of producing love or pride, *vice* and the power of producing humility or hatred. In every case, therefore, we must judge of the one by the other; and may pronounce any *quality* of the mind virtuous, which causes love or pride; and any one vicious, which causes hatred or humility.

SECT
I

Of the
origin of
the natural
virtues and
vices

If any *action* be either virtuous or vicious, 'tis only a sign of some quality or character. It must depend upon durable principles of the mind, which extend over the whole conduct, and enter into the personal character. Actions themselves, not proceeding from any constant principle, have no influence on love or hatred, pride or humility; and consequently are never consider'd in morality.

This reflection is self-evident, and deserves to be attended to, as being of the utmost importance in the present subject. We are never to consider any single action in our enquiries concerning the origin of morals; but only the quality or character from which the action proceeded. These alone are *durable* enough to affect our sentiments concerning the person. Actions are, indeed, better indications of a character than words, or even wishes and sentiments; but 'tis only so far as they are such indications, that they are attended with love or hatred, praise or blame.

To discover the true origin of morals, and of that love or hatred, which arises from mental qualities, we must take the matter pretty deep, and compare some principles, which have been already examin'd and explain'd.

We may begin with considering anew the nature and force of *sympathy*.[1] The minds of all men are similar in their feelings and operations; nor can any one be actuated by any affection, of which all others are not, in some degree, susceptible. As in strings equally wound up, the motion of one communicates itself to the rest; so all the affections readily pass from one person to another, and beget correspondent movements in every human creature. When I see the *effects* of passion in the voice and gesture of any person, my mind immediately passes from these effects to their causes, and forms such a lively idea of the passion, as is presently converted into the passion itself. In like manner, when I perceive the *causes* of any emotion, my mind is convey'd to

[¹ Introd sect 52.—Ed]

PART
III

Of the
other
virtues
and vices.

the effects, and is actuated with a like emotion. Were I present at any of the more terrible operations of surgery, 'tis certain, that even before it begun, the preparation of the instruments, the laying of the bandages in order, the heating of the irons, with all the signs of anxiety and concern in the patient and assistants, wou'd have a great effect upon my mind, and excite the strongest sentiments of pity and terror. No passion of another discovers itself immediately to the mind. We are only sensible of its causes or effects. From *these* we infer the passion: And consequently *these* give rise to our sympathy.

Our sense of beauty depends very much on this principle; and where any object has a tendency to produce pleasure in its possessor, it is always regarded as beautiful; as every object, that has a tendency to produce pain, is disagreeable and deform'd. Thus the conveniency of a house, the fertility of a field, the strength of a horse, the capacity, security, and swift-sailing of a vessel, form the principal beauty of these several objects. Here the object, which is denominated beautiful, pleases only by its tendency to produce a certain effect. That effect is the pleasure or advantage of some other person. Now the pleasure of a stranger, for whom we have no friendship, pleases us only by sympathy. To this principle, therefore, is owing the beauty, which we find in every thing that is useful. How considerable a part this is of beauty will easily appear upon reflection. Wherever an object has a tendency to produce pleasure in the possessor, or in other words, is the proper *cause* of pleasure, it is sure to please the spectator, by a delicate sympathy with the possessor. Most of the works of art are esteem'd beautiful, in proportion to their fitness for the use of man, and even many of the productions of nature derive their beauty from that source. Handsome and beautiful, on most occasions, is not an absolute but a relative quality, and pleases us by nothing but its tendency to produce an end that is agreeable.[1]

The same principle produces, in many instances, our sentiments of morals, as well as those of beauty. No virtue is more esteem'd than justice, and no vice more detested than

---

[1] Decentior equus cujus astricta sunt ilia, sed idem velocior. Pulcher aspectu sit athleta, cujus lacertos exercitatio expressit, idem certamini paratior. Nunquam vero *species* ab *utilitate* dividitur. Sed hoc quidem discernere, modici judicii est.

Quinct lib 8

injustice; nor are there any qualities, which go farther to the fixing the character, either as amiable or odious. Now justice is a moral virtue, merely because it has that tendency to the good of mankind; and, indeed, is nothing but an artificial invention to that purpose. The same may be said of allegiance, of the laws of nations, of modesty, and of good-manners. All these are mere human contrivances for the interest of society. And since there is a very strong senti-ment of morals, which in all nations, and all ages, has attended them, we must allow, that the reflecting on the tendency of characters and mental qualities, is sufficient to give us the sentiments of approbation and blame. Now as the means to an end can only be agreeable, where the end is agreeable; and as the good of society, where our own interest is not concern'd, or that of our friends, pleases only by sym-pathy: It follows, that sympathy is the source of the esteem, which we pay to all the artificial virtues.

SECT
I.

Of the
origin of
the natural
virtues and
vices

Thus it appears, *that* sympathy is a very powerful principle in human nature, *that* it has a great influence on our taste of beauty, and *that* it produces our sentiment of morals in all the artificial virtues. From thence we may presume, that it also gives rise to many of the other virtues; and that quali-ties acquire our approbation, because of their tendency to the good of mankind. This presumption must become a cer-tainty, when we find that most of those qualities, which we *naturally* approve of, have actually that tendency, and render a man a proper member of society: While the qualities, which we *naturally* disapprove of, have a contrary tendency, and render any intercourse with the person dangerous or disagreeable. For having found, that such tendencies have force enough to produce the strongest sentiment of morals, we can never reasonably, in these cases, look for any other cause of approbation or blame; it being an inviolable maxim in philosophy, that where any particular cause is sufficient for an effect, we ought to rest satisfied with it, and ought not to multiply causes without necessity. We have happily attain'd experiments in the artificial virtues, where the ten-dency of qualities to the good of society, is the *sole* cause of our approbation, without any suspicion of the concurrence of another principle. From thence we learn the force of that principle. And where that principle may take place, and the quality approv'd of is really beneficial to society, a true

PART
III

Of the
other
virtues
and vices.

'philosopher will never require any other principle to account for the strongest approbation and esteem.

That many of the natural virtues have this tendency to the good of society, no one can doubt of. Meekness, beneficence, charity, generosity, clemency, moderation, equity, bear the greatest figure among the moral qualities, and are commonly denominated the *social* virtues, to mark their tendency to the good of society. This goes so far, that some philosophers have represented all moral distinctions as the effect of artifice and education, when skilful politicians endeavour'd to restrain the turbulent passions of men, and make them operate to the public good, by the notions of honour and shame. This system, however, is not consistent with experience. For, *first*, there are other virtues and vices beside those which have this tendency to the public advantage and loss. *Secondly*, had not men a natural sentiment of approbation and blame, it cou'd never be excited by politicians; nor wou'd the words *laudable* and *praise-worthy*, *blameable* and *odious*, be any more intelligible, than if they were a language perfectly unknown to us, as we have already observ'd. But tho' this system be erroneous, it may teach us, that moral distinctions arise, in a great measure, from the tendency of qualities and characters to the interests of society, and that 'tis our concern for that interest, which makes us approve or disapprove of them. Now we have no such extensive concern for society but from sympathy; and consequently 'tis that principle, which takes us so far out of ourselves, as to give us the same pleasure or uneasiness in the characters of others, as if they had a tendency to our own advantage or loss.

The only difference betwixt the natural virtues and justice lies in this, that the good, which results from the former, arises from every single act, and is the object of some natural passion: Whereas a single act of justice, consider'd in itself, may often be contrary to the public good; and 'tis only the concurrence of mankind, in a general scheme or system of action, which is advantageous. When I relieve persons in distress, my natural humanity is my motive; and so far as my succour extends, so far have I promoted the happiness of my fellow-creatures. But if we examine all the questions, that come before any tribunal of justice, we shall find, that, considering each case apart, it wou'd as often be

an instance of humanity to decide contrary to the laws of
justice as conformable to them. Judges take from a poor man
to give to a rich ; they bestow on the dissolute the labour of
the industrious ; and put into the hands of the vicious the
means of harming both themselves and others. The whole
scheme, however, of law and justice is advantageous to the
society ; and 'twas with a view to this advantage, that men,
by their voluntary conventions, establish'd it. After it is
once establish'd by these conventions, it is *naturally* attended
with a strong sentiment of morals ; which can proceed from
nothing but our sympathy with the interests of society.
We need no other explication of that esteem, which attends
such of the natural virtues, as have a tendency to the public
good.[1]

SECT.
I

Of the
origin of
the natural
virtues and
vices

  I must farther add, that there are several circumstances,
which render this hypothesis much more probable with regard
to the natural than the artificial virtues. 'Tis certain, that
the imagination is more affected by what is particular, than
by what is general ; and that the sentiments are always
mov'd with difficulty, where their objects are, in any degree,
loose and undetermin'd : Now every particular act of justice
is not beneficial to society, but the whole scheme or system :
And it may not, perhaps, be any individual person, for whom
we are concern'd, who receives benefit from justice, but the
whole society alike. On the contrary, every particular act
of generosity, or relief of the industrious and indigent, is
beneficial ; and is beneficial to a particular person, who is
not undeserving of it. 'Tis more natural, therefore, to think,
that the tendencies of the latter virtue will affect our sentiments, and command our approbation, than those of the
former ; and therefore, since we find, that the approbation of
the former arises from their tendencies, we may ascribe, with
better reason, the same cause to the approbation of the latter.
In any number of similar effects, if a cause can be discover'd
for one, we ought to extend that cause to all the other effects,
which can be accounted for by it : But much more, if these
other effects be attended with peculiar circumstances, which
facilitate the operation of that cause.

  Before I proceed farther, I must observe two remarkable
circumstances in this affair, which may seem objections to
the present system. The first may be thus explain'd. When

[1 Introd sect. 53 and 54.—Ed.]

any quality, or character, has a tendency to the good of mankind, we are pleas'd with it, and approve of it; because it presents the lively idea of pleasure; which idea affects us by sympathy, and is itself a kind of pleasure. But as this sympathy is very variable, it may be thought, that our sentiments of morals must admit of all the same variations. We sympathize more with persons contiguous to us, than with persons remote from us: With our acquaintance, than with strangers: With our countrymen, than with foreigners. But notwithstanding this variation of our sympathy, we give the same approbation to the same moral qualities in *China* as in *England*. They appear equally virtuous, and recommend themselves equally to the esteem of a judicious spectator. The sympathy varies without a variation in our esteem. Our esteem, therefore, proceeds not from sympathy.

To this I answer: The approbation of moral qualities most certainly is not deriv'd from reason, or any comparison of ideas; but proceeds entirely from a moral taste, and from certain sentiments of pleasure or disgust, which arise upon the contemplation and view of particular qualities or characters. Now 'tis evident, that those sentiments, whenceever they are deriv'd, must vary according to the distance or contiguity of the objects; nor can I feel the same lively pleasure from the virtues of a person, who liv'd in *Greece* two thousand years ago, that I feel from the virtues of a familiar friend and acquaintance. Yet I do not say, that I esteem the one more than the other: And therefore, if the variation of the sentiment, without a variation of the esteem, be an objection, it must have equal force against every other system, as against that of sympathy. But to consider the matter a-right, it has no force at all; and 'tis the easiest matter in the world to account for it. Our situation, with regard both to persons and things, is in continual fluctuation; and a man, that lies at a distance from us, may, in a little time, become a familiar acquaintance. Besides, every particular man has a peculiar position with regard to others; and 'tis impossible we cou'd ever converse together on any reasonable terms, were each of us to consider characters and persons, only as they appear from his peculiar point of view. In order, therefore, to prevent those continual *contradictions*, and arrive at a more *stable* judgment of things, we fix on some *steady* and *general* points of view; and always, in our thoughts, place ourselves in them, whatever may be our present situation.   In like manner, external beauty is determin'd merely by pleasure; and 'tis evident, a beautiful countenance cannot give so much pleasure, when seen at the distance of twenty paces, as when it is brought nearer us.   We say not, however, that it appears to us less beautiful: Because we know what effect it will have in such a position, and by that reflection we correct its momentary appearance.

In general, all sentiments of blame or praise are variable, according to our situation of nearness or remoteness, with regard to the person blam'd or prais'd, and according to the present disposition of our mind.   But these variations we regard not in our general decisions, but still apply the terms expressive of our liking or dislike, in the same manner, as if we remain'd in one point of view.   Experience soon teaches us this method of correcting our sentiments, or at least, of correcting our language, where the sentiments are more stubborn and inalterable.   Our servant, if diligent and faithful, may excite stronger sentiments of love and kindness than *Marcus Brutus*, as represented in history; but we say not upon that account, that the former character is more laudable than the latter.   We know, that were we to approach equally near to that renown'd patriot, he wou'd command a much higher degree of affection and admiration.   Such corrections are common with regard to all the senses; and indeed 'twere impossible we cou'd ever make use of language, or communicate our sentiments to one another, did we not correct the momentary appearances of things, and overlook our present situation.[1]

'Tis therefore from the influence of characters and qualities, upon those who have an intercourse with any person, that we blame or praise him.   We consider not whether the persons, affected by the qualities, be our acquaintance or strangers, countrymen or foreigners.   Nay, we over-look our own interest in those general judgments; and blame not a man for opposing us in any of our pretensions, when his own interest is particularly concern'd.   We make allowance for a certain degree of selfishness in men; because we know it to be inseparable from human nature, and inherent in our frame and constitution.   By this reflection we correct those sentiments of blame, which so naturally arise upon any opposition.

[1 Introd. sect. 53 and 54 -- Ed]

PART
III.

Of the
other
virtues
and vices.

But however the general principle of our blame or praise may be corrected by those other principles, 'tis certain, they are not altogether efficacious, nor do our passions often correspond entirely to the present theory. 'Tis seldom men heartily love what lies at a distance from them, and what no way redounds to their particular benefit; as 'tis no less rare to meet with persons, who can pardon another any opposition he makes to their interest, however justifiable that opposition may be by the general rules of morality. Here we are contented with saying, that reason requires such an impartial conduct, but that 'tis seldom we can bring ourselves to it, and that our passions do not readily follow the determination of our judgment. This language will be easily understood, if we consider what we formerly said concerning that *reason*, which is able to oppose our passion; and which we have found to be nothing but a general calm determination of the passions, founded on some distant view or reflection. When we form our judgments of persons, merely from the tendency of their characters to our own benefit, or to that of our friends, we find so many contradictions to our sentiments in society and conversation, and such an uncertainty from the incessant changes of our situation, that we seek some other standard of merit and demerit, which may not admit of so great variation. Being thus loosen'd from our first station, we cannot afterwards fix ourselves so commodiously by any means as by a sympathy with those, who have any commerce with the person we consider. This is far from being as lively as when our own interest is concern'd, or that of our particular friends; nor has it such an influence on our love and hatred: But being equally conformable to our calm and general principles, 'tis said to have an equal authority over our reason, and to command our judgment and opinion. We blame equally a bad action, which we read of in history, with one perform'd in our neighbourhood t'other day: The meaning of which is, that we know from reflection, that the former action wou'd excite as strong sentiments of disapprobation as the latter, were it plac'd in the same position.

I now proceed to the *second* remarkable circumstance, which I propos'd to take notice of. Where a person is possess'd of a character, that in its natural tendency is beneficial to society, we esteem him virtuous, and are delighted with the view of his character, even tho' particular accidents prevent its operation, and incapacitate him from being serviceable to his friends and country. Virtue in rags is still virtue; and the love, which it procures, attends a man into a dungeon or desart, where the virtue can no longer be exerted in action, and is lost to all the world. Now this may be esteem'd an objection to the present system. Sympathy interests us in the good of mankind; and if sympathy were the source of our esteem for virtue, that sentiment of approbation cou'd only take place, where the virtue actually attain'd its end, and was beneficial to mankind. Where it fails of its end, 'tis only an imperfect means; and therefore can never acquire any merit from that end. The goodness of an end can bestow a merit on such means alone as are compleat, and actually produce the end.

To this we may reply, that where any object, in all its parts, is fitted to attain any agreeable end, it naturally gives us pleasure, and is esteem'd beautiful, even tho' some external circumstances be wanting to render it altogether effectual. 'Tis sufficient if every thing be compleat in the object itself. A house, that is contriv'd with great judgment for all the commodities of life, pleases us upon that account; tho' perhaps we are sensible, that no-one will ever dwell in it. A fertile soil, and a happy climate, delight us by a reflection on the happiness which they wou'd afford the inhabitants, tho' at present the country be desart and uninhabited. A man, whose limbs and shape promise strength and activity, is esteem'd handsome, tho' condemn'd to perpetual imprisonment. The imagination has a set of passions belonging to it, upon which our sentiments of beauty much depend. These passions are mov'd by degrees of liveliness and strength, which are inferior to *belief*, and independent of the real existence of their objects. Where a character is, in every respect, fitted to be beneficial to society, the imagination passes easily from the cause to the effect, without considering that there are still some circumstances wanting to render the cause a compleat one. *General rules* create a species of probability, which sometimes influences the judgment, and always the imagination.

'Tis true, when the cause is compleat, and a good disposition is attended with good fortune, which renders it really beneficial to society, it gives a stronger pleasure to the spectator, and is attended with a more lively sympathy.

PART
III.

Of the
other
virtues
and vices

We are more affected by it; and yet we do not say that it is more virtuous, or that we esteem it more. We know, that an alteration of fortune may render the benevolent disposition entirely impotent; and therefore we separate, as much as possible, the fortune from the disposition. The case is the same, as when we correct the different sentiments of virtue, which proceed from its different distances from ourselves. The passions do not always follow our corrections; but these corrections serve sufficiently to regulate our abstract notions, and are alone regarded, when we pronounce in general concerning the degrees of vice and virtue.

'Tis observ'd by critics, that all words or sentences, which are difficult to the pronunciation, are disagreeable to the ear. There is no difference, whether a man hear them pronounc'd, or read them silently to himself. When I run over a book with my eye, I imagine I hear it all; and also, by the force of imagination, enter into the uneasiness, which the delivery of it wou'd give the speaker. The uneasiness is not real; but as such a composition of words has a natural tendency to produce it, this is sufficient to affect the mind with a painful sentiment, and render the discourse harsh and disagreeable. 'Tis a similar case, where any real quality is, by accidental circumstances, render'd impotent, and is depriv'd of its natural influence on society.

Upon these principles we may easily remove any contradiction, which may appear to be betwixt the *extensive sympathy*, on which our sentiments of virtue depend. and that *limited generosity* which I have frequently observ'd to be natural to men, and which justice and property suppose, according to the precedent reasoning. My sympathy with another may give me the sentiment of pain and disapprobation, when any object is presented, that has a tendency to give him uneasiness; tho' I may not be willing to sacrifice any thing of my own interest, or cross any of my passions, for his satisfaction. A house may displease me by being ill-contriv'd for the convenience of the owner; and yet I may refuse to give a shilling towards the rebuilding of it. Sentiments must touch the heart, to make them controul our passions: But they need not extend beyond the imagination, to make them influence our taste. When a building seems clumsy and tottering to the eye, it is ugly and disagreeable; tho' we be fully assur'd of the solidity of the workmanship.

SECT
I.

Of the
origin of
the natural
virtues and
vices

'Tis a kind of fear, which causes this sentiment of disapprobation; but the passion is not the same with that which we feel, when oblig'd to stand under a wall, that we really think tottering and insecure. The *seeming tendencies* of objects affect the mind: And the emotions they excite are of a like species with those, which proceed from the *real consequences* of objects, but their feeling is different. Nay, these emotions are so different in their feeling, that they may often be contrary, without destroying each other; as when the fortifications of a city belonging to an enemy are esteem'd beautiful upon account of their strength, tho' we cou'd wish that they were entirely destroy'd. The imagination adheres to the *general* views of things, and distinguishes the feelings they produce, from those which arise from our particular and momentary situation.[1]

If we examine the panegyrics that are commonly made of great men, we shall find, that most of the qualities, which are attributed to them, may be divided into two kinds, *viz.* such as make them perform their part in society; and such as render them serviceable to themselves, and enable them to promote their own interest. Their *prudence, temperance, frugality, industry, assiduity, enterprize, dexterity,* are celebrated, as well as their *generosity* and *humanity*. If we ever give an indulgence to any quality, that disables a man from making a figure in life, 'tis to that of *indolence,* which is not suppos'd to deprive one of his parts and capacity, but only suspends their exercise; and that without any inconvenience to the person himself, since 'tis, in some measure, from his own choice. Yet indolence is always allow'd to be a fault, and a very great one, if extreme: Nor do a man's friends ever acknowledge him to be subject to it, but in order to save his character in more material articles. He cou'd make a figure, say they, if he pleas'd to give application: His understanding is sound, his conception quick, and his memory tenacious; but he hates business, and is indifferent about his fortune. And this a man sometimes may make even a subject of vanity; tho' with the air of confessing a fault: Because he may think, that this incapacity for business implies much more noble qualities; such as a philosophical spirit, a fine taste, a delicate wit, or a relish for pleasure and

[1 Introd. sect. 53 and 54.—Ed.]

PART
III

Of the
other
virtues
and vices

society. But take any other case : Suppose a quality, that without being an indication of any other good qualities, incapacitates a man *always* for business, and is destructive to his interest ; such as a blundering understanding, and a wrong judgment of every thing in life , inconstancy and irresolution ; or a want of address in the management of men and business : These are all allow'd to be imperfections in a character ; and many men wou'd rather acknowledge the greatest crimes, than have it suspected, that they are, in any degree, subject to them.

'Tis very happy, in our philosophical researches, when we find the same phænomenon diversified by a variety of circumstances ; and by discovering what is common among them, can the better assure ourselves of the truth of any hypothesis we may make use of to explain it. Were nothing esteem'd virtue but what were beneficial to society, I am persuaded, that the foregoing explication of the moral sense ought still to be receiv'd, and that upon sufficient evidence : But this evidence must grow upon us, when we find other kinds of virtue, which will not admit of any explication except from that hypothesis. Here is a man, who is not remarkably defective in his social qualities ; but what principally recommends him is his dexterity in business, by which he has extricated himself from the greatest difficulties, and conducted the most delicate affairs with a singular address and prudence. I find an esteem for him immediately to arise in me : His company is a satisfaction to me ; and before I have any farther acquaintance with him, I wou'd rather do him a service than another, whose character is in every other respect equal, but is deficient in that particular. In this case, the qualities that please me are all consider'd as useful to the person, and as having a tendency to promote his interest and satisfaction. They are only regarded as means to an end, and please me in proportion to their fitness for that end. The end, therefore, must be agreeable to me. But what makes the end agreeable ? The person is a stranger : I am no way interested in him, nor he under any obligation to him : His happiness concerns not me, farther than the happiness of every human, and indeed of every sensible creature . That is, it affects me only by sympathy. From that principle, whenever I discover his happiness and good, whether in its causes or effects, I enter so deeply into it, that it gives me a sensible emotion. The appearance of qualities, that have a *tendency* to promote it, have an agreeable effect upon my imagination, and command my love and esteem.

This theory may serve to explain, why the same qualities, in all cases, produce both pride and love, humility and hatred; and the same man is always virtuous or vicious, accomplish'd or despicable to others, who is so to himself. A person, in whom we discover any passion or habit, which originally is only incommodious to himself, becomes always disagreeable to us, merely on its account; as on the other hand, one whose character is only dangerous and disagreeable to others, can never be satisfied with himself, as long as he is sensible of that disadvantage. Nor is this observable only with regard to characters and manners, but may be remark'd even in the most minute circumstances. A violent cough in another gives us uneasiness; tho' in itself it does not in the least affect us. A man will be mortified, if you tell him he has a stinking breath; tho' 'tis evidently no annoyance to himself. Our fancy easily changes its situation; and either surveying ourselves as we appear to others, or considering others as they feel themselves, we enter, by that means, into sentiments, which no way belong to us, and in which nothing but sympathy is able to interest us. And this sympathy we sometimes carry so far, as even to be displeas'd with a quality commodious to us, merely because it displeases others, and makes us disagreeable in their eyes; tho' perhaps we never can have any interest in rendering ourselves agreeable to them.

There have been many systems of morality advanc'd by philosophers in all ages; but if they are strictly examin'd, they may be reduc'd to two, which alone merit our attention. Moral good and evil are certainly distinguish'd by our *sentiments*, not by *reason*: But these sentiments may arise either from the mere species or appearance of characters and passions, or from reflections on their tendency to the happiness of mankind, and of particular persons. My opinion is, that both these causes are intermix'd in our judgments of morals; after the same manner as they are in our decisions concerning most kinds of external beauty: Tho' I am also of opinion, that reflections on the tendencies of actions have by far the greatest influence, and determine all the great lines of our duty. There are, however, instances, in cases of less moment,

PART
III

Of the
other
virtues
and vices.

wherein this immediate taste or sentiment produces our approbation. Wit, and a certain easy and disengag'd behaviour, are qualities *immediately agreeable* to others, and command their love and esteem. Some of these qualities produce satisfaction in others by particular *original* principles of human nature, which cannot be accounted for: Others may be resolv'd into principles, which are more general. This will best appear upon a particular enquiry.

As some qualities acquire their merit from their being *immediately agreeable* to others, without any tendency to public interest; so some are denominated virtuous from their being *immediately agreeable* to the person himself, who possesses them. Each of the passions and operations of the mind has a particular feeling, which must be either agreeable or disagreeable. The first is virtuous, the second vicious. This particular feeling constitutes the very nature of the passion; and therefore needs not be accounted for.

But however directly the distinction of vice and virtue may seem to flow from the immediate pleasure or uneasiness, which particular qualities cause to ourselves or others; 'tis easy to observe, that it has also a considerable dependence on the principle of *sympathy* so often insisted on. We approve of a person, who is possess'd of qualities *immediately agreeable* to those, with whom he has any commerce; tho' perhaps we ourselves never reap'd any pleasure from them. We also approve of one, who is possess'd of qualities, that are *immediately agreeable* to himself; tho' they be of no service to any mortal. To account for this we must have recourse to the foregoing principles.

Thus, to take a general review of the present hypothesis: Every quality of the mind is denominated virtuous, which gives pleasure by the mere survey; as every quality, which produces pain, is call'd vicious. This pleasure and this pain may arise from four different sources. For we reap a pleasure from the view of a character, which is naturally fitted to be useful to others, or to the person himself, or which is agreeable to others, or to the person himself. One may, perhaps, be surpriz'd, that amidst all these interests and pleasures, we shou'd forget our own, which touch us so nearly on every other occasion. But we shall easily satisfy ourselves on this head, when we consider, that every particular person's pleasure and interest being different, 'tis impossible men cou'd ever agree in their sentiments and judgments, unless they chose some common point of view, from which they might survey their object, and which might cause it to appear the same to all of them.   Now in judging of characters, the only interest or pleasure, which appears the same to every spectator, is that of the person himself, whose character is examin'd; or that of persons, who have a connexion with him.   And tho' such interests and pleasures touch us more faintly than our own, yet being more constant and universal, they counter-ballance the latter even in practice, and are alone admitted in speculation as the standard of virtue and morality.   They alone produce that particular feeling or sentiment, on which moral distinctions depend.[1]

As to the good or ill desert of virtue or vice, 'tis an evident consequence of the sentiments of pleasure or uneasiness. These sentiments produce love or hatred; and love or hatred, by the original constitution of human passion, is attended with benevolence or anger; that is, with a desire of making happy the person we love, and miserable the person we hate. We have treated of this more fully on another occasion.

Sect. II.—*Of greatness of mind.*

It may now be proper to illustrate this general system of morals, by applying it to particular instances of virtue and vice, and shewing how their merit or demerit arises from the four sources here explain'd.   We shall begin with examining the passions of *pride* and *humility*, and shall consider the vice or virtue that lies in their excesses or just proportion. An excessive pride or over-weaning conceit of ourselves is always esteem'd vicious, and is universally hated; as modesty, or a just sense of our weakness, is esteem'd virtuous, and procures the good-will of every-one.   Of the four sources of moral distinctions, this is to be ascrib'd to the *third*; viz. the immediate agreeableness and disagreeableness of a quality to others, without any reflections on the tendency of that quality.

In order to prove this, we must have recourse to two principles, which are very conspicuous in human nature. The *first* of these is the *sympathy*, and communication of sentiments and passions above-mention'd.   So close and in-

SECT
I
Of the
origin of
the natural
virtues and
vices.

[¹ Introd sect 53 and 54 —Ed]

PART
III

Of the
other
virtues
and vices.

timate is the correspondence of human souls, that no sooner any person approaches me, than he diffuses on me all his opinions, and draws along my judgment in a greater or lesser degree.   And tho', on many occasions, my sympathy with him goes not so far as entirely to change my sentiments, and way of thinking, yet it seldom is so weak as not to disturb the easy course of my thought, and give an authority to that opinion, which is recommended to me by his assent and approbation.   Nor is it any way material upon what subject he and I employ our thoughts.   Whether we judge of an indifferent person, or of my own character, my sympathy gives equal force to his decision: And even his sentiments of his own merit make me consider him in the same light, in which he regards himself.

This principle of sympathy is of so powerful and insinuating a nature, that it enters into most of our sentiments and passions, and often takes place under the appearance of its contrary.   For 'tis remarkable, that when a person opposes me in any thing, which I am strongly bent upon, and rouzes up my passion by contradiction, I have always a degree of sympathy with him, nor does my commotion proceed from any other origin.   We may here observe an evident conflict or rencounter of opposite principles and passions.   On the one side there is that passion or sentiment, which is natural to me; and 'tis observable, that the stronger this passion is, the greater is the commotion.   There must also be some passion or sentiment on the other side; and this passion can proceed from nothing but sympathy.   The sentiments of others can never affect us, but by becoming, in some measure, our own; in which case they operate upon us, by opposing and encreasing our passions, in the very same manner, as if they had been originally deriv'd from our own temper and disposition.   While they remain conceal'd in the minds of others, they can never have any influence upon us: And even when they are known, if they went no farther than the imagination, or conception; that faculty is so accustom'd to objects of every different kind, that a mere idea, tho' contrary to our sentiments and inclinations, wou'd never alone be able to affect us.

The *second* principle I shall take notice of is that of *comparison*, or the variation of our judgments concerning objects, according to the proportion they bear to those with which we compare them. We judge more of objects by comparison, than by their intrinsic worth and value; and regard every thing as mean, when set in opposition to what is superior of the same kind. But no comparison is more obvious than that with ourselves; and hence it is that on all occasions it takes place, and mixes with most of our passions. This kind of comparison is directly contrary to sympathy in its operation, as we have observ'd in treating of *compassion* and *malice*. [1]*In all kinds of comparison an object makes us always receive from another, to which it is compar'd, a sensation contrary to what arises from itself in its direct and immediate survey. The direct survey of another's pleasure naturally gives us pleasure; and therefore produces pain, when compar'd with our own. His pain, consider'd in itself, is painful; but augments the idea of our own happiness, and gives us pleasure.*

Since then those principles of sympathy, and a comparison with ourselves, are directly contrary, it may be worth while to consider, what general rules can be form'd, beside the particular temper of the person, for the prevalence of the one or the other. Suppose I am now in safety at land, and wou'd willingly reap some pleasure from this consideration: I must think on the miserable condition of those who are at sea in a storm, and must endeavour to render this idea as strong and lively as possible, in order to make me more sensible of my own happiness. But whatever pains I may take, the comparison will never have an equal efficacy, as if I were really on[2] the shore, and saw a ship at a distance, lost by a tempest, and in danger every moment of perishing on a rock or sand-bank. But suppose this idea to become still more lively. Suppose the ship to be driven so near me, that I can perceive distinctly the horror, painted on the countenance of the seamen and passengers, hear their lamentable cries, see the dearest friends give their last adieu, or embrace with a resolution to perish in each other's arms: No man has so savage a heart as to reap any pleasure from such a spectacle, or withstand the motions of the tenderest compassion and sympathy. 'Tis evident, therefore, there is a medium in this case; and that if the idea be too faint, it

---

[1] Book II Part II Sect VIII
[2] Suave mari magno turbantibus æquora ventis
E terra magnum alterius spectare laborem;
Non quia vexari quenquam est jucunda voluptas,
Sed quibus ipse malis careas quia cernere suav' est.—*Lucret.*

PART
III.

Of the
other
virtues
and vices.

has no influence by comparison; and on the other hand, if it be too strong, it operates on us entirely by sympathy, which is the contrary to comparison. Sympathy being the conversion of an idea into an impression, demands a greater force and vivacity in the idea than is requisite to comparison.

All this is easily applied to the present subject. We sink very much in our own eyes, when in the presence of a great man, or one of a superior genius; and this humility makes a considerable ingredient in that *respect*, which we pay our superiors, according to our[1] foregoing reasonings on that passion. Sometimes even envy and hatred arise from the comparison; but in the greatest part of men, it rests at respect and esteem. As sympathy has such a powerful influence on the human mind, it causes pride to have, in some measure, the same effect as merit; and by making us enter into those elevated sentiments, which the proud man entertains of himself, presents that comparison, which is so mortifying and disagreeable. Our judgment does not entirely accompany him in the flattering conceit, in which he pleases himself; but still is so shaken as to receive the idea it presents, and to give it an influence above the loose conceptions of the imagination. A man, who, in an idle humour, wou'd form a notion of a person of a merit very much superior to his own, wou'd not be mortified by that fiction: But when a man, whom we are really persuaded to be of inferior merit, is presented to us; if we observe in him any extraordinary degree of pride and self-conceit; the firm persuasion he has of his own merit, takes hold of the imagination, and diminishes us in our own eyes, in the same manner, as if he were really possess'd of all the good qualities which he so liberally attributes to himself. Our idea is here precisely in that medium, which is requisite to make it operate on us by comparison. Were it accompanied with belief, and did the person appear to have the same merit, which he assumes to himself, it wou'd have a contrary effect, and wou'd operate on us by sympathy. The influence of that principle wou'd then be superior to that of comparison, contrary to what happens where the person's merit seems below his pretensions.

The necessary consequence of these principles is, that pride, or an over-weaning conceit of ourselves, must be

[1] Book II Part II Sect. X.

vicious; since it causes uneasiness in all men, and presents them every moment with a disagreeable comparison. 'Tis a trite observation in philosophy, and even in common life and conversation, that 'tis our own pride, which makes us so much displeas'd with the pride of other people; and that vanity becomes insupportable to us merely because we are vain. The gay naturally associate themselves with the gay, and the amorous with the amorous: But the proud never can endure the proud, and rather seek the company of those who are of an opposite disposition. As we are, all of us, proud in some degree, pride is universally blam'd and condemn'd by all mankind; as having a natural tendency to cause uneasiness in others by means of comparison. And this effect must follow the more naturally, that those, who have an ill-grounded conceit of themselves, are for ever making those comparisons, nor have they any other method of supporting their vanity. A man of sense and merit is pleas'd with himself, independent of all foreign considerations: But a fool must always find some person, that is more foolish, in order to keep himself in good humour with his own parts and understanding.

But tho' an over-weaning conceit of our own merit be vicious and disagreeable, nothing can be more laudable, than to have a value for ourselves, where we really have qualities that are valuable. The utility and advantage of any quality to ourselves is a source of virtue, as well as its agreeableness to others; and 'tis certain, that nothing is more useful to us in the conduct of life, than a due degree of pride, which makes us sensible of our own merit, and gives us a confidence and assurance in all our projects and enterprizes. Whatever capacity any one may be endow'd with, 'tis entirely useless to him, if he be not acquainted with it, and form not designs suitable to it. 'Tis requisite on all occasions to know our own force; and were it allowable to err on either side, 'twou'd be more advantageous to over-rate our merit, than to form ideas of it, below its just standard. Fortune commonly favours the bold and enterprizing; and nothing inspires us with more boldness than a good opinion of ourselves.

Add to this, that tho' pride, or self-applause, be sometimes disagreeable to others, 'tis always agreeable to ourselves; as on the other hand, modesty, tho' it give pleasure to every

SECT
II
Of greatness of mind.

PART
III.

Of the
other
virtues
and vices

one, who observes it, produces often uneasiness in the person endow'd with it. Now it has been observ'd, that our own sensations determine the vice and virtue of any quality, as well as those sensations, which it may excite in others.

Thus self-satisfaction and vanity may not only be allowable, but requisite in a character. 'Tis, however, certain, that good-breeding and decency require that we shou'd avoid all signs and expressions, which tend directly to show that passion. We have, all of us, a wonderful partiality for ourselves, and were we always to give vent to our sentiments in this particular, we shou'd mutually cause the greatest indignation in each other, not only by the immediate presence of so disagreeable a subject of comparison, but also by the contrariety of our judgments. In like manner, therefore, as we establish the *laws of nature*, in order to secure property in society, and prevent the opposition of self-interest; we establish the *rules of good-breeding*, in order to prevent the opposition of men's pride, and render conversation agreeable and inoffensive. Nothing is more disagreeable than a man's over-weaning conceit of himself: Every one almost has a strong propensity to this vice: No one can well distinguish *in himself* betwixt the vice and virtue, or be certain, that his esteem of his own merit is well-founded: For these reasons, all direct expressions of this passion are condemn'd; nor do we make any exception to this rule in favour of men of sense and merit. They are not allow'd to do themselves justice openly, in words, no more than other people; and even if they show a reserve and secret doubt in doing themselves justice in their own thoughts, they will be more applauded. That impertinent, and almost universal propensity of men, to over-value themselves, has given us such a *prejudice* against self-applause, that we are apt to condemn it, by a *general rule*, wherever we meet with it; and 'tis with some difficulty we give a privilege to men of sense, even in their most secret thoughts. At least, it must be own'd, that some disguise in this particular is absolutely requisite; and that if we harbour pride in our breasts, we must carry a fair outside, and have the appearance of modesty and mutual deference in all our conduct and behaviour. We must, on every occasion, be ready to prefer others to ourselves; to treat them with a kind of deference, even tho' they be our equals; to seem always the lowest and least in the company, where we are not very much distinguish'd above them : And if we observe these rules in our conduct, men will have more indulgence for our secret sentiments, when we discover them in an oblique manner.

I believe no one, who has any practice of the world, and can penetrate into the inward sentiments of men, will assert, that the humility, which good-breeding and decency require of us, goes beyond the outside, or that a thorough sincerity in this particular is esteem'd a real part of our duty. On the contrary, we may observe, that a genuine and hearty pride, or self-esteem, if well conceal'd and well founded, is essential to the character of a man of honour, and that there is no quality of the mind, which is more indispensibly requisite to procure the esteem and approbation of mankind. There are certain deferences and mutual submissions, which custom requires of the different ranks of men towards each other; and whoever exceeds in this particular, if thro' interest, is accus'd of meanness, if thro' ignorance, of simplicity. 'Tis necessary, therefore, to know our rank and station in the world, whether it be fix'd by our birth, fortune, employments, talents or reputation. 'Tis necessary to feel the sentiment and passion of pride in conformity to it, and to regulate our actions accordingly. And shou'd it be said, that prudence may suffice to regulate our actions in this particular, without any real pride, I wou'd observe, that here the object of prudence is to conform our actions to the general usage and custom; and that 'tis impossible those tacit airs of superiority shou'd ever have been establish'd and authoriz'd by custom, unless men were generally proud, and unless that passion were generally approv'd, when well-grounded.

If we pass from common life and conversation to history, this reasoning acquires new force, when we observe, that all those great actions and sentiments, which have become the admiration of mankind, are founded on nothing but pride and self-esteem. *Go,* says *Alexander* the Great to his soldiers, when they refus'd to follow him to the *Indies, go tell your countrymen, that you left Alexander compleating the conquest of the world.* This passage was always particularly admir'd by the prince of *Conde,* as we learn from *St. Evremond.* ' *Alexander,*' said that prince, ' abandon'd by his ' soldiers, among barbarians, not yet fully subdu'd, felt in

PART
III.

Of the
other
virtues
and vices.

'himself such a dignity and right of empire, that he cou'd
'not believe it possible any one cou'd refuse to obey him.
'Whether in *Europe* or in *Asia*, among *Greeks* or *Persians*,
'all was indifferent to him: Wherever he found men, he
'fancied he had found subjects.'

In general we may observe, that whatever we call *heroic
virtue*, and admire under the character of greatness and
elevation of mind, is either nothing but a steady and well-
establish'd pride and self-esteem, or partakes largely of that
passion. Courage, intrepidity, ambition, love of glory, magnanimity, and all the other shining virtues of that kind
have plainly a strong mixture of self-esteem in them, and
derive a great part of their merit from that origin. Accordingly we find, that many religious declaimers decry those
virtues as purely pagan and natural, and represent to us the
excellency of the *Christian* religion, which places humility
in the rank of virtues, and corrects the judgment of the
world, and even of philosophers, who so generally admire all
the efforts of pride and ambition. Whether this virtue of
humility has been rightly understood, I shall not pretend to
determine. I am content with the concession, that the
world naturally esteems a well-regulated pride, which
secretly animates our conduct, without breaking out into
such indecent expressions of vanity, as may offend the vanity
of others.

The merit of pride or self-esteem is deriv'd from two circumstances, *viz.* its utility and its agreeableness to ourselves; by which it capacitates us for business, and, at the
same time, gives us an immediate satisfaction. When it
goes beyond its just bounds, it loses the first advantage, and
even becomes prejudicial; which is the reason why we condemn an extravagant pride and ambition, however regulated
by the decorums of good-breeding and politeness. But as
such a passion is still agreeable, and conveys an elevated
and sublime sensation to the person, who is actuated by it,
the sympathy with that satisfaction diminishes considerably
the blame, which naturally attends its dangerous influence
on his conduct and behaviour. Accordingly we may observe,
that an excessive courage and magnanimity, especially when
it displays itself under the frowns of fortune, contributes, in
a great measure, to the character of a hero, and will render
a person the admiration of posterity; at the same time, that

it ruins his affairs, and leads him into dangers and difficulties, with which otherwise he wou'd never have been acquainted.

Heroism, or military glory, is much admir'd by the generality of mankind. They consider it as the most sublime
kind of merit. Men of cool reflection are not so sanguine in
their praises of it. The infinite confusions and disorder,
which it has caus'd in the world, diminish much of its merit
in their eyes. When they wou'd oppose the popular notions
on this head, they always paint out the evils, which this
suppos'd virtue has produc'd in human society; the subversion of empires, the devastation of provinces, the sack of
cities. As long as these are present to us, we are more
inclin'd to hate than admire the ambition of heroes. But
when we fix our view on the person himself, who is the
author of all this mischief, there is something so dazling in
his character, the mere contemplation of it so elevates the
mind, that we cannot refuse it our admiration. The pain,
which we receive from its tendency to the prejudice of
society, is over-power'd by a stronger and more immediate
sympathy.

Thus our explication of the merit or demerit, which
attends the degrees of pride or self-esteem, may serve as a
strong argument for the preceding hypothesis, by shewing
the effects of those principles above explain'd in all the
variations of our judgments concerning that passion. Nor
will this reasoning be advantageous to us only by shewing,
that the distinction of vice and virtue arises from the *four*
principles of the *advantage* and of the *pleasure* of the *person
himself*, and of *others* · But may also afford us a strong proof
of some under-parts of that hypothesis.

No one, who duly considers of this matter, will make any
scruple of allowing, that any piece of ill-breeding, or any expression of pride and haughtiness, is displeasing to us,
merely because it shocks our own pride, and leads us by
sympathy into a comparison, which causes the disagreeable
passion of humility. Now as an insolence of this kind is
blam'd even in a person who has always been civil to ourselves in particular: nay, in one, whose name is only known
to us in history; it follows, that our disapprobation proceeds
from a sympathy with others, and from the reflection, that

PART
III

Of the
other
virtues
and vices

such a character is highly displeasing and odious to every
one, who converses or has any intercourse with the person
possest of it. We sympathize with those people in their uneasiness; and as their uneasiness proceeds in part from a
sympathy with the person who insults them, we may here
observe a double rebound of the sympathy; which is a principle
very similar to what we have observ'd on another occasion.[1]

SECT. III.—*Of goodness and benevolence.*

Having thus explain'd the origin of that praise and approbation, which attends every thing we call *great* in human
affections; we now proceed to give an account of their
goodness, and shew whence its merit is deriv'd.

When experience has once given us a competent knowledge
of human affairs, and has taught us the proportion they bear
to human passion, we perceive, that the generosity of men is
very limited, and that it seldom extends beyond their friends
and family, or, at most, beyond their native country. Being
thus acquainted with the nature of man, we expect not any
impossibilities from him; but confine our view to that narrow
circle, in which any person moves, in order to form a judgment of his moral character. When the natural tendency of
his passions leads him to be serviceable and useful within his
sphere, we approve of his character, and love his person, by
a sympathy with the sentiments of those, who have a more
particular connexion with him. We are quickly oblig'd to
forget our own interest in our judgments of this kind, by
reason of the perpetual contradictions, we meet with in
society and conversation, from persons that are not plac'd in
the same situation, and have not the same interest with ourselves. The only point of view, in which our sentiments
concur with those of others, is, when we consider the tendency of any passion to the advantage or harm of those, who
have any immediate connexion or intercourse with the person
possess'd of it. And tho' this advantage or harm be often
very remote from ourselves, yet sometimes 'tis very near us,
and interests us strongly by sympathy. This concern we
readily extend to other cases, that are resembling; and when
these are very remote, our sympathy is proportionably weaker,

[1] Book II Part II Sect V.

and our praise or blame fainter and more doubtful. The case is here the same as in our judgments concerning external bodies. All objects seem to diminish by their distance : But tho' the appearance of objects to our senses be the original standard, by which we judge of them, yet we do not say, that they actually diminish by the distance ; but correcting the appearance by reflection, arrive at a more constant and establish'd judgment concerning them. In like manner, tho' sympathy be much fainter than our concern for ourselves, and a sympathy with persons remote from us much fainter than that with persons near and contiguous ; yet we neglect all these differences in our calm judgments concerning the characters of men. Besides, that we ourselves often change our situation in this particular, we every day meet with persons, who are in a different situation from ourselves, and who cou'd never converse with us on any reasonable terms, were we to remain constantly in that situation and point of view, which is peculiar to us. The intercourse of sentiments, therefore, in society and conversation, makes us form some general inalterable standard, by which we may approve or disapprove of characters and manners. And tho' the *heart* does not always take part with those general notions, or regulate its love and hatred by them, yet are they sufficient for discourse, and serve all our purposes in company, in the pulpit, on the theatre, and in the schools.

From these principles we may easily account for that merit, which is commonly ascrib'd to *generosity, humanity, compassion, gratitude, friendship, fidelity, zeal, disinterestedness, liberality,* and all those other qualities, which form the character of good and benevolent. A propensity to the tender passions makes a man agreeable and useful in all the parts of life ; and gives a just direction to all his other qualities, which otherwise may become prejudicial to society. Courage and ambition, when not regulated by benevolence, are fit only to make a tyrant and public robber. 'Tis the same case with judgment and capacity, and all the qualities of that kind. They are indifferent in themselves to the interests of society, and have a tendency to the good or ill of mankind, according as they are directed by these other passions.

As love is *immediately agreeable* to the person, who is actuated by it, and hatred *immediately disagreeable* ; this may also be a considerable reason, why we praise all the passions

PART
III

Of the
other
virtues
and vices.

that partake of the former, and blame all those that have any considerable share of the latter. 'Tis certain we are infinitely touch'd with a tender sentiment, as well as with a great one. The tears naturally start in our eyes at the conception of it; nor can we forbear giving a loose to the same tenderness towards the person who exerts it. All this seems to me a proof, that our approbation has, in those cases, an origin different from the prospect of utility and advantage, either to ourselves or others. To which we may add, that men naturally, without reflection, approve of that character, which is most like their own. The man of a mild disposition and tender affections, in forming a notion of the most perfect virtue, mixes in it more of benevolence and humanity, than the man of courage and enterprize, who naturally looks upon a certain elevation of mind as the most accomplish'd character. This must evidently proceed from an *immediate* sympathy, which men have with characters similar to their own. They enter with more warmth into such sentiments, and feel more sensibly the pleasure, which arises from them.

'Tis remarkable, that nothing touches a man of humanity more than any instance of extraordinary delicacy in love or friendship, where a person is attentive to the smallest concerns of his friend, and is willing to sacrifice to them the most considerable interest of his own. Such delicacies have little influence on society; because they make us regard the greatest trifles: But they are the more engaging, the more minute the concern is, and are a proof of the highest merit in any one, who is capable of them. The passions are so contagious, that they pass with the greatest facility from one person to another, and produce correspondent movements in all human breasts. Where friendship appears in very signal instances, my heart catches the same passion, and is warm'd by those warm sentiments, that display themselves before me. Such agreeable movements must give me an affection to every one that excites them. This is the case with every thing that is agreeable in any person. The transition from pleasure to love is easy: But the transition must here be still more easy; since the agreeable sentiment, which is excited by sympathy, is love itself; and there is nothing requir'd but to change the object.

Hence the peculiar merit of benevolence in all its shapes and appearances. Hence even its weaknesses are virtuous and amiable ; and a person, whose grief upon the loss of a friend were excessive, wou'd be esteem'd upon that account. His tenderness bestows a merit, as it does a pleasure, on his melancholy.

We are not, however, to imagine, that all the angry passions are vicious, tho' they are disagreeable. There is a certain indulgence due to human nature in this respect. Anger and hatred are passions inherent in our very frame and constitution. The want of them, on some occasions, may even be a proof of weakness and imbecillity. And where they appear only in a low degree, we not only excuse them because they are natural ; but even bestow our applauses on them, because they are inferior to what appears in the greatest part of mankind.

Where these angry passions rise up to cruelty, they form the most detested of all vices. All the pity and concern which we have for the miserable sufferers by this vice, turns against the person guilty of it, and produces a stronger hatred than we are sensible of on any other occasion.

Even when the vice of inhumanity rises not to this extreme degree, our sentiments concerning it are very much influenc'd by reflections on the harm that results from it. And we may observe in general, that if we can find any quality in a person, which renders him incommodious to those, who live and converse with him, we always allow it to be a fault or blemish, without any farther examination. On the other hand, when we enumerate the good qualities of any person, we always mention those parts of his character, which render him a safe companion, an easy friend, a gentle master, an agreeable husband, or an indulgent father. We consider him with all his relations in society ; and love or hate him, according as he affects those, who have any immediate intercourse with him. And 'tis a most certain rule, that if there be no relation of life, in which I cou'd not wish to stand to a particular person, his character must so far be allow'd to be perfect. If he be as little wanting to himself as to others, his character is entirely perfect. This is the ultimate test of merit and virtue.

SECT. IV.—*Of natural abilities.*

No distinction is more usual in all systems of ethics, than that betwixt *natural abilities* and *moral virtues*; where the

PART
III.

_Of the
other
virtues
and vices._

former are plac'd on the same footing with bodily endowments, and are suppos'd to have no merit or moral worth annex'd to them. Whoever considers the matter accurately, will find, that a dispute upon this head wou'd be merely a dispute of words, and that tho' these qualities are not altogether of the same kind, yet they agree in the most material circumstances. They are both of them equally mental qualities : And both of them equally produce pleasure; and have of course an equal tendency to procure the love and esteem of mankind. There are few, who are not as jealous of their character, with regard to sense and knowledge, as to honour and courage; and much more than with regard to temperance and sobriety. Men are even afraid of passing for good-natur'd; lest _that_ shou'd be taken for want of understanding : And often boast of more debauches than they have been really engag'd in, to give themselves airs of fire and spirit. In short, the figure a man makes in the world, the reception he meets with in company, the esteem paid him by his acquaintance; all these advantages depend almost as much upon his good sense and judgment, as upon any other part of his character. Let a man have the best intentions in the world, and be the farthest from all injustice and violence, he will never be able to make himself be much regarded, without a moderate share, at least, of parts and understanding. Since then natural abilities, tho', perhaps, inferior, yet are on the same footing, both as to their causes and effects, with those qualities which we call moral virtues, why shou'd we make any distinction betwixt them?

Tho' we refuse to natural abilities the title of virtues, we must allow, that they procure the love and esteem of mankind; that they give a new lustre to the other virtues; and that a man possess'd of them is much more intitled to our good-will and services, than one entirely void of them. It may, indeed, be pretended, that the sentiment of approbation, which those qualities produce, besides its being _inferior_, is also somewhat _different_ from that, which attends the other virtues. But this, in my opinion, is not a sufficient reason for excluding them from the catalogue of virtues. Each of the virtues, even benevolence, justice, gratitude, integrity, excites a different sentiment or feeling in the spectator. The characters of _Cæsar_ and _Cato_, as drawn by _Sallust_, are both of them virtuous, in the strictest sense of the word;

but in a different way : Nor are the sentiments entirely the same, which arise from them. The one produces love ; the other esteem : The one is amiable ; the other awful : We cou'd wish to meet with the one character in a friend ; the other character we wou'd be ambitious of in ourselves. In like manner, the approbation, which attends natural abilities, may be somewhat different to the feeling from that, which arises from the other virtues, without making them entirely of a different species. And indeed we may observe, that the natural abilities, no more than the other virtues, produce not, all of them, the same kind of approbation. Good sense and genius beget esteem : Wit and humour excite love.[1]

Those, who represent the distinction betwixt natural abilities and moral virtues as very material, may say, that the former are entirely involuntary, and have therefore no merit attending them, as having no dependence on liberty and free-will. But to this I answer, *first*, that many of those qualities, which all moralists, especially the antients, comprehend under the title of moral virtues, are equally involuntary and necessary, with the qualities of the judgment and imagination. Of this nature are constancy, fortitude, magnanimity ; and, in short, all the qualities which form the *great* man. I might say the same, in some degree, of the others ; it being almost impossible for the mind to change its character in any considerable article, or cure itself of a passionate or splenetic temper, when they are natural to it. The greater degree there is of these blameable qualities, the more vicious they become, and yet they are the less voluntary. *Secondly*, I wou'd have any one give me a reason, why virtue and vice may not be involuntary, as well as beauty and deformity. These moral distinctions arise from the natural distinctions of pain and pleasure ; and when we receive those feelings from the general consideration of any quality or character, we denominate it vicious or virtuous. Now I believe no one will assert, that a quality can never produce pleasure or pain to the person who considers it, unless it be perfectly

---

[1] Love and esteem are at the bottom the same passions, and arise from like causes. The qualities, that produce both, are agreeable, and give pleasure But where this pleasure is severe and serious ; or where its object is great, and makes a strong impression ; or where it produces any degree of humility and awe In all these cases, the passion, which arises from the pleasure, is more properly denominated esteem than love. Benevolence attends both · But is connected with love in a more eminent degree.

PART
III.

Of the
other
virtues
and vices.

voluntary, in the person who possesses it. *Thirdly*, As to free-will, we have shewn that it has no place with regard to the actions, no more than the qualities of men. It is not a just consequence, that what is voluntary is free. Our actions are more voluntary than our judgments; but we have not more liberty in the one than in the other.

But tho' this distinction betwixt voluntary and involuntary be not sufficient to justify the distinction betwixt natural abilities and moral virtues, yet the former distinction will afford us a plausible reason, why moralists have invented the latter. Men have observ'd, that tho' natural abilities and moral qualities be in the main on the same footing, there is, however, this difference betwixt them, that the former are almost invariable by any art or industry; while the latter, or at least, the actions, that proceed from them, may be chang'd by the motives of rewards and punishments, praise and blame. Hence legislators, and divines, and moralists, have principally applied themselves to the regulating these voluntary actions, and have endeavour'd to produce additional motives for being virtuous in that particular. They knew, that to punish a man for folly, or exhort him to be prudent and sagacious, wou'd have but little effect; tho' the same punishments and exhortations, with regard to justice and injustice, might have a considerable influence. But as men, in common life and conversation, do not carry those ends in view, but naturally praise or blame whatever pleases or displeases them, they do not seem much to regard this distinction, but consider prudence under the character of virtue as well as benevolence, and penetration as well as justice. Nay, we find, that all moralists, whose judgment is not perverted by a strict adherence to a system, enter into the same way of thinking; and that the antient moralists in particular made no scruple of placing prudence at the head of the cardinal virtues. There is a sentiment of esteem and approbation, which may be excited, in some degree, by any faculty of the mind, in its perfect state and condition; and to account for this sentiment is the business of *Philosophers*. It belongs to *Grammarians* to examine what qualities are entitled to the denomination of *virtue*; nor will they find, upon trial, that this is so easy a task, as at first sight they may be apt to imagine.

The principal reason why natural abilities are esteem'd, is

because of their tendency to be useful to the person, who is possess'd of them. 'Tis impossible to execute any design with success, where it is not conducted with prudence and discretion; nor will the goodness of our intentions alone suffice to procure us a happy issue to our enterprizes. Men are superior to beasts principally by the superiority of their reason; and they are the degrees of the same faculty, which set such an infinite difference betwixt one man and another. All the advantages of art are owing to human reason; and where fortune is not very capricious, the most considerable part of these advantages must fall to the share of the prudent and sagacious.

When it is ask'd, whether a quick or a slow apprehension be most valuable? whether one, that at first view penetrates into a subject, but can perform nothing upon study; or a contrary character, which must work out every thing by dint of application? whether a clear head, or a copious invention? whether a profound genius, or a sure judgment? in short, what character, or peculiar understanding, is more excellent than another? 'Tis evident we can answer none of these questions, without considering which of those qualities capacitates a man best for the world, and carries him farthest in any of his undertakings.

There are many other qualities of the mind, whose merit is deriv'd from the same origin. *Industry*, *perseverance*, *patience*, *activity*, *vigilance*, *application*, *constancy*, with other virtues of that kind, which 'twill be easy to recollect, are esteem'd valuable upon no other account, than their advantage in the conduct of life. 'Tis the same case with *temperance*, *frugality*, *œconomy*, *resolution* : As on the other hand, *prodigality*, *luxury*, *irresolution*, *uncertainty*, are vicious, merely because they draw ruin upon us, and incapacitate us for business and action.

As wisdom and good-sense are valued, because they are *useful* to the person possess'd of them; so *wit* and *eloquence* are valued, because they are *immediately agreeable* to others. On the other hand, *good humour* is lov'd and esteem'd, because it is *immediately agreeable* to the person himself. 'Tis evident, that the conversation of a man of wit is very satisfactory; as a chearful good-humour'd companion diffuses a joy over the whole company, from a sympathy with his gaiety. These qualities, therefore, being agreeable, they naturally

PART
III.

Of the
other
virtues
and vices

beget love and esteem, and answer to all the characters of virtue.

'Tis difficult to tell, on many occasions, what it is that renders one man's conversation so agreeable and entertaining, and another's so insipid and distasteful. As conversation is a transcript of the mind as well as books, the same qualities, which render the one valuable, must give us an esteem for the other. This we shall consider afterwards. In the mean time it may be affirm'd in general, that all the merit a man may derive from his conversation (which, no doubt, may be very considerable) arises from nothing but the pleasure it conveys to those who are present.

In this view, *cleanliness* is also to be regarded as a virtue; since it naturally renders us agreeable to others, and is a very considerable source of love and affection. No one will deny, that a negligence in this particular is a fault; and as faults are nothing but smaller vices, and this fault can have no other origin than the uneasy sensation, which it excites in others, we may in this instance, seemingly so trivial, clearly discover the origin of the moral distinction of vice and virtue in other instances.

Besides all those qualities, which render a person lovely or valuable, there is also a certain *je-ne-sçai-quoi* of agreeable and handsome, that concurs to the same effect. In this case, as well as in that of wit and eloquence, we must have recourse to a certain sense, which acts without reflection, and regards not the tendencies of qualities and characters. Some moralists account for all the sentiments of virtue by this sense. Their hypothesis is very plausible. Nothing but a particular enquiry can give the preference to any other hypothesis. When we find, that almost all the virtues have such particular tendencies; and also find, that these tendencies are sufficient alone to give a strong sentiment of approbation: We cannot doubt, after this, that qualities are approv'd of, in proportion to the advantage, which results from them.

The *decorum* or *indecorum* of a quality, with regard to the age, or character, or station, contributes also to its praise or blame. This decorum depends, in a great measure, upon experience. 'Tis usual to see men lose their levity, as they advance in years. Such a degree of gravity, therefore, and such years, are connected together in our thoughts. When we observe them separated in any person's character, this imposes a kind of violence on our imagination, and is disagreeable.

That faculty of the soul, which, of all others, is of the least consequence to the character, and has the least virtue or vice in its several degrees, at the same time that it admits of a great variety of degrees, is the *memory*. Unless it rise up to that stupendous height as to surprize us, or sink so low as, in some measure, to affect the judgment, we commonly take no notice of its variations, nor ever mention them to the praise or dispraise of any person. 'Tis so far from being a virtue to have a good memory, that men generally affect to complain of a bad one; and endeavouring to persuade the world, that what they say is entirely of their own invention, sacrifice it to the praise of genius and judgment. Yet to consider the matter abstractedly, 'twou'd be difficult to give a reason, why the faculty of recalling past ideas with truth and clearness, shou'd not have as much merit in it, as the faculty of placing our present ideas in such an order, as to form true propositions and opinions. The reason of the difference certainly must be, that the memory is exerted without any sensation of pleasure or pain; and in all its middling degrees serves almost equally well in business and affairs. But the least variations in the judgment are sensibly felt in their consequences; while at the same time that faculty is never exerted in any eminent degree, without an extraordinary delight and satisfaction. The sympathy with this utility and pleasure bestows a merit on the understanding; and the absence of it makes us consider the memory as a faculty very indifferent to blame or praise.

Before I leave this subject of *natural abilities*, I must observe, that, perhaps, one source of the esteem and affection, which attends them, is deriv'd from the *importance* and *weight*, which they bestow on the person possess'd of them. He becomes of greater consequence in life. His resolutions and actions affect a greater number of his fellow-creatures. Both his friendship and enmity are of moment. And 'tis easy to observe, that whoever is elevated, after this manner, above the rest of mankind, must excite in us the sentiments of esteem and approbation. Whatever is important engages our attention, fixes our thought, and is contemplated with satisfaction. The histories of kingdoms are more interesting

PART
III.

Of the
other
virtues
and vices

than domestic stories: The histories of great empires more than those of small cities and principalities: And the histories of wars and revolutions more than those of peace and order. We sympathize with the persons that suffer, in all the various sentiments which belong to their fortunes. The mind is occupied by the multitude of the objects, and by the strong passions, that display themselves. And this occupation or agitation of the mind is commonly agreeable and amusing. The same theory accounts for the esteem and regard we pay to men of extraordinary parts and abilities. The good and ill of multitudes are connected with their actions. Whatever they undertake is important, and challenges our attention. Nothing is to be over-look'd and despis'd, that regards them. And where any person can excite these sentiments, he soon acquires our esteem; unless other circumstances of his character render him odious and disagreeable.

SECT. V.—*Some farther reflections concerning the natural virtues.*

It has been observ'd, in treating of the passions, that pride and humility, love and hatred, are excited by any advantages or disadvantages of the *mind, body,* or *fortune*; and that these advantages or disadvantages have that effect by producing a separate impression of pain or pleasure. The pain or pleasure, which arises from the general survey or view of any action or quality of the *mind*, constitutes its vice or virtue, and gives rise to our approbation or blame, which is nothing but a fainter and more imperceptible love or hatred. We have assign'd four different sources of this pain and pleasure; and in order to justify more fully that hypothesis, it may here be proper to observe, that the advantages or disadvantages of the *body* and of *fortune*, produce a pain or pleasure from the very same principles. The tendency of any object to be *useful* to the person possess'd of it, or to others; to convey *pleasure* to him or to others; all these circumstances convey an immediate pleasure to the person, who considers the object, and command his love and approbation.

To begin with the advantages of the *body*; we may observe a phænomenon, which might appear somewhat trivial and ludicrous, if any thing cou'd be trivial, which fortified a conclusion of such importance, or ludicrous, which was employ'd in a philosophical reasoning. 'Tis a general remark, that those we call good *women's men*, who have either signaliz'd themselves by their amorous exploits, or whose make of body promises any extraordinary vigour of that kind, are well received by the fair sex, and naturally engage the affections even of those, whose virtue prevents any design of ever giving employment to those talents. Here 'tis evident, that the ability of such a person to give enjoyment, is the real source of that love and esteem he meets with among the females; at the same time that the women, who love and esteem him, have no prospect of receiving that enjoyment themselves, and can only be affected by means of their sympathy with one, that has a commerce of love with him. This instance is singular, and merits our attention.

Another source of the pleasure we receive from considering bodily advantages, is their utility to the person himself, who is possess'd of them. 'Tis certain, that a considerable part of the beauty of men, as well as of other animals, consists in such a conformation of members, as we find by experience to be attended with strength and agility, and to capacitate the creature for any action or exercise. Broad shoulders, a lank belly, firm joints, taper legs; all these are beautiful in our species, because they are signs of force and vigour, which being advantages we naturally sympathize with, they convey to the beholder a share of that satisfaction they produce in the possessor.

So far as to the *utility*, which may attend any quality of the body. As to the immediate *pleasure*, 'tis certain, that an air of health, as well as of strength and agility, makes a considerable part of beauty; and that a sickly air in another is always disagreeable, upon account of that idea of pain and uneasiness, which it conveys to us. On the other hand, we are pleas'd with the regularity of our own features, tho' it be neither useful to ourselves nor others; and 'tis necessary for us, in some measure, to set ourselves at a distance, to make it convey to us any satisfaction. We commonly consider ourselves as we appear in the eyes of others, and sympathize with the advantageous sentiments they entertain with regard to us.

How far the advantages of *fortune* produce esteem and approbation from the same principles, we may satisfy our-

PART
III.

Of the
other
virtues
and vices

selves by reflecting on our precedent reasoning on that subject. We have observ'd, that our approbation of those, who are possess'd of the advantages of fortune, may be ascrib'd to three different causes. *First,* To that immediate pleasure, which a rich man gives us, by the view of the beautiful cloaths, equipage, gardens, or houses, which he possesses. *Secondly,* To the advantage, which we hope to reap from him by his generosity and liberality. *Thirdly,* To the pleasure and advantage, which he himself reaps from his possessions, and which produce an agreeable sympathy in us. Whether we ascribe our esteem of the rich and great to one or all of these causes, we may clearly see the traces of those principles, which give rise to the sense of vice and virtue. I believe most people, at first sight, will be inclin'd to ascribe our esteem of the rich to self-interest, and the prospect of advantage. But as 'tis certain, that our esteem or deference extends beyond any prospect of advantage to ourselves, 'tis evident, that that sentiment must proceed from a sympathy with those, who are dependent on the person we esteem and respect, and who have an immediate connexion with him. We consider him as a person capable of contributing to the happiness or enjoyment of his fellow-creatures, whose sentiments, with regard to him, we naturally embrace. And this consideration will serve to justify my hypothesis in preferring the *third* principle to the other two, and ascribing our esteem of the rich to a sympathy with the pleasure and advantage, which they themselves receive from their possessions. For as even the other two principles cannot operate to a due extent, or account for all the phænomena, without having recourse to a sympathy of one kind or other; 'tis much more natural to chuse that sympathy, which is immediate and direct, than that which is remote and indirect. To which we may add, that where the riches or power are very great, and render the person considerable and important in the world, the esteem attending them, may, in part, be ascrib'd to another source, distinct from these three, *viz.* their interesting the mind by a prospect of the multitude, and importance of their consequences : Tho', in order to account for the operation of this principle, we must also have recourse to *sympathy*; as we have observ'd in the preceding section.

It may not be amiss, on this occasion, to remark the flexibility of our sentiments, and the several changes they so

readily receive from the objects, with which they are conjoin'd. All the sentiments of approbation, which attend any
particular species of objects, have a great resemblance to
each other, tho' deriv'd from different sources; and, on the
other hand, those sentiments, when directed to different
objects, are different to the feeling, tho' deriv'd from the
same source. Thus the beauty of all visible objects causes
a pleasure pretty much the same, tho' it be sometimes deriv'd from the mere *species* and appearance of the objects;
sometimes from sympathy, and an idea of their utility. In
like manner, whenever we survey the actions and characters
of men, without any particular interest in them, the pleasure,
or pain, which arises from the survey (with some minute
differences) is, in the main, of the same kind, tho' perhaps
there be a great diversity in the causes, from which it is deriv'd. On the other hand, a convenient house, and a virtuous
character, cause not the same feeling of approbation; even
tho' the source of our approbation be the same, and flow from
sympathy and an idea of their utility. There is something
very inexplicable in this variation of our feelings; but 'tis
what we have experience of with regard to all our passions
and sentiments.

SECT.
V.
Some
farther re-
flections
concerning
the natural
virtues.

SECT. VI.—*Conclusion of this book.*

Thus upon the whole I am hopeful, that nothing is wanting to an accurate proof of this system of ethics. We are
certain, that sympathy is a very powerful principle in human
nature. We are also certain, that it has a great influence on
our sense of beauty, when we regard external objects, as well
as when we judge of morals. We find, that it has force
sufficient to give us the strongest sentiments of approbation, when it operates alone, without the concurrence
of any other principle; as in the cases of justice, allegiance,
chastity, and good-manners. We may observe, that all the
circumstances requisite for its operation are found in most
of the virtues; which have, for the most part, a tendency to
the good of society, or to that of the person possess'd of
them. If we compare all these circumstances, we shall not
doubt, that sympathy is the chief source of moral distinctions; especially when we reflect, that no objection can be
rais'd against this hypothesis in one case, which will not

PART
III.

Of the
other
virtues
and vices.

extend to all cases. Justice is certainly approv'd of for no
other reason, than because it has a tendency to the public
good: And the public good is indifferent to us, except so far
as sympathy interests us in it. We may presume the like
with regard to all the other virtues, which have a like tendency to the public good. They must derive all their merit
from our sympathy with those, who reap any advantage from
them: As the virtues, which have a tendency to the good of
the person possess'd of them, derive their merit from our
sympathy with him.

Most people will readily allow, that the useful qualities of
the mind are virtuous, because of their utility. This way of
thinking is so natural, and occurs on so many occasions,
that few will make any scruple of admitting it. Now this
being once admitted, the force of sympathy must necessarily
be acknowledg'd. Virtue is consider'd as means to an end.
Means to an end are only valued so far as the end is valued.
But the happiness of strangers affects us by sympathy alone.
To that principle, therefore, we are to ascribe the sentiment
of approbation, which arises from the survey of all those
virtues, that are useful to society, or to the person possess'd
of them. These form the most considerable part of morality.

Were it proper in such a subject to bribe the reader's assent, or employ any thing but solid argument, we are here
abundantly supplied with topics to engage the affections.
All lovers of virtue (and such we all are in speculation, however we may degenerate in practice) must certainly be
pleas'd to see moral distinctions deriv'd from so noble a
source, which gives us a just notion both of the *generosity*
and *capacity* of human nature. It requires but very little
knowledge of human affairs to perceive, that a sense of
morals is a principle inherent in the soul, and one of the
most powerful that enters into the composition. But this
sense must certainly acquire new force, when reflecting on
itself, it approves of those principles, from whence it is
deriv'd, and finds nothing but what is great and good in its
rise and origin. Those who resolve the sense of morals into
original instincts of the human mind, may defend the cause
of virtue with sufficient authority; but want the advantage,
which those possess, who account for that sense by an ex-

tensive sympathy with mankind. According to their system, not only virtue must be approv'd of, but also the sense of virtue : And not only that sense, but also the principles, from whence it is deriv'd. So that nothing is presented on any side, but what is laudable and good.

This observation may be extended to justice, and the other virtues of that kind. Tho' justice be artificial, the sense of its morality is natural. 'Tis the combination of men, in a system of conduct, which renders any act of justice beneficial to society. But when once it has that tendency, we *naturally* approve of it ; and if we did not so, 'tis impossible any combination or convention cou'd ever produce that sentiment.

Most of the inventions of men are subject to change. They depend upon humour and caprice. They have a vogue for a time, and then sink into oblivion. It may, perhaps, be apprehended, that if justice were allow'd to be a human invention, it must be plac'd on the same footing. But the cases are widely different. The interest, on which justice is founded, is the greatest imaginable, and extends to all times and places. It cannot possibly be serv'd by any other invention. It is obvious, and discovers itself on the very first formation of society. All these causes render the rules of justice stedfast and immutable ; at least, as immutable as human nature. And if they were founded on original instincts, cou'd they have any greater stability?

The same system may help us to form a just notion of the *happiness*, as well as of the *dignity* of virtue, and may interest every principle of our nature in the embracing and cherishing that noble quality. Who indeed does not feel an accession of alacrity in his pursuits of knowledge and ability of every kind, when he considers, that besides the advantage, which immediately result from these acquisitions, they also give him a new lustre in the eyes of mankind, and are universally attended with esteem and approbation? And who can think any advantages of fortune a sufficient compensation for the least breach of the *social* virtues, when he considers, that not only his character with regard to others, but also his peace and inward satisfaction entirely depend upon his strict observance of them ; and that a mind will never be able to bear its own survey, that has been wanting in its part to mankind and society? But I forbear insisting on this subject. Such reflections require a work a-part, very different

PART
III.

Of the
other
virtues
and vices.

from the genius of the present. The anatomist ought never to emulate the painter; nor in his accurate dissections and portraitures of the smaller parts of the human body, pretend to give his figures any graceful and engaging attitude or expression. There is even something hideous, or at least minute in the views of things, which he presents; and 'tis necessary the objects shou'd be set more at a distance, and be more cover'd up from sight, to make them engaging to the eye and imagination. An anatomist, however, is admirably fitted to give advice to a painter; and 'tis even impracticable to excel in the latter art, without the assistance of the former. We must have an exact knowledge of the parts, their situation and connexion, before we can design with any elegance or correctness. And thus the most abstract speculations concerning human nature, however cold and unentertaining, become subservient to *practical morality*; and may render this latter science more correct in its precepts, and more persuasive in its exhortations.

DIALOGUES

CONCERNING

NATURAL RELIGION.

DIALOGUES

CONCERNING

NATURAL RELIGION.

___

PAMPHILUS TO HERMIPPUS.

It has been remarked, my Hermippus, that, though the ancient philosophers conveyed most of their instruction in the form of dialogue, this method of composition has been little practised in later ages, and has seldom succeeded in the hands of those, who have attempted it. Accurate and regular argument, indeed, such as is now expected of philosophical enquirers, naturally throws a man into the methodical and didactic manner; where he can immediately, without preparation, explain the point, at which he aims; and thence proceed, without interruption, to deduce the proofs, on which it is established. To deliver a SYSTEM in conversation scarcely appears natural; and while the dialogue-writer desires, by departing from the direct style of composition, to give a freer air to his performance, and avoid the appearance of *Author* and *Reader*, he is apt to run into a worse inconvenience, and convey the image of *Pedagogue* and *Pupil*. Or if he carries on the dispute in the natural spirit of good company, by throwing in a variety of topics, and preserving a proper balance among the speakers; he often loses so much time in preparations and transitions, that the reader will scarcely think himself compensated, by all the graces of dialogue, for the order, brevity, and precision, which are sacrificed to them.

There are some subjects, however, to which dialogue-writing is peculiarly adapted, and where it is still preferable to the direct and simple method of composition.

Any point of doctrine, which is so *obvious*, that it scarcely admits of dispute, but at the same time so *important*, that it cannot be too often inculcated, seems to require some such method of handling it; where the novelty of the manner may compensate the triteness of the subject, where the vivacity of conversation may enforce the precept, and where the variety of lights, presented by various personages and characters, may appear neither tedious nor redundant.

Any question of philosophy, on the other hand, which is so *obscure* and *uncertain*, that human reason can reach no fixed determination with regard to it; if it should be treated at all; seems to lead us naturally into the style of dialogue and conversation. Reasonable men may be allowed to differ, where no one can reasonably be positive : Opposite sentiments, even without any decision, afford an agreeable amusement : and if the subject be curious and interesting, the book carries us, in a manner, into company; and unites the two greatest and purest pleasures of human life, study and society.

Happily, these circumstances are all to be found in the subject of NATURAL RELIGION. What truth so obvious, so certain, as the BEING of a God, which the most ignorant ages have acknowledged, for which the most refined geniuses have ambitiously striven to produce new proofs and arguments? What truth so important as this, which is the ground of all our hopes, the surest foundation of morality, the firmest support of society, and the only principle, which ought never to be a moment absent from our thoughts and meditations? But in treating of this obvious and important truth; what obscure questions occur, concerning the NATURE of that divine being; his attributes, his decrees, his plan of providence? These have been always subjected to the disputations of men: Concerning these, human reason has not reached any certain determination: But these are topics so interesting, that we cannot restrain our restless enquiry with regard to them; though nothing but doubt, uncertainty and contradiction, have, as yet, been the result of our most accurate researches.

This I had lately occasion to observe, while I passed, as usual, part of the summer season with CLEANTHES, and was present at those conversations of his with PHILO and DEMEA, of which I gave you lately some imperfect account. Your curiosity, you then told me, was so excited, that I must of necessity enter into a more exact detail of their reasonings, and display those various systems, which they advanced with regard to so delicate a subject as that of Natural Religion. The remarkable contrast in their characters still farther raised your expectations; while you opposed the accurate philosophical turn of CLEANTHES to the careless scepticism of PHILO, or compared either of their dispositions with the rigid inflexible orthodoxy of DEMEA. My youth rendered me a mere auditor of their disputes; and that curiosity, natural to the early season of life, has so deeply imprinted in my memory the whole chain and connection of their arguments, that, I hope, I shall not omit or confound any considerable part of them in the recital.

PART I.

AFTER I joined the company, whom I found sitting in
CLEANTHES'S library, DEMEA paid CLEANTHES some com-
pliments, on the great care, which he took of my education,
and on his unwearied perseverance and constancy in all his
friendships. The father of PAMPHILUS, said he, was your
intimate friend: The son is your pupil, and may indeed be
regarded as your adopted son; were we to judge by the pains
which you bestow in conveying 'to him every useful branch
of literature and science. You are no more wanting, I am
persuaded, in prudence than in industry. I shall, therefore,
communicate to you a maxim, which I have observed with
regard to my own children, that I may learn how far it agrees
with your practice. The method I follow in their education
is founded on the saying of an ancient, 'That students of philosophy ought first to learn Logics, then Ethics, next Physics,
last of all, the Nature of the Gods.'[1] This science of Natural
Theology, according to him, being the most profound and
abstruse of any, required the maturest judgment in its students; and none but a mind, enriched with all the other
sciences, can safely be entrusted with it.

Are you so late, says PHILO, in teaching your children the
principles of religion? Is there no danger of their neglecting
or rejecting altogether those opinions, of which they have
heard so little, during the whole course of their education?
It is only as a science, replied DEMEA, subjected to human
reasoning and disputation, that I postpone the study of
Natural Theology. To season their minds with early piety
is my chief care; and by continual precept and instruction,
and I hope too, by example, I imprint deeply on their tender
minds an habitual reverence for all the principles of religion.
While they pass through every other science, I still remark
the uncertainty of each part, the eternal disputations of

---

[1] Chrysippus apud Plut. de repug Stoicorum

men, the obscurity of all philosophy, and the strange, ridiculous conclusions, which some of the greatest geniuses have derived from the principles of mere human reason. Having thus tamed their mind to a proper submission and self-diffidence, I have no longer any scruple of opening to them the greatest mysteries of religion, nor apprehend any danger from that assuming arrogance of philosophy, which may lead them to reject the most established doctrines and opinions.

Your precaution, says PHILO, of seasoning your children's minds with early piety, is certainly very reasonable ; and no more than is requisite, in this profane and irreligious age. But what I chiefly admire in your plan of education, is your method of drawing advantage from the very principles of philosophy and learning, which, by inspiring pride and self-sufficiency, have commonly, in all ages, been found so destructive to the principles of religion. The vulgar, indeed, we may remark, who are unacquainted with science and profound enquiry, observing the endless disputes of the learned, have commonly a thorough contempt for Philosophy ; and rivet themselves the faster, by that means, in the great points of Theology, which have been taught them. Those, who enter a little into study and enquiry, finding many appearances of evidence in doctrines the newest and most extraordinary, think nothing too difficult for human reason ; and presumptuously breaking through all fences, profane the inmost sanctuaries of the temple. But CLEANTHES will, I hope, agree with me, that, after we have abandoned ignorance, the surest remedy, there is still one expedient left to prevent this profane liberty. Let DEMEA's principles be improved and cultivated : Let us become thoroughly sensible of the weakness, blindness, and narrow limits of human reason : Let us duly consider its uncertainty and endless contrarieties, even in subjects of common life and practice : Let the errors and deceits of our very senses be set before us ; the insuperable difficulties, which attend first principles in all systems ; the contradictions, which adhere to the very ideas of matter, cause and effect, extension, space, time, motion ; and in a word, quantity of all kinds, the object of the only science, that can fairly pretend to any certainty or evidence. When these topics are displayed in their full light, as they are by some philosophers and almost all divines ; who can retain

such confidence in this frail faculty of reason as to pay any
regard to its determinations in points so sublime, so abstruse,
so remote from common life and experience? When the
coherence of the parts of a stone, or even that composition
of parts, which renders it extended; when these familiar
objects, I say, are so inexplicable, and contain circumstances
so repugnant and contradictory; with what assurance can
we decide concerning the origin of worlds, or trace their
history from eternity to eternity?

While PHILO pronounced these words, I could observe a
smile in the countenance both of DEMEA and CLEANTHES.
That of DEMEA seemed to imply an unreserved satisfaction
in the doctrines delivered: But in CLEANTHES'S features, I
could distinguish an air of finesse; as if he perceived some
raillery or artificial malice in the reasonings of PHILO.

You propose then, PHILO, said CLEANTHES, to erect religious faith on philosophical scepticism; and you think, that
if certainty or evidence be expelled from every other subject
of enquiry, it will all retire to these theological doctrines,
and there acquire a superior force and authority. Whether
your scepticism be as absolute and sincere as you pretend,
we shall learn by and by, when the company breaks up: We
shall then see, whether you go out at the door or the window;
and whether you really doubt, if your body has gravity, or
can be injured by its fall; according to popular opinion, derived from our fallacious senses and more fallacious experience. And this consideration, DEMEA, may, I think, fairly
serve to abate our ill-will to this humourous sect of the
sceptics. If they be thoroughly in earnest, they will not long
trouble the world with their doubts, cavils, and disputes: If
they be only in jest, they are, perhaps, bad ralliers, but can
never be very dangerous, either to the state, to philosophy,
or to religion.

In reality, PHILO, continued he, it seems certain, that
though a man, in a flush of humour, after intense reflection
on the many contradictions and imperfections of human
reason, may entirely renounce all belief and opinion; it is
impossible for him to persevere in this total scepticism, or
make it appear in his conduct for a few hours. External
objects press in upon him: Passions solicit him: His philosophical melancholy dissipates; and even the utmost violence
upon his own temper will not be able, during any time, to

preserve the poor appearance of scepticism. And for what reason impose on himself such a violence? This is a point, in which it will be impossible for him ever to satisfy himself, consistently with his sceptical principles: So that upon the whole nothing could be more ridiculous than the principles of the ancient PYRRHONIANS; if in reality they endeavoured, as is pretended, to extend throughout, the same scepticism, which they had learned from the declamations of their schools, and which they ought to have confined to them.

In this view, there appears a great resemblance between the sects of the STOICS and PYRRHONIANS, though perpetual antagonists: and both of them seem founded on this erroneous maxim, That what a man can perform sometimes, and in some dispositions, he can perform always, and in every disposition. When the mind, by Stoical reflections, is elevated into a sublime enthusiasm of virtue, and strongly smit with any *species* of honour or public good, the utmost bodily pain and sufferance will not prevail over such a high sense of duty; and 'tis possible, perhaps, by its means, even to smile and exult in the midst of tortures. If this sometimes may be the case in fact and reality, much more may a philosopher, in his school, or even in his closet, work himself up to such an enthusiasm, and support in imagination the acutest pain or most calamitous event, which he can possibly conceive. But how shall he support this enthusiasm itself? The bent of his mind relaxes, and cannot be recalled at pleasure: Avocations lead him astray: Misfortunes attack him unawares: and the *philosopher* sinks by degrees into the *plebeian*.

I allow of your comparison between the STOICS and SCEPTICS, replied PHILO. But you may observe, at the same time, that though the mind cannot, in Stoicism, support the highest flights of philosophy, yet even when it sinks lower, it still retains somewhat of its former disposition; and the effects of the Stoic's reasoning will appear in his conduct in common life, and through the whole tenor of his actions. The ancient schools, particularly that of ZENO, produced examples of virtue and constancy which seem astonishing to present times.

> Vain Wisdom all and false Philosophy
> Yet with a pleasing sorcery could charm
> Pain, for a while or anguish, and excite
> Fallacious Hope, or arm the obdurate breast
> With stubborn Patience as with triple steel

In like manner, if a man has accustomed himself to sceptical considerations on the uncertainty and narrow limits of reason, he will not entirely forget them when he turns his reflection on other subjects; but in all his philosophical principles and reasoning, I dare not say, in his common conduct, he will be found different from those, who either never formed any opinions in the case, or have entertained sentiments more favourable to human reason.

To whatever length any one may push his speculative principles of scepticism, he must act, I own, and live, and converse like other men; and for this conduct he is not obliged to give any other reason, than the absolute necessity he lies under of so doing. If he ever carries his speculations farther than this necessity constrains him, and philosophises, either on natural or moral subjects, he is allured by a certain pleasure and satisfaction, which he finds in employing himself after that manner. He considers besides, that every one, even in common life, is constrained to have more or less of this philosophy; that from our earliest infancy we make continual advances in forming more general principles of conduct and reasoning; that the larger experience we acquire, and the stronger reason we are endued with, we always render our principles the more general and comprehensive; and that what we call *philosophy* is nothing but a more regular and methodical operation of the same kind. To philosophise on such subjects is nothing essentially different from reasoning on common life; and we may only expect greater stability, if not greater truth, from our philosophy, on account of its exacter and more scrupulous method of proceeding.

But when we look beyond human affairs and the properties of the surrounding bodies: When we carry our speculations into the two eternities, before and after the present state of things; into the creation and formation of the universe; the existence and properties of spirits; the powers and operations of one universal spirit, existing without beginning and without end; omnipotent, omniscient, immutable, infinite, and incomprehensible: We must be far removed from the smallest tendency to scepticism not to be apprehensive, that we have here got quite beyond the reach of our faculties. So long as we confine our speculations to trade, or morals, or politics, or criticism, we make appeals, every moment, to common sense and experience, which strengthen our philosophical conclusions, and remove (at least, in part) the suspicion, which we so justly entertain with regard to every reasoning, that is very subtile and refined. But in theological reasonings, we have not this advantage; while at the same time we are employed upon objects, which, we must be sensible, are too large for our grasp, and of all others, require most to be familiarised to our apprehension. We are like foreigners in a strange country, to whom every thing must seem suspicious, and who are in danger every moment of transgressing against the laws and customs of the people, with whom they live and converse. We know not how far we ought to trust our vulgar methods of reasoning in such a subject; since, even in common life and in that province, which is peculiarly appropriated to them, we cannot account for them, and are entirely guided by a kind of instinct or necessity in employing them.

All sceptics pretend, that, if reason be considered in an abstract view, it furnishes invincible arguments against itself, and that we could never retain any conviction or assurance, on any subject, were not the sceptical reasonings so refined and subtile, that they are not able to counterpoise the more solid and more natural arguments, derived from the senses and experience. But it is evident, whenever our arguments lose this advantage, and run wide of common life, that the most refined scepticism comes to be upon a footing with them, and is able to oppose and counterbalance them. The one has no more weight than the other. The mind must remain in suspense between them; and it is that very suspense or balance, which is the triumph of scepticism.

But I observe, says CLEANTHES, with regard to you, PHILO, and all speculative sceptics, that your doctrine and practice are as much at variance in the most abstruse points of theory as in the conduct of common life. Where-ever evidence discovers itself, you adhere to it, notwithstanding your pretended scepticism; and I can observe too some of your sect to be as decisive as those, who make greater professions of certainty and assurance. In reality, would not a man be ridiculous, who pretended to reject NEWTON's explication of the wonderful phenomenon of the rainbow, because that explication gives a minute anatomy of the rays of light; a subject, forsooth, too refined for human comprehension?

And what would you say to one, who having nothing particular to object to the arguments of COPERNICUS and GALILÆO
for the motion of the earth, should with-hold his assent, on
that general principle, That these subjects were too magnificent and remote to be explained by the narrow and fallacious
reason of mankind?

There is indeed a kind of brutish and ignorant scepticism,
as you well observed, which gives the vulgar a general prejudice against what they do not easily understand, and makes
them reject every principle, which requires elaborate reasoning to prove and establish it. This species of scepticism is
fatal to knowledge, not to religion; since we find, that those
who make greatest profession of it, give often their assent,
not only to the great truths of Theism, and natural theology,
but even to the most absurd tenets, which a traditional
superstition has recommended to them. They firmly believe
in witches; though they will not believe nor attend to the
most simple proposition of Euclid. But the refined and
philosophical sceptics fall into an inconsistence of an opposite nature. They push their researches into the most abstruse corners of science; and their assent attends them in
every step, proportioned to the evidence which they meet
with. They are even obliged to acknowledge, that the most
abstruse and remote objects are those, which are best explained
by philosophy. Light is in reality anatomized: The true
system of the heavenly bodies is discovered and ascertained.
But the nourishment of bodies by food is still an inexplicable
mystery: The cohesion of the parts of matter is still incomprehensible. These sceptics, therefore, are obliged, in every
question, to consider each particular evidence apart, and proportion their assent to the precise degree of evidence, which
occurs. This is their practice in all natural, mathematical,
moral, and political science. And why not the same, I ask,
in the theological and religious? Why must conclusions of
this nature be alone rejected on the general presumption of
the insufficiency of human reason, without any particular
discussion of the evidence? Is not such an unequal conduct
a plain proof of prejudice and passion?

Our senses, you say, are fallacious, our understanding
erroneous, our ideas even of the most familiar objects, extension, duration, motion, full of absurdities and contradictions.
You defy me to solve the difficulties, or reconcile the repug-

nancies, which you discover in them. I have not capacity
for so great an undertaking: I have not leisure for it: I
perceive it to be superfluous. Your own conduct, in every
circumstance, refutes your principles; and shows the firmest
reliance on all the received maxims of science, morals, prudence, and behaviour.

I shall never assent to so harsh an opinion as that of a
celebrated writer,[1] who says, that the sceptics are not a sect
of philosophers: They are only a sect of liars. I may, however, affirm, (I hope without offence) that they are a sect of
jesters or ralliers. But for my part, whenever I find myself
disposed to mirth and amusement, I shall certainly chuse
my entertainment of a less perplexing and abstruse nature.
A comedy, a novel, or at most a history, seems a more
natural recreation than such metaphysical subtilties and abstractions.

In vain would the sceptic make a distinction between
science and common life, or between one science and another.
The arguments, employed in all, if just, are of a similar
nature, and contain the same force and evidence. Or if
there be any difference among them, the advantage lies
entirely on the side of theology and natural religion. Many
principles of mechanics are founded on very abstruse reasoning; yet no man, who has any pretensions to science, even
no speculative sceptic, pretends to entertain the least doubt
with regard to them. The COPERNICAN system contains the
most surprising paradox, and the most contrary to our natural conceptions, to appearances, and to our very senses:
yet even monks and inquisitors are now constrained to with-
draw their opposition to it. And shall PHILO, a man of so
liberal a genius, and extensive knowledge, entertain any
general undistinguished scruples with regard to the religious
hypothesis, which is founded on the simplest and most obvious arguments, and, unless it meets with artificial obstacles,
has such easy access and admission into the mind of man?

And here we may observe, continued he, turning himself
towards DEMEA, a pretty curious circumstance in the history
of the sciences. After the union of philosophy with the
popular religion, upon the first establishment of Christianity,
nothing was more usual, among all religious teachers, than
declamations against reason, against the senses, against every

---

[1] L'art de penser.

principle, derived merely from human research and enquiry. All the topics of the ancient Academics were adopted by the Fathers; and thence propagated for several ages in every school and pulpit throughout Christendom. The Reformers embraced the same principles of reasoning, or rather declamation; and all panegyrics on the excellency of faith were sure to be interlarded with some severe strokes of satire against natural reason. A celebrated prelate too,[1] of the Romish communion, a man of the most extensive learning, who wrote a demonstration of Christianity, has also composed a treatise, which contains all the cavils of the boldest and most determined PYRRHONISM. LOCKE seems to have been the first Christian, who ventured openly to assert, that *faith* was nothing but a species of *reason*, that religion was only a branch of philosophy, and that a chain of arguments, similar to that which established any truth in morals, politics, or physics, was always employed in discovering all the principles of theology, natural and revealed. The ill use, which BAYLE and other libertines made of the philosophical scepticism of the fathers and first reformers, still farther propagated the judicious sentiment of Mr. LOCKE: and it is now, in a manner, avowed, by all pretenders to reasoning and philosophy, that Atheist and Sceptic are almost synonymous. And as it is certain, that no man is in earnest, when he professes the latter principle; I would fain hope that there are as few, who seriously maintain the former.

Don't you remember, said PHILO, the excellent saying of Lord BACON on this head? That a little philosophy, replied CLEANTHES, makes a man an Atheist: a great deal converts him to religion. That is a very judicious remark too, said PHILO. But what I have in my eye is another passage, where, having mentioned DAVID's fool, who said in his heart there is no God, this great philosopher observes, that the Atheists now a days have a double share of folly: for they are not contented to say in their hearts there is no God, but they also utter that impiety with their lips, and are thereby guilty of multiplied indiscretion and imprudence. Such people, though they were ever so much in earnest, cannot, methinks, be very formidable.

But though you should rank me in this class of fools, I cannot forbear communicating a remark, that occurs to me,

[1] Mons. Huet.

from the history of the religious and irreligious scepticism, with which you have entertained us. It appears to me, that there are strong symptoms of priestcraft in the whole progress of this affair. During ignorant ages, such as those which followed the dissolution of the ancient schools, the priests perceived, that Atheism, Deism, or heresy of any kind, could only proceed from the presumptuous questioning of received opinions, and from a belief, that human reason was equal to everything. Education had then a mighty influence over the minds of men, and was almost equal in force to those suggestions of the senses and common understanding, by which the most determined sceptic must allow himself to be governed. But at present, when the influence of education is much diminished, and men, from a more open commerce of the world, have learned to compare the popular principles of different nations and ages, our sagacious divines have changed their whole system of philosophy, and talk the language of STOICS, PLATONISTS, and PERIPATETICS, not that of PYRRHONIANS and ACADEMICS. If we distrust human reason, we have now no other principle to lead us into religion. Thus, sceptics in one age, dogmatists in another; whichever system best suits the purpose of these reverend gentlemen, in giving them an ascendant over mankind, they are sure to make it their favourite principle, and established tenet.

It is very natural, said CLEANTHES, for men to embrace those principles, by which they find they can best defend their doctrines; nor need we have any recourse to priestcraft to account for so reasonable an expedient. And surely nothing can afford a stronger presumption, that any set of principles are true, and ought to be embraced, than to observe, that they tend to the confirmation of true religion, and serve to confound the cavils of Atheists, Libertines, and Freethinkers of all denominations.

PART II.

I MUST own, CLEANTHES, said DEMEA, that nothing can more surprise me, than the light, in which you have, all along, put this argument. By the whole tenor of your discourse, one would imagine that you were maintaining the Being of a God, against the cavils of Atheists and Infidels; and were necessitated to become a champion for that fundamental principle of all religion. But this, I hope, is not by any means a question among us. No man; no man, at least, of common sense, I am persuaded, ever entertained a serious doubt with regard to a truth, so certain and self-evident. The question is not concerning the BEING, but the NATURE of GOD. This, I affirm, from the infirmities of human understanding, to be altogether incomprehensible and unknown to us. The essence of that supreme mind, his attributes, the manner of his existence, the very nature of his duration; these and every particular, which regards so divine a Being, are mysterious to men. Finite, weak, and blind creatures, we ought to humble ourselves in his august presence, and, conscious of our frailties, adore in silence his infinite perfections, which eye hath not seen, ear hath not heard, neither hath it entered into the heart of man to conceive. They are covered in a deep cloud from human curiosity: It is profaneness to attempt penetrating through these sacred obscurities: And next to the impiety of denying his existence, is the temerity of prying into his nature and essence, decrees and attributes.

But lest you should think, that my *piety* has here got the better of my *philosophy*, I shall support my opinion, if it needs any support, by a very great authority. I might cite all the divines almost, from the foundation of Christianity, who have ever treated of this or any other theological subject: But I shall confine myself, at present, to one equally celebrated for piety and philosophy. It is Father MALEBRANCHE, who, I remember, thus expresses himself.[1] 'One ought not so much (says he) to call God a spirit, in order to express positively what he is, as in order to signify that he is not matter. He is a Being infinitely perfect: Of this we cannot doubt. But in the same manner as we ought not to imagine, even supposing him corporeal, that he is clothed with a human body, as the ANTHROPOMORPHITES asserted, under colour that that figure was the most perfect of any; so neither ought we to imagine, that the Spirit of God has human ideas, or bears any resemblance to our spirit; under colour that we know nothing more perfect than a human

---

[1] Recherche de la Verité, liv 3, chap 9

mind. We ought rather to believe, that as he comprehends the perfections of matter without being material . . . . . . he comprehends also the perfections of created spirits, without being spirit, in the manner we conceive spirit: That his true name is, *He that is*, or, in other words, Being without restriction, All Being, the Being infinite and universal.'

After so great an authority, DEMEA, replied PHILO, as that which you have produced, and a thousand more, which you might produce, it would appear ridiculous in me to add my sentiment, or express my approbation of your doctrine. But surely, where reasonable men treat these subjects, the question can never be concerning the *Being*, but only the *Nature* of the Deity. The former truth, as you well observe, is unquestionable and self-evident. Nothing exists without a cause; and the original cause of this universe (whatever it be) we call GOD; and piously ascribe to him every species of perfection. Whoever scruples this fundamental truth, deserves every punishment, which can be inflicted among philosophers, to wit, the greatest ridicule, contempt and disapprobation. But as all perfection is entirely relative, we ought never to imagine, that we comprehend the attributes of this divine Being, or to suppose, that his perfections have any analogy or likeness to the perfections of a human creature. Wisdom, Thought, Design, Knowledge; these we justly ascribe to him; because these words are honourable among men, and we have no other language or other conceptions, by which we can express our adoration of him. But let us beware, lest we think, that our ideas any wise correspond to his perfections, or that his attributes have any resemblance to these qualities among men. He is infinitely superior to our limited view and comprehension; and is more the object of worship in the temple, than of disputation in the schools.

In reality, CLEANTHES, continued he, there is no need of having recourse to that affected scepticism, so displeasing to you, in order to come at this determination. Our ideas reach no farther than our experience: We have no experience of divine attributes and operations: I need not conclude my syllogism: You can draw the inference yourself. And it is a pleasure to me (and I hope to you too) that just reasoning and sound piety here concur in the same conclusion, and both of them establish the adorably mysterious and incomprehensible nature of the Supreme Being.

Not to lose any time in circumlocutions, said CLEANTHES, addressing himself to DEMEA, much less in replying to the pious declamations of PHILO; I shall briefly explain how I conceive this matter. Look round the world: contemplate the whole and every part of it: You will find it to be nothing but one great machine, subdivided into an infinite number of lesser machines, which again admit of subdivisions, to a degree beyond what human senses and faculties can trace and explain. All these various machines, and even their most minute parts, are adjusted to each other with an accuracy, which ravishes into admiration all men, who have ever contemplated them. The curious adapting of means to ends, throughout all nature, resembles exactly, though it much exceeds, the productions of human contrivance; of human designs, thought, wisdom, and intelligence. Since therefore the effects resemble each other, we are led to infer, by all the rules of analogy, that the causes also resemble; and that the Author of Nature is somewhat similar to the mind of man; though possessed of much larger faculties, proportioned to the grandeur of the work, which he has executed. By this argument *a posteriori,* and by this argument alone, do we prove at once the existence of a Deity, and his similarity to human mind and intelligence.

I shall be so free, CLEANTHES, said DEMEA, as to tell you, that from the beginning, I could not approve of your conclusion concerning the similarity of the Deity to men; still less can I approve of the mediums, by which you endeavour to establish it. What! No demonstration of the Being of a God! No abstract arguments! No proofs *a priori!* Are these, which have hitherto been so much insisted on by philosophers, all fallacy, all sophism? Can we reach no farther in this subject than experience and probability? I will not say, that this is betraying the cause of a Deity: But surely, by this affected candor, you give advantage to Atheists, which they never could obtain, by the mere dint of argument and reasoning.

What I chiefly scruple in this subject, said PHILO, is not so much, that all religious arguments are by CLEANTHES reduced to experience, as that they appear not to be even the most certain and irrefragable of that inferior kind. That a stone will fall, that fire will burn, that the earth has solidity, we have observed a thousand and a thousand times; and when any new instance of this nature is presented, we draw without hesitation the accustomed inference. The exact similarity of the cases gives us a perfect assurance of a similar event; and a stronger evidence is never desired nor sought after. But where-ever you depart, in the least, from the similarity of the cases, you diminish proportionably the evidence; and may at last bring it to a very weak *analogy*, which is confessedly liable to error and uncertainty. After having experienced the circulation of the blood in human creatures, we make no doubt that it takes place in Titius and Mævius: but from its circulation in frogs and fishes, it is only a presumption, though a strong one, from analogy, that it takes place in men and other animals. The analogical reasoning is much weaker, when we infer the circulation of the sap in vegetables from our experience, that the blood circulates in animals; and those, who hastily followed that imperfect analogy, are found, by more accurate experiments, to have been mistaken.

If we see a house, CLEANTHES, we conclude, with the greatest certainty, that it had an architect or builder; because this is precisely that species of effect, which we have experienced to proceed from that species of cause. But surely you will not affirm, that the universe bears such a resemblance to a house, that we can with the same certainty infer a similar cause, or that the analogy is here entire and perfect. The dissimilitude is so striking, that the utmost you can here pretend to is a guess, a conjecture, a presumption concerning a similar cause; and how that pretension will be received in the world, I leave you to consider.

It would surely be very ill received, replied CLEANTHES; and I should be deservedly blamed and detested, did I allow, that the proofs of a Deity amounted to no more than a guess or conjecture. But is the whole adjustment of means to ends in a house and in the universe so slight a resemblance? The œconomy of final causes? The order, proportion, and arrangement of every part? Steps of a stair are plainly contrived, that human legs may use them in mounting; and this inference is certain and infallible. Human legs are also contrived for walking and mounting; and this inference, I allow, is not altogether so certain, because of the dissimilarity which you remark; but does it, therefore, deserve the name only of presumption or conjecture?

Good God! cried DEMEA, interrupting him, where are we?

Zealous defenders of religion allow, that the proofs of a Deity fall short of perfect evidence! And you, PHILO, on whose assistance I depended, in proving the adorable mysteriousness of the Divine Nature, do you assent to all these extravagant opinions of CLEANTHES? For what other name can I give them? Or why spare my censure, when such principles are advanced, supported by such an authority, before so young a man as PAMPHILUS?

You seem not to apprehend, replied PHILO, that I argue with CLEANTHES in his own way; and by showing him the dangerous consequences of his tenets, hope at last to reduce him to our opinion. But what sticks most with you, I observe, is the representation which CLEANTHES has made of the argument *a posteriori*; and finding, that that argument is likely to escape your hold and vanish into air, you think it so disguised, that you can scarcely believe it to be set in its true light. Now, however much I may dissent, in other respects, from the dangerous principles of CLEANTHES, I must allow, that he has fairly represented that argument; and I shall endeavour so to state the matter to you, that you will entertain no farther scruples with regard to it.

Were a man to abstract from every thing which he knows or has seen, he would be altogether incapable, merely from his own ideas, to determine what kind of scene the universe must be, or to give the preference to one state or situation of things above another. For as nothing which he clearly conceives, could be esteemed impossible or implying a contradiction, every chimera of his fancy would be upon an equal footing; nor could he assign any just reason, why he adheres to one idea or system, and rejects the others, which are equally possible.

Again; after he opens his eyes, and contemplates the world, as it really is, it would be impossible for him, at first, to assign the cause of any one event; much less, of the whole of things or of the universe. He might set his Fancy a rambling; and she might bring him in an infinite variety of reports and representations. These would all be possible; but being all equally possible, he would never, of himself, give a satisfactory account for his preferring one of them to the rest. Experience alone can point out to him the true cause of any phenomenon.

Now, according to this method of reasoning, DEMEA, it

follows (and is, indeed, tacitly allowed by Cleanthes himself) that order, arrangement, or the adjustment of final causes is not, of itself, any proof of design; but only so far as it has been experienced to proceed from that principle. For ought we can know *a priori*, matter may contain the source or spring of order originally, within itself, as well as mind does; and there is no more difficulty in conceiving, that the several elements, from an internal unknown cause, may fall into the most exquisite arrangement, than to conceive that their ideas, in the great, universal mind, from a like internal, unknown cause, fall into that arrangement. The equal possibility of both these suppositions is allowed. But by experience we find, (according to Cleanthes) that there is a difference between them. Throw several pieces of steel together, without shape or form; they will never arrange themselves so as to compose a watch: Stone, and mortar, and wood, without an architect, never erect a house. But the ideas in a human mind, we see, by an unknown, inexplicable œconomy, arrange themselves so as to form the plan of a watch or house. Experience, therefore, proves, that there is an original principle of order in mind, not in matter. From similar effects we infer similar causes. The adjustment of means to ends is alike in the universe, as in a machine of human contrivance. The causes, therefore, must be resembling.

I was from the beginning scandalised, I must own, with this resemblance, which is asserted, between the Deity and human creatures; and must conceive it to imply such a degradation of the Supreme Being as no sound Theist could endure. With your assistance, therefore, Demea, I shall endeavour to defend what you justly called the adorable mysteriousness of the Divine Nature, and shall refute this reasoning of Cleanthes, provided he allows, that I have made a fair representation of it.

When Cleanthes had assented, Philo, after a short pause, proceeded in the following manner.

That all inferences, Cleanthes, concerning fact, are founded on experience, and that all experimental reasonings are founded on the supposition, that similar causes prove similar effects, and similar effects similar causes; I shall not, at present, much dispute with you. But observe, I entreat you, with what extreme caution all just reasoners proceed in the transferring of experiments to similar cases. Unless the cases be exactly similar, they repose no perfect confidence in applying their past observation to any particular phenomenon. Every alteration of circumstances occasions a doubt concerning the event; and it requires new experiments to prove certainly, that the new circumstances are of no moment or importance. A change in bulk, situation, arrangement, age, disposition of the air, or surrounding bodies; any of these particulars may be attended with the most unexpected consequences: And unless the objects be quite familiar to us, it is the highest temerity to expect with assurance, after any of these changes, an event similar to that which before fell under our observation. The slow and deliberate steps of philosophers, here, if any where, are distinguished from the precipitate march of the vulgar, who, hurried on by the smallest similitudes, are incapable of all discernment or consideration.

But can you think, CLEANTHES, that your usual phlegm and philosophy have been preserved in so wide a step as you have taken, when you compared to the universe houses, ships, furniture, machines; and from their similarity in some circumstances inferred a similarity in their causes? Thought, design, intelligence, such as we discover in men and other animals, is no more than one of the springs and principles of the universe, as well as heat or cold, attraction or repulsion, and a hundred others, which fall under daily observation. It is an active cause, by which some particular parts of nature, we find, produce alterations on other parts. But can a conclusion, with any propriety, be transferred from parts to the whole? Does not the great disproportion bar all comparison and inference? From observing the growth of a hair, can we learn any thing concerning the generation of a man? Would the manner of a leaf's blowing, even though perfectly known, afford us any instruction concerning the vegetation of a tree?

But allowing that we were to take the *operations* of one part of nature upon another for the foundation of our judgement concerning the *origin* of the whole (which never can be admitted) yet why select so minute, so weak, so bounded a principle as the reason and design of animals is found to be upon this planet? What peculiar privilege has this little agitation of the brain which we call *thought*, that we must thus make it the model of the whole universe? Our partiality in our own favour does indeed present it on all occasions; but sound philosophy ought carefully to guard against so natural an illusion.

So far from admitting, continued PHILO, that the operations of a part can afford us any just conclusion concerning the origin of the whole, I will not allow any one part to form a rule for another part, if the latter be very remote from the former. Is there any reasonable ground to conclude, that the inhabitants of other planets possess thought, intelligence, reason, or any thing similar to these faculties in men? When Nature has so extremely diversified her manner of operation in this small globe; can we imagine, that she incessantly copies herself throughout so immense a universe? And if thought, as we may well suppose, be confined merely to this narrow corner, and has even there so limited a sphere of action; with what propriety can we assign it for the original cause of all things? The narrow views of a peasant, who makes his domestic œconomy the rule for the government of kingdoms, is in comparison a pardonable sophism.

But were we ever so much assured, that a thought and reason, resembling the human, were to be found throughout the whole universe, and were its activity elsewhere vastly greater and more commanding than it appears in this globe; yet I cannot see, why the operations of a world, constituted, arranged, adjusted, can with any propriety be extended to a world, which is in its embryo-state, and is advancing towards that constitution and arrangement. By observation, we know somewhat of the œconomy, action, and nourishment of a finished animal; but we must transfer with great caution that observation to the growth of a fœtus in the womb, and still more, in the formation of an animalcule in the loins of its male parent. Nature, we find, even from our limited experience, possesses an infinite number of springs and principles, which incessantly discover themselves on every change of her position and situation. And what new and unknown principles would actuate her in so new and unknown a situation as that of the formation of a universe, we cannot, without the utmost temerity, pretend to determine.

A very small part of this great system, during a very short time, is very imperfectly discovered to us: and do we then pronounce decisively concerning the origin of the whole?

Admirable conclusion! Stone, wood, brick, iron, brass,

have not, at this time, in this minute globe of earth, an order
or arrangement without human art and contrivance : therefore the universe could not originally attain its order and
arrangement, without something similar to human art. But
is a part of nature a rule for another part very wide of the
former ?   Is it a rule for the whole ?   Is a very small part a
rule for the universe ?   Is nature in one situation, a certain
rule for nature in another situation, vastly different from the
former ?

And can you blame me, CLEANTHES, if I here imitate the
prudent reserve of SIMONIDES, who, according to the noted
story, being asked by HIERO, *What God was ?* desired a day
to think of it, and then two days more ; and after that
manner continually prolonged the term, without ever
bringing in his definition or description ?   Could you even
blame me, if I had answered at first *that I did not know,* and
was sensible that this subject lay vastly beyond the reach of
my faculties ?   You might cry out sceptic and rallier as much
as you pleased : but having found, in so many other subjects,
much more familiar, the imperfections and even contradictions of human reason, I never should expect any success
from its feeble conjectures, in a subject, so sublime, and so
remote from the sphere of our observation.   When two *species*
of objects have always been observed to be conjoined together,
I can *infer*, by custom, the existence of one where-ever I *see*
the existence of the other : and this I call an argument from
experience.   But how this argument can have place, where
the objects, as in the present case, are single, individual,
without parallel, or specific resemblance, may be difficult to
explain.   And will any man tell me with a serious countenance, that an orderly universe must arise from some thought
and art, like the human ; because we have experience of it ?
To ascertain this reasoning, it were requisite, that we had
experience of the origin of worlds ; and it is not sufficient
surely, that we have seen ships and cities arise from human
art and contrivance .   .   .   .   .

PHILO was proceeding in this vehement manner, somewhat
between jest and earnest, as it appeared to me ; when he observed some signs of impatience in CLEANTHES, and then
immediately stopped short.   What I had to suggest, said
CLEANTHES, is only that you would not abuse terms, or make
use of popular expressions to subvert philosophical reason-

ings. You know, that the vulgar often distinguish reason from experience, even where the question relates only to matter of fact and existence; though it is found, where that *reason* is properly analyzed, that it is nothing but a species of experience. To prove by experience the origin of the universe from mind is not more contrary to common speech than to prove the motion of the earth from the same principle. And a caviller might raise all the same objections to the COPERNICAN system, which you have urged against my reasonings. Have you other earths, might he say, which you have seen to move? Have . . . .

Yes! cried PHILO, interrupting him, we have other earths. Is not the moon another earth, which we see to turn round its centre? Is not Venus another earth, where we observe the same phenomenon? Are not the revolutions of the sun also a confirmation, from analogy, of the same theory? All the planets, are they not earths, which revolve about the sun? Are not the satellites moons, which move round Jupiter and Saturn, and along with these primary planets, round the sun? These analogies and resemblances, with others, which I have not mentioned, are the sole proofs of the COPERNICAN system: and to you it belongs to consider, whether you have any analogies of the same kind to support your theory.

In reality, CLEANTHES, continued he, the modern system of astronomy is now so much received by all enquirers, and has become so essential a part even of our earliest education, that we are not commonly very scrupulous in examining the reasons upon which it is founded. It is now become a matter of mere curiosity to study the first writers on that subject, who had the full force of prejudice to encounter, and were obliged to turn their arguments on every side, in order to render them popular and convincing. But if we peruse GALILÆO's famous Dialogues concerning the system of the world, we shall find, that that great genius, one of the sublimest that ever existed, first bent all his endeavours to prove, that there was no foundation for the distinction commonly made between elementary and celestial substances. The schools, proceeding from the illusions of sense, had carried this distinction very far; and had established the latter substances to be ingenerable, incorruptible, unalterable, impassible; and had assigned all the opposite qualities to the former. But GALILÆO, beginning with the moon, proved its similarity in every particular to the earth; its convex figure, its natural darkness when not illuminated, its density, its distinction into solid and liquid, the variations of its phases, the mutual illuminations of the earth and moon, their mutual eclipses, the inequalities of the lunar surface, &c. After many instances of this kind, with regard to all the planets, men plainly saw, that these bodies became proper objects of experience; and that the similarity of their nature enabled us to extend the same arguments and phenomena from one to the other.

In this cautious proceeding of the astronomers, you may read your own condemnation, CLEANTHES; or rather may see, that the subject in which you are engaged exceeds all human reason and enquiry. Can you pretend to show any such similarity between the fabric of a house, and the generation of a universe? Have you ever seen nature in any such situation as resembles the first arrangement of the elements? Have worlds ever been formed under your eye? and have you had leisure to observe the whole progress of the phenomenon, from the first appearance of order to its final consummation? If you have, then cite your experience, and deliver your theory.

PART III.

How the most absurd argument, replied CLEANTHES, in the hands of a man of ingenuity and invention, may acquire an air of probability! Are you not aware, PHILO, that it became necessary for COPERNICUS and his first disciples to prove the similarity of the terrestrial and celestial matter; because several philosophers, blinded by old systems, and supported by some sensible appearances, had denied that similarity? But that it is by no means necessary, that Theists should prove the similarity of the works of Nature to those of Art; because this similarity is self-evident and undeniable? The same matter, a like form: what more is requisite to show an analogy between their causes, and to ascertain the origin of all things from a divine purpose and intention? Your objections, I must freely tell you, are no better than the abstruse cavils of those philosophers who denied motion; and ought to be refuted in the same manner, by illustrations, examples, and instances, rather than by serious argument and philosophy.

Suppose, therefore, that an articulate voice were heard in the clouds, much louder and more melodious than any which human art could ever reach: Suppose, that this voice were extended in the same instant over all nations, and spoke to each nation in its own language and dialect: Suppose, that the words delivered not only contain a just sense and meaning, but convey some instruction altogether worthy of a benevolent being, superior to mankind: could you possibly hesitate a moment concerning the cause of this voice? and must you not instantly ascribe it to some design or purpose? Yet I cannot see but all the same objections (if they merit that appellation) which lie against the system of Theism, may also be produced against this inference.

Might you not say, that all conclusions concerning fact were founded on experience: that when we hear an articulate voice in the dark, and thence infer a man, it is only the resemblance of the effects, which leads us to conclude that there is a like resemblance in the cause: but that this extraordinary voice, by its loudness, extent, and flexibility to all languages, bears so little analogy to any human voice, that we have no reason to suppose any analogy in their causes: and consequently, that a rational, wise, coherent speech proceeded, you know not whence, from some accidental whistling of the winds, not from any divine reason or intelligence? You see clearly your own objections in these cavils; and I hope too, you see clearly, that they cannot possibly have more force in the one case than in the other.

But to bring the case still nearer the present one of the universe, I shall make two suppositions, which imply not any absurdity or impossibility. Suppose, that there is a natural, universal, invariable language, common to every individual of human race, and that books are natural productions, which perpetuate themselves in the same manner with animals and vegetables, by descent and propagation. Several expressions of our passions contain a universal language: all brute animals have a natural speech, which, however limited, is very intelligible to their own species. And as there are infinitely fewer parts and less contrivance in the finest composition of eloquence, than in the coarsest organized body, the propagation of an *Iliad* or *Æneid* is an easier supposition than that of any plant or animal.

Suppose, therefore, that you enter into your library, thus peopled by natural volumes, containing the most refined reason and most exquisite beauty: could you possibly open one of them, and doubt, that its original cause bore the strongest analogy to mind and intelligence? When it reasons and discourses; when it expostulates, argues, and enforces its views and topics; when it applies sometimes to the pure intellect, sometimes to the affections; when it collects, disposes, and adorns every consideration suited to the subject: could you persist in asserting, that all this, at the bottom, had really no meaning, and that the first formation of this volume in the loins of its original parent proceeded not from thought and design? Your obstinacy, I know, reaches not that degree of firmness: even your sceptical play and wantonness would be abashed at so glaring an absurdity.

But if there be any difference, PHILO, between this supposed case and the real one of the universe, it is all to the advantage of the latter. The anatomy of an animal affords many stronger instances of design than the perusal of LIVY or TACITUS: and any objection which you start in the former case, by carrying me back to so unusual and extraordinary a scene as the first formation of worlds, the same objection has place on the supposition of our vegetating library. Chuse, then, your party, PHILO, without ambiguity or evasion; assert either that a rational volume is no proof of a rational cause, or admit of a similar cause to all the works of nature.

Let me here observe too, continued CLEANTHES, that this religious argument, instead of being weakened by that scepticism, so much affected by you, rather acquires force from it, and becomes more firm and undisputed. To exclude all argument or reasoning of every kind is either affectation or madness. The declared profession of every reasonable sceptic is only to reject abstruse, remote and refined arguments; to adhere to common sense and the plain instincts of nature; and to assent, where-ever any reasons strike him with so full a force, that he cannot, without the greatest violence, prevent it. Now the arguments for Natural Religion are plainly of this kind; and nothing but the most perverse, obstinate metaphysics can reject them. Consider, anatomize the eye; Survey its structure and contrivance; and tell me, from your own feeling, if the idea of a contriver does not immediately flow in upon you with a force like that of sensation. The most obvious conclusion surely is in favour of design; and it requires time, reflection and study, to summon up those frivolous, though abstruse objections, which can support Infidelity. Who can behold the male and female of each species, the correspondence of their parts and instincts, their passions and whole course of life before and after generation, but must be sensible, that the propagation of the species is intended by Nature? Millions and millions of such instances present themselves through every part of the universe; and no language can convey a more intelligible, irresistible meaning, than the curious adjustment of final causes. To what degree, therefore, of blind dogmatism must one have attained, to reject such natural and such convincing arguments?

Some beauties in writing we may meet with, which seem contrary to rules, and which gain the affections, and animate the imagination, in opposition to all the precepts of criticism, and to the authority of the established masters of art. And if the argument for Theism be, as you pretend, contradictory to the principles of logic; its universal, its irresistible influence proves clearly, that there may be arguments of a like irregular nature. Whatever cavils may be urged; an orderly world, as well as a coherent, articulate speech, will still be received as an incontestable proof of design and intention.

It sometimes happens, I own, that the religious arguments have not their due influence on an ignorant savage and barbarian; not because they are obscure and difficult, but because he never asks himself any question with regard to them. Whence arises the curious structure of an animal? From the copulation of its parents. And these whence? From *their* parents? A few removes set the objects at such a distance, that to him they are lost in darkness and confusion; nor is he actuated by any curiosity to trace them farther. But this is neither dogmatism nor scepticism, but stupidity; a state of mind very different from your sifting, inquisitive disposition, my ingenious friend. You can trace causes from effects: You can compare the most distant and remote objects: and your greatest errors proceed not from barrenness of thought and invention, but from too luxuriant a fertility, which suppresses your natural good sense, by a profusion of unnecessary scruples and objections.

Here I could observe, HERMIPPUS, that PHILO was a little embarrassed and confounded: But while he hesitated in delivering an answer, luckily for him, DEMEA broke in upon the discourse, and saved his countenance.

Your instance, CLEANTHES, said he, drawn from books and language, being familiar, has, I confess, so much more force on that account; but is there not some danger too in this very circumstance; and may it not render us presumptuous, by making us imagine we comprehend the Deity, and have some adequate idea of his nature and attributes? When I read a volume, I enter into the mind and intention of the author: I become him, in a manner, for the instant; and have an immediate feeling and conception of those ideas which revolved in his imagination while employed in that composition. But so near an approach we never surely can make to the Deity. His ways are not our ways. His attributes are perfect, but incomprehensible. And this volume of Nature contains a great and inexplicable riddle, more than any intelligible discourse or reasoning.

The ancient PLATONISTS, you know, were the most religious and devout of all the Pagan philosophers: yet many of them, particularly PLOTINUS, expressly declare, that intellect or understanding is not to be ascribed to the Deity, and that our most perfect worship of him consists, not in acts of veneration, reverence, gratitude or love; but in a certain mysterious self-annihilation or total extinction of all our faculties. These ideas are, perhaps, too far stretched; but still it must be acknowledged, that, by representing the Deity as so intelligible, and comprehensible, and so similar to a human mind, we are guilty of the grossest and most narrow partiality, and make ourselves the model of the whole universe

All the *sentiments* of the human mind, gratitude, resentment, love, friendship, approbation, blame, pity, emulation, envy, have a plain reference to the state and situation of man, and are calculated for preserving the existence, and promoting the activity of such a being in such circumstances. It seems therefore unreasonable to transfer such sentiments to a supreme existence, or to suppose him actuated by them; and the phenomena, besides, of the universe will not support us in such a theory. All our *ideas*, derived from the senses are confusedly false and illusive; and cannot, therefore, be supposed to have place in a supreme intelligence: And as the ideas of internal sentiment, added to those of the external senses, compose the whole furniture of human understanding, we may conclude, that none of the *materials* of thought are in any respect similar in the human and in the divine intelligence. Now, as to the *manner* of thinking; how can we make any comparison between them, or suppose them anywise resembling? Our thought is fluctuating, uncertain, fleeting, successive, and compounded; and were we to remove these circumstances, we absolutely annihilate its essence, and it would, in such a case, be an abuse of terms to apply to it the name of thought or reason. At least, if it appear more pious and respectful (as it really is) still to retain these terms, when we mention the Supreme Being, we ought to acknowledge, that their meaning, in that case, is totally incomprehensible; and that the infirmities of our nature do not permit us to reach any ideas, which in the least correspond to the ineffable sublimity of the divine attributes.

PART IV.

It seems strange to me, said CLEANTHES, that you, DEMEA, who are so sincere in the cause of religion, should still maintain the mysterious, incomprehensible nature of the Deity, and should insist so strenuously, that he has no manner of likeness or resemblance to human creatures. The Deity, I can readily allow, possesses many powers and attributes, of which we can have no comprehension: But if our ideas, so far as they go, be not just and adequate, and correspondent to his real nature, I know not what there is in this subject worth insisting on. Is the name, without any meaning, of such mighty importance? Or how do you MYSTICS, who maintain the absolute incomprehensibility of the Deity, differ from Sceptics or Atheists, who assert, that the first cause of all is unknown and unintelligible? Their temerity must be very great, if, after rejecting the production by a mind; I mean, a mind, resembling the human (for I know of no other) they pretend to assign, with certainty, any other specific, intelligible cause: And their conscience must be very scrupulous indeed, if they refuse to call the universal, unknown cause a God or Deity; and to bestow on him as many sublime eulogies and unmeaning epithets, as you shall please to require of them.

Who could imagine, replied DEMEA, that CLEANTHES, the calm, philosophical CLEANTHES, would attempt to refute his antagonists, by affixing a nick-name to them; and like the common bigots and inquisitors of the age, have recourse to invective and declamation, instead of reasoning? Or does he not perceive, that these topics are easily retorted, and that ANTHROPOMORPHITE is an appellation as invidious, and implies as dangerous consequences, as the epithet of MYSTIC, with which he has honoured us? In reality, CLEANTHES, consider what it is you assert, when you represent the Deity as similar to a human mind and understanding. What is the soul of man? A composition of various faculties, passions, sentiments, ideas; united, indeed, into one self or person, but still distinct from each other. When it reasons, the ideas, which are the parts of its discourse, arrange themselves in a certain form or order; which is not preserved entire for a moment, but immediately gives place to another arrangement. New opinions, new passions, new affections, new feelings arise, which continually diversify the mental scene, and produce in it the greatest variety, and most rapid succession imaginable. How is this compatible, with that perfect immutability and simplicity, which all true Theists ascribe to the Deity? By the same act, say they, he sees past, present, and future: His love and His hatred, his mercy and his justice, are one individual operation: He is entire in every point of space; and complete in every instant of duration. No succession, no change, no acquisition, no diminution. What he is implies not in it any shadow of distinction or diversity. And what he is, this moment, he ever has been, and ever will be, without any new judgement, sentiment, or operation. He stands fixed in one simple, perfect state; nor can you ever say, with any propriety, that this act of his is different from that other, or that this judgement or idea has been lately formed, and will give place, by succession, to any different judgement or idea.

I can readily allow, said CLEANTHES, that those who maintain the perfect simplicity of the Supreme Being, to the extent in which you have explained it, are complete MYSTICS, and chargeable with all the consequences which I have drawn from their opinion.   They are, in a word, ATHEISTS, without knowing it.   For though it be allowed, that the Deity possesses attributes, of which we have no comprehension; yet ought we never to ascribe to him any attributes, which are absolutely incompatible with that intelligent nature, essential to him.   A mind, whose acts and sentiments and ideas are not distinct and successive; one, that is wholly simple, and totally immutable; is a mind, which has no thought, no reason, no will, no sentiment, no love, no hatred; or in a word, is no mind at all.   It is an abuse of terms to give it that appellation; and we may as well speak of limited extension without figure, or of number without composition.

Pray consider, said PHILO, whom you are at present inveighing against.   You are honouring with the appellation of *Atheist* all the sound, orthodox divines almost, who have treated of this subject; and you will, at last, be, yourself, found, according to your reckoning, the only sound Theist in the world.   But if idolaters be Atheists, as, I think, may justly be asserted, and Christian Theologians the same; what becomes of the argument, so much celebrated, derived from the universal consent of mankind?

But because I know you are not much swayed by names and authorities, I shall endeavour to show you, a little more distinctly, the inconveniences of that Anthropomorphism, which you have embraced; and shall prove, that there is no ground to suppose a plan of the world to be formed in the divine mind, consisting of distinct ideas, differently arranged; in the same manner as an architect forms in his head the plan of a house which he intends to execute.

It is not easy, I own, to see, what is gained by this supposition, whether we judge of the matter by *Reason* or by *Experience*.   We are still obliged to mount higher, in order to find the cause of this cause, which you had assigned as satisfactory and conclusive.

If *Reason* (I mean abstract reason, derived from inquiries *a priori*) be not alike mute with regard to all questions concerning cause and effect; this sentence at least it will venture to pronounce, That a mental world, or universe of ideas, requires a cause as much, as does a material world, or universe of objects; and if similar in its arrangement must require a similar cause.   For what is there in this subject, which should occasion a different conclusion or inference?   In an abstract view, they are entirely alike; and no difficulty attends the one supposition, which is not common to both of them.

Again, when we will needs force *Experience* to pronounce some sentence, even on these subjects, which lie beyond her sphere; neither can she perceive any material difference in this particular, between these two kinds of worlds, but finds them to be governed by similar principles, and to depend upon an equal variety of causes in their operations. We have specimens in miniature of both of them. Our own mind resembles the one: A vegetable or animal body the other. Let Experience, therefore, judge from these samples. Nothing seems more delicate with regard to its causes than thought; and as these causes never operate in two persons after the same manner, so we never find two persons, who think exactly alike. Nor indeed does the same person think exactly alike at any two different periods of time. A difference of age, of the disposition of his body, of weather, of food, of company, of books, of passions; any of these particulars, or others more minute, are sufficient to alter the curious machinery of thought, and communicate to it very different movements and operations. As far as we can judge, vegetables and animal bodies are not more delicate in their motions, nor depend upon a greater variety or more curious adjustment of springs and principles.

How therefore shall we satisfy ourselves concerning the cause of that Being, whom you suppose the Author of Nature, or, according to your system of Anthropomorphism, the ideal world, into which you trace the material? Have we not the same reason to trace that ideal world into another ideal world, or new intelligent principle? But if we stop, and go no farther; why go so far? Why not stop at the material world? How can we satisfy ourselves without going on *in infinitum*? And after all, what satisfaction is there in that infinite progression? Let us remember the story of the INDIAN philosopher and his elephant. It was never more applicable than to the present subject. If the material world rests upon a similar ideal world, this ideal world must rest upon some other; and so on, without end. It were better, therefore, never to look beyond the present material world. By supposing it to contain the principle of its order within itself, we really assert it to be God; and the sooner we arrive at that divine Being, so much the better. When you go one step beyond the mundane system, you only excite an inquisitive humour, which it is impossible ever to satisfy.

To say, that the different ideas, which compose the reason of the Supreme Being, fall into order, of themselves, and by their own nature, is really to talk without any precise meaning. If it has a meaning, I would fain know, why it is not as good sense to say, that the parts of the material world fall into order, of themselves, and by their own nature. Can the one opinion be intelligible, while the other is not so?

We have, indeed, experience of ideas, which fall into order, of themselves, and without any *known* cause: But, I am sure, we have a much larger experience of matter, which does the same; as, in all instances of generation and vegetation, where the accurate analysis of the cause exceeds all human comprehension. We have also experience of particular systems of thought and of matter, which have no order; of the first, in madness; of the second, in corruption. Why then should we think, that order is more essential to one than the other? And if it requires a cause in both, what do we gain by your system, in tracing the universe or objects into a similar universe of ideas? The first step, which we make, leads us on for ever. It were, therefore, wise in us, to limit all our enquiries to the present world, without looking farther. No satisfaction can ever be attained by these speculations, which so far exceed the narrow bounds of human understanding.

It was usual with the PERIPATETICS, you know, CLEANTHES, when the cause of any phenomenon was demanded, to have recourse to their *faculties* or *occult qualities*, and to say, for instance, that bread nourished by its nutritive faculty, and senna purged by its purgative: But it has been discovered, that this subterfuge was nothing but the disguise of ignorance; and that these philosophers, though less ingenuous, really said the same thing with the sceptics or the vulgar, who fairly confessed, that they knew not the cause of these phenomena. In like manner, when it is asked, what cause produces order in the ideas of the Supreme Being, can any other reason be assigned by you, Anthropomorphites, than that it is a *rational* faculty, and that such is the nature of the Deity? But why a similar answer will not be equally satisfactory in accounting for the order of the world, without having recourse to any such intelligent creator, as you insist on, may be difficult to determine. It is only to say, that *such* is the nature of material objects, and that they are all originally possessed of a *faculty* of order and proportion. These are only more learned and elaborate ways of confessing our ignorance; nor has the one hypothesis any real advantage above the other, except in its greater conformity to vulgar prejudices.

You have displayed this argument with great emphasis, replied CLEANTHES: You seem not sensible, how easy it is to answer it. Even in common life, if I assign a cause for any event; is it any objection, PHILO, that I cannot assign the cause of that cause, and answer every new question, which may incessantly be started? And what philosophers could possibly submit to so rigid a rule? philosophers, who confess ultimate causes to be totally unknown, and are sensible, that the most refined principles, into which they trace the phenomena, are still to them as inexplicable as these phenomena themselves are to the vulgar. The order and arrangement of nature, the curious adjustment of final causes, the plain use and intention of every part and organ; all these bespeak in the clearest language an intelligent cause or author. The heavens and the earth join in the same testimony: The whole chorus of Nature raises one hymn to the praises of its creator: You alone, or almost alone, disturb this general harmony. You start abstruse doubts, cavils, and objections: You ask me, what is the cause of this cause? I know not; I care not; that concerns not me. I have found a Deity; and here I stop my enquiry. Let those go farther, who are wiser or more enterprising.

I pretend to be neither, replied PHILO: and for that very reason, I should never perhaps have attempted to go so far; especially when I am sensible, that I must at last be contented to sit down with the same answer, which, without farther trouble, might have satisfied me from the beginning. If I am still to remain in utter ignorance of causes, and can absolutely give an explication of nothing, I shall never esteem it any advantage to shove off for a moment a difficulty, which, you acknowledge, must immediately, in its full force, recur upon me. Naturalists indeed very justly explain particular effects by more general causes, though these general causes themselves should remain in the end totally inexplicable: but they never surely thought it satisfactory to explain a particular effect by a particular cause, which was no more to be accounted for than the effect itself. An ideal system, arranged of itself, without a precedent design, is not a whit more explicable than a material one, which attains its order in a like manner; nor is there any more difficulty in the latter supposition than in the former.

PART V.

But to show you still more inconveniencies, continued PHILO, in your Anthropomorphism; please to take a new survey of your principles. *Like effects prove like causes.* This is the experimental argument; and this, you say too, is the sole theological argument. Now it is certain, that the liker the effects are, which are seen, and the liker the causes, which are inferred, the stronger is the argument. Every departure on either side diminishes the probability, and renders the experiment less conclusive. You cannot doubt of the principle: neither ought you to reject its consequences.

All the new discoveries in astronomy, which prove the immense grandeur and magnificence of the works of Nature, are so many additional arguments for a Deity, according to the true system of Theism: but according to your hypothesis of experimental Theism, they become so many objections, by removing the effect still farther from all resemblance to the effects of human art and contrivance. For if Lucretius,[1] even following the old system of the world, could exclaim,

> Quis regere immensi summam, quis habere profundi
> Indu manu validas potis est moderanter habenas?
> Quis pariter cœlos omnes convertere? et omnes
> Ignibus ætheriis terras suffire feraces?
> Omnibus inque locis esse omni tempore præsto?

If *Tully*[2] esteemed this reasoning so natural, as to put it into the mouth of his EPICUREAN. *Quibus enim oculis animi intueri potuit vester Plato fabricam illam tanti operis, qua construi a Deo atque ædificari mundum facit? quæ molitio? quæ ferramenta? qui vectes? quæ machinæ? qui ministri tanti muneris fuerunt? quemadmodum autem obedire et parere voluntati architecti aer, ignis, aqua, terra potuerunt?* If this argument, I say, had any force in former ages; how much

[1] Lib. ii 1094   [2] De Nat. Deor. lib. i.

greater must it have at present; when the bounds of Nature are so infinitely enlarged, and such a magnificent scene is opened to us? It is still more unreasonable to form our idea of so unlimited a cause from our experience of the narrow productions of human design and invention.

The discoveries by microscopes, as they open a new universe in miniature, are still objections, according to you; arguments, according to me. The farther we push our researches of this kind, we are still led to infer the universal cause of all to be vastly different from mankind, or from any object of human experience and observation.

And what say you to the discoveries in anatomy, chymistry, botany? . . . . . These surely are no objections, replied CLEANTHES: they only discover new instances of art and contrivance. It is still the image of mind reflected on us from innumerable objects. Add, a mind *like the human*, said PHILO. I know of no other, replied CLEANTHES. And the liker the better, insisted PHILO. To be sure, said CLEANTHES.

Now, CLEANTHES, said PHILO, with an air of alacrity and triumph, mark the consequences. *First*, By this method of reasoning, you renounce all claim to infinity in any of the attributes of the Deity. For as the cause ought only to be proportioned to the effect, and the effect, so far as it falls under our cognisance, is not infinite; what pretensions have we, upon your suppositions, to ascribe that attribute to the divine Being? You will still insist, that, by removing him so much from all similarity to human creatures, we give in to the most arbitrary hypothesis, and at the same time weaken all proofs of his existence.

Secondly, You have no reason, on your theory, for ascribing perfection to the Deity, even in his finite capacity; or for supposing him free from every error, mistake, or incoherence in his undertakings. There are many inexplicable difficulties in the works of Nature, which, if we allow a perfect author to be proved *a priori*, are easily solved, and become only seeming difficulties, from the narrow capacity of man, who cannot trace infinite relations. But according to your method of reasoning, these difficulties become all real; and perhaps will be insisted on, as new instances of likeness to human art and contrivance. At least, you must acknowledge, that it is impossible for us to tell, from our limited views, whether this system contains any great faults, or deserves any considerable praise, if compared to other possible, and even real systems. Could a peasant, if the ÆNEID were read to him, pronounce that poem to be absolutely faultless, or even assign to it its proper rank among the productions of human wit; he, who had never seen any other production?

But were this world ever so perfect a production, it must still remain uncertain, whether all the excellences of the work can justly be ascribed to the workman. If we survey a ship, what an exalted idea must we form of the ingenuity of the carpenter, who framed so complicated, useful, and beautiful a machine? And what surprise must we feel, when we find him a stupid mechanic, who imitated others, and copied an art, which, through a long succession of ages, after multiplied trials, mistakes, corrections, deliberations, and controversies, had been gradually improving? Many worlds might have been botched and bungled, throughout an eternity, ere this system was struck out: much labour lost: many fruitless trials made: and a slow, but continued improvement carried on during infinite ages in the art of world-making. In such subjects, who can determine, where the truth; nay, who can conjecture where the probability, lies; amidst a great number of hypotheses which may be proposed, and a still greater number which may be imagined?

And what shadow of an argument, continued PHILO, can you produce, from your hypothesis, to prove the unity of the Deity? A great number of men join in building a house or ship, in rearing a city, in framing a commonwealth: why may not several deities combine in contriving and framing a world? This is only so much greater similarity to human affairs. By sharing the work among several, we may so much further limit the attributes of each, and get rid of that extensive power and knowledge, which must be supposed in one deity, and which, according to you, can only serve to weaken the proof of his existence. And if such foolish, such vicious creatures as man can yet often unite in framing and executing one plan; how much more those deities or dæmons, whom we may suppose several degrees more perfect?

To multiply causes, without necessity, is indeed contrary to true philosophy: but this principle applies not to the present case. Were one deity antecedently proved by your theory, who were possessed of every attribute, requisite to the production of the universe; it would be needless, I own (though not absurd) to suppose any other deity existent. But while it is still a question, Whether all these attributes are united in one subject, or dispersed among several independent beings: by what phenomena in nature can we pretend to decide the controversy? Where we see a body raised in a scale, we are sure that there is in the opposite scale, however concealed from sight, some counterpoising weight equal to it: but it is still allowed to doubt, whether that weight be an aggregate of several distinct bodies, or one uniform united mass. And if the weight requisite very much exceeds any thing which we have ever seen conjoined in any single body, the former supposition becomes still more probable and natural. An intelligent being of such vast power and capacity, as is necessary to produce the universe, or, to speak in the language of ancient philosophy, so prodigious an animal, exceeds all analogy, and even comprehension.

But farther, CLEANTHES; men are mortal, and renew their species by generation; and this is common to all living creatures. The two great sexes of male and female, says MILTON, animate the world. Why must this circumstance, so universal, so essential, be excluded from those numerous and limited deities? Behold then the theogony of ancient times brought back upon us.

And why not become a perfect Anthropomorphite? Why not assert the deity or deities to be corporeal, and to have eyes, a nose, mouth, ears, &c.? EPICURUS maintained, that no man had ever seen reason but in a human figure; therefore the gods must have a human figure. And this argument, which is deservedly so much ridiculed by Cicero, becomes, according to you, solid and philosophical.

In a word, CLEANTHES, a man, who follows your hypothesis, is able, perhaps, to assert, or conjecture, that the universe, sometime, arose from something like design: but beyond that position he cannot ascertain one single circumstance, and is left afterwards to fix every point of his theology, by the utmost licence of fancy and hypothesis. This world, for aught he knows, is very faulty and imperfect, compared to a superior standard; and was only the first rude essay of some infant deity, who afterwards abandoned it, ashamed of his lame performance: it is the work only of some dependent, inferior deity; and is the object of derision to his superiors:

it is the production of old age and dotage in some super-annuated deity; and ever since his death, has run on at adventures, from the first impulse and active force, which it received from him. You justly give signs of horror, DEMEA, at these strange suppositions: but these, and a thousand more of the same kind, are CLEANTHES's suppositions, not mine. From the moment the attributes of the Deity are supposed finite, all these have place. And I cannot, for my part, think, that so wild and unsettled a system of theology is, in any respect, preferable to none at all.

These suppositions I absolutely disown, cried CLEANTHES: they strike me, however, with no horror; especially, when proposed in that rambling way in which they drop from you. On the contrary, they give me pleasure, when I see, that, by the utmost indulgence of your imagination, you never get rid of the hypothesis of design in the universe; but are obliged, at every turn, to have recourse to it. To this concession I adhere steadily; and this I regard as a sufficient foundation for religion.

PART VI.

IT must be a slight fabric, indeed, said DEMEA, which can be erected on so tottering a foundation. While we are uncertain, whether there is one deity or many; whether the deity or deities, to whom we owe our existence, be perfect or imperfect, subordinate or supreme, dead or alive; what trust or confidence can we repose in them? What devotion or worship address to them? What veneration or obedience pay them? To all the purposes of life, the theory of religion becomes altogether useless: and even with regard to speculative consequences, its uncertainty, according to you, must render it totally precarious and unsatisfactory.

To render it still more unsatisfactory, said PHILO, there occurs to me another hypothesis, which must acquire an air of probability from the method of reasoning so much insisted on by CLEANTHES. That like effects arise from like causes: this principle he supposes the foundation of all religion. But there is another principle of the same kind, no less certain, and derived from the same source of experience; That where several known circumstances are observed to be similar, the unknown will also be found similar. Thus, if we see the limbs of a human body, we conclude, that it is also attended with a human head, though hid from us. Thus, if we see, through a chink in a wall, a small part of the sun, we conclude, that, were the wall removed, we should see the whole body. In short, this method of reasoning is so obvious and familiar, that no scruple can ever be made with regard to its solidity.

Now if we survey the universe, so far as it falls under our knowledge, it bears a great resemblance to an animal or organized body, and seems actuated with a like principle of life and motion. A continual circulation of matter in it produces no disorder: a continual waste in every part is incessantly repaired: the closest sympathy is perceived throughout the entire system: and each part or member, in performing its proper offices, operates both to its own preservation and to that of the whole. The world, therefore, I infer, is an animal, and the Deity is the SOUL of the world, actuating it, and actuated by it.

You have too much learning, CLEANTHES, to be at all surprised at this opinion, which, you know, was maintained by almost all the Theists of antiquity, and chiefly prevails in their discourses and reasonings. For though sometimes the ancient philosophers reason from final causes, as if they thought the world the workmanship of God; yet it appears rather their favourite notion to consider it as his body, whose organization renders it subservient to him. And it must be confessed, that as the universe resembles more a human body than it does the works of human art and contrivance; if our limited analogy could ever, with any propriety, be extended to the whole of nature, the inference seems juster in favour of the ancient than the modern theory.

There are many other advantages too, in the former theory, which recommend it to the ancient Theologians. Nothing more repugnant to all their notions, because nothing more repugnant to common experience than mind without body; a mere spiritual substance, which fell not under their senses nor comprehension, and of which they had not observed one single instance throughout all nature. Mind and body they knew, because they felt both: an order, arrangement, organization, or internal machinery in both they likewise knew, after the same manner: and it could not but seem reasonable to transfer this experience to the universe, and to suppose the divine mind and body to be also coeval, and to have, both of them, order and arrangement naturally inherent in them, and inseparable from them.

Here therefore is a new species of *Anthropomorphism*, CLEANTHES, on which you may deliberate; and a theory which seems not liable to any considerable difficulties. You are too much superior surely to *systematical prejudices*, to find any more difficulty in supposing an animal body to be, originally, of itself, or from unknown causes, possessed of order and organization, than in supposing a similar order to belong to mind. But the *vulgar prejudice*, that body and mind ought always to accompany each other, ought not, one should think, to be entirely neglected; since it is founded on *vulgar experience*, the only guide which you profess to follow in all these theological inquiries. And if you assert, that our limited experience is an unequal standard, by which to judge of the unlimited extent of nature; you entirely abandon your own hypothesis, and must thenceforward adopt our Mysticism, as you call it, and admit of the absolute incomprehensibility of the Divine Nature.

This theory, I own, replied CLEANTHES, has never before occurred to me, though a pretty natural one; and I cannot readily, upon so short an examination and reflection, deliver any opinion with regard to it. You are very scrupulous, indeed, said PHILO; were I to examine any system of yours, I should not have acted with half that caution and reserve, in starting objections and difficulties to it. However, if any thing occur to you, you will oblige us by proposing it.

Why then, replied CLEANTHES, it seems to me, that, though the world does, in many circumstances, resemble an animal body; yet is the analogy also defective in many circumstances, the most material: no organs of sense; no seat of thought or reason; no one precise origin of motion and action. In short, it seems to bear a stronger resemblance to a vegetable than to an animal, and your inference would be so far inconclusive in favour of the soul of the world.

But, in the next place, your theory seems to imply the eternity of the world; and that is a principle, which, I think, can be refuted by the strongest reasons and probabilities. I shall suggest an argument to this purpose, which, I believe, has not been insisted on by any writer. Those, who reason from the late origin of arts and sciences, though their inference wants not force, may perhaps be refuted by considerations, derived from the nature of human society, which is in continual revolution between ignorance and knowledge, liberty and slavery, riches and poverty; so that it is impossible for us, from our limited experience, to foretell with assurance what events may or may not be expected. Ancient learning and history seem to have been in great danger of entirely perishing after the inundation of the barbarous nations; and had these convulsions continued a little longer, or been a little more violent, we should not probably have now known what passed in the world a few centuries before us. Nay, were it not for the superstition of the Popes, who preserved a little jargon of Latin, in order to support the appearance of an ancient and universal church, that tongue must have been utterly lost: in which case, the Western world, being totally barbarous, would not have been in a fit disposition for receiving the Greek language and learning, which was conveyed to them after the sacking of Constantinople. When learning and books had been extinguished, even the mechanical arts would have fallen considerably to decay; and it is easily imagined, that fable or tradition might ascribe to them a much later origin than the true one. This vulgar argument, therefore, against the eternity of the world, seems a little precarious.

But here appears to be the foundation of a better argument. Lucullus was the first that brought cherry-trees from Asia to Europe; though that tree thrives so well in many European climates, that it grows in the woods without any culture. Is it possible, that, throughout a whole eternity, no European had ever passed into Asia, and thought of transplanting so delicious a fruit into his own country? Or if the tree was once transplanted and propagated, how could it ever afterwards perish? Empires may rise and fall; liberty and slavery succeed alternately; ignorance and knowledge give place to each other; but the cherry-tree will still remain in the woods of Greece, Spain and Italy, and will never be affected by the revolutions of human society.

It is not two thousand years since vines were transplanted

into FRANCE; though there is no climate in the world more favourable to them. It is not three centuries since horses, cows, sheep, swine, dogs, corn, were known in AMERICA. Is it possible, that, during the revolutions of a whole eternity, there never arose a COLUMBUS, who might open the communication between EUROPE and that continent? We may as well imagine, that all men would wear stockings for ten thousand years, and never have the sense to think of garters to tie them. All these seem convincing proofs of the youth, or rather infancy of the world; as being founded on the operation of principles more constant and steady, than those by which human society is governed and directed. Nothing less than a total convulsion of the elements will ever destroy all the EUROPEAN animals and vegetables, which are now to be found in the Western world.

And what argument have you against such convulsions? replied PHILO. Strong and almost incontestable proofs may be traced over the whole earth, that every part of this globe has continued for many ages entirely covered with water. And though order were supposed inseparable from matter, and inherent in it; yet may matter be susceptible of many and great revolutions, through the endless periods of eternal duration. The incessant changes, to which every part of it is subject, seem to intimate some such general transformations; though at the same time, it is observable, that all the changes and corruptions, of which we have ever had experience, are but passages from one state of order to another; nor can matter ever rest in total deformity and confusion. What we see in the parts, we may infer in the whole; at least, that is the method of reasoning on which you rest your whole theory. And were I obliged to defend any particular system of this nature (which I never willingly should do) I esteem none more plausible, than that which ascribes an eternal, inherent principle of order to the world; though attended with great and continual revolutions and alterations. Thus at once solves all difficulties; and if the solution, by being so general, is not entirely complete and satisfactory, it is, at least, a theory, that we must, sooner or later, have recourse to, whatever system we embrace. How could things have been as they are, were there not an original, inherent principle of order somewhere, in thought or in matter? And it is very indifferent to which of these we give the preference.

Chance has no place, on any hypothesis, sceptical or religious. Every thing is surely governed, by steady, inviolable laws. And were the inmost essence of things laid open to us, we should then discover a scene, of which, at present, we can have no idea. Instead of admiring the order of natural beings, we should clearly see that it was absolutely impossible for them, in the smallest article, ever to admit of any other disposition.

Were any one inclined to revive the ancient Pagan Theology, which maintained, as we learn from Hesiod, that this globe was governed by 30,000 deities, who arose from the unknown powers of nature : you would naturally object, CLEANTHES, that nothing is gained by this hypothesis ; and that it is as easy to suppose all men animals, beings more numerous, but less perfect, to have sprung immediately from a like origin. Push the same inference a step farther ; and you will find a numerous society of deities as explicable as one universal deity, who possesses, within himself, the powers and perfections of the whole society. All these systems, then, of Scepticism, Polytheism, and Theism, you must allow, on your principles, to be on a like footing, and that no one of them has any advantage over the others. You may thence learn the fallacy of your principles.

PART VII.

BUT here, continued PHILO, in examining the ancient system of the soul of the world, there strikes me, all on a sudden, a new idea, which, if just, must go near to subvert all your reasoning, and destroy even your first inferences, on which you repose such confidence. If the universe bears a greater likeness to animal bodies and to vegetables, than to the works of human art, it is more probable, that its cause resembles the cause of the former than that of the latter, and its origin ought rather to be ascribed to generation or vegetation than to reason or design. Your conclusion, even according to your own principles, is therefore lame and defective.

Pray open up this argument a little farther, said DEMEA.

For 1 do not rightly apprehend it, in that concise manner, in which you have expressed it.

Our friend CLEANTHES, replied PHILO, as you have heard, asserts, that since no question of fact can be proved otherwise than by experience, the existence of a Deity admits not of proof from any other medium. The world, says he, resembles the works of human contrivance : Therefore its cause must also resemble that of the other. Here we may remark, that the operation of one very small part of nature, to wit man, upon another very small part, to wit that inanimate matter lying within his reach, is the rule, by which CLEAN-THES judges of the origin of the whole ; and he measures objects, so widely disproportioned, by the same individual standard. But to wave all objections drawn from this topic ; I affirm, that there are other parts of the universe (besides the machines of human invention) which bear still a greater resemblance to the fabric of the world, and which therefore afford a better conjecture concerning the universal origin of this system. These parts are animals and vegetables. The world plainly resembles more an animal or a vegetable, than it does a watch or a knitting-loom. Its cause, therefore, it is more probable, resembles the cause of the former. The cause of the former is generation or vegetation. The cause, therefore, of the world, we may infer to be something similar or analogous to generation or vegetation.

But how is it conceivable, said DEMEA, that the world can arise from any thing similar to vegetation or generation ?

Very easily, replied PHILO. In like manner as a tree sheds its seeds into the neighbouring fields, and produces other trees ; so the great vegetable, the world, or this planetary system, produces within itself certain seeds, which, being scattered into the surrounding chaos, vegetate into new worlds. A comet, for instance, is the seed of a world ; and after it has been fully ripened, by passing from sun to sun, and star to star, it is at last tost into the unformed elements, which everywhere surround this universe, and immediately sprouts up into a new system.

Or if, for the sake of variety (for I see no other advantage) we should suppose this world to be an animal ; a comet is the egg of this animal ; and in like manner as an ostrich lays its egg in the sand, which, without any farther care, hatches the egg, and produces a new animal ; so . . . . . I understand you, says DEMEA : But what wild, arbitrary suppositions are these ? What *data* have you for such extraordinary conclusions ? And is the slight, imaginary resemblance of the world to a vegetable or an animal sufficient to establish the same inference with regard to both ? Objects, which are in general so widely different; ought they to be a standard for each other ?

Right, cries PHILO : This is the topic on which I have all along insisted. I have still asserted, that we have no *data* to establish any system of cosmogony. Our experience, so imperfect in itself, and so limited both in extent and duration, can afford us no probable conjecture concerning the whole of things. But if we must needs fix on some hypothesis ; by what rule, pray, ought we to determine our choice ? Is there any other rule than the greater similarity of the objects compared ? And does not a plant or an animal, which springs from vegetation or generation, bear a stronger resemblance to the world, than does any artificial machine, which arises from reason and design ?

But what is this vegetation and generation of which you talk ? said DEMEA. Can you explain their operations, and anatomize that fine internal structure, on which they depend?

As much, at least, replied PHILO, as CLEANTHES can explain the operations of reason, or anatomize that internal structure, on which *it* depends. But without any such elaborate disquisitions, when I see an animal, I infer, that it sprang from generation ; and that with as great certainty as you conclude a house to have been reared by design. These words, *generation, reason,* mark only certain powers and energies in nature, whose effects are known, but whose essence is incomprehensible ; and one of these principles, more than the other, has no privilege for being made a standard to the whole of nature.

In reality, DEMEA, it may reasonably be expected, that the larger the views are which we take of things, the better will they conduct us in our conclusions concerning such extraordinary and such magnificent subjects. In this little corner of the world alone, there are four principles, *Reason, Instinct, Generation, Vegetation,* which are similar to each other, and are the causes of similar effects. What a number of other principles may we naturally suppose in the immense extent and variety of the universe, could we travel from planet to planet and from system to system, in order to examine each part of this mighty fabric? Any one of these four principles above mentioned (and a hundred others which lie open to our conjecture) may afford us a theory, by which to judge of the origin of the world; and it is a palpable and egregious partiality, to confine our view entirely to that principle, by which our own minds operate. Were this principle more intelligent on that account, such a partiality might be somewhat excuseable: But reason, in its internal fabric and structure, is really as little known to us as instinct or vegetation; and perhaps even that vague, undeterminate word, *Nature*, to which the vulgar refer every thing, is not at the bottom more inexplicable. The effects of these principles are all known to us from experience: But the principles themselves, and their manner of operation are totally unknown: Nor is it less intelligible, or less conformable to experience to say, that the world arose by vegetation from a seed shed by another world, than to say that it arose from a divine reason or contrivance, according to the sense in which CLEANTHES understands it.

But methinks, said DEMEA, if the world had a vegetative quality, and could sow the seeds of new worlds into the infinite chaos, this power would be still an additional argument for design in its author. For whence could arise so wonderful a faculty but from design? Or how can order spring from any thing, which perceives not that order which it bestows?

You need only look around you, replied PHILO, to satisfy yourself with regard to this question. A tree bestows order and organization on that tree, which springs from it, without knowing the order: an animal, in the same manner, on its offspring: a bird, on its nest: and instances of this kind are even more frequent in the world, than those of order, which arise from reason and contrivance. To say, that all this order in animals and vegetables proceeds ultimately from design, is begging the question; nor can that great point be ascertained otherwise than by proving *a priori*, both that order is, from its nature, inseparably attached to thought, and that it can never, of itself, or from original unknown principles, belong to matter.

But farther, DEMEA; this objection, which you urge, can never be made use of by CLEANTHES, without renouncing a defence, which he has already made against one of my objections. When I enquired concerning the cause of that supreme reason and intelligence, into which he resolves every thing; he told me, that the impossibility of satisfying such enquiries could never be admitted as an objection in any species of philosophy. *We must stop somewhere, says he; nor is it ever within the reach of human capacity to explain ultimate causes, or show the last connections of any objects. It is sufficient, if any steps, so far as we go, are supported by experience and observation.* Now, that vegetation and generation, as well as reason, are experienced to be principles of order in nature, is undeniable. If I rest my system of cosmogony on the former, preferably to the latter, 'tis at my choice. The matter seems entirely arbitrary. And when CLEANTHES asks me what is the cause of my great vegetative or generative faculty, I am equally entitled to ask him the cause of his great reasoning principle. These questions we have agreed to forbear on both sides; and it is chiefly his interest on the present occasion to stick to this agreement. Judging by our limited and imperfect experience, generation has some privileges above reason: For we see every day the latter arise from the former, never the former from the latter.

Compare, I beseech you, the consequences on both sides. The world, say I, resembles an animal, therefore it is an animal, therefore it arose from generation. The steps, I confess, are wide; yet there is some small appearance of analogy in each step. The world, says CLEANTHES, resembles a machine, therefore it is a machine, therefore it arose from design. The steps are here equally wide, and the analogy less striking. And if he pretends to carry on *my* hypothesis a step farther, and to infer design or reason from the great principle of generation, on which I insist; I may, with better authority, use the same freedom to push farther his hypothesis, and infer a divine generation or theogony from his principle of reason. I have at least some faint shadow of experience, which is the utmost, that can ever be attained in the present subject. Reason, in innumerable instances, is observed to arise from the principle of generation, and never to arise from any other principle.

HESIOD, and all the ancient Mythologists, were so struck with this analogy, that they universally explained the origin of nature from an animal birth, and copulation. PLATO too, so far as he is intelligible, seems to have adopted some such notion in his Timæus.

The Brahmins assert, that the world arose from an infinite spider, who spun this whole complicated mass from his bowels, and annihilates afterwards the whole or any part of it, by absorbing it again, and resolving it into his own essence. Here is a species of cosmogony, which appears to us ridiculous; because a spider is a little contemptible animal, whose operations we are never likely to take for a model of the whole universe. But still here is a new species of analogy, even in our globe. And were there a planet wholly inhabited by spiders, (which is very possible) this inference would there appear as natural and irrefragable as that which in our planet ascribes the origin of all things to design and intelligence, as explained by Cleanthes. Why an orderly system may not be spun from the belly as well as from the brain, it will be difficult for him to give a satisfactory reason.

I must confess, Philo, replied Cleanthes, that of all men living, the task which you have undertaken, of raising doubts and objections, suits you best, and seems, in a manner, natural and unavoidable to you. So great is your fertility of invention, that I am not ashamed to acknowledge myself unable, on a sudden, to solve regularly such out-of-the-way difficulties as you incessantly start upon me: though I clearly see, in general, their fallacy and error. And I question not, but you are yourself, at present, in the same case, and have not the solution so ready as the objection; while you must be sensible, that common sense and reason is entirely against you, and that such whimsies as you have delivered, may puzzle, but never can convince us.

PART VIII.

What you ascribe to the fertility of my invention, replied Philo, is entirely owing to the nature of the subject. In subjects, adapted to the narrow compass of human reason, there is commonly but one determination, which carries probability or conviction with it; and to a man of sound judgement, all other suppositions, but that one, appear entirely absurd and chimerical. But in such questions, as the present, a hundred contradictory views may preserve a kind of imperfect analogy; and invention has here full scope to exert itself. Without any great effort of thought, I believe that I could, in an instant, propose other systems of cosmogony, which would have some faint appearance of truth; though it is a thousand, a million to one, if either yours or any one of mine be the true system.

For instance; what if I should revive the old Epicurean hypothesis? This is commonly, and I believe, justly, esteemed the most absurd system, that has yet been proposed; yet, I know not, whether, with a few alterations, it might not be brought to bear a faint appearance of probability. Instead of supposing matter infinite, as Epicurus did; let us suppose it finite. A finite number of particles is only susceptible of finite transpositions: and it must happen, in an eternal duration, that every possible order or position must be tried an infinite number of times. This world, therefore, with all its events, even the most minute, has before been produced and destroyed, and will again be produced and destroyed, without any bounds and limitations. No one, who has a conception of the powers of infinite, in comparison of finite, will ever scruple this determination.

But this supposes, said Demea, that matter can acquire motion, without any voluntary agent or first mover.

And where is the difficulty, replied Philo, of that supposition? Every event, before experience, is equally difficult and incomprehensible; and every event, after experience, is equally easy and intelligible. Motion, in many instances, from gravity, from elasticity, from electricity, begins in matter, without any known voluntary agent; and to suppose always, in these cases, an unknown voluntary agent, is mere hypothesis; and hypothesis attended with no advantages. The beginning of motion in matter itself is as conceivable à priori as its communication from mind and intelligence.

Besides; why may not motion have been propagated by impulse through all eternity, and the same stock of it, or nearly the same, be still upheld in the universe? As much is lost by the composition of motion, as much is gained by its resolution. And whatever the causes are, the fact is certain, that matter is, and always has been in continual agitation, as far as human experience or tradition reaches. There is not probably, at present, in the whole universe, one particle of matter at absolute rest.

And this very consideration too, continued PHILO, which we have stumbled on in the course of the argument, suggests a new hypothesis of cosmogony, that is not absolutely absurd and improbable. Is there a system, an order, an œconomy of things, by which matter can preserve that perpetual agitation, which seems essential to it, and yet maintain a constancy in the forms, which it produces? There certainly is such an œconomy: for this is actually the case with the present world. The continual motion of matter, therefore, in less than infinite transpositions, must produce this œconomy or order; and by its very nature, that order, when once established, supports itself, for many ages, if not to eternity. But where-ever matter is so poized, arranged, and adjusted as to continue in perpetual motion, and yet preserve a constancy in the forms, its situation must, of necessity, have all the same appearance of art and contrivance, which we observe at present. All the parts of each form must have a relation to each other, and to the whole: and the whole itself must have a relation to the other parts of the universe; to the element, in which the form subsists; to the materials, with which it repairs its waste and decay; and to every other form, which is hostile or friendly. A defect in any of these particulars destroys the form; and the matter, of which it is composed, is again set loose, and is thrown into irregular motions and fermentations, till it unite itself to some other regular form. If no such form be prepared to receive it, and if there be a great quantity of this corrupted matter in the universe, the universe itself is entirely disordered; whether it be the feeble embryo of a world in its first beginnings, that is thus destroyed, or the rotten carcass of one, languishing in old age and infirmity. In either case, a chaos ensues; till finite, though innumerable revolutions produce at last some forms, whose parts and organs are so adjusted as to support the forms amidst a continued succession of matter.

Suppose, (for we shall endeavour to vary the expression) that matter were thrown into any position, by a blind, unguided force; it is evident that this first position must in all probability be the most confused and most disorderly imaginable, without any resemblance to those works of human contrivance, which, along with a symmetry of parts, discover an adjustment of means to ends and a tendency to self-preservation. If the actuating force cease after this operation, matter must remain for ever in disorder, and continue an immense chaos, without any proportion or activity. But suppose, that the actuating force, whatever it be, still continues in matter, this first position will immediately give place to a second, which will likewise in all probability be as disorderly as the first, and so on, through many successions of changes and revolutions. No particular order or position ever continues a moment unaltered. The original force, still remaining in activity, gives a perpetual restlessness to matter. Every possible situation is produced, and instantly destroyed. If a glimpse or dawn of order appears for a moment, it is instantly hurried away, and confounded, by that never-ceasing force, which actuates every part of matter.

Thus the universe goes on for many ages in a continued succession of chaos and disorder. But is it not possible that it may settle at last, so as not to lose its motion and active force (for that we have supposed inherent in it) yet so as to preserve an uniformity of appearance, amidst the continual motion and fluctuation of its parts? This we find to be the case with the universe at present. Every individual is perpetually changing, and every part of every individual, and yet the whole remains, in appearance, the same. May we not hope for such a position, or rather be assured of it, from the eternal revolutions of unguided matter, and may not this account for all the appearing wisdom and contrivance, which is in the universe? Let us contemplate the subject a little, and we shall find, that this adjustment, if attained by matter, of a seeming stability in the forms, with a real and perpetual revolution or motion of parts, affords a plausible, if not a true solution of the difficulty.

It is in vain, therefore, to insist upon the uses of the parts in animals or vegetables and their curious adjustment to each other. I would fain know how an animal could subsist, unless its parts were so adjusted? Do we not find, that it immediately perishes whenever this adjustment ceases, and that its matter corrupting tries some new form. It happens, indeed, that the parts of the world are so well adjusted, that some regular form immediately lays claim to this corrupted matter: and if it were not so, could the world subsist?

Must it not dissolve as well as the animal, and pass through new positions and situations; till in a great, but finite succession, it falls at last into the present or some such order?

It is well, replied CLEANTHES, you told us, that this hypothesis was suggested on a sudden, in the course of the argument. Had you had leisure to examine it, you would soon have perceived the insuperable objections, to which it is exposed. No form, you say, can subsist, unless it possess those powers and organs, requisite for its subsistence: some new order or œconomy must be tried, and so on, without intermission; till at last some order, which can support and maintain itself, is fallen upon. But according to this hypothesis, whence arise the many conveniencies and advantages which men and all animals possess? Two eyes, two ears, are not absolutely necessary for the subsistence of the species. Human race might have been propagated and preserved, without horses, dogs, cows, sheep, and those innumerable fruits and products which serve to our satisfaction and enjoyment. If no camels had been created for the use of a man in the sandy deserts of AFRICA and ARABIA, would the world have been dissolved? If no loadstone had been framed to give that wonderful and useful direction to the needle, would human society and the human kind have been immediately extinguished? Though the maxims of Nature be in general very frugal, yet instances of this kind are far from being rare; and any one of them is a sufficient proof of design, and of a benevolent design, which gave rise to the order and arrangement of the universe.

At least, you may safely infer, said PHILO, that the foregoing hypothesis is so far incomplete and imperfect; which I shall not scruple to allow. But can we ever reasonably expect greater success in any attempts of this nature? Or can we ever hope to erect a system of cosmogony, that will be liable to no exceptions, and will contain no circumstance repugnant to our limited and imperfect experience of the analogy of Nature? Your theory itself cannot surely pretend to any such advantage; even though you have run into *Anthropomorphism*, the better to preserve a conformity to common experience. Let us once more put it to trial. In all instances which we have ever seen, ideas are copied from real objects, and are ectypal, not archetypal, to express myself in learned terms: You reverse this order, and give thought the precedence. In all instances which we have ever seen, thought has no influence upon matter, except where that matter is so conjoined with it, as to have an equal reciprocal influence upon it. No animal can move immediately any thing but the members of its own body; and indeed, the equality of action and re-action seems to be an universal law of Nature: But your theory implies a contradiction to this experience. These instances, with many more, which it were easy to collect, (particularly the supposition of a mind or system of thought that is eternal, or in other words, an animal ingenerable and immortal) these instances, I say, may teach, all of us, sobriety in condemning each other; and let us see, that as no system of this kind ought ever to be received from a slight analogy, so neither ought any to be rejected on account of a small incongruity. For that is an inconvenience, from which we can justly pronounce no one to be exempted.

All religious systems, it is confessed, are subject to great and insuperable difficulties. Each disputant triumphs in his turn; while he carries on an offensive war, and exposes the absurdities, barbarities, and pernicious tenets of his antagonist. But all of them, on the whole, prepare a complete triumph for the *Sceptic*; who tells them, that no system ought ever to be embraced with regard to such subjects: For this plain reason, that no absurdity ought ever to be assented to with regard to any subject. A total suspense of judgment is here our only reasonable resource. And if every attack, as is commonly observed, and no defence, among Theologians, is successful; how complete must be *his* victory, who remains always, with all mankind, on the offensive, and has himself no fixed station or abiding city, which he is ever, on any occasion, obliged to defend?

PART IX.

BUT if so many difficulties attend the argument *a posteriori*, said DEMEA; had we not better adhere to that simple and sublime argument *a priori*, which, by offering to us infallible demonstration, cuts off at once all doubt and difficulty? By this argument, too, we may prove the INFINITY of the divine attributes, which, I am afraid, can never be ascertained with certainty from any other topic. For how can an effect, which either is finite, or, for aught we know, may be so; how can such an effect, I say, prove an infinite cause? The unity too of the Divine Nature, it is very difficult, if not absolutely impossible, to deduce merely from contemplating the works of nature; nor will the uniformity alone of the plan, even were it allowed, give us any assurance of that attribute. Whereas the argument *a priori* . . . .

You seem to reason, DEMEA, interposed CLEANTHES, as if those advantages and conveniencies in the abstract argument were full proofs of its solidity. But it is first proper, in my opinion, to determine what argument of this nature you chuse to insist on; and we shall afterwards, from itself, better than from its *useful* consequences, endeavour to determine what value we ought to put upon it.

The argument, replied DEMEA, which I would insist on is the common one. Whatever exists must have a cause or reason of its existence; it being absolutely impossible for any thing to produce itself, or be the cause of its own existence. In mounting up, therefore, from effects to causes, we must either go on in tracing an infinite succession, without any ultimate cause at all; or must at last have recourse to some ultimate cause, that is *necessarily* existent: Now that the first supposition is absurd may be thus proved. In the infinite chain or succession of causes and effects, each single effect is determined to exist by the power and efficacy of that cause, which immediately preceded; but the whole eternal chain or succession, taken together, is not determined or caused by any thing: and yet it is evident that it requires a cause or reason, as much as any particular object, which begins to exist in time. The question is still reasonable, Why this particular succession of causes existed from eternity, and not any other succession, or no succession at all. If there be no necessarily-existent being, any supposition, which can be formed, is equally possible; nor is there any more absurdity in Nothing's having existed from eternity, than there is in that succession of causes, which constitutes the universe. What was it then, which determined something to exist rather than nothing, and bestowed being on a particular possibility, exclusive of the rest? *External causes*, there are supposed to be none. *Chance* is a word without a meaning. Was it *Nothing?* But that can never produce any thing.

We must, therefore, have recourse to a necessarily-existent Being, who carries the REASON of his existence in himself; and who cannot be supposed not to exist without an express contradiction. There is consequently such a Being, that is, there is a Deity.

I shall not leave it to PHILO, said CLEANTHES, (though I know that the starting objections is his chief delight) to point out the weakness of this metaphysical reasoning. It seems to me so obviously ill-grounded, and at the same time of so little consequence to the cause of true piety and religion, that I shall myself venture to show the fallacy of it.

I shall begin with observing, that there is an evident absurdity in pretending to demonstrate a matter of fact, or to prove it by any arguments *a priori*. Nothing is demonstrable, unless the contrary implies a contradiction. Nothing, that is distinctly conceivable, implies a contradiction. Whatever we conceive as existent, we can also conceive as non-existent. There is no being, therefore, whose non-existence implies a contradiction. Consequently there is no being, whose existence is demonstrable. I propose this argument as entirely decisive, and am willing to rest the whole controversy upon it.

It is pretended that the Deity is a necessarily-existent being; and this necessity of his existence is attempted to be explained by asserting, that, if we knew his whole essence or nature, we should perceive it to be as impossible for him not to exist as for twice two not to be four. But it is evident, that this can never happen, while our faculties remain the same as at present. It will still be possible for us, at any time, to conceive the non-existence of what we formerly conceived to exist; nor can the mind ever lie under a necessity of supposing any object to remain always in being; in the same manner as we lie under a necessity of always conceiving twice two to be four. The words, therefore, *necessary existence*, have no meaning; or, which is the same thing, none that is consistent.

But farther; why may not the material universe be the necessarily-existent Being, according to this pretended explication of necessity? We dare not affirm that we know all the qualities of matter; and for aught we can determine, it may contain some qualities, which, were they known, would make its non-existence appear as great a contradiction as that twice two is five. I find only one argument employed to prove, that the material world is not the necessarily-existent Being; and this argument is derived from the contingency both of the matter and the form of the world. 'Any particle of matter,' 'tis said,[1] 'may be *conceived* to be annihilated; and any form may be *conceived* to be altered. Such an annihilation or alteration, therefore, is not impossible.' But it seems a great partiality not to perceive, that the same argument extends equally to the Deity, so far as we have any conception of him; and that the mind can at least imagine him to be non-existent, or his attributes to be altered. It must be some unknown, inconceivable qualities, which can make his non-existence appear impossible, or his attributes unalterable: And no reason can be assigned, why these qualities may not belong to matter. As they are altogether unknown and inconceivable, they can never be proved incompatible with it.

Add to this, that in tracing an eternal succession of objects, it seems absurd to inquire for a general cause or first author. How can any thing, that exists from eternity, have a cause, since that relation implies a priority in time and a beginning of existence?

In such a chain too, or succession of objects, each part is caused by that which preceded it, and causes that which succeeds it. Where then is the difficulty? But the WHOLE, you say, wants a cause. I answer, that the uniting of these parts into a whole, like the uniting of several distinct counties into one kingdom, or several distinct members into one body, is performed merely by an arbitrary act of the mind, and has no influence on the nature of things. Did I show you the particular causes of each individual in a collection of twenty particles of matter, I should think it very unreasonable, should you afterwards ask me, what was the cause of the whole twenty. This is sufficiently explained in explaining the cause of the parts.

Though the reasonings, which you have urged, CLEANTHES, may well excuse me, said PHILO, from starting any farther difficulties; yet I cannot forbear insisting still upon another topic. 'Tis observed by arithmeticians, that the products of 9 compose always either 9 or some lesser product of 9; if you add together all the characters, of which any of the former products is composed. Thus, of 18, 27, 36, which are pro-

[1] Dr. Clarke.

ducts of 9, you make 9 by adding 1 to 8, 2 to 7, 3 to 6. Thus, 369 is a product also of 9; and if you add 3, 6, and 9, you make 18, a lesser product of 9.[1] To a superficial observer, so wonderful a regularity may be admired as the effect either of chance or design: but a skilful algebraist immediately concludes it to be the work of necessity, and demonstrates, that it must for ever result from the nature of these numbers. Is it not probable, I ask, that the whole œconomy of the universe is conducted by a like necessity, though no human algebra can furnish a key, which solves the difficulty? And instead of admiring the order of natural beings, may it not happen, that, could we penetrate into the intimate nature of bodies, we should clearly see why it was absolutely impossible, they could ever admit of any other disposition? So dangerous is it to introduce this idea of necessity into the present question! and so naturally does it afford an inference directly opposite to the religious hypothesis!

But dropping all these abstractions, continued PHILO; and confining ourselves to more familiar topics; I shall venture to add an observation, that the argument *a priori* has seldom been found very convincing, except to people of a metaphysical head, who have accustomed themselves to abstract reasoning, and who finding from mathematics, that the understanding frequently leads to truth, through obscurity, and contrary to first appearances, have transferred the same habit of thinking to subjects, where it ought not to have place. Other people, even of good sense and the best inclined to religion, feel always some deficiency in such arguments, though they are not perhaps able to explain distinctly where it lies. A certain proof, that men ever did, and ever will derive their religion from other sources than from this species of reasoning.

PART X.

IT is my opinion, I own, replied DEMEA, that each man feels, in a manner, the truth of religion within his own breast, and from a consciousness of his imbecility and misery, rather than from any reasoning, is led to seek protection from that Being, on whom he and all nature is dependent. So anxious

------

[1] République des Lettres, Août 1685.

or so tedious are even the best scenes of life, that futurity is still the object of all our hopes and fears. We incessantly look forward, and endeavour, by prayers, adoration, and sacrifice, to appease those unknown powers, whom we find, by experience, so able to afflict and oppress us. Wretched creatures that we are! what resource for us amidst the innumerable ills of life, did not Religion suggest some methods of atonement, and appease those terrors, with which we are incessantly agitated and tormented?

I am indeed persuaded, said PHILO, that the best and indeed the only method of bringing every one to a due sense of religion, is by just representations of the misery and wickedness of men. And for that purpose a talent of eloquence and strong imagery is more requisite than that of reasoning and argument. For is it necessary to prove, what every one feels within himself? 'Tis only necessary to make us feel it, if possible, more intimately and sensibly.

The people, indeed, replied DEMEA, are sufficiently convinced of this great and melancholy truth. The miseries of life, the unhappiness of man, the general corruptions of our nature, the unsatisfactory enjoyment of pleasures, riches, honours; these phrases have become almost proverbial in all languages. And who can doubt of what all men declare from their own immediate feeling and experience?

In this point, said PHILO, the learned are perfectly agreed with the vulgar; and in all letters, *sacred* and *profane*, the topic of human misery has been insisted on with the most pathetic eloquence that sorrow and melancholy could inspire. The poets, who speak from sentiment, without a system, and whose testimony has therefore the more authority, abound in images of this nature. From HOMER down to Dr. YOUNG, the whole inspired tribe have ever been sensible, that no other representation of things would suit the feeling and observation of each individual.

As to authorities, replied DEMEA, you need not seek them. Look round this library of CLEANTHES. I shall venture to affirm, that, except authors of particular sciences, such as chymistry or botany, who have no occasion to treat of human life, there is scarce one of those innumerable writers, from whom the sense of human misery has not, in some passage or other, extorted a complaint and confession of it. At least, the chance is entirely on that side; and no one author has ever, so far as I can recollect, been so extragavant as to deny it.

There you must excuse me, said PHILO: LEIBNITZ has denied it; and is perhaps the first,[1] who ventured upon so bold and paradoxical an opinion; at least, the first, who made it essential to his philosophical system.

And by being the first, replied DEMEA, might he not have been sensible of his error? For is this a subject, in which philosophers can propose to make discoveries, especially in so late an age? And can any man hope by a simple denial (for the subject scarcely admits of reasoning) to bear down the united testimony of mankind, founded on sense and consciousness?

And why should man, added he, pretend to an exemption from the lot of all other animals? The whole earth, believe me, PHILO, is cursed and polluted. A perpetual war is kindled amongst all living creatures. Necessity, hunger, want, stimulate the strong and courageous: Fear, anxiety, terror, agitate the weak and infirm. The first entrance into life gives anguish to the new-born infant and to its wretched parent: Weakness, impotence, distress, attend each stage of that life: and 'tis at last finished in agony and horror.

Observe too, says PHILO, the curious artifices of Nature, in order to imbitter the life of every living being. The stronger prey upon the weaker, and keep them in perpetual terror and anxiety. The weaker too, in their turn, often prey upon the stronger, and vex and molest them without relaxation. Consider that innumerable race of insects, which either are bred on the body of each animal, or flying about infix their stings in him. These insects have others still less than themselves, which torment them. And thus on each hand, before and behind, above and below, every animal is surrounded with enemies, which incessantly seek his misery and distruction.

Man alone, said DEMEA, seems to be, in part, an exception to this rule. For by combination in society, he can easily master lions, tygers, and bears, whose greater strength and agility naturally enable them to prey upon him.

On the contrary, it is here chiefly, cried PHILO, that the uniform and equal maxims of Nature are most apparent. Man, it is true, can, by combination, surmount all his *real*

---

[1] That sentiment had been maintained by Dr. King and some few others, before LEIBNITZ, though by none of so great fame as that GERMAN philosopher.

enemies, and become master of the whole animal creation: but does he not immediately raise up to himself *imaginary* enemies, the dæmons of his fancy, who haunt him with superstitious terrors, and blast every enjoyment of life? His pleasure, as he imagines, becomes, in their eyes, a crime: his food and repose give them umbrage and offence: his very sleep and dreams furnish new materials to anxious fear: and even death, his refuge from every other ill, presents only the dread of endless and innumerable woes. Nor does the wolf molest more the timid flock, than superstition does the anxious breast of wretched mortals.

Besides, consider, DEMEA; this very society, by which we surmount those wild beasts, our natural enemies; what new enemies does it not raise to us? What woe and misery does it not occasion? Man is the greatest enemy of man. Oppression, injustice, contempt, contumely, violence, sedition, war, calumny, treachery, fraud; by these they mutually torment each other: and they would soon dissolve that society which they had formed, were it not for the dread of still greater ills, which must attend their separation.

But though these external insults, said DEMEA, from animals, from men, from all the elements, which assault us, form a frightful catalogue of woes, they are nothing in comparison of those, which arise within ourselves, from the distempered condition of our mind and body. How many lie under the lingering torment of diseases? Hear the pathetic enumeration of the great poet.

> Intestine stone and ulcer, colic-pangs,
> Demoniac frenzy, moping melancholy,
> And moon-struck madness, pining atrophy,
> Marasmus and wide-wasting pestilence
> Dire was the tossing, deep the groans DESPAIR
> Tended the sick, busiest from couch to couch.
> And over them triumphant DEATH his dart
> Shook, but delay'd to strike, tho' oft invok'd
> With vows, as their chief good and final hope.

The disorders of the mind, continued DEMEA, though more secret, are not perhaps less dismal and vexatious. Remorse, shame, anguish, rage, disappointment, anxiety, fear, dejection, despair; who has ever passed through life without cruel inroads from these tormentors? How many have scarcely ever felt any better sensations? Labour and poverty, so abhorred by every one, are the certain lot of the far greater number; and those few privileged persons, who enjoy ease and opulence, never reach contentment or true felicity. All the goods of life united would not make a very happy man : but all the ills united would make a wretch indeed; and any one of them almost (and who can be free from every one) nay often the absence of one good (and who can possess all) is sufficient to render life ineligible.

Were a stranger to drop, on a sudden, into this world, I would show him, as a specimen of its ills, an hospital full of diseases, a prison crowded with malefactors and debtors, a field of battle strewed with carcases, a fleet floundering in the ocean, a nation languishing under tyranny, famine, or pestilence. To turn the gay side of life to him, and give him a notion of its pleasures ; whither should I conduct him? to a ball, to an opera, to court? He might justly think, that I was only showing him a diversity of distress and sorrow.

There is no evading such striking instances, said PHILO, but by apologies, which still farther aggravate the charge. Why have all men, I ask, in all ages, complained incessantly of the miseries of life? . . . . They have no just reason, says one : these complaints proceed only from their discontented, repining, anxious disposition. . . . . And can there possibly, I reply, be a more certain foundation of misery, than such a wretched temper?

But if they were really as unhappy as they pretend, says my antagonist, why do they remain in life? . . . .

Not satisfied with life, afraid of death.

This is the secret chain, say I, that holds us. We are terrified, not bribed to the continuance of our existence.

It is only a false delicacy, he may insist, which a few refined spirits indulge, and which has spread these complaints among the whole race of mankind. . . . . And what is this delicacy, I ask, which you blame? Is it any thing but a greater sensibility to all the pleasures and pains of life? and if the man of a delicate, refined temper, by being so much more alive than the rest of the world, is only so much more unhappy; what judgment must we form in general of human life?

Let men remain at rest, says our adversary; and they will be easy. They are willing artificers of their own misery. . . . . No! reply I; an anxious languor follows their repose : disappointment, vexation, trouble, their activity and ambition.

I can observe something like what you mention in some others, replied CLEANTHES : but I confess, I feel little or nothing of it in myself, and hope that it is not so common as you represent it.

If you feel not human misery yourself, cried DEMEA, I congratulate you on so happy a singularity. Others, seemingly the most prosperous, have not been ashamed to vent their complaints in the most melancholy strains. Let us attend to the great, the fortunate Emperor, CHARLES V, when, tired with human grandeur, he resigned all his extensive dominions into the hands of his son. In the last harangue, which he made on that memorable occasion, he publicly avowed, *that the greatest prosperities which he had ever enjoyed, had been mixed with so many adversities, that he might truly say he had never enjoyed any satisfaction or contentment.* But did the retired life, in which he sought for shelter, afford him any greater happiness ? If we may credit his son's account, his repentance commenced the very day of his resignation.

CICERO's fortune, from small beginnings, rose to the greatest lustre and renown ; yet what pathetic complaints of the ills of life do his familiar letters, as well as philosophical discourses, contain ? And suitably to his own experience, he introduces CATO, the great, the fortunate CATO, protesting in his old age, that, had he a new life in his offer, he would reject the present.

Ask yourself, ask any of your acquaintance, whether they would live over again the last ten or twenty years of their lives. No ! but the next twenty, they say, will be better :

> And from the dregs of life, hope to receive
> What the first sprightly running could not give.

Thus at last they find (such is the greatness of human misery ; it reconciles even contradictions) that they complain, at once, of the shortness of life, and of its vanity and sorrow.

And is it possible, CLEANTHES, said PHILO, that after all these reflections, and infinitely more, which might be suggested, you can still persevere in your Anthropomorphism, and assert the moral attributes of the Deity, his justice,

benevolence, mercy, and rectitude, to be of the same nature
with these virtues in human creatures? His power we allow
infinite: whatever he wills is executed: but neither man nor
any other animal are happy: therefore he does not will their
happiness. His wisdom is infinite: he is never mistaken in
chusing the means to any end: but the course of nature
tends not to human or animal felicity: therefore it is not
established for that purpose. Through the whole compass of
human knowledge, there are no inferences more certain and
infallible than these. In what respect, then, do his benevolence and mercy resemble the benevolence and mercy of men?

Epicurus's old questions are yet unanswered.

Is he willing to prevent evil, but not able? then is he impotent. Is he able, but not willing? then is he malevolent.
Is he both able and willing? whence then is evil?

You ascribe, Cleanthes, (and I believe justly) a purpose
and intention to Nature. But what, I beseech you, is the
object of that curious artifice and machinery, which she has
displayed in all animals? The preservation alone of individuals and propagation of the species. It seems enough
for her purpose, if such a rank be barely upheld in the
universe, without any care or concern for the happiness of
the members that compose it. No resource for this purpose:
no machinery, in order merely to give pleasure or ease: no
fund of pure joy and contentment: no indulgence without
some want or necessity accompanying it. At least, the few
phenomena of this nature are overbalanced by opposite phenomena of still greater importance.

Our sense of music, harmony, and indeed beauty of all
kinds gives satisfaction, without being absolutely necessary
to the preservation and propagation of the species. But
what racking pains, on the other hand, arise from gouts,
gravels, megrims, tooth-aches, rheumatisms; where the injury to the animal-machinery is either small or incurable?
Mirth, laughter, play, frolic, seems gratuitous satisfactions,
which have no farther tendency: spleen, melancholy, discontent, superstition, are pains of the same nature. How
then does the divine benevolence display itself, in the sense
of you Anthropomorphites? None but we Mystics, as you
were pleased to call us, can account for this strange mixture
of phenomena, by deriving it from attributes, infinitely perfect, but incomprehensible.

And have you at last, said CLEANTHES smiling, betrayed your intentions, PHILO? Your long agreement with DEMEA did indeed a little surprise me; but I find you were all the while erecting a concealed battery against me. And I must confess, that you have now fallen upon a subject, worthy of your noble spirit of opposition and controversy. If you can make out the present point, and prove mankind to be unhappy or corrupted, there is an end at once of all religion. For to what purpose establish the natural attributes of the Deity, while the moral are still doubtful and uncertain?

You take umbrage very easily, replied DEMEA, at opinions the most innocent, and the most generally received even amongst the religious and devout themselves: and nothing can be more surprising than to find a topic like this, concerning the wickedness and misery of man, charged with no less than Atheism and profaneness. Have not all pious divines and preachers, who have indulged their rhetoric on so fertile a subject; have they not easily, I say, given a solution of any difficulties, which may attend it? This world is but a point in comparison of the universe: this life but a moment in comparison of eternity. The present evil phenomena, therefore, are rectified in other regions, and in some future period of existence. And the eyes of men, being then opened to larger views of things, see the whole connection of general laws; and trace, with adoration, the benevolence and rectitude of the Deity, through all the mazes and intricacies of his providence.

No! replied CLEANTHES, No! These arbitrary suppositions can never be admitted, contrary to matter of fact, visible and uncontroverted. Whence can any cause be known but from its known effects? Whence can any hypothesis be proved but from the apparent phenomena? To establish one hypothesis upon another, is building entirely in the air; and the utmost we ever attain, by these conjectures and fictions, is to ascertain the bare possibility of our opinion; but never can we, upon such terms, establish its reality.

The only method of supporting divine benevolence (and it is what I willingly embrace) is to deny absolutely the misery and wickedness of man. Your representations are exaggerated: Your melancholy views mostly fictitious: Your inferences contrary to fact and experience. Health is more common than sickness: Pleasure than pain: Happiness than misery.

And for one vexation, which we meet with, we attain, upon computation, a hundred enjoyments.

Admitting your position, replied PHILO, which yet is extremely doubtful, you must, at the same time, allow, that, if pain be less frequent than pleasure, it is infinitely more violent and durable. One hour of it is often able to outweigh a day, a week, a month of our common insipid enjoyments: And how many days, weeks, and months are passed by several in the most acute torments? Pleasure, scarcely in one instance, is ever able to reach ecstacy and rapture: And in no one instance can it continue for any time at its highest pitch and altitude. The spirits evaporate; the nerves relax; the fabric is disordered; and the enjoyment quickly degenerates into fatigue and uneasiness. But pain often, good God, how often! rises to torture and agony; and the longer it continues, it becomes still more genuine agony and torture. Patience is exhausted; courage languishes; melancholy seizes us; and nothing terminates our misery but the removal of its cause, or another event, which is the sole cure of all evil, but which, from our natural folly, we regard with still greater horror and consternation.

But not to insist upon these topics, continued PHILO, though most obvious, certain, and important; I must use the freedom to admonish you, CLEANTHES, that you have put the controversy upon a most dangerous issue, and are unawares introducing a total Scepticism, into the most essential articles of natural and revealed theology. What! no method of fixing a just foundation for religion, unless we allow the happiness of human life, and maintain a continued existence even in this world, with all our present pains, infirmities, vexations, and follies, to be eligible and desireable! But this is contrary to every one's feeling and experience: It is contrary to an authority so established as nothing can subvert: No decisive proofs can ever be produced against this authority; nor is it possible for you to compute, estimate, and compare all the pains and all the pleasures in the lives of all men and of all animals: And thus by your resting the whole system of religion on a point, which, from its very nature, must for ever be uncertain, you tacitly confess, that that system is equally uncertain.

But allowing you, what never will be believed; at least, what you never possibly can prove, that animal, or at least, human happiness, in this life, exceeds its misery; you have yet done nothing: For this is not, by any means, what we expect from infinite power, infinite wisdom, and infinite goodness. Why is there any misery at all in the world? Not by chance surely. From some cause then. Is it from the intention of the Deity? But he is perfectly benevolent. Is it contrary to his intention? But he is almighty. Nothing can shake the solidity of this reasoning, so short, so clear, so decisive; except we assert, that these subjects exceed all human capacity, and that our common measures of truth and falsehood are not applicable to them; a topic, which I have all along insisted on, but which you have, from the beginning, rejected with scorn and indignation.

But I will be contented to retire still from this intrenchment: For I deny that you can ever force me in it: I will allow, that pain or misery in man is *compatible* with infinite power and goodness in the Deity, even in your sense of these attributes: What are you advanced by all these concessions? A mere possible compatibility is not sufficient. You must *prove* these pure, unmixt, and uncontrollable attributes from the present mixed and confused phenomena, and from these alone. A hopeful undertaking! Were the phenomena ever so pure and unmixt, yet being finite, they would be insufficient for that purpose. How much more, where they are also so jarring and discordant!

Here, CLEANTHES, I find myself at ease in my argument. Here I triumph. Formerly, when we argued concerning the natural attributes of intelligence and design, I needed all my sceptical and metaphysical subtilty to elude your grasp. In many views of the universe, and of its parts, particularly the latter, the beauty and fitness of final causes strike us with such irresistible force, that all objections appear (what I believe they really are) mere cavils and sophisms; nor can we then imagine how it was ever possible for us to repose any weight on them. But there is no view of human life or of the condition of mankind, from which, without the greatest violence, we can infer the moral attributes, or learn that infinite benevolence, conjoined with infinite power and infinite wisdom, which we must discover by the eyes of faith alone. It is your turn now to tug the labouring oar, and to support your philosophical subtilties against the dictates of plain reason and experience.

PART XI.

I scruple not to allow, said Cleanthes, that I have been apt to suspect the frequent repetition of the word, *infinite*, which we meet with in all theological writers, to savour more of panegyric than of philosophy, and that any purposes of reasoning, and even of religion, would be better served, were we to rest contented with more accurate and mo.e moderate expressions. The terms, *admirable, excellent, superlatively great, wise,* and *holy*; these sufficiently fill the imaginations of men; and any thing beyond, besides that it leads into absurdities, has no influence on the affections or sentiments. Thus, in the present subject, if we abandon all human analogy, as seems your intention, Demea, I am afraid we abandon all religion, and retain no conception of the great object of our adoration. If we preserve human analogy, we must for ever find it impossible to reconcile any mixture of evil in the universe with infinite attributes; much less can we ever prove the latter from the former. But supposing the Author of Nature to be finitely perfect, though far exceeding mankind; a satisfactory account may then be given of natural and moral evil, and every untoward phenomenon be explained and adjusted. A less evil may then be chosen, in order to avoid a greater; Inconveniencies be submitted to, in order to reach a desirable end : And in a word, benevolence, regulated by wisdom, and limited by necessity, may produce just such a world as the present. You, Philo, who are so prompt at starting views, and reflections, and analogies, I would gladly hear, at length, without interruption, your opinion of this new theory; and if it deserve our attention, we may afterwards, at more leisure, reduce it into form.

My sentiments, replied Philo, are not worth being made a mystery of; and therefore, without any ceremony, I shall deliver what occurs to me, with regard to the present subject. It must, I think, be allowed, that, if a very limited intelligence, whom we shall suppose utterly unacquainted with the universe, were assured, that it were the production of a very good, wise, and powerful being, however finite, he would, from his conjectures, form *beforehand* a different notion of it from what we find it to be by experience, nor would he ever imagine, merely from these attributes of the cause, of which he is informed, that the effect could be so full of vice and misery and disorder, as it appears in this life. Supposing now, that this person were brought into the world, still assured, that it was the workmanship of such a sublime and benevolent Being; he might, perhaps, be surprised at the disappointment; but would never retract his former belief, if founded on any very solid argument; since such a limited intelligence must be sensible of his own blindness and ignorance, and must allow, that there may be many solutions of those phenomena, which will for ever escape his comprehension. But supposing, which is the real case with regard to man, that this creature is not antecedently convinced of a supreme intelligence, benevolent, and powerful, but is left to gather such a belief from the appearances of things; this entirely alters the case, nor will he ever find any reason for such a conclusion. He may be fully convinced of the narrow limits of his understanding; but this will not help him in forming an inference concerning the goodness of superior powers, since he must form that inference from what he knows, not from what he is ignorant of. The more you exaggerate his weakness and ignorance, the more diffident you render him, and give him the greater suspicion, that such subjects are beyond the reach of his faculties. You are obliged, therefore, to reason with him merely from the known phenomena, and to drop every arbitrary supposition or conjecture.

Did I show you a house or palace, where there was not one apartment convenient or agreeable; where the windows, doors, fires, passages, stairs, and the whole œconomy of the building were the source of noise, confusion, fatigue, darkness, and the extremes of heat and cold; you would certainly blame the contrivance, without any farther examination. The architect would in vain display his subtilty, and prove to you, that if this door or that window were altered, greater ills would ensue. What he says, may be strictly true · The alteration of one particular, while the other parts of the building remain, may only augment the inconveniencies. But still you would assert in general, that, if the architect had had skill and good intentions, he might have formed such a plan of the whole, and might have adjusted the parts in such a manner, as would have remedied all or most of these inconveniencies. His ignorance, or even your own ignorance of such a plan, will never convince you of the impossibility of it. If you find any inconveniencies and deformities in the building, you will always, without entering into any detail, condemn the architect.

In short, I repeat the question: Is the world, considered in general, and as it appears to us in this life, different from what a man or such a limited Being would, *beforehand*, expect from a very powerful, wise, and benevolent Deity? It must be strange prejudice to assert the contrary. And from thence I conclude, that, however consistent the world may be, allowing certain suppositions and conjectures, with the idea of such a Deity, it can never afford us an inference concerning his existence. The consistence is not absolutely denied, only the inference. Conjectures, especially where infinity is excluded from the Divine attributes, may perhaps be sufficient to prove a consistence; but can never be foundations for any inference.

There seems to be *four* circumstances, on which depend all, or the greatest parts of the ills, that molest sensible creatures; and it is not impossible but all these circumstances may be necessary and unavoidable. We know so little beyond common life, or even of common life, that, with regard to the œconomy of a universe, there is no conjecture, however wild, which may not be just; nor any one, however plausible, which may not be erroneous. All that belongs to human understanding, in this deep ignorance and obscurity, is to be sceptical, or at least cautious; and not to admit of any hypothesis, whatever; much less, of any which is supported by no appearance of probability. Now this I assert to be the case with regard to all the causes of evil, and the circumstances, on which it depends. None of them appear to human reason, in the least degree, necessary or unavoidable; nor can we suppose them such, without the utmost license of imagination.

The *first* circumstance which introduces evil, is that contrivance or œconomy of the animal creation, by which pains, as well as pleasures, are employed to excite all creatures to action, and make them vigilant in the great work of self-preservation. Now pleasure alone, in its various degrees, seems to human understanding sufficient for this purpose. All animals might be constantly in a state of enjoyment; but when urged by any of the necessities of nature, such as thirst, hunger, weariness; instead of pain, they might feel a diminution of pleasure, by which they might be prompted to seek that object, which is necessary to their subsistence. Men pursue pleasure as eagerly as they avoid pain; at least, might have been so constituted. It seems, therefore, plainly possible to carry on the business of life without any pain. Why then is any animal ever rendered susceptible of such a sensation? If animals can be free from it an hour, they might enjoy a perpetual exemption from it; and it required as particular a contrivance of their organs to produce that feeling, as to endow them with sight, hearing, or any of the senses. Shall we conjecture, that such a contrivance was necessary, without any appearance of reason? and shall we build on that conjecture as on the most certain truth?

But a capacity of pain would not alone produce pain, were it not for the *second* circumstance, *viz.* the conducting of the world by general laws; and this seems nowise necessary to a very perfect being. It is true; if every thing were conducted by particular volitions, the course of nature would be perpetually broken, and no man could employ his reason in the conduct of life. But might not other particular volitions remedy this inconvenience? In short, might not the Deity exterminate all ill, where-ever it were to be found; and produce all good, without any preparation or long progress of causes and effects?

Besides, we must consider, that, according to the present œconomy of the world, the course of Nature, though supposed exactly regular, yet to us appears not so, and many events are uncertain, and many disappoint our expectations. Health and sickness, calm and tempest, with an infinite number of other accidents, whose causes are unknown and variable, have a great influence both on the fortunes of particular persons and on the prosperity of public societies: and indeed all human life, in a manner, depends on such accidents. A being, therefore, who knows the secret springs of the universe, might easily, by particular volitions, turn all these accidents to the good of mankind, and render the whole world happy, without discovering himself in any operation. A fleet, whose purposes were salutary to society, might always meet with a fair wind: Good princes enjoy sound health and long life: Persons, born to power and authority, be framed with good tempers and virtuous dispositions. A few such events as these, regularly and wisely conducted, would change the face of the world; and yet would no more seem to disturb the course of Nature or confound human conduct, than the present œconomy of things, where the causes are secret, and variable, and compounded. Some small touches, given to CALIGULA's brain in his infancy, might have converted him into a TRAJAN: one wave, a little higher than the rest, by burying CÆSAR and his fortune in the bottom of the ocean, might have restored liberty to a considerable part of mankind. There may, for aught we know, be good reasons, why Providence interposes not in this manner; but they are unknown to us: and though the mere supposition, that such reasons exist, may be sufficient to *save* the conclusion concerning the divine attributes, yet surely it can never be sufficient to *establish* that conclusion.

If every thing in the universe be conducted by general laws, and if animals be rendered susceptible of pain, it scarcely seems possible but some ill must arise in the various shocks of matter, and the various concurrence and opposition of general laws: But this ill would be very rare, were it not for the *third* circumstance, which I proposed to mention, *viz.* the great frugality, with which all powers and faculties are distributed to every particular being. So well adjusted are the organs and capacities of all animals, and so well fitted to their preservation, that, as far as history or tradition reaches, there appears not to be any single species, which has yet been extinguished in the universe. Every animal has the requisite endowments; but these endowments are bestowed with so scrupulous an œconomy, that any considerable diminution must entirely destroy the creature. Where-ever one power is encreased, there is a proportional abatement in the others. Animals, which excel in swiftness, are commonly defective in force. Those, which possess both, are either imperfect in some of their senses, or are oppressed with the most craving wants. The human species, whose chief excellency is reason and sagacity, is of all others the most necessitous, and the most deficient in bodily advantages; without cloaths, without arms, without food, without lodging, without any convenience of life, except what they owe to their own skill and industry. In short, Nature seems to have formed an exact calculation of the necessities of her creatures; and like a *rigid master*, has afforded them little more powers or endowments, than what are strictly sufficient to supply those necessities. An *indulgent parent* would have bestowed a large stock, in order to guard against accidents, and secure the happiness and welfare of the creature, in the most unfortunate concurrence of circumstances. Every course of life would not have been so surrounded with precipices, that the least departure from the true path, by mistake or necessity, must involve us in misery and ruin. Some reserve, some fund would have been provided to ensure happiness; nor would the powers and the necessities have been adjusted with so rigid an œconomy. The author of Nature is inconceivably powerful: his force is supposed great, if not altogether inexhaustible: nor is there any reason, as far as we can judge, to make him observe this strict frugality in his dealings with his creatures. It would have been better, were his power extremely limited, to have created fewer animals, and to have endowed these with more faculties for their happiness and preservation. A builder is never esteemed prudent, who undertakes a plan, beyond what his stock will enable him to finish.

In order to cure most of the ills of human life, I require not that man should have the wings of the eagle, the swiftness of the stag, the force of the ox, the arms of the lion, the scales of the crocodile or rhinoceros; much less do I demand the sagacity of an angel or cherubim. I am contented to take an encrease in one single power or faculty of his soul. Let him be endowed with a greater propensity to industry and labour; a more vigorous spring and activity of mind; a more constant bent to business and application. Let the whole species possess naturally an equal diligence with that which many individuals are able to attain by habit and reflection; and the most beneficial consequences, without any allay of ill, is the immediate and necessary result of this endowment. Almost all the moral, as well as natural evils of human life arise from idleness; and were our species, by the original constitution of their frame, exempt from this vice or infirmity, the perfect cultivation of land, the improvement of arts and manufactures, the exact execution of every office and duty, immediately follow; and men at once may fully reach that state of society, which is so imperfectly attained by the best-regulated government. But as industry is a power, and the most valuable of any, Nature seems deter-

mined, suitably to her usual maxims, to bestow it on men
with a very sparing hand; and rather to punish him severely
for his deficiency in it, than to reward him for his attain-
ments. She has so contrived his frame, that nothing but the
most violent necessity can oblige him to labour; and she
employs all his other wants to overcome, at least in part, the
want of diligence, and to endow him with some share of a
faculty, of which she has thought fit naturally to bereave
him. Here our demands may be allowed very humble, and
therefore the more reasonable. If we required the endowments of superior penetration and judgment, of a more delicate taste of beauty, of a nicer sensibility to benevolence and
friendship; we might be told, that we impiously pretend to
break the order of Nature, that we want to exalt ourselves
into a higher rank of being, that the presents which we require, not being suitable to our state and condition, would
only be pernicious to us. But it is hard; I dare to repeat
it, it is hard, that being placed in a world so full of wants
and necessities; where almost every being and element is
either our foe or refuses its assistance . . . we should also
have our own temper to struggle with, and should be de-
prived of that faculty, which can alone fence against these
multiplied evils.

The *fourth* circumstance, whence arises the misery and
ill of the universe, is the inaccurate workmanship of all the
springs and principles of the great machine of nature. It
must be acknowledged, that there are few parts of the universe, which seem not to serve some purpose, and whose
removal would not produce a visible defect and disorder in
the whole. The parts hang all together, nor can one be
touched without affecting the rest in a greater or less degree.
But at the same time, it must be observed, that none of these
parts or principles, however useful, are so accurately adjusted, as to keep precisely within those bounds, in which
their utility consists; but they are, all of them, apt, on every
occasion, to run into the one extreme or the other. One
would imagine, that this grand production had not received
the last hand of the maker; so little finished is every part,
and so coarse are the strokes, with which it is executed.
Thus, the winds are requisite to convey the vapours along
the surface of the globe, and to assist men in navigation:
but how oft, rising up to tempests and hurricanes, do they

become pernicious? Rains are necessary to nourish all the plants and animals of the earth: but how often are they defective? how often excessive? Heat is requisite to all life and vegetation; but is not always found in the due proportion. On the mixture and secretion of the humours and juices of the body depend the health and prosperity of the animal: but the parts perform not regularly their proper function. What more useful than all the passions of the mind, ambition, vanity, love, anger? But how oft do they break their bounds, and cause the greatest convulsions in society? There is nothing so advantageous in the universe, but what frequently becomes pernicious, by its excess or defect; nor has Nature guarded, with the requisite accuracy, against all disorder or confusion. The irregularity is never, perhaps, so great as to destroy any species; but is often sufficient to involve the individuals in ruin and misery.

On the concurrence, then, of these *four* circumstances does all, or the greatest part of natural evil depend. Were all living creatures incapable of pain, or were the world administered by particular volitions, evil never could have found access into the universe: and were animals endowed with a large stock of powers and faculties, beyond what strict necessity requires; or were the several springs and principles of the universe so accurately framed as to preserve always the just temperament and medium; there must have been very little ill in comparison of what we feel at present. What then shall we pronounce on this occasion? Shall we say, that these circumstances are not necessary, and that they might easily have been altered in the contrivance of the universe? This decision seems too presumptuous for creatures, so blind and ignorant. Let us be more modest in our conclusions. Let us allow, that, if the goodness of the Deity (I mean a goodness like the human) could be established on any tolerable reasons *a priori*, these phenomena, however untoward, would not be sufficient to subvert that principle; but might easily, in some unknown manner, be reconcilable to it. But let us still assert, that as this goodness is not antecedently established, but must be inferred from the phenomena, there can be no grounds for such an inference, while there are so many ills in the universe, and while these ills might so easily have been remedied, as far as human understanding can be allowed to judge on such a subject. I am Sceptic enough to allow, that the bad appearances, notwithstanding all my reasonings, may be compatible with such attributes as you suppose : But surely they can never prove these attributes. Such a conclusion cannot result from Scepticism ; but must arise from the phenomena, and from our confidence in the reasonings, which we deduce from these phenomena.

Look round this universe. What an immense profusion of beings, animated and organized, sensible and active ! You admire this prodigious variety and fecundity. But inspect a little more narrowly these living existences, the only beings worth regarding. How hostile and destructive to each other ! How insufficient all of them for their own happiness ! How contemptible or odious to the spectator ! The whole presents nothing but the idea of a blind Nature, impregnated by a great vivifying principle, and pouring forth from her lap, without discernment or parental care, her maimed and abortive children !

Here the MANICHÆAN system occurs as a proper hypothesis to solve the difficulty : and no doubt, in some respects, it is very specious, and has more probability than the common hypothesis, by giving a plausible account of the strange mixture of good and ill, which appears in life. But if we consider, on the other hand, the perfect uniformity and agreement of the parts of the universe, we shall not discover in it any marks of the combat of a malevolent with a benevolent being. There is indeed an opposition of pains and pleasures in the feelings of sensible creatures : but are not all the operations of Nature carried on by an opposition of principles, of hot and cold, moist and dry, light and heavy ? The true conclusion is, that the original source of all things is entirely indifferent to all these principles, and has no more regard to good above ill than to heat above cold, or to drought above moisture, or to light above heavy.

There may *four* hypotheses be framed concerning the first causes of the universe ; *that* they are endowed with perfect goodness, *that* they have perfect malice, *that* they are opposite and have both goodness and malice, *that* they have neither goodness nor malice. Mixt phenomena can never prove the two former unmixt principles. And the uniformity and steadiness of general laws seem to oppose the third. The fourth, therefore, seems by far the most probable.

What I have said concerning natural evil will apply to

moral, with little or no variation; and we have no more reason to infer, that the rectitude of the Supreme Being resembles human rectitude than that his benevolence resembles the human. Nay, it will be thought, that we have still greater cause to exclude from him moral sentiments, such as we feel them; since moral evil, in the opinion of many, is much more predominant above moral good than natural evil above natural good.

But even though this should not be allowed, and though the virtue, which is in mankind, should be acknowledged much superior to the vice; yet so long as there is any vice at all in the universe, it will very much puzzle you Anthropomorphites, how to account for it. You must assign a cause for it, without having recourse to the first cause. But as every effect must have a cause, and that cause another; you must either carry on the progression *in infinitum,* or rest on that original principle, who is the ultimate cause of all things . . . .

Hold! hold! cried DEMEA: Whither does your imagination hurry you? I joined in alliance with you, in order to prove the incomprehensible nature of the Divine Being, and refute the principles of CLEANTHES, who would measure every thing by a human rule and standard. But I now find you running into all the topics of the greatest libertines and infidels; and betraying that holy cause, which you seemingly espoused. Are you secretly, then, a more dangerous enemy than CLEANTHES himself?

And are you so late in perceiving it? replied CLEANTHES. Believe me, DEMEA; your friend PHILO, from the beginning, has been amusing himself at both our expence; and it must be confessed, that the injudicious reasoning of our vulgar theology has given him but too just a handle of ridicule. The total infirmity of human reason, the absolute incomprehensibility of the Divine Nature, the great and universal misery and still greater wickedness of men; these are strange topics surely to be so fondly cherished by orthodox divines and doctors. In ages of stupidity and ignorance, indeed, these principles may safely be espoused; and perhaps, no views of things are more proper to promote superstition, than such as encourage the blind amazement, the diffidence, and melancholy of mankind. But at present . . . . . .

Blame not so much, interposed PHILO, the ignorance of

these reverend gentlemen. They know how to change their
style with the times. Formerly it was a most popular theological topic to maintain, that human life was vanity and
misery, and to exaggerate all the ills and pains, which are
incident to men. But of late years, divines, we find, begin
to retract this position, and maintain, though still with some
hesitation, that there are more goods than evils, more pleasures than pains, even in this life. When religion stood
entirely upon temper and education, it was thought proper
to encourage melancholy; as indeed, mankind never have
recourse to superior powers so readily as in that disposition.
But as men have now learned to form principles, and to draw
consequences, it is necessary to change the batteries, and to
make use of such arguments as will endure, at least some
scrutiny and examination. This variation is the same (and
from the same causes) with that which I formerly remarked
with regard to Scepticism.

Thus PHILO continued to the last his spirit of opposition,
and his censure of established opinions. But I could observe,
that DEMEA did not at all relish the latter part of the discourse; and he took occasion soon after, on some pretence or
other, to leave the company.

PART XII.

AFTER DEMEA'S departure, CLEANTHES and PHILO continued the conversation in the following manner. Our
friend, I am afraid, said CLEANTHES, will have little inclination to revive this topic of discourse, while you are in company; and to tell truth, PHILO, I should rather wish to
reason with either of you apart on a subject, so sublime and
interesting. Your spirit of controversy, joined to your
abhorrence of vulgar superstition, carries you strange lengths,
when engaged in an argument; and there is nothing so
sacred and venerable, even in your own eyes, which you spare
on that occasion.

I must confess, replied PHILO, that I am less cautious on
the subject of Natural Religion than on any other; both
because I know that I can never, on that head, corrupt the
principles of any man of common sense, and because no one,

I am confident, in whose eyes I appear a man of common sense, will ever mistake my intentions. You, in particular, CLEANTHES, with whom I live in unreserved intimacy; you are sensible, that, notwithstanding the freedom of my conversation, and my love of singular arguments, no one has a deeper sense of religion impressed on his mind, or pays more profound adoration to the Divine Being, as he discovers himself to reason, in the inexplicable contrivance and artifice of Nature. A purpose, an intention, a design strikes everywhere the most careless, the most stupid thinker; and no man can be so hardened in absurd systems, as at all times to reject it. *That Nature does nothing in vain*, is a maxim established in all the schools, merely from the contemplation of the works of Nature, without any religious purpose; and, from a firm conviction of its truth, an anatomist, who had observed a new organ or canal, would never be satisfied, till he had also discovered its use and intention. One great foundation of the COPERNICAN system is the maxim, *That Nature acts by the simplest methods, and chuses the most proper means to any end;* and astronomers often, without thinking of it, lay this strong foundation of piety and religion. The same thing is observable in other parts of philosophy: And thus all the sciences almost lead us insensibly to acknowledge a first intelligent Author; and their authority is often so much the greater, as they do not directly profess that intention.

It is with pleasure I hear GALEN reason concerning the structure of the human body. The anatomy of a man, says he,[1] discovers above 600 different muscles; and whoever duly considers these, will find, that in each of them Nature must have adjusted at least ten different circumstances, in order to attain the end which she proposed; proper figure, just magnitude, right disposition of the several ends, upper and lower position of the whole, the due insertion of the several nerves, veins, and arteries: So that in the muscles alone, above 6000 several views and intentions must have been formed and executed. The bones he calculates to be 284: The distinct purposes, aimed at in the structure of each, above forty. What a prodigious display of artifice, even in these simple and homogeneous parts! But if we consider the skin, ligaments, vessels, glandules, humours, the several

[1] De formatione Fœtus.

limbs and members of the body; how must our astonishment rise upon us, in proportion to the number and intricacy of the parts so artificially adjusted! The farther we advance in these researches, we discover new scenes of art and wisdom: But descry still, at a distance, farther scenes beyond our reach; in the fine internal structure of the parts, in the œconomy of the brain, in the fabric of the seminal vessels. All these artifices are repeated in every different species of animal, with wonderful variety, and with exact propriety, suited to the different intentions of Nature, in framing each species. And if the infidelity of GALEN, even when these natural sciences were still imperfect, could not withstand such striking appearances; to what pitch of pertinacious obstinacy must a philosopher in this age have attained, who can now doubt of a Supreme Intelligence?

Could I meet with one of this species (who, I thank God, are very rare) I would ask him: Supposing there were a God, who did not discover himself immediately to our senses; were it possible for him to give stronger proofs of his existence, than what appear on the whole face of Nature? What indeed could such a divine Being do, but copy the present œconomy of things; render many of his artifices so plain, that no stupidity could mistake them; afford glimpses of still greater artifices, which demonstrate his prodigious superiority above our narrow apprehensions; and conceal altogether a great many from such imperfect creatures? Now according to all rules of just reasoning, every fact must pass for undisputed, when it is supported by all the arguments, which its nature admits of; even though these arguments be not, in themselves, very numerous or forcible: How much more, in the present case, where no human imagination can compute their number, and no understanding estimate their cogency!

I shall farther add, said CLEANTHES, to what you have so well urged, that one great advantage of the principle of Theism, is, that it is the only system of cosmogony, which can be rendered intelligible and complete, and yet can throughout preserve a strong analogy to what we every day see and experience in the world. The comparison of the universe to a machine of human contrivance is so obvious and natural, and is justified by so many instances of order and design in Nature, that it must immediately strike all unprejudiced apprehensions, and procure universal approbation. Whoever attempts to weaken this theory, cannot pretend to succeed by establishing in its place any other, that is precise and determinate : It is sufficient for him, if he start doubts and difficulties; and by remote and abstract views of things, reach that suspense of judgement, which is here the utmost boundary of his wishes. But besides, that this state of mind is in itself unsatisfactory, it can never be steadily maintained against such striking appearances, as continually engage us into the religious hypothesis. A false, absurd system, human nature, from the force of prejudice, is capable of adhering to, with obstinacy and perseverance : But no system at all, in opposition to theory, supported by strong and obvious reason, by natural propensity, and by early education, I think it absolutely impossible to maintain or defend.

So little, replied PHILO, do I esteem this suspense of judgement in the present case to be possible, that I am apt to suspect there enters somewhat of a dispute of words into this controversy, more than is usually imagined. That the works of Nature bear a great analogy to the productions of art is evident: and according to all the rules of good reasoning, we ought to infer, if we argue at all concerning them, that their causes have a proportional analogy. But as there are also considerable differences, we have reason to suppose a proportional difference in the causes; and in particular ought to attribute a much higher degree of power and energy to the supreme cause than any we have ever observed in mankind. Here then the existence of a DEITY is plainly ascertained by reason ; and if we make it a question, whether, on account of these analogies, we can properly call him a *mind* or *intelligence*, notwithstanding the vast difference, which may reasonably be supposed between him and human minds ; what is this but a mere verbal controversy ? No man can deny the analogies between the effects : To restrain ourselves from enquiring concerning the causes is scarcely possible : From this enquiry, the legitimate conclusion is, that the causes have also an analogy : And if we are not contented with calling the first and supreme cause a GOD or DEITY, but desire to vary the expression; what can we call him but MIND or THOUGHT, to which he is justly supposed to bear a considerable resemblance ?

All men of sound reason are disgusted with verbal disputes,

which abound so much in philosophical and theological enquiries; and it is found, that the only remedy for this abuse
must arise from clear definitions, from the precision of those
ideas which enter into any argument, and from the strict and
uniform use of those terms which are employed. But there
is a species of controversy, which, from the very nature of
language and of human ideas, is involved in perpetual ambiguity, and can never, by any precaution or any definitions,
be able to reach a reasonable certainty or precision. These
are the controversies concerning the degrees of any quality
or circumstance. Men may argue to all eternity, whether
HANNIBAL be a great, or a very great, or a superlatively
great man, what degree of beauty CLEOPATRA possessed, what
epithet of praise LIVY or THUCYDIDES is intitled to, without
bringing the controversy to any determination. The dis-
putants may here agree in their sense, and differ in the
terms, or *vice versa*; yet never be able to define their terms,
so as to enter into each other's meaning: Because the degrees
of these qualities are not, like quantity or number, susceptible of any exact mensuration, which may be the standard
in the controversy. That the dispute concerning Theism is of
this nature, and consequently is merely verbal, or perhaps, if
possible, still more incurably ambiguous, will appear upon the
slightest enquiry. I ask the Theist, if he does not allow, that
there is a great and immeasurable, because incomprehensible,
difference between the *human* and the *divine* mind: The
more pious he is, the more readily will he assent to the
affirmative, and the more will he be disposed to magnify
the difference: He will even assert, that the difference is of
a nature which cannot be too much magnified. I next turn
to the Atheist, who, I assert, is only nominally so, and can
never possibly be in earnest; and I ask him, whether, from
the coherence and apparent sympathy in all the parts of this
world, there be not a certain degree of analogy among all the
operations of Nature, in every situation and in every age;
whether the rotting of a turnip, the generation of an animal,
and the structure of human thought be not energies that
probably bear some remote analogy to each other: It is
impossible he can deny it: He will readily acknowledge it.
Having obtained this concession, I push him still farther
in his retreat; and I ask him, if it be not probable, that the
principle which first arranged, and still maintains order in

this universe, bears not also some remote inconceivable analogy to the other operations of Nature, and among the rest to the œconomy of human mind and thought? However reluctant, he must give his assent. Where then, cry I to both these antagonists, is the subject of your dispute? The Theist allows, that the original intelligence is very different from human reason: The Atheist allows, that the original principle of order bears some remote analogy to it. Will you quarrel, Gentlemen, about the degrees, and enter into a controversy, which admits not of any precise meaning, nor consequently of any determination? If you should be so obstinate, I should not be surprised to find you insensibly change sides; while the Theist on the one hand exaggerates the dissimilarity between the Supreme Being, and frail, imperfect, variable, fleeting, and mortal creatures; and the Atheist on the other magnifies the analogy among all the operations of Nature, in every period, every situation, and every position. Consider then, where the real point of controversy lies, and if you cannot lay aside your disputes, endeavour, at least, to cure yourselves of your animosity.

And here I must also acknowledge, CLEANTHES, that, as the works of Nature have a much greater analogy to the effects of *our* art and contrivance, than to those of *our* benevolence and justice; we have reason to infer that the natural attributes of the Deity have a greater resemblance to those of man, than his moral have to human virtues. But what is the consequence? Nothing but this, that the moral qualities of man are more defective in their kind than his natural abilities. For, as the Supreme Being is allowed to be absolutely and entirely perfect, whatever differs most from him departs the farthest from the supreme standard of rectitude and perfection.[1]

---

[1] It seems evident, that the dispute between the Sceptics and Dogmatists is entirely verbal, or at least regards only the degrees of doubt and assurance, which we ought to indulge with regard to all reasoning. And such disputes are commonly, at the bottom, verbal, and admit not of any precise determination. No philosophical Dogmatist denies, that there are difficulties both with regard to the senses and to all science, and that these difficulties are in a regular, logical method, absolutely insolveable. No Sceptic denies, that we lie under an absolute necessity, notwithstanding these difficulties, of thinking, and believing, and reasoning with regard to all kind of subjects, and even of frequently assenting with confidence and security. The only difference, then, between these sects, if they merit that name is, that the Sceptic, from habit, caprice, or inclination, insists most on the difficulties; the Dogmatist, for like reasons, on the necessity.

These, CLEANTHES, are my unfeigned sentiments on this subject; and these sentiments, you know, I have ever cherished and maintained. But in proportion to my veneration for true religion, is my abhorrence of vulgar superstitions; and I indulge a peculiar pleasure, I confess, in pushing such principles, sometimes into absurdity, sometimes into impiety. And you are sensible, that all bigots, notwithstanding their great aversion to the latter above the former, are commonly equally guilty of both.

My inclination, replied CLEANTHES, lies, I own, a contrary way. Religion, however corrupted, is still better than no religion at all. The doctrine of a future state is so strong and necessary a security to morals, that we never ought to abandon or neglect it. For if finite and temporary rewards and punishments have so great an effect, as we daily find; how much greater must be expected from such as are infinite and eternal?

How happens it then, said PHILO, if vulgar superstition be so salutary to society, that all history abounds so much with accounts of its pernicious consequences on public affairs? Factions, civil wars, persecutions, subversions of government, oppression, slavery; these are the dismal consequences which always attend its prevalency over the minds of men. If the religious spirit be ever mentioned in any historical narration, we are sure to meet afterwards with a detail of the miseries, which attend it. And no period of time can be happier or more prosperous, than those in which it is never regarded, or heard of.

The reason of this observation, replied CLEANTHES, is obvious. The proper office of religion is to regulate the heart of men, humanize their conduct, infuse the spirit of temperance, order, and obedience; and as its operation is silent, and only enforces the motives of morality and justice, it is in danger of being overlooked, and confounded with these other motives. When it distinguishes itself, and acts as a separate principle over men, it has departed from its proper sphere, and has become only a cover to faction and ambition.

And so will all religion, said PHILO, except the philosophical and rational kind. Your reasonings are more easily eluded than my facts. The inference is not just, because finite and temporary rewards and punishments have so great influence, that therefore such as are infinite and eternal must have so much greater. Consider, I beseech you, the attachment, which we have to present things, and the little concern which we discover for objects, so remote and uncertain. When divines are declaiming against the common behaviour and conduct of the world, they always represent this principle as the strongest imaginable (which indeed it is) and describe almost all human kind as lying under the influence of it, and sunk into the deepest lethargy and unconcern about their religious interests. Yet these same divines, when they refute their speculative antagonists, suppose the motives of religion to be so powerful, that, without them, it were impossible for civil society to subsist; nor are they ashamed of so palpable a contradiction. It is certain, from experience, that the smallest grain of natural honesty and benevolence has more effect on men's conduct, than the most pompous views suggested by theological theories and systems. A man's natural inclination works incessantly upon him; it is for ever present to the mind, and mingles itself with every view and consideration: whereas religious motives, where they act at all, operate only by starts and bounds; and it is scarcely possible for them to become altogether habitual to the mind. The force of the greatest gravity, say the philosophers, is infinitely small, in comparison of that of the least impulse; yet it is certain, that the smallest gravity will, in the end, prevail above a great impulse; because no strokes or blows can be repeated with such constancy as attraction and gravitation.

Another advantage of inclination: It engages on its side all the wit and ingenuity of the mind; and when set in opposition to religious principles, seeks every method and art of eluding them: in which it is almost always successful. Who can explain the heart of man, or account for those strange salvos and excuses, with which people satisfy themselves, when they follow their inclinations in opposition to their religious duty! This is well understood in the world; and none but fools ever repose less trust in a man, because they hear, that, from study and philosophy, he has entertained some speculative doubts with regard to theological subjects. And when we have to do with a man, who makes a great profession of religion and devotion; has this any other effect upon several, who pass for prudent, than to put them on their guard, lest they be cheated and deceived by him?

We must farther consider, that philosophers, who cultivate reason and reflection, stand less in need of such motives to keep them under the restraint of morals; and that the vulgar, who alone may need them, are utterly incapable of so pure a religion, as represents the Deity to be pleased with nothing but virtue in human behaviour. The recommendations to the Divinity are generally supposed to be either frivolous observances, or rapturous ecstasies, or a bigotted credulity. We need not run back into antiquity, or wander into remote regions, to find instances of this degeneracy. Amongst ourselves, some have been guilty of that atrociousness, unknown to the EGYPTIAN and GRECIAN superstitions, of declaiming, in express terms, against morality, and representing it as a sure forfeiture of the Divine favour, if the least trust or reliance be laid upon it.

But even though superstition or enthusiasm should not put itself in direct opposition to morality; the very diverting of the attention, the raising up a new and frivolous species of merit, the preposterous distribution, which it makes of praise and blame; must have the most pernicious consequences, and weaken extremely men's attachment to the natural motives of justice and humanity.

Such a principle of action likewise, not being any of the familiar motives of human conduct, acts only by intervals on the temper, and must be rouzed by continual efforts, in order to render the pious zealot satisfied with his own conduct, and make him fulfil his devotional task. Many religious exercises are entered into with seeming fervour, where the heart, at the time, feels cold and languid: A habit of dissimulation is by degrees contracted: and fraud and falsehood become the predominant principle. Hence the reason of that vulgar observation, that the highest zeal in religion and the deepest hypocrisy, so far from being inconsistent, are often or commonly united in the same individual character

The bad effects of such habits, even in common life, are easily imagined: but where the interests of religion are concerned, no morality can be forcible enough to bind the enthusiastic zealot. The sacredness of the cause sanctifies every measure, which can be made use of to promote it.

The steady attention alone to so important an interest as that of eternal salvation is apt to extinguish the benevolent affections, and beget a narrow, contracted selfishness. And when such a temper is encouraged, it easily eludes all the general precepts of charity and benevolence.

Thus the motives of vulgar superstition have no great influence on general conduct; nor is their operation favourable to morality, in the instances, where they predominate.

Is there any maxim in politics more certain and infallible, than that both the number and authority of priests should be confined within very narrow limits, and that the civil magistrate ought, for ever, to keep his *fasces* and *axes* from such dangerous hands? But if the spirit of popular religion were so salutary to society, a contrary maxim ought to prevail. The greater number of priests, and their greater authority and riches will always augment the religious spirit. And though the priests have the guidance of this spirit, why may we not expect a superior sanctity of life, and greater benevolence and moderation, from persons who are set apart for religion, who are continually inculcating it upon others, and who must themselves imbibe a greater share of it? Whence comes it then, that in fact, the utmost a wise magistrate can propose with regard to popular religions, is, as far as possible, to make a saving game of it, and to prevent their pernicious consequences with regard to society? Every expedient which he tries for so humble a purpose is surrounded with inconveniencies. If he admits only one religion among his subjects, he must sacrifice, to an uncertain prospect of tranquillity, every consideration of public liberty, science, reason, industry, and even his own independency. If he gives indulgence to several sects, which is the wiser maxim, he must preserve a very philosophical indifference to all of them, and carefully restrain the pretensions of the prevailing sect; otherwise he can expect nothing but endless disputes, quarrels, factions, persecutions, and civil commotions.

True religion, I allow, has no such pernicious consequences: but we must treat of religion, as it has commonly been found in the world; nor have I any thing to do with that speculative tenet of Theism, which, as it is a species of philosophy, must partake of the beneficial influence of that principle, and at the same time must lie under a like inconvenience, of being always confined to very few persons.

Oaths are requisite in all courts of judicature; but it is a question whether their authority arises from any popular religion. 'Tis the solemnity and importance of the occasion, the regard to reputation, and the reflecting on the general interests of society, which are the chief restraints upon mankind. Custom-house oaths and political oaths are but little regarded even by some who pretend to principles of honesty and religion : and a Quaker's asseveration is with us justly put upon the same footing with the oath of any other person. I know, that POLYBIUS[1] ascribes the infamy of GREEK faith to the prevalency of the EPICUREAN philosophy; but 1 know also, that PUNIC faith had as bad a reputation in ancient times, as IRISH evidence has in modern : though we cannot account for these vulgar observations by the same reason. Not to mention, that GREEK faith was infamous before the rise of the EPICUREAN philosophy; and EURIPIDES,[2] in a passage which I shall point out to you, has glanced a remarkable stroke of satire against his nation, with regard to this circumstance.

Take care, PHILO, replied CLEANTHES, take care; push not matters too far : allow not your zeal against false religion to undermine your veneration for the true. Forfeit not this principle, the chief, the only great comfort in life ; and our principal support amidst all the attacks of adverse fortune. The most agreeable reflection, which it is possible for human imagination to suggest, is that of genuine Theism, which represents us as the workmanship of a Being perfectly good, wise, and powerful; who created us for happiness, and who, having implanted in us immeasureable desires of good, will prolong our existence to all eternity, and will transfer us into an infinite variety of scenes, in order to satisfy those desires, and render our felicity compleat and durable. Next to such a Being himself (if the comparison be allowed) the happiest lot which we can imagine, is that of being under his guardianship and protection.

These appearances, said PHILO, are most engaging and alluring ; and with regard to the true philosopher, they are more than appearances. But it happens here, as in the former case, that, with regard to the greater part of mankind, the appearances are deceitful, and that the terrors of religion commonly prevail above its comforts.

[1] Lib 6, cap 54   [2] Iphigenia in Tauride.

It is allowed, that men never have recourse to devotion so readily as when dejected with grief or depressed with sickness. Is not this a proof, that the religious spirit is not so nearly allied to joy as to sorrow?

But men, when afflicted, find consolation in religion, replied CLEANTHES. Sometimes, said PHILO: but it is natural to imagine, that they will form a notion of those unknown beings, suitably to the present gloom and melancholy of their temper, when they betake themselves to the contemplation of them. Accordingly, we find the tremendous images to predominate in all religions; and we ourselves, after having employed the most exalted expressions in our description of the Deity, fall into the flattest contradiction, in affirming, that the damned are infinitely superior in number to the elect.

I shall venture to affirm, that there never was a popular religion, which represented the state of departed souls in such a light, as would render it eligible for human kind, that there should be such a state. These fine models of religion are the mere product of philosophy. For as death lies between the eye and the prospect of futurity, that event is so shocking to Nature, that it must throw a gloom on all the regions which lie beyond it; and suggest to the generality of mankind the idea of CERBERUS and FURIES; devils, and torrents of fire and brimstone.

It is true; both fear and hope enter into religion; because both these passions, at different times, agitate the human mind, and each of them forms a species of divinity, suitable to itself. But when a man is in a chearful disposition, he is fit for business or company or entertainment of any kind; and he naturally applies himself to these, and thinks not of religion. When melancholy, and dejected, he has nothing to do but brood upon the terrors of the invisible world, and to plunge himself still deeper in affliction. It may, indeed, happen, that after he has, in this manner, engraved the religious opinions deep into his thought and imagination, there may arrive a change of health or circumstances, which may restore his good humour, and raising chearful prospects of futurity, make him run into the other extreme of joy and triumph. But still it must be acknowledged, that, as terror is the primary principle of religion, it is the passion, which always predominates in it, and admits but of short intervals of pleasure.

Not to mention, that these fits of excessive, enthusiastic joy, by exhausting the spirits, always prepare the way for equal fits of superstitious terror and dejection; nor is there any state of mind so happy as the calm and equable. But this state, it is impossible to support, where a man thinks, that he lies, in such profound darkness and uncertainty, between an eternity of happiness and an eternity of misery. No wonder, that such an opinion disjoints the ordinary frame of the mind, and throws it into the utmost confusion. And though that opinion is seldom so steady in its operation as to influence all the actions; yet it is apt to make a considerable breach in the temper, and to produce that gloom and melancholy, so remarkable in all devout people.

It is contrary to common sense to entertain apprehensions or terrors, upon account of any opinion whatsoever, or to imagine that we run any risk hereafter, by the freest use of our reason. Such a sentiment implies both an *absurdity* and an *inconsistency*. It is an absurdity to believe that the Deity has human passions, and one of the lowest of human passions, a restless appetite for applause. It is an inconsistency to believe, that, since the Deity has this human passion, he has not others also; and, in particular, a disregard to the opinions of creatures, so much inferior.

To know God, says Seneca, *is to worship him.* All other worship is indeed absurd, superstitious, and even impious. It degrades him to the low condition of mankind, who are delighted with intreaty, solicitation, presents, and flattery. Yet is this impiety the smallest of which superstition is guilty. Commonly, it depresses the Deity far below the condition of mankind; and represents him as a capricious dæmon, who exercises his power without reason and without humanity! And were that divine Being disposed to be offended at the vices and follies of silly mortals, who are his own workmanship; ill would it surely fare with the votaries of most popular superstitions. Nor would any of the human race merit his *favour*, but a very few, the philosophical Theists, who entertain, or rather indeed endeavour to entertain, suitable notions of his divine perfections: as the only persons, intitled to his *compassion* and *indulgence*, would be the philosophical Sceptics, a sect almost equally rare, who, from a natural diffidence of their own capacity, suspend, or endeavour to suspend all judgement with regard to such sublime and such extraordinary subjects.

If the whole of Natural Theology, as some people seem to maintain, resolves itself into one simple, though somewhat ambiguous, at least undefined proposition, *That the cause or causes of order in the universe probably bear some remote analogy to human intelligence* · If this proposition be not capable of extension, variation, or more particular explication: If it affords no inference that affects human life, or can be the source of any action or forbearance: And if the analogy, imperfect as it is, can be carried no farther than to the human intelligence; and cannot be transferred, with any appearance of probability, to the qualities of the mind: If this really be the case, what can the most inquisitive, contemplative, and religious man do more than give a plain, philosophical assent to the proposition, as often as it occurs; and believe that the arguments, on which it is established, exceed the objections, which lie against it? Some astonishment indeed will naturally arise from the greatness of the object: Some melancholy from its obscurity: Some contempt of human reason, that it can give no solution more satisfactory with regard to so extraordinary and magnificent a question. But believe me, CLEANTHES, the most natural sentiment, which a well-disposed mind will feel on this occasion, is a longing desire and expectation, that heaven would be pleased to dissipate, at least alleviate this profound ignorance, by affording some particular revelation to mankind, and making discoveries of the nature, attributes, and operations of the divine object of our faith. A person, seasoned with a just sense of the imperfections of natural reason, will fly to revealed truth with the greatest avidity: While the haughty Dogmatist, persuaded, that he can erect a complete system of Theology by the mere help of philosophy, disdains any farther aid, and rejects this adventitious instructor. To be a philosophical Sceptic is, in a man of letters, the first and most essential step towards being a sound, believing Christian; a proposition, which I would willingly recommend to the attention of PAMPHILUS: And I hope CLEANTHES will forgive me for interposing so far in the education and instruction of his pupil.

CLEANTHES and PHILO pursued not this conversation much farther; and as nothing ever made greater impression on me, than all the reasonings of that day; so I confess, that, upon a serious review of the whole, I cannot but think, that PHILO's principles are more probable than DEMEA's; but that those of CLEANTHES approach still nearer to the truth.

INDEX

TO

THE SECOND VOLUME.

s. refers to the Sections of the Introduction; p to the Pages of Hume's text;
f means 'and following sections' or 'pages.'

LONDON PRINTED BY
SPOTTISWOODE AND CO, NEW-STREET SQUARE
AND PARLIAMENT STREET

THE

PHILOSOPHICAL WORKS

OF

DAVID HUME

VOL II.

LONDON PRINTED BY
SPOTTISWOODE AND CO, NEW-STREET SQUARE
AND PARLIAMENT STREET

THE

PHILOSOPHICAL WORKS

OF

DAVID HUME

EDITED BY

T. H. GREEN   AND   T. H. GROSE

LATE FELLOW AND TUTOR OF BALLIOL   FELLOW AND TUTOR OF QUEEN'S
COLLEGE, OXFORD   COLLEGE, OXFORD

IN FOUR VOLUMES

VOL II

NEW EDITION

LONDON

LONGMANS, GREEN, AND CO.

1882

Catalogue of Books

PUBLISHED BY

MESSRS. LONGMANS, GREEN, & CO.

39 PATERNOSTER ROW, LONDON, E.C.

———◆———

Abbott.—*THE ELEMENTS OF LOGIC* By T. K ABBOTT, B.D 12mo 2s 6d sewed, or 3s cloth.

Acton. — *MODERN COOKERY FOR PRIVATE FAMILIES*, reduced to a System of Easy Practice in a Series of carefully tested Receipts By ELIZA ACTON With upwards of 150 Woodcuts. Fcp. 8vo. 4s 6d.

Æschylus. — *THE EUMENIDES OF ÆSCHYLUS*· a Critical Edition, with Metrical English Translation. By JOHN F DAVIES, M A Univ. Dub Lit D. Q.U.I. F.R.U I Professor of Latin in the Queen's College, Galway 8vo 7s.

A. K. H. B.—*THE ESSAYS AND CONTRIBUTIONS OF A K. H B*—Uniform Cabinet Editions in crown 8vo.

Autumn Holidays of a Country Parson, 3s. 6d

Changed Aspects of Unchanged Truths, 3s. 6d.

Commonplace Philosopher, 3s. 6d.

Counsel and Comfort from a City Pulpit, 3s. 6d.

Critical Essays of a Country Parson, 3s. 6d.

Graver Thoughts of a Country Parson. Three Series, 3s 6d each.

Landscapes, Churches, and Moralities, 3s 6d

Leisure Hours in Town, 3s 6d.

Lessons of Middle Age, 3s 6d

Our Little Life Two Series, 3s. 6d. each

Present Day Thoughts, 3s. 6d

Recreations of a Country Parson. Three Series, 3s. 6d each

Seaside Musings, 3s 6d.

Sunday Afternoons in the Parish Church of a University City, 3s. 6d.

Aldridge. — *RANCH NOTES IN KANSAS, COLORADO, THE INDIAN TERRITORY AND NORTHERN TEXAS.* By REGINALD ALDRIDGE Crown 8vo. with 4 Illustrations engraved on Wood by G. Pearson, 5s.

Allen.—*FLOWERS AND THEIR PEDIGREES.* By GRANT ALLEN. With 50 Illustrations engraved on Wood. Crown 8vo. 5s.

Alpine Club (The).—*GUIDES AND MAPS.*

THE ALPINE GUIDE By JOHN BALL, M R I A. Post 8vo. with Maps and other Illustrations :—

THE EASTERN ALPS, 10s 6d

CENTRAL ALPS, including all the Oberland District, 7s 6d.

WESTERN ALPS, including Mont Blanc, Monte Rosa, Zermatt, &c. 6s. 6d.

THE ALPINE CLUB MAP OF SWITZERLAND, on the Scale of Four Miles to an Inch. Edited by R. C. NICHOLS, F R G S 4 Sheets in Portfolio, 42s. coloured, or 34s. uncoloured

ENLARGED ALPINE CLUB MAP OF THE SWISS AND ITALIAN ALPS, on the Scale of Three English Statute Miles to One Inch, in 8 Sheets, price 1s 6d each.

ON ALPINE TRAVELLING AND THE GEOLOGY OF THE ALPS. Price 1s. Either of the Three Volumes or Parts of the 'Alpine Guide' may be had with this Introduction prefixed, 1s. extra.

Amos.—*WORKS BY SHELDON AMOS, M.A.*

A PRIMER OF THE ENGLISH CONSTITUTION AND GOVERNMENT. Crown 8vo. 6s.

A SYSTEMATIC VIEW OF THE SCIENCE OF JURISPRUDENCE. 8vo, 18s.

A

Anstey.—*THE BLACK POODLE*, and other Stories. By F. ANSTEY, Author of 'Vice Versâ' With Frontispiece by G Du Maurier and Initial Letters by the Author. Crown 8vo 6s.

Antinous.—An Historical Romance of the Roman Empire By GEORGE TAYLOR (Professor HAUSRATH). Translated from the German by J. D. M. Crown 8vo. 6s.

Aristophanes.—*THE ACHARNIANS OF ARISTOPHANES.* Translated into English Verse by ROBERT YELVERTON TYRRELL, M A. Dublin. Crown 8vo. 2s. 6d.

Aristotle.—*THE WORKS OF.*

THE POLITICS, G Bekker's Greek Text of Books I III IV. (VII.) with an English Translation by W. E. BOLLAND, M.A. ; and short Introductory Essays by A. LANG, M A. Crown 8vo. 7s 6d

THE ETHICS ; Greek Text, illustrated with Essays and Notes By Sir ALEXANDER GRANT, Bart M.A LL D. 2 vols. 8vo. 32s

THE NICOMACHEAN ETHICS, Newly Translated into English By ROBERT WILLIAMS, Barrister-at-Law. Crown 8vo. 7s. 6d.

Arnold. — *WORKS BY THOMAS ARNOLD, D D. Late Head-master of Rugby School.*

INTRODUCTORY LECTURES ON MODERN HISTORY, delivered in 1841 and 1842 8vo 7s. 6d.

SERMONS PREACHED MOSTLY IN THE CHAPEL OF RUGBY SCHOOL. 6 vols. crown 8vo 30s or separately, 5s. each.

MISCELLANEOUS WORKS 8vo 7s. 6d.

Arnold.—*A MANUAL OF ENGLISH LITERATURE*, Historical and Critical By THOMAS ARNOLD, M.A. Crown 8vo. 7s. 6d.

Arnott.—*THE ELEMENTS OF PHYSICS OR NATURAL PHILOSOPHY* By NEIL ARNOTT, M D Edited by A BAIN, LL D and A. S. TAYLOR, M D F R S. Woodcuts. Crown 8vo. 12s. 6d.

Ashby. — *NOTES ON PHYSIOLOGY FOR THE USE OF STUDENTS PREPARING FOR EXAMINATION.* With 120 Woodcuts. By HENRY ASHBY, M D. Lond. Fcp. 8vo. 5s.

Bacon.—*THE WORKS AND LIFE OF.*

COMPLETE WORKS. Collected and Edited by R. L. ELLIS, M.A . J. SPEDDING, M.A. and D. D. HEATH. 7 vols. 8vo. £3. 13s. 6d.

LETTERS AND LIFE INCLUDING ALL HIS OCCASIONAL WORKS. Collected and Edited, with a Commentary, by J. SPEDDING. 7 vols. 8vo. £4. 4s.

THE ESSAYS , with Annotations. By RICHARD WHATELY, D.D., sometime Archbishop of Dublin. 8vo 10s 6d.

THE ESSAYS , with Introduction, Notes, and Index. By E. A. ABBOTT, D D. 2 vols. fcp. 8vo price 6s The Text and Index only, without Introduction and Notes, in 1 vol. fcp. 8vo. price 2s. 6d.

THE PROMUS OF FORMULARIES AND ELEGANCIES, illustrated by Passages from SHAKESPEARE By Mrs H. POTT. Preface by E A. ABBOTT, D.D 8vo. 16s

The BADMINTON LIBRARY

of Sports and Pastimes, edited by His Grace the DUKE OF BEAUFORT, K.G., assisted by ALFRED E T. WATSON. Dedicated to H R H. the Prince of Wales.

HUNTING By His Grace the DUKE OF BEAUFORT, K.G., and MOWBRAY MORRIS. With Contributions by the Earl of Suffolk and Berkshire, Rev. E. W. L. Davies, Digby Collins, and Alfred E T. Watson. With Coloured Frontispiece and 53 Illustrations by J. Sturgess, J Charlton, and Agnes M. Biddulph. Crown 8vo. 10s. 6d.

FISHING. By. H. CHOLMONDELEY-PENNELL, late H M Inspector of Sea Fisheries. With Contributions by the Marquis of Exeter, Henry R Francis, M A , Major John P Traherne, and G. Christopher Davies Fully Illustrated.

Vol. I Salmon, Trout, and Grayling. Crown 8vo. 10s 6d.

Vol. II Pike and other Coarse Fish. Crown 8vo. 10s. 6d.

Racing { Flat Racing The EARL OF SUFFOLK and W. G. CRAVEN Steeplechasing A COVENTRY and A. E. T. WATSON.
[*In the press*

Riding and Driving Riding (including Military Riding and Ladies' Riding) · R WEIR. Driving Major DIXON, with an Introduction by E. L. Anderson
[*In the press.*

*** Other volumes in preparation.

Bagehot.—WORKS BY WALTER BAGEHOT, M.A.

BIOGRAPHICAL STUDIES. 8vo 12s.

ECONOMIC STUDIES. 8vo. 10s. 6d.

LITERARY STUDIES. 2 vols 8vo. Portrait. 28s.

THE POSTULATES OF ENGLISH POLITICAL ECONOMY. Student's Edition With a Preface by Alfred Marshall, Professor of Political Economy, Cambridge Crown 8vo 2s. 6d.

Bagwell.—IRELAND UNDER THE TUDORS, with a Succinct Account of the Earlier History. Compiled from the State Papers and other authentic sources. By RICHARD BAGWELL, M A. Vols I and II From the first invasion of the Northmen to the year 1578. With Maps and Index 2 vols 8vo. 32s.
Vol. III., completing the work, is in preparation.

Bailey.—FESTUS, A POEM. By PHILIP JAMES BAILEY. Crown 8vo. 12s. 6d.

Bain.—WORKS BY ALEXANDER BAIN, LL.D.

MENTAL AND MORAL SCIENCE; a Compendium of Psychology and Ethics Crown 8vo. 10s. 6d.

THE SENSES AND THE INTELLECT. 8vo. 15s.

THE EMOTIONS AND THE WILL. 8vo. 15s.

PRACTICAL ESSAYS. Crown 8vo. 4s. 6d.

LOGIC, DEDUCTIVE AND INDUCTIVE. PART I Deduction, 4s. PART II. Induction, 6s. 6d.

JAMES MILL; a Biography. Crown 8vo. 5s.

JOHN STUART MILL, a Criticism, with Personal Recollections. Crown 8vo. 2s 6d.

Baker.—WORKS BY SIR SAMUEL W. BAKER, M.A.

EIGHT YEARS IN CEYLON. Crown 8vo Woodcuts. 5s.

THE RIFLE AND THE HOUND IN CEYLON. Crown 8vo. Woodcuts. 5s

Beaconsfield.—WORKS BY THE EARL OF BEACONSFIELD, K.G.

NOVELS AND TALES. The Hughenden Edition. With 2 Portraits and 11 Vignettes 11 vols Crown 8vo. 42s.
Endymion.

Lothair.	Henrietta Temple
Coningsby.	Contarini Fleming, &c.
Sybil.	Alroy, Ixion, &c.
Tancred	The Young Duke, &c.
Venetia	Vivian Grey, &c.

NOVELS AND TALES Cheap Edition, complete in 11 vols Crown 8vo 1s. each, sewed, 1s 6d. each, cloth.

SELECTED SPEECHES With Introduction and Notes, by T. E KEBBEL, M A. 2 vols. 8vo Portrait, 32s.

THE WIT AND WISDOM OF BENJAMIN DISRAELI, EARL OF BEACONSFIELD. Crown 8vo. 3s. 6d.

THE BEACONSFIELD BIRTHDAYBOOK With 2 Portraits and 11 Views of Hughenden Manor and its Surroundings. 18mo. 2s. 6d. cloth, gilt, 4s. 6d. bound.

Becker.—WORKS BY PROFESSOR BECKER, translated from the German by the Rev F. METCALFE

GALLUS; or, Roman Scenes in the Time of Augustus. Post 8vo. 7s. 6d.

CHARICLES, or, Illustrations of the Private Life of the Ancient Greeks Post 8vo. 7s. 6d.

Bent.—THE CYCLADES; or, Life among the Insular Greeks. By J. THEODORE BENT, B A Oxon; with Map. Crown 8vo. 12s. 6d.

Boultbee.—WORKS BY THE REV. T. P BOULTBEE, LL.D.

A COMMENTARY ON THE 39 ARTICLES of the Church of England. Crown 8vo 6s

A HISTORY OF THE CHURCH OF ENGLAND, Pre-Reformation Period 8vo. 15s.

Bourne.—WORKS BY JOHN BOURNE, C E.

A TREATISE ON THE STEAM ENGINE, in its application to Mines, Mills, Steam Navigation, Railways, and Agriculture. With 37 Plates and 546 Woodcuts. 4to. 42s.

CATECHISM OF THE STEAM ENGINE in its various Applications in the Arts, to which is now added a chapter on Air and Gas Engines, and another devoted to Useful Rules, Tables, and Memoranda. Illustrated by 212 Woodcuts. Crown 8vo. 7s. 6d. [Continued on next page.

Bourne. — *WORKS BY JOHN BOURNE, C E.*—continued.

HANDBOOK OF THE STEAM ENGINE, a Key to the Author's Catechism of the Steam Engine. With 67 Woodcuts Fcp. 8vo 9s.

RECENT IMPROVEMENTS IN THE STEAM ENGINE. With 124 Woodcuts. Fcp. 8vo. 6s.

EXAMPLES OF STEAM AND GAS ENGINES, with 54 Plates and 356 Woodcuts 4to. 70s

Brabourne.—*FRIENDS AND FOES FROM FAIRYLAND* By the Right Hon LORD BRABOURNE, Author of 'Higgledy-Piggledy,' 'Whispers from Fairyland,' &c With 20 Illustrations by Linley Sambourne Crown 8vo 6s.

Bramston & Leroy.—*HISTORIC WINCHESTER*, England's First Capital By A R BRAMSTON and A. C. LEROY. Cr 8vo 6s.

Brande's *DICTIONARY OF SCIENCE, LITERATURE, AND ART* Re-edited by the Rev. Sir G. W. Cox, Bart, M A. 3 vols. medium 8vo 63s.

Brassey. — *WORKS BY LADY BRASSEY.*

A VOYAGE IN THE 'SUNBEAM,' OUR HOME ON THE OCEAN FOR ELEVEN MONTHS With Map and 65 Wood Engravings. Library Edition, 8vo. 21s Cabinet Edition, crown 8vo 7s 6d. School Edition, fcp. 2s Popular Edition, 4to. 6d.

SUNSHINE AND STORM IN THE EAST, or, Cruises to Cyprus and Constantinople With 2 Maps and 114 Illustrations engraved on Wood. Library Edition, 8vo. 21s. Cabinet Edition, cr. 8vo. 7s 6d.

IN THE TRADES, THE TROPICS, AND THE 'ROARING FORTIES'; or, Fourteen Thousand Miles in the *Sunbeam* in 1883 With 292 Illustrations engraved on Wood from drawings by R T. Pritchett, and Eight Maps and Charts Édition de Luxe, imperial 8vo £3 13s 6d Library Edition, 8vo. 21s

Bray. — *PHASES OF OPINION AND EXPERIENCE DURING A LONG LIFE* an Autobiography By CHARLES BRAY, Author of 'The Philosophy of Necessity' &c. Crown 8vo. 3s. 6d.

Browne.—*AN EXPOSITION OF THE 39 ARTICLES*, Historical and Doctrinal. By E. H. BROWNE, D.D., Bishop of Winchester. 8vo. 16s.

Buckle.—*WORKS BY HENRY THOMAS BUCKLE.*

HISTORY OF CIVILISATION IN ENGLAND AND FRANCE, SPAIN AND SCOTLAND. 3 vols. crown 8vo. 24s.

MISCELLANEOUS AND POSTHUMOUS WORKS A New and Abridged Edition. Edited by GRANT ALLEN 2 vols crown 8vo. 21s.

Buckton.—*WORKS BY MRS. C. M. BUCKTON*

FOOD AND HOME COOKERY, a Course of Instruction in Practical Cookery and Cleaning With 11 Woodcuts. Crown 8vo 2s 6d.

HEALTH IN THE HOUSE · Twenty-five Lectures on Elementary Physiology. With 41 Woodcuts and Diagrams. Crown 8vo. 2s.

OUR DWELLINGS. Healthy and Unhealthy With 39 Illustrations. Crown 8vo. 3s. 6d.

Bull.—*WORKS BY THOMAS BULL, M.D.*

HINTS TO MOTHERS ON THE MANAGEMENT OF THEIR HEALTH during the Period of Pregnancy and in the Lying-in Room. Fcp. 8vo. 1s. 6d.

THE MATERNAL MANAGEMENT OF CHILDREN IN HEALTH AND DISEASE. Fcp. 8vo. 1s. 6d.

Cabinet Lawyer, The; a Popular Digest of the Laws of England, Civil, Criminal, and Constitutional. Fcp. 8vo 9s.

Carlyle. — *THOMAS AND JANE WELSH CARLYLE.*

THOMAS CARLYLE, a History of the first Forty Years of his Life, 1795–1835 By J A FROUDE, M.A With 2 Portraits and 4 Illustrations, 2 vols. 8vo. 32s.

THOMAS CARLYLE, a History of his Life in London from 1834 to his death in 1881. By JAMES A. FROUDE, M.A., with Portrait. 2 vols 8vo. 32s

LETTERS AND MEMORIALS OF JANE WELSH CARLYLE Prepared for publication by THOMAS CARLYLE, and edited by J A. FROUDE, M.A. 3 vols. 8vo 36s

Cates. — *A DICTIONARY OF GENERAL BIOGRAPHY.* Fourth Edition, with Supplement brought down to the end of 1884 By W L. R. CATES. 8vo. 28s cloth, 35s. half-bound russia.
The Supplement, 1881–4, 2s. 6d.

Chesney.—*WATERLOO LECTURES;* a Study of the Campaign of 1815. By Col. C. C. CHESNEY, R E. 8vo. 10s. 6d.

Cicero.—*THE CORRESPONDENCE OF CICERO.* a revised Text, with Notes and Prolegomena—Vol. I, The Letters to the end of Cicero's Exile. By ROBERT Y. TYRRELL, M A., Fellow of Trinity College, Dublin, 12s.

Coats.—*A MANUAL OF PATHOLOGY.* By JOSEPH COATS, M.D. Pathologist to the Western Infirmary and the Sick Children's Hospital, Glasgow. With 339 Illustrations engraved on Wood. 8vo. 31s. 6d.

Colenso.—*THE PENTATEUCH AND BOOK OF JOSHUA CRITICALLY EXAMINED.* By J. W. COLENSO, D.D, late Bishop of Natal. Crown 8vo. 6s.

Conder. — *A HANDBOOK TO THE BIBLE,* or Guide to the Study of the Holy Scriptures derived from Ancient Monuments and Modern Exploration. By F. R. CONDER, and Lieut. C. R CONDER, R.E. Post 8vo. 7s. 6d.

Conington. — *WORKS BY JOHN CONINGTON, M.A.*

THE ÆNEID OF VIRGIL. Translated into English Verse Crown 8vo. 9s.

THE POEMS OF VIRGIL. Translated into English Prose. Crown 8vo. 9s.

Conybeare & Howson. — *THE LIFE AND EPISTLES OF ST PAUL* By the Rev. W. J. CONYBEARE, M A, and the Very Rev. J. S. HOWSON, D D. Dean of Chester.

Library Edition, with Maps, Plates, and Woodcuts. 2 vols. square crown 8vo 21s.

Student's Edition, revised and condensed, with 46 Illustrations and Maps. 1 vol. crown 8vo. 7s. 6d.

Cooke. — *TABLETS OF ANATOMY.* By THOMAS COOKE, F.R C S Eng. B.A. B.Sc. M.D. Paris. Fourth Edition, being a selection of the Tablets believed to be most useful to Students generally. Post 4to. 7s 6d.

Cox. — *THE FIRST CENTURY OF CHRISTIANITY* By HOMERSHAM COX, M.A. 8vo 12s.

Cox.—*WORKS BY THE REV. SIR G. W. COX, BART., M.A.*

A GENERAL HISTORY OF GREECE from the Earliest Period to the Death of Alexander the Great; with a Sketch of the History to the Present Time. With 11 Maps and Plans. Crown 8vo. 7s. 6d.

LIVES OF GREEK STATESMEN. Vol I *SOLON-THEMISTOCLES;* Vol. II. *EPHIALTES-HERMOKRATES.* Fcp. 8vo. 2s. 6d. each.

*** For other Works, *see* 'Epochs of History,' p. 24.

Crawford.—*ACROSS THE PAMPAS AND THE ANDES.* By ROBERT CRAWFORD, M A With Map and 7 Illustrations. Crown 8vo. 7s. 6d.

Creighton. — *HISTORY OF THE PAPACY DURING THE REFORMATION.* By the Rev. M. CREIGHTON, M.A. Vols. I. and II. 8vo 32s.

Crookes. — *SELECT METHODS IN CHEMICAL ANALYSIS* (chiefly Inorganic). By WILLIAM CROOKES, F R S V P C S. With 37 Illustrations. 8vo. 24s

Crozier.—*CIVILIZATION AND PROGRESS;* being the Outline of a New System of Political, Religious, and Social Philosophy. By J. BEATTIE CROZIER 8vo 14s.

Crump.—*A SHORT ENQUIRY INTO THE FORMATION OF POLITICAL OPINION,* from the Reign of the Great Families to the Advent of Democracy. By ARTHUR CRUMP. 8vo 7s. 6d.

Culley.—*HANDBOOK OF PRACTICAL TELEGRAPHY* By R. S. CULLEY, M Inst. C.E. Plates and Woodcuts. 8vo. 16s.

Dante.—*THE DIVINE COMEDY OF DANTE ALIGHIERI* Translated verse for verse from the Original into Terza Rima. By JAMES INNES MINCHIN. Cr 8vo. 15s.

Davidson.—*AN INTRODUCTION TO THE STUDY OF THE NEW TESTAMENT.* Critical, Exegetical, and Theological By the Rev. S. DAVIDSON, D.D. LL.D. Revised Edition. 2 vols. 8vo. 30s.

Davidson.—*THE LOGIC OF DEFINITION EXPLAINED AND APPLIED* By WILLIAM L. DAVIDSON, M.A. Crown 8vo 6s.

Dead Shot, The, OR SPORTSMAN'S COMPLETE GUIDE; a Treatise on the Use of the Gun, with Lessons in the Art of Shooting Game of all kinds, and Wild-Fowl, also Pigeon-Shooting, and Dog-Breaking. By MARKSMAN. With 13 Illustrations. Crown 8vo 10s 6d

Decaisne & Le Maout. — A GENERAL SYSTEM OF BOTANY. Translated from the French of E. LE MAOUT, M D , and J. DECAISNE, by Lady HOOKER; with Additions by Sir J D HOOKER, C.B F.R.S. Imp. 8vo. with 5,500 Woodcuts, 31s. 6d.

Dent. — ABOVE THE SNOW LINE: Mountaineering Sketches between 1870 and 1880. By CLINTON DENT, Vice-President of the Alpine Club. With Two Engravings by Edward Whymper and an Illustration by Percy Macquoid. Crown 8vo. 7s. 6d

D'Eon de Beaumont. — THE STRANGE CAREER OF THE CHEVALIER D'EON DE BEAUMONT, Minister Pleni-potentiary from France to Great Britain in 1763. By Captain J. BUCHAN TELFER, R.N F S.A. F. R.G S. With 3 Portraits 8vo 12s.

De Tocqueville. — DEMOCRACY IN AMERICA By ALEXIS DE TOCQUE-VILLE. Translated by H. REEVE, C B. 2 vols. crown 8vo. 16s.

Dewes. — THE LIFE AND LETTERS OF ST. PAUL. By ALFRED DEWES. M A LL.D. D D Vicar of St. Augus-tine's, Pendlebury. With 4 Maps. 8vo 7s. 6d.

Dickinson. — ON RENAL AND URINARY AFFECTIONS By W HOWSHIP DICKINSON, M.D. Cantab F.R.C P &c. With 12 Plates and 122 Woodcuts. 3 vols. 8vo. £3 4s. 6d.

*** The Three Parts may be had sepa-rately PART I —Diabetes, 10s 6d. sewed, 12s. cloth PART II. Albuminuria, 20s sewed, 21s cloth. PART III.—Mis-cellaneous Affections of the Kidneys and Urine, 30s. sewed, 31s. 6d. cloth.

Dixon. — RURAL BIRD LIFE, Essays on Ornithology, with Instructions for Preserving Objects relating to that Science. By CHARLES DIXON. With 45 Woodcuts. Crown 8vo. 5s.

Dowell. — A HISTORY OF TAXA-TION AND TAXES IN ENGLAND, FROM THE EARLIEST TIMES TO THE PRESENT DAY. By STEPHEN DOWELL, Assistant Solicitor of Inland Revenue. 4 vols. 8vo 48s.

Doyle. — THE OFFICIAL BARONAGE OF ENGLAND. By JAMES E DOYLE Showing the Succession, Dignities, and Offices of every Peer from 1066 to 1885 Vols I to III With 1,600 Portraits, Shields of Arms, Badges, and Auto-graphs. 3 vols 4to £5. 5s. Large Paper Edition, Imperial 4to. £15. 15s.

Dresser. — JAPAN; ITS ARCHITEC-TURE, ART, AND ART MANUFACTURES. By CHRISTOPHER DRESSER, Ph.D. F.L S &c With 202 Illustrations. Square crown 8vo 31s. 6d

Dunster. — HOW TO MAKE THE LAND PAY; or. Profitable Industries connected with the Land, and suitable to all Occupations, Large or Small. By HENRY P. DUNSTER, M.A. Crown 8vo. 5s.

Eastlake. — HINTS ON HOUSEHOLD TASTE IN FURNITURE, UPHOLSTERY, &c. By C. L. EASTLAKE, F R I B A. With 100 Illustrations. Square crown 8vo 14s.

Edersheim. — WORKS BY THE REV. ALFRED EDERSHEIM, D D.

THE LIFE AND TIMES OF JESUS THE MESSIAH 2 vols 8vo 42s.

PROPHECY AND HISTORY IN RELA-TION TO THE MESSIAH. the Warburton Lectures, delivered at Lincoln's Inn Chapel, 1880–1884. 8vo. 12s.

Edwards. — OUR SEAMARKS. By E. PRICE EDWARDS With numerous Illustrations of Lighthouses, &c engraved on Wood by G. H Ford. Crown 8vo. 8s. 6d.

Ellicott. — WORKS BY C. J. ELLICOTT, D.D., Bishop of Gloucester and Bristol.

A CRITICAL AND GRAMMATICAL COMMENTARY ON ST PAUL'S EPISTLES. 8vo. Galatians, 8s 6d. Ephesians, 8s. 6d. Pastoral Epistles, 10s. 6d. Philip-pians, Colossians, and Philemon, 10s. 6d. Thessalonians, 7s. 6d. I. Corinthians
[Nearly ready.

HISTORICAL LECTURES ON THE LIFE OF OUR LORD JESUS CHRIST. 8vo. 12s

English Worthies. Edited by AN-
DREW LANG, M A. Fcp. 8vo price
2s. 6d. each

DARWIN By GRANT ALLEN.

MARLBOROUGH. By GEORGE SAINTS-
BURY.

The following Volumes are in preparation —
Steele. By Austin Dobson
Sir T. More. By J. Cotter Morison
Wellington. By R. Louis Stevenson.
Lord Peterborough By Walter Besant.
Claverhouse. By Mowbray Morris
Laumer. By Canon Creighton.
Shaftesbury. By H. D Traill.
Garrick. By W H Pollock.
Admiral Blake By David Hannay.
Raleigh. By Edmund Gosse
Ben Jonson. By J. A Symonds.
Isaak Walton. By Andrew Lang.
Canning By Frank H Hill.

Epochs of Ancient History.
Edited by the Rev Sir G. W Cox, Bart.
M.A. and C SANKEY, M.A 10 vols.
fcp 8vo 2s 6d each *See* p. 24

Epochs of Modern History.
Edited by C. COLBECK, M A 17 vols.
fcp. 8vo. 2s. 6d each *See* p 24

Erichsen.—*WORKS BY JOHN ERIC
ERICHSEN, F.R.S.*

*THE SCIENCE AND ART OF SUR-
GERY*· Being a Treatise on Surgical Injuries, Diseases, and Operations. Illustrated by Engravings on Wood. 2 vols.
8vo. 42s. ; or bound in half-russia, 60s.

*ON CONCUSSION OF THE SPINE, NER-
VOUS SHOCKS,* and other Obscure Injuries
of the Nervous System in their Clinical
and Medico-Legal Aspects. Crown 8vo.
10s. 6d.

Evans.—*THE BRONZE IMPLEMENTS,
ARMS, AND ORNAMENTS OF GREAT
BRITAIN AND IRELAND.* By JOHN
EVANS, D C L LL.D. F.R.S. With
540 Illustrations. 8vo. 25s

Ewald. — *WORKS BY PROFESSOR
HEINRICH EWALD,* of Gottingen.

THE ANTIQUITIES OF ISRAEL
Translated from the German by H. S.
SOLLY, M.A. 8vo 12s. 6d.

THE HISTORY OF ISRAEL. Translated from the German Vols I.–V 8vo
63s. Vol. VI *Christ and his Times*, 8vo.
16s. Vol. VII. *The Apostolic Age*, 8vo.
21s.

Fairbairn.—*WORKS BY SIR W.
FAIRBAIRN, BART, C E*

*A TREATISE ON MILLS AND MILL-
WORK,* with 18 Plates and 333 Woodcuts.
1 vol. 8vo 25s.

*USEFUL INFORMATION FOR ENGI-
NEERS* With many Plates and Woodcuts. 3 vols crown 8vo. 31s 6d.

Farrar. — *LANGUAGE AND LAN-
GUAGES* A Revised Edition of *Chapters
on Language and Families of Speech.* By
F. W FARRAR, D D. Crown 8vo. 6s.

Fitzwygram. — *HORSES AND
STABLES.* By Major-General Sir F.
FITZWYGRAM, Bart. With 39 pages of
Illustrations. 8vo. 10s. 6d.

Fox.—*THE EARLY HISTORY OF
CHARLES JAMES FOX* By the Right
Hon. G. O. TREVELYAN, M P. Library
Edition, 8vo. 18s. Cabinet Edition,
cr 8vo. 6s.

Francis.—*A BOOK ON ANGLING;*
or, Treatise on the Art of Fishing in every
branch ; including full Illustrated Lists
of Salmon Flies. By FRANCIS FRANCIS.
Post 8vo. Portrait and Plates, 15s.

Freeman.—*THE HISTORICAL GEO-
GRAPHY OF EUROPE* By E A. FREE-
MAN, D.C.L. With 65 Maps. 2 vols.
8vo. 31s. 6d.

French. — *NINETEEN CENTURIES
OF DRINK IN ENGLAND,* a History.
By RICHARD VALPY FRENCH, D C L.
LL D. F S A ; Author of ' The History
of Toasting ' &c. Crown 8vo. 10s. 6d.

Froude.—*WORKS BY JAMES A.
FROUDE, M A.*

THE HISTORY OF ENGLAND, from
the Fall of Wolsey to the Defeat of the
Spanish Armada.
Cabinet Edition, 12 vols. cr 8vo. £3. 12s
Popular Edition, 12 vols cr 8vo. £2. 2s.

*SHORT STUDIES ON GREAT SUB-
JECTS.* 4 vols. crown 8vo 24s.

*THE ENGLISH IN IRELAND IN THE
EIGHTEENTH CENTURY.* 3 vols. crown
8vo. 18s.

*OCEANA, OR, ENGLAND AND HER
COLONIES* With 9 Illustrations. 8vo. 18s.

THOMAS CARLYLE, a History of the
first Forty Years of his Life, 1795 to
1835. 2 vols. 8vo 32s.

THOMAS CARLYLE, a History of His
Life in London from 1834 to his death in
1881. By JAMES A. FROUDE, M.A. with
Portrait engraved on steel. 2 vols. 8vo.
32s.

Ganot. — *WORKS BY PROFESSOR GANOT.* Translated by E. ATKINSON, Ph D. F C S.

ELEMENTARY TREATISE ON PHYSICS, for the use of Colleges and Schools. With 5 Coloured Plates and 898 Woodcuts. Large crown 8vo. 15*s.*

NATURAL PHILOSOPHY FOR GENERAL READERS AND YOUNG PERSONS. With 2 Plates and 471 Woodcuts. Crown 8vo 7*s* 6*d.*

Gardiner. — *WORKS BY SAMUEL RAWSON GARDINER, LL.D.*

HISTORY OF ENGLAND, from the Accession of James I to the Outbreak of the Civil War, 1603–1642 Cabinet Edition, thoroughly revised. 10 vols. crown 8vo. price 6*s* each

OUTLINE OF ENGLISH HISTORY, B.C. 55–A D. 1880 With 96 Woodcuts, fcp. 8vo. 2*s.* 6*d.*

*** For other Works, *see* 'Epochs of Modern History,' p 24

Garrod. — *WORKS BY ALFRED BARING GARROD, M.D. F.R.S*

A TREATISE ON GOUT AND RHEUMATIC GOUT (RHEUMATOID ARTHRITIS). With 6 Plates, comprising 21 Figures (14 Coloured), and 27 Illustrations engraved on Wood 8vo. 21*s.*

THE ESSENTIALS OF MATERIA MEDICA AND THERAPEUTICS. New Edition, revised and adapted to the New Edition of the British Pharmacopœia, by NESTOR TIRARD, M D. Crown 8vo. 12*s* 6*d.*

Garrod. — *AN INTRODUCTION TO THE USE OF THE LARYNGOSCOPE* By ARCHIBALD G GARROD, M A M R C.P. With Illustrations. 8vo. 3*s* 6*d.*

Goethe. — *FAUST* Translated by T. E WEBB, LL D 8vo 12*s* 6*d.*

FAUST A New Translation, chiefly in Blank Verse; with Introduction and Notes. By JAMES ADEY BIRDS, B A. F.G S. Crown 8vo 12*s* 6*d.*

FAUST. The German Text, with an English Introduction and Notes for Students By ALBERT M. SELSS, M.A. Ph D. Crown 8vo 5*s.*

Goodeve. — *WORKS BY T. M. GOODEVE, M A.*

PRINCIPLES OF MECHANICS. With 253 Woodcuts Crown 8vo 6*s.*

THE ELEMENTS OF MECHANISM.

Grant. — *WORKS BY SIR ALEXANDER GRANT, BART. LL D D C.L &c*

THE STORY OF THE UNIVERSITY OF EDINBURGH during its First Three Hundred Years. With numerous Illustrations. 2 vols. 8vo. 36*s.*

THE ETHICS OF ARISTOTLE. The Greek Text illustrated by Essays and Notes. 2 vols. 8vo. 32*s.*

Gray. — *ANATOMY, DESCRIPTIVE AND SURGICAL.* By HENRY GRAY, F.R S late Lecturer on Anatomy at St. George's Hospital. With 557 large Woodcut Illustrations Re-edited by T. PICKERING PICK, Surgeon to St. George's Hospital. Royal 8vo. 30*s*

Green. — *THE WORKS OF THOMAS HILL GREEN,* late Fellow of Balliol College, and Whyte's Professor of Moral Philosophy in the University of Oxford. Edited by R. L. NETTLESHIP, Fellow of Balliol College, Oxford. In 3 vols. Vol. I.—Philosophical Works. 8vo. 16*s.*

Greville. — *WORKS BY C C F. GREVILLE.* Edited by H REEVE, C B

A JOURNAL OF THE REIGNS OF KING GEORGE IV AND KING WILLIAM IV 3 vols. 8vo. 36*s.*

A JOURNAL OF THE REIGN OF QUEEN VICTORIA, from 1837 to 1852. 3 vols 8vo 36*s.*

Grimston. — *THE HON. ROBERT GRIMSTON* a Sketch of his Life. By FREDERICK GALE. With Portrait. Crown 8vo. 10*s.* 6*d.*

Gwilt. — *AN ENCYCLOPÆDIA OF ARCHITECTURE.* By JOSEPH GWILT, F.S.A. Illustrated with more than 1,100 Engravings on Wood. Revised, with Alterations and Considerable Additions, by WYATT PAPWORTH. 8vo 52*s* 6*d.*

Grove. — *THE CORRELATION OF PHYSICAL FORCES.* By the Hon. Sir W. R. GROVE, F.R.S. &c. 8vo. 15*s.*

Halliwell-Phillips. — *OUTLINES OF THE LIFE OF SHAKESPEARE* By J. O HALLIWELL-PHILLIPPS, F.R.S. Royal 8vo. 7*s.* 6*d.*

Hamilton. — *LIFE OF SIR WILLIAM R HAMILTON,* Kt LL D. D C.L M R I.A. &c. Including Selections from his Poems, Correspondence, and Miscellaneous Writings By the Rev. R. P. GRAVES, M.A. (3 vols) Vols I. and

Hartwig.—*WORKS BY DR. G. HARTWIG.*

THE SEA AND ITS LIVING WONDERS. 8vo. with many Illustrations, 10s 6d

THE TROPICAL WORLD. With about 200 Illustrations 8vo. 10s. 6d.

THE POLAR WORLD, a Description of Man and Nature in the Arctic and Antarctic Regions of the Globe. Maps, Plates, and Woodcuts. 8vo. 10s. 6d.

THE ARCTIC REGIONS (extracted from the 'Polar World'). 4to. 6d. sewed.

THE SUBTERRANEAN WORLD. With Maps and Woodcuts. 8vo. 10s. 6d.

THE AERIAL WORLD; a Popular Account of the Phenomena and Life of the Atmosphere. Map, Plates, Woodcuts. 8vo. 10s. 6d.

Harte.—*WORKS BY BRET HARTE.*

IN THE CARQUINEZ WOODS. Fcp. 8vo. 2s. boards, 2s. 6d. cloth.

ON THE FRONTIER. Three Stories 16mo. 1s.

BY SHORE AND SEDGE Three Stories. 16mo. 1s.

Hassall.—*WORKS BY ARTHUR HILL HASSALL, M.D.*

THE INHALATION TREATMENT OF DISEASES OF THE ORGANS OF RESPIRATION, including Consumption, with 19 Illustrations of Apparatus Cr. 8vo. 12s 6d.

SAN REMO, climatically and medically considered. With 30 Illustrations. Crown 8vo. 5s.

Haughton.—*SIX LECTURES ON PHYSICAL GEOGRAPHY*, delivered in 1876, with some Additions. By the Rev SAMUEL HAUGHTON, F.R.S. M D D C L. With 23 Diagrams. 8vo. 15s.

Havelock.—*MEMOIRS OF SIR HENRY HAVELOCK, K.C.B.* By JOHN CLARK MARSHMAN. Crown 8vo. 3s. 6d.

Haward.—*A TREATISE ON ORTHOPÆDIC SURGERY.* By J WARRINGTON HAWARD, F.R C S Surgeon to St. George's Hospital. With 30 Illustrations engraved on Wood. 8vo. 12s. 6d.

Helmholtz.—*WORKS BY PROFESSOR HELMHOLTZ.*

ON THE SENSATIONS OF TONE AS A PHYSIOLOGICAL BASIS FOR THE THEORY OF MUSIC Translated by A J. ELLIS, F.R.S. Royal 8vo. 28s.

POPULAR LECTURES ON SCIENTIFIC SUBJECTS. Translated and edited by EDMUND ATKINSON, Ph D. F.C.S. With a Preface by Professor TYNDALL, F.R S and 68 Woodcuts 2 vols. Crown 8vo. 15s. or separately, 7s. 6d. each.

Herschel.—*OUTLINES OF ASTRONOMY.* By Sir J. F. W HERSCHEL, Bart M.A. With Plates and Diagrams. Square crown 8vo 12s.

Hewitt.—*WORKS BY GRAILY HEWITT, M.D*

THE DIAGNOSIS AND TREATMENT OF DISEASES OF WOMEN, INCLUDING THE DIAGNOSIS OF PREGNANCY. New Edition, in great part re-written and much enlarged, with 211 Engravings on Wood, of which 79 are new in this Edition. 8vo 24s.

THE MECHANICAL SYSTEM OF UTERINE PATHOLOGY. With 31 Life-size Illustrations prepared expressly for this Work. Crown 4to. 7s 6d

Hickson.—*IRELAND IN THE SEVENTEENTH CENTURY*, or, The Irish Massacres of 1641-2, their Causes and Results. By MARY HICKSON With a Preface by J A. Froude, M.A 2 vols. 8vo. 28s.

Hiley.—*THE INSPIRATION OF SCRIPTURE* · an Examination into its Meaning, Origin, and Theories thereon. By the Rev R W HILEY, D.D., Vicar of Wighill, Yorkshire. Crown 8vo 2s. 6d.

Hobart.—*THE MEDICAL LANGUAGE OF ST. LUKE.* a Proof from Internal Evidence that St. Luke's Gospel and the Acts were written by the same person, and that the writer was a Medical Man. By the Rev. W. K. HOBART, LL.D. 8vo. 16s.

Holmes.—*A SYSTEM OF SURGERY*, Theoretical and Practical, in Treatises by various Authors. Edited by TIMOTHY HOLMES, M A. and J. W. HULKE, F.R S. 3 vols. royal 8vo. £4. 4s.

Homer.—*THE ILIAD OF HOMER*, Homometrically translated by C. B CAYLEY. 8vo. 12s 6d

THE ILIAD OF HOMER. The Greek Text, with a Verse Translation, by W. C. GREEN, M A. Vol. I. Books I.–XII. Crown 8vo. 6s.

Hopkins.—*CHRIST THE CONSOLER;* a Book of Comfort for the Sick By ELLICE HOPKINS. Fcp. 8vo. 2s 6d

Horses and Roads; or How to Keep a Horse Sound on His Legs. By FREE-LANCE. Crown 8vo. 6s.

Hort.—*THE NEW PANTHEON*, or an Introduction to the Mythology of the Ancients By W. J. HORT 18mo. 2s. 6d.

Howitt.—*VISITS TO REMARKABLE PLACES*, Old Halls, Battle-Fields, Scenes illustrative of Striking Passages in English History and Poetry. By WILLIAM HOWITT With 80 Illustrations engraved on Wood. Crown 8vo. 7s. 6d.

Howley. — *THE OLD MORALITY, TRACED HISTORICALLY AND APPLIED PRACTICALLY* By EDWARD HOWLEY, Barrister-at-Law. With Frontispiece, Raffaelle's School at Athens Crown 8vo. 3s.

Hudson & Gosse.—*THE ROTIFERA OR 'WHEEL-ANIMALCULES'* By C. T. HUDSON, LL D. and P H GOSSE, F.R S. With 30 Coloured Plates. In 6 Parts 4to 10s 6d. each. [Pt 1 *now ready*

Hullah.—*WORKS BY JOHN HULLAH, LL D.*

COURSE OF LECTURES ON THE HISTORY OF MODERN MUSIC 8vo 8s 6d.

COURSE OF LECTURES ON THE TRANSITION PERIOD OF MUSICAL HISTORY 8vo. 10s. 6d.

Hume.—*THE PHILOSOPHICAL WORKS OF DAVID HUME* Edited by T. H GREEN, M A. and the Rev. T. H GROSE, M A 4 vols 8vo. 56s Or separately, Essays, 2 vols. 28s. Treatise of Human Nature. 2 vols. 28s.

In the Olden Time —A Novel. By the Author of 'Mademoiselle Mori.' Crown 8vo. 6s.

Ingelow.—*WORKS BY JEAN INGELOW*

POETICAL WORKS Vols 1 and 2 Fcp. 8vo. 12s. Vol 3. Fcp. 8vo 5s

THE HIGH TIDE ON THE COAST OF LINCOLNSHIRE With 40 Illustrations, drawn and engraved under the supervision of GEORGE T. ANDREW Royal 8vo 10s. 6d. cloth extra, gilt edges.

Jackson.—*AID TO ENGINEERING SOLUTION.* By LOWIS D'A. JACKSON, C E. With 111 Diagrams and 5 Woodcut Illustrations 8vo. 21s.

Jameson.—*WORKS BY MRS. JAMESON*

LEGENDS OF THE SAINTS AND MARTYRS. With 19 Etchings and 187 Woodcuts. 2 vols 31s. 6d.

LEGENDS OF THE MADONNA, the Virgin Mary as represented in Sacred and Legendary Art. With 27 Etchings and 165 Woodcuts. 1 vol. 21s.

LEGENDS OF THE MONASTIC ORDERS. With 11 Etchings and 88 Woodcuts. 1 vol. 21s.

HISTORY OF THE SAVIOUR, His Types and Precursors Completed by Lady EASTLAKE. With 13 Etchings and 281 Woodcuts. 2 vols 42s.

Jeans.—*ENGLAND'S SUPREMACY*. its Sources, Economics, and Dangers. By J. S. JEANS. 8vo. 8s 6d

Jefferies. — *RED DEER.* By RICHARD JEFFERIES. Crown 8vo. 4s. 6d.

Johnson.—*THE PATENTEE'S MANUAL*, a Treatise on the Law and Practice of Letters Patent, for the use of Patentees and Inventors By J JOHNSON and J. H JOHNSON. 8vo. 10s. 6d.

Johnston.—*A GENERAL DICTIONARY OF GEOGRAPHY*, Descriptive, Physical, Statistical, and Historical; a complete Gazetteer of the World. By KEITH JOHNSTON. Medium 8vo. 42s.

Jones — *THE HEALTH OF THE SENSES. SIGHT, HEARING, VOICE, SMELL AND TASTE, SKIN*, with Hints on Health, Diet, Education, Health Resorts of Europe, &c By H MACNAUGHTON JONES, M D Crown 8vo. 3s. 6d.

Jordan. — *WORKS BY WILLIAM LEIGHTON JORDAN, F.R.G.S.*

THE OCEAN a Treatise on Ocean Currents and Tides and their Causes 8vo 21s

THE NEW PRINCIPLES OF NATURAL PHILOSOPHY a Defence and Extension of the Principles established by the Author's treatise on Ocean Currents With 13 plates 8vo 21s.

THE WINDS an Essay in Illustration of the New Principles of Natural Philosophy. Crown 8vo 2s.

THE STANDARD OF VALUE. Crown 8vo. 5s.

Jukes.— *Works by Andrew Jukes.*

The New Man and the Eternal Life Crown 8vo. 6s.

The Types of Genesis. Crown 8vo. 7s 6d.

The Second Death and the Restitution of all Things. Crown 8vo. 3s. 6d.

The Mystery of the Kingdom. Crown 8vo. 2s. 6d.

Justinian.— *The Institutes of Justinian*, Latin Text, chiefly that of Huschke, with English Introduction, Translation, Notes, and Summary. By Thomas C. Sandars, M A. 8vo. 18s.

Kalisch. — *Works by M. M. Kalisch, M.A*

Bible Studies. Part I. The Prophecies of Balaam. 8vo. 10s. 6d. Part II. The Book of Jonah. 8vo. 10s. 6d.

Commentary on the Old Testament; with a New Translation. Vol. I Genesis, 8vo. 18s. or adapted for the General Reader, 12s. Vol. II Exodus, 15s. or adapted for the General Reader, 12s. Vol III. Leviticus, Part I. 15s. or adapted for the General Reader, 8s. Vol. IV. Leviticus, Part II. 15s. or adapted for the General Reader, 8s.

Hebrew Grammar. With Exercises. Part I 8vo. 12s 6d. Key, 5s. Part II. 12s. 6d.

Kant.— *Works by Emmanuel Kant.*

Critique of Practical Reason. Translated by Thomas Kingsmill Abbott, B.D. 8vo. 12s. 6d.

Introduction to Logic, and his Essay on the Mistaken Subtilty of the Four Figures. Translated by Thomas Kingsmill Abbott, B D With a few Notes by S. T. Coleridge. 8vo. 6s.

Kerl.—*A Practical Treatise on Metallurgy* By Professor Kerl. Adapted from the last German Edition by W. Crookes, F R.S. &c. and E. Rohrig, Ph.D. 3 vols. 8vo with 625 Woodcuts, £4. 19s.

Killick.— *Handbook to Mill's System of Logic* By the Rev. A. H. Killick, M.A. Crown 8vo. 3s. 6d.

Kolbe.—*A Short Text-book of Inorganic Chemistry.* By Dr Hermann Kolbe. Translated from the German by T. S Humpidge, Ph.D. With a Coloured Table of Spectra and 66 Illustrations. Crown 8vo. 7s. 6d.

Lang.— *Works by Andrew Lang, M.A. late Fellow of Merton College.*

Custom and Myth, Studies of Early Usage and Belief. With 15 Illustrations. Crown 8vo. 7s. 6d.

The Princess Nobody a Tale of Fairyland. After the Drawings by Richard Doyle, printed in colours by Edmund Evans. Post 4to. 5s. boards.

Latham.— *Works by Robert G. Latham, M A. M D*

A Dictionary of the English Language. Founded on the Dictionary of Dr Johnson. Four vols 4to £7.

A Dictionary of the English Language Abridged from Dr. Latham's Edition of Johnson's Dictionary. One Volume. Medium 8vo. 14s.

Handbook of the English Language. Crown 8vo. 6s.

Lecky.— *Works by W. E. H. Lecky.*

History of England in the 18th Century. 4 vols. 8vo. 1700–1784, £3 12s.

The History of European Morals from Augustus to Charlemagne. 2 vols. crown 8vo. 16s.

History of the Rise and Influence of the Spirit of Rationalism in Europe. 2 vols. crown 8vo. 16s.

Leaders of Public Opinion in Ireland. — Swift, Flood, Grattan, O'Connell. Crown 8vo. 7s. 6d.

Lewes.—*The History of Philosophy*, from Thales to Comte. By George Henry Lewes. 2 vols. 8vo. 32s.

Liddell & Scott. — *A Greek-English Lexicon* Compiled by Henry George Liddell, D D Dean of Christ Church ; and Robert Scott, D D Dean of Rochester. 4to 36s.

List.— *The National System of Political Economy.* By Friedrich List. Translated from the Original German by Sampson S. Lloyd, M.P. 8vo. 10s. 6d.

Little.— *On In-knee Distortion* (Genu Valgum) Its Varieties and Treatment with and without Surgical Operation. By W. J. Little, M D. Assisted by Muirhead Little, M.R.C.S. With 40 Illustrations. 8vo. 7s. 6d.

Liveing.— *WORKS BY ROBERT LIVE-ING, M.A. and M.D. Cantab.*

HANDBOOK ON DISEASES OF THE SKIN With especial reference to Diagnosis and Treatment Fcp 8vo. 5s

NOTES ON THE TREATMENT OF SKIN DISEASES. 18mo. 3s.

ELEPHANTIASIS GRÆCORUM, OR TRUE LEPROSY. Crown 8vo. 4s. 6d.

Lloyd.—*A TREATISE ON MAGNET-ISM,* General and Terrestrial By H. LLOYD, D.D. D.C.L. 8vo. 10s. 6d

Lloyd.—*THE SCIENCE OF AGRICUL-TURE.* By F. J. LLOYD. 8vo 12s

Longman.—*WORKS BY WILLIAM LONGMAN, F.S.A.*

LECTURES ON THE HISTORY OF ENGLAND from the Earliest Times to the Death of King Edward II. Maps and Illustrations. 8vo. 15s

HISTORY OF THE LIFE AND TIMES OF EDWARD III With 9 Maps, 8 Plates, and 16 Woodcuts 2 vols 8vo. 28s.

Longman.—*WORKS BY FREDERICK W. LONGMAN, Balliol College, Oxon.*

CHESS OPENINGS. Fcp. 8vo 2s 6d

FREDERICK THE GREAT AND THE SEVEN YEARS' WAR. With 2 Coloured Maps. 8vo. 2s. 6d

A NEW POCKET DICTIONARY OF THE GERMAN AND ENGLISH LAN-GUAGES Square 18mo. 2s. 6d.

Longman's Magazine. Published Monthly Price Sixpence
Vols. 1–6, 8vo price 5s each.

Longmore.— *GUNSHOT INJURIES;* Their History, Characteristic Features, Complications, and General Treatment By Surgeon-General T. LONGMORE, C.B. F.R.C.S With 58 Illustrations. 8vo. price 31s. 6d.

Loudon — *WORKS BY J. C. LOUDON, F.L.S*

ENCYCLOPÆDIA OF GARDENING; the Theory and Practice of Horticulture, Floriculture, Arboriculture, and Landscape Gardening. With 1,000 Woodcuts. 8vo. 21s.

ENCYCLOPÆDIA OF AGRICULTURE; the Laying-out, Improvement, and Management of Landed Property; the Cultivation and Economy of the Productions of Agriculture. With 1,100 Woodcuts. 8vo. 21s.

ENCYCLOPÆDIA OF PLANTS; the Specific Character, Description, Culture, History, &c. of all Plants found in Great

Lubbock.—*THE ORIGIN OF CIVILI-ZATION AND THE PRIMITIVE CONDITION OF MAN.* By Sir J LUBBOCK, Bart. M.P. F.R.S. 8vo. Woodcuts, 18s

Lyra Germanica ; Hymns Translated from the German by Miss C. WINKWORTH. Fcp. 8vo. 5s

Macalister.— *AN INTRODUCTION TO THE SYSTEMATIC ZOOLOGY AND MORPHOLOGY OF VERTEBRATE ANI-MALS.* By A. MACALISTER, M.D. With 28 Diagrams 8vo. 10s 6d.

Macaulay.—*WORKS AND LIFE OF LORD MACAULAY.*

HISTORY OF ENGLAND FROM THE ACCESSION OF JAMES THE SECOND
Student's Edition, 2 vols crown 8vo 12s.
People's Edition, 4 vols crown 8vo. 16s.
Cabinet Edition, 8 vols post 8vo. 48s.
Library Edition, 5 vols. 8vo. £4.

CRITICAL AND HISTORICAL ESSAYS, with LAYS of ANCIENT ROME, in 1 volume
Authorised Edition, crown 8vo. 2s. 6d. or 3s. 6d gilt edges
Popular Edition, crown 8vo 2s 6d.

CRITICAL AND HISTORICAL ESSAYS :
Student's Edition, 1 vol crown 8vo. 6s.
People's Edition, 2 vols crown 8vo. 8s.
Cabinet Edition, 4 vols. post 8vo. 24s.
Library Edition, 3 vols. 8vo 36s.

ESSAYS which may be had separately price 6d. each sewed, 1s. each cloth
Addison and Walpole.
Frederick the Great
Croker's Boswell's Johnson.
Hallam's Constitutional History.
Warren Hastings. 3d sewed, 6d cloth.
The Earl of Chatham (Two Essays).
Ranke and Gladstone
Milton and Machiavelli.
Lord Bacon.
Lord Clive.
Lord Byron, and The Comic Dramatists of the Restoration.

The Essay on Warren Hastings annotated by S. HALES, 1s 6d
The Essay on Lord Clive annotated by H. COURTHOPE-BOWEN, M.A. 2s. 6d.

SPEECHES ·
People's Edition, crown 8vo. 3s. 6d

MISCELLANEOUS WRITINGS
Library Edition, 2 vols. 8vo. Portrait, 21s.
People's Edition, 1 vol crown 8vo 4s. 6d

Macaulay—WORKS AND LIFE OF LORD MACAULAY—continued.

LAYS OF ANCIENT ROME, &c.

Illustrated by G. Scharf, fcp. 4to. 10s 6d.
——————— Popular Edition, fcp. 4to 6d. sewed, 1s. cloth.
Illustrated by J. R. Weguelin, crown 8vo. 3s. 6d cloth extra, gilt edges.
Cabinet Edition, post 8vo. 3s. 6d.
Annotated Edition, fcp. 8vo. 1s. sewed, 1s. 6d. cloth, or 2s. 6d. cloth extra, gilt edges.

SELECTIONS FROM THE WRITINGS OF LORD MACAULAY. Edited, with Occasional Notes, by the Right Hon G O TREVELYAN, M.P. Crown 8vo. 6s.

MISCELLANEOUS WRITINGS AND SPEECHES

Student's Edition, in ONE VOLUME, crown 8vo 6s.
Cabinet Edition, including Indian Penal Code, Lays of Ancient Rome, and Miscellaneous Poems, 4 vols post 8vo. 24s.

THE COMPLETE WORKS OF LORD MACAULAY Edited by his Sister, Lady TREVELYAN

Library Edition with Portrait, 8 vols demy 8vo £5.5s.
Cabinet Edition, 6 vols post 8vo £4. 16s.

THE LIFE AND LETTERS OF LORD MACAULAY. By the Right Hon. G. O. TREVELYAN, MP.

Popular Edition, 1 vol crown 8vo 6s.
Cabinet Edition, 2 vols. post 8vo. 12s.
Library Edition, 2 vls 8vo. with Portrait, 36s.

Macdonald.—WORKS BY GEORGE MACDONALD, LL D

UNSPOKEN SERMONS. Second Series. Crown 8vo. 7s. 6d

A BOOK OF STRIFE, IN THE FORM OF THE DIARY OF AN OLD SOUL Poems. 12mo. 6s.

HAMLET. A Study with the Text of the Folio of 1623. 8vo 12s.

Macfarren.—LECTURES ON HARMONY, delivered at the Royal Institution. By Sir G. A. MACFARREN. 8vo. 12s.

Mackenzie.—ON THE USE OF THE LARYNGOSCOPE IN DISEASES OF THE THROAT, with an Appendix on Rhinoscopy. By MORELL MACKENZIE, M.D Lond. With 47 Woodcut Illustrations. 8vo. 6s.

Macleod.—WORKS BY HENRY D. MACLEOD, M A.

PRINCIPLES OF ECONOMICAL PHILOSOPHY. In 2 vols Vol. I. 8vo. 15s. Vol. II. PART I 12s

THE ELEMENTS OF ECONOMICS. In 2 vols. Vol I crown 8vo 7s. 6d. Vol. II. crown 8vo

THE ELEMENTS OF BANKING. Crown 8vo 5s.

THE THEORY AND PRACTICE OF BANKING Vol. 1. 8vo. 12s. Vol. II.

ELEMENTS OF POLITICAL ECONOMY. 8vo 16s

Macnamara. — HIMALAYAN AND SUB-HIMALAYAN DISTRICTS OF BRITISH INDIA, their Climate, Medical Topography, and Disease Distribution By F N MACNAMARA, M D. With Map and Fever Chart. 8vo. 21s.

McCulloch. — THE DICTIONARY OF COMMERCE AND COMMERCIAL NAVIGATION of the late J R. McCULLOCH, of H.M. Stationery Office. Latest Edition, containing the most recent Statistical Information by A J. WILSON 1 vol. medium 8vo. with 11 Maps and 30 Charts, price 63s. cloth, or 70s strongly halfbound in russia

Mahaffy.—A HISTORY OF CLASSICAL GREEK LITERATURE By the Rev. J. P. MAHAFFY, M A Crown 8vo. Vol I. Poets, 7s. 6d. Vol. II Prose Writers, 7s 6d

Malmesbury. — MEMOIRS OF AN EX-MINISTER an Autobiography. By the Earl of MALMESBURY, G C B Cheap Edition. Crown 8vo 7s. 6d.

Manning.—THE TEMPORAL MISSION OF THE HOLY GHOST; or, Reason and Revelation. By H E MANNING, D.D Cardinal-Archbishop. Crown 8vo. 8s. 6d.

The Maritime Alps and their Seaboard. By the Author of 'Véra,' 'Blue Roses,' &c. With 14 Full-page Illustrations and 15 Woodcuts in the Text. 8vo. 21s.

Martineau—WORKS BY JAMES MARTINEAU, D D

HOURS OF THOUGHT ON SACRED THINGS. Two Volumes of Sermons. 2 vols. crown 8vo. 7s. 6d each.

ENDEAVOURS AFTER THE CHRISTIAN LIFE. Discourses Crown 8vo. 7s. 6d.

Maunder's Treasuries.

BIOGRAPHICAL TREASURY. Reconstructed, revised, and brought down to the year 1882, by W. L. R. CATES. Fcp. 8vo. 6s.

TREASURY OF NATURAL HISTORY, or, Popular Dictionary of Zoology. Fcp. 8vo. with 900 Woodcuts, 6s.

TREASURY OF GEOGRAPHY, Physical, Historical, Descriptive, and Political With 7 Maps and 16 Plates. Fcp. 8vo. 6s.

HISTORICAL TREASURY: Outlines of Universal History, Separate Histories of all Nations. Revised by the Rev. Sir G. W. Cox, Bart. M.A. Fcp 8vo 6s.

TREASURY OF KNOWLEDGE AND LIBRARY OF REFERENCE. Comprising an English Dictionary and Grammar, Universal Gazetteer, Classical Dictionary, Chronology, Law Dictionary, &c. Fcp. 8vo. 6s

SCIENTIFIC AND LITERARY TREASURY a Popular Encyclopædia of Science, Literature, and Art. Fcp. 8vo. 6s.

THE TREASURY OF BIBLE KNOWLEDGE, being a Dictionary of the Books, Persons, Places, Events, and other matters of which mention is made in Holy Scripture. By the Rev J AYRE, M A. With 5 Maps, 15 Plates, and 300 Woodcuts. Fcp. 8vo. 6s.

THE TREASURY OF BOTANY, or Popular Dictionary of the Vegetable Kingdom Edited by J. LINDLEY, F R S. and T. MOORE, F.L.S. With 274 Woodcuts and 20 Steel Plates. Two Parts, fcp. 8vo. 12s.

Maxwell.—*DON JOHN OF AUSTRIA,* or, Passages from the History of the Sixteenth Century, 1547–1578. By the late Sir WILLIAM STIRLING MAXWELL, Bart K T With numerous Illustrations engraved on Wood Library Edition. 2 vols. royal 8vo 42s.

May—*WORKS BY THE RIGHT HON. SIR THOMAS ERSKINE MAY, K.C B.*

THE CONSTITUTIONAL HISTORY OF ENGLAND SINCE THE ACCESSION OF GEORGE III 1760–1870. 3 vols. crown 8vo. 18s.

DEMOCRACY IN EUROPE, a History. 2 vols. 8vo. 32s.

Melville.—*THE NOVELS OF G. J WHITE MELVILLE.* 1s each, sewed; or 1s. 6d cloth.

The Gladiators.	Holmby House.
The Interpreter.	Kate Coventry.
Good for Nothing.	Digby Grand

Mendelssohn.—*THE LETTERS OF FELIX MENDELSSOHN.* Translated by Lady WALLACE. 2 vols. crown 8vo. 10s.

Merivale.—*WORKS BY THE VERY REV. CHARLES MERIVALE, D.D. Dean of Ely.*

HISTORY OF THE ROMANS UNDER THE EMPIRE. 8 vols. post 8vo 48s.

THE FALL OF THE ROMAN REPUBLIC: a Short History of the Last Century of the Commonwealth. 12mo 7s. 6d.

GENERAL HISTORY OF ROME FROM B C. 753 TO A.D. 476. Crown 8vo. 7s. 6d.

THE ROMAN TRIUMVIRATES. With Maps. Fcp 8vo 2s. 6d

Miles. — *WORKS BY WILLIAM MILES.*

THE HORSE'S FOOT, AND HOW TO KEEP IT SOUND. Imp. 8vo 12s. 6d.

STABLES AND STABLE FITTINGS. Imp. 8vo with 13 Plates 15s

REMARKS ON HORSES' TEETH, addressed to Purchasers. Post 8vo. 1s. 6d.

PLAIN TREATISE ON HORSE-SHOEING. Post 8vo. Woodcuts, 2s. 6d.

Mill.—*ANALYSIS OF THE PHENOMENA OF THE HUMAN MIND* By JAMES MILL. With Notes, Illustrative and Critical. 2vols. 8vo. 28s.

Mill.— *WORKS BY JOHN STUART MILL.*

PRINCIPLES OF POLITICAL ECONOMY. Library Edition, 2vols. 8vo 30s. People's Edition, vol crown 8vo. 5s.

A SYSTEM OF LOGIC, Ratiocinative and Inductive. Library Edition, 2vols. 8vo. 25s. People's Edition, crown 8vo. 5s.

ON LIBERTY. Crown 8vo 1s. 4d.

ON REPRESENTATIVE GOVERNMENT. Crown 8vo. 2s

AUTOBIOGRAPHY, 8vo. 7s. 6d.

ESSAYS ON SOME UNSETTLED QUESTIONS OF POLITICAL ECONOMY. 8vo. 6s 6d.

UTILITARIANISM. 8vo 5s.

THE SUBJECTION OF WOMEN Crown 8vo 6s.

EXAMINATION OF SIR WILLIAM HAMILTON'S PHILOSOPHY 8vo. 16s

DISSERTATIONS AND DISCUSSIONS. 4 vols 8. £2 6s 6d.

NATURE, THE UTILITY OF RELIGION, AND THEISM. Three Essays. 8vo.

Miller.—*Works by W. Allen Miller, M.D. LL.D.*

The Elements of Chemistry, Theoretical and Practical. Re-edited, with Additions, by H. Macleod, F.C.S. 3 vols 8vo.

Part I CHEMICAL PHYSICS, 16s.
Part II. INORGANIC CHEMISTY, 24s.
Part III. ORGANIC CHEMISTRY, 31s. 6d.

An Introduction to the Study of Inorganic Chemistry. With 71 Woodcuts. Fcp. 8vo. 3s 6d.

Miller.—*Readings in Social Economy.* By Mrs. F. Fenwick Miller. Crown 8vo. 2s.

Mitchell.—*A Manual of Practical Assaying.* By John Mitchell, F.C.S Revised, with the Recent Discoveries incorporated. By W. Crookes, F.R.S 8vo Woodcuts, 31s 6d

Modern Novelist's Library (The). Price 2s. each boards, or 2s. 6d. each cloth :—
By the Earl of Beaconsfield, K.G.

Endymion.

Lothair.	Henrietta Temple.
Coningsby.	Contarini Fleming, &c.
Sybil.	Alroy, Ixion, &c
Tancred.	The Young Duke, &c.
Venetia.	Vivian Grey.

By Mrs. OLIPHANT.
  In Trust.

By JAMES PAYN
  Thicker than Water

By BRET HARTE.
  In the Caiquinez Wods.

By ANTHONY TROLLOPE.
  Barchester Towers.
  The Warden.

By VARIOUS WRITERS
  The Atelier du Lys. By the Author of 'Mademoiselle Mori.'
  Atherstone Priory. By N. Comyn.
  The Burgomaster's Family. By E. C. W Van Walrée.
  Elsa and her Vulture. By W. Van Hillern.
  Mademoiselle Mori By the Author of 'The Atelier du Lys.'
  The Six Sisters of the Valley By Rev. W. Bramley-Moore, M A.
  Unawares By the Author of The Rose-Garden.'

Monsell.—*Spiritual Songs for the Sundays and Holidays throughout the Year.* By J. S. B. Monsell, LL D. Fcp 8vo. 5s. 18mo. 2s

Moore.—*Lalla Rookh* By Thomas Moore Tenniel's Edition, with 68 Woodcut Illustrations. Crown 8vo. 10s. 6d.

Morehead.—*Clinical Researches on Disease in India.* By Charles Morehead, M D. Surgeon to the Jamsetjee Jcejeebhoy Hospital. 8vo. 21s.

Mozley.—*Works by the Rev. Thomas Mozley, M A.*

Reminiscences chiefly of Oriel College and the Oxford Movement. 2 vols crown 8vo. 18s.

Reminiscences chiefly of Towns, Villages, and Schools. 2 vols. crown 8vo. 18s.

Mulhall.—*History of Prices since the Year 1850.* By Michael G. Mulhall. Crown 8vo. 6s.

Müller.—*Works by F. Max Muller, M.A.*

Biographical Essays. Crown 8vo. 7s. 6d.

Selected Essays on Language, Mythology and Religion. 2 vols. crown 8vo. 16s.

Lectures on the Science of Language. 2 vols crown 8vo 16s.

India, What Can it Teach Us? A Course of Lectures delivered before the University of Cambridge. 8vo. 12s 6d.

Hibbert Lectures on the Origin and Growth of Religion, as illustrated by the Religions of India Crown 8vo. 7s 6d

Introduction to the Science of Religion Four Lectures delivered at the Royal Institution. Crown 8vo. 7s. 6d

A Sanskrit Grammar for Beginners, in Devanagari and Roman Letters throughout. Royal 8vo. 7s. 6d.

Murchison.—*Works by Charles Murchison, M D. LL D. &c.*

A Treatise on the Continued Fevers of Great Britain. Revised by W. Cayley, M D. Physician to the Middlesex Hospital. 8vo. with numerous Illustrations, 25s.

Clinical Lectures on Diseases of the Liver, Jaundice, and Abdominal Dropsy Revised by T Lauder Brunton, M.D. and Sir Joseph Fayrer, M.D. 8vo. with 43 Illustrations, 24s.

Neison.—*THE MOON*, and the Condition and Configurations of its Surface By E. NEISON, F.R.A.S. With 26 Maps and 5 Plates. Medium 8vo. 31s. 6d.

Nevile.—*WORKS BY GEORGE NEVILE, M.A.*

HORSES AND RIDING With 31 Illustrations. Crown 8vo 6s

FARMS AND FARMING. With 13 Illustrations. Crown 8vo. 6s

Newman.—*WORKS BY CARDINAL NEWMAN*

APOLOGIA PRO VITA SUA. Crown 8vo. 6s

THE IDEA OF A UNIVERSITY DEFINED AND ILLUSTRATED. Crown 8vo 7s

HISTORICAL SKETCHES. 3 vols. crown 8vo 6s. each

DISCUSSIONS AND ARGUMENTS ON VARIOUS SUBJECTS Crown 8vo. 6s.

AN ESSAY ON THE DEVELOPMENT OF CHRISTIAN DOCTRINE. Crown 8vo. 6s

CERTAIN DIFFICULTIES FELT BY ANGLICANS IN CATHOLIC TEACHING CONSIDERED. Vol 1, crown 8vo 7s 6d; Vol 2, crown 8vo. 5s. 6d.

THE VIA MEDIA OF THE ANGLICAN CHURCH, ILLUSTRATED IN LECTURES &c 2 vols. crown 8vo. 6s each.

ESSAYS, CRITICAL AND HISTORICAL. 2 vols crown 8vo. 12s

ESSAYS ON BIBLICAL AND ON ECCLESIASTICAL MIRACLES. Crown 8vo. 6s.

AN ESSAY IN AID OF A GRAMMAR OF ASSENT 7s. 6d.

New Testament (The) of our Lord and Saviour Jesus Christ Illustrated with Engravings on Wood after Paintings by the Early Masters chiefly of the Italian School. New and Cheaper Edition. 4to. 21s cloth extra, or 42s morocco.

Noble.—*THE RUSSIAN REVOLT* its Causes, Condition, and Prospects By EDMUND NOBLE. Fcp 8vo 5s.

Northcott.—*LATHES AND TURNING,* Simple, Mechanical, and Ornamental By W. H NORTHCOTT. With 338 Illustrations. 8vo 18s.

O'Hagan.—*SELECTED SPEECHES AND ARGUMENTS OF THE RIGHT HON. THOMAS BARON O'HAGAN.* Edited by GEORGE TEELING With Portrait 8vo. 16s

Oliphant.—*MADAM* A Novel. By Mrs OLIPHANT. Crown 8vo. 3s. 6d.

Overton.—*LIFE IN THE ENGLISH CHURCH (1660–1714).* By I H. OVER-

Owen.—*THE COMPARATIVE ANATOMY AND PHYSIOLOGY OF THE VERTEBRATE ANIMALS.* By Sir RICHARD OWEN, K.C.B &c. With 1,472 Woodcuts. 3 vols. 8vo. £3 3s. 6d.

Paget.—*WORKS BY SIR JAMES PAGET, BART F.R.S. D.C.L. &c.*

CLINICAL LECTURES AND ESSAYS. Edited by F HOWARD MARSH, Assistant-Surgeon to St. Bartholomew's Hospital. 8vo 15s.

LECTURES ON SURGICAL PATHOLOGY. Re edited by the AUTHOR and W. TURNER, M.B. 8vo. with 131 Woodcuts, 21s.

Pasolini. — *MEMOIR OF COUNT GIUSEPPE PASOLINI, LATE PRESIDENT OF THE SENATE OF ITALY* Compiled by his SON Translated and Abridged by the DOWAGER-COUNTESS OF DALHOUSIE. With Portrait 8vo. 16s.

Pasteur.—*LOUIS PASTEUR*, his Life and Labours By his SON-IN-LAW. Translated from the French by Lady CLAUD HAMILTON. Crown 8vo 7s. 6d.

Payn —*THE LUCK OF THE DARRELLS* a Novel. By JAMES PAYN, Author of 'By Proxy,' 'Thicker than Water,' &c. Crown 8vo. 3s. 6d

Pears.—*THE FALL OF CONSTANTINOPLE* being the Story of the Fourth Crusade By EDWIN PEARS, LL B. Barrister-at-Law, late President of the European Bar at Constantinople, and Knight of the Greek Order of the Saviour 8vo. 6s

Peel. — *A HIGHLAND GATHERING* By E. LENNOX PEEL With 31 Illustrations engraved on Wood by E. Whymper. Crown 8vo 10s. 6d.

Pennell.—'*FROM GRAVE TO GAY*' a Volume of Selections from the complete Poems of H CHOLMONDELEY-PENNELL, Author of Puck on Pegasus' &c. Fcp. 8vo. 6s.

Pereira.—*MATERIA MEDICA AND THERAPEUTICS.* By Dr. PEREIRA. Edited by Professor R. BENTLEY, M.R.C. F.L.S and by Professor T. REDWOOD, Ph D. F.C.S. With 126 Woodcuts, 8vo. 25s.

Perry.—*A POPULAR INTRODUCTION O THE HISTORY OF GREEK AND ROMAN SCULPTURE,* designed to Promote the knowledge and Appreciation of the Remains of Ancient Art. By WALTER C. PERRY. With 268 Illustrations.

Piesse.—*THE ART OF PERFUMERY*, and the Methods of Obtaining the Odours of Plants; with Instructions for the Manufacture of Perfumes, &c. By G W S. PIESSE, Ph D F.C.S With 96 Woodcuts, square crown 8vo. 21*s*.

Pole.—*THE THEORY OF THE MODERN SCIENTIFIC GAME OF WHIST.* By W. POLE, F R.S. Fcp. 8vo. 2*s*. 6*d*.

Pontalis.—*JOHN DE WITT, GRAND PENSIONARY OF HOLLAND*; or, Twenty Years of a Parliamentary Republic. By M ANTONIN LEFÈVRE PONTALIS Translated from the French by S. E and A. Stephenson. 2 vols 8vo. 36*s*.

Proctor.—*WORKS BY R. A. PROCTOR*

THE SUN, Ruler, Light, Fire, and Life of the Planetary System With Plates and Woodcuts Crown 8vo. 14*s*.

THE ORBS AROUND US; a Series of Essays on the Moon and Planets, Meteors and Comets. With Chart and Diagrams, crown 8vo 5*s*.

OTHER WORLDS THAN OURS, The Plurality of Worlds Studied under the Light of Recent Scientific Researches. With 14 Illustrations, crown 8vo. 5*s*.

THE MOON, her Motions, Aspects, Scenery, and Physical Condition. With Plates, Charts, Woodcuts, and Lunar Photographs, crown 8vo. 10*s* 6*d*.

UNIVERSE OF STARS, Presenting Researches into and New Views respecting the Constitution of the Heavens With 22 Charts and 22 Diagrams, 8vo. 10*s*. 6*d*.

LARGER STAR ATLAS for the Library, in 12 Circular Maps, with Introduction and 2 Index Pages. Folio, 15*s* or Maps only, 12*s* 6*d*.

NEW STAR ATLAS for the Library, the School, and the Observatory, in 12 Circular Maps (with 2 Index Plates). Crown 8vo. 5*s*

LIGHT SCIENCE FOR LEISURE HOURS, Familiar Essays on Scientific Subjects, Natural Phenomena, &c. 3 vols. crown 8vo. 5*s* each.

STUDIES OF VENUS-TRANSITS; an Investigation of the Circumstances of the Transits of Venus in 1874 and 1882. With 7 Diagrams and 10 Plates. 8vo 5*s*.

PLEASANT WAYS IN SCIENCE, with numerous Illustrations. Crown 8vo 6*s*

MYTHS AND MARVELS OF ASTRONOMY, with numerous Illustrations. Crown 8vo 6*s*.

The 'KNOWLEDGE' LIBRARY. Edited by RICHARD A. PROCTOR.

HOW TO PLAY WHIST· WITH THE LAWS AND ETIQUETTE OF WHIST. By R. A PROCTOR. Crown 8vo 5*s*.

HOME WHIST an Easy Guide to Correct Play By R A PROCTOR 16mo 1*s*

THE POETRY OF ASTRONOMY. A Series of Familiar Essays By R A. PROCTOR. Crown 8vo. 6*s*

NATURE STUDIES. Reprinted from *Knowledge* By GRANT ALLEN, A. WILSON, T. FOSTER, E. CLODD, and R. A. PROCTOR. Crown 8vo. 6*s*.

LEISURE READINGS. Reprinted from *Knowledge.* By E CLODD, A. WILSON, T FOSTER, A C. RUNYARD, and R. A. PROCTOR. Crown 8vo. 6*s*.

THE STARS IN THEIR SEASONS. An Easy Guide to a Knowledge of the Star Groups, in 12 Large Maps. By R. A. PROCTOR. Imperial 8vo. 5*s*

STAR PRIMER. Showing the Starry Sky Week by Week, in 24 Hourly Maps. By R A PROCTOR. Crown 4to 2*s*. 6*d*

THE SEASONS PICTURED IN 48 SUN-VIEWS OF THE EARTH, and 24 Zodiacal Maps, &c By R A PROCTOR. Demy 4to. 5*s*.

STRENGTH AND HAPPINESS. By R. A. PROCTOR. Crown 8vo. 5*s*

ROUGH WAYS MADE SMOOTH. A Series of Familiar Essays on Scientific Subjects. By R. A. PROCTOR. Crown 8vo. 6*s*.

OUR PLACE AMONG INFINITES A Series of Essays contrasting our Little Abode in Space and Time with the Infinites Around us. By R. A. PROCTOR Crown 8vo. 5*s*.

THE EXPANSE OF HEAVEN. A Series of Essays on the Wonders of the Firmament By R. A PROCTOR. Crown 8vo 5*s*.

Quain's Elements of Anatomy. The Ninth Edition. Re-edited by ALLEN THOMSON, M D. LL. D. F R S S L. & E. EDWARD ALBERT SCHAFER, F R S. and GEORGE DANCER THANE. With upwards of 1,000 Illustrations engraved on Wood, of which many are Coloured. 2 vols. 8vo. 18*s*. each.

Quain.—*A Dictionary of Medicine.* By Various Writers Edited by R. Quain, M D F R S &c. With 138 Woodcuts Medium 8vo 31s 6d. cloth, or 40s. half-russia, to be had also in 2 vols 34s. cloth.

Rawlinson. — *The Seventh Great Oriental Monarchy;* or, a History of the Sassanians. By G Rawlinson, M A. With Map and 95 Illustrations. 8vo. 28s.

Reader.—*Works by Emily E. Reader.*

Voices from Flower-Land, in Original Couplets. A Birthday-Book and Language of Flowers. 16mo 2s. 6d. limp cloth, 3s 6d. roan, gilt edges, or in vegetable vellum, gilt top.

Fairy Prince Follow-my-Lead, or, the *Magic Bracelet.* Illustrated by WM Reader Cr. 8vo. 5s. gilt edges; or 6s. vegetable vellum, gilt edges.

Reeve. — *Cookery and Housekeeping* By Mrs. Henry Reeve. With 8 Coloured Plates and 37 Woodcuts. Crown 8vo. 7s 6d

Rich.—*A Dictionary of Roman and Greek Antiquities.* With 2,000 Woodcuts By A Rich, B A Cr. 8vo 7s. 6d.

Rivers. — *Works by Thomas Rivers.*

The Orchard-House Crown 8vo. with 25 Woodcuts, 5s.

The Rose Amateur's Guide. Fcp. 8vo 4s 6d.

Robinson. — *The New Arcadia,* and other Poems By A. Mary F Robinson Crown 8vo. 6s.

Rogers.—*Works by Hy. Rogers.*

The Eclipse of Faith, or, a Visit to a Religious Sceptic Fcp. 8vo 5s.

Defence of the Eclipse of Faith. Fcp. 8vo. 3s 6d.

Roget. — *Thesaurus of English Words and Phrases.* By Peter M. Roget, M D. Crown 8vo 10s. 6d.

Ronalds. — *The Fly-Fisher's Entomology* By Alfred Ronalds. With 20 Coloured Plates. 8vo. 14s.

Salter.—*Dental Pathology and Surgery.* By S J. A. Salter, M B. F.R.S With 133 Illustrations 8vo 18s.

Schafer. — *The Essentials of Histology, Descriptive and Practical* For the use of Students By E. A Schafer, F R S. With 281 Illustrations. 8vo. 6s or Interleaved with Drawing Paper, 8s. 6d.

Schellen. — *Spectrum Analysis in its Application to Terrestrial Substances,* and the Physical Constitution of the Heavenly Bodies. By the late Dr H Schellen. Translated by Jane and Caroline Lassell. Edited, with Notes, by Capt. W. De W Abney, R E. Second Edition. With 14 Plates (including Ångström's and Cornu's Maps) and 291 Woodcuts 8vo 31s 6d

Seebohm.—*Works by Frederic Seebohm.*

The Oxford Reformers—John Colet, Erasmus, and Thomas More; a History of their Fellow-Work. 8vo. 14s.

The English Village Community Examined in its Relations to the Manorial and Tribal Systems, &c, 13 Maps and Plates. 8vo. 16s

The Era of the Protestant Revolution. With Map. Fcp 8vo. 2s. 6d.

Sennett. — *The Marine Steam Engine,* a Treatise for the use of Engineering Students and Officers of the Royal Navy. By Richard Sennett, Chief Engineer, Royal Navy. With 244 Illustrations. 8vo. 21s

Sewell. — *Stories and Tales.* By Elizabeth M. Sewell Cabinet Edition, in Eleven Volumes, crown 8vo 3s. 6d each, in cloth extra, with gilt edges —

> Amy Herbert.
> The Earl's Daughter.
> The Experience of Life
> A Glimpse of the World.
> Cleve Hall.
> Katharine Ashton.
> Margaret Percival.
> Laneton Parsonage.
> Ursula.
> Gertrude.
> Ivors.

Shakespeare. — *Bowdler's Family Shakespeare.* Genuine Edition, in 1 vol medium 8vo. large type, with 36 Woodcuts, 14s. or in 6 vols. fcp. 8vo 21s.

Outlines of the Life of Shakespeare. By J. O Halliwell-Phillipps, F.R S. Royal 8vo 7s 6d.

Short.—*Sketch of the History of the Church of England to the Revolution of 1688* By T. V Short, D.D Crown 8vo. 7s 6d

Simcox.—*A History of Latin Literature.* By G A. Simcox, M.A. Fellow of Queen's College, Oxford. 2 vols. 8vo. 32s.

Smith, Rev. Sydney.— THE WIT AND WISDOM OF THE REV. SYDNEY SMITH. Crown 8vo. 3s 6d.

Smith, R. Bosworth. — CARTHAGE AND THE CARTHAGINIANS By R. BOSWORTH SMITH, M.A. Maps, Plans, &c Crown 8vo. 10s. 6d.

Smith, R. A.—AIR AND RAIN; the Beginnings of a Chemical Climatology. By R A. SMITH, F.R.S 8vo. 24s.

Smith, James.—THE VOYAGE AND SHIPWRECK OF ST. PAUL By JAMES SMITH, of Jordanhill. With Dissertations on the Life and Writings of St. Luke, and the Ships and Navigation of the Ancients. With numerous Illustrations. Crown 8vo 7s. 6d.

Smith, T.—A MANUAL OF OPERATIVE SURGERY ON THE DEAD BODY By THOMAS SMITH, Surgeon to St. Bartholomew's Hospital. A New Edition, re-edited by W J WALSHAM. With 46 Illustrations. 8vo. 12s.

Smith, H. F.—THE HANDBOOK FOR MIDWIVES. By HENRY FLY SMITH, M.B. Oxon. M R C.S. late Assistant-Surgeon at the Hospital for Sick Women, Soho Square. With 41 Woodcuts. Crown 8vo. 5s.

Sophocles. — SOPHOCLIS TRAGŒDIÆ superstites; recensuit et brevi Annotatione instruxit GULIELMUS LINWOOD, M A. Ædis Christi apud Oxonienses nuper Alumnus. Editio Quarta, auctior et emendatior. 8vo. 16s.

Southey—THE POETICAL WORKS OF ROBERT SOUTHEY, with the Author's last Corrections and Additions. Medium 8vo. with Portrait, 14s.

Stanley. — A FAMILIAR HISTORY OF BIRDS. By E. STANLEY, D.D Revised and enlarged, with 160 Woodcuts. Crown 8vo. 6s.

Steel.—A TREATISE ON THE DISEASES OF THE OX, being a Manual of Bovine Pathology specially adapted for the use of Veterinary Practitioners and Students By J. H. STEEL, M.R C V S. F.Z S. With 2 Plates and 116 Woodcuts 8vo. 15s.

Stephen. — ESSAYS IN ECCLESIASTICAL BIOGRAPHY. By the Right Hon. Sir J STEPHEN, LL.D. Crown 8vo. 7s 6d

Stevenson.—WORKS BY ROBERT LOUIS STEVENSON.
A CHILD'S GARDEN OF VERSES Small fcp 8vo. 5s.
THE DYNAMITER. Fcp. 8vo. 1s. swd. 1s 6d. cloth.
STRANGE CASE OF DR JEKYLL AND MR HYDE. Fcp. 8vo 1s sewed; 1s. 6d. cloth.

'Stonehenge. '—THE DOG IN HEALTH AND DISEASE. By 'STONEHENGE.' With 78 Wood Engravings. Square crown 8vo. 7s 6d.
THE GREYHOUND. By 'STONEHENGE.' With 25 Portraits of Greyhounds, &c. Square crown 8vo. 15s.

Stoney. — THE THEORY OF THE STRESSES ON GIRDERS AND SIMILAR STRUCTURES With Practical Observations on the Strength and other Properties of Materials By BINDON B STONEY, LL D F.R.S. M.I.C.E. New Edition, Revised, with numerous Additions of Graphic Statics, Pillars, Steel, Wind Pressure, Oscillating Stresses, Working Loads, Riveting, Strength and Tests of Material. With 5 Plates, and 143 Illustrations in the Text Royal 8vo 36s.

Sully.—OUTLINES OF PSYCHOLOGY, with Special Reference to the Theory of Education By JAMES SULLY, M.A. 8vo. 12s. 6d.

Supernatural Religion ; an Inquiry into the Reality of Divine Revelation Complete Edition, thoroughly revised. 3 vols 8vo 36s.

Swinburne. — PICTURE LOGIC; an Attempt to Popularise the Science of Reasoning By A. J. SWINBURNE, B A Post 8vo. 5s.

Swinton. — THE PRINCIPLES AND PRACTICE OF ELECTRIC LIGHTING. By ALAN A. CAMPBELL SWINTON. With 54 Illustrations engraved on Wood. Crown 8vo. 5s.

Taylor.—AUTOBIOGRAPHY OF SIR HENRY TAYLOR, K.C M.G. 2 vols. 8vo. 32s

Taylor. — STUDENT'S MANUAL OF THE HISTORY OF INDIA, from the Earliest Period to the Present Time. By Colonel MEADOWS TAYLOR, C.S.I. Crown 8vo. 7s. 6d

Taylor.—THE COMPLETE WORKS OF BISHOP JEREMY TAYLOR. With Life by Bishop Heber Revised and corrected by the Rev. C. P. EDEN. 10 vols. £5 5s.

Text-Books of Science: a Series of Elementary Works on Science, adapted for the use of Students in Public and Science Schools. Fcp. 8vo. fully illustrated with Woodcuts. *See p. 23.*

'That Very Mab.' Fcp. 8vo 5*s*
*** A Critical and Satirical Romance, dealing with modern theology and philosophy, and social life and character.

Thompson.—*A System of Psychology* By Daniel Greenleaf Thompson. 2 vols 8vo 36*s*.

Thomson.—*An Outline of the Necessary Laws of Thought*, a Treatise on Pure and Applied Logic. By W. Thomson, D.D. Archbishop of York. Crown 8vo. 6*s*.

Thomson's Conspectus. New Edition *Adapted to the New Edition of the British Pharmacopœia* By Nestor Tirard, M.D. [*In preparation.*

Three in Norway. By Two of Them. With a Map and 59 Illustrations on Wood from Sketches by the Authors. Crown 8vo. 6*s*

Trevelyan. — *Works by the Right Hon G O Trevelyan, M P*

The Life and Letters of Lord Macaulay By the Right Hon G. O. Trevelyan, M P.
Library Edition, 2 vols 8vo. 36*s*
Cabinet Edition, 2 vols. crown 8vo. 12*s*
Popular Edition, 1 vol. crown 8vo. 6*s*.

The Early History of Charles James Fox Library Edition, 8vo 18*s*. Cabinet Edition, crown 8vo 6*s*

Tulloch. — *Movements of Religious Thought in Britain during the Nineteenth Century* being the Fifth Series of St. Giles' Lectures. By John Tulloch, D.D. LL D. 8vo 10*s*. 6*d*. half-bound, Roxburgh

Twiss.—*Works by Sir Travers Twiss*

The Rights and Duties of Nations, considered as Independent Communities in Time of War. 8vo. 21*s*

The Rights and Duties of Nations in Time of Peace. 8vo. 15*s*.

Tyndall. — *Works by John Tyndall, F.R.S &c.*

Fragments of Science 2 vols. crown 8vo. 16*s*

Heat a Mode of Motion. Crown 8vo. 12*s*.

Sound. With 204 Woodcuts. Crown 8vo. 10*s*. 6*d*.

Essays on the Floating-Matter of the Air in relation to Putrefaction and Infection With 24 Woodcuts. Crown 8vo. 7*s*. 6*d*.

Lectures on Light, delivered in America in 1872 and 1873. With 57 Diagrams Crown 8vo. 5*s*.

Lessons in Electricity at the Royal Institution, 1875-76. With 58 Woodcuts. Crown 8vo. 2*s*. 6*d*.

Notes of a Course of Seven Lectures on Electrical Phenomena and Theories, delivered at the Royal Institution Crown 8vo 1*s* sewed, 1*s*. 6*d* cloth.

Notes of a Course of Nine Lectures on Light, delivered at the Royal Institution. Crown 8vo. 1*s*. sewed, 1*s*. 6*d*. cloth.

Faraday as a Discoverer. Fcp. 8vo 3*s* 6*d*.

Ure.—*A Dictionary of Arts, Manufactures, and Mines.* By Dr. Ure. Seventh Edition, re-written and enlarged by R. Hunt, F R S With 2,064 Woodcuts. 4 vols. medium 8vo. £7. 7*s*.

Verney. — *Chess Eccentricities* Including Four-handed Chess, Chess for Three, Six, or Eight Players, Round Chess for Two, Three, or Four Players, and several different ways of Playing Chess for Two Players. By Major George Hope Verney. Crown 8vo 10*s*. 6*d*.

Verney.—*Cottier Owners, Little Takes, and Peasant Properties.* A Reprint of 'Jottings in France, Germany, and Switzerland By Lady Verney With Additions. Fcp 8vo. 1*s*. sewed.

Ville.—*On Artificial Manures*, their Chemical Selection and Scientific Application to Agriculture. By Georges Ville Translated and edited by W. Crookes, F.R.S With 31 Plates. 8vo. 21*s*.

Virgil.—*PUBLI VERGILI MARONIS BUCOLICA, GEORGICA, ÆNEIS ;* the Works of VIRGIL, Latin Text, with English Commentary and Index By B. H. KENNEDY, D D Crown 8vo 10s 6d.

THE ÆNEID OF VIRGIL Translated into English Verse. By J. CONINGTON, M A. Crown 8vo 9s.

THE POEMS OF VIRGIL. Translated into English Prose. By JOHN CONINGTON, M A Crown 8vo. 9s.

Walker.—*THE CORRECT CARD,* or, How to Play at Whist ; a Whist Catechism. By Major A CAMPBELL-WALKER, F R G.S. Fcp 8vo. 2s. 6d.

Walpole.—*HISTORY OF ENGLAND FROM THE CONCLUSION OF THE GREAT WAR IN 1815 TO THE YEAR 1841.* By SPENCER WALPOLE. 3 vols. 8vo. £2. 14s

Watson.—*LECTURES ON THE PRINCIPLES AND PRACTICE OF PHYSIC,* delivered at King's College, London, by Sir THOMAS WATSON, Bart. M D. With Two Plates. 2 vols. 8vo 36s.

Watt.—*ECONOMIC ASPECTS OF RECENT LEGISLATION* the Newmarch Memorial Essay By WILLIAM WATT, Fellow of the Statistical Society Cr 8vo 4s 6d.

Watts.—*A DICTIONARY OF CHEMISTRY AND THE ALLIED BRANCHES OF OTHER SCIENCES.* Edited by HENRY WATTS, F.R.S. 9 vols. medium 8vo £15. 2s. 6d

Webb.—*THE REV T W WEBB*

CELESTIAL OBJECTS FOR COMMON TELESCOPES Map, Plate, Woodcuts. Crown 8vo. 9s.

THE SUN With 17 Diagrams. Fcp. 8vo 1s.

Webb.—*THE VEIL OF ISIS ·* a Series of Essays on Idealism. By THOMAS W. WEBB, LL D 8vo. 10s. 6d

Wellington.—*LIFE OF THE DUKE OF WELLINGTON.* By the Rev. G. R. GLEIG, M A. Crown 8vo. Portrait, 6s.

West.—*WORKS BY CHARLES WEST,* M D &c. Founder of, and formerly Physician to, the Hospital for Sick Children.

LECTURES ON THE DISEASES OF INFANCY AND CHILDHOOD. 8vo. 18s

THE MOTHER'S MANUAL OF CHILDREN'S DISEASES Crown 8vo. 2s. 6d.

Whately.—*WORKS BY R WHATELY, D.D.*

ELEMENTS OF LOGIC. Crown 8vo. 4s. 6d.

ELEMENTS OF RHETORIC. Crown 8vo. 4s. 6d

LESSONS ON REASONING. Fcp. 8vo. 1s. 6d.

BACON'S ESSAYS, with Annotations. 8vo. 10s 6d.

Whately.—*ENGLISH SYNONYMS.* By E. JANE WHATELY. Edited by her Father, R. WHATELY, D.D Fcp. 8vo 3s

White and Riddle.—*A LATIN-ENGLISH DICTIONARY* By J T. WHITE, D D. Oxon. and J. J. E. RIDDLE, M A. Oxon. Founded on the larger Dictionary of Freund. Royal 8vo 21s.

White.—*A CONCISE LATIN-ENGLISH DICTIONARY,* for the Use of Advanced Scholars and University Students By the Rev. J. T. WHITE, D D Royal 8vo. 12s.

Wilcocks.—*THE SEA FISHERMAN* Comprising the Chief Methods of Hook and Line Fishing in the British and other Seas, and Remarks on Nets, Boats, and Boating. By J. C. WILCOCKS. Profusely Illustrated New and Cheaper Edition, much enlarged, crown 8vo 6s.

Williams.—*MANUAL OF TELEGRAPHY.* By W WILLIAMS, Superintendent of Indian Government Telegraphs Illustrated by 93 Wood Engravings. 8vo. 10s 6d.

Willich.—*POPULAR TABLES* for giving Information for ascertaining the value of Lifehold, Leasehold, and Church Property, the Public Funds, &c. By CHARLES M. WILLICH Edited by MONTAGU MARRIOTT. Crown 8vo. 10s.

Wilson.—*A MANUAL OF HEALTH-SCIENCE.* Adapted for Use in Schools and Colleges, and suited to the Requirements of Students preparing for the Examinations in Hygiene of the Science and Art Department, &c. By ANDREW WILSON, F R S E F L S &c. With 74 Illustrations. Crown 8vo. 2s. 6d.

Witt.—*Works by Prof. Witt.* Translated from the German by Frances Younghusband.

The Trojan War. With a Preface by the Rev. W. G. Rutherford, M.A. Head-Master of Westminster School. Crown 8vo 2*s.*

Myths of Hellas; or, Greek Tales. Crown 8vo. 3*s* 6*d.*

The Wanderings of Ulysses. Crown 8vo. 3*s* 6*d*

Wood.—*Works by Rev. J. G. Wood.*

Homes Without Hands, a Description of the Habitations of Animals, classed according to the Principle of Construction With about 140 Vignettes on Wood 8vo. 10*s* 6*d.*

Insects at Home, a Popular Account of British Insects, their Structure, Habits, and Transformations. 8vo. Woodcuts, 10*s* 6*d*

Insects Abroad; a Popular Account of Foreign Insects, their Structure, Habits, and Transformations. 8vo. Woodcuts, 10*s.* 6*d.*

Bible Animals; a Description of every Living Creature mentioned in the Scriptures. With 112 Vignettes. 8vo. 10*s.* 6*d.*

Strange Dwellings, a Description of the Habitations of Animals, abridged from 'Homes without Hands.' With Frontispiece and 60 Woodcuts Crown 8vo. 5*s.* Popular Edition, 4to. 6*d.*

Horse and Man their Mutual Dependence and Duties. With 49 Illustrations. 8vo. 14*s.*

Illustrated Stable Maxims To be hung in Stables for the use of Grooms, Stablemen, and others who are in charge of Horses On Sheet, 4*s*

Out of Doors; a Selection of Original Articles on Practical Natural History With 6 Illustrations Crown 8vo. 5*s.*

Common British Insects. Beetles, Moths, and Butterflies Crown 8vo with 130 Woodcuts, 3*s* 6*d*

Petland Revisited With numerous Illustrations, drawn specially by Miss Margery May, engraved on Wood by G. Pearson. Crown 8vo. 7*s.* 6*d.*

Wylie. — *History of England under Henry the Fourth.* By James Hamilton Wylie, M.A one of Her Majesty's Inspectors of Schools. (2 vols.) Vol. 1, crown 8vo. 10*s.* 6*d*

Wylie. — *Labour, Leisure, and Luxury;* a Contribution to Present Practical Political Economy By Alexander Wylie, of Glasgow Crown 8vo. 6*s.*

Year's Sport (The). A Review of British Sports and Pastimes for the Year 1885 Edited by A. E. T. Watson. 8vo. 21*s.* half-bound.

Youatt. — *Works by William Youatt.*

The Horse. Revised and enlarged by W. Watson, M R C V.S. 8vo. Woodcuts, 7*s* 6*d.*

The Dog Revised and enlarged. 8vo. Woodcuts 6*s.*

Zeller. — *Works by Dr. E. Zeller.*

History of Eclecticism in Greek Philosophy. Translated by Sarah F Alleyne. Crown 8vo. 10*s* 6*d.*

The Stoics, Epicureans, and Sceptics Translated by the Rev. O. J Reichel, M A. Crown 8vo 15*s*

Socrates and the Socratic Schools. Translated by the Rev. O. J. Reichel, M.A. Crown 8vo. 10*s.* 6*d.*

Plato and the Older Academy Translated by S. Frances Alleyne and Alfred Goodwin, B A. Crown 8vo. 18*s.*

The Pre-Socratic Schools; a History of Greek Philosophy from the Earliest Period to the time of Socrates. Translated by Sarah F. Alleyne. 2 vols. crown 8vo. 30*s.*

Outlines of the History of Greek Philosophy Translated by S. Frances Alleyne and Evelyn Abbott. Crown 8vo 10*s.* 6*d.*

TEXT-BOOKS OF SCIENCE.

ADAPTED FOR THE USE OF STUDENTS IN PUBLIC AND SCIENCE SCHOOLS.

PHOTOGRAPHY By Captain W. DE WIVE-LESLIE ABNEY, F.R S late Instructor in Chemistry and Photography at the School of Military Engineering, Chatham With 105 Woodcuts. 3s 6d

ON THE STRENGTH OF MATERIALS AND Structures the Strength of Materials as depending on their quality and as ascertained by Testing Apparatus, the Strength of Structures, as depending on their form and arrangement, and on the materials of which they are composed By Sir J ANDERSON, C.E. &c. 3s 6d.

INTRODUCTION TO THE STUDY OF ORGANIC Chemistry the Chemistry of Carbon and its Compounds By HENRY E ARMSTRONG, Ph.D. F C S With 8 Woodcuts 3s 6d

ELEMENTS OF ASTRONOMY. By R. S. BALL, II D F R S Andrews Professor of Astronomy in the Univ of Dublin, Royal Astronomer of Ireland. With 136 Figures and Diagrams 6s

RAILWAY APPLIANCES A Description of Details of Railway Construction subsequent to the completion of Earthworks and Masonry, including a short Notice of Railway Rolling Stock By J. W BARRY With 207 Woodcuts 3s 6d

SYSTEMATIC MINERALOGY. By HILARY BAUERMAN, F G S Associate of the Royal School of Mines. With 373 Diagrams 6s

DESCRIPTIVE MINERALOGY. By the same Author With 236 Woodcuts and Diagrams 6s

METALS, THEIR PROPERTIES AND TREAT-ment By C L BLOXAM and A. K HUNTINGTON, Professors in King's College, London With 130 Wood Engravings 5s.

PRACTICAL PHYSICS. By R. T. GLAZE-BROOK, M A F.R S and W N SHAW, M A With 62 Woodcuts 6s.

PHYSICAL OPTICS By R. T. GLAZEBROOK, M.A F.R S Fellow and Lecturer of Trin Coll Demonstrator of Physics at the Cavendish Laboratory, Cambridge With 183 Woodcuts of Apparatus, &c 6s

THE ART OF ELECTRO-METALLURGY, including all known Processes of Electro-Deposition By G GORE, LL D F R S With 56 Woodcuts. 6s

ALGEBRA AND TRIGONOMETRY By the Rev. WILLIAM NATHANIEL GRIFFIN, B D 3s 6d

NOTES ON THE ELEMENTS OF ALGEBRA and Trigonometry. With Solutions of the more difficult Questions By the Rev W N GRIFFIN, B D 3s 6d

ELECTRICITY AND MAGNETISM. By FLEEM-ING JENKIN, F R SS L & E Professor of Engineering in the University of Edinburgh. 3s 6d

THEORY OF HEAT. By J. CLERK MAXWELL, M A II.D Edin F R SS L & E With 41 Woodcuts 3s 6d

TECHNICAL ARITHMETIC AND MENSUR-tion By CHARLES W MERRIFIELD, F R S. 3s 6d.

KEY TO MERRIFIELD'S TEXT-BOOK OF Technical Arithmetic and Mensuration By the Rev JOHN HUNTER, M A. formerly Vice-Principal of the National Society's Training College, Battersea 3s 6d

INTRODUCTION TO THE STUDY OF INOR-ganic Chemistry By WILLIAM ALLEN MILLER, M D. LL D F R S. With 71 Woodcuts 3s. 6d

TELEGRAPHY. By W H. PREECE, C E and J. SIVEWRIGHT, M A With 160 Woodcuts. 5s.

THE STUDY OF ROCKS, an Elementary Text-Book of Petrology By FRANK RUTLEY, F G S of Her Majesty's Geological Survey With 6 Plates and 88 Woodcuts 4s 6d

WORKSHOP APPLIANCES, including Descriptions of some of the Gauging and Measuring Instruments—Hand Cutting Tools, Lathes, Drilling, Planing, and other Machine Tools used by Engineers By C P B SHELLEY, M I C E With 292 Woodcuts 4s 6d

STRUCTURAL AND PHYSIOLOGICAL BOTANY By Dr. OTTO WILHELM THOMÉ, Professor of Botany, School of Science and Art, Cologne Translated by A W BENNETT, M A B.Sc. F L S. With 600 Woodcuts 6s

QUANTITATIVE CHEMICAL ANALYSIS By T E THORPE, F R S E Ph D Professor of Chemistry in the Andersonian University, Glasgow With 88 Woodcuts. 4s. 6d

MANUAL OF QUALITATIVE ANALYSIS AND Laboratory Practice By T E THORPE, Ph D. F R S E Professor of Chemistry in the Andersonian University, Glasgow, and M. M. PATTISON MUIR. 3s. 6d.

INTRODUCTION TO THE STUDY OF CHEM-ical Philosophy, the Principals of Theoretical and Systematical Chemistry By WILLIAM A TILDEN, B Sc London, F C S With 5 Woodcuts 3s 6d. With Answers to Problems, 4s 6d.

ELEMENTS OF MACHINE DESIGN; an Introduction to the Principles which determine the Arrangement and Proportion of the Parts of Machine, and a Collection of Rules for Machine Designs By W CAWTHORNE UNWIN, B Sc. Assoc Inst C F With 325 Woodcuts. 6s.

PLANE AND SOLID GEOMETRY By the Rev. H W WATSON, formerly Fellow of Trinity College, Cambridge 3s 6d

EPOCHS OF HISTORY.

EPOCHS OF ANCIENT HISTORY.

Edited by the Rev Sir G. W. Cox, Bart M A and by C. SANKEY, M A 10 Volumes, fcp 8vo. with Maps, price 2s. 6d. each vol.

THE GRACCHI, MARIUS, AND SULLA By A H BEESLY, M A Assistant Master Marlborough College. With 2 Maps.

THE EARLY ROMAN EMPIRE. From the Assassination of Julius Cæsar to the Assassination of Domitian By the Rev W WOLFE CAPES, M A With 2 Coloured Maps

THE ROMAN EMPIRE OF THE SECOND CENTURY, or the Age of the Antonines By the Rev W. WOLFE CAPES, M A With 2 Coloured Maps

THE ATHENIAN EMPIRE FROM THE FLIGHT of Xerxes to the Fall of Athens By the Rev Sir G W Cox, Bart M A Joint-Editor of the Series With 5 Maps.

THE GREEKS AND THE PERSIANS By the Rev Sir G W Cox, Bart M A Joint Editor of the Series With 4 Coloured Maps

THE RISE OF THE MACEDONIAN EMPIRE. By ARTHUR M CURTEIS, M A formerly Fellow of Trinity College, Oxford With 8 Maps

ROME TO ITS CAPTURE BY THE GAULS. By WILHELM IHNE, Author of 'History of Rome' With a Coloured Map.

THE ROMAN TRIUMVIRATES By the Very Rev CHARLES MERIVALE, D D Dean of Ely With a Coloured Map.

THE SPARTAN AND THEBAN SUPREMACIES. By CHARLES SANKEY, M A Joint-Editor of the Series, Assistant-Master in Marlborough College. With 5 Maps

ROME AND CARTHAGE, THE PUNIC WARS. By R BOSWORTH SMITH, M A Assistant-Master, Harrow School. With 9 Maps and Plans

EPOCHS OF MODERN HISTORY.

Edited by C COLBECK, M A. 17 vols. fcp 8vo with Maps, price 2s. 6d. each vol.

THE NORMANS IN EUROPE. By Rev. A. H JOHNSON, M A late Fellow of All Souls College, Oxford Historical Lecturer to Trinity St John's, Pembroke, and Wadham Colleges With 3 Maps

THE CRUSADES By the Rev Sir G W Cox, Bart M A late Scholar of Trinity College, Oxford Author of the 'Aryan Mythology,' &c With a Coloured Map

THE BEGINNING OF THE MIDDLE AGES. By the Very Rev RICHARD WILLIAM CHURCH, M A &c Dean of St Paul's and Honorary Fellow of Oriel College, Oxford With 3 Coloured Maps

THE EARLY PLANTAGENETS By the Right Rev W STUBBS, D D Bishop of Chester With 2 Coloured Maps

EDWARD THE THIRD By the Rev. W WARBURTON, M A late Fellow of All Souls College, Oxford. Her Majesty's Senior Inspector of Schools With 3 Coloured Maps and 3 Genealogical Tables

THE HOUSES OF LANCASTER AND YORK, with the Conquest and Loss of France By JAMES GAIRDNER, of the Public Record Office, Editor of 'The Paston Letters,' &c With 5 Coloured Maps

THE ERA OF THE PROTESTANT REVOLUTION By F SEEBOHM, Author of 'The Oxford Reformers—Colet, Erasmus, More' With 4 Coloured Maps and 12 Diagrams on Wood

THE AGE OF ELIZABETH. By the Rev M CREIGHTON, M A I L D Dixie Professor of Ecclesiastical History in the University of Cambridge With 5 Maps and 4 Genealogical Tables

THE FIRST TWO STUARTS AND THE PURITAN Revolution, 1603-1660 By SAMUEL RAWSON GARDINER, Author of 'The Thirty Years War, 1618-1648' With 4 Coloured Maps.

THE FALL OF THE STUARTS, AND WESTERN Europe from 1678 to 1697 By the Rev EDWARD HALE, M A Assistant Master at Eton With 11 Maps and Plans

THE AGE OF ANNE. By E E MORRIS, M A of Lincoln College, Oxford Professor of English, &c at the University of Melbourne With 7 Maps and Plans

THE THIRTY YEARS' WAR, 1618-1648 By SAMUEL RAWSON GARDINER, Fellow of All Souls College. With a Coloured Map

THE EARLY HANOVERIANS By E. E. MORRIS, M A Professor of English, &c at the University of Melbourne

FREDERICK THE GREAT AND THE SEVEN Years' War By F W LONGMAN, of Balliol College, Oxford With 2 Maps

THE WAR OF AMERICAN INDEPENDENCE, 1775-1783 By J M LUDLOW, Barrister at-Law With 4 Coloured Maps

THE FRENCH REVOLUTION, 1789-1795. By Mrs S R GARDINER, Author of 'The Struggle Against Absolute Monarchy' With 77 Maps

THE EPOCH OF REFORM, 1830-1850. By JUSTIN M'CARTHY, M P. Author of 'A History of Our Own Times'

Lightning Source UK Ltd.
Milton Keynes UK
UKOW040202210112

185753UK00002B/100/P

9 781172 833818